Modern English Handbook

Prentice-Hall, Inc., Englewood Cliffs, N. J.

Modern

FOURTH EDITION

English

ROBERT M. GORRELL
University of Nevada

CHARLTON LAIRD
University of Nevada

Handbook

15558

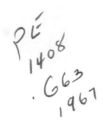

Printed in the United States of America

Library of Congress Catalog Card Number: 67-15172

Current printing (last number):

10   9   8   7   6   5   4   3

PRENTICE-HALL INTERNATIONAL, INC., *London*
PRENTICE-HALL OF AUSTRALIA, PTY. LTD., *Sydney*
PRENTICE-HALL OF CANADA, LTD., *Toronto*
PRENTICE-HALL OF INDIA PRIVATE LTD., *New Delhi*
PRENTICE-HALL OF JAPAN, INC., *Tokyo*

Preface

But easy writing's curst hard reading.

—*Richard Brinsley Sheridan*

Writing is hard work, but this book assumes that it becomes easier and better with serious study. The book is based on the following beliefs:

1. Writing grows from expression and is intended to communicate; good writing says something. and develops from clear thinking.

2. Writing improves more readily through understanding than through correction. Some correction is essential, but many so-called errors diminish when the student learns to construct a sentence or a paragraph.

3. Basic principles can be discovered, learned, and applied— some by analyzing examples of successful prose and by learning how language works.

Because of these beliefs we have approached writing with two major emphases: rhetorical and linguistic. Rhetoric we have taken to be a study of how to develop ideas through language and how to choose among available means of expression, that is, how to build sentences and groups of sentences so that they will achieve the results the writer wants. We have accordingly offered the student writer information about available means of expression, about the varied devices for communication. We have also attempted to help him learn to distinguish among these by anticipating their effects, learning which tools will do which jobs.

Since the basic tool of writing is language, we have rested discussion upon it. The native language is obviously worthy of study for itself, but language study is also practically important for writing because it describes the tools with which the writer works. The book treats English grammar because grammatical principles show how words work together and thus define constructions available to the writer, but it limits grammatical discussions to problems having direct impact on writing and speaking. The book discusses usage differences as linguistic phenomena because the traditions of standard English influence the effect of any piece of writing. We have attempted through such approaches to make the book practical, to teach the essentials of linguistics and rhetoric while applying these to the modern student's daily writing needs.

In this fourth edition we have retained the principles of earlier editions, but we have tried to implement those principles more thoroughly, notably by expanding rhetorical discussions at all levels and by adding illustrations. We have tried, also, to simplify portions of the book especially concerned with revision, continuing the "Guide for Revision" as the second part of most sections but including many grammatical terms along with common problems in usage in an enlarged alphabetically arranged Glossary (Section 27). We hope that this system will give instructors and students a direct reference system for isolating both broad rhetorical principles and more specific questions of grammar and usage. The student should refer to Section 28 on revising and correcting the theme for directions in using the reference system.

We are grateful for many criticisms and suggestions which helped in the preparation of this edition, especially to Ralph Boettcher and James P. Beymer, Duquesne University; Louis B. Hall, Alfred University; Samuel W. Jones, The Ohio State University; Harold D. Kelling, University of Colorado; Richard L. Larson, University of Hawaii; D. Judson Milburn, Oklahoma State University; and Alois J. Schieber, Marquette University. The staff of Prentice-Hall, Inc., has continued to provide guidance and careful editing; for help with this edition we thank especially Paul O'Connell and Cecil Yarbrough. We have had innumerable helpful suggestions from our colleagues at the University of Nevada, especially from some of the teaching assistants. From several generations of students we have gained good as well as horrible examples, but, more important, we have had evidence that teaching English is not entirely futile. To our wives, Johnnie Belle Gorrell and Helene Laird, we are grateful for patience and practical assistance; we had need of both.

ROBERT M. GORRELL
CHARLTON LAIRD

Acknowledgments

The authors are grateful for permission to quote from the following copyrighted works:

Sherwood Anderson, *Winesburg, Ohio.* Used by permission of the publisher, The Viking Press, Inc.

Jacques Barzun, "What Is Teaching?" *The Atlantic,* 174 (December, 1944), 85–86. Used by permission of the publisher.

Albert C. Baugh, *A History of the English Language,* 2nd ed. Used by permission of the publisher, Appleton-Century-Crofts, Inc.

Monroe Beardsley, *Thinking Straight: A Guide for Readers and Writers.* Copyright 1950, 1956 by Prentice-Hall, Inc. Used by permission of the publisher.

Ruth Benedict, *Patterns of Culture.* Used by permission of the publisher, Houghton Mifflin Company.

Franz Boas, *The Mind of Primitive Man.* Used by permission of the publisher, The Macmillan Company.

Van Wyck Brooks, *The World of Washington Irving,* Everyman's Library. Reprinted by permission of the publishers, E. P. Dutton & Co., Inc., and J. M. Dent & Sons, Ltd.

James Bryant Conant, "Force and Freedom," *The Atlantic,* 183 (January, 1949), 19. Used by permission of the publisher.

Norman Cousins, "History Is Made by Headlines," *Saturday Review,* July 25, 1953, pp. 20–21. Used by permission of the publisher.

Robert M. Estrich and Hans Sperber, *Three Keys to Language.* Used by permission of the publisher, Holt, Rinehart & Winston, Inc.

Bergen Evans, *The Natural History of Nonsense.* Used by permission of the publisher, Alfred A. Knopf, Inc.

Worthington C. Ford, *Letters of Henry Adams.* Used by permission of the publisher, Houghton Mifflin Company.

Robert A. Hume, *Runaway Star.* Used by permission of the publisher, Cornell University Press.

Arthur Keith, *Man: A History of the Human Body* (New York:

Oxford University Press, 1912). Used by permission of the publisher.

Jack Kerouac, *On the Road.* Copyright © 1957 by Jack Kerouac. Reprinted by permission of the publishers, The Viking Press, Inc., and André Deutsch, Ltd.

Louis Kronenberger, *Company Manners.* Copyright © 1951, 1953, 1954 by Louis Kronenberger. Reprinted by special permission of the publishers, The Bobbs-Merrill Company, Inc.

Susanne Langer, *Philosophy in a New Key: A Study in the Symbolism of Reason, Rite, and Art.* Copyright 1942, 1951 by Harvard University Press. Used by permission of the publisher.

John Livingston Lowes, *Convention and Revolt in Poetry.* Used by permission of the publisher, Houghton Mifflin Company.

Russell Lynes, "Highbrow, Middlebrow, Lowbrow," *Harper's Magazine,* February, 1949. Used by permission of the author.

Arthur Machen, *Hieroglyphics: A Note upon Ecstasy in Literature.* Used by permission of the publisher, Alfred A. Knopf, Inc.

Archibald MacLeish, "What Is 'Realism' Doing to American History?" *Saturday Review,* July 3, 1965, pp. 10–11. Used by permission of the publisher.

Marya Mannes, "The 'Night of Horror' in Brooklyn," from *But Will It Sell?* Copyright © 1955 by Marya Mannes. Reprinted by permission of the publishers, J. B. Lippincott Company and Victor Gallancz, Ltd., London.

Somerset Maugham, *Rain.* Used by permission of the publisher, Doubleday & Company, Inc.

The MLA Style Sheet, revised edition, compiled by William Riley Parker. Used by permission of the Modern Language Association.

Thomas Clark Pollock, "Misspelling in the Twelfth Grade" (*Teachers Service Bulletin in English*). Used by permission of The Macmillan Company.

Simeon Potter, *Our Language.* Used by permission of the publisher, Penguin Books, Ltd.

Kenneth Rexroth, "Gargantua and Pantagruel," *Saturday Review,* August 28, 1965, p. 20; "Le Morte d'Arthur," *Saturday Review,* July 10, 1965, p. 19. Used by permission of the publisher.

Carl Sandburg, *Abraham Lincoln: The Prairie Years.* Copyright 1926 by Harcourt, Brace and Company. Used by permission of the publisher.

Edward Sapir, *Language: An Introduction to the Study of Speech.* Copyright 1921 by Harcourt, Brace & World, Inc.; renewed 1949 by Jean Sapir. Reprinted by permission of the publisher.

Hilary St. George Saunders, "Can France Come Back?" *The Atlantic,* 183 (March, 1949), 54. Used by permission of the publisher.

John Steinbeck and Edward F. Ricketts, *Sea of Cortez.* Used by permission of the publisher, The Viking Press, Inc.

John Updike, "On the Sidewalk," *The New Yorker,* February 21, 1959. Used by permission of the publisher.

Nesta H. Webster, *The French Revolution.* Used by permission of the publisher, E. P. Dutton & Co., Inc.

A. N. Whitehead, *Science and the Modern World.* Used by permission of the publisher, The Macmillan Company.

Peter Winch, "Universities and the State," *Universities Quarterly,* XII (November, 1957), 14–23. Used by permission of the publisher.

Thomas Wolfe, *Of Time and the River.* Used by permission of the publisher, Charles Scribner's Sons.

Larzer Ziff, "The Other Lost Generation," *Saturday Review,* March 20, 1965, p. 15. Used by permission of the publisher.

Contents

3 ¶

4

Adequate Development 52

4 Dev

5

Coherence and Continuity 70

5 Coh

Sections 6–8: Organization

6

Analysis and Classification 90

phasis and Sound; Sentence Rhythm, 311. *4.* Emphasis Through Structure, 313. *5.* The Periodic Sentence and Special Devices, 314. *6.* The Cumulative Sentence, 315. *7.* Inversion, 317. *8.* Emphasis by Subordination, 318

18 Em

a. Inverted Sentences, 321. *b.* Minor Words to Provide Emphasis, 321. *c.* Rhetorical Questions, 322. Exercises, 322.

Point of View, Tone, and Style   326   **19**

1. Point of View, 328. *2.* Tone—Attitude Toward Material and Audience, 330. *3.* Varieties of Tone, 331. *4.* Appropriateness of Style and Tone, 334.

19 PV; Tone

a. Consistency in Point of View, 337 *b.* Appropriateness in Tone, 338. Exercises, 341.

Sections 20–21: Words

Language, the Means of Being Human   350   **20**

1. The Miracle of Language, 350. *2.* The Ancestry of English, 352. *3.* Indo-European and Its Descendants, 354. *4.* The Growth of English, 357. *5.* Semantic Change, 361. *6.* Indo-European Bases and Modern Cognates, 363. Exercises, 365.

Vocabulary, Meaning, Word Choice   367   **21**

1. Word Hoards and Dictionaries, 368. *2.* Increasing a Writing Vocabulary, 369. *3.* The Meaning of Meaning, 370. *4.* Symbols and Word Choice, 372. *5.* Abstract and Concrete, 373.

21 W

Sections 22–24: The Research Paper

22 *Taking Notes; Plagiarism* *400*

23 *Collecting Material* *418*

24 *Writing a Research Report* *440*

Sections 25–26: The Writing System

Modern English Handbook

Rhetoric and the Paragraph

Rhetoric is the art by which discourse is adapted to its end.
—George Campbell

She was long deaf to all the sufferings of her lovers, till . . . the rhetoric of John the hostler, with a new straw hat and a pint of wine, made a second conquest over her.
—Henry Fielding, *Joseph Andrews*

The practical end to which John the hostler adapted his discourse is probably not the goal of most student writing. But John's triumph, along with Campbell's definition, suggests the extent and inclusiveness of rhetoric, why for 2000 years it has been central in the curriculum of the liberal arts. Rhetoric, considered broadly as the art of discourse, as the technique of effective communication, is fundamental in education and is the main subject of this book.

Rhetoric has an honorable ancestry, but it has also its modern uses. It stems from Classical Greece and Rome, where it throve in the courts and in the Forum; for centuries, as part of the medieval trivium of grammar, logic, and rhetoric, it was one of the pillars of education. Later it was expanded to include all forms of discourse and, in recent years, to emphasize writing. In the broader sense in which it is conceived today, rhetoric embraces such related subjects as grammar, logic, and usage. This book discusses rhetoric, especially the rhetoric of modern standard written English, attempting to provide guides for writing and to show how the principles of good writing can be derived from the analysis of successful prose.

Usually, learning to do involves studying what others have done. By taking an engine apart, a beginning mechanic learns how to put one together; and by studying a house under construction, an apprentice carpenter can see how to frame a building. So with writing, and especially since writing problems are varied and complex, student writers profit from analyzing the techniques of other writers. The goal of this study is not necessarily imitation—although imi-

1

tation is often fruitful; the goal is learning workable methods of composition.

Such analysis, which seeks to identify techniques, to reveal how the writer has accomplished something as well as what he has accomplished, is called rhetorical analysis. As a means of learning the taste of editors, one textbook on the short story advocates using colored pencils to underline key words in magazines—presumably if a magazine averages fifty instances of the word *love* per story, a writer submitting to that magazine should get in fifty *loves*. Even without colored pencils and lists of supposedly marketable words, however, rhetorical analysis can become complex. It can include speculation about the audience whom the author addresses, and the tone of voice he adopts. It can study relationships within and between sentences, the patterns of sentences and the best use of these patterns, the appropriateness of sentence length, and the characteristics of diction. By making such analysis the student can expand his working stock of techniques.

A major problem in the study of writing is knowing where to begin. A practicing writer needs all his skills all the time; a student of writing needs to study everything at once. A writer produces words, sentences, paragraphs, and extended compositions all at the same time; words must be spelled, sentences punctuated, and paragraphs unified. A writer may be studying the meanings of words; meanwhile, to practice what he is learning, he must use sentences and paragraphs. But inevitably writing begins with thinking. Nobody can write unless he has something to say.

Section 1 therefore begins by considering what we mean by an "idea for a theme," what constitutes something worth writing about. Sections 2 and 3 discuss how such an idea can be presented and how it can control the structure of a unit of discourse, particularly the paragraph. Section 4 concerns the development of ideas, the fleshing out of the skeleton to produce meaningful and interesting prose. And Section 5 considers some of the ways in which a piece of prose leads the thought of the reader, giving the writing continuity and coherence.

The Topic;
The Main Idea

For
Guide to Revision
see page 12.

Writing animates a purpose; it develops something the writer has to say about a specific topic.

To suit varying circumstances and purposes, communication takes many forms. One friend says to another, "What have you been doing?" and receives the reply, "Nothing much." In the circumstances, for a casual conversation, the answer is adequate and possibly more or less accurate. In a more serious conversation, the friend might have answered more thoughtfully: "As I get older, I seem to accomplish less and less, becoming steadily slower to protest, more contented, and more lazy." Such an answer does more with the idea; a sentence like this might become the basis for an organized paragraph in a friendly letter (see 2-3). Other circumstances might require a much fuller answer; Robert Louis Stevenson, for example, wrote an extended essay called *An Apology for Idlers.*

Circumstances and purposes vary so widely, in fact, that no formula will suffice for writing. If formulas were possible at all, the many different kinds of writing would require many formulas. Older rhetorical statements recognized broad divisions sometimes called the forms of discourse: exposition, narration, description, and argumentation. These distinctions have their use, but they indicate only very generally the many kinds of writing that modern society can require. Consider, for example, the different demands of an assignment to write a newspaper story, to make a formal report to a government commission, to amuse a lodge group with an account of a trip, to explain a professional philosophy in an application for a scholarship, to prepare a new constitution for a club, to write a letter of sympathy. Each of these would require different approaches and different writing techniques. This book is mainly concerned with exposition and argumentation—that is, with explanation and clarification and sometimes with persuasion—but even within these limitations, no rules can be absolute or all-inclusive.

1-1 The Topic

The old recipe for rabbit stew begins with the obvious—"first catch the rabbit"—but it begins wisely. The rabbit is essential, and the essential must not be overlooked just because it is obvious. Thinking of a possible topic is not so difficult; the problem is thinking of something to say. Ideas are more elusive than rabbits, and writing is more complicated than rabbit stew.

Writing requires thinking, and thinking is always complicated and hard; but the student writer, facing the practical problem of turning blank paper and chewed fingernails into a theme, may agonize needlessly in the mistaken notion that he can solve all his problems by finding a novel or exciting topic—new rocket fuels, piranha fish, or Turkish harems. In reality, he has topics all around him—in his past life, his relations with other people, his courses, his reading, or the library. He can start—and one sure way not to learn to write is not to start—by thinking about relatively simple or familiar subjects which he knows about or wants to investigate. If he disciplines his thinking, he may readily find what students often refer to as an "idea for a theme."

1-2 An "Idea for a Theme"; Topic plus Comment

In some ways the college theme is an artificial exercise, but it provides a way of practicing some of the kinds of writing that the many audiences and the varied situations of modern society demand. Like other types of writing, the theme gets its individuality not just from its topic but from the writer's "idea." Dozens of sportsmen have written essays on fishing, but they are not necessarily repetitious, because each writer can narrow the general subject to a topic which interests him and can write about this restricted topic for his own purposes, focusing on his own ideas. A letter, a newspaper editorial, a political speech, a legal brief, or a report on a business inspection trip may have its subject dictated by orders or circumstances; but its distinction and its impact grow from its individual focus and purpose. Furthermore, the deadlines of the world are at least as rigorous as those of the classroom, and editors or juries or vice-presidents are more ruthless critics than are instructors.

An "idea for a theme" may develop in many ways—from reading, from disciplined thinking, or even in a sudden flash of insight; but it must be more than a general inclination toward a topic: "I think I might write something about icebergs" or "The whooping crane might be an interesting subject." The starting place for a composition as for all communication in language is a topic plus a comment about it, or a subject and a predicate. The motive for expression is an observation or thought about a topic, not just the topic. We do not say "Dogs smell" because we select the topic *dogs* and then look for something to say about it. What we have observed about the topic motivates the expression. "Dogs smell," if not an especially promising theme idea, is usable. A more inventive idea, like the following topic sentence of a paragraph, indicates the importance of a comment as well as a topic:

Sometimes the Scandinavians gave a fresh lease of life to obsolescent or obsolete native words.

The subject of the sentence, the topic being discussed, is *Scandinavians,* but the comment on this topic furnishes the idea to be expanded in the paragraph. The paragraph will not be a discussion of Scandinavians; it will concern certain words and what happened to them. What the Scandinavians did is the important part of the sentence, and the remainder of the paragraph provides specific illustrations of what they did to certain words (see 2-3).

The student trying to find something to write about, then, is working toward more than a topic, toward a topic plus a comment which can be profitably expanded, toward a predication, toward a statement of a main idea. Sometimes he reaches this starting place readily—because of an assignment, because he has a conviction he wants to express, because he has read an essay and disagrees with some point in it, or because he has some notion about the central meaning of a poem. Usually, however, he has to think. Orderly thinking is likely to be more fruitful and more efficient than the most determined daydreaming.

1-3   Ideas for Writing; A Journal

One good way to collect ideas for writing is to keep a thoughtful journal. The student who takes a little time every night to ask and answer the following question is never at a loss for a subject: "What was the most interesting thing I did, heard, thought, read, observed, or experienced today?" He may answer to himself: "For the first time today I understood what *calculus* means"; "I am beginning to observe that my roommate is a complex person"; "Lunch in the dining hall is unpleasant, even though the food is good, because the constant noise and confusion make conversation impossible"; "Looking about this afternoon, I noticed that I can detect about three generations of style in the campus architecture"; "What Professor Whitsmall said today about Freud's theory of the unconscious seems to me to contradict what he said day before yesterday"; "I cannot study efficiently and watch television at the same time." If the student can tell himself in some detail what he means by one of these generalizations and can collect evidence or illustrations to develop it, he has most of the raw material he needs to write a brief composition. The instructor may control assigned material in composition more or less rigidly, but the student who is thrown on his own need never lack for something to write about if he keeps a tolerably full journal.

1-4   Limiting the Topic

Analysis applied to a subject to narrow or limit it can stimulate orderly thinking. For example, a student recalls that he has been thinking about extracurricular activities in college and decides to write on the subject. Since he realizes that "Extracurricular Activities in College" is too broad for a 750-word paper, he decides to narrow the topic by considering one activity. He breaks the general subject into athletics, music, drama, social affairs, campus politics. He might, of course, have thought of more subtopics, but he knows something of campus politics. "Campus Politics," however, is not specific enough for a relatively short paper. The student considers various aspects of campus politics: graft in campus politics, relations of campus politics to academic work, methods for succeeding in campus politics, the value of campus politics. He decides on the last, but as he considers ways in which campus politics is valuable, he recognizes that political activity has more than one value, and he sees he must subdivide his topic. Re-examining his ideas, he finds that he considers campus politics valuable to the nation as training in democracy, valuable to the school, and valuable to the individual student. He sees that these subtopics partially overlap, but he also sees the advantage of separating them and selecting one for his paper. Because he feels he is best able to discuss the value of politics to the student, he works down to a topic specific enough so that he can hope to do something with it: "Campus Politics as Education." The process, then, whereby a specific topic can be drawn from a general subject is roughly pictured in the following chart:

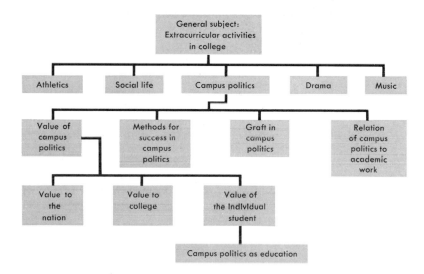

The process is essentially that of analysis (see Section 6), breaking a subject into its parts in an orderly manner and then selecting a specific part to be discussed in detail.

Even when a subject is assigned, the writer can usually improve his paper by narrowing the topic. After class study of an essay on language, the instructor might ask for a paper recording some of the student's observations or attitudes on language, but the student would need to restrict the subject for his individual purposes. He might ask himself questions and rule out large portions of the subject, such as the history of English, comparison of different languages, or changes in modern studies of grammar, as too complicated or outside his knowledge and interest; he might decide to write on some aspect of modern usage. Again he could think of various narrower possibilities: dialect peculiarities, modern "errors" in usage, current slang. He could pick any one of these and narrow it; modern "errors" in usage might be restricted to current attitudes toward *like* and *as* or *lie* and *lay*. Or current slang might be narrowed as the student remembers his experiences with a dance orchestra, decides to write about musicians' slang, and then realizes that he can restrict still further and write about musicians' slang for naming instruments. With his topic restricted he can recall pertinent details from his experience, fill in by reading, and write an interesting paper. Or he might turn the assignment in a quite different way. He might recall that dictionaries provide exciting information and decide to do something on word history or word origins. He could then start working toward something specific and develop a good paper on meaning variations in a single word— "Do You Dig *Dig*?" or "*Nice* Was Not Always Nice."

A final title may differ from the descriptive topic that a writer selects for his own guidance, but a writer can help himself by restricting his thinking to a topic narrow enough to be manageable and descriptive enough to serve as a guide. He need not, of course, proceed as formally as the chart above suggests, but he needs to ask himself questions until he can focus on a topic in which he is interested, about which he has some knowledge, and which he can develop in the space allotted.

1-5   Asking Questions

Thinking about writing can be a kind of question-and-answer dialogue between the writer and himself. The kind of analysis suggested above to limit a topic implies such a dialogue: "What are the parts or kinds of . . .?" Similarly, a student assigned to write a critical comment on a poem he has studied might ask himself questions like the following:

Which of the poems in the text do I find most interesting?
What does the poem I have chosen say?
What devices does the poet use to give the poem its individuality?
Is the poem serious, ironic, flippant? What is its tone?
How do the sound patterns of the poem contribute to its effect?
What is the rhythmic pattern of the poem? Does it have rhymes or other repetitions of sounds?

Are the qualities of individual words, the poet's choices, important to the final effect of the poem?

What are some of the characteristics of the poem's imagery? What are the subjects of the images? Are metaphors simple or complex?

Such questions could go on, with each answer provoking a new question or series of questions. From this sort of mental exercise the student might isolate a central topic and develop a comment on it —for example:

John Donne's poem *Love's Alchemy* is a complex elaboration of a comparison between a lover's attempts to discover the essence of love and an alchemist's efforts to find the elixir of life.

A Main Idea 1-6

Such a topic and comment, developing together as the writer thinks, might serve as the main idea for a paper. A student, for example, may be told to write on Milton's *Paradise Lost*. He may narrow his subject to something about religious attitudes in the poem and then, further, to Puritanism in the poem, but he has something to say, an idea for a paper, only after he decides from his study of the poem that Milton does not sound like the Puritan he is called in the introduction to his text. He then has something to say about his topic. Or a student may experience a month of college social life and find he wants to talk about it—describe it, criticize it, suggest changes, praise it. If he narrows a topic to some manageable aspect of college social life and then decides from his month of experience what he thinks about it, he has an idea for a theme, something to say. An idea for a paper may come from long-held convictions of the writer, from study and research, from questions the writer asks himself about his experiences, from all sorts of sources, and even from prejudices. It may grow or change as actual writing progresses, but a main idea is essential in writing that has purpose and unity.

Almost any unit of writing, from a sentence to a book, focuses on a main idea. The main idea may be a highly important interpretive statement or a highly personal point of view. Frederick Jackson Turner in his influential essay *The Significance of the Frontier in American History* marshals evidence to support the view that

. . . the existence of an area of free land, its continuous recession, and the advance of American settlement westward, explain American development.

Well-known facts of history are seen in a new light when interpreted on the basis of this central idea. On the other hand, Robert Louis Stevenson in an entirely different kind of essay, *Walking Tours,* offers no profound conclusions; he holds his facts together with a central theme that walking tours, well-conducted, are a source of genuine delight and satisfaction. Both essays give clear evidence that the writers had thought about the central meaning of what they had to say, and had selected and organized their material with a main idea or purpose in mind.

Usually student writing will center on main ideas that are less ambitious than those which govern the full-length essays mentioned above. In fact, this book suggests that the student can best begin by working to unify a very brief composition about a main idea stated in a topic sentence (see Section 2).

1-7   Commitment and the Main Idea

Even for a brief composition, the student trying to improve his writing can profitably develop the habit of *writing down his main idea in a complete sentence.* The sentence need not appear in the finished paper, although some version of it usually does. It may change as the writing progresses; but writing such a statement is a useful exercise in planning, because it specifies the writer's commitment to his material and to his reader.

When a writer frames this statement—which might be called a theme sentence or thesis sentence—he commits or obligates himself to develop his paper in certain ways. As he narrows his topic, he is thinking of what he may say about it. When he writes his comment in a sentence, he focuses his attention still more precisely. The student who decided to write on "Campus Politics as Education" will have had reasons for his selection—his attitude toward the subject and his purpose in writing. He might now adopt a controversial point of view and phrase his main idea as:

Campus politics provides the opportunities for practical education that are lacking in formal courses in political science.

Such a statement commits and limits the writer in a number of ways. He will need to list specific educational opportunities provided by campus politics; furthermore he must show that courses in political science cannot provide these opportunities. Another student might phrase his idea as:

Campus politics, because it deals with artificial situations and insignificant problems, has no place in an educational institution.

This student has committed himself quite differently, to show artificiality and insignificance in campus political activity and still further to maintain the rather awkward logical assumption that anything artificial or insignificant has no place in an educational institution. A third student might decide to take no controversial stand, to describe and not argue:

Campus politics is sometimes educational and sometimes a waste of time, but it is almost always exciting for the participating student.

At first glance, this student may seem to have committed himself less because his statement is broader; actually he has given himself a considerable task: to illustrate both the educational and the wasteful aspects of campus politics and then to show that campus politics is always exciting. All of these statements, because they commit the writer so extensively, suggest papers of some length. For the kind of paper usually required in college classes, the student would need to limit his main idea, restrict his commitment, still further. The first student, for example, might think of specific opportunities for education in campus politics, using a process of dividing and selecting like that outlined above for limiting a topic. His statement might become one of the following, more specific and more workable:

Campus politics teaches students the psychological principles of political campaigning.

Campus politics is a practical way of teaching a student public speaking

Campus politics teaches the methods of organizing a large group of people and directing their efforts toward a single goal.

Campus politics gives students practice in operating the machinery of government.

Campus politics tests the student's integrity because it often requires him to choose between his selfish interests and the general good.

As he writes, the student may, of course, change his mind or collect new evidence which will result in a modification of his main idea; but until he can tie himself down to some tentative view, he has not thought enough. Before he starts he should be able to make a statement of the main idea which has the following qualities:

1. It should be a complete sentence. The statement should not be merely a wordier version of the topic.

11

2. It should be specific, the more specific the better. "This paper describes a house I knew in my childhood" only postpones the necessary thinking. "An old house had an important influence on my childhood" is better. "An old house in our block, because it reminded me of the man in the Charles Addams cartoons, gave me a horror of dark rooms" is still better.

3. It should be exact; an inexact statement usually results from cloudy thinking. For instance, the first topic mentioned above might have been phrased as follows: "Campus politics provides more opportunities for practical education than all the formal courses in political science in the university." This is a possible subject, but the student probably has no intention of writing on it. Has he taken "all the formal courses in political science"? Probably not, and even if he has he probably has no intention of contrasting them systematically with what a student can learn from campus politics.

4. It should make a commitment which the writer can hope to fulfill. A statement like "Campus politics is the most important part of any student's college career" probably commits the writer to more than he realizes. Any topic statement should be considered in the light of what it promises the reader.

1 *Guide to Revision*

Consider your purposes in the paper and frame a statement of the main idea, limiting the topic if necessary; then rewrite to focus attention on the main idea.

A sufficiently restricted topic and a significant main idea for a paper usually develop together; the topic limits itself as the main idea emerges more sharply. Usually, therefore, the paper that attempts to discuss a broad subject can be improved by some attention to a main idea.

1a The Topic   Top

Many student themes are doomed at the outset; a workable main idea is almost impossible because the themes attempt too much. Students try to discuss in 500 words "The Culture of the

Middle West"; they strive in a page or two to analyze "America's Foreign Policy" or "University Education in America." These are, of course, worthy general subjects, but they are topics for books or series of books, not for short essays. A theme on any one of them would be only a string of unsubstantiated generalities.

The writer must limit himself, must focus on the aspect of his general subject to which he can make an individual contribution. He might, for example, narrow a subject like "The Culture of the Middle West" geographically, restricting his topic to the culture of one state or to the culture of a city or a section of a city. He might narrow the subject still more to various aspects of culture—the literature or the religion or the art of a restricted area. Religion could then be restricted to some attitude toward religion. A possible working topic might be "Fundamentalism in Religion in Midtown, Michigan."

ORIGINAL	REVISION
Fishing	How to Tie a Fly
Interesting People I Have Known	My Temperamental Music Teacher
Athletics	How to Play First Base
Photography	Photographing Against the Sun
Newspapers in the United States	The Editorial Attitude of *The Daily News* Toward Expansion of the School System
War Between the States	A Problem in Tactics at the Battle of Bull Run

Preliminary restriction of the topic can prevent the theme from rambling. The writer can break a larger topic into its parts, select the one on which he wants to concentrate, and eliminate the others from his discussion in a single sentence of his introduction.

ORIGINAL

The accomplished skier has many means of negotiating steep country. The beginner, of course, cannot hope to learn them all at once, and he does not need to, although they are all worth learning, and anyone who loves to ski will keep learning new ones. Some maneuvers are important for safety, even though they are not much used by experts interested in

REVISION

The accomplished skier learns many means of negotiating steep country, but for the beginner the snowplow is the most useful. With this simple skill even a novice can come down any slope without breaking his neck.

[*More or less consciously the writer has divided maneuvers into those suitable for experts and those for beginners, then di-*

13

ORIGINAL (*Cont.*)

speed.

[*The writer has not broken the broad subject of skiing maneuvers into its parts and selected one to write about.*]

REVISION (*Cont.*)

vided the latter group again and selected the snowplow for his topic.]

1b   The Main Idea   MI

A paper without a main idea is almost certain to become a purposeless jumble. Clarity of organization depends on a unifying central idea; materials introduced for development and expansion can be relevant only if they can be related to a central idea.

ORIGINAL

Reading

It is said that we learn to read in order to learn by reading. And because reading is the greatest individual means of acquiring knowledge, it is easy to understand why the person who lets himself hang back in the shadows of illiteracy can never attain anything in life worth shouting about.

Many of the happiest hours of my childhood were passed in reading. I can remember when I found my father's discarded stories of Frank Merriwell in a box in the garage and found them more exciting than the batch of comic books I had acquired. It was from those books that I learned how much fun reading could be. I used to push myself back into a corner of the garage and sit for hours while Frank Merriwell struck out the entire Harvard team or rescued Elsie from the head-hunters.

Many people I know say that they do not like to read. I do not understand their point of view, because most of the knowledge of the world can be acquired from reading. In some countries of the world today people are not so fortunate, because there is no freedom of the press and they cannot acquire knowledge so

REVISION

Reading to Learn

There are so many reasons for reading that we sometimes overlook the obvious one—that reading is our most important single means of acquiring knowledge. We talk nostalgically of childhood hours spent with Frank Merriwell among the head-hunters, or we cite the emotional power of a great poem, and we forget some of the more pedestrian uses of printed language.

Even our most common day-to-day activities require some ability in reading. The worker has to read signs to drive his car to the plant in the morning. The careful shopper reads labels as she compares the quality of the products she is considering. Telegrams, memoranda, letters are read every second, and important matters turn on the communication they carry. Lives often depend on the ability of a military officer to read orders accurately. Our daily lives turn on communication, much of which requires skillful reading.

Almost equally important is our use of reading to acquire more general but equally practical information. We read to find out how to bake a cake or make a model airplane or

ORIGINAL *(Cont.)*

easily. In America we need only to read in order to become educated.

A reader should not be content to read something he is already an authority on, but he should tackle books about subjects of which he is relatively ignorant. It is true that a good book can teach a lesson, one which you can profit from, if you will think how pleasant and easy it is to read. . . .

[*The paper continues generally in the same vein. Much is wrong with it, but at the bottom of most of the trouble is the absence of a main idea. One cannot say that the paper wanders from the point; there just is no point. To begin with, the title is too broad; it needs to be narrowed. Then the writer needs to decide what he wants to say about reading and start over.*]

I like Walt Kelly's comic strip, *Pogo*. One of my favorite characters is Albert the Alligator; good old lazy Albert is somewhat of a big, conceited show-off. And of course everybody loves Pogo. As for Deacon Muskrat and the Buzzard, they are anything but lovable, though they are not so short-tempered as Albert, who though he is loyal to his friends and even sentimental on occasion will sometimes throw a towering tantrum. His friend, Churchy La Femme. . . .

[*At the beginning this composition threatens to become confused because it lacks any unifying main idea.*]

REVISION *(Cont.)*

identify a horned lark. Words describe the cast of a play, tell us when and where to find a meeting, help us order a meal or catch a train. More complex reading can make a student an expert in chemistry or philosophy. And in a very real sense, reading can make a democracy work. Only reading can create an informed electorate in a world as complex as ours.

In still another way, however, reading is the route to valuable information. By reading literature we begin to learn what life is about. . . .

[*With a main idea—that reading is necessary because it is our most important means of acquiring knowledge—the theme makes more sense. The topic is still too broad, but the writer can collect illustrative details because he knows what he is trying to illustrate.*]

Walt Kelly's comic strip, *Pogo*, gains part of its charm from the fact that each of the swamp creatures becomes a satire on some recognizable type of human being. Albert the Alligator is an irresponsible but genial ne'er-do-well, a lazy, rather cowardly show-off, short-tempered enough to throw a towering tantrum, but loyal to his friends and even, on occasion, sentimental. Deacon Muskrat, on the other hand. . . .

[*With the unifying idea that each of Kelly's creatures can be equated with a human type, the writer can give order to his composition.*]

Exercise 1

A. Each of the following sentences appears early in an essay or book and may be taken as an expression of the main idea of some part of the composition. Describe what each sentence commits the writer to do.

1. Probably the most powerful effect of literature on us is a moral effect, and this effect, rightly appreciated, is what gives literature its unique value.

2. One of the most precise clues to what is actually going on psychologically in a culture is its use of language.

3. The question of form in language presents itself under two aspects.

4. As an undergraduate Kittredge had acquired a taste for clubs and societies, and the taste proved lasting.

5. The English drama arose out of two compulsions: the natural instinct to imitate and the evangelical desire to teach.

6. *Winnie-the-Pooh* is, as practically everyone knows, one of the greatest books ever written, but it is also one of the most controversial.

B. Criticize the following topics and statements of main ideas; which are suitable for student themes? Consider what commitments are implied in the statements of ideas; do the statements suggest any devices for unity?

1. TOPIC: Orientation
   MAIN IDEA: This theme will show various problems of the freshman at a large university and how his courses are different from his high school work and something should be done to remedy the situation.

2. TOPIC: Sweaters in the College Wardrobe
   MAIN IDEA: Uses of sweaters in a girl's wardrobe. Many kinds. Sizes, colors, styles, etc. What will go with what? How many should a girl have? Styles. Goods from which made.

3. TOPIC: Improving Bus Service
   MAIN IDEA: Bus service in my city could be made better, and even profitable, if the bus company would change some of the routes to fit shifts in population, adjust schedules to popular need, and teach drivers some common courtesy.

4. TOPIC: Learning American History from Stamps
   MAIN IDEA: Collecting American stamps is a painless but profitable way to learn the facts of American history.

5. TOPIC: Making Your Own Drapes
   MAIN IDEA: Making drapes for your room requires consideration of

texture and color in choosing material, selection of a suitable and practical style, patience, and a sense of humor.

6. TOPIC: Woodchucks as Game Animals
   MAIN IDEA: Hunting woodchucks provides good sport; woodchucks
   are plentiful and never out of season, and properly dressed
   the flesh is excellent food.

7. TOPIC: Sutphen's Mansion
   MAIN IDEA: An hour wandering through the ruins of the old mansion
   makes one feel a sense of loss for a way of life that has disappeared from the South.

8. TOPIC: Ballet
   MAIN IDEA: I would expect to give a brief sketch of the invention, history, and development of ballet, say something about the
   recent popularity of ballet in this country, the leading ballet companies, especially the New York City Ballet, and
   the amateur and semiprofessional groups that are growing
   up everywhere, very much like the Little Theater Movement of the last generation, the ballet in movies and TV,
   and give some of my own opinions of ballet as an art,
   based on my lessons in ballet.

9. TOPIC: Becky Thatcher's Home
   MAIN IDEA: When we visited Hannibal, Mo., we went to see it.

C. From the following list of subjects select those appropriate for treatment
in a theme 500 to 1000 words long:

1. Ideal Communities in New
   York State in the Nineteenth
   Century
2. My First Lost Tooth
3. Should Medicine Be Social-
   ized?
4. How to Poison Coyotes

5. How to Ride a Subway
6. The Monroe Doctrine
7. A Major Weakness of the Sales
   Tax
8. Prejudice in a Small Town
9. Making Automobiles Safe
10. Clam Chowder

D. From the list below, select five general subjects. Then (a) narrow each of
the five to a topic which might be managed in a theme of about 500
words, (b) for each restricted topic write a sentence stating a main idea
which you might develop if you were to write a theme on the topic, and
(c) for each restricted topic write a still more specific statement which
might serve as the main idea of a single paragraph of 100–200 words
within the longer paper.

1. Advertising
2. Television programs
3. Magazines
4. Desserts
5. Regional prejudices

6. College sports
7. Snobs
8. International tensions
9. Southern industry
10. Farming

17

1

Exercises

E. The following is part of a paragraph from Van Wyck Brooks, *The World of Washington Irving,* concerning David Crockett, a picturesque frontier figure who got himself elected to Congress, partly by his outrageously tall tales.

> ... He [Crockett] was quite willing to have it known that he had waded the Mississippi and whipped his weight in wildcats and leaped over the Ohio, that he salted his bear-steaks with hail and peppered them with buckshot and broiled them with a flash of lightning, after riding on it. He had hugged a bear out of breath and caught and tamed an alligator and set him up beside his cabin and used him as a bench, and his little boy brought bear-cubs home in his pocket. He even wrote the story of his life, in which a friend helped him to "classify the matter." He liked the kind of real life that made a book "jump out of the press like a new dollar fresh from a mint-hopper," he said; and this *Narrative,* with its fresh images and homespun style, at once became, and remained, a frontier classic.

Obviously, Brooks has set limits to this piece of writing; it is about Crockett, and furthermore it is about a certain aspect of Crockett. Discuss each of the following as a theme sentence which will make clear the limitations that Brooks has imposed upon this passage:

1. Crockett had his own means of attracting attention.
2. Crockett had a language of his own, a mixture of fantasy, poetry, and backwoods wit.
3. Crockett had quite a career, and even got himself elected to Congress.
4. Crockett, son of a tavern keeper, was hunter, trapper, scout, and itinerant farmer.
5. Crockett never tired of recounting his truly remarkable exploits.

F. Select an essay from a reader used in your course or an article from a magazine like *Harper's* or *The Atlantic* or *The Reporter* and state in a sentence what seems to you to be its main idea. Then choose a topic for a paper which you might write, suggested by the article, and write a statement of the main idea of the paper.

Unity;
The Topic Sentence

*For
Guide to Revision
see page 31.*

Unity requires focus on a purpose and a main idea; the standard paragraph, a brief composition, is unified around a topic sentence.

A motion picture cameraman photographing a crowd faces a problem like the writer's. He attempts to present a large number of details in such a way that they will make a unified impression. He often provides views from a distance which give a general impression of the large scene, then turns his camera to details, to pictures of individuals and smaller scenes; and almost always he helps his audience to keep these more concentrated scenes in order by focusing attention on some central object. A tree or a building or an important character becomes a focal point, and the camera swings back to it and then away from it so that the audience can keep the great mass of details in order by relating them to this point of focus. Similarly, the skillful writer keeps his reader's attention turned toward a main idea or to central objects which he can use as focal points.

Devices for Unity   2-1

Usually the main idea or central proposition becomes the focal point, the unifying device of the paper. A student writing a theme on the educational value of student self-government might take as his theme sentence a statement that student government provides experience in democracy. He could then unify his paper by relating subsidiary facts and arguments to this thesis. Other devices may help to focus the reader's attention. In his famous essay *On a Piece of Chalk,* Thomas Henry Huxley develops the main idea that the earth "has been the theatre of a series of changes," that physical characteristics and living inhabitants of the earth have been affected by evolution. The essay is unified around a specific example, the story of the changes embodied in a piece of chalk.

Similarly, Esmé Wingfield Stratford labels a chapter of his *History of British Civilization* "Gothic Christianity." He wishes to describe the particular qualities of the growth of religious ardor in thirteenth century England. To unify his chapter he relates his ideas to the development of the Gothic architecture which distinguished English cathedrals built during the period. These cathedrals become a symbol for the thesis of the chapter.

A student theme on the value of student self-government might use a similar device for unity. Its central thesis could be that student government improves efficiency and justice in handling student affairs. Let us assume that the arguments in the paper rely upon a story of how a student government acquired a university bookstore and improved its service and management. The paper could make such general points as these: students are better aware of their own needs than are other groups; they are capable of sensible management; they are stimulated by the challenge of the problems of regulating their own affairs. The paper might connect all these by relating them to the specific instance of the development of the bookstore.

Unity can be furthered by keeping the reader's attention focused. A textbook explanation of the working of a gasoline engine provides a good example. The explanation follows the fuel from the storage tank through the carburetor into the cylinders and finally, as waste, out the exhaust. By explaining the working of each part of the engine in terms of its effect on the fuel, the writer makes a clear and unified explanation. An account of the workings of the houses of Congress gains unity by centering attention on the progress of a bill from its original drafting through readings and committee reports and votes and conferences to its final signing.

Some devices for unity, invented solely to hold the composition together, are more artificial than these. A bridge game unifies one mystery novel, for instance; it has no relation to the plot of the story, but ties it together. The murder takes place during a bridge game, and subsequent events are talked about, sometimes whimsically, as if they were parts of a game. A chapter in which the women characters do some expert investigating is called "Queens are Trumps"; the device gets mixed in a chapter called "One-eyed Jacks Wild," but the book returns to the original game and concludes with "The

Last Trick." Even so contrived a device as this may unify writing, but simpler devices, which focus on a topic sentence, are usually adequate.

The Standard Expository Paragraph 2-2

A sentence can develop an idea, but most ideas exceed the limits of a single sentence. Accordingly, in serious, adult communication, paragraphs usually become the working units. Paragraphs, indicated by about a half inch of indentation in script or five spaces on the typewriter, are not mainly devices for breaking up a page, although single sentences may take the form of paragraphs in dialogue or in the narrow columns of newspapers. Nor are paragraphs any arbitrary number of words or sentences. A few types of paragraphs, cast in the form of transitions, introductions, or conclusions, may be brief, relatively undeveloped guides for the reader, but most good expository paragraphs are organized units of composition, planned discussions of one topic or one part of a larger topic.

Paragraphs can be written in many ways, with different methods of development and organization. They cannot be constructed by formula. But the paragraph is so important to successful composition that the student writer can profit from consciously practicing a few common patterns. The basic pattern, one which occurs with variations time after time in any writing, is so useful that we are calling it the *standard expository paragraph*.

This standard paragraph, which might be called the "workhorse paragraph," centers upon a topic. Normally the paragraph includes (1) some topical material introducing the subject, (2) development which may break into divisions and even subdivisions, and (3) sometimes a conclusion. Of these, the first, the topical material, is usually brief; it may consist only of a topic sentence, often the first sentence in the paragraph, which sometimes is supported by restatement or amplifying comments at various points throughout the paragraph. The development is likely to comprise the bulk of an expository or argumentative paragraph. In very informal or unsophisticated prose it may comprise only a sentence or two presenting relatively few details in support of the topic sentence, but most closely reasoned or adequately developed paragraphs are likely to include a hundred or perhaps several hundred words of development. The conclusion, if one is required, is almost always

21

brief, and often is merely implied in the topical material opening the next paragraph.

2-3   **Topic plus Details**

Section 3 considers some relatively complicated problems of paragraph structure, and succeeding sections discuss further the development and control of ideas, but the student can begin practicing perhaps the simplest—and one of the most useful—patterns for unifying material in a paragraph. The pattern is simple: the paragraph begins with a topic sentence, usually a generalization of some sort, and then presents a series of details that illustrate that topic. Consider, for example, the following:

I am no better than a procrastinating cuss, and since being married I do less than ever before. Here is another winter gone and I am again nursing nasturtiums and feeding mosquitoes. I am going on to thirty-eight years old, the yawning gulf of middle-age. Another, the fifth, year of professordom is expiring this week. I am balder, duller, more pedantic, and more lazy than ever. I have lost my love of travel. My fits of wrath and rebellion against the weaknesses and shortcomings of mankind are less violent than they were, though grumbling has become my favorite occupation. I have ceased to grow rapidly either in public esteem or in mental development. One year resembles another, and if it weren't for occasional disturbing dreams of decay, disaster, or collapse, I should consider myself as having attained as much of Nirwana as a man of my race and temperament can expect to do.

The paragraph is from a letter by Henry Adams, one of America's most cogent writers. For other purposes and more subtle ideas, Adams often wrote more complicated paragraphs. Here he needs only to announce a subject, develop it with a series of details having no expressed order, and finish with a more general illustration of the topic to serve as conclusion.

The same pattern will work for more formal material, as the following paragraph developed from a topic sentence used in Section 1 (see 1-2) illustrates:

Sometimes the Scandinavians gave a fresh lease of life to obsolescent or obsolete native words. The preposition *till*, for instance, is found only once or twice in OE. texts belonging to the pre-Scandinavian period, but after that time it begins to be exceedingly common in the North, from whence it spreads southward; it was used as in Danish with regard to both time and space, and it is still so used in Scotch. Similarly *dale* (OE. *dæl*) "appears to have been reinforced from Norse (*dal*), for it is in the North that the word is a living geographical name" (NED.), and *barn*, Scotch *bairn* (OE. *bearn*) would probably have disappeared in the North, as it did in the South, if it had not been strengthened by the Scandinavian word. The verb *blend*, too, seems to owe its vitality (as well as its vowel) to Old Norse, for *blandan* was very rare in Old English. —OTTO JESPERSEN, *Growth and Structure of the English Language*

The author follows his opening topic sentence with others presenting four words as examples of his opening generalization. The following illustrates the same pattern:

His folks talked like other folks in the neighborhood. They called themselves "pore" people. A man learned in books was "eddicated." What was certain was "sartin." The syllables came through the nose; "joints" were "j'ints"; fruit "spiled" instead of spoiling; in corn-planting time they "drapped" the seeds. They went on errands and "brung" things back. Their dogs "follered" the coons. Flannel was "flannen," a bandanna a "banddanner," a chimney a "chimbly," a shadow a "shadder," and mosquitoes plain "skeeters." They "gethered" crops. A creek was a "crick," a cover a "kiver."
—CARL SANDBURG, *Abraham Lincoln: The Prairie Years*

The paragraph begins by summarizing the main idea. The remainder of the paragraph lists particular instances to illustrate and support the opening statement. No conclusion is needed.

In some paragraphs the two or three parts are not sharply distinct, and the organization of the development may be rather loose. In brief paragraphs, particularly those that are quasi-narrative, little organization may be needed. The details may be in chronological order, for example, and the author may be endeavoring to record no more than the details and their order. Notice the following consecutive paragraphs from Robert A. Hume's *Runaway Star*, a study of Henry Adams as an intellectual and artistic figure.

Henry Adams's first venture into published scholarly writing was an essay entitled "Captain John Smith," appearing in the January, 1867, issue of the *North American Review*, then edited by Charles Eliot Norton. As candidly admitted in *The Education*, the young man was eager "to make a position for himself," and such an article seemed calculated for an effect, since it struck at the Pocahontas legend, particularly precious to self-conscious exemplars of Virginian chivalry. Adams had done some research on Smith as early as 1861, after hints obtained in conversation from John Gorham Palfrey, author of *A History of New England*, but he owed most to Charles Deane, whose edition of Wingfield's *Discourse of Virginia* contained notes casting doubt on Captain John Smith's veracity. Adams finished a draft of his study in 1862 but laid it aside until 1866, when at Palfrey's urging he revised and sent it to the *North American*.

In essence the article virtually establishes that the famous story of Smith's rescue by Pocahontas is not history but hoax, invented by Smith in his later years, presumably to call attention to himself so that he might mend his tattered fortunes. At least it is highly suspicious that Smith's first account of the

23

incident was that in his *General Historie of Virginia,* published in 1624, seven years after the death of the Indian maiden who was said to have laid her head upon his when the clubs of her father's warriors were about to fall. In his *True Relation* (1608) and subsequent writings, published before 1624, Smith had not mentioned the episode.

Here Hume is attempting nothing very complicated; in the first paragraph he is recounting the details of the publication of an article, and in the second he is summarizing the import of the article. He is laying the groundwork for more serious writing to come; the material is not difficult, and much of it is narrative with chronology making the order clear. He needs no elaborate organization; as a matter of fact the organization of the two paragraphs is similar, although as usual this basic similarity does not seem repetitious because it is obscured by minor differences. In each paragraph the topic is announced at once, in the first part of the first sentence, but the topical material is brief enough so that the author can use part of the sentence to add details. Thereafter more details are presented in a few sentences and the details are kept in order by chronology, in the first paragraph through the chronology of the writing, revising, and printing of the article, in the second paragraph through the chronology of Smith's published works. The first paragraph has a sort of conclusion; it starts with the implication that the paragraph is to concern the publication of an article, and the last sentence sees the study published. The second paragraph has nothing much that can be called conclusion; the topic sentence had made the subject quite precise, that the Pocahontas legend was "not history but hoax." Hume then presents the evidence, and presumably assumes that in so brief a paragraph he need not remind his reader of the subject, particularly since this is all background as far as Hume's book is concerned, and whether Smith was or was not a genial liar makes little difference in his discussion.

Elsewhere, Hume feels he must make points more precisely. Consider the following:

A man's birth is indispensable to his physical existence but is intellectually unimportant, belonging on the same level with his conception about nine months earlier, or with his taking successive breaths and imbibing maternal milk. It is difficult, therefore, to identify the author of *The Education of Henry Adams* with a certain helpless, presumably intractable male brat that appeared on February 18, 1838, in Boston, Massachusetts, to be promptly designated the fourth child and third son of Charles Francis Adams, who was the son of John Quincy Adams, who was the son of John Adams. That complicated entity Henry Brooks Adams—diffident, contemptuous; energetic, indolent; rebellious, tradition-conscious; eye-twinkling, dour—did not indubitably emerge for a number of years, just how many it is hard to say.

The structure is still relatively simple. Again, the topical element is in the first part of the first sentence—birth is physically indispensable but not intellectually important. The remainder of the first sentence and the second sentence provide development of this idea, that for a time Adams was more brat than brain. The final sentence pins down the conclusion rather sharply, that Adams as an entity did not emerge for some time. The one-two-three sequence that we have noticed above is here sharper, but not much more complicated.

The Topic Sentence   2-4

Most paragraphs focus on a central idea or unifying device expressed in topical material. Occasionally this topical matter is complex, involving more than one sentence and some subtopics; sometimes it carries over from a previous paragraph and is assumed to be understood or is referred to briefly; but usually it simply takes the form of a sentence, sometimes amplified or made more specific in a sentence or two following it. This topic sentence may appear at the end of the paragraph as a kind of summary or somewhere within the paragraph, but most frequently it opens the paragraph or follows an opening introduction or transition. The topic sentence has the following main functions:

1. It provides transition (see 8-2). One of the most common types of topic sentence opens with a reference to what has preceded, a repetition of it, or even a kind of summary, and then goes on to introduce a new topic. Notice, for example, how the following sentence from an essay of W. H. Hudson links what has preceded and what is to follow:

Although the potato was very much to me in those early years, it grew to be more when I heard its history.

The opening subordinate clause summarizes generally what has preceded, a narrative comment on the author's interest in the potato; the second clause introduces a new topic, the history of the potato, which is the subject of the paragraph the sentence introduces. The following from a *Time* report on the telephone business does the same kind of thing less directly but succinctly:

Not all calls end so happily.

The paragraph that preceded had reported pleasant experiences with the telephone; the sentence itself introduces a paragraph listing less fortunate incidents. Often, as in the following, the first sentence of a paragraph is almost entirely transitional material:

The return of fatalism in our modern world leads us to another general question.

The preceding material discussed the return of fatalism; the sentence presents the transition directly, and a second topic sentence states the question to be discussed.

2. The topic sentence often suggests an organization or structure for the paragraph (see 3-3). Another sentence from Hume's *Runaway Star,* for example, introduces two subjects:

Once more, then, Henry Adams was not an unalloyed pessimist.

The sentence commits the writer to discuss pessimism and the fact that it was "alloyed." It points to a two-part pattern treating each subject in turn, and the paragraph does develop in this way. The first half summarizes what has apparently been mentioned earlier, that Adams was pessimistic. Then a sentence, "He never gave up," introduces the second division, which asserts that the pessimism was alloyed.

3. The topic sentence presents a topic. The manner in which the topic sentence introduces the subject for the paragraph varies, of course, with the nature of the subject, but most commonly the topic sentence either names or introduces a subject or presents a proposition or thesis for discussion.

2-5   Topic Sentences That Introduce Subjects

Topic sentences may be mainly utilitarian, introducing a subject and anticipating what is to follow. Notice, for instance, the following, which is almost entirely transitional and structural:

The opposition also has its arguments.

The writer uses the topic sentence almost like a title, directly telling the reader that he will now describe the arguments of the opposition. More complicated sentences may work in much the same way:

The sudden development of these attitudes is not easy to analyze, but we must begin by recognizing what has happened.

As for the social theorists, here, too, I think we can discern two main tendencies.

These paragraphs open with a sentence which not only mentions a topic but also suggests what the paragraph will do.

Topic Sentences as Propositions   2-6

Often, the topic sentence is a proposition that commits the writer to support it in some way (see 1-7).

A paragraph can provide such support only if the proposition is manageable—only if it makes a commitment the writer can hope to fulfill. Propositions may take many forms and each may obligate the writer in a different way. Among the most common characteristics and types of propositions are the following:

1. *Generalization.* Most propositions involve generalization: that is, they result from observing facts and discovering something worth recording that is common to all of them. The student writing on campus politics, for example, might check the files of the student paper for five years and produce a generalization, a proposition, like the following:

During the past five years every campaign for student body president has turned about trivialities rather than issues of educational policy.

The generalization identifies a characteristic that the student considers common to all the campaigns he has examined. Used as the topic sentence of a paragraph, the proposition would commit the writer to provide illustrations and examples of the trivialities. More serious and more extensive study did in fact produce the following generalization, which serves as topic sentence of a paragraph:

First of all, it is certain that we of Western society have never, in our five thousand years of recorded history, kept peace for long within an area save by bringing that area within the authority of a single government.

The proposition is one of a series which serve as topic sentences of paragraphs that provide background for another generalization used as a topic sentence: that there is

in the past of our civilization little—indeed, no—precedent for the immediate success of the kind of effort well-meaning men and women are now making in the cause of world government and a sovereign world-state.

2. *Definition, Classification, Description.* A proposition may characterize a topic and thus commit the writer to explain it in more detail. As a topic sentence, such a proposition usually is specific enough to stimulate further comment. A definition like "A diction-

ary is a book" is so broad that it tends to end discussion, but consider the following:

A dictionary is a book which lists a selection of the words of a language, providing information about their spelling, pronunciation, meaning, and uses.

The fuller definition refines the proposition and gives the writer some basis for continuing, suggesting that subsequent sentences illustrate each of the dictionary's functions. Other propositions, although they take the form of definitions or classifications, may express opinions which require support:

Campus politics is one of our most successful methods of miseducation.

Such a topic sentence would commit the writer to illustration and perhaps to argument. Descriptive propositions may require lists of the kinds of details on which the generalization is based:

The room was a garden of wax fruit and plastic flowers.

A paragraph based on this topic sentence would mention specific things: the bowl of pink and lavender grapes on the table, the shiny calla lilies on the piano, the planting area with its imitation tropical greenery.

Propositions which describe may also include implied judgment or opinion:

Ten minutes of his conversation was enough to convince the girls that they should have stayed at home.

Such a topic sentence would require the writer to describe this conversation more fully.

3. *Relational Propositions.* Propositions may develop from a writer's speculations about how things or events are related—how one thing may be a part of another or the cause or effect of another. Such propositions often open paragraphs which list reasons, cite evidence, develop an argument. For example:

Campus politics persists mainly as an outlet for the energies of a few students who need to build their egos and are incapable of doing it in athletics or scholarship.

Such a proposition, involving a fairly complicated causal relationship, might be hard to support in a single paragraph. Consider:

Our Town is popular as a school play mainly because it can be staged easily.

The proposition obligates the writer to supply some support for both ideas—that the play is easily staged and is popular—and to argue that the easy staging leads to the popularity.

4. *Practical Propositions.* Propositions may be called practical when they advocate action, indicate something that should exist or should happen.

Campus politics should be reformed by strict university regulations and faculty control.

Actually, propositions of this sort introduce paragraphs less frequently than might be imagined, probably because they require argument as support. Writers are often more successful with propositions that introduce factual support.

There are, of course, many other kinds of propositions and other ways than these of describing them. Many topic sentences can be considered as propositions of some sort. The nature of the proposition used as a topic sentence—the way it is framed and the degree to which it obligates the writer—has much to do with determining the ultimate success of the paragraph.

Topic Sentences and Precision   2-7

For either of his sentences in 2-3 above, Hume might have written something like the following:

We must now consider another aspect of Adams's character, one that we have not as yet treated, but one which we surely should not ignore in any extensive treatment of our subject's character.

This sentence is not bad; it would serve. But it postpones deciding what is to be said in each paragraph. It gets much less done than Hume's brief but precisely thought and carefully worded statement.

Although a topic sentence may contain some routine transitional material, its excellence is likely to reflect clear thinking, to rest on definition in the etymological sense of that word, thereby setting up boundaries. A good topic sentence blocks out enough space for the paragraph and sets limits to it. It is general enough to provide scope for the idea in the paragraph, but it should restrict the subject in order to exclude other materials.

For variety, we might consider a paragraph from Gilbert Highet's *The Classical Tradition:*

Nineteenth-century writers admired this culture for two chief reasons: because it was beautiful, and because it was not Christian. They saw their own civilizaton as squalid and greedy; they praised the Greeks and Romans as noble and spiritual. They felt contemporary Christianity to be mean, ugly, and repressive; they admired the cults of antiquity as free, strong, and graceful. Looking at the soot-laden sky, pierced by factory chimneys and neo-Gothic steeples, they exclaimed

> Great God! I'd rather be
> A Pagan suckled in a creed outworn.

Highet wishes to say that nineteenth-century writers admired the Greek and Roman culture for two reasons, "it was beautiful" and "it was not Christian," and his topic sentence restricts the discussion to just these subjects, although he carries them parallel through the paragraph. He might have written:

> In this connection it is interesting to note that earlier periods exerted a certain charm over many of the more sensitive spirits of the nineteenth century and that among the reasons for this charm were the differences between theirs and an earlier day. They saw in their own civilization. . . .

As a topic sentence this could have been worse. It would have permitted the writer to say almost anything he pleased; but it is clearly a worse topic sentence than Highet's, partly because it is less exact, less precise. It tells the reader too little of what he should know; it does not restrict the paragraph to just that material which is to be its content.

Similarly, Highet might have begun his paragraph in this manner:

> Nineteenth-century writers resented living under a soot-laden sky. They resented the growing ugliness of an industrial society. They disliked the factory chimneys that thrust up everywhere, and not only the factories but the neo-Gothic spires, which suggested that the Christianity of the day, like the industry, was ugly. They saw in their own civilization. . . .

Again, he did not, and the reason is obvious. He would have been starting with material so specific that it provides no proper introduction to the whole.

Topic sentences may appear anywhere, or even be omitted. For any of a number of reasons the writer may wish to have the topic sentence at the end; for example, he may wish to develop a paragraph inductively, doing no more than hint at the subject until he has developed it, and summarizing it when it is developed. Or the topic sentence may be pivotal, somewhere about the middle of the paragraph, with details developing toward it and conclusions drawn from it. Some paragraphs have nothing that can clearly be called topic sentences, particularly in rather chatty writing on a light subject broken into small units. Such writing may ramble on without much organization and be none the worse for its loose-jointed manner, but most modern, carefully constructed prose rests on standard paragraphs, most of which have topic sentences to open them. The student will do well to write one standard paragraph after another until he can produce them easily, inevitably, and naturally before he experiments with variations and before he tries to write without the discipline of drafting standard paragraphs carefully.

Guide to Revision **2**

Unify paragraphs by focusing on a main idea, usually expressed in a topic sentence.

The paragraph is a basic structural unit in expository writing; difficulties in paragraphing usually are symptoms of several weaknesses. Often, therefore, a number of difficulties can be overcome by revising paragraphs according to a standard pattern, unifying them under topic sentences. Such revision may be necessary because the writer has allowed minor issues, which he never intends to develop, to appear as if they are main propositions.

ORIGINAL

There was an oval mirror on one wall with a heavy black frame containing fat angels carved into the wood. I have never much cared for representations of angels. The insipid ones on Sunday-school cards seemed to me dull even when I was a child, and fat ones are not very attractive, to say the least. There was a faint

REVISION

The contents of the room seemed to exhale the faint scent of violet that hung over it. The oval mirror, framed heavily with fat angels carved into blackened wood, the silver brush and comb on the massive walnut dresser, the faded lace curtains, the high walnut bed, the bad print of a Rosa Bonheur picture all

ORIGINAL (*Cont.*)

tinge of violet perfume hanging over the room. A bad print of a Rosa Bonheur picture was hanging on the wall over the high walnut bed. Faded lace curtains bordered the high, narrow windows, which contrasted with a mantel that had been recently dusted; they were rather dirty. Some books sat on the table.

[*Presumably the details are accurately recorded, but they produce no unified effect because they are set down one after the other with no apparent main idea controlling the selection.*]

[1] The success of the American educational system can be traced directly to freedom of speech. American instructors are not mouthpieces for the government. [2] Their job is to teach a sound doctrine, one not influenced by a person or group of persons. [3] And what about the students? [4] Very few students have ever been condemned for expressing their ideas in the classroom. [5] In Germany, when Hitler was dictator, the fellow who dared criticize the system of government was promptly executed or rushed to a concentration camp. [6] It is not like that in this great land of ours. [7] The man in the street is granted by constitutional law the privilege of saying what he pleases without fear of prosecution. [8] Newspapers in the United States are at liberty to present their readers with local, national, and world news without dictation from the government. [9] Radio broadcasting, though censored to a certain degree by the Federal Communications Commission, is another example of freedom of speech in this country.

[*This paragraph fails, partly because*

REVISION (*Cont.*)

seemed part of the odor of the mildly sickening perfume. A few volumes, propped between bookends painted with roses, were slim and gold-lettered; one sensed that they concerned well-dressed gentlemen, very properly courting demure but willing ladies in crinoline.

[*The writer has focused upon a main idea, supplying a topic sentence. He has furthered unity by rearranging his materials, removing the irrelevant comment on his personal reaction to angels, and, by closer observation, describing the details to show how they relate to the main idea.*]

America, unlike Hitler's Germany, enjoys freedom of speech. The man in the street is granted by constitutional law the privilege of saying what he pleases without fear of prosecution. Education is generally free from censorship. Instructors in America are not mouthpieces for the government. Their job is to teach a sound doctrine, one not influenced by a person or group. And very few students have ever been condemned for expressing their ideas in the classroom. Newspapers in the United States are at liberty to present their readers with local, national, and world news without dictation from the government. Radio broadcasting, though censored to a certain degree by the Federal Communications Commission, provides another example of freedom of speech.

[*The writer's selection of details suggests that he probably intended the paragraph's main purpose to be the presentation of evidence that freedom of speech exists in America. Perhaps in another place he intends to show also that this freedom distinguishes America from other nations, such as Hitler's Germany. The revision supplies a proposition, apparently the one*

ORIGINAL *(Cont.)*

it does not fulfill what the first sentence seems to promise. The reader assumes he will learn how freedom of speech has caused the success of education. He learns something else. Probably the writer did not intend this sentence as a proposition, but he has written as if he did.]

REVISION *(Cont.)*

intended, then lists the details already available in the paragraph to support the proposition; sentences 5 and 6, irrelevant, are reduced to parts of the opening sentence.]

Topic sentences may be more or less adequate to the paragraphs they serve.

ORIGINAL

I shall always remember an experience I had last summer; it was the most exciting thing that has ever happened to me.

[*This has the earmarks of a poor topic sentence. The writer probably does not intend to demonstrate that he will remember this incident while forgetting others, or to make a comprehensive study of his exciting moments.*]

REVISION

Last summer, while I was trying out my new skin-diving equipment, I blacked out and nearly drowned.

[*This sentence, although it may have no great virtues as a topic sentence, says something, and what it says is to the point. It is briefer than the original, does not mislead the reader, and introduces the subject with some exactness.*]

A topic sentence may fail to provide sufficient evidence of the relationship of the paragraph to other paragraphs or to the whole composition.

ORIGINAL

. . . My mother's graduation present was tied up in two neatly ironed strips of gingham, which I recognized as her apron strings.

I got the job I had applied for, and I also received a letter saying I had been admitted to the University.

[*The lack of transition leaves the reader wondering where the account is going.*]

REVISION

. . . My mother's graduation present was tied up in two neatly ironed strips of gingham, which I recognized as her apron strings.

These apron strings soon became a symbol for the new life which, I discovered, I was now beginning to lead.

[*Not all topic sentences require repetition of words but most of them require some transitional material.*]

Exercise 2

A. The following are examples of the kind of standard paragraph described in this section. Analyze each, pointing out the topic sentence and describing how it functions in the paragraph.

It is an evening of many muted sounds. In the trees the birds are making drowsy last efforts at chirruping, but obviously their hearts are elsewhere. There is the slow chug-chug of the motor ferry blown over the water, but you only imagine the sound of water swirling away from its bow. Now there is the quicker pant of a motor launch, and the launch itself can soon be seen, white and slick, exulting skittishly over the river. Before long there is the croak of the frogs, not so muted. And from time to time, without warning, there is the snort of the hippo, and if you focus quickly in the direction from which the noise comes, you see a small arm of water rise above the surrounding placidity and fall quickly back.
—JOHN NAGENDA, *The Hippos*

As a matter of fact, we are all of us original in our expression until our wings are clipped. I know a three-year-old boy who calls an automobile a "cadeúga." It is, both to him and in point of fact, an excellently descriptive term, based, like many a word in the pristine days of speech, on the sound the thing makes. But you can't go to the telephone and ask for a "cadeúga" with any valid hope of seeing it appear. And since the world with which the young adventurer must communicate prefers to call the affair a motor, or a car, or a machine (incomparably less exact and fitting terms), he will infallibly drop his own fresh and vivid coinage, and conform. The tangential energy of the individual beats its wings in vain against the centripetal force of the community, and every infant anarchist in speech yields at last to the usage of that world by which, if he is to live, he must be understood.
—JOHN LIVINGSTON LOWES, *Convention and Revolt in Poetry*

Today our point of view is so remote from Rabelais's that it requires a special effort of will even to know what he is talking about. Our science of the mind is founded on the study of the behavior of the mentally ill; our Public Health on epidemiology; our practical sociology on a kind of social workers' criminology; our economics on Marx. It has been said of America that its philosophy of life, like that of the ancient Greeks, is medically oriented. The ethics or the politics or the psychology of Aristotle or Plato are founded on a clear concept of the fully healthy man. Our parallel disciplines begin with pathology. Psychiatrists say we are all neurotics. Rabelais would not have known what they are talking about.
—KENNETH REXROTH, *Gargantua and Pantagruel*

Proud of his wonderful achievements, civilized man looks down upon the humbler members of mankind. He has conquered the forces of nature and compelled them to serve him. He has transformed inhospitable forests into fertile fields. The mountain fastnesses are yielding their treasures to his demands. The fierce animals which are obstructing his progress are being exterminated, while others which are useful to him are made to increase a thousand-fold. The waves of the ocean carry him from land to land, and towering mountain-ranges set him no bounds. His genius has moulded inert matter into powerful machines which await a touch of his hand to serve his manifold demands.

—FRANZ BOAS, *The Mind of Primitive Man*

B. Consider the following topic sentences:

1. Mrs. Jones was even stingier than her daughter.
2. Mrs. Jones was the stingiest woman I ever knew.
3. Mrs. Jones's name was a synonym for *stingy* in our town, and everybody had some anecdote to tell about her.

Each of these sentences might serve as a topic sentence, but each makes a different sort of commitment to what is to follow. The first implies that the daughter's stinginess has been discussed in a previous paragraph. The second seems to imply that Mrs. Jones is to be compared with all other stingy women the writer has known; probably he has no such intention, and the reader would probably assume that these words mean no more than "Mrs. Jones was very stingy," but the writer would do well to say what he means. The last sentence could suitably introduce a paragraph of tales told about Mrs. Jones. Now examine the following groups of possible topic sentences and distinguish the implications of each.

1. *a*) Janet is the most tiresome salesgirl I ever dealt with in my whole life.
   b) I do not like Janet as a salesgirl.
   c) Obviously, Janet is a poor salesgirl.
   d) Janet is a poor salesgirl because she wants to do all the talking.
   e) Janet is a poor salesgirl because she has never learned to let the customer do a little healthy griping.
   f) Janet is the worst salesgirl in the store.
   g) Janet would be a better salesgirl if she would cultivate a little interest in her customers.
   h) Janet would be a better salesgirl if she were a kind and sympathetic person who could take a natural interest in her customer's wishes.
   i) Janet might be a better salesgirl if she would read a book on selling.
   j) Janet would not be such a bad salesgirl if she would remember what she was told in her course in salesmanship.

2. *a*) The American attitude toward Chinese affairs is wholly wrong.

   b) The American attitude toward Chinese affairs seems to me wrong.

   c) The American attitude toward Chinese affairs seems to me un-realistic.

   d) The American attitude toward Chinese affairs seems to me shrewd but dangerous.

   e) Washington does not understand the Chinese problem.

   f) If Washington understands the Chinese problem, our recent moves do not reveal the fact.

   g) Washington may or may not understand Chinese problems, but we are endeavoring to give the impression of knowledge, not to say clairvoyance.

   h) Washington cannot be expected to reveal its Chinese policy until we have studied the reactions of London and Moscow.

3. *a*) All that I can now remember learning in high school I gained from playing basketball.

   b) Until I started playing basketball, I had no interest in high school.

   c) Chemistry is now my major interest, but I got started in chemistry only through my high school basketball coach.

   d) For me, basketball was a bridge between bumming around town and studying chemistry.

   e) If I ever become a chemical engineer, one reason is to be sought in a tricky backhand shot I have, which brought me to the coach's attention.

   f) I think basketball should be a required course for every student.

   g) Basketball is an American invention, and the more people live in cities where there is no room for baseball diamonds, the more basketball becomes our national sport, and that was my experience, that it changed my life.

   h) The lessons learned on the basketball court are the factors needed for success in the classroom and in the world of today.

   i) For all-around fun and character building, give me basketball.

   j) Basketball, so called because the first games were played with a peach basket with the bottom knocked out, provided a turning point in my life.

C. The following paragraph—minus its topic sentence—is taken from a letter from an officer in the Second Iowa Regiment describing what he saw and heard of the Battle of Shiloh, April 6, 1862. Construct topic and closing sentences which, taken together, will give the paragraph unity.

"What was the plan of the battle, General?" asked Gen. Buell of Acting Brig. Gen. Tuttle. "By God, sir, I don't know!" he replied. Gen.

Sweeney on our right said he gave all his orders on his own hook, and so of many others. The army was scattered over about twenty miles. The greenest regiments were on the outposts, and not a shovel full of dirt thrown up to protect them until they could be reinforced from the interior of the camp. As a natural consequence, they were panic stricken and retreated in, reporting their regiments "all cut to pieces." Col. Peabody's brigade, on the left, had none but green regiments, viz.: the 12th Michigan, 16th Wisconsin, and the 23d and 25th Missouri. They lost both their batteries, which soon were turned upon us. Sherman's regiments on the right and Prentiss in the centre had few troops that had ever seen a fight.

D. Each of the following might serve as the topic sentence for a paragraph like the standard paragraphs described above; that is, each might be developed by enumerating examples or listing details. The first might rely upon specific examples of difficulties of registration day, the second on personally important recollections of a home town, and so on.

Select sentences in the list which interest you and develop them into simple standard paragraphs. Then write a brief analysis of each of your paragraphs, describing the general pattern and pointing out the relationship of each sentence to the whole.

1. For me, registration day was a series of confusions and misunderstandings.
2. Much of what I remember about my home town has only personal importance.
3. My sixth-grade teacher's methods of getting the class to work were certainly not conventional.
4. The buildings on the campus seemed designed to illustrate as many different kinds of architecture as possible.
5. Almost every piece of furniture in the room had been constructed out of scraps and salvaged material.
6. A college newspaper has certain clear obligations to the student body.
7. A few snatches of my childhood reading still stick in my mind.
8. Students have developed a variety of techniques to conceal inadequate study from their teachers.
9. While I was ill, I learned that there is more than one way to spend a quiet afternoon.
10. Many current terms of college slang describe aspects of academic work.
11. A student expects to find certain qualities in a good classroom lecture.
12. A few basic ingredients are part of the recipe for almost every Western movie.

3

Paragraph Patterns

For
Guide to Revision,
see page 45.

Paragraphs can be constructed from basic units in a variety of patterns of coordination and subordination.

As suggested at the beginning of this book, writing can be thought of as a process of addition, of adding comments to topics and extending them. Sentences, paragraphs, entire essays, or units within any of these usually develop by addition: predicates and modifiers are added to subjects in the typical English sentence; when sentences occur in groups, one sentence may introduce a topic to be amplified in those that follow. The paragraphs analyzed in Section 2 comprise such a series of comments on a single topic.

Obviously all paragraphs in English prose cannot be as simple in their structure as those in Section 2. But the pattern—a topic followed by explanation, instances, illustrations—is basic in many kinds of more complicated paragraphs. That is, patterns like those in the simple standard paragraph can be combined and ordered in a variety of ways to meet the demands of more complex subject matter. To examine some of these more complex patterns, we should observe how these topic-comment units are combined; we should consider patterns in terms of coordination and subordination.

3-1   Topic-Comment Units

The following paragraph combines two basic units:

[1] At the moment, as for many years past, the chances to see silent comedy are rare. [2] There is a smattering of it on television—too often treated as something quaintly archaic, to be laughed at, not with. [3] Some two hundred comedies—long and short—can be rented for home projection. [4] And a lucky minority has access to the comedies in the collection of New York's Museum of Modern Art, which is still incomplete but which is probably the best in the world. [5] In the near future, however, something of this lost art will return to regular theaters. [6] A thick straw in the wind is the big business now being done by a series of revivals of W. C. Fields's memorable

movies, a kind of comedy more akin to the old silent variety than anything which is being made today. [7] Mack Sennett now is preparing a sort of potpourri variety show called *Down Memory Lane* made up out of his old movies, featuring people like Fields and Bing Crosby when they were movie beginners, but including also interludes from the silents. [8] Harold Lloyd has re-released *Movie Crazy,* a talkie, and plans to revive four of his best silent comedies (*Grandma's Boy, Safety Last, Speedy* and *The Freshman*). [9] Buster Keaton hopes to make at feature length, with a minimum of dialogue, two of the funniest short comedies ever made, one about a porous homemade boat and one about a prefabricated house.   —JAMES AGEE, *Agee on Film*

The paragraph divides into two parts, closely related as aspects of the general topic—not directly expressed—the accessibility of silent comedies. Sentence 1 presents the first topic, that there are now only rare chances to see silent comedy; sentences 2, 3, and 4 list three of these opportunities. Sentence 5 presents a second topic, that silent comedy will return, and sentences 6-9 provide four examples of coming events. Sentences 1-4 and 5-9 each constitute a structural unit in the simple paragraph pattern.

Another paragraph from Hume's book on Henry Adams is similar in that it combines two topic-comment units, but it is different in that these units join as comments on an opening topic.

[1] He [Adams] knew, surely, what any competent scientist is aware of: that no one method or set of experiments can be regarded as final. [2] The scientist works not in terms of certain, ultimate cause (though in the name of human dignity he holds this forever before him as an ideal), but in terms of probability. [3] Probability arises from the findings in one experiment. [4] If the findings in a second experiment are at least roughly equivalent, the probability becomes stronger. [5] It becomes still stronger with similar findings in a third experiment, and so on. [6] If findings in continual and repeated experiments all point to the same end, the scientist gains confidence in his original hypothesis and eventually may cease to regard it as a mere hypothesis but as something so strongly impregnated with probability that it can be adopted for convenience as a workable fact. [7] But the scientist, if he be worthy of his name, will never quite lose sight of the lurking latency of error. [8] He will be sufficiently a philosopher to feel the force of David Hume's contention that causation is never established in a manner answerable to logic. [9] To invoke the humdrum instance, although the sun has punctually risen on a hundred thousand successive days, it may not rise tomorrow.

The main idea of this paragraph, that Adams understood that probability can become a workable "fact" but never an absolute fact, breaks naturally into two parts: the first exploring the nature of probability and the second defining the scientist's responsibility to the possibility of error. The pattern might be analyzed somewhat as follows:

TOPIC: (1) Adams knew as a scientist that no set of experiments can be final.

SUBTOPIC 1: (2) Scientist works in terms of probability. *(In this second sentence, the writer selects one aspect of the topic for detailed explanation.)*

DEVELOPMENT: (3-5) How probability becomes stronger with additional experiments.

CONCLUSION: (6) When probability becomes strong enough, in practice it can be considered workable fact. *(This first unit, 2-6, illustrates a logical progression in thought as the writer adds to the topic of probability introduced in 2, so that he can come to the conclusion in 6, which looks back to 1, the original topic sentence of the paragraph.)*

SUBTOPIC 2: (7) Scientist must beware of lurking latency of error. *(After the conclusion of 6, the writer must look at the other side of the coin: 7 partly repeats 1, the original topic.)*

DEVELOPMENT: (8) Justifying 7 by citing a general contention of David Hume and (9) providing a familiar instance.

Obviously, patterns of this sort can vary widely, but the most common and most useful system for building paragraphs relies on topic-comment units. The single-unit pattern described in Section 2 may be adequate, but often the topic of a paragraph lends itself to subdivision and is followed by two or three units in which subtopics are supported by details. Furthermore, the units themselves may vary; sometimes, for example, the supporting details precede a summary topic statement, and in longer compositions further variations may develop as paragraphs that are themselves subdivisions of larger topics or main ideas (see Section 7).

3-2 Coordination and Subordination

Two structural devices for handling ideas and using the English language, coordination and subordination, underlie paragraph patterns. These two devices appear constantly in discourse—in organizing large units of composition (see Section 7) or in creating sentences or parts of sentences (see Sections 15 and 16). They are used naturally by even the most unsophisticated speakers or writers, but like most relational concepts they are not easy to define. They do not depend on something inherent in ideas or things themselves, but in what we want to say about ideas or things, the kinds of relationships we want to give them. Ham and eggs, to take an oversimple example, are often coordinated in sentences—*He ate ham and scrambled eggs.* Here the two are put into a coordinate pattern; that is, they are presented in such a way that the reader finds them bearing the same—an equal— relationship to the rest of the sentence. Nothing in the nature of the two foods requires this sort of comment, however, and the sentence with equal logic might be *He ate eggs scrambled with ham,* in which *ham* is subordinate to *eggs,* or *He ate ham garnished with scrambled eggs,* in which *eggs* is subordinate. In the second and third sentences, ham and eggs are not shown to be coordinate; they are not listed as two items of equal rank, independent of each other, as they are in the first sentence. One is subordinate to the other, not because one is less important, but because the writer wants to talk about them differently—about eggs as they are prepared in a particular way involving ham, or about ham as it is served along with eggs. The sentence with coordination is like *He ate ham and cabbage;* the sentence with subordination is like *He ate poached eggs on whole wheat toast.* The writer has signaled the coordination by using *and* to connect the two items; he has signaled the subordination by putting one item into the pattern and position for modifiers (see 16-2).

Words in sentences, sentences in paragraphs, or paragraphs in longer compositions follow patterns of coordination and subordination—more complex than the relationships between ham and eggs described above, but essentially the same. In the kinds of paragraphs illustrated in Section 2, for instance, the sentences following the topic statement are usually all subordinate to the topic sentence and coordinate with each other. In the paragraph by James Agee, sentences 1 and 5 are coordinate, related in the same way to the general subject of the paragraph. Sentences 2, 3, and 4 are coordinate with one another but are all subordinate to 1; and 6, 7, 8, and 9 are similarly coordinate with one another but subordinate to 5. Or consider another paragraph arranged so that coordinate sentences have the same left margin, but indentation indicates subordination (coordination and subordination within the sentences are not indicated, although obviously there).

[1] The intellectual life of the nineteenth century was more complex than that of any previous age.
    [2] This was due to several causes.

[3] First: The area concerned was larger than ever before; America and Russia made important contributions, and Europe became more aware than formerly of Indian philosophies, both ancient and modern.

[4] Second: Science, which had been a chief source of novelty since the seventeenth century, made new conquests, especially in geology, biology, and organic chemistry.

[5] Third: Machine production profoundly altered the social structure, and gave men a new conception of their powers in relation to the physical environment.

[6] Fourth: A profound revolt, both philosophical and political, against traditional systems in thought, in politics, and in economics, gave rise to attacks upon many beliefs and institutions that had hitherto been regarded as unassailable.

[7] This revolt had two very different forms, one romantic, the other rationalistic.

[8] (I am using these words in a liberal sense.)

[9] The romantic revolt passes from Byron, Schopenhauer, and Nietzsche to Mussolini and Hitler; the rationalistic revolt begins with the French philosophers of the Revolution, passes on, somewhat softened, to the philosophical radicals in England, then acquires a deeper form in Marx and issues in Soviet Russia.

—BERTRAND RUSSELL, *A History of Western Philosophy*

The patterns stand out partly because the writer has used obvious, almost over-formal, signals to help the reader. Sentences 3–6, for instance, are shown to be coordinate not only by their parallel form but by the introductory words which label them as items in a list of coordinate clauses. Similarly, the repetition of *revolt* from sentence 6 to open 7 helps the reader see that 7 will expand 6 and be subordinate to it, that it will not be coordinate and offer a fifth cause. The same device relates 9 to 7.

Paragraphs do not always, of course, follow the sequences of most of the examples above; coordination and subordination can be shown in a wide variety of patterns. The following, more complicated paragraph indicates one of many possible arrangements:

[1] It is sometimes said to be characteristic of our time that we undo the spiritual structures of our ancestors; whatever they sacralized we desacralized. [2] They retreated from the evident unholiness of the world into images which stored up the strength of those moments when it seemed holy or terrible in a different way. [3] They built in order to make space sacred, and in their rites they abolished the terrors of time, as spring kills winter and St. George the dragon. [4] They made books which were compact of all the world and of all its history, syllabically inspired and, like nature itself, signed

with the secret meanings of a god. [5] We build to serve human functions, and not to make models of a divine world: cathedrals that were living bibles, churches proportioned as the music of the spheres. [6] We live, more than any of our ancestors, in a time become linear and patternless. [7] Our books inform or divert in a purely human sense. [8] Where a book continues to be venerable, we attribute its power to different causes; we demythologize, find reasons in nature for its being as it is; we see it as figuring not the whole world of knowledge but dead men's knowledge of the world. [9] It sinks into history, becomes the victim of our perspectival trick, falls under the rule of time. [10] So we desacralize the world. —FRANK KERMODE, *The Patience of Shakespeare*

The paragraph is more difficult than those cited above, partly because it remains relatively abstract, occupied with ideas. It is logically organized, however, with materials coordinated and sub-ordinated to show the relationships the writer wishes to emphasize. The topic sentence makes a proposition relating past and present, requiring explanation of both if its contention is to convince. Sentences 2–4 are subordinate to one part of the topic sentence—what our ancestors did. Sentences 5–9 are subordinate to the second part —what we do in our time. Sentence 10 repeats the proposition of the topic sentence briefly but at the same time more broadly as it extends the desacralizing to the world. The coordination and sub ordination might be outlined as follows:

TOPIC, PART 1	TOPIC, PART 2
2	5
3	6
4	7
	8
	9
10	

The writer, developing a complex abstract argument, uses coordination and subordination to keep his ideas in order.

Revealing the Plan of the Paragraph 3-3

Since a paragraph takes its plan or its structure in order to express relationships between ideas, the writer should help the reader see his plan. Usually the topic sentence provides the first guideposts, especially when a paragraph falls into parts, as many expository paragraphs do. A paragraph may begin with such obvious structural markers as in the following:

These results can be accounted for in any of three ways.

The writer will then treat the three ways one after the other and will indicate when the first stops and the second begins; he may even label them, *first, second, third.* He may feel no occasion to be so pedestrian; but if he is a careful, orderly writer he will still keep his three parts separate and will let his reader know when he passes from one to the other, as the author does in the following description of a neighboring genial maniac whom he had known as a child.

> One of Mrs. Sedley's inner convictions was that she was the nymph of the spring in the valley which provided our drinking water. This conviction usually smote her in the evening shortly after sundown. Once she had been smitten, Mrs. Sedley got into a white nightgown, let down her stringy gray hair, and walked to the spring. She then washed her feet in the water and sang original little songs as she dabbled about the rim of the pool. If anyone came near her, she called a cheery greeting and said: "I am the nymph of this spring. Won't you be a nymph too?" No one ever accepted her invitation, but that didn't trouble Mrs. Sedley. She stuck a few flowers in her hair, sang another song, and went on being the nymph of the spring until someone from her house missed her and sent a servant down to lead her home. There were rumors afloat that if the servant didn't get to the spring soon enough, Mrs. Sedley was smitten by a conviction that a nymph wore no clothes, but my sister and I, though we watched her a number of evenings, never saw anything to confirm this. —JOHN J. ESPEY, *Minor Heresies*

The paragraph runs so smoothly that it can be read with no more than a vague awareness of its organization, but it is developed in three parts as carefully controlled as though Espey had marked them *first, second, third.* The first sentence is clearly the topic sentence, after which the first portion begins with "This conviction," the second with "If anyone came near," and the third with "There were rumors afloat."

If the paragraph dealt with difficult material, such easy-going indications of plan would probably be insufficient; the writer might well feel that he needed what would amount to three minor paragraphs within his paragraph, each with its own clear topic sentence, perhaps each with its own conclusion. The organization should be adapted to the material, but all careful writing should have plan, and within the paragraph it should contain sufficient evidence of this plan, the subject matter and the reader being what and who they are.

Guide to Revision **3** ¶

Organize paragraphs into logical units, using coordination and subordination to relate ideas.

¶ a   Choppy Paragraphing   3a

For reasons unrelated to the logical development of a paragraph—reasons of appearance and quick readability—newspaper writers customarily start a new paragraph every few lines, often at the end of every sentence. In writing that does not follow the special forms of journalism, however, choppy paragraphing usually indicates that sentences are not organized to reveal coordination and subordination. A series of short paragraphs is usually symptomatic of either weak organization or lack of development; that is, the writer has not worked out the relationships among his ideas, or he is writing down one topic sentence after another without development.

ORIGINAL

[1] In the suburbs and on the highways of many large American cities, young men are killing themselves by the thousands.

[2] Many of the accidents could be avoided if a little common sense were used. When a boy gets behind the steering wheel of a car, the first thing he thinks of is how fast he can go.

[3] Speed is the reason for so many deaths. The teen-ager does not seem to realize that his car is dangerous if it is not used sensibly.

[4] There is another reason for a large number of teen-age automobile accidents.

[5] This is the playing of games with cars. These senseless games kill

REVISION

On the highways in and around many large American cities, young men are killing themselves by the thousands in automobile accidents which could be avoided by the use of a little common sense. First, young drivers must learn to be sensible about speed. When a boy gets behind a steering wheel, the first thing he thinks of is how fast he can go. He does not seem to realize that his car is dangerous if it is not used sensibly. Second, young drivers must learn some sense about the senseless games played with cars which kill hundreds of teen-agers each year.

The most popular game is "Ditch 'Em." Two or more cars. . . .

[*Five paragraphs have been combined*

45

ORIGINAL (*Cont.*)

hundreds of teen-agers every year.
[6] The most popular game is
"Ditch 'Em." Two or more cars. . . .
[*The body of the theme concerns the
game mentioned in paragraph 6, but the
preceding matter is broken into what appear as five paragraphs. This introduction
is not well planned or closely knit, but such
plan as it has is obscured by the meaningless indentations.*]

REVISION (*Cont.*)

*into one, but the revision has involved
more than removing the indentations. For
example, the first two sentences have become a single sentence, with elements subordinated. The three sentences of paragraphs 4 and 5 have become a single sentence. Sentences have been reworked to provide continuity between them, and the remark of the original about common sense
has been exploited to provide unity.*]

3b   Revealing the Plan of the Paragraph   ¶ b

A paragraph should be built upon a conscious plan, and this
plan should be apparent to the reader. There are many methods
of making a plan clear; the most common employ a topic sentence,
supplemented with other transitional material at various points
through the paragraph.

ORIGINAL

Gail McDermott is likely to win
the election as president of the Associated Students. He is both a quarterback and an actor, and has support from organizations all over the
campus. Meanwhile, some candidates for offices are running unopposed or are opposed by candidates
who have little support. The widest
interest in the election is being drawn
by the races for the three vacant seats
in the Student Senate. Many campaigners believe that the election of
so many as one candidate for the
Senate supported by the Associated
Resident Halls Party, known as The
Barbs, will assure the decline or
abolishment of football at State University. The reasons for this belief are
complicated and will later require
some analysis. Meanwhile, Nancy
Jenkins and Dorothy Cochran are
leading a lively field of candidates for
the presidency of AWS. That race is
attracting no attention off the cam-

REVISION

Interest in the State University
student elections this year centers in
the race for the three vacant seats in
the Student Senate. The other contests are likely to be side shows. Gail
McDermott, known as both an actor
and a quarterback, has support from
so many organizations that his election as president of the Associated
Students is practically conceded.
Some of the class officers are running
unopposed, and other races are attracting little attention. None of the
freshman candidates, for instance, is
well known or widely supported. For
the presidency of AWS, Nancy Jenkins and Dorothy Cochran are leading a lively field of candidates, but
the race is attracting no attention off
the campus and relatively little on
the campus. The election of three
members to the Senate, on the other
hand, has become a question of interest throughout the state and has
led to so much electioneering that

ORIGINAL *(Cont.)*

pus, and very little on the campus, though the question of who is to be elected to the Student Senate has become a statewide issue. The other contests, except for the race for the Student Senate, are side-shows. None of the freshman candidates, for instance, is well known or widely supported. But the Senate race has raised questions of such interest and has stimulated so much electioneering that billboard space is getting scarce on the campus, with placards plastered all the way from the President's gate to the back door of the Aggie Greenhouse.

[*Much of the effect of this paper is lost for lack of apparent plan. The topic sentence is inadequate as an introduction, and although the nature of the material suggests division into two or more parts, these parts do not become readily clear. Furthermore, since this is an opening paragraph, it should lead naturally to the next paragraph, which it does not.*]

REVISION *(Cont.)*

placards are plastered all the way from the President's gate to the back door of the Aggie Greenhouse. The issue, of course, is the future of football at State University, and many campaigners believe that the election of so many as one candidate from the Associated Resident Halls Party, known as The Barbs, will assure the decline or the abolishment of football at State University. The reasons for this belief are complicated and will require some analysis.

[*The paragraph now has a clear plan. The topic sentence announces the purpose. A subtopic sentence introduces the campaigns of minor interest. The discussion of candidates is tied together by synonyms. The second half of the paragraph is introduced by "The election of three members to the Senate, on the other hand. . . ." It leads to a conclusion and a transition to the succeeding paragraph.*]

¶ c   Dialogue Paragraphs   3c

To help the reader identify speakers, writers of dialogue—especially in fiction—have adopted the convention of beginning a new paragraph whenever the speaker changes, as indicated in the version on the right below.

"Good evening. It's a cold night," said Holmes. The salesman nodded, and shot a questioning glance at my companion. "Sold out of geese, I see," continued Holmes, pointing at the bare slabs of marble. "Let you have 500 tomorrow morning." "That's no good."

"Good evening. It's a cold night," said Holmes.

The salesman nodded, and shot a questioning glance at my companion.

"Sold out of geese, I see," continued Holmes, pointing at the bare slabs of marble.

"Let you have 500 tomorrow morning."

"That's no good."

Exercise 3

A. The following paragraphs vary in structure, some of them being more complex than the examples in Section 2. Analyze each: describe its structure in an outline like those in 3-1 or 3-2 and observe how general and specific comments are used. Sentences are numbered for reference.

1. [1] There were two ancient Greek philosophers, long before even Socrates haunted the streets of Athens, who had diametrically opposed views about reality. [2] There was Parmenides, who argued that all change is illusory, transitory, imperfect, unreal. [3] And later there was Heraclitus, who saw reality as a flowing river, apparently the same but never the same, to whom all was constant flux and change, and who dismissed the permanent as unreal, as evidence of human imperfection, as a distortion of reality.

   —EMMANUEL G. MESTHENE, *Learning to Live with Science*

2. [1] I do not mean to suggest that this portrait of America, composed by fifty years of history and two world wars, was wholly flattering. [2] No nation is universally admired until time has left it 3,000 years behind, and even then there will be Alcibiades in the stern of the ship and Socrates' murderers. [3] We had our critics—as many critics, indeed, as we had contemporaries. [4] We were too rich. [5] We talked in a rather childish way about brinkmanship, like two boys daring each other to walk out on a railroad trestle. [6] Our principal exports —tourists and Coca-Cola—were not everywhere well received. [7] Nevertheless, the essential figure was still the figure Wilson had presented—Wilson and that innocent doughboy of the First World War. [8] We still talked in the vocabulary of the vast ideal and backed it up with enormous gifts of goods and money. [9] And above all, though we had more power than any nation in the history of the world had ever had, we still refrained from the use of power except as a deterrent.

   —ARCHIBALD MACLEISH, *What Is "Realism" Doing to American History?*

3. [1] I have been emphasizing the importance of study and investigation as ends in themselves and insisting that the *raison d'être* of the universities is to further those ends for their own sakes and not as means to anything else. [2] But I am not advocating that academic work should be treated as a closed mystery, or that every undergraduate should be regarded as carrying a professorial chair in his knapsack. [3] To say that study is an attitude of mind and way of life with criteria and interests peculiar to itself is not to deny that someone who has been trained in that way of life may for that very reason be the more successful in quite different walks of life. [4] To bring this out

it is necessary to distinguish between the concept of the "life of an individual" and that of the "life of an institution." [5] To speak of the life of an institution is, I have suggested, to speak of a specific tradition, a definite way of doing things, involving interests, methods, and criteria peculiar to itself. [6] But it would be a mistake to regard the life of an individual person in this circumscribed way. [7] Just as a society contains many different ways of life, so does an individual participate in many different ways of life. [8] And the ways in which the various kinds of activity in which a person participates influence each other (and therefore him) in the course of life may be compared to the ways in which different forms of activity may influence each other within a whole society. [9] Only if academic institutions maintain the integrity of their own specific ways of working will academic training continue to be of value to someone who proposes to devote most of his life to the service of some other institution.

—PETER WINCH, *Universities and the State*

B. The following paragraphs are not well planned; they lack topic sentences and do not have any logical pattern of coordination and subordination. Rewrite each into a logical, well-organized paragraph, supplying topical material as necessary.

1. There are many dictionaries on the market, and some of these are reprints of older dictionaries. Some are good and some are bad. Some of these reprints reproduce books which were badly prepared when they were new, and some of them are reprints of books which were once good, but are now out of date. Many of them carry the name *Webster* on the title page. In fact, more than 140 dictionaries have that name on the cover, and the word *Webster* has been declared by the Supreme Court as part of public domain. Thus anyone can now use the word if he wants to, although anyone who uses it must be able to show that he follows principles laid down by Noah Webster. This, however, is not hard, and thus the word *Webster* does not tell much about what is inside a dictionary.

2. Although it is far from the largest museum in New York, the Cloisters is one of the most interesting for its size in the city, well arranged and well managed. It provides ready and revealing insight into the Middle Ages. Here, within a few miles of the greatest industrial concentration in the world, is a little bit of the Middle Ages. Parts of five French cloisters, with their ancient stonework from corbels to statues, have been taken down stone by stone and re-erected here.

3. The electric saw is certainly one invention which has helped the modern carpenter. With an electric saw a carpenter can cut the frame for a small house in a few hours. Or with an electric drill an electrician can drill the frame for wiring in a short time. In the old days, cutting framing timbers by hand was a long and tedious job, in spite of a sharp saw. Today few people are alive who know how to sharpen a

saw properly. And drilling was always a long and hard job. In the same manner the sanding and finishing of hardwood floors has been simplified by electrical tools.

C. A rather ignorant and illogical woman visited the Comstock Lode during the mining boom and wrote a description of the mines. It reads in part as follows:

In many of the mines the miners cannot strike the pick more than three blows before they have to go to the cooling station and stay double the time they are at work.

The cooling stations are where they have a free circulation of air. These stations are on every level. They have large tanks or reservoirs to hold the water that is pumped from one level to another. These vats are often full of boiling water. In many of the mines the water is so hot that if a person slips into one of these tanks, he is generally scalded to death before he can be rescued.

If he is rescued alive, it is only to linger a few days, suffering the most intense agony, till death relieves him of his sufferings. He is often so completely cooked in the scalding vats that the flesh drops from the bones while taking him out. His suffering and agony are terrible to witness.

The heat of the mines is very great. In some mines it is almost unendurable. In such mines it is almost impossible to work, while in others they can work without such excessive heat.

Miners are brought to the surface almost daily from overheat.

There is scarcely a day in the year that there is not from one to two funerals among the miners; and I have known of there being five in one day.

There are a great many different causes of death. Sometimes death is caused by the caving in of rock, or by falling into the scalding tanks, or by a misstep, by falling hundreds of feet down the shafts or inclines.

—MRS. M. M. MATHEWS, *Ten Years in Nevada,
or Life on the Pacific Coast*

This writing is not without promise. It contains concrete observation and some significant generalization, but the whole is jotted down in a scatterbrained way. Try to make a good paragraph of this material, expressing a central idea in a topic sentence, developing the paragraph in accordance with some orderly plan, and omitting extraneous matter.

D. The following sentences might serve as topic sentences for paragraphs. Use the list for practice. Try to write different sorts of paragraphs on the same topic sentence, and select different sentences as the basis for paragraphs with varying patterns.

1. The word *tradition* often takes on new and special meanings in campus life.

2. General misunderstanding of teen-agers can develop from a variety of causes.
3. Fashions in popular music have changed considerably during the past few years.
4. Styles in campus clothing seem to grow more from the student's desire for comfort and convenience than from his interest in being attractive.
5. Students have come to accept and even to like regimentation.
6. I am still interested in many of the books I read as a child, but for new reasons.
7. Attending a small college has advantages as well as disadvantages.
8. Our educational system has become too dependent on test scores.
9. One problem for the entering freshman is learning a new vocabulary of campus slang.
10. It is hard to believe that large masses of people can take television advertising seriously.

Adequate Development

*For
Guide to Revision,
see page 61.*

Facts support judgments; details clarify generalizations.

We have all heard the kind of fruitless conversation which is a string of vociferously maintained opinions:

"Modern music is no good. It isn't worth listening to. You have to go back to the old masters if you want to hear something."

"You don't know what you're talking about. There's a lot of good modern music."

"No, there isn't. The moderns just turn out popularized tripe."

"Oh, no, they don't. It's the long-hairs that turn out tripe."

Such dialogue, obviously unproductive as communication, can only exaggerate confusion or lead to a fistfight. Similarly, much bad writing fails because it consists mainly of unsubstantiated judgments or opinions.

Paragraphs like those described in Sections 2 and 3—as well as longer units of composition—require not only topic sentences or main ideas but elaboration, explanation, development, or support for them. Preceding discussions have already emphasized that writing can be thought of as a process of addition and that a topic statement usually makes a commitment, obligating the writer to further comment (see 2-4). Section 4 suggests means of meeting the commitment implied in a main idea, of expanding or supporting a proposition.

4-1 Distinguishing Fact and Judgment

Compare the following sets of statements:

JUDGMENT: Martha is a bad girl.
FACT: Martha took two pieces of candy without asking.
JUDGMENT: Snidhart is a murderer.

FACT: Two witnesses saw Snidhart shoot twice at the cashier who died in the hospital this morning.
JUDGMENT: Smith's dog kills sheep.
FACT: I saw Smith's dog kill a sheep.
JUDGMENT: College football is on the way out.
FACT: In many major universities, football costs are increasing more rapidly than gate receipts.

The judgments are opinions, decisions, pronouncements. They characterize or classify; they express approval or disapproval; they make a general statement. Their truth or falsity cannot finally be demonstrated. The facts report what has happened or exists; they result from observation or measurement or calculation; they can be tested or verified.

Most statements, however, cannot be distinguished so sharply as these examples. A comment like "I believe that Martha is a bad girl" can be called fact—presumably the writer knows what he believes—but it obviously includes a judgment. Or a primarily factual statement like "We saw the murderer Snidhart shoot the cashier" includes a judgment in the label *murderer*. Furthermore, judgments are not always so nearly final as those above. They often are plausible opinions which provoke thought or lead to factual development:

A little learning is a dangerous thing.
Athletics are a valuable part of an educational program.

Many statements are somewhere between, seemingly factual but not clearly verifiable. They often introduce substantiating evidence or illustrative fact.

The trouble with youth is that it belongs to those who are too young to enjoy it.
College football has ceased to have any relation to education.

Obviously, not all statements can be clearly classified, but fact and judgment can usually be distinguished as products of different kinds of thinking, and judgments and facts have different uses in writing.

Judgments are deceptively easy to come by. We hear them all about us; and often, especially if we think uncritically, we accept them because other people do. When we need to put words on paper, judgments and opinions often occur to us first, but they impair writing unless they introduce factual material. Facts are harder to collect than judgments, but judgments are useless without them.

Furthermore, accepted at face value, judgments impede the writer because they tend to bring his thinking to a dead end. In serious writing, judgments as nearly final as those cited above leave the reader only two choices: agreement or denial. Confronted by "John is a fool" a reader can only agree or say, "He is not." The judgment opens no further discussion. It begins by settling the matter. Such a judgment, in other words, is so sweeping that it cannot be substantiated, even by evidence that John behaved foolishly. The writer can only reassert his opinion, and repetition does not convince. The successful writer, therefore, recognizes the limited usefulness of judgments, preferring statements which he can develop with facts.

4-2 General and Specific

Judgments are usually more general than facts, although *general* and *specific* are relative terms. That is, things or expressions are not absolutely or finally general or specific, but only more general or more specific than something else. *Animal* is more general than *horse* but more specific than *creature,* and *horse* is more general than *Dobbin.* The general expression is broader, more inclusive; it tends to refer to a whole class, a type, or a group. As a statement becomes more specific it approaches pointing to a particular, to a single individual object. *Man* is more specific than *living being; American citizen* is more specific than *man; John Jones* is more specific than *American citizen.* Compare the following examples:

College activities are bad.
Extracurricular activities in college are harmful to the student.
Extracurricular activities in college prevent good academic work.
Bill Jones failed chemistry because he spent too much time in dramatics.

Each statement is more specific than the one preceding it.

4-3 Specification and Development

This direction of thought, pushing toward the specific, is the characteristic pattern of expository writing. Generalization has its uses, since the idea that ranges widely often expresses the purpose or point of a piece of writing; but understanding sharpens as the writer explains his general observations in specific terms the reader can grasp. Modern prose, even in a unit as small as the single sentence, develops in large part through specification (see 21-10). The following sequence of sentences illustrates a typical movement.

[1] Change in meaning is frequently due to ethical, or moral, considerations. [2] A word may, as it were, go downhill, or it may rise in the world; there is no way of predicting what its career may be. [3] *Politician* has had a downhill development in American English; in British English it is still not entirely without honor.

— THOMAS PYLES, *The Origin and Development of the English Language*

The three sentences open a paragraph by moving successively toward greater specificity. Sentence 2 moves to a level of greater specificity than 1 by pointing out a precise way in which a word may change for ethical or moral reasons—by going up or down hill. Then 3 moves to another stage with a particular illustration of meaning change in the word *politician*. The paragraph continues at the same level of specification, using other words as examples of the kind of change described in 2.

The following opening of a paragraph begins in the same way:

[1] Like most of the American Indians, except those of the Southwest pueblos, the tribes of the Northwest Coast were Dionysian. [2] In their religious ceremonies the final thing they strove for was ecstasy. [3] The chief dancer, at least at the high point of his performance, should lose normal control of himself and be rapt into another state of existence. [4] He should froth at the mouth, tremble violently and abnormally, do deeds which would be terrible in a normal state. — RUTH BENEDICT, *Patterns of Culture*

The paragraph begins with a general statement. The second sentence explains the first, and the term *Dionysian,* with a statement a little more specific. The third illustrates the second and the meaning of *ecstasy.* The fourth becomes more specific still in illustrating the third. As it becomes more specific, the writing becomes more vivid.

The same general movement toward specification may appear in more complex paragraphs.

[1] Viewed from the scrolled wooden veranda of a middle-class home in any one of a thousand towns on a buzzing summer twilight when ice cream was being served from the freezer, the 1890s were gay. [2] This home in its small town still gave the tone to the nation, as Howells's fiction comprehensively reveals. [3] From the factories in a hundred cities, however, and from the drought-stricken, mortgage-ridden farms of the great Plains, the age had a

different look. [4] The unchecked stream of immigration kept industrial wages low. [5] The wheat-growing states, beginning in 1887, suffered from ten consecutive years of drought; for five of those years there was practically no crop at all. [6] Meanwhile, the centralization of capital combined with advancing technology to make millionaires by the hundreds with an amazing swiftness. —LARZER ZIFF, *The Other Lost Generation*

The paragraph divides into two parts, with sentences 1 and 2 presenting a view to be contradicted in 3-6. Structurally, 2 seems subordinate to 1, an extension of the first topic that the 1890s were gay; but a large portion of 1 is a specification of *this home* in 2, and thus the paragraph opens with an unusual pattern. The second portion of the paragraph, however, approaches standard structure, with 3 presenting a topic and 4-6 subordinate to it and coordinate with one another.

As these paragraphs illustrate, specification characterizes the development in the paragraph patterns described in Sections 2 and 3. The standard paragraph in Section 2 opens with a topic statement, usually relatively general; and is followed by particulars that move toward specification. The topic-comment units combined in Section 3 might be described as generalization and specification. Furthermore, levels of subordination and levels of specification usually coincide so that subordinate sentences or parts of sentences tend to be relatively specific.

The basis of development in writing, then, is specification; adequate development requires the writer to find specific details or illustrations for his topic. This is not easy; it requires thinking and often reading or investigation, but any writer who has a judgment or generalization worth stating can find specific details with which to develop it. If, for example, the participants in the conversation about music that opens this section wanted to become serious and discuss their views, they could ask themselves questions about specific composers, specific compositions, or observable characteristics of the music, such as instrumentation, complexity of harmony, or range of subject matter. If they know enough even to justify the judgments they have been making, the answers to such questions will give them the specific details needed to develop their ideas.

4-4   Methods of Development

As indicated in 2-4, different subjects or different statements of main ideas commit a writer to different sorts of development. In fact, every composition, every paragraph requires its individual development, and no general principles or methods can be applied literally. Like the structural patterns of paragraphs (see Section 3), patterns of logic and meaning vary. Although the development almost always involves some degree of specificaton, many kinds of specifying materials may be used. The following types are only samples of some of the kinds of development that differing sorts of topic sentence require, and even the examples here are not entirely typical. Most paragraphs do not concentrate as closely as these on any one procedure, but combine approaches as the subject dictates.

1. *Citing particulars, instances, examples, illustrations.* Topic sentences, whether they state propositions or prescribe the structure of the paragraph, may lead to particulars or illustrations. The following paragraph has a structural topic sentence; that is, it simply introduces the list of examples that follow it:

> The foregoing are particularly striking examples, but hundreds of others could be cited. We find generalization in such everyday words as *picture*, once restricted, as the etymology would suggest (compare: the Picts, "painted ones"), to a *painted* representation of something seen, but now applicable to photography, crayon drawing, and so forth; *butcher*, who once slew one animal only, the goat (French *bouc*); the verb *sail*, which has been transferred to steam navigation, just as *drive* has been transferred to self-propelled vehicles . . . . —STUART ROBERTSON and FREDERIC G. CASSIDY, *The Development of Modern English*

The paragraph continues with examples, as the topic sentence promises it will. The writer cannot, of course, collect all possible examples or instances, but he has enough to illustrate what he means by his generalization. Similarly, the following paragraph begins with a topic sentence that introduces what is to follow:

> From the moment that one doesn't take composing for granted in our country, a dozen questions come to mind. What is the composer's life in America? Does it differ so very much from that of the European or even the Latin American composer of today? Or from the life of United States composers in other periods? Are our objectives and purposes the same as they have always been? —AARON COPLAND, *Music and Imagination*

The writer does not complete the dozen he has promised, but he does develop by listing particulars. The following paragraph opens with a sentence which less obviously dictates structure but introduces two topics—the evening and the crowds—each developed by citing specific characteristics of the scene.

> It was early evening of a day in the late fall and the Winesburg County Fair had brought crowds of country people into town. The day had been clear and the night came on warm and pleasant. On the Trunion Pike, where the road after it left town stretched away between berry fields now covered with dry brown leaves, the dust from passing wagons arose in clouds. Children, curled into little balls, slept on the straw scattered on wagon beds. Their hair was full of dust and their fingers black and sticky. The dust rolled away over the fields and the departing sun set it ablaze with colors.
> —SHERWOOD ANDERSON, *Winesburg, Ohio*

Often, as in the following, the topic sentence offers a proposition that can be illustrated by specific instances.

> But, indeed, the dictum that truth always triumphs over persecution is one of those pleasant falsehoods which men repeat after one another till they pass into commonplaces, but which all experience refutes. History teems with instances of truth put down by persecutions. If not suppressed forever, it may be thrown back for centuries. To speak only of religious opinions: the Reformation broke out at least twenty times before Luther, and was put down. Arnold of Brescia was put down. Fra Dolcino was put down. Savonarola was put down. The Lollards were put down. The Hussites were put down.
> —JOHN STUART MILL, *On Liberty*

The paragraph uses two sentences to expand the topic sentence and make it more specific, then shifts to one kind of opinion—religious —and cites specific instances. Often the particulars cited provide reasons or explanations to support an opening thesis.

> The Yellow or Silver Pine is more frequently overturned than any other tree on the Sierra, because its leaves and branches form the largest mass in proportion to its height, while in many places it is planted sparsely, leaving long, open lanes, through which storms may enter with full force. Furthermore, because it is distributed along the lower portion of the range, which was the first to be left bare on the breaking up of the ice-sheet at the close of the glacial winter, the soil it is growing upon has been longer exposed to post-glacial weathering, and consequently is in a more crumbling, decayed condition than the fresher soils farther up the range, and therefore offers a less secure anchorage for the roots.   —JOHN MUIR, *The Passes of the Sierra*

The development presents a series of sentences justifying the opening assertion that the Yellow Pine is most frequently overturned.

2. *Incident, extended illustration.*   Instead of offering a series of instances, a writer may make his point by telling a story or describing a single illustration in some detail. Ruth Benedict, supporting the proposition that happiness depends upon social customs, begins

her book *Patterns of Culture* by recounting her conversations with a chief of the Digger Indians of California. The following paragraph uses one event in the life of Adolf Hitler to illustrate a more general observation about his tactics.

> Surprise was a favourite gambit of Hitler's, in politics, diplomacy, and war: he gauged the psychological effect of sudden, unexpected hammer-blows in paralysing opposition. An illustration of his appreciation of the value of surprise and quick decision, even when on the defensive, is the second presidential campaign of 1932. It had taken Goebbels weeks to persuade Hitler to stand for the Presidency at all. The defeat in the first ballot brought Goebbels to despair; but Hitler, now that he had committed himself, with great presence of mind dictated the announcement that he would stand a second time and got it on to the streets almost before the country had learned of his defeat. In war the psychological effect of the *Blitzkrieg* was just as important in Hitler's eyes as the strategic: it gave the impression that the German military machine was more than life-size, that it possessed some virtue of invincibility against which ordinary men could not defend themselves. —ALAN BULLOCK, *Hitler: A Study In Tyranny*

The first sentence generalizes about Hitler's reliance on surprise; the second introduces an illustration; the next three describe what happened in 1932; the final sentence generalizes again, relating the incident of 1932 to the general proposition of the first sentence.

3. *Analogy.* In analogy, a special kind of illustration, the writer draws a parallel, explaining the unknown by something familiar. The device is common; to explain the rotation of the earth to a child, we might use a rubber ball or a top. Victor Hugo describes the Battle of Waterloo as a giant letter *A*. Thomas Henry Huxley in a famous analogy says that life is like a game of chess. The following paragraph uses a literary analogy to begin its discussion of man's failure to resist mass pressures that can drive him back toward savagery.

> Of all the sad experiences of these last twelve years this is perhaps the most dreadful one. It may be compared to the experience of Odysseus on the island of Circe. But it is even worse. Circe had transformed the friends and companions of Odysseus into various animal shapes. But here are men, men of education and intelligence, honest and upright men who suddenly give up the highest human privilege. They have ceased to be free and personal agents. Performing the same prescribed rites they begin to feel, to think, and to speak in the same way. . . .
> —ERNST CASSIRER, *The Myth of the State*

4. *Comparison and contrast.* The paragraph of analogy above demonstrates also another technique of development, in which the writer cites similarities and differences. A proposition like

59

"Boston is not a small New York" would require noting differences between the cities. The following paragraph uses the method in a rather complex pattern, citing contrasting incidents:

> But there is another side to the War and one that it would be wrong to ignore or minimize—the side of glory. There was glory enough for each side. The North has its legends (true legends) as well as the South. There is the desperate and fruitless courage of Fredericksburg; there is the rush by Missionary Ridge; there are the heroic stories of units like the 20th Maine at Gettysburg; there is Sheridan riding on to the field at Cedar Creek and turning the tide of battle like Desaix at Marengo. There is most impressive of all, the disciplined and despairing advance at Cold Harbor. Here is glory. But whether the South has more glory than the North or not (I think it has), it needs it more and, as is right, cherishes it more. It cherishes the fame of the most Plutarchian (and greatest) American soldier, "Marse Robert." It cherishes or should cherish, with Pickett's attack, the memory of Hood's men advancing to their doom at Franklin. And for the individual heroic actions, their name is legion. It should remember with pride, not that there were so few under arms to surrender with Lee or Johnston, but that there were still so many.   —D. W. BROGAN, *A Fresh Appraisal of the Civil War*

The first three sentences develop the topic, establishing parallels and contrasts between legends of the North and South; then the paragraph breaks into two divisions providing particulars.

5. *Restatement and amplification.*   Almost all the examples above are variations on the use of particulars to support a topic or a proposition. Most paragraphs do develop in such patterns, illustrating the general with the more specific. Sometimes, however, a paragraph—especially an introductory paragraph or a short summary paragraph—may need mainly to restate or amplify an idea, sometimes revealing varying implications of the topic. Consider the following:

> Another obvious practical point is that the goal of education, in a cognitive world as eclectic, as ignorant, as accidental, as disorganized as ours inevitably will be, needs very much to be rethought. We need, certainly in higher education, to be sure that some genuine experience of discovery and rediscovery is a part of the life of everyone who is educated; we need to be sure that some genuine appreciation of the gulf which separates knowledge and ignorance is also a part of it. I say this because only people who have been through these experiences are intellectually prepared to live in a world in which they are surrounded by knowledge of which they will largely remain ignorant, prepared not to take the vulgar and superficial account of knowledge for the reality.   —J. ROBERT OPPENHEIMER, *ACLS Annual Lecture*

Even here the movement is primarily toward specification; the second sentence restates the first somewhat more specifically, and the third produces a reason.

Guide to Revision **4**   Dev

Rewrite, eliminating repetitious or undeveloped judgments or supplying adequate development with facts and specific details.

The writer who cannot finish a paper because "he has said everything he knows" may be partly right; he has stated every conclusion, every judgment or opinion, that he can relate to his topic. In another sense, the writer is stalled because he has not really started, he is repeating judgments but has not thought of anything to say about them. Usually writing which lacks adequate development requires two types of revision.

First, the generalizations need to be reconsidered—limited or revised so that they can be supported (see 2-4). The generalizations may be too inclusive, so sweeping that they cannot be illustrated. The writer who begins by saying "American teachers are uneducated" may shock his readers into interest, but he also makes logical development of his paper almost impossible. How can he obtain convincing data on all teachers? Unless he wishes merely to repeat judgments, he must modify his assertion by suggesting that he means "many teachers" and "inadequately educated"; and when he modifies in this way, only a rather obvious comment remains. If he makes his general statement more specific—for instance, "Many American teachers have not been trained for the jobs they are required to do"—he opens the way for illustration.

Second, the generalizations need to be developed—not merely restated or repeated. The writer must marshal the facts he knows or must look up new material to clarify or illustrate what he has asserted. With his more specific statement on teachers, for instance, the writer mentioned above might cite examples of teachers he has known who have been put into jobs for which they have not been prepared. Such illustrations would not prove the generalization, but they would show the reader more specifically what the generalization means. Or the writer might find statistics about teacher training—the numbers who are not teaching the subject of their college major, for example.

ORIGINAL

College education is much too expensive in America, and it is getting worse every day. Many deserving students either have to postpone college indefinitely or work so much of the time that they neglect their studies. If democracy is to survive, the government must provide some method for enabling more capable students to get college educations. Scholarship awards are unfair because they put a premium on memory and mental ability and not on character and need. If our country is to survive, something must be done about this problem.

[*It is no wonder that this paper stopped short of the required number of words; except for the second sentence, the paragraph is made up of undeveloped judgments, so broad that they discourage development. The writer should begin by abandoning the unnecessary judgments.*]

The old Union Building at Winnemac University must be replaced. We must have a modern building which will be worthy of an institution like Winnemac. The present building is a disgrace and a shame, far from providing any beneficial college atmosphere. Both inside and out the building is inadequate. It does not, even in the most elementary way, fulfill the needs of student body and faculty. The building stands out on the campus like a sore thumb.

REVISION

The cost of a college education in the United States has almost doubled in the last fifteen years. It is no longer easy for a young man to save enough from his paper route and a job in the soda fountain on Saturdays to see him through four years at a university. Tuition costs in many private institutions have doubled, and many state universities have had to increase fees substantially. The textbook that cost $5.00 a few years ago is likely to be $10.00 or $12.00 now. Inflated food prices have affected college cafeterias, and even the soft drink or cup of coffee which used to provide a couple of hours of afternoon recreation for a nickel is now ten or fifteen cents. . . .

[*The revision narrows the scope of the paragraph; instead of broad judgments, it uses a general factual statement which can be illustrated. It leaves the writer with a chance to develop his topic.*]

The old Union Building at Winnemac University is not meeting the needs of the student body. Its cafeteria offers only 75 seats to a student body of 8,000 residents. Its dance floor is so small that a hundred couples crowd it; as a result, Union dances are becoming more and more unpopular. The bookstore is so crowded that it cannot keep texts in stock. Furthermore, many important activities are entirely neglected. No rooms are available for meetings of student or faculty groups. There is

ORIGINAL (*Cont.*)

[*The writer of this paper also had trouble finishing, probably because he found a limit to the number of times he could say the same thing in different words. The paper fails because no idea is developed; it is a series of judgments—or repetitions of one judgment.*]

Obviously, the theater was everything that a university theater should be. It had all the qualities that one wants to find in a campus playhouse. In size and equipment it was almost perfect. It is no wonder that drama was so popular on the campus and that plays were so well attended. We should attempt to get something like it for our university. And the responsibility for action rests in part with the students themselves.

[*Like most examples of inadequate development, this passage from a student theme is general rather than specific; it repeats judgments; it includes in one short paragraph material which could be developed into a long theme. The writer gets into trouble at the beginning by failing to illustrate. The writer may be willing to make his obvious statement on the basis of his knowledge, but the reader does not have enough information to accept it.*]

More than one American statesman has revealed aptitude in fields quite unrelated to politics and diplomacy. It is possible to find men in our history who were capable of all sorts of tasks, ranging from manual labor to technical science. Many men were not only skillful in political affairs but really achieved a great deal in such occupations as printing, medicine, science, agriculture, finance. Among the men with broad interests in addition to their interests in affairs of state were Washington, Jefferson, Franklin, and others.

REVISION (*Cont.*)

no space for accommodation of guests of the University. There is no theater, no auditorium, no office space for publications or other activities.

[*The addition of some facts makes the judgments more plausible.*]

The theater was everything that a university theater should be. It was small and intimate, holding only about 250, and you could hear and see from every seat. The seats were comfortable but not new, and an occasional rip in the leather gave the place an atmosphere of permanence; it did not have the kind of polish that makes you expect to smell fresh paint when you walk in. There was no revolving stage or other complex machinery, but the stage was large and there was plenty of room to get around backstage. There was enough equipment to make possible all kinds of experiments—good and bad—but there was not enough to keep the stage crew from using ingenuity.

[*The first sentence of the original can be developed into a paragraph. If the other general statements of the original are to remain, they need similar illustration.*]

More than one American statesman has revealed aptitude in fields quite unrelated to politics and diplomacy. There was Jefferson, for example. An astute politician, he was also an important political philosopher, developing in his writing his theories that government should rest in the hands of the producing class. His interest in science was practical as well as theoretical; he is credited with a mathematical formula that still governs the shape of plowshares, with the invention of the swivel chair, and with the design of a

ORIGINAL *(Cont.)*

Many such men were always doing things not directly connected with national or foreign affairs.

[*The paragraph begins to develop at times, but it remains general and repetitious. Even a single well-developed example would illustrate better than do these general statements.*]

REVISION *(Cont.)*

leather buggy top. He contributed to the University of Virginia not only his knowledge as an educator but also the plans for the campus, one of the most beautifully arranged in America. He studied language and was one of the first Americans to learn Anglo-Saxon. His was the kind of inquisitive mind that found interest and new ideas in many subjects.

Exercise 4

A. Which of the following statements are mainly fact and which mainly judgment? Some may be considered more or less factual, depending upon the circumstances. For instance, if an entomologist says, "That is a golden-eyed fly," he may be identifying a tabanid of the genus Chrysopa, but if a five-year-old child makes the same remark he may be implying much less fact.

1. William James, elder brother of Henry James and one of America's most significant philosophers, was born in 1842 and died in 1910.
2. Water freezes at 32 degrees Fahrenheit.
3. The early bird catches the worm.
4. The road was a ribbon of moonlight across the purple moor.
5. Patriotism is the last refuge of a scoundrel.
6. If a man in someone else's house calls another a perjurer or accosts him insultingly with scandalous words, he shall pay 1*s.* to the householder, 6*s.* to the man whom he insulted, and 12*s.* to the king.
   —Anglo-Saxon Law, A.D. 685–86.
7. In the seventeenth century, although three hundred crimes in English law were punishable by death, the Massachusetts Body of Liberties listed only ten, and in some of the other states there were fewer.
8. Being in a ship is being in a jail—with the chance of being drowned
9. We cannot continue to support the nations of Europe forever.
10. Parallel lines will never meet, no matter how far extended.

B. Rearrange the roughly synonymous expressions in each of the following groups in order of their specificity, with the most general first and the most specific last.

1. *a*) dark dress
   b) Mary's black jersey shift
   c) wearing apparel
   d) garment contrived for the purpose of covering the female figure

2. *a*) drum
   b) musical instrument
   c) percussion instrument
   d) band instrument

3. *a*) It was a lovely scene.
   b) The western sky was deep blue-green with feathered gold spots where the sun broke through.
   c) The sky was bright-colored and lovely.
   d) The greenish western sky was mottled with gold spots.

4. *a*) The three major composers of the postromantic revolution are like the three brothers in the fairy tale who set off in different directions, follow divergent paths, and after sundry adventures arrive at much the same destination.
   b) The three major composers of the postromantic revolution used different methods and different procedures to achieve their ends but finally achieved new types of music.
   c) The three major composers of the postromantic period sought to move away from what they considered the sterility of nineteenth century music—Schoenberg through mathematics, Bartók through ethnography, Stravinsky through history.
   d) The changes which characterize the postromantic revolution in music came about through varying influences on composition.

5. *a*) The statue sat in the Museum of Modern Art garden impressive in its utilization of unusual materials and its effective symbolism, combining life and space in a complex symphony of light and shadow.
   b) Reuben Nakian's statue "Rape of Lucrece," in the Museum of Modern Art garden, is two interacting abstract figures constructed of variously shaped, movable plates of steel mounted on a skeleton of black pipe.
   c) Nakian's statue in the Museum of Modern Art garden was not a simple cubist construction but a complex play of light, shadow, and reflection, combining steel plates mounted in different planes.
   d) The statue in the garden was exciting and moving because of the sculptor's unusual approach to its subject matter and his skillful handling of its materials.

C. The following groups of sentences are from actual paragraphs but are not necessarily in their original order. Arrange them according to increasing specificity; that is, so that the most specific is last. Then decide whether this order seems the most logical one for the sentences within their paragraph.

1. *a*) All our energies ought to be going into the attempt to get world attention for this objective, so that a framework will be created within which sources of income will not depend on voluntary offerings or payments, any more than individual citizens may decide when, how, and if their taxes are to be paid.

   b) The United Nations is not a country club for privileged members who have access to the facilities so long as they keep up their dues.

   c) The United Nations is, or should be, a world constitutional body with complete jurisdiction in those matters concerning the common safety of the world's peoples.　　　　　　　—NORMAN COUSINS

2. *a*) However, the Chinese are a proud people.

   b) They are not partial to foreigners, and they are thoroughly confident of the superiority of their age-old culture.

   c) They have not yet recovered from the wounds and indignities which the Western world unjustly and arrogantly inflicted upon them during the last century.　　　　　　　—JAMES S. DUNCAN

3. *a*) *Huckleberry Finn* deals directly with the virtue and depravity of man's heart.

   b) *Tom Sawyer* has the truth of honesty—what it says about things and feelings is never false and always both adequate and beautiful.

   c) It is more intense truth, fiercer and more complex.

   d) The truth of *Huckleberry Finn* is of a different kind from that of *Tom Sawyer*.　　　　　　　—LIONEL TRILLING

D. The following selections concern change in language. Which contain broad judgments? Which judgments are buttressed by fact?

1. The worst vulgarism in English speech is a habit of prefixing a neutral vowel . . . to all the vowels and diphthongs. . . . When I pass an elementary school and hear the children repeating the alphabet in unison, and chanting unrebuked "Ah-yee, Be-yee, Ce-yee, De-yee," I am restrained from going in and shooting the teacher only by the fact that I do not carry a gun and by my fear of the police.

   　　　　—GEORGE BERNARD SHAW, *The Miraculous Birth of Language*

2. A happier expedient than the use of discarded meanings by modern writers would appear to be functional shift, which also figures largely in the creation of words and has been a source of fine poetic effects in the work of our greatest poets, including Shakespeare and Keats. Since poetry may frequently be called "double talk," that is, saying one thing in terms of another, a poetic image, the change in word usage which is called functional shift would appear to have its merits.

   　　　　—MARGARET BRYANT, *Modern English and Its Heritage*

3. All languages being imperfect, it does not follow that one should change them. One must adhere absolutely to the manner in which the

15558

good authors have spoken them; and when one has a sufficient number of approved authors, a language is fixed.

—VOLTAIRE, *Philosophical Dictionary*

4. As used in the title of this work, "Americanism" means a word or expression that originated in the United States. The term includes: outright coinages, as *appendicitis, hydrant, tularemia;* such words as *adobe, campus, gorilla,* which first became English in the United States; and terms such as *faculty, fraternity, refrigerator,* when used in senses first given them in American usage.

—MITFORD M. MATHEWS, *A Dictionary of Americanisms*

5. The mechanism of the English language would also be improved by the adoption or invention of some indefinite pronoun other than *one* to correspond in meaning and usage to French *on,* deriving from Latin *homo, hominem* "man," and to German *man,* which is readily distinguishable from *der Mann* both in speech (because, like *man* in the Scandinavian languages and like *men* in Dutch, it is pronounced with weaker stress and with reduced vowel) and in writing (since it has one final *n* and no initial capital).   —SIMEON POTTER, *Our Language*

E. Study the following student theme and determine which statements are primarily judgment and which primarily fact. Then select two judgments, rewrite them as generalizations limited enough to permit illustration, and make a list of facts which you might use in a paragraph illustrating each of your generalizations.

A good campus newspaper can be a great asset to any college or university. However, it must be truly a campus paper, and it should be very outstanding. Many campus papers are more concerned about national or international news than about the affairs right on the campus. They are all ill-advised. It is much more desirable for a campus paper to concentrate its efforts on local matters and leave major news stories to larger papers, which have the advantages of a huge staff and expensive news services.

Local news is just as important as the events that make the headlines in the large dailies. Students are often more interested in the campus prom queen election than in the election of a representative to Congress. Interest in local affairs is highly desirable. Everyone should be interested in what goes on in his immediate surroundings.

A paper which is primarily concerned with campus events also provides better training for budding journalists. This country, and every country in the world today, has need for good journalists. Journalism has much to do with the formation of public opinion, and in a democracy public opinion is very important. It is therefore of the greatest significance for a country like ours that papers should train the best type of journalist.

A local paper is also more interesting because it does not pretend to be something more important than it is. Any pretension is always unpleasant. We can, however, really be interested in a campus paper which tells us the things we want to hear about.

4

Exercises

> For these reasons I believe that a campus newspaper should be concentrated on reporting campus news.

F. Rewrite each of the following in specific terms, inventing specific details to develop the general statements:

> EXAMPLE: Later Milly and her mother were sitting outside looking as usual at the flowers.
>
> After lunch Milly and her mother were sitting as usual on the balcony beyond the salon, admiring for the five-hundredth time the stocks, the roses, the small, bright grass beneath the palm, and the oranges against a wavy line of blue.
> —KATHERINE MANSFIELD, *The Dove's Nest*

1. When we rose in the morning, we could see all over the streets the signs of the storm of the night.
2. Mary was always doing the kind of thing which gave her the reputation of being a girl you could not trust.
3. The shelves were packed with books of a great many kinds and varieties.
4. The pond was bordered by very beautiful patches of lovely flowers and shrubs.
5. The kitchen was well equipped with all the modern conveniences.
6. The white tablecloth was almost invisible because it was so thoroughly covered with so many good things to eat.
7. The children came to the Halloween party in the many kinds of costumes customary to such celebrations of an old holiday.
8. The desk was piled in high confusion with numerous evidences of Wendy's varied interests.
9. When Sue sat down to study, she always found her thoughts wandering off to many unrelated subjects.
10. Before he started in college, Phil had not realized that he would constantly be needing money for a variety of incidental and miscellaneous expenses.

G. List fifteen specific details which you might use in describing any three of the list below. Make the details concrete; prefer "the soiled brown chair with protruding springs" to "the furniture in the room."

1. A college room
2. A favorite restaurant
3. A teacher I know
4. A classroom
5. The lake front
6. A campus politician

List specific details which you might use to illustrate each of the following statements:

1. A university provides wide opportunities for wasting time.

2. Drugstores have become more than places that sell drugs.
3. The modern automobile has developed with concern for the comfort of driver and passengers.
4. Members of theater audiences are guilty of a variety of discourtesies.
5. Comic books are not designed exclusively for children.

Describe a specific instance which might be used to illustrate any five of the following statements:

1. Abraham Lincoln had great respect for the feelings of others.
2. Incidents of childhood may have profound effects on human beings.
3. Not all beautiful places in America have been discovered by tourists.
4. Athletes are not necessarily poor students.
5. Proverbs are not always applicable.
6. Pets can be nuisances.
7. Emergency measures sometimes become permanent parts of a social system.
8. Economy does not always pay
9. Newspaper columnists are not always right in their prophecies.
10. Individuals may profit from a war.

H. If you wish to discuss the fact that the lever action of a typewriter forces the typewriter key to travel at considerable speed, you might make your meaning clear by giving the ratio of the lever action in a specific typewriter and estimating the speed a key might attain under normal touch; that is, you might give an example. Or you might try to explain the lever action and its effect by comparing the typewriter key assembly to the human forearm; that is, you might use an analogy. For each of the following statements, supply (a) a possible example and (b) a possible analogy.

1. As modern furniture becomes more popular, prices are likely to drop.
2. A rocket attains its great speed through the propulsive powers of discharging gas.
3. The central portion of the United States is a great, shallow bowl.
4. An end run can be a deceptive play.
5. A personnel manager should have training as well as experience.
6. Animals can be taught more with kindness than with whipping.
7. Race prejudice should be discouraged in the public schools.
8. This year's automobiles are designed more to sell cars than to improve transportation.

Coherence
and Continuity

For
Guide to Revision,
see page 76.

Good writing has continuity; the parts of a paragraph cohere.

Proficiency with the kinds of patterns illustrated in Sections 1-4 will help any writer; the ability to construct logically planned paragraphs is a fundamental skill. But writing does not always follow patterns as neatly as the examples cited here might suggest. A topic sentence may extend its influence over more than one paragraph, or a paragraph may contain no stated topic sentence, with elements unified around an understood idea. For kinds of writing different from the expository prose this book emphasizes—narration, for example—quite different patterns may be appropriate. Accordingly, we may observe the movements of expository prose from another direction—as a sequence of linked assertions moving from point to point. Whether organized in orderly paragraphs or not, all good writing has some kind of continuity leading the reader. Consider the following remarks about the American opossum, which could constitute a list of particulars or details for the development of a paragraph.

The opossum has survived in definitely hostile surroundings for 70 million
    years.
The opossum is small; it can easily find hiding places.
The opossum can always find a little food, where big animals starve.
The individual opossum is not very delicate; it can stand severe punishment.
It "plays 'possum" when it gets into trouble.
It can go without food for a long time.
Many different things are food to an opossum.
Traits of the opossum have a high survival value.
The opossum is a survivor from the Age of Reptiles.

This list has been abstracted from a paragraph in the order of the original, but merely running the items together would not produce a paragraph. The material would be there; and it would even have a kind of unity, because the details all refer to the same topic, the opossum, but the whole lacks coherence. Compare the original:

> The reasons our opossum has survived in definitely hostile surroundings for 70 million years are evident. One is his small size: small animals always find hiding places, they always find a little food, where the big ones starve. Another of its assets was its astounding fecundity: if local catastrophes left only a few survivors, it did not take long to re-establish a thriving population. Also the individual opossum is not exactly delicate: it can stand severe punishment during which it "plays 'possum" and then scampers away—and it can go without food for a considerable time. Finally, a great many different things are "food" to an opossum. Each of these traits has a high survival value, and their combination has presented the United States with a survivor from the Age of Reptiles.
>
> —WILLY LEY, *The Lungfish and the Unicorn*

The paragraph differs from the list largely because it has continuity and coherence. It gains coherence partly, of course, because it has been put into a standard expository form with a topic sentence followed by specification leading to a conclusion. It gains coherence also however, because ideas are linked, because thoughts move in a discernible progression.

Commitment and Response   5-1

The movement of expository prose can be considered as a flow or sequence with every unit making a commitment for the future while responding to what has preceded. Or, to put it another way, every time we use a word or a clause or a sentence we commit ourselves; we limit or restrict in some ways the possible words or sentences that can follow. The choice we make of a sentence subject, for instance, does much to dictate what the remainder of the sentence will be like (see 12-2); and every sentence we write determines in some way what the next sentence is to be—or if it is a topic sentence, what several sentences are to be. In the generation of prose, we tend to move from sentence to sentence in a series of commitments and responses. Consider the following:

[1] We do not learn to frame sentences instinctively, as we learn to breathe or to walk. [2] We repeat sentences from memory and we vary them by analogy. [3] Imagine for a moment that all the sentences you have uttered during the course of the last two weeks are somewhere accurately recorded and that you can now scrutinize them at leisure. [4] You will probably find them to be surprisingly varied: long and short; simple, double, multiple, and complex; statements, commands, wishes, questions, and exclamations; bal-

ance, periodic, and loose. [5] The words have been largely of your own choosing, but the sentences have seldom been of your own making. [6] You have inherited them from the immediate, the distant, and the long-distant past. [7] You have carried with you in your mind a certain number of sentence-patterns, few or many according to your individual linguistic capacity, and into these patterns you have fitted and varied the words expressing your thoughts and desires. —SIMEON POTTER, *Our Language*

The paragraph does coordinate and subordinate different elements in a structural pattern, and it does demonstrate the cooperation of generality and specificity; but it also has continuity. One idea implies the next.

The opening sentence commits the writer to relatively few possible responses in sentence 2. He might repeat the general idea of 1 more specifically:

Sentences are not a gift of nature, like the five senses.

Such a sentence would be mainly waste motion, only postponing a response to the idea of sentence 1. The writer might write a parallel sentence, moving toward another general topic:

And we do not learn the words of a particular language because of some mysterious patriotic genes.

This sentence would turn the discussion and shift the emphasis of the paragraph. Such a shift would be possible, but the most likely response to sentence 1 is the one that appears—sentence 2—telling us how we *do* learn to frame sentences. Sentence 2 then makes another commitment; it is a proposition requiring sentence 3 to proceed with explanation or illustration or evidence, as it does. Sentence 3 shows the way to 4, asking the reader to imagine something and then in 4 indicating the likely results of his imagining.

For the writer the lesson is clear enough. He should so phrase each sentence that it commits him to what he wants and to no more, and so that it makes a plausible response to what precedes.

5-2   Repetition of Words and Ideas

Structural devices smooth this flow of ideas through sequences of sentences. For one thing, almost every sentence in clear prose is linked with the sentences around it by direct or implied references. Pronouns in one sentence may refer to words in the sentence before. The idea of one sentence may be briefly rephrased in another. Repeated references to the central idea of the paragraph may serve to bind sentences together. These central ideas echoing through the composition—along with transitional expressions—make the parts of the writing cohere and draw the reader effortlessly along the trail of the writer's thoughts. The following passage indicates how parts of clear writing are linked together.

A driver doesn't have to look at his road map once he starts on a highway, as long as he doesn't come to any intersections. He doesn't have to worry about which way to go if he has no choice about it. But when he comes to a crossroads, with signs pointing in various directions—then he can't just let the road decide where he is to go; he has to make up his mind. He has to stop and think. —MONROE C. BEARDSLEY, *Thinking Straight*

The passage carries through a single subject, *driver*, designated by the pronoun *he* after the first mention. Sentences cohere, also, by the repetition of patterns like *doesn't have to* and *has to, intersections* and *crossroads;* the connective *but* holds the two main parts of the paragraph together, marking the contrast between them.

Another passage relies on different echoes of meaning:

In time of peace in the modern world, if one is thoughtful and careful, it is rather more difficult to be killed or maimed in the outland places of the globe than it is in the streets of our great cities, but the atavistic urge toward danger persists and its satisfaction is called adventure. However, your adventurer feels no gratification in crossing Market Street in San Francisco against the traffic. Instead, he will go to a good deal of trouble and expense to get himself killed in the South Seas. (In reputedly rough water, he will go in a canoe; he will expose his tolerant and uninoculated blood to strange viruses.) This is adventure. It is possible that his ancestor, wearying of the humdrum attacks of the saber-tooth, longed for the good old days of pterodactyl and triceratops.

—JOHN STEINBECK and EDWARD F. RICKETTS, *Sea of Cortez*

A pronoun subject, standing for *adventurer,* carries through, but references to adventure and danger also hold the paragraph together. *However* and *instead* mark shifts in the thought.

5-3   Continuity and Word Order

The links between sentences, the structural indicators of the commitment-response patterns of ideas, are usually reinforced by word order.

Repetitions of sentence patterns emphasize parallels or contrasts in ideas and help the reader move smoothly from paragraph to paragraph, from sentence to sentence. In both paragraphs above, the sentence subjects link one sentence to the next, mainly because each sentence repeats the order of the preceding one. The following two sentences are linked, even though the subjects differ, because the subjects appear in the same relative place in each:

An old man stood in front of the monkey cage excitedly throwing peanuts at a score of begging arms. A small boy only a few feet away sat with his face buried in a comic book.

The repetition of sentence order sharpens the contrast between the two main actions, and the contrast helps link the sentences. On the other hand, variations from usual word order may provide bridges, carrying special emphasis from one sentence to another:

In front of the monkey cage stood an old man, excitedly throwing peanuts at a score of begging arms. A few feet away sat a small boy, his face buried in a comic book.

The shift in order throws emphasis on the location, heightens the contrast in the actions by stressing the nearness of the two persons, and helps link the sentences through the repetition of the reversed pattern. There is some loss of continuity when the word order pattern is not repeated, as in the following:

In front of the monkey cage stood an old man, excitedly throwing peanuts at a score of begging arms. A small boy only a few feet away sat with his face buried in a comic book.

Consider another sentence. Standing alone, it seems unnecessarily backward:

This heifer they sold in despair.

When the sentence is put into its context, the reasons for the irregular order are clear.

One heifer refused to stay in the farm close. This heifer they sold in despair.

Consider the following, which at first seems an unjustifiable inversion:

The ashes Daniel spread over the floor.

Compare the sentence in its context:

The servant brought a gleaming torch and a sack of ashes. He set the torch in a bracket on the wall. The ashes Daniel spread over the floor.

Sometimes coherence and continuity may justify quite unusual word order or variations on usual sentence patterns (see 18-4). Most frequently, however, continuity is enforced by the repetition of standard sentence patterns beginning with a subject and verb, as in the following:

Dr. Woods looked his *creed* more decidedly, perhaps, than any of the professors. *He* had the firm *fibre* of a theological athlete, and *lived* to be old without ever mellowing, I think, into a kind of half-heterodoxy, as old ministers of stern creed are said to do now and then,—just as old doctors grow to be sparing of the more exasperating drugs in their later days. *He had manipulated* the *mysteries* of the Infinite so long and so exhaustively that he would have seemed more at home among the mediaeval schoolmen than amidst the working clergy of our own time.
—OLIVER WENDELL HOLMES, *The Autocrat of the Breakfast Table*

The reader moves easily from sentence to sentence, because the sentence pattern continues.

Words of Transition 5-4

Relationships can be clarified further by transitional words, words which identify the relationships between the parts of a paragraph and improve continuity. Notice, for example, the use of the words *also* and *finally* in the paragraph on the opossum. The following are some of the most useful transitional words:

To mark an addition: *and, furthermore, next, moreover, in addition, again, also, likewise, similarly, finally, second*

To introduce or emphasize a contrast or alternative: *but, or, nor, still, however, nevertheless, on the contrary, on the other hand, conversely*

To mark a conclusion: *therefore, thus, then, in conclusion, consequently, as a result, in other words, accordingly*

To introduce an illustration or example: *thus, for example, for instance, that is, namely*

Others indicate shifts of time or introduce clauses; almost all connectives can provide transitions. Overuse of transitional expressions makes stiff prose; careful use of them helps make clear prose.

Coh   **5** *Guide to Revision*

> *Revise so that all elements of the composition cohere, so that the continuity is clear from one idea to another.*

All the parts of a composition must stick together—must cohere—and each word or sentence must lead clearly to the next.

5a   **Continuity**   **Coh a**

Ideas in a composition must "track"—that is, they must follow easily one upon another. If the writer does not fulfill commitments, does not do what a preceding sentence has promised he would do, his prose is hard to follow.

ORIGINAL

[1] A genuinely humorous television commercial is not funny just by accident. [2] There are many pitfalls and traps in creating an amusing commercial which if not avoided will cause the television viewer to become psychologically adverse to the product being advertised. [3] First, if possible, violence should be avoided or cut down to a minimum. [4] The brand of humor used on a successful commercial such as the beer commercial centering about playful bears is warmly amusing, and al-

REVISION

[1] A humorous television commercial can be successful only if it draws its amusement from subjects and incidents which do not antagonize the viewer and turn him against the product being advertised. [2] Violence, for example, should not be used as a device for humor in commercials. [3] Nor should humor be used which is insipid and, as in the case of the laughing beer bottles, relies on its loudness rather than its psychological appeal. [4] A successful commercial, such as the beer

ORIGINAL *(Cont.)*

though they actually incorporate violence, it does not become objectionable because no one is hurt. [5] Sometimes the humor used in a commercial is insipid and, as in the case of the laughing beer bottles, relies on its loudness rather than its psychological appeal. [6] The humor used in the most effective advertisements is usually the happy type, the carefree type with no undertones of objectional material. [7] The formula that is most successful in producing a good humorous commercial is really very simple. [8] The ideas and material used should always be of the clean and happy type which more often than not constitutes a really refreshing advertisement.

[The paragraph is bad in a variety of ways, but notably it lacks continuity from idea to idea. Sentence 1, for instance, commits the writer to limited kinds of responses: he might follow the last part of the sentence which seems to promise to tell us how the commercial is funny, if not by accident; he might tell us more specifically something about the genuinely humorous commercial; he might even shift to a parallel but contrasting sort of topic— "A genuinely serious television commercial is. . . ." But sentence 2 makes none of these likely responses. It introduces a new kind of topic, one which commits the writer to a discussion of "pitfalls and traps." Sentence 3 responds more plausibly with what might be considered an example of a "pitfall," but the example in 4 is not related to 3 in any clear way. And so on. The paragraph needs complete rewriting.]

REVISION *(Cont.)*

advertisement about the playful bears, is warmly amusing; although it may include some violence, it does not become objectionable because no one is hurt. [5] It is typical of the successful humorous commercial, which uses clean and happy ideas and materials to produce a refreshing advertisement.

[The revision is still a weak paragraph, producing no real support for its pronouncements about what should not be done in humorous commercials. A good paragraph would require more thought, more evidence. But some of the major faults of the original have been corrected, and the revision can at least be followed from point to point. For one thing, the revision is shorter. Useless repetition, especially in the beginning and in sentences 7-9, has been omitted as sentences have been combined. The paragraph has also been given a topic sentence which can be developed and has been organized in a two-part plan. Finally, sentences have been rewritten and rearranged to provide some continuity. Sentence 1 of the original, for instance, has been rewritten so that it does not make a commitment that the writer cannot or does not fulfill. With 1 rewritten, 2 can respond logically with a more specific example of what 1 asserts, and 3 can follow with another example. Sentence 4 of the original does not follow 3 at all, although it perhaps could have been related as a qualification of the concept of violence. In the revision it has been moved to provide illustration for the second topic of the paragraph, what makes a good commercial— a topic only inadequately developed.]

Coh b   Coherence Through Words and Constructions   5b

Especially within paragraphs, the repetition of words, of ideas through synonyms, and of grammatical structures promotes coherence.

ORIGINAL

[1] A fraternity pledge finds life during the week preceding his initiation complex and not very pleasant. [2]This week is commonly known as hell week, and there are many good reasons for the name. [3] The pledge cannot speak to any person without first begging for permission in a long and difficult set oration. [4] Any member can make the pledge do his bidding. [5] He can make him shine anybody's shoes, and the pledge must sing, dance, and generally entertain at all meals and sleep under the dining room tables at night. [6] An infraction of any of the rules brings any number of swats from the members' paddles. [7] The swats are not administered gently and are by no means soothing to the receiver. [8] Why it is called hell week is a question never asked by any pledge. [9] Since it is the last test and marks the end of months of trial, most freshmen look forward to it.

[Some of the weaknesses of this paragraph result from failure to subordinate secondary ideas (see Section 16); 6 and 7, for instance, might be combined. The choppiness, however, is evidence that sentences are not arranged and linked so that continuity is smooth. For example, 4 and 5 might be recast so as to continue the subject in 3; wih some transition and recasting, 7 could be constructed so that it carries on the subject of earlier sentences.]

REVISION

[1] For a week preceding his initiation a fraternity pledge finds life complex and not very pleasant. [2] The week is commonly known as hell week, and there are good reasons for the name. [3] For seven days the pledge cannot speak to any person without first begging for permission in a long and difficult set oration. [4] He must do the bidding of any member; shine the shoes of anybody a member designates; sing, dance, and generally entertain at all meals; and sleep under the dining room table at night. [5] An infraction of any of these rules brings swats from the members paddles, not administered gently and by no means soothing to the receiver. [6] No pledge ever asks why the week is called hell week. [7] Nevertheless, most pledges look forward to it as their last test and the end of months of trial.

[Suggested changes have been made; 1 has been revised, and a transition has been prefixed to 3 so that week *holds the three sentences together.* These rules *in 5 refers to the two preceding sentences.]*

Clumsy repetition produces awkward, wordy writing. Useless repetition of the same idea produces only redundancy (see Glossary). Skillful repetition, however—particularly skillful use of synonyms—will give writing a coherence which can be obtained in no other way.

ORIGINAL

Modern scholars now agree that the ancestor of the Romance languages is not now much taught in our schools. It was Vulgar Latin, which is usually taught today only in the graduate schools. The kind of language that was written by Virgil and Cicero is the kind that is usually taught both in high school and in college, but that is not the kind from which French or any other language of that sort has come. In English we have words from the language of the Romans, and some of those words did come from the language written by the famous Romans. However, what are called Romance languages did not. The working men were the ones who determined the language in the various countries which had been conquered by Caesar and the other classical generals. Church Latin is still spoken but is not much taught. Vulgar Latin is made up of words spoken by the common people, or *vulgus*.

[*This paragraph is confused, partly because of faulty order, but partly also because sentences are not linked by synonyms and repeated words. Three ideas run parallel in the paragraph: the kinds of Latin, the descent of the Romance languages, the teaching of Latin in the schools. These ideas should be distinct, but should also be tied together.*]

REVISION

The modern Romance languages descended from Latin, but not from the Latin usually taught in the schools. There are several Latins, notably Classical Latin, Church Latin, and Vulgar Latin. Of these three divisions of the Latin language, Classical Latin is taught almost exclusively. Church Latin is still spoken but is seldom taught to undergraduates. Vulgar Latin is taught only in a few graduate schools. Yet Vulgar Latin is the ancestor of all modern Romance languages—Italian, French, Spanish, Portuguese, and Romanic. Classical Latin has accounted for words borrowed into these languages, as it accounted for words borrowed into English, but all scholars now agree that the Romance languages did not come from the classical speech of Virgil and Cicero. French and Italian and Spanish came from the Latin speakers who were working in France and Italy and Spain, the soldiers, the merchants, the laboring men, that is, the *vulgus* whose speech is known as Vulgar Latin.

[*The three ideas are carried through the paragraph by repetition of words like* Latin, *and the generous use of synonyms and partial synonyms like* Vulgar Latin *and* the classical speech of Virgil and Cicero.]

Similar constructions in consecutive sentences help to tie a paragraph together.

ORIGINAL

Most co-eds at State University did not come here to get married,

REVISION

Whatever the administration may imply, the co-eds at State University

ORIGINAL (*Cont.*)

though the president did make a joke something like that. We didn't come to get dates, either, at least not mainly, though the Dean kind of hinted that. And I suppose the profs think we are just being nice to them to get good grades without working.

[*This paragraph is not completely incoherent, but the reader is given little help in moving through it.*]

REVISION (*Cont.*)

have not come here mainly to get married. Whatever the Dean of Women may say, they have not come mainly to get dates. And whatever the faculty may think, they have not come mainly to get good grades by flashing their smiles at professors.

[*With sentences having similar constructions and similar or contrasting words, the paragraph moves to a cumulative effect.*]

Especially within a paragraph, material can be cemented by a subject continued from sentence to sentence.

ORIGINAL

I can remember when tires were quite different from what they are today. Twenty to thirty thousand miles is not now considered unusual tire mileage, provided tires are kept at proper inflation and are not run at excessive speeds. Also, anybody can change a tire with ease now. The modern tire is a marvel and a joy. A good tire, when it is new, will turn most nails and almost any old tire ought to zip through broken glass from milk bottles without a scratch. You can buy tires in nonskid, high-speed, and antisnow types.

[*The reader is needlessly confused because the subject shifts from sentence to sentence.*]

REVISION

To anyone who knew touring in the old days, the modern automobile tire is a marvel and a joy. It will run, with proper care, twenty thousand to thirty thousand miles. It will zip through smashed milk bottles without a scratch. When new, it will spurn most tacks and nails. At reasonable speeds and with proper pressure, it is almost blow-out-proof. It is available in nonskid, high-speed, and snow types. Best of all, it can be changed in a few minutes.

The ancestor of the modern tire, however, was quite different. . . .

[*The paragraph gains coherence because the subject of discussion, modern tires, has become the grammatical subject of the individual sentences.*]

Exercise 5

A. Describe methods used in the following paragraphs to gain continuity, and point out specific examples of each method. Then select at least one of the paragraphs and analyze in detail the commitment each sentence makes to what is to follow and the way in which each sentence responds to this commitment.

1. The story of Galahad and the Grail quest may well have been included by Malory as a metaphor of the transcendence of the epic's war and adultery, hate and lust. It serves that function in any theoretical analysis of the book. But in the act of reading and appreciation it does not. It separates itself out as a different story. However carefully Malory strives to connect the main story of Launcelot, Arthur, and Gawain with their failure in the Grail quest, and however symbolical the relation of Launcelot and his bastard son, Galahad, may be, the two plots are really incongruous. The story of the Grail stands best alone. In spite of tedious detail and naïve style, the medieval French Grail romances transmit more of the mystery that has attracted generations of cranky interpreters and spinners of learned fantasy as well as the whole tribe of occultists to the Grail legends. However, Malory's version is all most modern readers are likely to read and it is sufficiently awe-inspiring. In *Le Morte d'Arthur* the major actors in the drama of King Arthur's court will find their transcendence, not in supernatural vision, but in the common human illumination that comes with the acceptance of tragedy.
   —KENNETH REXROTH, *Le Morte d'Arthur*

2. The doctrine of energy has to do with the notion of quantitative permanence underlying change. The doctrine of evolution has to do with the emergence of novel organisms as the outcome of chance. The theory of energy lies in the province of physics. The theory of evolution lies mainly in the province of biology, although it had previously been touched upon by Kant and Laplace in connection with the formation of suns and planets.
   —A. N. WHITEHEAD, *Science and the Modern World*

3. I have already given you a summary account of the manner in which young misses are educated in this country. They are all sent early to school; where they are taught to spell, and read, and write. From parochial schools, many of them are transferred to boarding-schools and academics. Here they learn to understand arithmetic, which indeed is usually taught them in parochial schools, and study English grammar, geography, history to some extent, criticism, and composi-

tion. In a few instances they are taught moral science, and in some ascend to higher branches of mathematics, the Latin and French languages. To these are added embroidery, drawing, and music.
—TIMOTHY DWIGHT, *Travels in New England and New York*

4. I am therefore led to my final assumption, that the admission of a principle of relativity and uncertainty should not be simply depressing. It does not destroy all possibility of knowledge and judgment. Rather, it is the outcome of comprehensive knowledge, and the means to further knowledge of man's history. It enables a higher objectivity, a fuller understanding of present and past. It enables wiser choices among the possibilities open to us—among goods that are no less real because they are relative, and that are more relevant than arbitrary absolutes. Above all, this principle encourages a positive faith in positive values: of liberality, of breadth of spirit, hospitality to new ideas, willingness to adventure, humility in admitting one's own fallibility and the limitations of the human mind—of the tolerance that is indispensable for the pursuit of truth, for social harmony, and for simple humanity. If these are not the highest values, none are more essential to the hopes of world order and peace.
—HERBERT J. MULLER, *The Uses of the Past*

B. Following are sentences taken from actual paragraphs. Frame a sentence which might follow each, one which seems to you a possible response to the commitment made by the sentence quoted. Your instructor can tell you what sentence actually did follow in the original paragraph.

1. The American, probably more than any other man, is prone to be apologetic about the trade he follows.
2. The vanishing father is perhaps the central fact of the changing American family structure.
3. Not only were the potatoes of that land as large as any in the world, but they were probably the best in the world to eat.
4. We humans have had very little experience in any environment save one in which we can travel in any path at any speed we wish.
5. The human animal has survived by virtue of his ability to perceive, decide, and react.
6. Teen-agers could hardly live without the telephone—and many parents can hardly live with it.
7. It does not take a linguist to know that language changes.
8. Football is a game which simply does not lend itself to intelligent spectatordom.
9. In one large city, the principals of the junior high schools and the superintendent are now holding firm against interscholastic games.
10. Almost no feature of the interior design of our current car provides safeguards against injury in the event of collision.

C. Rewrite the following paragraphs from student themes, attempting to improve the continuity from sentence to sentence:

1. The mythology and folkways of a primitive people are the basis of their society. Wise men and priests explain the mysteries of the universe. Folkways are learned by the young by imitation and under the pressure of authority. Traditions of a different society are sometimes imposed on a primitive group, and then the old folkways are submerged and covered by superficial acquired habits. The dress and language of the new society are adopted. You have to probe beneath the surface to find the old beliefs persisting.

2. What to wear was a very important problem to me. Blue was the color which my mother considered most flattering to me, but I liked red. I was only in the seventh grade. It was very hard for me to find a formal that fit me. Dress designers apparently did not take sufficient account of the special problems of seventh-graders. Many dresses, both blue and red, were presented. I did not seem to have curves in the right places. When I did find a suitable dress, the alterations turned out to be more complicated than making the dress could have been.

D. Select a paragraph from a theme you have written. Using the paragraphs in 5-2 as models, draw lines tracing the continuity from key word to key word. Then revise the paragraph, attempting to improve its continuity, and draw lines on the revision to test whether more ideas carry from sentence to sentence.

E. The following paragraphs can be used for analysis to apply the principles discussed in the first five sections of this book. A full analysis would attempt to answer questions like the following: What is the main idea of the paragraph? Is there a topic sentence; what is it and to what does it commit the writer? What is the plan of the paragraph; which parts are coordinate and which subordinate? How does the writer reveal the plan of the paragraph to the reader? Does the paragraph have adequate development? What are the relations between general and specific material in the paragraph? Does the paragraph cohere? What devices are used to give the paragraph continuity? Can you think of ways in which the sentences could be improved by better organization or continuity? Sentences are numbered for reference.

1. [1] Their sufferings, they told him, were too great to be endured. [2] All the men had received one, most of them two or three wounds. [3] More than fifty had perished, in one way or another, since leaving Vera Cruz. [4] There was no beast of burden but led a life preferable to theirs. [5] For when the night came, the former could rest from his labors; but they, fighting or watching, had no rest, day or night.
   —WILLIAM H. PRESCOTT, *Conquest of Mexico*

2. [1] Then it is said of the American woman that, in order to satisfy her ambition, she urges men to killing extremes of competition. [2] Undoubtedly, there are greedy women in America, just as there are lazy men. [3] But they are the exception, not the rule. [4] The economic rat race, as men like to call it, far from being a female creation, terrifies the American woman, who by and large would make almost any sacrifice to reduce the work pressure on her husband and keep him healthy. [5] But the American man is certain he is loved for his money, not for himself—he brings this idea into marriage, and nothing his wife can do will disabuse him of it. [6] It is he, far more than his wife, who is the victim of the materialism he deplores in her. [7] The American man, unlike the American woman, doesn't have to be conspicuously shallow, he has only to be average in his society, to measure his personal worth by the kind of house he lives in, the car he drives, the show his family makes in the community.

—DIANA TRILLING, *Look Magazine*

3. [1] In any event, it might be useful for the newspapers themselves to undertake a scientific survey of the effects on public opinion of headlines and news angling. [2] It might be useful, too, to look into specific cases in which members of Congress or Government officials have spoken or acted on the basis of spot headline news rather than the full story. [3] One such instance comes to mind. [4] Two weeks ago the State Department issued a new statement of policy on its book and library program overseas. [5] That statement was carefully worded and attempted to state the basic principles governing the acquisition and retention of books. [6] It tried to deal with the complexities of the library program. [7] Yet one sentence from the statement was featured in the news lead of one of the wire services to make it appear that the State Department had gone "soft on Red writers." [8] A number of headlines emphasized this erroneous, out-of-context reference. [9] Within minutes Congressmen were publicly denouncing the statement, though admittedly they had not read it in full. [10] Public investigations were ordered and the library program was again in jeopardy.   —NORMAN COUSINS, *Saturday Review*

4. [1] The development of language is the history of the gradual accumulation and elaboration of verbal symbols. [2] By means of this phenomenon, man's whole behavior-pattern has undergone an immense change from the simple biological scheme, and his mentality has expanded to such a degree that it is no longer comparable to the minds of animals. [3] Instead of a direct transmitter of coded signals, we have a system that has sometimes been likened to a telephone-exchange, wherein messages may be relayed, stored up if a line is busy, answered by proxy, perhaps sent over a line that did not exist when they were first given, *noted down and kept* if the desired number gives no answer. [4] Words are the plugs in this super-switchboard; they connect impressions and let them function together; sometimes they cause lines to become crossed in funny or disastrous ways.

—SUSANNE K. LANGER, *Philosophy in a New Key*

5. [1] Among medieval and modern philosophers, anxious to establish the religious significance of God, an unfortunate habit has prevailed of paying to Him metaphysical compliments. [2] He has been conceived as the foundation of the metaphysical situation with its ultimate activity. [3] If this conception be adhered to, there can be no alternative except to discern in Him the origin of all evil as well as of all good. [4] He is then the supreme author of the play, and to Him must therefore be ascribed its shortcomings as well as its success. [5] If He be conceived as the supreme ground for limitation, it stands in His very nature to divide the Good from the Evil, and to establish Reason "within her domination supreme."

—A. N. WHITEHEAD, *Science and the Modern World*

6. [1] As for our brand of humor, the tall tale of the nineteenth century, being the expression of a young, healthy, hell-raising frontier people, gave something new and exhilarating to the humor of the world. [2] Our contributions in the twentieth century—the gag, the wisecrack, the comeback, the nifty, the clincher are nowhere so good. [3] As long as it was expertly used indeed, scrupulously stylized—in old vaudeville routine; as long, too, as it represented a second stage of the American humor, a kind of retort on the tall tale's boastfulness, the American gag had its real virtues. [4] But we have turned the gag into a mechanical, ubiquitous, incessant national tool so brassy as to be vulgar, so unchanging as to be dull. [5] As for the comeback, though fond of it, we have never been very good at it; in terms of cussing and repartee alike, our truck drivers are mere duffers by comparison with even the average cockney. [6] After all, the essence of a good comeback is a certain delayed sting, a certain perfection of surface politeness. [7] Two Frenchmen who had been brilliant and bitterly hostile rivals at school went on to become a famous general and a distinguished cardinal. [8] The cardinal, seeing the general, after many years, on a railway platform, approached him haughtily and said, "Mr. Stationmaster, when does the next train leave for Bordeaux?" [9] The general paused, smiled, and said, "At half past two, madame," [10] By comparison, how very American at bottom is the most famous of modern comebacks; how lacking in all subtlety and in any final wit is Whistler's "You will, Oscar, you will."

—LOUIS KRONENBERGER, *Company Manners*

7. [1] There are, however, one or two minor points in Rabelais that may be worth notice. [2] I might, you know, analyze it as I attempted to analyze *Don Quixote*. [3] There is in *Gargantua* and *Pantagruel* that same complexity of thought and construction: you may note, first of all, the great essence which is common to these masterpieces as to all literature—ectasy, expressed in the one case under the similitude of knight-errantry, in the other by the symbol of the vine. [4] Then, in Rabelais you have another symbolism of ecstasy—the shape of *gauloiseries*, of gross, exuberant gaiety, expressing itself by outrageous tales, outrageous words, by a very cataract of obscenity, if you please, if only you will notice how the obscenity of Rabelais transcends the

obscenity of common life; how grossness is poured out in a sort of mad torrent, in a frenzy, a very passion of the unspeakable. [5] Then, thirdly, there is the impression one collects from the book: a transfigured picture of that wonderful age; there is the note of the vast, interminable argument of the schools, and for a respond, the clear, enchanted voice of Plato; there is the vision, there is the mystery of the vast, farlifted Gothic quire; and those fair, ornate, and smiling *chateaux* rise smiling from the rich banks of the Loire and the Vienne. [6] The old tales told in the farmhouse kitchens in the Chinonais, the exultation of the new learning, of lost beauty recovered, the joy of the vintage, the old legends, the ancient turns of speech, the new style and manner of speaking: so too the old world answers the new. [7] Then one has the satire of clergy and lawyers—the criticism of life—analogous, as I said, with much that is in Cervantes, and so from divers elements you see how a literary masterpiece is made into a whole.

—ARTHUR MACHEN, *Hieroglyphics: A Note Upon Ecstasy in Literature*

F. Below are paragraphs from student themes which are faulty because they lack plan, fail to turn about a topic sentence, include irrelevant material, or lack continuity. Criticize each paragraph; then supply a plausible topic sentence for each, and rewrite it into a coherent unit.

1. In his story *The Devil and Daniel Webster,* Stephen Vincent Benét uses the Devil, or Mr. Scratch, to stand for evil. There is entirely too much evil in this world of ours. Mainly the story teaches a very important rule, that evil can win over almost anything but not over goodness. This appears at the end of the story. Daniel Webster has been losing almost all the time in the trial, because he is not dealing with a fair judge or a fair opponent. In the beginning of the trial a legal battle is fought between Mr. Scratch and Daniel Webster, with Webster trying to argue fine legal points with the Devil. Finally Daniel Webster realized that he could not fight his opponents with their own weapons. You cannot win fighting evil with evil. The tactics of Daniel Webster changed, and a long speech about the good things in the world was the next order of business. "The simple things that everybody's known and felt" were what he talked about. The rule has been taught to society in many ways, but this method of teaching it through fiction is one of the most effective. Evil cannot conquer goodness is the rule which is the main theme of the story.

2. For one thing, cotton had to be picked by hand in the eighteenth century. The pickers had to spend long hours working with the cotton if they were to get anywhere. Cotton is an example of how the Industrial Revolution developed in the eighteenth century. From the fields the cotton went to the home. Here seeds were removed from the cotton by hand. This job required a considerable amount of time and patience. Then the cotton was spun into thread and woven into cloth. Men finally became tired of slow and tedious manual labor, and they began to seek new methods of producing cotton textiles. It was about the mid-

dle of the century when a number of inventions appeared which tended to shift the cotton industry from the home to the factory. Hundreds of workers could be replaced by the new machinery. Factories were built in order to house this machinery.

3. She has native aptitude as a literary critic, or at least as a critic of current magazines. Unless restrained, she literally devours *The Atlantic,* concentrating on the front and back covers, if she can stuff them into her mouth. My young brother attributes this preference for *The Atlantic* to the whisky advertisements on the back page, but I am convinced she genuinely has taste for a good thing, something solid enough so that she can get her teeth into it. This theory of mine gains support from her other tastes. She prefers the woodpulp of *The New York Times* to that of the local paper, and I confess that I prefer the *Times,* also, to read as well as to swat flies. She will have none of the sleazy magazine digests. She throws them on the floor with a squawk of disgust. The *Saturday Evening Post* and Mother's home-building magazine intrigue her for short periods—she likes to chew the square binding at the back, for there is a certain four-square practicality in Barbara—but not for long. I gather she finds them jargonic and repetitious, lacking in the sort of body required by a young woman with three teeth. *The New Yorker* she toys with, but never consumes. I suspect that it is too brittle for her taste, caviar to the nursery. Mother, I am happy to report, encourages Barbara in her literary leanings; Mother approves of *The Atlantic,* partly because the covers are so tough that Barbara can seldom chew anything loose. Think what might happen to her taste and her stomach if she were some day to swallow a chunk of a true confession magazine.

Organization

Order is Heaven's first law.

—Alexander Pope

The ancient world had a pleasant if erroneous idea that divine order regulated the entire universe. Planets, stars, angels, men, animals, or stones all fit set places, and each of these had order within it. The pattern for order was established and clear, and it fit man or beast or the heavens. The great world, for example, the macrocosm—*macro-* meaning great and *cosmus* a universe—comprised the earth and heavens with all the stars and planets. Man, the microcosm, was a little universe, supposed by early thinkers to be like the physical universe in nature and organization, with some necessary variations for size. Arteries and veins, they observed, were like the rivers of the greater world; the seven openings in man's head—two eyes, two ears, two nostrils, and a mouth—corresponded to the seven planets. While this order was preserved, all went well. When it was violated in any part, chaos prevailed.

As a scientific explanation, this elaborate analogy has long been abandoned; there are differences between blood and river water. As a description of expository composition, the old system is still at least interesting, both for its insistence on the importance of order and its enthusiasm for correspondences in patterns.

For composition is, in essence, a process of imposing order, of organization. All writers have the same words at their disposal. The problem is to put them into patterns—sentences, paragraphs, chapters, books. "To write," says Jean Cocteau, "is to disarrange the dictionary." Furthermore, in expository prose, at least, the writer does not invent material or make up facts; rather, he finds them and puts them in order and thus expresses his individual view of their relationships. He converts his raw material into a creation of his own by organizing details to suit his particular purposes. The new insights he reveals by his selection and arrangement give the composition its individuality or originality or significance. Hundreds of worthwhile books can be written about the Elizabethan theater or the French Revolution because the material can be ordered in almost infinite ways to suit the purposes and main ideas of different writers.

There is, of course, no single plan of organization; the Almighty was not so systematic about composition as the ancients thought He was about the universe. But the old analogy between the small and great worlds can be applied to composition in another way, to a correspondence in general patterns of order between small and larger units of composition. For example, one can think of the paragraph as a kind of "microcomposition," reflecting in miniature the same sorts of order that govern longer pieces of writing. The same general principles for ordering ideas apply to sentences, to paragraphs, and to larger units. Organization, furthermore, is implicit in the very beginning stages of composition, in the "pre-writing" that produces an "idea" for a paper (see 1-2); organizing an idea is part of the process of getting an idea. Thus, the student approaching problems of organization discussed in the following sections has already learned basic principles.

Like the paragraph, a longer composition is unified about main ideas, governed by specific purposes (see Section 1). The main idea may be simple or complex, clearly stated or left for the reader to infer, but it is almost inevitably clear in the writer's mind. Moreover, in the longer composition the writer orders paragraphs into a pattern much as he orders sentences to focus on the topic sentence of a paragraph. And just as the writer seeks coherence in a paragraph, he uses transitions and other topical devices to give his longer paper continuity and coherence.

Most of the following discussions, then, extend and elaborate basic principles already considered, but introduce techniques particularly useful in organizing materials too extensive for treatment in a single paragraph. Section 6 suggests procedures for finding the parts or subdivisions of a topic and for putting the parts in order— analysis and classification. Section 7 discusses practical machinery useful in organization, particularly the outline. Section 8 presents further practical devices of organization, those with which the writer can make his plan clear, start the reader in the right direction, lead him easily from point to point, and bring him to a satisfactory conclusion.

Analysis and
Classification

For
Guide to Revision,
see page 96.

Organization of a composition develops from analysis and classification of materials.

Analysis and classification can make order out of chaos. Indeed, they work even in so ordinary an activity as cleaning a room after a Saturday night party. The student can analyze the mess, breaking it into its elements or parts; he discovers clothes, books and papers, food, dirty dishes, trash. Then he considers each of these parts of the confusion as if it labeled a class, and classifies individual items under one or another head—clothes in a pile for the closet, dishes in another pile for the kitchen, trash in the wastebasket, and so on.

These processes—actually different ways of looking at the same process—constantly work together. By analysis, wholes are divided into parts—directions into north, east, south, and west; colors into primary and secondary, and then primary colors into red, yellow, and blue. By classification we may attain the same result by a reverse process, by bringing like things together. Given a number of colors we can assort them on the basis of one of their characteristics into primary and secondary. These two approaches supplement each other, and both are fundamental techniques for handling ideas, underlying many of the processes already discussed. Analysis, for instance, provides a method for focusing on a topic or main idea (see 1-4). A topic statement is likely to commit the writer to some specific kind of analysis (see 2-5, 2-6). Classification establishes coordinate or subordinate relationships among ideas (see 3-2). When the chemist classifies aluminum, argon, arsenic, and calcium under the heading *elements,* he presents them as coordinate with one another but subordinate to the general idea of elements. For the writer, analysis and classification strengthen organization by clarifying patterns of coordination and subordination.

Scientific and Literary Analysis   6-1

Roughly speaking, analysis is of two sorts: scientific or formal, and literary or informal. The first, scientific analysis, attempts to be complete and exact. A biologist making an analysis of animals, for instance, would endeavor to include every sort that exists: he would establish the families, the subfamilies, the genera, and the species, and continue his subdivisions until every known sort of animal is accounted for. For example, the Canadian lynx, which clearly belongs in the cat family or Felidae, is placed within the genus *Lynx* and becomes *Lynx canadensis* to distinguish it from *Lynx rufus,* the bay lynx. If a new sort of lynx were now to be discovered, a Canadian lynx but different from previous known lynxes of the species, a new category within *Lynx canadensis* would be required to differentiate it from the first. This sort of analysis is useful in bringing permanent order into a complex subject, but it is necessarily exacting and time consuming.

Literary or informal analysis, being less exacting, is usually used for practical and relatively immediate ends. The same ornithologist who spends his lifetime endeavoring to correct and complete the classification of Pacific Ocean birds may open a lecture as follows: "Birds that frequent the Hawaiian Islands represent several aquatic species in such families and subfamilies as the Sternidae, the Pelecanidae, the Sulidae, but I am concerned this morning with only *Pterodroma phaeopygia sandwichensis,* the Hawaiian race of the dark-rumped petrel." He is using literary analysis. He feels no obligation to enumerate all the main categories of Pacific birds or to pursue any category to its final subdivision. He has said enough to indicate that there are a number of sorts of birds and to center attention upon the subject of his lecture. A lecturer in history may say, "Land fighting in the War Between the States divides roughly into campaigns in the East and those in the West. The western campaigns were important, but by the very nature of Southern population distribution they could never be decisive." He has been systematic so far as he has gone, but he will certainly feel no obligation to analyze either campaign to the last skirmish—he would have few students left if he did—and he has provided, in his word *roughly,* for the fact that he has ignored minor actions like raids into the North and Indian action in the far West. Furthermore, some subjects are not amenable to scientific analysis. A lecturer on recent American literature, for instance, might mention the Southern school of novelists, the Midwestern regionalists, the proletarian novelists, the psychological novelists, the novelists concerned with race problems. This rough, informal analysis would be adequate for his purposes, but it is not, because of the nature of the material, a scientific analysis. What would the lecturer do, for instance, about a novel written by a Southern writer and concerned with psychological problems of a Negro steel worker? Literary or informal analysis is not so detailed or so systematic as scientific analysis, but it is much more common and, for most purposes, more useful. In this book we shall be concerned with some common types of literary or informal analysis.

6-2 Analysis and Writing

Almost any topic can be approached analytically. The following paragraphs suggest how analysis can be applied to a few common sorts of writing problems.

1. *Division in time.* The history of English literature is traditionally approached in chronological stages—the heroic age, the medieval age, the early Renaissance, and so on. An account of a fire might consider the discovery, the alarm, the arrival of the fire trucks, the fire fighting, and then 'the scene after the fire is controlled. Almost any narrative, report of an event, or historical account can be divided by analysis into periods of time.

2. *Parts of a system or institution or mechanism.* A writer analyzing the government of the United States might begin by considering three branches: legislative, executive, and judiciary. In sections treating each of these branches he could analyze further, perhaps dividing the discussion of the executive branch into chapters on the President, the cabinet, and the executive bureaus. One writer discusses the weather by considering each of the "seven American airs." Another, discussing jet propulsion, treats each of four types of power units. Analysis can break anything complex into its parts.

3. *Parts of an argument.* A student preparing an appeal for more lenient dormitory regulations might describe practical problems presented by existing rules, make comparisons with rules in other schools, and discuss possible effects of the proposed changes.

Analysis of a logical discussion can produce divisions to make the case orderly.

4. *Parts of a process.*   Description of a simple process like building a campfire might proceed in chronological steps—selecting and preparing a site, gathering fuel, building the fire. Jacques Barzun in a more complicated discussion of how a teacher conducts a class analyzes the problem into methods: "The three basic ways are the lecture, the discussion group, and the tutorial hour."

5. *Aspects of a character.*   A writer planning a sketch of a character from fiction or from life might use analysis to isolate such subjects as personal appearance, attitudes and prejudices, activities and accomplishments, and family background.

6. *Characteristics of a literary work.*   Criticizing a story, a writer might consider its theme, its imagery, its characterization, and its diction. Or he might examine the story through its parts   its introduction, its early development, its climax, its denouement.

Analysis, in other words, need not be scientifically thorough to be useful, especially in the pre-writing stages of gathering material and planning and in keeping ideas in order.

The Basis of Classification   6-3

Classification relies on similarities and differences. For example, considering all living things on earth, we could observe that some are similar in that they have four feet. We could group them as quadrupeds. But within this class, brought together because of a particular similarity, we would also find differences, and distinguish cows, horses, sheep, pigs, and lions. Furthermore, each of these subclasses could again be subdivided—cows into Guernseys, Jerseys, Holsteins, Herefords.

The same items may be grouped in a number of ways by using different points of similarity as the basis of classification. Consider the following items: fire truck, bluebird, violet, yellow convertible, goldfinch, poinsettia, sunflower, blue bicycle, cardinal. They can obviously be classified by kind, as follows.

Vehicles	Birds	Flowers
fire truck	bluebird	violet
yellow convertible	goldfinch	poinsettia
blue bicycle	cardinal	sunflower

But a painter might classify them by color:

Red	*Blue*	*Yellow*
fire truck	blue bicycle	yellow convertible
cardinal	bluebird	goldfinch
poinsettia	violet	sunflower

The students in a classroom may be classified by the registrar as freshmen, sophomores, juniors, and seniors; by a minister as Baptists, Catholics, Episcopalians, Methodists; by the instructor as A students, B students, C students; by the football coach as potential spectators, potential halfbacks, potential linemen; by a boy in the back row as men and possible "dates." The important consideration is that *material can be classified on only one basis at one time.* The women in a class may be classified by the color of their hair as blondes, brunettes, and redheads. The redheads can be reclassified on the basis of their grades, and the B-student redheads can be classified into Pan Hellenics, members of local sororities, and independents. They cannot be classified on any two of these bases at one time, since some students would belong to both classes and some to neither.

The interests of the classifier determine the basis for the classification. There is an old story of a college dean who had no trouble dealing with a parrot that had become a nuisance in a dormitory, even though its presence did not violate any existing rule. "I suggest," he told the owner of the offending bird, "that you dispose of your parrot before I am forced to classify it as a dog or a television set."

6-4 Analysis and Classification in Planning a Composition

In planning a composition, analysis and classification work together. Notice, for example, the Barzun paragraph referred to above:

Let me explain. The three basic ways are the lecture, the discussion group, and the tutorial hour. In a lecture, a silent class is addressed, more or less like a public meeting. In a discussion group, comprising from five or six to not more than thirty students, the members of the class speak freely, putting or answering questions on points which the teacher organizes so as to form a coherent account of some topic. It may be that for this purpose discussion by the class is broken at intervals by lecturettes from him. In a tutorial hour, the instructor is really holding a conversation, usually with one student, certainly with not more than three or four. This is in the best sense a free-for-all and it presupposes a good stock of knowledge on the part of the students.

—JACQUES BARZUN, *What Is Teaching?*

By analysis the main topic, ways of conducting a class, is broken into three divisions. The paragraph develops through discussing each of these. Specific facts about what happens in a class are classified under the three methods. In the book from which the paragraph is taken, however, the uses of analysis and classification are much more complex. The three kinds of classes constitute only one of many subjects discussed in the book; classroom method is classified as coordinate with selection of subject matter, administrative procedures, and other topics that contribute to the general topic, *What Is Teaching?* Similarly, coordinate topics are analyzed; for example, subjects for lectures are subdivided and provide topics for a half dozen paragraphs.

In a longer composition, in other words, analysis and classification have varied uses. For example, a historian trying to find out why Lee's army lost at Gettysburg considers Longstreet's failure to move as he was ordered, Stuart's failure to arrive until the battle was essentially over, the questionable tactic of Lee in ordering Pickett to charge, and a number of other factors, and decides to consider the question of the unexpected effectiveness of the Union artillery. He has now narrowed his subject by analysis, but he is not done. He has now to ask himself why the Union batteries wrought such havoc. Another analysis suggests that the key reason was that Brigadier General Henry J. Hunt had managed to trick the Confederate command into believing he was out of ammunition, although he was not. How did he manage to do this? Of all the artillery actions, of all the evidence from spies and skirmishers, which will be significant and which will not be significant for this question? Now the job becomes one of classification; evidence must be sorted, rejected if it is not pertinent, and grouped with other like evidence if it is pertinent. This process may become complicated, with new analysis of minor questions, new categories into which evidence must be classified, and with the historian moving as his evidence and his interpretation of this evidence lead him. Through it all he will be using analysis and classification, sometimes one, sometimes the other, and often both.

6 *Guide to Revision*

Use analysis and classification to provide clear organization for a composition.

The writer who merely records material in the order in which it occurs to him usually reveals more about his own mental processes than about his subject. Analysis and classification are twin processes which can bring order to disorganized material.

6a
Analysis to Clarify Organization   An

Often analysis of the topic provides the pattern necessary to convert a chaotic jumble of material to a readable discussion.

ORIGINAL

What is a hot rod? Ask this question of the average person. It is almost a certainty that he will picture it as an old vintage roadster less fenders and paint. Furthermore, he will think that the driver is incompetent. In reality, the hot rod has changed tremendously during the past decade, even if the public's conception of it has not.

The public is unaware that the present-day hot rod is really a complex mechanism, involving a good deal of hard work on the part of the boy constructing it. It is really a complete rebuilding of many of the most important parts of a car, not just a heap of junk put in temporary running order.

Such things as the body and engine are thoroughly overhauled and put into shape for greater speed and better lines. The car, therefore, is made lighter and more compact.

REVISION

What is a hot rod? Most people would answer this question by describing an old-vintage roadster, lacking fenders, paint, and a competent driver. Actually a modern hot rod is a complex automobile, embodying a series of improvements over the ordinary stock car.

A hot rod varies most obviously from an ordinary car in the structure of its body. The body of a hot rod is likely to begin as that of a discarded light car; this body is first rebuilt so that it sits several inches down over the chassis and lowers the center of gravity of the car. Then excess parts of the body, especially chrome ornaments, are removed, and the doors are welded shut and smoothed in to fit the lines of the rest of the body.

More important to the actual running of the car, however, are the extensive changes in the running gear. The hot rod builder improves wheels,

ORIGINAL (*Cont.*)

Moreover, the engine is a better engine than the original car because it has greater horsepower. The hot rod does not look like an ordinary car, but it does not look like a dilapidated car either. Hot rods often resemble more nearly the custom-built sport cars that one sometimes sees.

It is a mistake to look on the hot rod as a dangerous toy for careless boys, because it is not that. It is really good training for young men to work with hot rods, because they can feel pride in accomplishing a good job of remodeling.

[*The weaknesses of this theme can be described in many ways: the main idea is forgotten as the paper wanders from point to point; there are too many unsubstantiated judgments; statements are general and not specific. Analysis and classification provide one way of avoiding most of those difficulties. If the writer would break his subject into parts, he would give his paper some order and would probably find that he could classify specific material to substantiate his judgments.*]

REVISION (*Cont.*)

axles, brakes, and differential assembly as extensively as his pocketbook will allow; safety requires some changes. He must, for example, change the size of the wheels and use regulation high-speed tires. He must install modern brakes, either hydraulic or disc type. He may lower the center of gravity by dropping the front axle, and he may change the differential to an assembly with a lower ratio.

Changes in the engine vary with the ingenuity and patience of the builder, but they provide the extra speed characteristic of the modern hot rod. They may be as fundamental as a modernized carburetor or as nonessential as chrome plate on the exhaust manifold, but improvements in the engine increase the power of the average motor by thirty five to fifty horsepower.

Changes like these, rather than those the public imagines, distinguish the modern hot rod.

[*By analyzing the hot rod, breaking the subject into three main groups, the writer finds something to say.*]

The basis of even informal analysis should be clear to the reader, and the writer may need to indicate what items have been eliminated and on what basis the analysis was made.

ORIGINAL

Prior to the Communist occupation there were more than four million Christians of all denominations in China. Matthew Ricci, S.J., who arrived in the sixteenth century was one of them. . . .

[*The writer has used analysis, although not in an orderly manner, and he has not made the basis of his analysis clear.*]

REVISION

Christianity has been introduced into China three times, but the missionary ventures of the seventh and thirteenth centuries proved abortive. Not until Matthew Ricci, S.J., arrived in 1582 to replant the faith of the West did Christianity play a leading part in Chinese life. . . .

[*The chronological analysis is now clear to the reader.*]

6b   Consistent Classification; Cross-ranking   Class

Although long compositions sometimes can accommodate more than one set of classes of material, usually items in each rank should be classified on a single basis. Otherwise classes overlap, and the material of the paper is confused rather than organized. Apples cannot be classified as green, yellow, red, small, winter; the bases for classifications—color, size, time of ripening—differ, and the classes overlap.

ORIGINAL

During the period 1932–1936, the government of the United States created a large number of temporary bureaus and agencies. In this paper I shall be concerned with the question of why some of the supposedly temporary agencies were accepted permanently. I shall consider four groups of agencies: agricultural agencies, financial agencies, agencies established after 1936, and agencies that exist today. . . .

[*Classes have been established on different bases. The first two depend on matter the agencies dealt with; the third is based on time of establishment of the agency, and the fourth on permanence of the agency. The material needs to be reclassified on a consistent basis—probably a basis indicated by the central purpose of the paper.*]

REVISION

During the period 1932–1936, the government of the United States created a large number of temporary bureaus and agencies. In this paper I shall be concerned primarily with the question of why some agencies were accepted permanently whereas others were soon abandoned. I shall consider the agencies in four groups: those abandoned after a short trial, those replaced by other agencies, those abandoned because their purpose was accomplished, and those still in existence.

[*The classification of the final sentence is changed to one which depends on a single principle—the permanence of the agencies. The basis for classification in the revision is the one suggested by the paragraph's statement of the purpose of the paper.*]

Exercise 6

A. Select any five of the following general topics and list subdivisions— parts, elements, stages, etc.—revealed by analysis.

1. A football team
2. A newspaper
3. A storm
4. Building a tree house
5. A university
6. Snobbishness
7. Registration day
8. A gasoline engine
9. Learning to swim
10. A garden

B. Consider the following subjects; obviously they are much too broad for brief papers. Limit these subjects by analysis, and then write a theme sentence for each in which you announce the subject of the proposed essay and give sufficient indication of the basis on which the analysis was made. Review of Section 1 will help.

1. Political tension in Asia
2. The teacher shortage
3. A recent political campaign
4. The economic problems of the emerging African nations
5. Automation and the labor problem
6. Juvenile delinquency
7. The farmer in the modern world
8. Picking the right college
9. Summer vacations
10. Modern music

C. Make two separate classifications for the items in each of the following groups, classifying each time on a different basis and being sure to classify on only one basis at a time:

1. canned peas, frozen pears, canned peaches, a can of wax, a dozen clothes pins, 10 pounds of potatoes, a dozen oranges, frozen peaches, a can of kitchen cleanser

2. baseball, tennis, swimming, basketball, diving, skiing

3. advanced economics, freshman chemistry, beginning history, physics seminar, beginning German, first-year Italian, freshman biology, senior French

D. Indicate one item in each of the following classifications which is inconsistent because it has not been classified on the same basis as the other items:

1. Books: *into* novels, collections of poems, collections of short stories, leather-bound books, collections of plays, histories, textbooks

2. Shoes: *into* leather shoes, canvas shoes, horseshoes

3. Dresses: *into* evening dresses, afternoon dresses, sports dresses, cotton dresses, dinner dresses.

4. Criminals: *into* burglars, murderers, incorrigibles, arsonists, embezzlers

5. Literature: *into* novels, poetry, drama, pastorals, short fiction

E. The following paragraph is confused for a number of reasons, but it can be put in order if it is revised after clear analysis of the problem. What light do our presidents throw on the question of humor as an asset in politics? Analyze the problem, classify the evidence on the basis of your analysis, and rewrite the paragraph with a central idea and clear evidence of organization.

Neither Richard Nixon nor John F. Kennedy was devoid of a sense of humor, but neither was notable for it; Kennedy's victory seems to provide little evidence one way or the other. Calvin Coolidge did have a sense of humor, a salty Vermont wit. Very few people liked it much. George Washington was a great general and a great president. He had dignity, but apparently not much sense of humor. William Howard Taft is said to have been a very genial man in private, but he was also a very heavy man, and thus in public life he was more frequently the butt of humor than the creator of it. Most of our presidents, if they do not illustrate the assertion "The people expect their statesmen to be solemn asses," give us little reason to suppose that a sense of humor is a political asset. Woodrow Wilson had a sense of humor, which he used in his scholarly writing and in the privacy of his home. John Adams and John Quincy Adams were men of subtle mind, but they seem not to have enjoyed laughing. Adlai Stevenson, who convulsed his audiences when he was campaigning against Dwight D. Eisenhower, was defeated twice, whether because of his humor or in spite of it. Of the early presidents, only Thomas Jefferson seems to have enjoyed a joke, a very quiet joke well screened from public view. Theodore Roosevelt was perhaps not subtle enough to have much humor; as Professor T. V. Smith has said, "He exclaimed 'bully' from the larynx more often than he laughed from the belly." Franklin Roosevelt used his humor sparingly and for calculated effects. When Peter Cartwright, a frontier evangelist, was campaigning against Lincoln for Congress, he accused Lincoln of not knowing where he wanted to go because he would stand neither with those who were certain they would go to heaven nor with those who expected to go to hell. "I aim, of course, to go to Congress," Lincoln drawled. More recently, both Lyndon B. Johnson and Barry Goldwater could crack jokes, but Goldwater's wit did not save him and Johnson's homely humor probably brought him few votes. Presidents like Zachary Taylor and Andrew Jackson were blunt, almost humorless men, but they were triumphant vote getters and popular presidents. Even Madison and Monroe were notably solemn. Abraham Lincoln, whose sense of humor became legend, offers the only notable exception to the general rule that our presidents have not been characterized by their sense of humor. Some presidents seem to have had some sense of humor, but hesitated to use it in politics, or in any connection suggestive of state affairs. Harding probably lacked the liveliness of mind either to engender or to appreciate much humor.

Organization; the Outline

For Guide to Revision, see page 111.

Organization, planned in the outline, reveals the relationships among ideas, the essentials of the composition.

Analysis, as Section 6 indicates, can expose the parts or elements of a subject; but even after analysis the writer faces the problem of ordering these parts. Which is to come first, which last? Often the order can be readily determined by following a chronological or a spatial pattern; sometimes the problem of order is more complex and depends on the logical relationships which the writer wants to establish.

Chronological Organization 7-1

In the following sentences, order shows a chronological relationship:

A yellow convertible flashed by the billboard and screamed around the curve. A traffic policeman wheeled his motorcycle from its hiding place and roared into the highway.

Because one sentence precedes the other, the reader assumes that the event it describes precedes the other event. Reversing the order of the sentences would reverse the order of events and save a fine for the driver of the convertible.

Any record of happenings can almost always be planned around related times—often by the simple procedure of putting first things first. The following description of Mary Stuart's preparation for execution is organized in this way:

She laid her crucifix on her chair. The chief executioner took it as a perquisite, but was ordered instantly to lay it down. The lawn veil was lifted carefully off, not to disturb the hair, and was hung upon the rail. The black robe was next removed. Below it was a petticoat of crimson velvet. The black jacket followed, and under the jacket was a bodice of crimson satin. One of her ladies handed her a pair of crimson sleeves, with which she hastily covered her arms; and thus she stood on the black scaffold with the black figures all around her, blood-red from head to foot.

—JAMES ANTHONY FROUDE, *History of England*

7-2   Spatial Organization

Order can show relationship in space as well as in time. To help the reader picture relative positions, the writer reflects spatial arrangement by the arrangement of his sentences. For example, a writer describing a scene can arrange details as they meet the eye.

The ship turned sharply and steamed slowly in. It was a great landlocked harbour big enough to hold a fleet of battleships; and all around it rose, high and steep, the green hills. Near the entrance, getting such breeze as blew from the sea, stood the governor's house in a garden. The Stars and Stripes dangled languidly from a flag staff.   —SOMERSET MAUGHAM, *Rain*

Even though the writer's purpose may be to set a scene and center attention on a particular object, the method may be by spatial arrangement, as in the following, where relationship words are notably those of space—*on, among, removed, near, above, under,* and *where.*

On the shelving bank of the river, among the slimy stones of a causeway— not the special causeway of the Six Jolly Fellowships, which had a landing place of its own, but another, a little removed, and very near to the old windmill which was the denounced man's dwelling-place—were a few boats; some, moored and already beginning to float; others, hauled up above the reach of the tide. Under one of these latter Eugene's companion disappeared. And when Eugene had observed its position with reference to the other boats, and had made sure that he could not miss it, he turned his eyes upon the building, where, as he had been told, the lonely girl with the dark hair sat by the fire.   —CHARLES DICKENS, *Our Mutual Friend*

7-3   Logical Organization

In much expository writing, the chronological and spatial patterns common in narrative and descriptive writing are inadequate. The writer must reveal complicated relationships between the elements of his main idea, relationships that can be loosely described as "logical"—such as cause and effect, conclusion and reasons, comparison or contrast, or the steps in a chain of reasoning. Sometimes organization is logical in relatively strict senses; Commander X receives unexpected reinforcements just at the time the river freezes over between him and his enemy, and his scouts report that the opposing forces have been decimated by a plague. Commander X decides to attack; the organization of a description of this decision is clearly that of cause to effect. Conversely, consider the situation of a householder who discovers water leaking into his living room. The leak is an effect; what is the cause? He checks the flashing of the chimney, the calking around essential nails, the flue, and the concrete cap on the chimney. All seem to be in order. Then he remembers that although the chimney is built of porous blocks it has never been waterproofed. He concludes that the chimney needs waterproofing. The order here is clearly that of effect back to cause.

Most writing is essentially logical if only loosely so. Consider the following, in which Thomas Jefferson is writing to a young student friend of his, urging him to examine objectively the claims of truth made by different religions.

> For example, in the book of Joshua, we are told, the sun stood still several hours. Were we to read that fact in Livy or Tacitus, we should class it with their showers of blood, speaking of statues, beasts, etc. But is it said, that the writer of that book was inspired. Examine, therefore, candidly, what evidence there is of his having been inspired. The pretension is entitled to inquiry, because millions believe it. On the other hand, you are astronomer enough to know how contrary it is to the law of nature that a body revolving on its axis, as the earth does, should have stopped, should not, by that sudden stoppage, have prostrated animals, trees, buildings, and should after a certain time have resumed its revolutions, and that without a second general prostration. Is this arrest of the earth's motion, or the evidence which affirms it, most within the law of probabilities?   —THOMAS JEFFERSON, *Letter to Peter Carr*

Jefferson is presenting a problem logically, and he orders his material with respect to logic, stating a proposition, breaking it into parts, presenting evidence, moving toward a conclusion.

The following paragraph is essentially logical, but less strictly so because the logical requirements are less rigid. The authors have said that language grows, and in this paragraph they are providing an example; their presentation, however, differs from Jefferson's in that they are presenting evidence, not balancing one set of evidence against another set.

> The history of *torpedo* offers a good illustration. It was originally the name of a fish of the ray family (*torpedinidae*), capable of emitting electric discharges. The name is derived from Latin *torpere,* "to be numb or stiff." There existed

in English names for this fish, as for instance, *cramp-fish, cramp-ray,* and *numb-fish,* which, however, were early superseded by the Latin term. The fish's curious electric power provided an atmosphere of mystery to a people who knew nothing of electricity. Naturally they regarded it as venomous and thought of it with horror. The *Oxford Dictionary* illustrates the use of the word in the sixteenth century with the quotation (1589), "like the fish Torpedo, which being towchd sends her venime alongst line and angle rod, till it cease on the finger, and so mar a fisher for euer." The traditionally dangerous nature of the fish made it early a suitable source of metaphor. Christopher Marlowe applied it to a dangerous human being:

> Fair queen, forbear to angle for the fish
> Which, being caught, strikes him that takes it dead;
> I mean that vile torpedo, Gaveston,
> That now I hope floats on the Irish seas.

Another metaphorical use is illustrated by Dr. Johnsons's remark, "Tom Birch is as brisk as a bee in conversation; but no sooner does he take a pen in his hand, than it becomes a torpedo to him, and benumbs all his faculties."

—ROBERT M. ESTRICH and HANS SPERBER, *Three Keys to Language*

The organization of the material is to a degree chronological, but mainly logical, telling how the word came from Latin, how it acquired new implications by superstition, and then how it developed metaphorical uses.

7-4   The Outline

For the word, for the paragraph, for the whole composition, various devices can be used to show classifications and relationships. For an extensive composition, the most useful tool for these purposes is the outline. With it, the writer can organize his material, coordinating it, subordinating it, arranging it. With the outline he can also test the results of his organization.

Student writers often resist the suggestion that they should write from an outline. An outline, they insist, is too limiting; it "stifles inspiration." Usually such students either have the wrong notion of what an outline should be or have found that outlining requires clear thinking and do not want to think. Actually, an outline provides the easiest method of doing preliminary thinking well, and good writing requires clear thinking. An outline is a means of saving time—provided the writer is trying to write well.

For a single paragraph or a short theme, one may keep his plan in mind without a written record, and an experienced writer knows basic patterns so well that he can compose still larger units without a written outline. A skilled carpenter can put together a considerable structure without a blueprint. But a contractor is not likely to start construction on a house without a set of carefully worked-out plans. A writer working seriously on an extensive piece of writing will not proceed without an outline.

The outline is a means to an end, not an end in itself. Since it is practical, it should have the most useful form the writer can devise. For a paragraph or two or for an answer to an essay question on an examination, a few scribbled headings may be sufficient. For longer compositions, however, the writer should follow the procedures described below because they will produce the kind of outline that will be most helpful.

Classification, Coordination, and Subordination   7-5

The basic processes necessary to successful outlining have already been discussed. The outline records the classification of material (see 6-3) and the arrangement of material to reveal coordination and subordination (see 3-2). Outlining can proceed only as a development of a main idea (see Section 1). A statement of the main idea, in a clear, complete sentence, is the first step in preparing an outline. For example, a writer thinking through a possible theme on "Women at State University" tentatively decides that he wants to show that "At State University women do not have rights and privileges equal to those of the men." He begins his outline with this statement. He then jots down ideas; let us assume that he produces something like the following:

1. Rules requiring women to live in dormitories
2. Rules regulating hours women must come in at night
3. The paragraph in the University Catalog concerning equal rights for all students
4. Women in student-body offices
5. Men's lounge in Union Building, but no women's lounge
6. As many women on campus as men
7. Women not willing to assert their rights
8. Rules requiring women to eat in dining hall
9. Swimming pool privileges
10. Rules on leaving campus
11. Intercollegiate athletics
12. College women just as responsible as college men
13. Attitudes of parents

14. The time Anne Wilkins was expelled but the boy who was equally guilty was not
15. Women not interested in student government
16. Gymnasium and athletic facilities
17. Modern women taking equal responsibilities in the world
18. Military service of women

The list is a beginning, a record of random thoughts about a subject; it is not a record of organized thinking. To organize his material, the writer needs to analyze his subject and classify his details.

He may do so in a more or less systematic way. He may ask himself: What are the principal aspects of the life of women on the campus, and which of these do I wish to consider? That is, he may start by analyzing his subject and stating a main idea which can be used as the basis of classification. Or, he can start by examining his jottings to see whether he can observe any general groups and by classifying material under general headings. He can check his findings later by asking himself whether the headings he gets do or do not constitute an adequate analysis. As a matter of practice, of course, most writers use analysis and classification pretty much unconsciously as twin means of restricting a subject, ordering it, and developing it.

The student may now appropriately look over his jottings. If he is to write on discrimination against women at State University, some material is obviously inappropriate and can be thrown out, items 4 and 17, for instance. On the other hand, items 1 and 2 begin a list of discriminatory rules. Items 5 and 9 suggest a class of inequalities in university facilities. Items 3 and 6 might suggest reasons for equality. Item 7 might suggest a class which would require new material, reasons for inequalities. Some items would seem inappropriate to the main idea and should therefore be stricken out. The list, then, could be rearranged and expanded by classification somewhat as follows:

Rules that discriminate against women

1. Rules requiring women to live in dormitories
2. Rules regulating hours women must come in at night
8. Rules requiring women to eat in dining hall
10. Rules on leaving campus
14. Expulsion of Anne Wilkins (might fit here as example of use of rules)
     Rules for sororities stricter than those for fraternities [*The writer thinks of a new point as he is making the classification.*]

Inequalities in university facilities

5. Men's lounge in Union Building
9. Swimming pool privileges
11. Intercollegiate athletics
16. Gymnasium and athletic facilities

Reasons why there should be equality

3. The statement of the University Catalog
6. As many women on campus as men
12. College women just as responsible as college men
17. Modern women taking equal responsibilities in the world
18. Military service of women

Causes for inequalities

7. Women not willing to assert their rights
15 Women not interested in student government
Tradition in colleges and world
Prevalence of men in administration and on faculties
Old prejudices against educating women
[*The writer adds new items.*]

Such classification is the beginning of an outline, but the writer must still give the outline form by considering the classes in terms of the main idea and in terms of the proposed length of his paper. Strictly speaking, only the first two of the classes listed above apply to the proposed subject. Reasons for equality and causes of inequalities could be incorporated, but they would expand the paper beyond manageable length. The writer therefore limits his main headings to:

I. Rules that discriminate against women
II. Inequalities in university facilities

He then subordinates details to these main headings, thinks of further details to support his ideas, and chooses an order for his topics.

The writer should never hesitate to add to his outline any kind of note that may help him later. Often as he works he has useful ideas for a transition, for a striking introduction, for an incident for illustration, for an apt phrase. He can jot them down on his outline so that he will not forget to use them in the appropriate places.

The degrees of subordination are conventionally indicated in an outline by indenting and by labeling subdivisions alternately with numbers and letters. A conventional form is shown below.

I. _____
   A. _____
      1. _____
      2. _____
   B. _____
II. _____
   A. _____
   B. _____
      1. _____
         a. _____
            (1) _____
            (2) _____
         b. _____
      2. _____
         a. _____
         b. _____
   C. _____

7-6   The Complete Outline

The final outline, then, includes a statement of the main idea, a note on the introduction and conclusion, and a summary of the main topics to be discussed in the body of the paper, with relationships between them indicated by numbers and indentation. The following outline might be developed from the materials collected above for a paper on "Women in State University."

STATEMENT OF MAIN IDEA: At State University, women do not have rights and privileges equal to those of the men.

INTRODUCTION: Use the statement in the University Catalog that all students have equal rights and privileges and point out that the paper will show the statement to be false.

[*A detail that the writer recalled when first thinking about the topic seems to provide a possible introduction. The writer gives himself a reminder.*]

  I. Rules that discriminate against women
     A. Dormitory rules (begin paragraph with story of expulsion of Anne Wilkins)

[*Again the writer sees a place to use a detail and makes a note.*]

    1. Rules requiring women to live in dormitories
    2. Rules on hours
    3. Registration and signout system
    4. Rules forbidding leaving dormitory and campus

  B. Sorority rules — regulations stricter than those for fraternities

  C. Rules requiring women to eat in dining hall
    1. Expense of dining hall
    2. Quality of food

II. Inequalities in university facilities. (Possible transition pointing out that above rules can be justified on ground that they are for students' "own good" but that other inequalities cannot.)

  A. Social facilities
    1. Lack of meeting places for women's organizations
    2. Lack of a room comparable to the men's lounge in the Union Building

  B. Athletic facilities
    1. Lack of women's activity comparable to men's intercollegiate athletic program
    2. Lack of equal swimming-pool privileges
    3. Restriction on women's use of gymnasium

CONCLUSION: Use idea that there are as many women on the campus as men, that they will have equal responsibilities in the world, and that they should have equal rights and privileges in college.

[The writer sees need for classification more detailed than in preliminary organization.]

[The expansion of point B is not illogically made a single subdivision.]

[A lengthy note for future use records an idea that occurs to the writer as he makes the outline.]

[Coordination of topics is indicated by parallel form.]

[A possible conclusion is suggested by another of the groups of details rejected in preparing the body of the outline.]

The outline is a working guide. It should be used but should not be followed slavishly. Obviously a writer cannot visualize a paper perfectly. He will change his mind as he works out paragraphs and sentences, and he will think of new material. He should use his outline as a preliminary sketch, constantly subject to revision and expansion as the writing proceeds.

7-7 The Sentence Outline

Many writers prefer a sentence outline, which differs from the sample outline above only in that it employs sentences rather than topics. The outline above, put in the form of a sentence outline, would start as something like the following:

STATEMENT OF MAIN IDEA—At State University, women do not have rights and privileges equal to those of the men.

INTRODUCTION—The University Catalog includes the statement that all students have equal rights, but this statement is not true, either in light of the regulations or the interpretation of regulations.

I. University rules discriminate against women.
   A. Dormitory rules discriminate against women, as is apparent in the case of Anne Wilkins.
      1. Rules require that all freshmen women live in dormitories, sororities, or private dwellings approved by the dean.

A respect for form and parallelism in an outline requires either that all headings in the outline be sentences or that none of them be, and certainly any outline used for itself should use one form or the other consistently. An outline, however, is usually practical; when the paper is written the outline has become useless, and many a competent writer pays little attention to whether his headings are parallel or not. The extra thinking required to make items parallel certainly does no harm, and most writers find it useful, even for a strictly utilitarian outline.

7-8 Utilizing the Outline to Check Logic

Obviously, an outline provides an orderly guide to writing, but it can have other uses as well. We have already noticed that it encourages thinking prior to writing; it also encourages continuity in thinking and in collecting material. Weeks, months, or even years may elapse during the preparation of an extensive piece of writing, but if the author has prepared a good outline with which to refresh his memory he can always return to his original plan. More immediately, the writer can use his outline to check the adequacy and logic of his planning or to guide him in revision of his first draft. Checking the finished draft against the outline or sketching a new outline of the draft can help the writer test for adequate planning, proportion, and logical relationships among items.

Guide to Revision **7**   **Org**

Rewrite to improve organization. Usually revision of the outline is a first step.

Faulty organization almost always results from a combination of difficulties, including faulty classification (see Section 6), lack of proper subordination (see 3-2), inadequate development (see Section 4), and lack of a main idea (see Section 1). Usually the writer should go back to the outline stage and reorganize and rewrite the entire paper.

Org a   Clear Planning   **7a**

Every piece of writing should have a clear, orderly plan.

ORIGINAL

A word not only indicates an object but can also suggest an emotional meaning. The essence of poetry depends upon words that arouse the emotions of the reader. An experiment may be conducted to prove how much words mean in poetry. Replace the emotionally filled words with neutral ones, and all the poetic value will be knocked out of the poem by the change. Poli-

REVISION

A word not only "means"; it conveys emotion. If we refer to a dog as a *mongrel,* we objectively define his pedigree, but we also reveal an attitude toward the dog.

The emotional meanings of words are useful, especially if the writer's purpose is to sway opinion. Poetry, for example, depends on words that arouse the emotions of the reader, as anyone may demonstrate if he will

111

ORIGINAL (*Cont.*)

ticians are apt at changing the public's opinion merely by the use of words. "Bolshevik," "Fascist," "reactionary," "revolutionary" are examples of emotional words used by politicians. Emotional words find their place in poetry but are out of place in modern science where exact thinking is required. The scientist wants only the facts. He does not want to be swayed by words, only facts. This type of straight scientific thinking results in new discoveries. Science has worked hard ridding their books and discussions of emotional words; politics should do the same. The use of emotional words makes it hard for us to think straight in national and social problems. If clear unemotional words were used by people in the government, it would benefit our civilization. People would then be able to form their opinions by facts, not words.

Emotion-filled words are used not only by politicians but also by critics. By the use of words a critic can sway the public opinion against a writer, simply because he does not like the work.

We need to be careful not to form opinions on emotionally filled words.

[*The student theme printed above contains many inaccuracies. (As a review exercise, the student might profitably see how many errors he can find in it.) Worse, the paper lacks any clear plan. An attempt to outline the theme reveals its weakness, for a meaningful outline proves to be almost impossible. An attempt might look like this:*

INTRODUCTION: *Words have emotional as well as denotative meaning.*

    I. *Importance of emotional words to poetry*
  II. *Use of emotional words by politicians*

REVISION (*Cont.*)

replace the emotion-filled words of a poem with neutral ones; all the poetic value will be knocked out of the poem by the change.

Emotional words have their place in poetry, but they are misleading when we are concerned with facts rather than attitudes. The scientist, for example, wants facts; he does not want to be swayed by words. He has worked to rid his books and discussion of emotional words, and by straight scientific thinking has made important discoveries. Politicians have not done the same. They are apt at changing the public's opinion merely by the use of such emotional words as *Bolshevik, Fascist, reactionary,* or *revolutionary.* They prevent straight thinking about national and social problems. If people in the government would use clear, unemotional words, we could form opinions on facts, not words, and society would benefit.

Emotional words can present a danger as well as an advantage, and we need to be careful not to form opinions on them.

[*The theme is still undeveloped, in spite of the addition of an illustration or two. But it does come nearer than the original to showing how ideas are related. The revision involved first of all a new outline:*

STATEMENT OF MAIN IDEA: *Emotion-filled words are a handicap to scientific thinking.*

INTRODUCTION: *Words not only "mean"; they convey emotions.*

  I. *Usefulness of emotional words*
    A. *Usefulness in swaying opinions*
    B. *Usefulness in poetry*
  II. *Dangers of emotional words*
    A. *Use in science*
    B. *Use in politics*

ORIGINAL (*Cont.*)

III. *Avoidance of emotional words by scientists*

IV. *Danger of emotional words in politics*

V. *Use of emotional words by critics*

CONCLUSION: *We need to be careful in using emotion-filled words.*

Topic II is out of order. The outline reveals the lack of classification of material and the failure to subordinate minor to major topics.]

REVISION (*Cont.*)

CONCLUSION: *We should avoid emotion-filled words to form opinions.*

The new outline classifies topics under two main headings and organizes the paper around a central idea. It changes the illogical order revealed by the original outline. The writing follows the outline, corrects the obvious errors in accuracy, revises many of the sentences, and leaves out the undeveloped and nonessential example of the critic.]

Org b   Proportion   **7b**

Inadequate planning leads to badly proportioned compositions. The writer who puts words on paper without a good outline may find that he has used half his space without reaching the center of his topic; he may become so much interested in one example that he has no space for other topics. A writer must plan so that secondary matters do not steal space needed for main ideas. The following outline of a 2,000-word investigative paper reveals the difficulty:

ORIGINAL

Marijuana and Juvenile Delinquency

STATEMENT OF MAIN IDEA: Marijuana is not an important cause of juvenile delinquency in our society.   .

I. The history of marijuana
   A. American Indians
   B. Europe
   C. The United States
II. Methods of growth and preparation of marijuana
   A. Growth of the hemp plant
      1. Ease of cultivation
      2. Extent of cultivation
   B. Extraction of the drug
   C. Commercial uses of the plant
III. Use and effects of marijuana
   A. Methods of taking drug

REVISION

Marijuana and Juvenile Delinquency

STATEMENT OF MAIN IDEA: Marijuana is not an important cause of juvenile delinquency in our society.

INTRODUCTION: Current concern about use of marijuana by juveniles and widespread opinion that it is a major cause of juvenile delinquency

I. Use of drugs by juveniles
   A. Methods of distribution of marijuana
      1. Distribution by amateurs
      2. Professional dope rings
   B. Marijuana and music
   C. Control of distribution
      1. Control by schools and welfare groups

113

ORIGINAL (*Cont.*)

    B. Characteristic behavior of users

    C. Question of habit formation

IV. Use of drugs by juveniles

    A. Methods of distribution of marijuana

    B. Control of distribution

    C. Marijuana and music

    D. Studies of extent and use

       1. Government statistics

       2. Recent studies of New York schools

CONCLUSION: Marijuana is not one of the major causes of juvenile delinquency in the United States today.

[*The outline suggests a superficial discussion of questions not pertinent to the main idea. Sections I, II, and III are out of proportion. Part IV is the central part of the paper, and should be built up. As the revision shows, I and II could be omitted and other sections developed to illustrate the main idea.*]

REVISION (*Cont.*)

    2. Law enforcement

    D. Cost of drugs to juveniles

    E. Studies of extent of use

       1. Government statistics

       2. Recent studies of New York schools

II. Effects of marijuana on juveniles

    A. Characteristic behavior of users of drug

       1. Actions while under influence of drug

       2. Aftereffects

    B. Habit formation

    C. Limited use of the drug

       1. Numbers of addicts in recent years

       2. Improved methods of restricting use

       3. Areas in which drug is used

CONCLUSION: Marijuana is not one of the major causes of juvenile delinquency in the United States today.

[*The revised outline needs further development, but at least it improves proportions.*]

7c   Individual Items in the Outline   Org c; Out

Individual items in the outline should be specific enough to be useful, should be parallel in form, should be arranged with due consideration for coordination and subordination, and, taken with other items, should approximate the item of which they are subdivisions.

Items should be as specific as the treatment of the subject allows. Notice the following:

Getting a Deer

I. Planning the hunt

    A. Reasons

    B. Methods

[*The writer has done almost nothing to plan his paper beyond deciding on what is apparently a chronological arrangement*

II. Finding the deer
A. Methods
B. Incidents
III. The kill
A. Incidents
B. Results

in three main stages. There is no main idea. And none of the material has been classified or arranged. One suspects that the writer has just not thought much about what the "methods" and "incidents" are.]

An outline permits the writer to record his thinking before he writes and to assure himself that his plan is adequate and orderly. Consider the following, which is the first part of a sentence outline:

TOPIC: Satire in Washington Irving's *Knickerbocker's Hisory of New York.*

[*The outline starts well; clearly, the author has thought his subject through. He has a main idea and he has phrased it with some care.*]

STATEMENT OF MAIN IDEA: The character of the satire in Irving's *History* changed as the work progressed and as the author matured, from genial persiflage and parody in the earlier section chapters, to salty high comedy toward the middle, and to trenchant, even bitter satire after the death of Irving's fiancée.

INTRODUCTION: Writing is inevitably associated with the writer; Irving's *History* seems to provide a good example, reflecting the changing emotions of a brilliant but disturbed young man.
1. The early chapters reflect Irving as an impudent young litterateur in a provincial city.
A. In the early years of the nineteenth century, Irving was one of a group who wrote gay, witty articles.
1. The pieces were intended to poke good-natured fun at the stodgy burghers and to flaunt a zeal for the arts.
a. The pieces were published as the *Salmagundi Papers.*
(1) A salmagundi is a sort of stew.

[*After the introductory material an outline should reveal levels of subordination and coordination. That is, I should be parallel with II and III, which should approximate the whole of the main idea. In this outline they will, if III reads something like the following:*
III. The latter chapters, written after the shock which followed his fiancée's death, are feverish, bitter, and a little sad.]

[*Similarly, A and B should approximate I.*]

[*Obviously a and (1) are illogical; nothing can be subdivided into fewer than two. If there is no b, that is, if there was no second group of published papers, a can be incorporated within 1. Certainly (1) can be incorporated, if it is not so trivial as to be omitted.*]

2. Irving and his bachelor friends had gay parties in which they planned the next "paper" and laughed hilariously at the effect it would have.
   a. They delighted in listening to the lively speculation as to who the authors were.
   b. The authors, members of socially prominent families, knew all the important gossip, but wrote under pseudonyms.
   c. Irving and his friends like James K. Pauling thought these satirical pieces great good fun.

[Clearly, something is wrong here; 1 and 2 do not add up to A. Furthermore, a, b, and c do not add up to 2. Examination of the entries will reveal that the difficulty arises from the handling of what is now 2. If what is now 2 is made subordinate as c, and what is now c is made coordinate with 1 as 2, the whole will become relatively logical.]

B. The earlier chapters of the *History* read like an extended *Salmagundi* paper.
   1. There is a tendency to try to be funny by using learned words to say nothing and to parody local history writers.
   2. The content is similar; here we find the same twitting of important people, especially venerated Dutchmen.
   3. Style.
      a. Irving seems to be trying to show off and to be funny—even when he is funny.
      b. Irving one of great American writers.

[Again, something is wrong. A and B do add up roughly to I, but 1, 2, and 3 do not add up to B. The trouble is that B should apparently have two parts, one for content, one for style. The present 1 is not parallel with the present 2 and 3, which should become 1 and 2. Then the present 1 will find its appropriate place along with the present a under 3. The present b probably has no business in the outline, at least not here. Number 3 should be rewritten; it is not a sentence and hence not parallel with the other sentences.]

II. The body of the work reflects Irving as an unwilling law student, who took out some of his hatred of law by satirizing the foibles of officialdom.

[The last two thirds of the outline are omitted. To round it out, II should be developed and III should read something like the proposed heading above.]

Exercise 7

A. Below are preliminary notes for a theme called "Education for Women Today." They are not complete and are not necessarily pertinent or sufficiently specific. Using the list as a start, select a main idea for a possible theme and then construct an outline for it, using the notes which are pertinent. You will probably need to eliminate some notes, revise others, and add new ones to fit your main purpose.

1. Women in industry
2. Practical or cultural education
3. Education for successful marriage
4. Dormitory regulations for women
5. Women's physical education
6. Extracurricular activities for women
7. Discrimination between the sexes
8. Beauty shop apprenticeship
9. Teacher-training courses
10. Liberal arts training
11. Special course for social workers
12. Nurses' training
13. Laboratory technology for women
14. Preparation for life
15. Home economics
16. Courses in preparation for marriage
17. General culture
18. Business courses
19. The importance of English composition for the secretary
20. Number of women in college last year
21. Adult education
22. Music and dancing schools
23. Business colleges
24. The old-fashioned finishing school

B. Comment on the weaknesses of the following outlines.

TOPIC: Satire in Moving Picture Cartoons

STATEMENT OF MAIN IDEA: The satire in cartoons which appear today on the moving picture screen

7

Exercises

I. Introduction
   A. Increasing tendency toward satire in the cartoons
II. Caricatures of human beings
   A. Caricatures of types
      1. The man who loses his temper
         a. Donald Duck
      2. The pedant
         a. Examples
      3. Sentimental lovers
         a. Examples
   B. Particular individuals may appear in cartoons
III. Satire on situations in life
   A. Domestic life
   B. National affairs
IV. Conclusion
   A. General quality of satire
   B. Conforms to attitudes already present in most people

TOPIC: Success in the American University

STATEMENT OF MAIN IDEA: To write about success at the university

I. Introduction
   A. The purpose of a university
      1. Details of the purpose
      2. Further details
   B. The organization of a university
      1. Schools and colleges
      2. The campus
      3. The administration
      4. Registrar's office, comptroller, etc.
      5. Fraternities and sororities
   C. Types of students in a university
      1. Men
      2. Women
      3. Foreign students
      4. Negro students
      5. Independents
      6. Alumni organizations
II. Methods of attaining success in a university
   A. Attaining social success
      1. Fraternities and sororities
      2. Dances
      3. Games and athletic events
      4. Snack bars, soda fountains, etc.
         1. Make new friends, get dates, etc.
      5. The library
      6. Contacts which will be valuable in afterlife

      B. Athletic successes
         1. Major sports
         2. Minor sports
         3. Passing your courses
            1. Choosing courses you can pass
              a. Advice about choosing courses
  III. Conclusion
     A. Success in college and social activity

C. Below are numbered sentences that might be arranged into a short essay describing the group of sea animals which includes squids and octopuses. Make an outline arranging the sentences in the order they might have in a theme. Do not copy the statements, refer to them by number.

1. Among the animal's most interesting characteristics is its system of jet propulsion.
2. With this jet engine the cephalopod attains extraordinary speed.
3. They are octopuses, cuttlefish, and squids, and they are remarkable organisms in a variety of ways.
4. Among the thousands of creatures that inhabit the oceans of the world none is more interesting than those known as *Cephalopoda* or "head-footed ones."
5. The cephalopod can protect itself not only with its speed and remarkable strength for its size; it also has two physical properties with which it can become almost invisible.
6. Some of the tiny, slim varieties streak through the water as fast as flies move through the air.
7. They can leap from the water and dart by so fast that the eye cannot follow them.
8. Cephalopods may not live up to all the fantastic yarns about them told by ancient mariners, but they are certainly among the most interesting of the animals of the sea.
9. First, it developed the technique of the smoke screen long before modern navies.
10. The cephalopod is encased in a long, slim cloak, with a muscular collar that rings its neck and a funnel that sticks up in front.
11. Larger varieties, it is estimated, move over the surface of the ocean faster than the fastest speedboat.
12. The cephalopods have little ink sacs which manufacture and store ink, and they can squirt sepia cloud screens to shield them from their enemies.
13. It can then close the collar and squeeze its body suddenly and violently.
14. Swimming on its belly, the octopus or squid can pump water into its body cavity through the space between this collar and its neck.

15. They also can hide themselves because of their chameleon-like ability to change colors.

16. The water shoots out the funnel, propelling the animal backward.

17. The propulsion system of the squid or octopus is no more remarkable than its special devices for defense.

18. They can turn purple when annoyed, or on white sand they can pale to near invisibility.

D. Use the following as a main idea: "The story of the letter *A* reflects the history of the alphabet." Construct a suitable outline by classifying, co-ordinating, and subordinating. Reject any material not pertinent, and note any main divisions which need to be further divided or developed and any details which have no general heading. Remember that Greek and Roman times are often referred to as *classical,* that the Egyptians, Babylonians, and Semites were preclassical peoples, and that the period between classical and modern times is often called the Middle Ages, for which the adjective is *medieval.*

Changes in Latin
Sounds of the various letters
Early known forms of *A*
Introduction—story of how I learned letter *A*
Changes during the Middle Ages leading to modern upper-case *A*
Lost Greek forms of *A*
Greek reversal of the letter
Development of North Semite *A* into Phoenician *A*
The North Semites and the earliest known form of *A*
Modern upper-case *A* from the medieval book hand
Difference between *a* and *an*
Contributions of medieval Irish scribes to modern upper-case *A*
Changes in Greek
Interesting details about *U* and *V*
Medieval and modern forms of the letter
Influence of Greek "boustrophedon" writing on *A*
Symbol for Egyptian sacred bull as possible ancestor of *A*
Contributions of medieval French scribes to modern upper-case *A*
Hypothetical origins of *A*
Modern upper-case *A* from medieval court hand
Developments in classical times
Babylonian aleph as possible ancestor of *A*
Preclassical history of *A*

Transitions, Introductions,
Conclusions

For
Guide to Revision,
see page 131.

Transitions, introductions, and conclusions reveal the organization of a composition.

Readers can be compared to persons following a trail through a strange land, with the writer as guide. If the trail is long, the guide must break the journey into stages, so that the travelers do not become exhausted, but have places to stop for rest or food. If there are obstacles in the trail—rivers, mountains, or swamps—the guide must provide methods for coping with them. There must be a plan in the whole route and in the parts. Similarly, the writer must give adequate instructions at the start and must give warning every time the trail turns. He should even give occasional assurance that the reader is still on the trail, just as the markers of highways occasionally put up a sign, U. S. 30, even though there has been little opportunity to get off the road.

Devices for guiding the reader, for marking the trail, give continuity and coherence. They show how the thought continues from one element to another and how the parts cohere, stick together. Coherence depends in part on devices within the paragraph—transitional words, repetition of words and ideas, word order (see Section 5). A longer composition, moreover, may require more elaborate machinery to reveal its plan and outline—transitional sentences or paragraphs, introductions, conclusions.

Revealing the Main Outline   8-1

A writer should give the reader signposts or indications of the main plan of the composition. Without necessarily relying on the formal "first, second, and third," he can naturally and directly keep the reader aware of where the discourse is headed. Following, for example, are guides included by Sir Arthur Keith in an essay on studying the human body.

In all the medical schools of London a notice is posted over the door leading to the dissecting room forbidding strangers to enter. I propose, however, to push the door open and ask the reader to accompany me within. . . . We propose to watch them [the students] at work. Each student is at his allotted part, and if we observe them in turn we shall, in an hour or less, obtain an idea of the main tissues and structures which enter into the composition of the human body.

[These passages appear in the opening paragraph and show the reader the overall purpose of the essay and the writer's plan for achieving it—by observing the students as they dissect.]

By good fortune a dissection is in progress in front of the wrist, which displays, amongst other structures, the radial artery. . . .

[The second paragraph locates the reader near the first student.]

Lying side by side with the sinews of the wrist there is another cord. . . . It is the median nerve. . . .

[The third paragraph tells the reader that the essay is turning to another part of the wrist dissection.]

We propose to observe the dissector as he traces the radial artery to the heart. . . .

[The reader is guided to a further observation.]

Before leaving the dissection we have been surveying it will be well to see one of those marvelously contrived structures known as a joint. . . .

[The reader is led to another stage in this dissection and is also warned of a change to come.]

We have surveyed the anatomy at the wrist in some detail and with a very distinct purpose. . . .

[A summary or transitional paragraph marks the end of this episode; the reader is led to a turn in the trail.]

We now propose to transfer our attention for a short time to two students who are uncovering the parts in front of the neck between the chin and breastbone or sternum. . . .

[The writer indicates a major shift to a new dissection.]

Our time with the students in the dissection room has almost expired; there remains only a moment to glance at a dissection which is exposing the important organs which are enclosed within the thorax and abdomen. . . .

[The writer marks another turn and also prepares the reader for the end of the trail.]

Our cursory visit to the dissecting room has not been in vain if the reader has realized how complex the structure of the human body really is, and how necessary it is that those who have to cure its disorders should try to understand the intricacy of its mechanism. . . .
—*Man: A History of the Human Body*

[*The conclusion reminds the reader of the purpose of the discussion.*]

The essay includes even more guides to its general pattern than have been excerpted here, but these samples, most of them opening sentences of paragraphs, illustrate the importance of such aids. These passages outline the complete essay:

MAIN IDEA: A visit to the dissecting room reveals the complexity of the human body and the importance of studying it.

 I. The anatomy at the wrist: the first dissection
   A. The radial artery
   B. The median nerve
   C. Tracing the radial artery to the heart
   D. The joint
 II. The parts in front of the neck
 III. Organs within the thorax and abdomen

The reader can follow clearly and easily because the writer has revealed his outline step by step.

Topic Sentences as Transitions   **8-2**

As the selections above indicate, the topic sentence (see 2-4) is the most useful guide from paragraph to paragraph. It introduces the topic of its own paragraph, but it can also link its paragraph with preceding material, providing a transition. Consider, for example, the following three topic sentences, taken at random from a discussion of the formation of a national government in America:

This solution was achieved under the Articles of Confederation, a formal agreement which had loosely unified the colonies since 1781. . . .

Thus a new colonial policy based upon the principle of equality was inaugurated. . . .

Unfortunately, however, in the solution of other problems the Articles of Confederation proved disappointing.

In the first of the topic sentences, *This solution* refers directly to what has preceded; then the sentence goes on to introduce the Articles of Confederation as the topic of its paragraph. The second sentence refers with the word *Thus*, but it provides continuity also because it summarizes the entire preceding paragraph, putting the material into new terms which emphasize the new aspect of the topic to be considered, the use of equality as a basis of the policy. The third provides a transition in two ways, by echoing the word *solution* from the first sentence and by referring to previous material with *other problems*.

Frequently, in order to clarify a transition, a writer uses two sentences, making his transition in the first sentence of the paragraph and stating his topic in the second. For example, DeWitt H. Parker moves to a new section of an essay on aesthetics as follows:

> In our discussion thus far, we have been assuming the possibility of aesthetic theory. But what shall we say in answer to the mystic who tells us that beauty is indefinable?

The first sentence summarizes what has preceded. The second introduces the topic of the paragraph, the possibilities of defining beauty.

8-3   Transitional Paragraphs

For brief papers, well-written topic sentences can supply all the transitional material necessary. Longer compositions may be broken into large divisions containing several paragraphs with transitions important enough to require brief transitional paragraphs. Thomas Henry Huxley, in an essay on the method of scientific investigation, moves from a series of examples of how we behave "scientifically" in everyday life to a more serious discussion of causal relationships, relying on the following relatively formal paragraph:

> So much, then, by way of proof that the method of establishing laws in science is exactly the same as that pursued in common life. Let us now turn to another matter (though really it is but another phase of the same question), and that is, the method by which, from the relations of certain phenomena, we prove that some stand in the position of causes toward the others.
>
> —*Darwiniana*

The paragraph has the qualities of a good topic sentence used transitionally, although it is developed more fully. Its first sentence summarizes what has preceded; the second tells us precisely and directly what is to follow.

The Introduction   8-4

"The beginning," Plato wrote long ago, "is the most important part of the work." It is important because it fixes the reader's attention, sets the tone of the paper, and suggests what the composition is to be about. It may also, of course, in a longer work, provide any necessary background information about the subject or the circumstances of the writing or the validity of the material. It need not be long; in fact, papers suffer more frequently from top-heavy, rambling introductions than from brevity in the beginning. But whatever else it does, the introduction must introduce.

In order to introduce, an introduction usually presents the main idea of the paper, either in a direct statement or by implication. Like the topic sentence in a paragraph, it makes the commitment which the remainder of the paper is to fulfill (see 5-1). It identifies the subject and leads gracefully into the body of the discussion. There is no recipe for introductions; various approaches may serve, and the writer may change his introduction half a dozen times before he finishes the final draft. He may prepare a very formal introduction which he knows he will discard, go on to complete the writing, and then return to work out a more interesting beginning. Or he may hit upon an idea for an introduction when he is first considering his subject. The following paragraphs illustrate some common ways of getting a paper started:

1. *Statement of proposition.* Often a direct statement of the proposition to be defended provides a good introduction.

The Growing Power of Admen

America's advertising industry is moving into a commanding role in our society. Its executives are becoming masters of our economic destiny, the engineers behind some of our most successful political campaigns, . . . —VANCE PACKARD

[*Here Packard begins with his general thesis, continues with general illustrations, and goes on to more specific evidence.*]

2. *Presentation of factual background.* An opening offering factual statements to provide some justification or background or reason for the proposition of the composition is one of the most common and most successful.

What Every Writer Must Learn

The teaching of writing has become practically a profession by now. There is hardly a college in the land that does not offer at least one course in "creative writing" (whatever that is) by some "teacher of writing" (whoever he is). There are, moreover, at least fifty annual writers' conferences now functioning among us with something like fifty degrees of competence. And there seems to be no way of counting the number of literary counselors, good and bad, who are prepared to promise that they can teach a writer what he needs to know. —JOHN CIARDI

[*The introduction continues, after this opening, to assert that writing requires inventiveness and then to consider six ways in which the writer's talents for creation may be realized.*]

The Pittsburgh Story

Six years ago, insiders were wondering if Pittsburgh was a used-up community. For a variety of reasons, the oldest, biggest, and most powerful center of heavy industry, the leading steelmaker for all the world, was shriveling away. . . .

Then, suddenly, something happened. —KARL SCHRIFTGIESSER

[*The essay describing the plan on which a city is being developed begins by describing the situation which stimulated development of the plan.*]

3. *Questions to isolate a problem.* Opening a paper with a series of questions to lead to the main topic can be effective, but this device must be used with caution, for in unskilled hands it can seem overoratorical and affected.

Force and Freedom

Can there be a moral basis for freedom in a world of force? This is one of the ugly questions which disturb many intelligent people at this moment. Can we reconcile the doctrine of military force—the idea of killing men in war—with a moral purpose? As a matter of history, freedom has often emerged from the successful use of force; yet we abominate war as intensely as we love free-

[*A series of questions leads to the basic problem of the paper: the relationship between force and freedom. The first question is the main one the writer will try to answer.*]

dom. How are we to resolve this
paradox? —JAMES BRYANT CONANT

4. *Analysis.* The introduction may divide the subject into its
parts and indicate which parts will have emphasis (see Section 6).

The words "prospects in the arts
and sciences" mean two quite different things to me. One is prophecy:
What will the scientists discover and
the painters paint, what new forms
will alter music, what parts of experience will newly yield to objective
description? The other meaning is
that of a view: What do we see when
we look at the world today and compare it with the past? I am not a
prophet; and I cannot very well
speak to the first subject, though in
many ways I should like to. I shall
try to speak to the second, because
there are some features of this view
which seem to me so remarkable, so
new and so arresting, that it may be
worth turning our eyes to them; it
may even help us create and shape
the future better, though we cannot
foretell it.

—J. ROBERT OPPENHEIMER

[*The introduction is an excellent model
of the careful analytic opening. It divides
the topic into two parts, "prophecy" and
"view," announces that it will consider
only the second of these, and tells the
reader why.*]

5. *Statement of view the writer is to oppose.* The writer may begin
by describing a popular opinion he thinks erroneous; he may comment on earlier writings with which he expects to disagree; he may
mention a person with whom he differs. With this device the writer
can gain the interest that always attaches to an argument and at
the same time define his own stand by its opposite.

Roosevelt and the Far East

Even the most friendly of the
many Roosevelt biographers have a
tendency to imply that the President
gave little thought to foreign affairs
before 1939. The impression created
is far from accurate.

—SUMNER WELLES

[*The introduction moves the writer—
and the reader—quickly into the main
matter of the essay: a defense of Roosevelt's
understanding of foreign policy.*]

6. *Justification or explanation of paper.* The writer may have been an eyewitness to an important event; he may have done exhaustive research; he may have conducted controlled experiments. Many research papers begin with a presentation which allows the reader to judge the validity of the material presented.

Thomas Couture

My first meeting with Couture, who became one of my best and dearest friends, was odd and characteristic. It was in 1834; I was not yet one and twenty, and had just arrived from the United States, well provided for in the way of courage and determination, with a stock of youthful illusions, and very little besides. —GEORGE P. A. HEALY

[*The introduction has the easy grace of familiar narration, but it also lets the reader know that the writer is speaking on the basis of long and intimate acquaintance with his subject.*]

7. *A striking illustration or relevant incident.* An amusing anecdote which illustrates an attitude important to the theme catches the interest of the reader.

Can France Come Back?

Some time ago Monsieur Schuman, French Foreign Minister, was taking an early morning walk in the gardens of his official residence on the Quai d'Orsay. In the course of it he met an elderly gardener at work upon a flower bed. "Be off with you," said the gardener, "the public are not allowed in these gardens." "But I am the Minister." The gardener gazed distastefully at Monsieur Schuman. "Oh, well," he said at last, "if you're the Minister . . ." and turning his back, went on with his work.

Such an attitude may betoken. . . .
—HILARY ST. GEORGE SAUNDERS

[*Note that the second paragraph proceeds at once to explain the significance of the incident for the purposes of the essay and to lead the reader from it into the main matter to be discussed.*]

8. *A quotation.* A quotation may serve as a starting point because it illustrates the main idea to be presented.

The Uses of Flexibility

Thackeray wrote, "The wicked are wicked, no doubt, and they go astray and they fall, and they come by their desserts; but who can tell the mischief which the very virtuous do?"   —J. WILLIAM FULBRIGHT

[*Fulbright goes on to discuss the dangers of inflexible and intolerant attitudes growing from the purest of motives.*]

The Conclusion   8-5

Like introductions, conclusions vary widely, from long summaries to brief suggestions, from formal deductions to illustrative incidents. Even a short paper, however, will profit from evidence that the discussion is finished, that the writer has completed what he had to say—not stopped because he heard a bell or came to the end of a page. Usually this concluding comment recalls what the composition has done, reinforces its theme or argument; sometimes it adds final suggestions or advice that the writer wants to emphasize. The following paragraphs exemplify some possible types of conclusion:

1. *Restatement of main idea.* Modern exposition tends to conclude with a restatement of the main idea of the composition— usually not a formal summary but a fresh presentation of the idea.

The Illusion of the Two Cultures

Today we hold a stone, the heavy stone of power. We must perceive beyond it, however, by the aid of the artistic imagination, those humane insights and understandings which alone can lighten our burden and enable us to shape ourselves, rather than the stone, into the forms which great art has anticipated.
   —LOREN EISELEY

[*A scientist uses a prehistoric shaped stone as a unifying device for his essay and turns his conclusion about it, emphasizing his point that the artistic and the practical can work together.*]

2. *A supplementary comment.* A writer may reinforce his argument by adding a new but related observation, which serves to emphasize what the essay has said.

Walt Whitman: He Had His Nerve

Let me finish by mentioning another quality of Whitman's—a

[*The essay has discussed a variety of aspects of Whitman's poetry. The final*

129

quality, delightful to me, that I have said nothing of. If some day a tourist notices, among the ruins of New York City, a copy of *Leaves of Grass*, and stops and picks it up and reads some lines in it, she will be able to say to herself: "how very American! If he and his country had not existed, it would have been possible to imagine them." —RANDALL JARRELL

comment, although technically presenting a new quality, actually epitomizes the attitude of the essay.]

3. *Statement of importance, plea for change.* Many kinds of conclusions suggest the importance of what has been presented (for example, 1 above). They may also make a plea for a change of attitude or for specific action.

The Technique of the Modern Political Myths

We should carefully study the origin, the structure, the methods, and the technique of the political myths. We should see the adversary face to face in order to know how to combat him.   —ERNST CASSIRER

[*After describing the nature and importance of political myths, the writer concludes by suggesting what we should do—which is what his essay does.*]

Moonlight and Poison Ivy

Better marriage relations in this country await an extensive revaluation of our attitude towards life and living. If our values are shabby and our attitudes adolescent, how can American marriage, made in our image, be anything but a monumental failure?   —DAVID COHN

[*An essay on the weaknesses of our attitudes toward marriage ends by suggesting that we change and by pointing out the necessity for change.*]

The conclusion, then, is designed chiefly to make sure that the reader leaves the essay with its main point clearly in mind. It helps the reader recall the pattern of ideas the essay has followed; and it may make a final effort to show him the special significance of the whole.

Trans
Guide to Revision **8**
Intro
Conc

Rewrite the introduction, transition, or conclusion so that it contributes to the interest and coherence of the writing as a whole.

Topical materials, whether in long or short compositions, should be adequate and so coordinated that they become a frame for the development of the ideas in the composition. Topical material within the paragraph is usually brief (see Section 5). For longer compositions topical material must be more extensive, and may require paragraphs or whole chapters as introductions, as transitions within the composition, and as conclusions.

Trans   **Transitions**   **8a**

Transitions are essential to clear writing. Often topic sentences provide them (see 2-4 and 8-2), but sometimes transitional paragraphs are required.

ORIGINAL

REVISION

Derring-do is an example of a meaning that has developed from misunderstanding, the original being something like "He was one of few daring do it."

Edward Sapir, in his book, *Language,* makes use of the English word *foot, feet* to illustrate linguistic change, what he calls *drift.*

[*This transition is clumsy; concluding and topic sentences would smooth it out, but since this is a turning point in the discussion, a transitional paragraph like that in the revision is useful. The writer is discussing two books on language. In the section with which the passage above opens, he has said that the first of the books is concerned with stories about odd words. He is now ready to turn to a more penetrating book by Sapir.*]

Derring-do is an example of a meaning that has developed from misunderstanding, the original being something like "He was one of few daring do it."

Thus, the first of the two books under discussion is mainly concerned with telling engaging stories about the origin or growth of odd words. The second, Edward Sapir's *Language,* is quite different; Sapir studies words—common words more than odd ones—to try to understand the nature and working of language.

Take, for example, his illustrations for his theory of linguistic change of the sort he calls *drift.* He starts with the common English words *foot* and *feet,* and by tracing these to such early forms as *foti* in Gothic. . . .

131

8b   Introduction That Introduces   Intro

Perhaps the most common weakness of beginnings in student papers is that they fail to show the reader what the paper is to be about—they do not introduce. The introduction should present the subject. Sometimes the opening paragraph can best be omitted.

ORIGINAL

Proper Feeding of Cattle

I have always been interested in cattle, and I have noticed the growing importance of the cattle industry in all parts of the country. Not only has the quality of American beef improved in recent years, but the raising of beef cattle has spread throughout the nation.

The first requirement of proper feeding for beef cattle is. . . .

[*The main idea of the paper is that scientific feeding of cattle has improved the entire beef industry.*]

REVISION

Proper Feeding of Cattle

The American beef industry has shown important developments in recent years. Not only has cattle raising been introduced in areas formerly thought unsuitable; at the same time the quality of beef has improved. The progress is due primarily to the introduction of scientific feeding.

The first requirement of. . . .

[*The revision omits superfluous, confusing material and tells what the paper is about; it introduces.*]

An introduction may fail because the writer does not show how it is related to the main body of the discussion. The writer sees the connection, but he forgets that the reader may not see it unless he is shown how to see it.

ORIGINAL

College Humor

[*The main idea of this paper is that practical joking in college has remained about the same for many years.*]

Last week four mechanical engineering students dismantled a Model-T Ford, carried the parts quietly up the back stairs of the dormitory one night, and reassembled the car in the third-floor hall. It was an interesting example of college humor, of the practical variety, as it exists in colleges today.

[*The incident attracts the reader's attention, but the second sentence does not relate it to the main idea of the paper.*]

REVISION

College Humor

Last week four mechanical engineering students dismantled a Model-T Ford, carried the parts quietly up the back stairs of the dormitory one night, and reassembled the car in the third-floor hall. Undergraduates admired, janitors were puzzled, and the incident made the national news reports, but it was only a repetition of a pattern that has characterized practical jokes in college for many years.

[*The new transitional sentence interprets the introduction in terms of the main idea of the paper.*]

The introduction should be independent of the title, partly because the title may be changed or may be dropped from a paper submitted for publication. Especially, a pronoun or adjective like *this* or *these* referring to the title should not begin the paper.

ORIGINAL	REVISION
Freedom of Speech	*Freedom of Speech*
This subject is basic to the survival of democracy in America.	Freedom of speech is basic to the survival of democracy in America.
[*The reference to the title destroys the independence of the introduction and betrays the writer into imprecise diction.* Freedom, *not the* subject, *is basic.*]	[*Repetition of the title makes the introduction independent, and also more accurate.*]

Better be dull than confusing or misleading; a reader will usually forgive dullness in an introduction or a conclusion if the writing is clear and direct, especially in very practical writing. A skillful writer, however, can be at once interesting and exact. In many kinds of writing an interesting introduction is imperative.

ORIGINAL	REVISION
I am going to tell you what happened the last time I went out with our truck. It was quite a rainy day, and we live quite a ways out in the country, and I had a big load of hogs to haul.	It was stuck, hub down in the black gumbo, a great hulking five ton truck, loaded with a couple dozen grunting, squealing sows. I was alone. I was still weak from influenza. And I had lost a chain, somewhere back in the sea of mud.
[*After a fashion this introduces, though not very exactly. We do not yet know that anything interesting is to happen, and the wordiness of the passage leads us to believe it will not.*]	[*The introduction has become dramatic, and we know that the driver, in a very unpleasant situation, must somehow try to get out of it.*]

Conc   The Adequate Conclusion   8c

The paper that seems to stop in the middle of things is usually less effective than one that stops because the writer has completed his job. Frequently a single sentence is enough to conclude a theme.

ORIGINAL	REVISION
[*The paper attempts to show that football is a business in this student's university.*]	I may be condemned for lack of school spirit or for idealism or for something worse, but I cannot help

ORIGINAL (*Cont.*)

All too frequently scholastic standards have been subordinated to football. I know of one instance in which an important player was allowed to take a final examination over twice, for no reason except that it took him that long to pass it. All of us have heard of exceptions to entrance requirements made for athletes.

[*The final sentences concern only one aspect of the theme; they do not return the reader to the main idea.*]

REVISION (*Cont.*)

hoping that someday football in State University may become a sport instead of a business.

[*The addition of a concluding paragraph which returns to the central topic rounds out the composition. It suggests that the writer has concluded, not just stopped. The conclusion here presents the point of view which the writer has explained by the evidence already submitted.*]

A conclusion is illogical if it makes a statement not justified by the body of the paper. The trouble may lie in the paper itself; difficulty in finding a logical conclusion suggests that the writer has not proved his case.

ORIGINAL

[*The body of the paper presents reasons to justify the heavy expenditures on modern college football.*]

On Saturday afternoon in the crowded stadium twenty-two young men are fighting for the kinds of ideals that have made this country great. May the best team win!

[*The conclusion is a string of stock statements that happen to fit football, but it has no intimate relationship with the point of the paper.*]

REVISION

Football may have become big business, but it is a business worth preserving because its aims are the aims of education.

[*When the writer starts thinking about what he has said—not just vaguely putting together sentences that happen to get associated in his mind with the subject of football—he finds that he can make a general statement that sums up his main argument and effectively concludes his theme.*]

8d — Proportion in Introduction or Conclusion — Intro d; Conc d

Most student themes are so short that they require little introduction or conclusion; the writer is wise to start what he wants to say as quickly as he can and to stop when he is finished. An introduction that uses, say, 200 words of a 500-word paper is obviously out of proportion (see 7b); often it merely multiplies judgments or generalities (see 4-1) and postpones development of the writer's ideas. A rambling, repetitious ending is no better.

ORIGINAL

Decorating a Living Room

As a hobby, I draw house plans, one of which I hope to have blue-printed and built in the near future. I have been working on various plans for many years, and I find the hobby fascinating. It is instructive as well as pleasant, and I have learned many things from my experiments. My first plans were amateurish and impractical. The plans I draw now are more detailed and more concerned with functional requirements. I have been especially interested in plans for decorating living rooms because actually the living room sets the theme for the rest of the house.

REVISION

Decorating a Living Room

Decorating the living room is the most important step in decorating a house, since the living room sets the theme for all the other rooms. . . .

[*The introduction was obviously too long for a paper of 300 words. The solution, as usually, is to omit material not relevant to the main purpose of the paper. The omission makes the paper more direct as well as better proportioned. The student might appropriately write, on another occasion, a paper detailing his experiences as an amateur architect, but the material is not appropriate here.*]

Apologetic Introduction or Conclusion   Intro e; Conc e   8e

Out of what may be commendable motives of modesty, a writer may be tempted to begin or conclude by protesting his own inability to deal with his topic or by apologizing for the topic itself. Such apologies should be avoided. The reader sees that if the apologetic writer means what he says, he should have kept his pen in his pocket. If he does not mean it, and is being falsely modest, the reader sees the deception.

ORIGINAL

Illegal Gambling

I have no firsthand knowledge of illegal gambling, and perhaps I should not write about it. But I do have some opinions. . . .

[*One suspects that the writer's first impulse was right; he should have changed his topic.*]

REVISION

Illegal Gambling

Illegal gambling is dangerous to our society mainly because of the other crimes which accompany it.

[*The writer has thought of the "opinion," which is what he planned to discuss, and he has used it to start the paper.*]

Exercise 8

A. Of the following sentences, assume that *a* is the concluding sentence of one paragraph and that *b* is the topic sentence of the next paragraph. Consider the following pair:

a) Thus a thundershower saved us from losing the first baseball game of the season, and gave us another week in which to tighten our team play.

b) A week later our pitchers were in better condition.

This is not a good transition. The opening of the second sentence, *a week later,* does something by setting the time; but the end of the preceding paragraph had seemed to promise some account of the practice during the week to develop team work, and sentence *b* does not fulfill the promise. Something like the following would be better:

c) The next Monday afternoon the coach started a series of drills intended to show us how to work together.

Now consider the following sequences of sentences. Which provide good transitions? Which are inadequate, and why?

1. *a*) Let me now come to closer grips with my assignment by asking three questions and then attempting to answer them.

   b) First, what kinds of librarians are needed by academic libraries?

2. *a*) The poll to assess student sentiment showed overwhelming enthusiasm for the proposed Student Union Association.

   b) They decided I should be chairman of the membership drive committee.

3. *a*) Here with a view of the mountains on three sides and the tiny creek near the center of the area was a perfect site for the new school.

   b) The site was nearly fifty miles from a sizable town. Supplies and help would be a problem. Building costs would be high.

4. *a*) Everybody had left by midnight, and we went to bed.

   b) I put the coffee on and started to mix batter for pancakes.

5. *a*) Literary merit is, then, a possible attribute, not essential but also not wholly casual, of any nonfictional writing.

   b) But isn't this also true of what goes more strictly by the names of literature itself: . . .

6. *a*) Thus for a century or two, the natives of Southeast Asia have associated extortion, brutality, and bad manners with white men.

   b) They are making white men pay—all white men, from whatever country they come and whatever their previous connection with Asia—for the mistakes and crimes of a few.

7. *a*) Interpreting local news, therefore, is perhaps the most important single function of the college newspaper.

   b) National affairs should be of interest to college students and college journalists.

8. *a*) In such ways are college traditions useful as laws or regulations which help students to live together.

   b) The tradition of fraternity hazing does not, it seems to me, have any reason for continued existence.

B. The following opening sentences of paragraphs from essays on language provide various sorts of transitional material. Study each one and try to determine what has preceded the sentence and what is to follow. Some reveal more than others.

   1. In addition to the great stock of Latin words that have entered our language through the French, or under its influence, we have a huge mass of words and phrases taken directly from the Latin without change.

   2. At no point is the intelligent traveller inconvenienced by these hitherto unfamiliar, but easily assimilable, expressions. The more difficult task is to understand the living and ever-changing idioms of American slang

   3. From yet another Romance language, Italian, English has acquired a good many words, including much of our musical terminology.

   4. A third premise arising from the two just discussed is that the difference between the way educated people talk and the way they write is a dialectal difference.

   5. There are two other types of constructions which are marked by end punctuation or intonation.

C. Below are beginning paragraphs, with the sentences that follow them, taken from papers discussing the general subject of fraternities and sororities in college. Comment specifically on the effectiveness of each as an introduction.

   1. In this theme I shall consider fraternities and sororities. There are both disadvantages and advantages to fraternities and sororities. . . .

   2. College fraternities obviously fail in a number of ways, but I believe that they are essentially valuable to our educational system because they contribute to the social development of the individual student.

8

Exercises

First of all, they help the student learn how to get along with other human beings. . . .

3. Fraternities have long been an essential part of the educational system of the United States. Most major colleges and universities now have many chapters on their campuses.

   The first reason that they should be retained is that they provide living quarters for many students. . . .

4. When Bill Jones came to college he was one of my closest friends, the kind of person everybody liked. Then he joined a fraternity. Now he hardly speaks to his old friends.

   This is just one of the reasons for abolishing fraternities and sororities. . . .

5. Birds of a feather flock together. In the same way those who want to join sororities join, and those who do not stay out.

   It is obvious, therefore, that there is no reason for changing the sorority system on our campuses. . . .

6. Not being a member of a fraternity, this is a subject about which I have little information, but I will write about it as well as I can.

   I am sure, however, that there needs to be a drastic change in the way fraternities operate on this campus. . . .

7. I have been a pledge to a national sorority for nearly three months, and I am sure that most of the criticisms that one hears about sororities are not true. These criticisms that sororities are snobbish and that they do not encourage study certainly do not apply to my sorority.

   The first advantage of sororities which I want to consider is . . .

8. When I first proudly attached my fraternity pledge pin to my lapel, I dreamed happily of the days the rush chairman had described for me—days of scholarly companionship, of good food and superior lodging, of brotherly love, of the cultural benefits of sophisticated social life. After three months of waxing floors and reaching for my toes my dreams are the same, but they are no longer connected with the fraternity.

   I dream, for instance, of the scholarly companionship, but I have not found it. . . .

D. Below are concluding paragraphs taken from papers discussing the general subject of fraternities and sororities in college. Comment specifically on the effectiveness of each as a conclusion.

1. [*The paper cites instances from the writer's experience which seem to him to show disadvantages of living in a fraternity.*]

   It took me only three months as a pledge to learn that there is a wide difference between the stories pledges hear during rush week and the realities of life in a fraternity house.

2. [*The paper cites evidence intended to show that living in a sorority is really no more expensive than living in a dormitory and that one gets more for her money in the sorority.*]

Sororities, therefore, should be encouraged on our campuses in America. They give a girl the kind of college life which prepares her for real-life situations.

3. [*The paper maintains that sororities aid education because they provide necessary supplements to academic work.*]

My sorority includes the nicest group of girls I have ever known. It is a pleasure and an honor to be associated with them.

4. [*The paper maintains that fraternities are undemocratic in their methods of selecting members and should therefore be banned from campuses of state institutions.*]

Instances like those I have presented could be multiplied to show that fraternities discriminate against certain races and religions. I believe that such organizations should not be recognized by colleges and universities in a democratic country.

5. [*The paper presents a logical argument to establish the idea that democracy is based on individual freedom and that any organization should be given freedom to choose its members as it pleases.*]

Of course, there may be other arguments, and this is a big subject which requires further investigation, but I see no reason for discriminating against fraternities.

Controlling Ideas

*Since it is reason which shapes and regulates all other things, it
ought not itself to be left in disorder.*

—Epictetus

*The labours of generations of logicians have added maze upon
maze to a terrain initially labyrinthine enough.*

—I. A. Richards

Implicit in preceding sections of this book is the association of
writing and thinking. The composing process stretches back long
before anything appears on paper, to observation and reading and
thinking. Much of writing grows from pre-writing, the invention
of approaches to a subject, the perception of relationships. Writing
requires thinking, but to think, we must think *about* something.

Something can be learned about thinking—especially about the
difference between good and bad thinking. Either because of the
way the human mind works or because of centuries of agreement
among human beings of Western society, most people accept the
same general principles of reasoning, the same means of controlling
ideas. They agree about what is "logical." Even though communication may achieve its ends without being logical—in advertising,
for instance—anyone attempting to write seriously should know
the accepted principles for regulating and testing thought.

These principles can get complicated. The terrain of thought
is labyrinthine; attempts to chart the maze may add new mazes,
but at least some of the principles are also practical. Everyone
either uses or violates them whenever his mind works. For instance,
the student who remarks on registration day, "I'm not going to take
that course; it's not practical," may be unaware that he has thought
much at all. Probably he has not thought very thoroughly, but
complicated reasoning, however inadequate, must lie behind his
decision.

The student has been involved with the difficult processes of definition, and the wisdom of his decision turns on his definition of *practical.* An advisor hearing the comment is likely to ask, "What do you *mean* by practical?" The student's answer will not be easy, for definition is not easy. But the adequacy of the definition may determine whether or not the advisor approves the student's decision. Orderly reasoning requires definition, the subject of Section 9, below.

Another kind of reasoning, also, lies behind the student's remark. Somehow he has reached the conclusion that the course is not practical. His conclusion may rest on no better evidence than a comment of his roommate, who took the course the year before. It may rest on random hearsay comments, or it may grow from careful examination of the course syllabus, the textbook, and the roommate's lecture notes. If the student has arrived at his generalization about the course in some such way, he has been thinking inductively. He has been pulling together particulars and drawing a general conclusion from them.

His decision, however, involves still another reasoning process. The remark assumes a still different kind of generalization to justify the final decision, the first step in a thought process which might be formalized something like this:

I should not take any course that is not practical.
This course is not practical.
I should not take this course.

The student is here thinking deductively. That is, he is applying a general principle to a particular instance and coming to a practical conclusion. If the advisor were to analyze the remark in this way, the student might want to think again.

These three processes—definition, induction, and deduction—can be separated for discussion, but they all work together in actual practice. The first generalization in the formalized deduction above, for example, came from somewhere. It may have developed inductively, from various kinds of reliable or unreliable evidence that anything not practical is a waste of time. Or it may have developed deductively from some previously conceived generalization; for example:

Education is practical training.
I should get an education.
I should not take an impractical course.

This reasoning is hardly perfect; it complicates questions of definition, for instance, with *education*. But regardless of how a particular conclusion is reached, the processes are present and are working together. They are essential to the kinds of techniques considered earlier in this book—the framing of a main idea or the establishment of a proposition (see 1-5 and 1-6, 2-4 through 2-7), the development of an idea (see Section 4). They combine to make thought a kind of chain of reasoning. Only by keeping the links untangled can we produce clear writing.

Definition

For
Guide to Revision,
see page 148.

Definition may both control and develop an idea.

The Romans were great extenders of boundaries. They found that boundaries have at least two uses: they keep something out and they provide an area for development within. Boundaries have these same uses in writing; in fact, we have adopted the Latin word for setting up limits, *definire*, for one important process in writing, definition. That is, definition in writing can set limits to an idea, even the main idea of a composition; and such limitation as this often becomes a way of developing or controlling an idea. For purposes of writing, then, definition is often more than the kind of formal delineation of a term to be found in a dictionary or in a science handbook. A definition of a university or of relativity may become a book.

Definition and Development   9-1

We have already observed that writing can be looked on as two essential—and inseparable—processes: establishing a main idea or central purpose and then controlling and developing it. Definition is useful in both. For example, a proposition serving as a topic sentence may be a definition or partial definition (see 2-6). Or, notice the way in which Elbridge Colby describes the purpose of his book *Army Talk: A Familiar Dictionary of Soldier Speech*. The first sentence of the preface reads:

This is an attempt to put in a book the language that lives on the lips of fighting men in the army of the United States.

This is a statement of the book's purpose, but it is mainly a definition, a clarification of what the writer means by *army talk* in the title. The definition limits his subjects, specifying that he will in-

143

clude in his book only words used orally, words used by men who did the fighting, words common enough so that they "lived on the lips." That is, he will eliminate words used by officers in making reports, words used in a spectacular way by one individual, and technical words not common in speech. Definition also extends beyond the opening sentence, to govern the development of the entire opening paragraph. The development of the paragraph, in fact, mainly extends the definition, with specific examples of what he will include as army talk. He explains that "A 'recoil spring rod' and a 'magazine floor plate' do not enter conversation unless a man is talking shop." He points out that he includes slang, but not all slang: "To be army slang, a phrase must either have originated in or be peculiar to the army."

Or consider the following paragraph in which definition controls and develops the main idea:

> It is this association of culture with every aspect of daily life, from the design of his razor to the shape of the bottle that holds his sleeping pills, that distinguishes the highbrow from the middlebrow or the lowbrow. Spiritually and intellectually the highbrow inhabits a precinct well up the slopes of Parnassus, and his view of the cultural scene is from above. His vision pinpoints certain lakes and quarries upon which his special affections are concentrated —a perturbed lake called Rilke or a deserted quarry called Kierkegaard— but he believes that he sees them, as he sees the functional design of his razor, always in relation to the broader cultural scene. There is a certain air of omniscience about the highbrow, though that air is in many cases the thin variety encountered on the tops of high mountains from which the view is extensive but the details are lost.
>
> —RUSSELL LYNES, *Highbrow, Lowbrow, Middlebrow*

The writer uses definition, telling what something is, as the basis of the topic sentence, the main idea, of his paragraph. He wishes to "distinguish" the highbrow from others, and as a distinguishing characteristic to be discussed in this paragraph he uses "association of culture with every aspect of daily life." Definition provides the purpose, the point of focus, for the paragraph. It also suggests the material for development. The writer builds his paragraph by reporting some of the specific ways in which the highbrow associates culture with daily life; each sentence contributes something toward clarifying the writer's definition of his concept of the highbrow, so that the entire essay becomes an extended definition or series of definitions.

W. H. Auden organizes a discussion of detective stories by various sorts of definition:

The vulgar definition, "a Whodunit," is correct. The basic formula is this: a murder occurs; many are suspected; all but one suspect, who is the murderer, are eliminated; the murdered is arrested or dies.

This definition excludes:

(1) studies of murderers whose guilt is known, e.g., *Malice Aforethought.* There are borderline cases in which the murderer is known and there are no false suspects, but the proof is lacking, e.g., many of the stories of Freeman Wills Crofts. Most of these are permissible.

(2) thrillers, spy stories, stories of master crooks, etc., when the identification of the criminal is subordinate to the defeat of his criminal designs.

The interest in the thriller is the ethical and eristic conflict between good and evil, between Us and Them. The interest in the study of a murderer is the observation, by the innocent many, of the sufferings of the guilty one. The interest in the detective story is the dialectic of innocence and guilt.

As in the Aristotelian description of tragedy, there is Concealment. . . .
　　　　　　　　　　　　　　　　　　　—*The Guilty Vicarage*

The writer is not attempting to establish a scientifically accurate definition of the detective story; he is defining rhetorically, using devices of definition to develop. In the passage above he uses a synonym, lists basic characteristics identifying his subject, excludes things which might be confused with his subject, and then moves on to discuss the basis of interest in the detective story. The essay is much more than a definition, but definition directs both its organization and its development. Similarly, when Cardinal Newman became rector of the new Dublin University, he needed a statement of purpose under which he, his faculty, and his students could work together. He prepared a series of lectures now called *The Idea of a University Defined,* in which he tried to determine what a university should do by asking himself what education is. He found that he could explain and even persuade by defining. Structurally, the work is an extended definition.

Methods of Definition　9-2

As indicated above, definitions may have various purposes. They may be needed to limit a term so that it can be used with absolute precision in a scientific discussion. Formal or logical definitions often have this purpose. Or they may be what are often called rhetorical definitions, which a writer may use to clarify or explain or develop or even amuse. In the essay mentioned above, Russell Lynes quotes A. P. Herbert's definition of a highbrow:

A highbrow is the kind of person who looks at a sausage and thinks of Picasso.

The statement is not a scientifically precise definition, but it makes its point; it is useful rhetorically. The following are some of the most useful kinds of definition for both logical and rhetorical purposes:

1. *Logical or formal definition.* This method, used by logicians since Aristotle, places a term in a general class and distinguishes it from others within the class. Man can be classified as an animal, and distinguished from other animals by his reason.

Man is a rational animal. A triangle is a plane figure with three sides. Materialism is a philosophical theory which holds that the existence and nature of matter sufficiently account for the universe.

This is the most precise type of definition, but not always the most readily understood. Carelessly used, it can become what is called circular definition, in which a concept is defined in terms of itself. "A washing machine is a machine that washes" does little to inform the reader.

2. *Definition by description.* Some terms can be at least partly defined by their physical qualities, by telling how they look, where they are, what they are made of, how big they are, what color they are. Often this sort of definition is less conclusive than logical definition, because it does not distinguish a term from others in its class. "A firetruck has ladders and hoses on it and is usually fairly large and painted red" provides understanding but does not adequately define. Other descriptive definitions are more precise:

A circle is the figure covered by a line fixed at one end and moving in a plane.

3. *Definition by example.* Examples often help to clarify, and hence to define. Children learn meanings of words by repeated examples, but the method does not usually provide a complete definition.

Epics are poems like *The Iliad, Beowulf,* and *The Song of Roland.*

The comment helps anyone who knows the poems mentioned, but even for him it does not establish a basis for deciding whether *Paradise Lost* is an epic. A definition like "Nouns are words like *horse, typewriter, disease,* and *happiness*" may be practical for teaching purposes, but it could have scientific validity only if it listed all the thousands of words in the class.

4. *Definition by synonyms.* Some terms can be defined by synonyms, other words which have similar meanings.

To masticate is to chew. Osculation is kissing. To define is to distinguish.

This type of definition has the virtue of brevity. Inevitably, most definitions are longer than the words they define, but a synonym may be only one word. Definition by synonyms has its limitation however, since no two synonyms ever have exactly the same meaning; hence the definition can be no more than approximate, and often it is not even that.

5. *Comparative and metaphorical definition.* Figures of speech, metaphors, similes, or analogies (see 19-8) may help definition. Although comparisons can never be exact, they may be revealing. If we say that a girl is catty we may be suggesting that she has some of the characteristics of a cat, but we are not suggesting that she has four legs or long whiskers. More extensively, if we define slang as "language that takes off its coat, spits on its hands, and goes to work," we may reveal one aspect of slang in a picturesque way. If we add that "slang is to language what an elevator is to a stair; it may get you there quickly and easily but it exercises neither your mind nor your legs," we may reveal another aspect of slang, but we are not so defining it that a reader can tell when *square* is or is not slang. But, used for clarity and not for restrictive definition, metaphors can be extremely useful.

6. *Definition by contrast or negation.* Defining something by telling what it is not can seldom be exact or adequate because it cannot be exhaustive, but it may be revealing. Consider the problem of defining a word like *bobbysoxer,* as it was popular in the 1940's. "A female who wears bobbysox" will not do; some wearers of short socks would not qualify, and a genuine bobbysoxer often wore something else. For similar reasons, "an American female teenager" will not suffice. Neither will the following statement define adequately, but it helps: "A bobbysoxer is a girl no longer young enough to act like a child but not yet old enough to take more than a fluttery interest in the opposite sex." It does not define in any exact sense, but it tells us something about what a bobbysoxer is by telling us what she is not.

7. *Definition by origin, process, or growth.*   A two-cycle motor can be distinguished from a four-cycle motor by explaining the process by which one motor achieves an explosion for each revolution of the crankshaft, whereas the other requires two complete revolutions for one explosion. Like definitions involving comparisons or contrasts, definitions which account for something by telling how it came to be or how it works may be unusually useful in defining a complicated or difficult subject. For example, what is a *wool-hat politician?* To say that he is a politician who represents one of the more rural and economically backward parts of the deep South may be tolerably accurate, but it may not mean much until the statement is supplemented with some explanation of how these areas have developed in contrast with some other areas. The definition would need to consider the aftermath of military defeat and carpetbag rule, the conflict between the white and Negro peoples, the declining role of agriculture in society, trends in education, the impacts of certain religious beliefs, and the like. The wool-hat politician can be defined revealingly if not exactly by the society that has helped to culture his ideals and his prejudices.

Def

9 *Guide to Revision*

Supply or revise definitions, to control the main idea, to clarify unfamiliar terms, or to provide development.

Writing can be vague, confusing, or inadequate because a writer has not defined key terms or taken advantage of an opportunity to develop by definition. A statement, for example, like "The United States is not a democracy" can be intelligently discussed only in the light of some agreement about a meaning for *democracy.* Such a definition might serve to clarify a main idea and also to provide material for development. If the writer is using definition rhetorically, primarily to describe or clarify, he does not require complete logical accuracy, but if he pretends to valid logical definition, he should provide it. Circular definition (a statement that has the form of definition but only repeats itself, taking the reader in a circle), for example, does not define:

A clothes drier is a drier to dry damp clothes.

And a definition by inadequate synonyms neither defines nor clarifies:

Democracy refers to the American way of life as we all conceive it.

The statement merely substitutes one confusion for another.

ORIGINAL

In the true sense of the word, a conservative is the person who really keeps our society from disaster. He is the man we should honor as the preserver of our traditions, not vilify as a foe to progress. . . .
[*The opening sentence appears to define, but does not. The remainder of the paper suffers because the reader does not understand a key term in the writer's special sense.*]

College football is no longer a sport. Coaches are hired for their ability to win games. Players are hired from whatever coal mines develop the biggest muscles, and stadiums are built or not built depending upon whether or not they will "pay off." Rooters go to the games as they would go to the movies, to see a hired actor put on a show. And collegiate sport promotes school spirit, but commercialized athletics does not.

We may define luxury commodities as those commodities which are not necessary. Necessary commodities are those which are not luxuries.
[*The definition is circular, defining with the terms to be defined.*]

REVISION

If we consider a conservative as the person who is reluctant to change until he is convinced that the new is better than the old, we can see that the conservative keeps our society from disaster. He is. . . .
[*A definition, distinguishing the term conservative as a type of person, clarifies the remainder of the discussion. The reader may not agree, but he at least understands.*]

College football is no longer a sport, at least not in the sense that a sport is an activity engaged in for fun. Coaches are hired for their ability to win games. Players are hired. . . .
[*The original is unclear; most of what it says would apply, for instance, to professional baseball, usually called a sport. The addition of a definition, specifying the particular sense in which the word sport is used, clarifies the paragraph.*]

We may define luxury commodities as those articles of commerce which are unnecessary to life and health.
[*A logical definition helps the reader to understand an essential term.*]

Exercise 9

A. Indicate which of the methods of definition described above (9-2) are used in each of the following statements. Comment on the adequacy of each as a definition.

1. Man is a two-legged animal without feathers.
2. Mental agility is not necessarily jumping at conclusions.
3. Rhetoric is speech designed to persuade.
4. Persuasion involves choice, will; it is directed to a man only insofar as he is *free.*—KENNETH BURKE
5. A narcotic is a drug which in moderate doses allays sensibility, relieves pain, and produces profound sleep, but in poisonous doses produces stupor, coma, or convulsions.
6. A chocolate éclair is like a cream puff stretched oblong and frosted or glazed with chocolate.
7. A concierge is a doorkeeper.
8. A hammer is what you use to drive nails or break rocks or beat smooth the dented fender of a car.
9. An example of a palindrome is "Able was I ere I saw Elba."
10. In other words, education is the instruction of the intellect in the laws of Nature, under which name I include not merely things and their forces, but men and their ways; and the fashioning of the affections and of the will into an earnest and loving desire to move in harmony with those laws.—THOMAS HENRY HUXLEY
11. Moreover, man is the sole possessor of language. It is true that a certain degree of power of communication, sufficient for the infinitely restricted needs of their intercourse, is exhibited also by some of the lower animals. Thus, the dog's bark and howl signify by their difference, and each by its various style and tone, very different things; the domestic fowl has a song of quiet enjoyment of life, a clutter of excitement and alarm, a cluck of maternal anticipation or care, a cry of warning—and so on. But these are not only greatly inferior in their degree to human language; they are also so radically diverse in kind from it, that the same name cannot justly be applied to both.
    —WILLIAM DWIGHT WHITNEY, *The Life and Growth of Language*
12. Aircraft carriers are the backbone of a Naval task force. They are slower than planes, but, of course, faster than fixed land installations.
    —U.S. Navy pamphlet

B. Consider the adequacy as definitions of the statements below. Describe any fault you find in them.

1. Experience is the name everyone gives to their mistakes.
2. A good book is the precious lifeblood of a master spirit embalmed and treasured upon purpose to a life beyond life.
3. A genealogist is one who traces your family back as far as your money will go.
4. *Toves* are something like badgers—they're something like lizards—and they're something like corkscrews.
5. A straight line is the shortest distance between two points.
6. Network: anything reticulated or decussated at equal intervals, with interstices between the intersections.
7. Liberty is the right to do anything which does not interfere with the liberty of others.
8. History is the lengthened shadow of one man.
9. History is philosophy teaching by examples.
10. A highbrow is a man who has found something more interesting than women.
11. A tie rack is a rack for holding ties.
12. A fallacious argument is an argument used by somebody else to prove a conclusion you do not agree with.

C. Define each of the following terms by putting it into a class and then adding characteristics which differentiate it from other members of the class.

1. river	4. revolver	7. botany
2. basketball	5. sonnet	8. rectangle
3. pan	6. asphalt	9. chuckle

D. Define the following terms, using three different methods for each term:

1. freshman	3. psychology	5. hair-styling
2. examinations	4. dates	6. campus clothes

Evidence:
Inductive Reasoning

*For
Guide to Revision,
see page 157.*

*Support generalizations with sound, adequate, appropriate evidence, or
avoid the generalizations.*

A city council in the Midwest recently considered a series of requests for rent controls. Representatives of landlords protested that
they could not meet their bills and asserted that there was no real
housing shortage. A hastily organized committee of renters appeared at the next meeting declaring that renters could not meet
their bills either and asserting that there was a severe housing shortage in the area. The council, understandably, was puzzled. Finally
an astute newspaperman took a list of all the apartments, real
estates offices, and rental agencies in the city and started telephon-
ing, pretending he had just arrived in the city and needed a place
to live. After three hours he located only two available apartments,
both at very high rents. His story was instrumental in the council's
decision to establish rent controls. It was convincing; it was "logical"; it was based on evidence.

The newspaperman's process was inductive. He collected data
which led to a generalization. He proceeded from specific instances
to a general conclusion.

10-1 Types of Induction; Generalization, Hypothesis

We use induction every day, to reach conclusions, to determine
causation, to make decisions. We must work with varying kinds of
evidence; as a result our conclusions vary in reliability and in usefulness. For example, a man goes out in the yard on a cool morning
in spring wondering whether a frost the night before has killed the

cherries. He examines a dozen blossoms in different parts of his tree and finds black spots in the center of each where the fruit should be forming. A neighbor's tree shows similar black spots. He believes that he has found enough specific instances to warrant the generalization that there has been a killing frost. He has noticed a number of unharmed cherries on a small tree partially protected by an overhanging porch roof, but he rejects these because they are not typical examples. The generalization is reliable because it is induced from a sufficient number of typical relevant instances.

Other generalizations develop in much the same way, but less directly. For example, we can generalize that if we flip a light switch the light will turn on, even though we are aware that current is sometimes off and bulbs burn out. The generalization rests on evidence of a pattern of occurrences; although it is a prediction, a statement of probability, it is practically useful. With less assurance, but on the same basis, we can generalize that if we pull a cat's tail we shall provoke some kind of noise.

Similarly we can generalize from statistical probability. If statistics record 607 traffic deaths during the Fourth of July holiday last year and reveal that holiday traffic deaths have tended to increase annually, we can predict with some assurance that there will be more than 607 traffic deaths over the holiday this year. But statistical evidence is likely to be dubious, subject to many variables. The political candidate who relaxes in his campaign when he discovers that 58 per cent of the voters are registered in his party may be surprised.

Analogy provides another type of evidence for inductive generalization. We may conclude, for example, that the chukkar partridge will flourish in western American semideserts because it lives in parts of India which have similar climate. The generalization may be useful if the two areas are sufficiently similar. That is, analogy is reliable as evidence if the instances compared are similar in all important respects and if any differences between them can be explained. Most often, it serves best to illustrate or clarify (see Section 4), not as evidence.

Arguments involving causation also employ induction. Usually they lead to hypotheses which are useful but require further testing. For example, a girl comes into her dormitory room late at night and finds her roommate's clothes spread about. She sees an empty flower box on the dresser. She finds a new bottle of perfume open. She remembers that this is the night of a formal dance. She discovers that her roommate's new gown is missing from the closet. She forms a hypothesis to explain the facts she has observed: that her roommate received a last-minute invitation and has gone to the dance. A hypothesis is usable if it provides a better explanation for all known facts than does any alternative; but it can be only a tentative explanation, requiring verification from the observation of more data.

10-2 Induction in Writing

The writer may use as the main idea of a composition or as the topic sentence of a paragraph a generalization based on observed evidence. He may develop this idea by citing more evidence. For example, Ruth Benedict, in *Patterns of Culture,* suggests that there is wide diversity in social habits and attitudes, but she does not leave the statement as an unsubstantiated judgment. She examines various cultures in terms of customs concerning adulthood, warfare, and marriage. The facts gathered lead to conclusions which lead in turn to a main idea. The whole structure might be described as a pyramid, a pyramid which is solid and convincing because its foundation is factual. Specific details support each general statement, and the analysis could be carried down to even smaller units of composition, supported by even more specific details. The lower left block of the pyramid below, for example, is the paragraph which follows it.

Adulthood in central North America means warfare. Honour in it is the great goal of all men. The constantly recurring theme of the youth's coming-of-age, as also of preparation for the warpath at any age, is a magic ritual for success in war. They torture not one another, but themselves; they cut strips of skin from their arms and legs, they strike off their fingers, they drag heavy weights pinned to their chests or leg muscles. Their reward is enhanced prowess in deeds of warfare.

The paragraph also resembles a pyramid, with details supporting statements which support another more general statement.

In the scheme of the whole chapter, however, as shown above, the apex of this pyramid becomes another statement which the writer uses to document further conclusions.

Tests of Evidence 10-3

To be reliable, evidence must be adequate, relevant, typical, and accurate. If the man examining his cherry trees had looked at only one blossom, he might have seen one damaged by the neighbor boy's baseball; his evidence would have been inadequate. If he had considered only the size or color of the blossoms, or even whether the petals had dropped off, his evidence would have been irrelevant to his conclusion. If he had looked at only the tree protected from frost, he would not have seen typical instances. If the man had taken his information from the testimony of a nearsighted neighbor, who had mistaken a dead bee for a frozen blossom, his evidence would have been inaccurate. To be useful to the writer in developing his ideas, evidence should be able to withstand tests of its authority:

1. *Is the evidence adequate?* A generalization that all cows are black and white, made by a city boy after his first visit to a farm specializing in Holstein-Frisian cattle, is not reliable; it is based on too few instances. A visitor's "firsthand account" of the attitude of the Chinese toward the United States, based on a two-day guided tour of Peking, is not trustworthy; his evidence is inadequate.

2. *Is the evidence relevant?* A writer who uses statistics about football gate receipts as evidence that football builds character is not

convincing; his evidence is not relevant to his generalization. It might be pertinent to some other proposition—that football helps finance college athletic programs, for instance. Testimony of a large number of students that examinations should be abolished is not evidence for the proposition that examinations are not fair tests of knowledge.

3. *Is the evidence typical?* A poll of its subscribers conducted by a business magazine is not likely to provide reliable evidence on the attitudes of Americans toward taxing corporations. The instances considered would not be typical. The kind of student paper which begins "Cats can never be trusted. I once had a cat that . . ." is probably unconvincing both because the instance cited is not typical and because the evidence is inadequate.

4. *Is the evidence up to date?* National statistics from ten years ago do not provide a reliable basis for determining present salary scales. The Battle of Bull Run does not necessarily provide evidence for current military strategy.

5. *Is the evidence unprejudiced?* A biography commissioned by a political party for its major candidate is suspect as evidence. A probable partner in crime is not a reliable character witness for an alleged criminal.

6. *Does the evidence come from a reliable witness?* If a nine-year-old reports that his neighbor is a political spy, his evidence must be discounted because of his limited knowledge and experience. A baseball fan in the right-field bleachers probably has less reliable information than the umpire about the last pitch.

7. *Is the relationship between events causal or coincidental?* When possibly related events occur near each other in time, both the careless and the unscrupulous are tempted to jump to the conclusion that the first caused the second. Mere sequence in time does not provide evidence of causation, even though superstitions, false political claims, and false accusations are often based on such a sequence. Establishing a causal relation requires direct evidence that one event led to the other. The fact that a bomb was tested just before a storm broke does not prove that the explosion caused the storm.

Guide to Revision **10**

Supply adequate evidence for generalizations or modify the generalizations.

Development of an idea in composition always must be clear, adequate, and reliable; but especially when it should provide evidence for a generalization, it must be sound as inductive reasoning. The writer who says that he thinks Swedes are stubborn, or policemen have big feet, or coyotes are cowardly, and then assumes that he can *prove* such statements by citing one incident from his experience, is not likely to convince anyone whose mind is working. Unsupported generalizations are unconvincing.

Ev a; Rel   Adequate and Relevant Evidence   10a

Human beings readily jump to conclusions without adequate evidence. A mother, quite innocently, indulges in what is known as wishful thinking to select only a small part of the evidence and conclude that her child has been grossly wronged by a teacher. Reporters from newspapers of rival political parties, perhaps not innocently, make different generalizations by selecting only part of the facts in their report of a mass meeting. Sometimes the generalization should be abandoned or rephrased (see 2-6); sometimes adequate and relevant evidence should be supplied.

ORIGINAL

Purebred dogs are essentially stupid. When I was a child, I had a fine pedigreed Dalmatian. I tried for months to teach him to shake hands. I succeeded only in encouraging him to jump up and wipe his front feet on anyone who came in sight. An expensive spaniel which succeeded him was no better. I tried to teach him to bring in the newspaper; he learned only to chew the paper to bits.

REVISION

I never expect to own another purebred dog; my experiences have prejudiced me thoroughly in favor of curs. When I was a child. . . .
[*The sweeping pronouncement about dogs in the original is unjustified and also unnecessary. With an opening like that in the revision, the writer can use his details as illustrations, avoid the problem of proof, and write a convincing paragraph.*]

157

Even material that has emotional appeal or some other sort of first-glance attraction works as evidence only if it is relevant to the generalization it pretends to support. Name-calling is one variety. Slipping in a clever—but irrelevant—comment or slogan is another. Advertising relies heavily on information that pretends dramatically to relevance and significance but often is quite beside the point. The number of ingredients in a headache tablet is not necessarily relevant to the efficacy of the medication. Neither the absence nor presence of suds guarantees that a soap cleanses well. Charming girls in bathing suits are not relevant evidence for the virtues of cigars, beer, or automobiles. Juries are cautioned to avoid such irrelevancies as the diction of the defense attorney or the dress worn by the defendant.

ORIGINAL

The Windhover is obviously not a good poem. I read it twice and was unable to make any sense at all of it. Many of the words were unclear to me, and some of them are run together in unusual ways. I do not see any reason for this kind of writing. . . .

[*The comments following the opening sentence are not relevant to the topic introduced. They are pertinent only to some kind of confession by the writer about his difficulties in reading; they tell nothing of the quality or excellence of the poem.*]

(1) Early in the morning they began chanting prayers and dancing around a large fire in the clearing. (2) The monotonous beat of the drums and the rhythm of the voices were punctuated by loud whoops. (3) The sound of the women beating sticks together, keeping time with the drums, blended with the barking of the dogs and the yelling of the children. (4) This celebration is carried on much as it was centuries ago. (5) They dance from morning until late at night. (6) The bright feathers of the war-bonnets made weird shadows on the trees.

REVISION

The diction of Hopkins in *The Windhover* causes much of the poem's complexity. His description of the falcon's wing as *wimpling,* for example, combines effects of meaning, sound, and a slightly archaic flavor. Or the compounded *dapple-dawn-drawn.* . . .

[*The writer should try to collect evidence relevant to the topic, not merely to his own feelings, or he should revise his topic sentence so that it becomes more specific and more susceptible to proof with relevant evidence.*]

Early in the morning they began chanting prayers and dancing around a large fire in the clearing. The monotonous beat of the drums and the rhythm of the voices were punctuated by loud whoops. The sound of the women beating sticks together, keeping time with the drums, blended with the barking of the dogs and the yelling of the children. The bright feathers of the war-bonnets made weird shadows on the trees.

[*Sentences (4) and (5) are irrelevant and have been omitted, perhaps to appear elsewhere in the composition.*]

Ev b   Pertinent Statistics   10b

Statistics can be useful evidence, but incomplete or unanalyzed statistics can lead to false conclusions. A campus newspaper once reported, quite accurately, that during the year fifty per cent of the women in one college of the university had married their instructors. Outraged conclusions had to be withdrawn when it was revealed that the college was the college of engineering and the total number of women students for the year was two.

ORIGINAL

Statistics show that everyone in the office is making enough money to live comfortably. The average salary, computed on certified figures for last year, was a little more than $7,000 per year per employee.

[*The statistics cited are not relevant to the first statement, although they may, at first glance, seem to be.*]

REVISION

Although the average salary for workers in the office last year was more than $7,000, many employees were not making a living wage. Only three salaries, those of executives at $35,000, were as high as the average figure; whereas five clerks received only $1920 per year.

[*Completed statistics require a different generalization.*]

Ev c   Typical and Reliable Evidence   10c

If we take a room in a city's best hotel, spend a week looking out the window, and then conclude from our observations that the city has no slums and no poverty, we are likely to be wrong. We have looked at some evidence, but it has not been typical. Or if we conclude from a vote of fraternity members that weekly all-campus dances in the Union Building should be discontinued, we have not examined typical evidence.

ORIGINAL

Required physical education courses tend to improve study habits and raise grade point averages for college students. A poll of physical education majors at State College reveals that more than 90 per cent testified that they studied better and made better grades while they were taking the required physical education courses.

[*Obviously the evidence is not typical, and the conclusion is not justified.*]

REVISION

Physical education majors at State College believe that the required physical education courses improve their study habits and help their grade averages, according to a recent poll. More than ninety per cent . . .

[*The most likely revision is to change the topic sentence to something factual. The generalization might be maintained with sufficient evidence.*]

159

To be reliable, evidence must be based on facts. Hearsay, legend, opinion, or speculation is not sufficient to support a generalization.

ORIGINAL

Some of the most important discoveries of modern times have been the result of accidents. For instance, according to the story, the great strike at Goldfield, which uncovered more than three billion dollars in gold and silver, resulted from the random kick of a bad-tempered jackass. Old Jim, while he was prospecting the area, had made camp, and was boiling his nightly coffee. The coffee pot tipped over, and splashed some boiling water on the jackass, which kicked at the pot, missed, but hit a ledge of rock instead. Old Jim stood staring, and with good reason. The sharp little hoof of the jackass had knocked loose a chunk of high-grade gold ore.

[*The writer admits that his story, improbable on the face of it, has no reliable authority; yet he proceeds to use it as evidence.*]

REVISION

In spite of the great advance in science, individual curiosity and even pure luck still play a part in important discoveries. As a matter of course the so-called "miracle drugs" have in the main resulted from careful planning, deliberate search, and vast technical knowledge. But even here, chance observations have helped make pharmaceutical history and save lives. Consider, for instance, penicillin. . . .

[*To substantiate his serious generalization about important discoveries, the writer needs a more reliable instance than the kind of folk legend which can be given no more authority than "according to the story." If he knows the interesting story of the development of penicillin, he can proceed to write a convincing paper, with authoritative support for his generalization.*]

10d Causation Ev d

A person dealing with causes may be tempted to generalize quickly, or to admit as evidence material that is not properly evidence at all. He sits in a draft Monday night, wakes up with a cold Tuesday morning, and concludes, too readily, that the draft "caused" the cold. It may, of course, have caused it or helped to cause it, but a little reflection shows that the evidence does not warrant the conclusion. He plays with a toad on Monday and discovers a wart on his finger on Friday. He finds a horseshoe at ten o'clock, throws it over his left shoulder at 10:02, and finds a $10 bill at noon. If he concludes that playing with the toad caused his wart or that finding the horseshoe was responsible for his good luck, he is making the error known as the *post hoc ergo propter hoc* fallacy, "after this therefore because of this." It is not a sound method of determining cause.

ORIGINAL

Governor Jones was elected two years ago. Since that time constant examples of corruption and subversion in government have been unearthed. It is time we got rid of the man responsible for this kind of corrupt government.

[*The assumption that Governor Jones caused the corruption exemplifies the* post hoc *fallacy.*]

REVISION

Governor Jones was elected two years ago. Since that time frequent examples of corruption and subversion in government have been unearthed. It is time to see whether a new administration can clean up the government.

[*The revision is equally sweeping in its assertions, but it avoids the illogical causal concluson.*]

Ev e   **Analogy**   **10e**

Analogy is a useful device for development, often illustrating or explaining vividly (see 4-4). The writer, however, must be aware of the limitations of analogy; it is usually not valid as evidence, as proof. A writer trying to explain the breeds of horses to city children might wish to say that just as racing automobiles have light wheels and chassis, and trucks have very heavy running gear, racing horses are relatively light and draft horses very heavy. This is an analogy. But a horse is not a machine, and an automobile is not an organism, even though the two have common use and some common qualities. The writer cannot prove anything about a horse by evidence from an automobile, but he may be able to promote understanding of the structure of the horse by noting similarities. An analogy can be a useful device, but it should not be misused.

ORIGINAL

The modern corporate businessman, in his use of ingenuity, is like the Indians of western Canada. Needing light during their foggy winters, they discovered a new use for the candlefish, which had long been a staple of their diets. This fish is so fat when it swims inland to spawn in the spring that the Indian has only to stick a rush into the fish's back and light it. The fish will then burn like a candle. It is evident, therefore, that modern business owes its success to the ability of Americans to take advantage of their natural resources.

[*The comparison of the ingenuity of the*

REVISION

The modern businessman, in his use of American natural resources, has often shown ingenuity comparable to that of the Indians of western Canada. The Indians had long included in their diet a fatty smelt called the candlefish. Finding that they had too little light through the foggy winter, they discovered that they could stick rushes in the backs of the oily fish and burn them like candles. Similarly the great oil companies have found more uses for oil than to furnish fuel for power and heat. From petroleum they have developed many kinds of synthetic rubbers, and plastics by the hundred.

161

ORIGINAL *(Cont.)*

businessman with that of the Indian may make a useful analogy, but it does not warrant the conclusion.]

REVISION *(Cont.)*

[*Used as an analogy, not as a proof, the story of the candlefish aids explanation.*]

Exercise 10

A. The passages given below contain generalizations which are illustrated or supported by evidence. Comment on the reliability of each generalization, indicating whether it is merely illustrated or is supported by evidence and pointing out especially instances of inadequate or unreliable evidence, of misused analogies, or of faulty causation. Examine each passage in light of the requirements listed in 10-3.

1. The Japanese people are completely in accord with American democratic principles. This is the conclusion of Mr. J who has just returned after spending a week in Tokyo visiting his son who has been in Japan for some time as the American representative of a large corporation. Mr. J reports that in spite of his handicap in not knowing the Japanese language he was able to collect many favorable opinions about this country in his conversations.

2. "People of discrimination smoke Foggs," says beautiful debutante Debbie Dune, "because scientific tests have proved that they are easier on the throat."

3. The enclosed manuscript contains about 22,000 words. In order to arrive at this figure I counted the words on ten typical pages, computed from this total the average number of words per page, and multiplied this average by the number of pages.

4. If the Jews are legally or morally entitled to Israel, then Mussolini would have been entitled to claim Britain as a colony of the ancient Roman Empire.

5. Some people think there is nothing in spiritualism, but they have never seen any of the proofs. I was convinced last year when a friend of mine told me what he had actually seen. He had been to a meeting where a woman went into a trance, and then pretty soon people all over the room started trying to talk with spirits out of the other world. It couldn't have been faked, because the spirits knew the people they were talking to and could remember things that happened a long time ago. And a couple of the spirits even materialized and floated around the room. They didn't look much like real people,

of course, because they were spirits, but you could see them so plainly there was no doubt about them.

6. The newspapers are full of nothing but stories about sex and crime. In last night's paper, for instance, there were five crime stories on the first page.

7. The learned man will say, for instance, "The natives of Mumbo-jumbo Land believe that the dead man can eat and will require food upon his journey to the other world. This is attested by the fact that they place food in the grave, and that any family not complying with this rite is the object of the anger of the priests and the tribe." To anyone acquainted with humanity this way of talking is topsy-turvy. It is like saying, "The English in the twentieth century believed that a dead man could smell. This is attested by the fact that they always covered his grave with lilies, violets, or other flowers."

—G. K. CHESTERTON, *Heretics*

8. Clearly Mr. B cannot be guilty of using his business offices to disguise the headquarters of a world wide syndicate distributing illegal drugs. Two of his business partners testify without reservation to his honesty and good character.

9. The Roman Empire collapsed when Rome became too prosperous. We should be sure to avoid too much prosperity for the United States.

10. During the past month living costs in America have risen .4 per cent. This figure is based on statistics compiled by governmental bureaus through sampling prices of selected commodities, and on rents in important areas throughout the United States. It does not take any account of changes in federal or state taxes.

11. A woman preaching is like a dog's walking on his hind legs. It is not done well, but you are surprised to find it done at all.

—JAMES BOSWELL, *Life of Samuel Johnson*

12. There is no doubt that the students at State University want football to be continued. The campus newspaper in a recent issue invited letters showing why the present sports program should be continued, and more than 200 students replied. Every letter favored retention of football.

B. Select any three of the following generalizations and list various sorts of evidence which might be used in support of each:

1. Extracurricular activities in college require a great deal of the student's time.

2. Fraternities and sororities are valuable parts of college life.

3. Fraternities and sororities foster snobbishness.

4. Television advertising is often misleading.

5. Lobbies may discourage honest legislation.

6. Convenience does not dictate fashions.

Exercises

    7. Comic books encourage juvenile delinquency.

    8. The mass media handicap education.

C. What evidence would be required to establish the following assertions?

    1. Interpretive dancing has a great future on television.

    2. Knute Rockne was the greatest football coach of all time.

    3. The Mississippi and Missouri drain the world's largest river basin.

    4. International treaties can be relied upon.

    5. Lemmings march by hordes to drown themselves in the sea.

    6. The airplane was invented, not by the Wright Brothers, but by Samuel P. Langley.

    7. The Dodgers will win the next world championship.

    8. There are 5,280 feet in a mile.

    9. Taxes are high because of corruption in government.

    10. Using a filter on cigarettes will prevent lung cancer.

D. The following table gives statistics on school-age population, school enrollments, and numbers and average salaries of teachers. Using inductive reasoning, draft three generalizations based upon the table.

School year ended in	Population 5 to 17 years	Pupils enrolled	Male teachers*	Female teachers*	Average salary† per member
1900	21,404,322	15,503,110	126,588	296,474	$ 325
1910	24,239,948	17,813,852	110,481	412,729	485
1920	27,728,788	21,578,316	95,654	583,648	871
1930	31,571,322	25,678,015	141,771	712,492	1,420
1940	29,805,259	25,433,542	194,725	680,752	1,441
1945	. . .	23,225,784	127,102	699,271	. . .
1950	30,788,000	25,111,427	194,968	718,703	3,010
1960	43,881,000	36,086,771	392,700	962,300	5,174
1962	45,380,000	38,253,000	436,575	1,021,389	5,700
1964	48,005,000	41,025,000	480,800	1,070,200	6,240

    * Prior to 1954, includes other nonsupervisory instructional staff (librarians and guidance and psychological personnel).

    † Average annual salary per member of instructional staff.

    SOURCE: U.S. Office of Education; salaries cover supervisors, principals, and teachers.

E. Each of the following generalizations is followed by four other statements, some of which might be relevant as supporting evidence for it, some of which would not. Comment on the suitability of each of the proposed supporting statements as relevant evidence.

1. In the half century preceding World War I, the United States came of age.

   a) In fifty years it was transformed from a rural republic to an urban state.

   b) Woodrow Wilson, who brought the Democrats into power at the end of the period, after three Republican administrations, was a native of Virginia.

   c) Great factories, steel mills, and railroad systems developed throughout the land.

   d) The Civil War, according to one writer, "cut a great white gash through the land."

2. The first quarter of the twentieth century in America brought a flood of important inventions.

   a) The principle of the dynamo was developed as early as 1831 and held great interest for Henry Adams.

   b) The first successful motor-driven airplane was invented in 1903 by the Wright brothers.

   c) Nearly a million patents were issued in the United States between 1900 and 1925.

   d) The X-ray tube was invented in the United States in 1916.

3. After the first rush of gold mining in the West, cattle raising developed as a major industry in many states.

   a) Between 1866 and 1888 some six million cattle were driven from Texas to winter on the high plains of Colorado, Montana, and Wyoming.

   b) In the late 1860's and 1870's cattle raising spread from Texas throughout much of the western territory, and herds moved annually on the "long drive" to shipping points in Kansas.

   c) Theodore Roosevelt, twenty-fifth President of the United States, worked on a cattle ranch in the Dakota territory.

   d) The cowboy was one of the most picturesque figures of American life in the nineteenth century.

Logic:
Deductive Reasoning

*For
Guide to Revision,
see page 174.*

"To begin with," said the Cat, "a dog's not mad. You grant that?"
"I suppose so," said Alice.
*"Well, then," the Cat went on, "you see a dog growls when it's angry,
and wags its tail when it's pleased. Now I growl when I'm pleased, and
wag my tail when I'm angry. Therefore, I'm mad."*

The logic of the Cheshire Cat, revealed above, would fool few
people outside Wonderland. The absurdity more than the validity
of his argument suggests his madness; but consider this:

Nobody would accuse American industry of communistic tendencies.
American business traditionally supports the Republican party and the interests of investors. On the other hand, labor traditionally supports the Democratic party and seeks the welfare of the worker rather than the prosperity
of the investor. Naturally, therefore, labor tends toward communism.

The paragraph is not obviously silly. Some persons reading it might
agree with the final controversial statement, but they could not
have formed their opinion on the basis of the argument presented
in the paragraph. The information does no more to establish that
labor tends toward communism than the argument above does to
prove that the Cheshire Cat is mad. The illogicalness in both examples involves the same sort of faulty deduction.

11-1 Induction and Deduction

Thinking almost always combines more than one process. For
example, the man described in 10-1 recognizing a frost in the blossoms of his cherry tree could not have reached his conclusion by
induction alone. He could observe that the blossoms had turned

black in the center, but he could interpret this change in color only with the aid of another process. He had to call on his experience or his knowledge to give him inductively a generalization: that blossoms which have turned black in the center may have been frozen. Then he could apply this generalization to a specific instance—that the blossoms on his trees were black—and reach the hypothesis that the blossoms he had examined had been frozen. Testing this hypothesis by his knowledge of recent weather and his further investigation, he could generalize that there had been a killing frost. The process by which he interpreted the meaning of the blackened blossoms is deduction, carrying understanding farther by applying generalizations to specific cases in order to learn more about the specific cases.

Thinking, in other words, progresses by chain reaction, in which induction and deduction constantly work together. By induction we examine specific instances until we are justified in making a generalization. Then we can apply this generalization to specific instances and understand the instances more fully. Even though we do not consciously follow steps in formal logic, we use logical procedures to reach dozens of everyday conclusions. By induction we learn that the dormitory dining hall always serves macaroni and cheese for lunch on Mondays. Since it is Monday, we can deductively apply the general principle to the specific instance, conclude that macaroni and cheese will be on the menu, and decide whether to go to lunch.

A lawyer building a case to prove that Elbridge Dangerfield is guilty of murder uses inductive reasoning to collect evidence which will lead to a generalization. He observes that a victim was shot through the heart; Mr. Dangerfield was found in the victim's room just after the shooting with a smoking revolver in his hand; the bullet taken from the victim's body was fired from the gun Mr. Dangerfield was holding; the victim had been blackmailing Mr. Dangerfield; therefore Mr. Dangerfield is probably guilty of murder. He has reasoned inductively, but an insurance agent sitting in the courtroom as the jury announces its verdict uses deduction to conclude that Elbridge Dangerfield is a bad insurance risk.

Deduction   11-2

Fully understood, deduction is a complicated process, but viewed simply it consists in putting two and two together. It applies generalizations—the results of induction, or general principles, or laws, or even definitions—to specific cases. The reasoning of the insurance agent making a professional estimate of Mr. Dangerfield might be formalized as follows, in a series of patterns known as syllogisms:

MAJOR PREMISE: Any man judged guilty of murder has an excellent chance of hanging.

MINOR PREMISE: Elbridge Dangerfield has been judged guilty of murder.

CONCLUSION: Elbridge Dangerfield has an excellent chance of hanging.

MAJOR PREMISE: Any man who has an excellent chance of hanging is a bad insurance risk.

MINOR PREMISE: Elbridge Dangerfield has an excellent chance of hanging.

CONCLUSION: Elbridge Dangerfield is a bad insurance risk.

The insurance man has seen the relationship between generalizations he knows about and has been able to reach a valid conclusion.

Deduction operates by putting together ideas or statements with a common term, called in logic *the middle term*. In the first group of statements above, the element common to each premise is *has been judged guilty of murder;* in the second group each premise contains *has an excellent chance of hanging.* Oversimplified, then, deduction is sometimes like the algebraic formula: if a equals b and b equals c, then a equals c. Two terms a and c can be related on the basis of the common term b. If John is the same age as Bill and Bill is the same age as George, then John is the same age as George. Or, we know that Sir Philip Sidney was killed in the Battle of Zutphen, and we know that the Battle of Zutphen occurred in 1586. We know the date of Sidney's death. We know that all students who do not have medical excuses must take physical education. We know that John Atlas is a student and does not have a medical excuse. We know that he must take physical education. Or we know that no student with a medical excuse needs to take physical education. We know that Wilfred Atlas is a student who has a medical excuse. We know that he does not have to take physical education.

We can look at deduction in another way by thinking of it as a process of relating groups or classes. The statement "Daisy, as she is a cow, is a ruminant" involves three elements or terms, which might be represented by three circles varying in size according to the relative sizes of the classes they name.

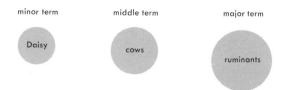

The minor term indicates the small class, the major term the large class, and the middle term the class somewhere between the other two in size. When the statement about the terms is put into its logical steps, it reads:

MAJOR PREMISE: All cows are ruminants.
MINOR PREMISE: Daisy is a cow.
CONCLUSION: Daisy is a ruminant.

The statements say something about how the terms are related or, if we think of the terms as circles, about which term includes the others. By the authority of the major premise, the middle circle can go into the larger one; but the minor premise puts the small circle into the middle one. Necessarily, therefore, the small circle must also be included in the large one.

Clearly Daisy belongs among the class of ruminants; the conclusion is *valid* because it follows logically from the premises stated. It is *true* if the premises are true.

Controlling the Middle Term 11-3

Reasoning turns about a middle term; if conclusions are to be valid, the middle term must be clear and stable. It must have the same meaning each time it appears. *Cow*, the middle term of the statements above, refers to the same thing in both the major and the minor premise. But consider the following:

All acts which threaten the American way of life are treasonable.
The new bill on civil rights threatens the American way of life.
The new bill on civil rights is treasonable.

The common element, *threatens the American way of life,* is vague to begin with, and its meaning changes from one sentence to the next. When Mark Twain says, "It is easy to give up smoking. I have done it thousands of times," he is shifting the meaning of *give up.* The effect is humorous but not logical.

The middle term must also be "distributed" at least once in any valid logical statement. A term that is distributed includes or excludes all members of the class it denotes; *all cows* or *no cows* is a distributed term. That is, in *All cows are ruminants,* cows is distributed, made by *all* to embrace an entire class. Similarly, in the following syllogism *no cows* is distributed: *No cows read books; this female student is reading a book; this female student is not a cow.* The following syllogism is not valid because the middle term is not distributed: *Cows have horns; this animal has horns; this horned toad is a cow.* The middle term is not distributed; the syllogism does not say either that all cows have horns or that all animals that have horns are cows. In any logical pattern, one premise must say something about all members of a class or no members of a class.

To be valid, then, a syllogism must contain a firm middle term distributed at least once. To be true, a syllogism must be valid and contain premises that are true. The following is valid, though not necessarily true.

All communists read Karl Marx.
Mr. Jones is a communist.
Mr. Jones reads Karl Marx.

The middle term, *communists,* is distributed in the first statement. Or *reads Karl Marx* could be distributed once and used as the middle term.

Anyone who reads Karl Marx is a communist.
Mr. Jones reads Karl Marx.
Mr. Jones is a communist.

Reads Karl Marx, the middle term, is distributed in the major prem-ise. The conclusion is valid, though untrue; but it would not be valid if the middle term were undistributed.

All communists read Karl Marx.
Mr. Jones reads Karl Marx.
Mr. Jones is a communist.

One term, *all communists,* is distributed, but it is not the middle term. The middle term, *read(s) Karl Marx,* is not distributed, and the con-clusion is not valid. Although arguments like the above are often accepted—especially when there are emotional reasons for liking the conclusion—they are no more valid than the following:

All chickens have feathers.
This canary has feathers.
This canary is a chicken.

Development by Deduction   11-4

If every statement in writing had to be analyzed into logical patterns like those above, writing would be both wordy and dull. Deductive patterns, however, are basic to writing, even though they are not labeled premises and conclusions. The following sen-tences, for example, develop mainly by deductive reasoning.

As enemy territory becomes more thoroughly protected by fighter planes during daylight hours, it becomes increasingly difficult to take the desired reconnaissance photographs each day. Therefore, the trend is toward more night photography, when darkness lends to planes increased safety from anti-aircraft fire and aerial pursuit.
—GEORGE RUSSELL HARRISON, *Atoms in Action*

The logic behind the development of the passage might be put as follows:

MAJOR PREMISE: Pictures cannot be safely taken over areas protected by fighter planes.
MINOR PREMISE: In daylight, areas are protected by fighter planes.
CONCLUSION: Pictures cannot be safely taken in daylight.

MAJOR PREMISE: The trend is toward photography in periods of increased safety.
MINOR PREMISE: Darkness is a period of increased safety.
CONCLUSION: The trend is toward photography in darkness.

The reasoning could be described in other ways and broken down more completely, but clearly the paragraph develops as a series of syllogisms.

11-5 Assumptions; Major Premises

These syllogisms, however, are not formally expressed. In fact, the major premises are not stated at all. They are assumed by the writer, and if the reader is to accept the ideas of the paragraph he must accept these assumed premises. In actual practice—in development in writing or in everyday thinking—deduction usually works in this way. Assumptions which are not formally expressed are used as the major premises of the reasoning. Both the writer and the reader, therefore, need to be able to distinguish assumptions from the discussion based on them.

Assumptions lie behind almost everything we do or say. We plan tomorrow and next week on the assumption that the sun will continue to rise, that there will be a tomorrow, that the earth will not burst into a shower of meteorites. This is a tolerably safe assumption. Students go to class on the assumption that the instructor will be there. This assumption is somewhat less certain, and is more or less reliable depending upon a number of conditions, including the instructor's health. Formerly, everybody assumed that if a line looked straight it was, for all practical purposes, straight. Then Einstein demonstrated that all lines curve. Now we have two assumptions. Philosophically we assume that all lines curve. Meanwhile, carpenters work on the assumption that a plumb bob or a square will provide a straight line.

Often assumptions in writing are as reliable and acceptable as that of the carpenter. An editorial writer states: "Police records prove that the old pool hall on Jones Street is encouraging juvenile delinquency; it should be closed." He is assuming, as a major premise, that anything that encourages juvenile delinquency is bad. Probably most readers will accept his assumption and therefore his argument. Or a writer states: "The sight-seeing tour into the mountains should begin at five so that it can be completed before dark." His assumption that sight-seeing is better in daylight than darkness will probably not meet serious opposition.

Suppose, however, that a student writes a theme recommending geology as a liberal arts subject because it promotes an understanding of the world in which we live. He is making many assumptions, among them that knowing about the physical world is so good that it is helpful to everybody. A reader says, "Yes, but geology casts doubt on the truth of Genesis, and anyone who does not believe every word of the Bible will be damned. Saving our souls is the only purpose in life, and thus geology does more harm than good." The reader has not accepted the assumption. For him the discussion proposed by the theme is not adequate, and if discussion with him is to continue, the earlier assumption—that knowledge of the physical world is absolutely good—must itself become the subject for discussion. Or a writer comments, "The man had been on relief for three years; he was obviously lazy." His assumption, the major premise of his argument, that only lazy men are on relief, is questionable, and therefore his argument is questionable.

Clearly, the writer needs to be aware of the assumptions on which he is basing his statements. He needs to change his argument if the assumed major premise is untenable. Or sometimes he needs to state his assumption so that the reader can judge its acceptability. By 1946, a writer on military tactics could assume, perhaps without comment, that the *blitzkrieg* would be part of any subsequent war; but if he was to assume, also, that atomic weapons would determine strategy, he had to say so in order to make the basis of his discussion clear. By 1967, the writer could assume silently that subsequent weapons would be atomic; but if he assumed that an aggressor nation would attack from a space platform, he would need to state his assumption. Sometimes a writer may even adopt an unreal assumption for the sake of discussion. A writer on child psychology, for instance, might begin an article: "Let us assume that you are only three months old."

Stated or not, however, assumptions are the basis of deduction, and therefore of much of our thinking and writing. Both writer and reader need to be aware of them, to distinguish the assumptions from the discussion based on them.

Log

11 *Guide to Revision*

Writing should be logical in its whole plan and in its parts.

Even though a writer may not employ the formal terminology of logic, his work should be logical. Since writing is always complicated, being logical in expression involves many reasoning processes, but much of logic can be comprised within the general process of deduction. Some of the troublesome aspects of deduction are considered here.

11a   Assumptions; Tenable Premises   Log a

Since reasoning seldom appears in the neat formal patterns of the syllogism, assumptions behind statements are not always apparent. The methods of deduction can be used to reveal and test assumptions.

Consider, for instance, the following from a student theme:

Although there have been a few highly publicized instances of serious injury, football is not really harmful to students and should be retained as part of every university program.

The statement appears in valid form, and some readers might accept it without question. When, however, the basic assumption of the statement appears as the major premise in a syllogism, it is absurd:

Anything not harmful should be on a university program.
Football is not harmful.
Football should be part of every university program.

The syllogism is valid, but it is not true because it is based on an untenable major premise; even the writer probably would not maintain that anything harmless—eating a cream puff, for instance —belongs on all university programs. Consider another statement of the same type:

It is difficult to take your eyes off this magnificent lamp since it is a hundred years old.

Faced with a bald statement of his assumption—that anything a hundred years old must be worth attention—the writer would probably be less positive. Or consider a less obvious example:

He found himself actually enjoying the plays of Shakespeare.

The statement does not explicitly state a logical proposition, but behind it is the assumption that Shakespeare's plays are dull.

A logical statement is true only if its premises are true, and reader and writer must be aware of the assumptions on which statements depend.

ORIGINAL	REVISION
A liberal arts course is a waste of time because it trains for no profession. [*The assumption that any course which does not train for a profession is a waste of time may be more doubtful than the writer realized.*]	1. A liberal arts course trains for no profession. 2. A liberal arts course is a waste of time. [*The writer should select one of the two statements combined in the original, or perhaps drop the whole idea.*]
Fraternities are obviously valuable parts of college life. Consider how long they have existed. [*Is the implied reason one the writer would try to maintain? Gangs of hoodlums also have a long history.*]	1. Fraternities contribute to college life. 2. Fraternities have been a valuable part of college life for many years.

Log b   Distributing and Stabilizing the Middle Term   11b

A conclusion is invalid if it is deduced from statements in which the middle term is undistributed (see 11-3). Attempts to establish "guilt by association" are among the most common examples of the fallacy of the undistributed middle: Communists oppose antistrike legislation; Mr. M opposes antistrike legislation; therefore, Mr. M is a communist. The middle term, *opposes antistrike legislation,* is not distributed, not made to include a class or group with the words *all* or *no.* If the middle term were distributed   Everyone who opposes antistrike legislation is a communist; Mr. M opposes antistrike legislation; Mr. M is a communist—the conclusion would be valid; but it would obviously not be true because the major premise is not true. The fallaciousness of an argument with an undistributed middle term should be apparent, but often emotional reaction to the conclusion tends to hide its invalidity. Compare the following:

All the students cheating lived in Miss Goodge's rooming house.
Walter lived in Miss Goodge's rooming house.
Walter must have been cheating.

All goats have beards.
Santa Claus has a beard.
Santa Claus is a goat.

Conclusions like that in the first argument are accepted every day; whereas the absurdity of the second is obvious. Actually, the argument of the second is just as good as that of the first; in both patterns the middle term is undistributed.

ORIGINAL

All the gangs of juvenile delinquents in our part of the city had a kind of uniform—a leather jacket and dark trousers. The boy on the corner, with his black leather jacket hanging open, was obviously from one of the gangs.
[*The argument exhibits the fallacy of the undistributed middle:*
All juvenile delinquents wear leather jackets.
The boy on the corner is wearing a leather jacket.
The boy is a juvenile delinquent.]

Great poetry becomes richer on successive reading. This must be a great poem, since it has revealed so much more to me on each reading.
[*The argument implied is:*
Great poetry becomes richer on successive readings.
This poem becomes richer on successive readings.
This poem is a great poem.
The statement does not exclude the possibility that bad poems also become richer on successive readings and that this is a bad poem.]

REVISION

The boy on the corner wore a black leather jacket, like those that were part of the uniform of the gangs of juvenile delinquents in our part of the city.
[*The original does not distribute the common term,* wear leather jackets, *and the argument is invalid. The revision, even though it still has dubious implications, avoids the invalid conclusion. Distributing the middle term would have required the writer to reveal his untenable premise:* All wearers of leather jackets are juvenile delinquents.]

Only great poetry becomes richer on successive reading. This must be a great poem because it has revealed more to me on each reading.
[*The addition of* only *distributes the middle term in the major premise and makes the conclusion valid. There is, of course, a question about the truth of the major premise and therefore of the conclusion. The writer needs to rethink his main idea.*]

Log c   Equivocation   **11c**

An argument is fallacious if it uses the same term with different meanings. The difficulty with this fallacy, often called equivocation, is that it seldom appears in a single sentence or even paragraph; it is likely to develop over the course of a longer composition. Especially susceptible are abstract terms like *democracy* or *freedom* or *moral,* which sometimes are used in one way at the beginning of a paper and in another way later on. For example, a paper which starts out as a criticism of *liberal* education and then uses the term to refer to political *liberals* in his argument is making a bad pun rather than an argument.

ORIGINAL

The things which have real educational value should obviously be the core of a college curriculum. Nobody who has ever tried to get a job will deny that typing is valuable. Certainly, then, all students should be required to take typing.

[*The terms, especially the middle term* value, *shift and slide.*

Courses of value should be required.

Typing has value.

Typing should be required.

The term value, *as it is used in the passage, changes from a vague general idea to a more specific practical idea.*]

REVISION

I think that typing, because of its practical value, should be a required course in the college curriculum.

[*Making the conclusion both true and valid is probably impossible. Revised so that the middle term is tied down, the statement is logical:*

All courses with practical value should be required.

Typing has practical value.

Typing should be required.

But the major premise—and thus the truth of the conclusion—is now in doubt. Few college curricula could find room for every practical subject.]

Log d   Consistency   **11d**

If a writer asserts in the first paragraph of a paper that freedom of speech must be preserved as a basic tenet of our democracy and then in the fourth paragraph insists that an opposition newspaper should stop criticizing the administration, he is obviously inconsistent. He is applying principles only when they suit his convenience. Statements are logically incompatible when one implies that the other is false.

ORIGINAL

Democracy can succeed only with an educated citizenry. It is of the greatest importance that our schools

REVISION

Democracy can succeed only with an educated citizenry. Our schools must be as good as possible and

ORIGINAL (*Cont.*)

be as good as possible and that teachers' salaries be high enough to attract our best citizens.

The city of B has always been proud of its schools, which have stood high in comparison with those of other communities. The city has also been proud of its financial record, its freedom from debt and its willingness to live within its means. It is regrettable, therefore, that the school board in its meeting last night should have seen fit to authorize a bond issue for the sake of expanding our school system and increasing salary scales. . . .

[*The writer of the editorial is trying to support two incompatible propositions at the same time; he cannot logically do it. He cannot at once support the extension of education and object to the extension of education.*]

REVISION (*Cont.*)

teachers' salaries must be high enough to attract our best citizens.

The city of B has always been proud of its schools, but the city has also been proud of its financial record, its freedom from debt and its willingness to live within its means. The school board, therefore, should not have authorized a bond issue in its meeting last night but should have found ways to meet the educational needs of the city through taxation and more efficient use of funds. We must expand our school system and increase salary scales, but we must pay for it as we go.

[*The revision shifts the ground of the argument in a manner which the original writer would probably not accept, but if he is to be logical, he must change one of his basic attitudes or shift the basis of his complaint.*]

11e   Arguing in a Circle   Log e

A circular argument assumes or implies whatever it purports to prove. The reader remains no wiser than he was at the beginning, except in his knowledge of the unreliability of the writer.

ORIGINAL

There is a kind of basic sense or voice within everyone which tells him to be careful and resist when a possible act is wrong. Cheating is that kind of act. Cheating is wrong, because our consciences tell us so.

[*The statement, purporting to be an argument, merely turns in a circle.*]

REVISION

Cheating is one of the acts which our consciences tell us are wrong.

[*There was no material for a logical conclusion in the original, but with a general statement which says what he wishes to say, the writer can try to substantiate his main idea with facts or arguments.*]

11f   Including Steps in the Argument   Log f

A writer may fail to carry the reader with him through the steps of his argument, either because the argument is confused in his own mind or because he forgets the need to show the reader his reasoning processes.

ORIGINAL

When clarinets are not playing, a band sounds dull, because the notes of the clarinet are so high and shrill.
[*The sentence makes no sense as it stands, although the reader can guess that the writer had some logical notion in mind. The reader cannot see how highness and shrillness prevent the band from being dull.*]

Apparently the *Titanic* had been built very well, for the crew did not know the lifeboat assignments.
[*The ignorance of the crew about lifeboat assignments is not conceivably a reason for believing that the ship had been well built. The writer has jumped so many steps that his thinking seems confused.*]

REVISION

The high and shrill tones of the clarinets are needed in a band to give it life and color. Therefore, when the clarinets are not playing, a band sounds dull.
[*With all the steps of the argument stated, the conclusion is valid, although many readers might reject the premise, and hence the conclusion.*]

Everyone on the ship considered the *Titanic* so well built that she was unsinkable. Members of the crew were so confident of the ship's safety that they had not even learned their lifeboat assignments.
[*An orderly presentation clarifies the relationship between the building of the ship and the lifeboat assignments.*]

Exercise 11

A. Indicate which of the sets of premises and conclusions given below are valid and which are true. Give reasons for your decisions.

1. All athletes eat Crumples for breakfast.
   Jerry is an athlete.
   Jerry eats Crumples for breakfast.

2. Men of distinction drink Old Overshoe.
   I drink Old Overshoe.
   I am a man of distinction.

3. All cats have nine lives.
   Tabby is a cat.
   Tabby has nine lives.

4. All good citizens vote.
   Al Capone voted.
   Al Capone was a good citizen.

Exercises

    5. Money is the root of all evil.
       Time is money.
       Time is the root of all evil.

    6. No tigers have wings.
       This creature has wings.
       This creature is not a tiger.

    7. Sixty men require one-sixtieth the time required by one man.
       One man can remove an automobile tire in sixty seconds.
       Sixty men can remove the same tire in one second.

    8. No cat has eight tails.
       One cat has one more tail than no cat.
       One cat has nine tails.

    9. Any golfer who makes a hole in one is lucky.
       Francis made a hole in one.
       Francis was lucky.

   10. Man is the only creature capable of reason.
       Mary is not a man.
       Therefore Mary is incapable of reason.

B. Discuss the logical truth and validity of the reasoning in the following passages:

    1. Students, like all young people with active minds, are easily susceptible to any idea like communism, which seems to be advanced and at first glance may hold out hope for the impractical idealist. It is easy to see why our colleges should be shot through with communism.

    2. People who are poor lack ambition; if they did not lack ambition they would not be poor.

    3. The editorial in the last student newspaper says that only a student can understand the need for a better intramural program on the campus. Well, I am a student, and I certainly think that the program we now have is all anyone could ask for. The editorial writer should be more logical about what he says.

    4. The money was taken between 11 o'clock and noon from the desk in this room. Nobody has left the room since eleven o'clock. One of the persons who have been present in the room must have taken the money. John was in the room. Obviously, he took the money.

    5. All governments, for reasons of security, must deceive the public from time to time. This bulletin issued by the government therefore must be false.

    6. Houses with shallow foundations should be avoided at all costs; but since this house has an unusually deep, reinforced foundation, you can have no reason for rejecting it.

    7. It was plain as a pikestaff. Anyone traveling on the African mailboat would be three days late. Mr. Sims was three days late. Therefore he must be on the mailboat from Africa.

8. We ought to be guided by the opinion of our ancestors, for old age is wiser than youth.

9. Of course, art is dying. The capacity of one man among ten million to create, whether in art or thought, whether in science or invention, is the hallmark of men's inequality, so that democracies, which aim at equality, have neither reward nor honor to offer to genius.

10. "There's more evidence to come yet, please your Majesty," said the White Rabbit, jumping up in a great hurry; "this paper has just been picked up."

"What's in it?" said the Queen.

"I haven't opened it yet," said the White Rabbit, "but it seems to be a letter, written by the prisoner to—to somebody." . . . He unfolded the paper as he spoke, and added, "It isn't a letter after all: it's a set of verses."

"Are they in the prisoner's handwriting?" asked another of the jurymen.

"No, they're not," said the White Rabbit, "and that's the queerest thing about it." (The jury all looked puzzled.)

"He must have imitated somebody else's hand," said the King. (The jury all brightened up again.)

"Please, your Majesty," said the Knave, "I didn't write it, and they can't prove I did: there's no name signed at the end."

"If you didn't sign it," said the King, "that only makes the matter worse. You *must* have meant some mischief, or else you'd have signed your name like an honest man. . . ."

"That *proves* his guilt," said the Queen.

LEWIS CARROLL, Alice in Wonderland

C. Each of the statements below assumes a major premise that is not stated. Supply the assumption behind each statement.

1. She must be intelligent if she is on the honor roll.

2. All high school students should have courses in driver education; careful driving is something they should know about.

3. The people next door go to church regularly; they will want to make a contribution to the Red Cross.

4. Many comic books are bad for children as they deal with wild and improbable adventures.

5. It is ridiculous to suppose that we can ever get rid of anything that has existed in our society as long as nationalism has.

6. He cannot be expected to be in sympathy with American ideas of democracy; he was born in Europe.

7. It should be a good dress; it cost more than any dress in the store.

8. You could tell she was a gossip because she criticized some of the most important clubwomen in town.

9. General B is certain to make a good university president; look how successful he was during the war.

10. Socialists really support the American system of government, for they believe in government by the people.

D. In this selection from *Macbeth,* Lady Macbeth is berating her husband because, having proposed murdering the king, he now prefers not to do so. Upon what general assumptions (major premises) is Lady Macbeth relying, even though she does not express all of them, but assumes their truth?

Lady M.   Was the hope drunk
Wherein you dressed yourself? and hath it slept since?
And wakes it now, to look so green and pale
At what it did so freely? From this time
Such I account thy love. Art thou afeard
To be the same in thine own act and valour
As thou art in desire? Wouldst thou have that
Which thou esteems the ornament of life,
And live a coward in thine own esteem,
Letting "I dare not" wait upon "I would,"
Like the poor cat i' the adage?
Macb.   Prithee, peace:
I dare do all that may become a man;
Who dares do more is none.
Lady M.   What beast was't then,
That made you break this enterprise to me?
When you durst do it, then you were a man;
And, to be more than what you were, you would
Be so much more the man.

Sentence Rhetoric

The congruent and harmonious fitting of parts in a sentence hath almost the fastning and force of knitting and connexion: As in stones well squar'd, which will rise strong a great way without mortar.
—Ben Jonson

"Language is the armory of the human mind," Samuel Taylor Coleridge wrote; "and at once contains the trophies of its past, and the weapons of its future conquests." From the earliest civilized times, man has seen that these trophies in the "armory of the mind" are worth studying for themselves, and that they help us forge mental weapons for the future. The Egyptian and Chinese systems of education were founded upon the study of the use of language; and others, like the Classical Greek and Roman and the Continental European and British systems, have made much of language study.

All languages are composed of units of various sizes, most frequently of three sorts: small units of meaning (conventionally in English they are called words), extended compositions, and intermediate combinations of words or other semantic units. In English these intermediate groups are called sentences; they are the subject of Sections 12-17. On the whole they can be studied in two ways: the way they are made and the way they work, a study which we call *grammar,* or the way they may be appropriately used to suit the needs of speaker or writer, a study which we call *rhetoric.*

Since this book concerns problems of writing, it discusses grammar only as grammar illuminates rhetoric. Rhetoric involves choice; it examines probable effects of different sorts of expressions in order to help a writer select from the many patterns available. Because grammar describes what is available (particularly in the sentence), we obviously need to understand it if we are to make wise rhetorical choices.

Furthermore, understanding the working of a grammar is usually quite easy, once we have the key to it. Languages—all languages, not only English—are extremely complicated, and understanding the grammar in all its details requires long and exacting study, but the basic principles are likely to be few and relatively easy to grasp. Fortunately, for those of us who are trying to learn to write, usually only the basic principles are fundamental for rhetoric. We shall need to understand the basis of English grammar, and know it well, but we can ignore most abstruse and technical problems.

On the whole, languages include two sorts of things, units of language and ways of using these units. The latter is what we call grammar. The units may be of several sorts, perhaps most frequently units of sound or meaning or both. In English, for example, we usually think of words as units of meaning, but a word has also a characteristic sound or a form in writing which distinguishes it from other words. Nobody confuses *pig* with *extrapolate,* on whatever basis we distinguish them. English can be broken, also, into units smaller than words. For example, the *s*-sound in *cups* could be thought of as a sound and at the same time as a unit of use or meaning, indicating plural number. Since sounds are often identified by putting a symbol between slant lines, we could rewrite the word *cups* as sound by writing it /cup/ + /s/. Thus, whatever the units in a language, or however we conceive them, all languages have some kind of units, the sort of thing that most of us think of as vocabulary in English.

These units can be changed or left unchanged. If we change them we can change them variously; for example, starting with the word *capital* we can add something to it and make it *capitalize.* In conventional terminology we have made a noun or a modifier into a verb, but however we describe this change, the fact is that *capital* and *capitalize* work differently in a sentence and they do so because we have added something to one of them. We can also change a word internally; *write, wrote,* and *written* work differently, and we know they should work differently because of differences within the words. This procedure, revealing grammar by changes in form, is called *inflection* or *synthesis.* It is very common in the languages of the world; it was characteristic of the ancient ancestor of English, Indo-European, and it survived extensively in Classic Latin and Greek, and in Old English. In recent centuries, however, it has been going out of fashion in many languages, especially in Modern English, so that it survives only scatteringly in distinctions like the following: "The player*s* play," but "The player play*s*."

Similarly, if linguistic units remain unchanged we can do various things with them. For example, we can change the order of the words; in the sentences *Man the pump* and *Pump the man* we know how the words *man* and *pump* work because of the words that come before and after them. We can also reveal grammar by using some words to show relationships; for example, in *hundreds of students* the construction can work only because the word *of,* which here has little semantic use, shows how *students* and *hundreds* work together. The system of revealing grammar by the order of words or by the use of words showing relationships is called *analysis, isolation,* or *distribution.* It is characteristic of Modern English. In fact, the grammar of Modern American speech can be roughly defined as the grammar of a language that has been moving from synthesis toward analysis, and this fact has implications for modern rhetoric and for modern sentence structure.

Thus far we have been using *grammar* to mean the way a language works, but this word, like most words, can be used in other ways, also. It can be used in the sense of *grammar book,* as a description of the way the language works. For clarity, we might call a grammar book a grammatical statement; that is, a statement that attempts to describe the way the language works. Of course, ideally, the grammatical statement should describe the grammar of the language exactly, but in fact it never does. In the first place, grammatical statements are made by human beings, and all human statements are more or less wrong, more or less inaccurate. Furthermore, language is always changing, so that even if a grammarian could devise a perfect statement about a language, by the time the statement had been worked out and published, it would be inaccurate. More important is the fact that, if by *grammar* we mean a grammatical statement, there is no such thing as *the* grammar, the one and only grammar, of English or of any other language.

This assertion may need explaining. As we have seen above, languages can work in various ways, can make use of various grammatical principles, and can use various devices to reveal these principles. Scholars have never found any language that used one grammatical device and only one. Accordingly, the grammatical statement will vary depending upon which of the grammatical devices in a language we accept as the most important. For example, in the sentence *Some plays play to large audiences,* we all know that *plays* is a noun and the subject of the sentence, and that *play* is a verb, involved in the predication. But how do we know? Do we know this because *plays* has an *s* in the printed form and a /z/ in the spoken form, and that these are characteristics of nouns, or do we know it because *plays* comes before *play,* and the standard English sentence pattern is subject–verb–complement? In practice, both principles may be working (perhaps not equally for all users of the language), but in preparing a grammatical statement a grammarian is likely to have to prefer one principle to the other. The result is that two grammarians can produce two somewhat different grammatical statements, depending upon which principles each assumes to be primary and which secondary.

The older grammatical statement, which is still taught in many schools, started with the assumption that English would be best described by identifying the parts of speech. This approach was based upon Latin grammars, and led to parsing; in Latin it worked fairly well, because Latin made much use of inflection, and thus the parts of speech could be identified by their endings. Few English words, however, now have endings, and modern grammarians tend to become unhappy when they try to apply Latin grammar to English. They find that a grammatical statement based upon the parts of speech is often inaccurate, generally inadequate, and subtly confusing. In short, it does not tell us enough.

On the other hand, this approach cannot be entirely invalid. Modern grammarians believe that in all languages certain locutions have what they call "privilege of occurrence." That is, some linguistic units can occur in certain ways but not in certain other ways. Take the word *the.* Practically speaking, it cannot occur as subject; we do not say *The is the brightest boy in class.* Neither can *the* be a verb; we do not say *He can the the problem. The* is not privileged to occur as subject or verb. Whenever the word *the* occurs we know it is the first word of a sequence that must end with a word like *man,* as in the following: *the man; the public-spirited man; the slovenly, slack-jawed, moronic, sack-of-potatoes sort of man.* Once the word *the* appears, we know that a word like *man* must come eventually, and that only certain sorts of words can intervene between them. That is, in the sense that all words have some sorts of privilege of occurrence, parts of speech must be a very real part of English grammar if not the whole of it.

Modern grammarians, therefore, have attempted to describe parts of speech or classes of words more precisely than did traditional grammar. They have observed, for example, the inadequacy of a definition like "A verb is a word that expresses action, being, or condition"; applied literally it suggests that *collision, game,* and *violently* might all be verbs since they express action. They have substituted two kinds of descriptive criteria: form and function. For example, a noun can be distinguished by its form as a word that can have an *s* or *es* plural or a possessive form with *'s* or *s'*. Some nouns can also be distinguished by derivational endings like the *–tion* or *–ness* or *–dom* in *prevention, happiness,* and *kingdom.* A verb can be distinguished as a word that changes its form to mark the difference between present and past tenses. Functional or positional definitions can supplement these. A noun can be described as a word that can be put into the blank in a test frame like *The ——— seemed ready.* Or an adjective can fit into a frame like *The ——— house.* Such definitions do not solve all problems, and they become more complicated as they become more inclusive.

Consideration of the function of parts of speech or words of different classes can lead to another approach to grammar. That is, grammarians recognized that not only was a noun a noun, but that it acted as *subject* of a sentence; it might be the "subject" in the sense that it was the subject under discussion. A verb was a verb as a part of speech, but it acted as *verb* in predication. It might be incomplete itself, and if so, the words that followed it, whatever their parts of speech, functioned as what could be called *complements.* The verb along with whatever accompanied it, often including a complement, constituted a predication about the subject, and thus could be called a *predicate.* Accordingly, from the point of view of function, a sentence was seen to consist of a subject and a predication about it, or a predicate, and the whole followed the subject–verb–complement pattern. Perhaps we should notice here that any one of these parts could be zero, could be missing; a sentence might have no expressed subject (*Get out!*), no verb (*John, a hero?*), or no complement (*I wonder*), or even lack of two or more of the usual parts (*Fire! What?*). Usually, however, in connected discourse, most sentences contain all three parts, and thus *subject–verb–complement* becomes a revealing description of a sentence.

These are some of the answers a grammarian will get if he assumes that English will be best described by starting with the parts of speech or with the functioning of words, but he can start with other assumptions. He can, for example, notice that all languages employ sound; in fact, all languages existed as speech long before anybody wrote or read, and languages seem still to change on an oral basis. Grammar must be basically oral. Further, all languages have some kind of structure. Thus, the grammarian may plausibly break a language into its sounds and observe their structure. This is essentially what we were doing earlier, when we broke *cups* into /cup/ + /s/—although, to be more exact, we should have used phonemic symbols and produced /kəp/ and /s/. Each of these symbols represent what is called a *phoneme,* a working unit of sound, and each working group of sounds is called a *morpheme,* a unit of language. The structuralist starts with a segment of language, usually a sentence. He cuts this into its *immediate constituents,* that is, into the two parts of which it is made, and then cuts each of those into its two most important parts, and so on until only phonemes are left.

This kind of analysis has been very successful. It has been used to analyze primitive, unwritten languages, to teach strange languages to the armed forces, and to teach English and other tongues as a second language, especially to primitive or uneducated people. It is being used in some schools to teach composition to Americans. It can provide a very interesting description of a language, because it can record the stress, pitch, and pauses within a sentence that reveal the grammar orally. It is sometimes called *structural analysis, phonemic analysis,* or *structural linguistics.* It is too complicated to treat in any detail here, but we might notice that when a structuralist makes his first immediate constituent cut (called an IC cut), he divides the sentence into the two conventional parts, the subject and the predicate. The next cut in the predicate cuts the verb from the complement.

The grammatical statements we have considered thus far start with language in existence, with a written sentence or with a recorded oral sentence. But of course grammar exists as speech coming to be, as sentences being written and as words being spoken and building into sentences. What is the grammar that allows language to come into existence? In an attempt to answer this question, some scholars are producing what is called *generative grammar,* which is a set of relatively simple rules that will account for the generation of all sentences. They produce a basic rule like the following:

$$S \longrightarrow NP \text{ plus } VP$$

In this formula, S stands for *sentence,* for any sentence. The symbol $\longrightarrow$ stands for "write as." NP stands for *noun phrase* and VP for *verb phrase.* Thus the formula means, "A sentence is written as a noun phrase plus a verb phrase." A noun phrase is defined roughly as any word or combination of words that users of the language would recognize as a subject. Thus NP could be *students, all the students, any group of students that you happen to be thinking of,* or anything else that could be a subject along with whatever goes along with the subject. Similarly, VP is a verb, a verb plus one or more complements, and anything that may go along with the verb or the complements. With this start the generative grammarian can go on to writing more specialized rules; one of the first will inevitably look something like the following:

$$VP \longrightarrow V \quad \text{plus} \quad \begin{cases} NP \\ mod \\ zero \end{cases}$$

Anyone who knows the conventional grammatical statement about sentences may be able to read this as "A verb phrase can be written as a verb plus a noun phrase, a modifier, or nothing." The first alternative would include predicates containing direct objects (*Fran watched television*), predicates containing predicate adjectives (*Fran looked bored*), and predicates having no complement (*Fran sulked*).

The generative grammar now attracting the most attention is called *transform* or *transformational* grammar, since it makes use of what are called *transforms.* For example, the sentence *Bruce does look like his sister* can be thought of as another way to say *Bruce looks like his sister.* In grammatical terms, *Bruce looks like his sister* is called a *kernel sentence,* because it is conceived to be the basic form of this sort of statement, using the simple SVC pattern. *Bruce does look like his sister* is a transform of this kernel; so is *Does Bruce look like his sister?* along with a number of others. This same sort of procedure can be used to reduce a sentence to a clause, a phrase, a verbal construction, or even a single modifier. *Karen has a blue hat* can become the transform *Karen's blue hat.*

Thus far, these are the main approaches to English grammar. If we were to pursue any of them very far, we should become involved in many complexities, and in contradictions between the

189

approaches, but viewed in their elements, we may observe that the four sorts of grammatical statements produce remarkably similar results. Whether we start by naming parts of speech, by identifying the functions of words, by splitting sentences up according to their structures, or by generating sentences in accordance with formulas, we get much the same answers. The core of English grammar, and probably of English sentence structure, is to be sought in the way in which the subject, the verb, and the complement work together. Of course the whole job of writing must be more complicated than this makes it sound; thought and life are complex and language is a subtle and variable instrument, but we shall do well to make the use of language as simple and orderly as we can. Apparently the subject–verb–complement pattern should be a good place to start, for the pattern must be central, yet it must have variations, and these variations must be important. What a writer does or does not do with this pattern must have much to do with what makes good writing good, and bad writing bad.

The Kernel Sentence

For
Guide to Revision,
see page 201.

The basic sentence is a comment about a topic.

Communication is cumulative; that is, it develops through what might be called a process of addition. Typically, the writer introduces a topic and then adds comments about it, which may extend through a paragraph or a chapter or may be completed in a single sentence. The pattern, topic plus comment, provides the framework for the paragraph or for a longer composition (see 1–2); it provides also the framework for the sentence.

Consider the following paragraph, in which some key words are in italics.

[1] *Government* in America *has always regarded* the *operation* of industry as a purely private function. [2] To return to an earlier example, even the *newest-biggest* of all governmental agencies, born in the early days of the Atomic age and the Fair Deal—the AEC—*operates* its vast, complex, "monopolistic," and largely secret *domain* through private industrial contractors. [3] But *business has* yet *to show* a comparably broad and tolerant *understanding* of the legitimate domain of government. [4] In fact, some *sections* of the business community *could not do better than follow,* in this regard, Dr. Johnson's *advice,* and *clear* their *minds* of cant and prejudiced misinformation, not to say the downright nonsense about "governmental dictatorship," and, of course, "creeping Socialism" that all too often, as a species of businessman's groupthink, takes the place of responsible consideration of the proper functions of government in free society.

—ADLAI STEVENSON, *My Faith in Democratic Capitalism*

The paragraph can be thought of as extended comments on two topics, government and business. Within the paragraph each of the four sentences introduces a topic and then adds a comment. The italicized words establish a framework for each sentence:

	Subject	*Verb*	*Complement*
[1]	Government	has regarded	operation
[2]	newest-biggest	operates	domain
[3]	business	has to show	understanding
[4]	sections	could not do better than follow	advice
		clear	minds

Sentences in English develop about patterns like these, in which a subject introduces a topic, and a verb and, usually, a complement comment on it.

12-1 Kernel Sentence Patterns

In English even the most complicated sentences can be generated by established grammatical procedures from a relatively small number of frameworks or kernel sentences. English kernel sentences have the following patterns:

Subject	*Verb*
Fish	swim.
Blue	fades.

Subject	*Verb*	*Object Complements*
Tam	sang	a sonnet.
Jack	threw	Evelyn the orchid.
The children	consider	her stupid.
The voters	made	him an ex-president.

Subject	*Linking Verb*	*Subject Complement or Modifier*
The moon	was	a ship.
The pumpkin	became	a coach.
Life	is	real.
The coat	felt	warm.
Nobody	was	there.

12-2 Developing Patterns

Most adult writers find few uses for sentences as simple as *Fish swim,* but one adult writer did produce

Most fish of which we have any record, either contemporary or geologic, swim with the digestive organs downward.

The precise grammatical rules by which *Fish swim* can generate a longer sentence like the above are the materials of modern grammars; in general the processes involved are the following:

1. Groups of words rather than single words function as any of the main parts of the kernel, especially the complement.

Jack hated *washing the car.*
Jerry learned *how to retouch the photographs.*
The new boss promised *that nobody would be fired.*
Where you find the parrot is not my concern.
The meeting *should be starting* now.

In the first three the italicized word group serves as a complement, in the fourth as a subject, in the last as a verb.

2. Words or groups of words can be combined or coordinated to serve as any of the main parts of the pattern.

Music and *poetry* can open *hearts* but not *purses.*
The children *ran out the door* and *jumped on their bicycles.*
They knew *what they wanted* and *what they could get.*

In the first example *music* and *poetry* are joined by *and* as the subject and *hearts* and *purses* are joined as compound object complements. In the second, two predicates, verb–complement combinations, are joined by *and.* In the third, two word groups are joined as object complements. Furthermore, complete patterns can be joined to develop complicated sentences.

Tam sang a sonnet, but his wife made him change his tune.

Almost infinite combinations of patterns and parts of patterns are possible.

3. Any part of the pattern may be modified by a word or group of words subordinated to it.

When it is exposed to strong sunlight, blue often fades into a dull gray.

The basic pattern is *blue fades;* the beginning word group modifies the whole pattern and *often* and *into a dull gray* modify the verb *fades.*

For the last two of these processes, coordination and subordination, see Sections 15 and 16; following are further illustrations of the composition of each of the main parts of the sentence kernel.

12-3   The Subject

We recognize a subject in English mainly from its position, at the beginning of the kernel sentence, except in a few inverted patterns (see Section 14). The order is so nearly standard in English that we identify it even without anything that can be called words, as in the following:

The quigquig obled a biscum.

We know at once, because it is preceded by the determiner *The*, that *quigquig* is a symbol like *girl* or *wind* and not a word like *off*. From its position and the absence of any signs that identify it as not the subject we assume that it is, that it obled the biscum.

Most frequently subjects are what modern grammarians call *noun phrases*, composed of a pronoun or a noun and its modifiers. *Salesgirls*, or *the salesgirl*, or *the new salesgirl with the motheaten wig* may be a noun phrase working as a subject. Pronouns may make good subjects, since they indicate specific persons or things and by referring to an antecedent provide continuity with what has preceded; for forms of pronouns suitable for subjects, see the Glossary. Various verbal constructions may serve as subjects. They include clauses, which themselves include subjects and verbs, and are usually distinguished by an introductory word like *that, how, what, whether, whoever*.

What you decide to do is your own business.
That he pocketed the commission himself seemed obvious.

A verbal (see 12-5) which is not a finite verb, usually a verbal and its object, may be used as a subject.

Watching television was his only recreation.
To solve that problem will take more than a slide rule.

12-4   The Verb

The second main part of the kernel sentence, the verb, is the focal point of the comment about the topic; its nature and function provide the distinctions among the types of kernels listed above. That is, the following three types of verbs are characteristic of the three general types of kernels:

1. *Intransitive.*   An intransitive verb has no complement. It does

not *transfer* or *transmit* meaning; along with modifiers it can complete the comment on the topic.

The tide *turned.*
She *sang.*
In spite of her incipient laryngitis, the drafty old barn in which she was asked
to perform, and the handicap of a foreign audience, she *sang* very well,
reaching high C with scarcely a suggestion of a squeak.

2. *Transitive.* The transitive verb takes at least one object complement.

The car *turned* the corner.
Johnny *gave* his mother a green apple.
Johnny *ate* an apple.

3. *Linking.* A linking verb, usually some form of *be*, carries
little meaning but links a subject with a subject complement.

The milk *turned* sour.
Life *is* real, life *is* earnest.
The man *was* a traitor.

In each example, the verb is primarily a function word; *turned* joins
milk and a complement that modifies it, *sour; was* joins *man* and
traitor, a subject complement that restates the subject in other terms.

Notice that *turned* appears in all three groups, with some change
of meaning in its different functions. Most verbs can function as
either transitive or intransitive, and some may also function as linking verbs (*seem, appear, look, get, become, feel, taste, smell, sound.*) Notice
also that *turned* can function also in sentences like the following:

The car *turned over.*
The cook *turned off* the gas.

The verbs in these sentences may be called *separable suffix verbs* or
merged verbs. Verbs of this type have been developing rapidly in the
English language, apparently as combinations of verbs with various
sorts of words that are not verbal. Compare the following:

Frankie looked over the transom.
Frankie looked over the contract.

In the first, *looked* can be thought of as the verb with *over the transom*   **195** telling where Frankie looked. In the second, this kind of interpretation obviously will not work; the contract is not a barrier over which Frankie cast her glance. *Look over* has become a verb, and a single synonym like *examined* might be substituted for it. Or consider other sentences:

The globe turned on its axis.
The cook turned on the stove.
Agnes called up the dumb waiter.
The airplane blew up.

In the first, the verb is *turned,* modified by *on its axis.* But in the second, the verb must be *turned on,* unless the family can expect broiled cook for dinner. In the third, we do not know whether the verb is *called* or *called up* unless we know the intended meaning. If Agnes put her head into the dumb waiter shaft and said "Yoo-hoo," the verb is *called,* and *up the dumb waiter* prescribes direction. If Agnes went to a telephone and tried to speak with a waiter who was either unable to talk or not very bright, then the verb is *called up.* In the final sentence a new verb has been created in which both parts have lost original meanings. *Up* certainly does not have its usual meaning; the plane, or what was left of it, came down. And *blew* in the combination does not mean the same thing as *blew* without the suffix. The two words have become a new word meaning *explode.*

New verb combinations reflect a significant historical change in the English verb, part of the shift in the nature of the language. As we have noticed before, English comes from an ancient language known as Indo-European, which was heavily inflected. Different forms of the verb indicated different uses. We retain remnants of these forms, as in *I write, I wrote, I have written.* English, however, has been losing its inflected forms and stringing words together to increase the varieties of meaning possible in verbs. Compare the following:

Janet   is going   to Europe.
Janet   is going   to marry Walter.

Divided this way, to indicate that the verb is *is going,* the second sentence apparently means that Janet is walking or riding and at the end of her journey will have arrived at the church or wherever the wedding is to take place. In most contexts this meaning would

not be intended; in modern English, sense dictates that the words
be divided as:

Janet   is going to marry   Walter.

The verb seems to be *is going to marry,* a future of the verb *marry.* In
recent centuries such forms have increased in number and complexity, so that we now find word groups like those in the following
which serve as verbs:

We *look forward to being able to consider* your plan.
They *should be trying to maneuver* the space capsule.
The dean *expects to get around to offering* them some advice.

These combinations have become very numerous, with different
combinations making distinctions in time or *tense.* Forms like *I eat,
I am eating, I am to eat* indicate present or future time, depending on
context (*I am eating now. I am eating a light lunch tomorrow.*) Forms like
I ate, I was eating, I had eaten, I have been eating indicate various stages
of past time. These same forms and others may indicate much more.
They may indicate the speaker's concepts of the sentence, the *mood*
(see Glossary). *He ate the cake* is indicative; *If he were to eat the cake*
is conditional; *He could have eaten the cake* is subjunctive; *Eat that cake*
is imperative. Or verbs may indicate the *aspect* from which the action is viewed. *I eat in the cafeteria* implies customary action; *I keep
eating too much* suggests that an action repeats itself; *I am about to start
eating* implies that an action is to begin.

Verbals **12-5**

Two types of verb forms need attention here because they will
not serve in the second position in the kernel sentence. They retain
enough of their characteristics as verbs to take subjects and objects
but function generally as nouns or modifiers. The two types are
those usually characterized by the separable prefix *to* and those
with the endings *-ing* or *-d* or *-ed.* They appear frequently as parts
of combinations that predicate as complete verbs. Outside such
combinations, however, these forms are not complete verbs and are
called *verbals.* Compare:

Verb: They *are going to prove* the theorem.
Verbal: We asked the students *to prove* the theorem.

Verb: Somebody *has been proving* the theorem.
Verbal: Proving the theorem was their assignment.

The first of these forms is the *infinitive,* one of the principal parts of the verb often distinguishable by its sign, *to,* and it may be used as a verbal noun or sometimes as a verbal modifier. The following six forms are relatively common in modern English:

	Active	*Passive*	*Progressive Active*
Present	to lose	to be lost	to be losing
Past	to have lost	to have been lost	to have been losing

The second type of verbal is called a *gerund* when it is used as a verbal noun and a *participle* when it is a verbal modifier. The most common forms of this verbal are:

	Active	*Passive*
Present	proving	being proved
Past	proved, having proved	having been proved

The simple past form *proved* is common for the participle but is not used for the gerund.

12-6   The Complement

Complements are not always easy to define or to distinguish from complex verbs, but in general they are of two sorts, as indicated in the last two groups of kernel sentences in 12-1.

The *object complement* completes the verb by introducing the name of something which is not the subject and which receives the predication of the verb.

Tam saw a *witch.*
He admired her short *skirt.*
The devil was going to roast *him.*
His wife was nursing her *wrath* to keep it warm.

These object complements are highly varied, and a complete analysis of them is not easy. For instance, in the sentences *Mary made a cake* and *The cake made Jimmie sick,* the cake, clearly, did not make Jimmie in the same sense that Mary made the cake. Fortunately, however, the student need not be able to distinguish all the different sorts of object complements in order to understand fundamental English sentence structure, or to write correct and vigorous sentences.

The *subject complement* completes predication but also elaborates or modifies the idea expressed in the subject. It may give another name for the subject, mention a class which includes the subject, or include the subject in a group and sharpen our understanding of it.

Tam O'Shanter was a *Scotsman.*
He was an old *soak.*

The student may know this type of complement as a *predicate noun* or *predicate nominative,* since it is the name of something and it appears in the predicate. The subject complement may also give a characteristic or quality of the subject.

Tam seemed *thirsty.*
He was *drunk* every Saturday night.

The student may know this type of complement under such names as *predicate adjective, predicate attribute,* or *attribute complement.*

The distinction between these two kinds of complements has practical importance in usage because pronouns used as subjective complements traditionally take the subjective or nominative forms.

Completing the Pattern 12-7

Often in conversation and sometimes in writing, some parts of the basic sentence are not expressed; they are understood from the context. They are incomplete in form, but they can stand independently in their contexts and are punctuated as sentences. Among the most common are exclamations, like *Oh, wonderful!* or *Incredible!* or *Good morning,* and replies to questions, like *No, Yes,* or *Of course.* Also used in both speaking and writing is the command, in which no subject is expressed: *Go wash the dishes* or *Let sleeping dogs lie.* Our feeling for usual word order is so firm, moreover, that other types of incomplete sentences can make complete statements in context. *How old are you?* might be answered by the complete sentence *I am twenty years old,* but the incomplete sentence *Twenty* is more likely. *Years old* can be omitted because we habitually state ages in years (we could specify *two decades*), and *I am* can be omitted because it is so obvious a part of the regular word order that the question implies it. The following from Dicken's *Pickwick Papers* concludes with a properly independent incomplete sentence:

> But bless our editorial heart, what a long chapter we have been betrayed into. We had quite forgotten all such petty restrictions as chapters, we solemnly declare. So here goes, to give the goblin a fair start in a new one. A clear stage, and no favour for the goblins, ladies and gentlemen, if you please.

A paragraph from Wolfe's *Of Time and the River* illustrates a modern writer's use of the incomplete sentence, punctuated like a complete sentence and making a statement.

> The coming on of the great earth, the new lands, the enchanted city, the approach, so smoky, blind and stifled, to the ancient web, the old grimed thrilling barricades of Boston. The streets and buildings that slid past that day with such a haunting strange familiarity, the mighty engine steaming to its halt, and the great trainshed dense with smoke and acrid with its smell and full of the slow pantings of a dozen engines, now passive as great cats, the mighty station with the ceaseless throngings of its illimitable life, and all of the murmurous, remote and mighty sounds of time forever held there in the station, together with a tart and nasal voice, a hand'sbreadth off that said: "There's hahdly time, but try it if you want."

Such sentences are incomplete as grammatical units because they omit one of the essential elements, subject or verb, but they may be successful, because basic word order has become standard in English. We anticipate missing elements, and in successful incomplete sentences we automatically supply them. The writer establishes a pattern in his style which helps the reader perceive unexpressed thoughts. The incomplete sentences in the Wolfe paragraph above are subjects; the reader can understand what the writer means to say about these subjects—that they were observed or were part of his experience. Most writers, however, use the incomplete sentence sparingly, except in reports of conversation. It is a special device, to be used for special effects. In the hands of anyone but an expert, it usually causes trouble because basic patterns have not been established, and missing ideas cannot be supplied.

Quite different are the incomplete sentences which result from carelessness or ignorance of the English sentence pattern. For instance, the writer who intends to write an independent complete sentence confuses his reader if he begins with a word which signals that the subsequent material is subordinate to something else. *We were eating dinner* is a complete and independent sentence, but *When we were eating dinner* is not. Such unsuccessful incomplete sentences, sentence fragments, are common; and they are serious, partly because they impede communication and partly because they are commonly looked upon as evidence of ignorance or stupidity.

Guide to Revision 12 Frag

Complete an incomplete sentence mistakenly used as complete, or join it to another sentence.

The kernel sentences described in this section have at least two elements, a subject and a verb. Since more complex sentences are derived from these kernels, they also must contain at least one independent basic sentence pattern with a subject and a verb. Sentences carry the burden of most standard writing, and the use of fragments—except, of course, in reports of conversation or other special uses—is a serious error. Unless fragments result from carelessness, they are symptoms of basic confusion about sentence structure and the relating of ideas.

As the following examples illustrate, fragments may mar student writing because a series of words constructed for use as only part of a sentence is punctuated as if it were the whole sentence. The series lacks subject or verb; or an incomplete combination of words, usually a verbal, replaces the verb. Usually fragments are best corrected not merely by supplying missing elements but by more extensive revision in which the fragment is combined with other elements to build a more revealing sentence.

ORIGINAL	REVISION
A communistic government attempts to distribute the products of	(1) A communistic government attempts to distribute the products of

ORIGINAL (*Cont.*)

industry equally. It often restricts individual liberty, however. The system requiring careful control of the means of production.

[*The final group of words contains no verb.* Requiring *could work as part of a combination of verbs,* is requiring *or* had been requiring, *but alone it is not a verb. Here it seems only a modifier of* system, *a verbal. The fault can be corrected, as the revisions show, by making the fragment dependent (1); changing the part of a verb to a verb (2); making the fragment a modifying phrase (3).*]

The actor had to strap his ankle to his thigh. In this manner giving the impression that he had only one leg.

REVISION (*Cont.*)

industry equally, but since the system requires careful state control of the means of production, it often restricts individual liberty.

[*Often this method of revision is best, since it clarifies relationships of ideas although it may require, as does this sentence, that the author rethink his statement and subordinate some of it.*]

(2) The system requires careful control of the means of production.

(3) It often restricts individual liberty, however, requiring careful state control of the means of production.

The actor had to strap his ankle to his thigh in order to give the impression that he had only one leg.

A fragment may lack an essential portion of the basic sentence pattern, usually the subject or the verb, or both.

ORIGINAL

He failed the course in physics. Either because of laziness or because of stupidity.

[*The final group of words fills no basic sentence pattern. The writer probably only mispunctuated, having meant something like (1). He could revise also by adding a verb (2) or by making the subordination clearer (3), which is often preferable.*]

With the knowledge that, although the documents have been stolen, they have not yet been seen by a foreign agent.

[*The group of words lacks a kernel sentence.*]

REVISION

(1) He failed the course in physics, either because of laziness or because of stupidity.

(2) He failed the course in physics. Either laziness or stupidity was his trouble.

(3) Because of either laziness or stupidity, he failed the course in physics.

We know that, although the documents have been stolen, they have not yet been seen by a foreign agent.

[*The revision adds a subject and verb to complete the sentence pattern.*]

Even an expression containing all elements of a basic pattern cannot stand independently if a subordinating word signals its dependence.

ORIGINAL

In the morning Thoreau was released from jail. Although he still refused to pay the tax.

[Although *labels the second group of words as dependent, incapable of standing as an independent sentence. The fragment can be joined to the independent clause it depends upon (1); or it can be made independent by removing* although *(2).*]

REVISION

(1) Although he still refused to pay the tax, Thoreau was released from jail in the morning.

(2) In the morning Thoreau was released from jail, but he still refused to pay the tax.

[*The second revision alters the meaning, but the meaning of the fragment itself is uncertain—just because it is a fragment.*]

Names may be mistaken for sentences.

ORIGINAL

Looking out toward the horizon, she saw only the old cabin in which Mary had been born. A single cottonwood that had escaped the drought. The apparently boundless expanse of sunburned prairie.

[*The last two groups are actually additional objects of* saw; *they name and do not tell anything about what they name. They are not complete. They can be placed in usual order as complements (1), or they can be made sentences by adding verbs (2).*]

REVISION

(1) Looking out toward the horizon, she saw only the old cabin in which Mary had been born, a single cottonwood that had escaped the drought, and the apparently boundless expanse of sunburned prairie.

(2) Looking out toward the horizon, she saw the old cabin in which Mary had been born. A single cottonwood that had escaped the drought stood near it. The apparently boundless expanse of sunburned prairie spread into the distance.

Exercise 12

A. Sentences developed from the different types of kernels described in 12-1 have different uses. The following paragraphs have been rewritten—often distorted—by changing sentences from one pattern to another, so that patterns with linking verbs predominate. Rewrite each paragraph, changing sentences to subject-verb or subject-verb-object patterns whenever you think you can make the writing more direct. Your instructor can supply the original paragraphs for comparison.

12

Exercises

1. [1] My father was as unmechanical a man as ever lived, and the gasoline engine was a complete mystery to him. [2] Sometimes as far as he went was to lift the hood and stare at the engine, or maybe it was to reach in and wiggle a wire to see whether it would wiggle. [3] But mostly his procedure was to confine himself to kicking the tires. [4] It was never clear to me, and I doubt that it was clear to him, what he expected to learn from this, but he was very serious and professional about it. [5] His attitude was that of thumping a patient's chest. [6] It is a wonder to me that he never placed a stethoscope to the casing or stuck a fever thermometer down the valve stem.

2. [1] The fact that courses are the means by which information is made available to students is one reason for there being textbooks. [2] Knowing where you are going in a class is easier for both student and teacher if there is a textbook available to them. [3] That is, to make the point briefly we could say that a textbook helps to show where the course is going and that it provides a kind of record of how the teacher and the class are getting on. [4] A lot of people are going to have their feelings hurt by this statement, especially those teachers that are liberal and progressive, who are the same ones who deplore there being any kind of prescription in teaching, and who may also have various reasons for not wanting textbooks, perhaps partly because of the name, textbook, because the word *text* has echoes of scripture and authority.

3. [1] The great migratory wave in American life is from country to city. [2] What happens to tens of thousands of children is that they are swept up in this wave and transplanted from a rural variety of poverty to the more oppressive urban ghetto. [3] Something from which they suffer is what social scientists call "cultural shock." [4] Little conception of what happens in cities or even what they look like is the rule for such children. [5] Trips to and around the city, routine for more privileged children, are the instruments whereby it is possible to help equalize the impoverished child's knowledge of modern realities.

4. [1] One of the important features of Boston today is a fairly stimulating atmosphere for the banker, the broker, for doctors and lawyers. [2] "Open-end" investments are prosperous, a major product at the dock is still fish, the wool market is still good, and employment is available for workers in the shoe factories in the nearby towns. [3] For the engineer, the physicist, the industrial designer, for all the highly trained specialists of the electronic age, Boston and its area are of seemingly unlimited promise. [4] Sleek, well-designed factories and research centers popping up everywhere are characteristic of the area; in the Sunday papers are pleas from the companies for more chemists, more engineers, and humble expressions of the executive benefits of salary and pension and advancement the companies are prepared to offer.

5. [1] Internationally, in the Fifties, intellectuals in Europe and America were the counter force to a dull, blatant Communist cultural offensive in a long weary effort. [2] They were what might be called successful, in a kind of Korean success. [3] Whether it was the boring quality of the enemy, the boring quantity of the support received at home—or

the boring quality of home itself, which in those years, was after all being defended—this conflict was one which can scarcely be said to have produced much in the way of intellectual monuments. [4] Those who engaged in this battle of the books and journals became possessors of what knowledge about the matter was available years before. [5] There were no new positions, only long heavings at the mired axles of cultural lag. [6] It was a stalemate, painful to some, boring to others, to some few, death; very like the Korean War. [7] Hungary in 1956 was a proof that there was no real point to it, but it went on.

B. Analyze the sentences in a theme you have written recently, underlining subject, verbs, and complements in the main kernels of each. Which of the main patterns appear most frequently? Try changing any of the sentences you can to another pattern, and decide whether the original or the revision is better.

C. The passage below contains a number of fragments used as sentences. Revise the passage, using methods outlined above, to make the fragments complete sentences or combine the fragments with other sentences.

[1] Catherine II, called Catherine the Great, came to the throne of Russia in 1762. [2] Her reign being the most notable of those which followed the long rule of Peter the Great. [3] Although she was actually not a Russian by birth, Catherine remained on the Russian throne for thirty-four years. [4] Since she was a German princess whose marriage to Peter III had been arranged by Frederick the Great. [5] Peter III being half-insane when he took the throne.

[6] Catherine, a despot who wished to be regarded as an "enlightened" despot like Frederick II of Prussia, more concerned actually with maintaining prestige than spreading culture through her country. [7] She continued some of the work of Peter the Great, ruling the country firmly and strengthening the central authority by administrative reorganization. [8] Divisions of the government under appointed governors and vice-governors, all responsible to the tsarina. [9] A church dependent for its property and power on the desires of the central authority. [10] By maintaining a strong foreign policy and striking her rivals when they were weak, she established the international position of the Russian empire. [11] A war against the Ottoman Empire, 1768–1774, was highly successful. [12] Which led to navigation rights for Russian ships and added considerably to Russian territory. [13] Poland, weakened by internal strife, and easily preyed upon by surrounding empires. [14] By 1795 Poland had virtually ceased to exist as an independent state. [15] Her territory partitioned among Austria, Prussia, and Russia. [16] With Catherine getting the lion's share.

[17] Catherine's internal policies did bring about a number of reforms. [18] The establishment, for example, of schools and academics. [19] Reform, however, being carefully regulated. [20] In order to prevent genuine enlightenment of the masses which might weaken the position of the aristocracy.

Predication

*For
Guide to Revision,
see page 214.*

Subject, verb, and complement must interact logically.

Predication is the relationship expressed when subject, verb, and complement interact; the kernel sentence predicates. Selection of the subject, verb, and complement, therefore, directs the course of the sentence—determines its structure, controls its plausibility. Consider, for example, a student attempting to tell why he came to college. If the first word that comes to his mind is *reason* and he writes it down as a subject, he restricts what is to follow. He cannot very easily use a verb like *growls* or *objects* or *admires*. He is almost committed to *is* or a verb like it. One student, starting in this way, muddled on to the following:

> The reason why I came to college is because, there being a law you have to have a degree for a license in the field of embalming in this state, which is my goal in life.

This production, of course, is not a sentence at all, and a much better sentence might have been written even with *reason* as the subject, but the writer's troubles began when he chose to begin with the relatively abstract word.

He might have chosen another abstraction: "My desire to meet the state requirements for an embalming license. . . ." He would have had a somewhat larger group of verbs to select from—*cause* or *make* or *influence*, as well as *is*—but he would still have been likely to write an indirect and perhaps wordy sentence. In conversation, if the student had been asked why he came to college, he probably would have stayed out of trouble. He would have said something like "I want to be a mortician" or "I need a degree so I can get a mortician's license." He would have chosen the actor as the subject and produced a straightforward, clear sentence.

Choosing Subjects   13-1

Usually, a writer chooses the subject as the first important word in a prospective sentence, and the subject, once it is chosen, does much to chart the predication. The verb must work with the subject, and the complement must follow from the verb. Thus, when a writer chooses a subject, he limits his choice of subsequent words and structures, and unless he chooses a subject which can be developed with an appropriate verb, he is likely to be led into a clumsy, rambling sentence.

The principle applies most readily to descriptions of events or acts. If a pencil drops off the table and a speaker wishes to comment, he is likely to say "The pencil dropped" or "The pencil fell on the floor." He picks the actor for the subject and uses the verb to specify what the actor did. Writers of fiction draft most of their sentences so that someone or something does, says, or is something. Writers of factual, expository prose may have to use abstractions, but the following illustrates how even a scholarly subject may be discussed mainly in sentences with the actor as subject.

> Two sages of a later day actually preached that the independent growth of American English was not only immoral but a sheer illusion. They were Richard Grant White, for long the most widely read writer upon language questions, and Thomas R. Lounsbury, for thirty-five years professor of English language and literature in the Sheffield Scientific School at Yale. White's "Words and Their Uses" (1872) and his "Everyday English" (1880) were mines of erudition. Lounsbury effectively attacked the follies of the grammarians; his two books "The Standard of Usage in English" and "The Standard of Pronunciation in English," not to mention his excellent "History of the English Language" and his numerous magazine articles, showed a sound knowledge of the early history of the language, and an admirable spirit of free inquiry. But when these laborious scholars turned from English proper to American English, they tried to deny its existence altogether, and to support that denial brought a critical method that was anything but scientific.   —H. L. MENCKEN and RAVEN I. MC DAVID, JR., *The American Language*

A less skillful writer might have been tempted to start sentences differently, to begin the first one, for example, with "A major contribution to the study of. . . ." or "The attitude of two sages of a later day. . . ." The resulting sentences would have been less direct and less clear.

Expository writing sometimes requires relatively abstract subjects followed by a form of *be*—to fit a context, for introductory matter, or in topic sentences, for example. The following sentences, for good reason, all have subjects that take the verb *be:*

Our lives are the creation of memory and the accompanying power to extend ourselves outward into ideas and relive them.

At the other pole, the spread of attitudes is wider.

This polarization is sheer loss to us all.

These are good sentences. The student writer, however, can do nothing more important to improve his writing than try whenever possible to pick a subject that will allow him to use a vigorous verb rather than *be.* Compare the following:

The origin of the classic prose which Mark Twain developed was his knowledge of the actual speech of America.

Out of his knowledge of the actual speech of America Mark Twain forged a classic prose.

The second sentence is obviously stronger and more direct than the first, which is a bad remolding of the original. Or compare another distortion with its original:

The demand for creation in science is a high level of imaginative insight and intuitive perception.

Creation in science demands a high level of imaginative insight and intuitive perception.

Again, the second sentence, the original with the subject–verb–object pattern, seems stronger. Although the writing may attempt only to inform the reader of the existence of facts and ideas, sentences turning about an actor and an action usually say more and say it more briefly.

Even within subject–verb–object sentences a specific subject usually works better than a more general one. Abstract nouns (*heroism, nutrition, importance, reason*) tend to require more general, less active verbs than concrete nouns (*quarterback, candle, creek*). In many confused sentences the trouble starts with the selection of abstract subjects that betray the writer into indiscriminate use of verbs like *mean, provide, result, prove.* Because transitional sentences and topic sentences may need to deal in abstractions, they are particularly susceptible to weakening through imprecise subjects.

Since the sentence begins to take shape when a possible subject gets on paper, the following practical suggestions can save the student from verbal quagmires:

1. On the whole, make the subject the actor if there is one; or use as the grammatical subject the actual subject, what the sentence is mainly about.

2. Whenever possible, prefer concrete, specific subjects to abstract or general ones. Especially treacherous are abstract words which usually must be followed by *is* or *was*—words like *reason, explanation, conclusion, situation,* and *attitude.* Often, of course, a context demands a sentence beginning with such a subject, but more often a better sentence emerges when the writer avoids abstract subjects.

3. Choose the subject in light of the verb that is to follow it, for the subject alone cannot make the sentence, but usually a concrete, precise subject will permit the choosing of an appropriate verb.

4. If a sentence causes trouble, try finding a new subject and starting over. Often you can ask yourself, "What am I trying to say?" and make the simplest answer you can. The subject in your answer often makes the best subject for the sentence you are trying to write.

Choosing Verbs   13-2

Even with a good subject, an inadequate verb may weaken the sentence. The verb provides the distinction among kernel sentences (see 12-1); thus the choice of the verb determines whether the most appropriate sentence pattern will develop. Consider the following:

Johnny is a dropout.

The writer begins with the actor as subject, but *is* does little more than fill the sentence pattern and link *Johnny* and *dropout.* If the writer has no more to say than to establish this connection, the sentence is adequate; but usually a writer has more to say. He could go on with the same pattern:

Johnny is a dropout. He was the owner of convertible.
It was new. But he was in a wreck with it.

This sounds wordy and immature largely because verbs carry none of the meaning. Compare:

Johnny, a dropout, wrecked his new convertible.

With an expressive verb, *wrecked,* for the main predication, *is* and *was* can be dropped and *dropout* and *new* can be subordinated (see Section 16).

Furthermore, sensitive choice of verbs permits subtle distinctions. In the example above, the devastation to Johnny's car could be altered by changing *wrecked* to *scratched, dented, crumpled, smashed,* or *demolished.* Such precision through verb choice characterizes poetry and much narrative writing, but verbs can specify also in the sort of exposition that students need to write. For example, students quoting material often overuse the verb *state,* when they might gain at once variety and exactness by judicious use of dozens of synonyms like *write, declare, assert, imply, infer, admit, insist, concede, suggest, explain, postulate, amplify, propose, conclude, reveal, doubt, argue, point out, wonder if, question whether, add, continue.*

13-3 Logical Predication

The following have the kinds of patterns described in Section 12; they look like possible kernel sentences:

The prejudice ambushed inconsequentials.
The lampshade promised Albert.
The person meant the failure.
Wilbur seemed the artichoke.

The words in each position have privilege of occurrence where they are used; that is, the "sentences" differ from *Wilbur artichokes seem,* which makes no sense because *artichoke* does not have privilege of occurrence as a verb nor *seem* as a complement. They also differ from grammatical sentences which err factually, like *Rabbits eat elephants.* Nevertheless, these groups of words obviously do not work as kernel sentences. Modern grammarians would call them "ungrammatical," because the words chosen to be subject, verb, and complement in each example do not represent meanings that can conceivably work together. The predication, the interaction of the main sentence parts, is here not logical.

Nobody is likely to write a sentence like any of the absurdities above: *The person meant the failure,* for example. The following sentence, however, was taken from a student paper:

Any person ill on the day of that first performance would have meant the failure of the entire summer theater.

Embedded in the longer sentence, the basic pattern does not parade its lack of sense so obviously. The reader can guess at what the writer intended to say, even though the sentence appears confused and obscure, but essentially the longer sentence is as illogical as the pattern on which it is based. The writer has not produced a meaningful predication, has not combined a compatible subject, verb, and object. He probably meant:

The illness of any member of the cast on the day of that first performance would have caused the failure of the entire summer theater.

The sentence remains awkward, however, and in most contexts the following would be better:

The entire summer theater would probably have failed if any member of the cast had been ill on the day of that first performance.

A better subject allows the use of a more vigorous verb, and permits a more vigorous sentence. Or consider another sentence:

The basis for the continuing unrest, which was partly misunderstanding and partly understanding too well what our motives were, held little hope among our representatives for success in negotiating new treaties.

The words seem at first glance to communicate; they sound like a sentence. But they communicate only confusion because the basic pattern is confused: *The basis held little hope.* The subject, verb, and complement do not make sense together, even though the length of the sentence momentarily obscures the confusion. With a new subject and verb the sentence comes nearer sense:

Our representatives had little hope of negotiating new treaties because of the continuing unrest, based partly on misunderstanding our motives and partly on understanding them too well.

Clear communication requires a basic sentence pattern that makes a plausible predication.

Subjects, Verbs, and Predication   13-4

A plausible predication requires first of all a subject and verb that make sense together, and obviously not all combinations work. The possible subjects for *sparkle* are numerous, but they are also limited; *gold, eyes,* and *hair* would work, and metaphorically even *wit* and *conversation,* but *clamor, participation, sneeze,* and *appetite* are not likely. In a broad way certain classes of nouns point toward different kinds of verbs. For example, animate nouns (*boy, dog, captain*) can be followed by verbs that will not work with inanimate nouns (*book, opinion, cup*). A clear sentence must derive from a plausible kernel; when the writer loses sight of his main predication he may produce sentences like the following:

If present trends continue, by next year the applicants who want to be considered for the benefits of free advanced education will have doubled.
Many people may find homes there and expand into towns.

Isolating the kernels from which the two sentences derive, *applicants double* and *people expand* reveals the basic absurdity—with applicants splitting like amoebas and people becoming balloons.

13-5   Complements and Predication

Like subjects and verbs, verbs and complements must fit together logically. Consider the following sentence:

The king lost his composure and reverted himself to a frightened and hesitant man.

Revert cannot here work with *king*. Although one can revert to a condition, a belief, or a practice, he cannot revert to a person. In the following, a passive structure disguises a similar inconsistency between a verb and its complement:

They let the discussion continue until after midnight in order that a consensus might be garnered.

Extraction of the kernel of the final clause, *they garnered a consensus,* points up the awkwardness. The following produces an impossible complement in a modifying clause:

He tried to borrow money from everybody in the room that he was acquainted.

As the sentence stands, the final clause derives from *he was acquainted everybody;* presumably the writer intended *with whom he was acquainted* or *he was acquainted with.*

13-6   Be and Predication

The verb *be*—which appears most frequently as *am, is, was, were* or in combinations like *will be* and *has been*—presents special problems in predication, partly because of the variety of ways in which it may link the subject and verb. It may carry some meaning, as in *To be or not to be* and *Whatever is, is right,* where it can mean to exist. It may imply definition or classification (*Music is an art*), supply a name (*This is John*), connect a subject with a modifier (*The apple is ripe*), or act as part of another verb (*The picture is being made now*). In all these the "meaning" of the verb is relatively insignificant; the verb mainly joins or links other meanings. Used in this way, to link a subject and a complement, the verb *be* almost always implies some kind of identity between subject and complement. Compare the following:

The coat is in the closet.
Happiness is where you find it.
Happiness is oblivion.
Two and two is four.
My sister is a trained nurse.
Alcoholism is the root of his trouble.
Beauty is truth.
Life is a dream.

In the first two examples the verb is modified by *in the closet* and *where you find it;* it retains much of the meaning of *exists* and does not link the subject with a complement. In the other sentences, however, the verb *be* resembles the equals sign in mathematics; the sentences form a kind of equation. Whatever comes before the verb is conceived to be equal, from at least one point of view, with what comes after it.

Frame Sentences and Predication 13-7

In most of the sentences we have considered, the main predication, the central kernel, has carried the important part of the meaning of the sentence. Consider, however, the following:

The most important thing to remember is that nobody has ever reached the peak without oxygen tanks.
The first matter to consider is how far we can go without letting the administration express its attitude.
I think that somebody must have picked the lock and taken the examinations long enough to have copies made.

Each of these sentences has a standard kernel, subject–verb–subject   **213** complement, with the complement slot filled by a clause. But the three subjects, *thing, matter,* and *I,* are not what the sentences mainly concern, and the verbs *be* and *think* do not embody significant assertions. In each sentence the complement makes the important comment; the main kernel works only as a kind of "frame" to present the idea in the complement.

Such sentences are useful, especially in introductions and transitions. Often context requires them, to carry on a subject or provide special emphasis, as in the following, which use a possible object to construct a frame:

Algebra was the only course John studied last year.
This quarrel with his son was now his only regret.

All of these, however, are indirect and carry the hazards of the *be* sentence, with its need for a logical equation. Often the more direct sentence, with the actor as subject, can improve the writing:

John studied only algebra last year.
Now he regretted only this quarrel with his son.

Pred

13 *Guide to Revision*

Examine the subject, verb, and complement basic to the sentence and revise so that their meanings work together to make sense.

Sentences work only if the kernel sentences from which they develop are clear. If subject, verb, and complement do not relate logically and plausibly—even if their relationship is buried in the complexities of a long sentence—the writing limps on its way. Often a badly selected abstract subject, an inexpressive verb, or an inappropriately used frame sentence weakens predication. The solution is usually to pick a new subject and start over.

ORIGINAL

The important thing is that shifting your weight is necessary on a turn if the centrifugal force is to be accommodated for.

[*The abstract subject and the unnecessary frame lead to a clumsy construction.*]

REVISION

You must shift your weight to accommodate for the centrifugal force developed in the turn.

[*With a pronoun as the subject the sentence becomes simpler and clearer.*]

The reason for Gary's wanting to major in molecular physics was because of his interest in a graduate degree in rocket engineering.

Gary wanted to major in molecular physics as preparation for a graduate degree in rocket engineering.

Pred a   Fitting Subject to Verb to Complement   13a

The meaning of the subject must fit logically with the verb and the complement. Often when sentences are not clear, the writer has not chosen the subject he intends to talk about or has buried the real subject in a modifier.

ORIGINAL

My mother being unable to resist installment buying meant the difference between a comfortable existence and constant fear of poverty.

[Mother *makes no sense as a subject for* meant. *The subject probably intended is buried as a modifier.*]

REVISION

My mother's inability to resist installment buying meant the difference between a comfortable existence and constant fear of poverty.

[*Not* mother, *but* mother's weakness *was probably intended as the subject.*]

The cowboy's job seems about to be replaced in many areas by helicopters and jeeps.

The cowboy seems about to be replaced in many areas by helicopters and jeeps.

[*Not the job but the cowboy is being replaced.*]

The setting of this picturesque little town was filled with a colorful history.

[*The setting was not filled. The writer should pick an appropriate subject and start over.*]

This picturesque little town had a colorful history.

[*The writer may have meant this or something else, but the revision at least makes sense.*]

The lack of a proper diet and work as heavy as lumbering demanded a man with a strong body.

[*The second part of the compound subject fits logically with the verb, but the first does not.*]

Work as heavy as lumbering, carried on without a proper diet, demanded a man with a strong body.

[*The main subject is selected and the inappropriate idea becomes a modifier.*]

It inserted as a dummy subject does not remedy a faulty predication in which the logical subject appears as a modifier.

ORIGINAL

I believe that with a knowledge of a word's past, it would enable one to read with keener understanding much of the literature written in preceding ages.

REVISION

I believe that a knowledge of a word's history would enable one to read much early literature with keener understanding.

The verb must not stand for some action which the subject is logically incapable of performing. Errors of this sort may result from careless diction (see Section 21).

ORIGINAL

They should not have allowed such tragedies to exist in their community.
[*Tragedies* do not exist.]

REVISION

(1) They should not have allowed conditions in their community which further such tragedies.
(2) They should not have allowed such tragedies to occur in their community.

Mr. Johnson's disagreement with Wilde was apparently done after a good deal of thought.
[*A disagreement is not done. The writer should be careful of the verb,* do, *which is often misused.*]

(1) Mr. Johnson's disagreement with Wilde was apparently entered into after a good deal of thought.
(2) Apparently, Mr. Johnson broke with Wilde only after a good deal of thought.

The central idea of the poem shows how in youth all is beautiful.

The central idea of the poem is that in youth all is beautiful.

Especially when verbs refer to subjects in another clause, the writer must be careful that they do not represent actions inappropriate for the remainder of the sentence.

ORIGINAL

Perhaps there are omissions which should have been included.
[*Even though the verb* should have been included *is in a subordinate clause, it must make sense with* omissions, *represented by* which.]

REVISION

(1) Perhaps there are omissions which should have been remedied.
(2) Perhaps material has been omitted which should have been included.
[*The second revision is clearer.*]

A complement must have a meaning which makes it logically capable of receiving the action of the verb.

ORIGINAL	REVISION
He managed during his life to defy all the traditional qualities of an outstanding politician. [To defy qualities *makes no sense.*]	He managed during his life to defy all the traditions associated with success in politics.
Economists are still piecing together the over-all situation. [*One cannot piece together a situation.*]	(1) Economists are still piecing together a picture of the period. (2) Economists do not yet understand all that occurred.

Pred b; Eq   Equations With Verb Be   13b

Sentences based on kernels with the verb *be* need not be mathematical equations; life is not literally a dream. But a sentence in the form of an equation must link ideas that can be plausibly identified with each other. Abstractions in such sentences are especially treacherous.

Ranching is an idea that has always attracted me.

Ranching is not an idea; the implausible equation spoils the sentence. It could be made accurate.

Ranching is a profession that has always attracted me.

But even this better equation does little but add words; the sentence is clearer without the equation:

Ranching has always attracted me.

When a sentence implies an equation with *be*, the equation should be plausible. Eliminating the equation often improves the sentence.

ORIGINAL	REVISION
The only knowledge I have had about horses is living on a farm and raising them. [Knowledge *is not* living.]	The only knowledge I have of horses comes from living on a farm and raising them. [*Changing the verb makes the sentence logical.*]
Perhaps the most important action	(1) Perhaps the most important

regarding the teacher's technique of adjusting behavior problems in the classroom is her attitude toward the problem child.

[*An* action *is not an* attitude, *and the sentence is further complicated by other inexact constructions. Various revisions are possible.*]

decisions for the teacher facing problems of classroom behavior grow out of her attitude toward the problem child.

(2) The teacher who wishes to solve her problems of classroom behavior should be careful of the attitude she adopts toward the problem child.

Sentences are usually awkward if they contain plural and singular expressions carelessly equated.

ORIGINAL

The trouble was the many difficulties which complicated the sending of the invitations.

[Trouble *is singular and* difficulties *plural. As a result the meaning is not precise.*]

REVISION

(1) The trouble was that many difficulties complicated the sending of the invitations.

(2) The trouble grew out of complications in sending the invitations.

The list of kernel sentences above (see 12-1) includes three types with the verb *be:*

Subject–*be*–subject complement—Integrity is a virtue.
Subject–*be*–modifier of subject—Violets are blue.
Subject–*be*–place adverb—Jerry is outside.

That is, the only kind of sentence with *be* which does not in some sense equate a subject and complement is the third type, in which a modifier after *be* designates place or area: *Love is where you find it. The moon was over his left shoulder.* Other kinds of adverbial modifiers —like *quickly, prominently, with gay abandon, whenever he was ready,* will not work in the third position in this pattern. If such modifiers are used after *is,* they often produce ambiguity, because the reader tends to relate them to the subject, not the predication. Consider the following:

The method of holding a club that some golfers find produces the longest drives is with the hands locked together.

The sentence derives from *method is with the hands locked;* the adverb of manner, *with the hands locked,* will not work as a subject complement nor as an adverb of place. The pattern is not characteristic of the language. As usual, choosing a different subject, the actor, begins the best revision:

Some golfers find that they can get their longest drives if they grip the club with the hands locked together.

ORIGINAL	REVISION
The process of cutting hay in the early days was by means of the scythe, which was manipulated by hand.	(1) In the early days hay was cut by hand with a scythe. (2) Pioneers mowed with a scythe.
The only uniform I have been issued was in camp last August. [*The sentence is unclear because* was *links no complement with* uniform. *Either supply a complement (1) or change the verb (2).*]	(1) The only uniform I have been issued is the one I received in camp last August. (2) I have been issued only one uniform, which I received in camp last August.
The way in which Mary wore her clothes was with an air of sophistication.	Mary wore her clothes with an air of sophistication.

In conversation and some informal writing a few constructions usually used as adverb modifiers are treated as if they were subject complements. *Because, when, where,* in particular, traditionally introduce modifying clauses, but in sentences like the following they introduce noun clauses used as complements:

Radicalism is when you jump to conclusions.
The study of mathematics is where I get my lowest grades.
The reason Johnson wrote *Rasselas* was because he needed money for his
    mother's funeral.

None of these presents much danger of serious misunderstanding, but the equations are hardly precise. Whatever radicalism may be, it is not time, and study is not place. Furthermore, *that,* not *because,* is the standard introduction for a noun clause. Sentences of this sort are almost always wordier and less precise than more direct constructions:

Radicalism usually involves jumping to conclusions.

I get my lowest grades in mathematics.

Johnson wrote *Rasselas* because he needed money for his mother's funeral.

ORIGINAL	REVISION
A syllogism is where you use a major and minor premise to get a logical answer. [*A syllogism is not a place.*]	In a syllogism, you use a major and minor premise to obtain a logical answer.
The reason I do not like herring is because they taste so fishy.	I do not like herring because they taste fishy.
Probation is when you are not eligible for competition.	On probation you are not eligible for competition.

13c   Shifts in Structure   Pred c; Shift

Among the most confusing disruptions of the subject–verb–complement relationship are those which result from careless shifting of the structure or some part of it. The same sort of forgetfulness probably causes unnecessary shifts in patterns from one clause to the succeeding one.

ORIGINAL	REVISION
For information concerning almost any happening which is too minor to be found in periodical articles may be located through *The New York Times Index.* [*The writer starts with one construction and shifts to another; thus the "sentence" never acquires a subject.*]	(1) For information concerning almost any happening which is too minor to be found in periodical articles the research worker may use *The New York Times Index.* (2) *The New York Times Index* will serve to locate information concerning almost any happening too minor to be reported in periodicals.
Any passage that pleased him he tried to write something in the same style. [*What promises to be the subject,* passage, *never becomes one.*]	(1) Any passage which pleased him was likely to become the model for a composition in the same style. (2) He would imitate any passage which pleased him.

Shifts from one pattern to another in successive clauses or from one subject to another can be confusing.

ORIGINAL	REVISION
I looked out over the pines toward the tiny lake a thousand feet below us. You could hardly see the cabin where we had spent the night.	I looked out over the pines toward the tiny lake a thousand feet below us. I could hardly see the cabin where we had spent the night.
After the textbook had been mastered, he had no trouble with chemistry.	After he had mastered the textbook, he had no trouble with chemistry.
[*The impersonal passive construction shifts awkwardly to the active with the subject* he.]	[*Both structures are now active.*]

Exercise 13

A. Revise each of the following sentences by choosing a new subject and following it with a verb other than a form of *be*.

1. The reason for the confusion of the people with the new regulations was the ambiguous way in which they were written.
2. The influence which he had over his wife was only in regard to her political attitudes.
3. The way in which he taught his daughter to swim was by throwing her into the middle of the lake without her water wings.
4. The answer which he gave was reluctant and was to the effect that he had not expected the firecrackers to go off while anybody was sitting on them.
5. Because he was stalking her calf was why Bryan was chased by the moose.
6. Saturday night was the occasion of the defeat of our basketball team at the hands of the team from State College.
7. The information which we needed to discredit the first witness was from an old man who had seen the accident occur.
8. The method by which the fence was built by the new gardener was by the use of plum saplings planted and twisted so that they would grow together.
9. The result he hoped to achieve was frightening the girls by holding the skull on a stick outside their window.

10. By promising everybody everything they might ever want was the system by which it was his hope that he would be victorious in the election.

B. Try writing sentences in which you use each of the pairs of subjects below with each of the verbs following it. Some of the subjects may not work with some of the verbs; for these be able to discuss why you could not write a grammatical sentence.

Possible Subjects	*Possible Verbs*
1. Andrew, intention	was, implicated, smiled
2. sharks, conclusions	conspired, jumped, indicated
3. water, book	presented, fell, promised
4. tendency, painter	splashed, developed, forced
5. nutrition, horse	saved, prevented, occupied
6. play, actor	frightened, awoke, broke
7. Breaking the appointment, Jeremy	was, called, contributed
8. What I want to know, happiness	is, requires, smashed

C. The sentences below contain faulty predication; that is, the basic sentence in each is illogical. Point out the main kernel in each sentence, analyze relationships, and revise each sentence so that the subject, verb, and complement work together.

1. The sidewalk, being old and broken in many places, made our progress slow.

2. He did not recognize how difficult were the many facets he must play in his role as director.

3. In two years in the club she managed to break every situation required by the rules.

4. As soon as they are corrected these disadvantages will improve the club a great deal.

5. Children playing with matches could be prevented if parents were cautious.

6. Everyone was aware of the exceptional influence played by the United States in the early days of Japanese relations with foreign nations.

7. My mother objected to everybody whom I associated.

8. Roads covered with gravel or ice double the stopping distance.

9. A parrot can be stroked on the chest, but anywhere else usually costs the admirer a sore finger.

10. Her mental attitude is disturbed and may not return for several hours.

11. For a person to not obey the Duke's wishes would mean the person's death.

12. The friends that you make often result from your manners.
13. A girl may have some classes after lunch, but if there isn't she may study.
14. This method took as long as three days to plant three hundred acres.
15. For a rifle team to become a success, many points must be accomplished.
16. The amount of money lost by both the strikers and the employers took a matter of years in order to regain them.
17. The main idea of Donne's *Song* seems to be about a man who has been jilted by his mistress.
18. Many citizens practiced an anti-Christian cult during the period.
19. After intensive courses in hairdressing at the new college, everyone on our staff is trained to accentuate your beauty needs.
20. Constant experimentation with different techniques of painting increased her versatility and incidentally her composition.

D. The sentences below contain equations with the verb *be*. Identify subjects and complements. Then revise each sentence, changing subject or complement to make them work more logically together or using a more expressive verb than *be*.

1. The nature of the adult illiterate has been one who has not had a chance to go to school and has never learned to read and write.
2. The unique aspect of ballet is the fastness it is growing within the United States today.
3. College spirit is an experience long remembered after school is over.
4. In the play, the weavers' situation, which in broad terms is a people born into a society where they must struggle to develop in all ways, is a basic problem of humanity.
5. Journalism is not a romantic life as some books play it up to be, and as some people believe; it is a hard job for anyone to undertake.
6. It can clearly be seen from the story that the desire to return Cassio to her husband's favor was because she honestly felt that it was best for him.
7. The source of my material is from two books.
8. A tragedy is when all the main characters die at the end.
9. The plans of a log cabin should be very compact and not too roomy.
10. The value of this book, in my opinion, was in the fact that it showed more than one cause of juvenile delinquency.
11. The story is where a group of men find themselves the sole survivors of a civilization destroyed by war.
12. A fireplace planned from a diagram is the best clue to a comfortable living room.
13. A person's education is a very important task and one that may decide his whole future.

14. The purpose of a Geiger counter is with it you can find uranium.
15. The subject of *The Washerwoman's Day* is about the situation in which a girl finds herself.
16. One other example of Shakespeare's humor being portrayed in his characters was Bottom.
17. A basic method of binding books is the use of cords to which each signature is stitched.
18. The primary purpose of colleges was intended to be an institution of higher learning.
19. The most outstanding of their rivalries were over a woman.
20. A follower and a leader are both qualities he must possess to enable him to achieve his goals.

Variations in Patterns;
Expletive, Passive

For
Guide to Revision,
see page 230.

Basic sentence patterns can be varied for special purposes.

Most of the sentences in contemporary prose expand and combine the basic patterns described in Section 12-1, following the subject–verb–complement order. Language and thought are complicated, however, and particular uses may call for other structures that can be thought of as variations on the basic patterns, as transformations of kernel sentences. For example, *The children are happy* readily changes to *Are the children happy?* for the purpose of asking a question. Or *Horses eat grass* can be changed to a question, *Do horses eat grass?* Variations like these present no significant rhetorical problems, but two more complicated patterns need attention because undiscriminating use of them may mar writing.

Postponed Subject; Expletives   14-1

The following sentence combines kernels which vary from those described in 12-1:

It is simply impossible to exhaust the variety of significant change in linguistic growth: there is no conceivable direction in which a transfer may not be made; there is no assignable distance to which a word may not wander from its primitive meaning.   —WILLIAM DWIGHT WHITNEY

In each of these three patterns *it* or *there* serves as an expletive. That is, in each clause *it* or *there* fills the subject slot, although it is not a noun and carries no meaning. The expletive is not a subject like those in kernel sentences; it serves as a function word to fill the sentence pattern. The ideas being talked about, the usual material for the subject, appear in the complement position after *is*.   **225**

This sentence is unusual in the book from which it is taken, since Whitney relies mainly on sentences utilizing subject–verb–complement patterns. Here, however, he has good reasons for the variations. Sentences of this sort, with the expletive used in the subject slot, can be derived from sentence kernels, most frequently from the subject–is–adverb kernel. That is, a sentence like *There was a mouse in the soup* could be derived from the kernel sentence *A mouse was in the soup*. Whitney's opening clause could be derived from a different sort of kernel: *To exhaust the variety is impossible*. For each of these variations, Whitney could have employed a basic pattern, but he was doubtless aware of the main uses of expletives:

1. The expletive provides a simple means of saying that something exists, as in the following:

There are two reasons for doubting his word.
There will be time for one more question.

These ideas could be expressed in other ways as in *We could find two reasons* . . . and *Two reasons are apparent* . . ., but for most purposes such devices would offer no improvement. For Whitney's second and third sentence, *No direction is* . . . and *No distance is* . . . would have been awkward. Whitney could have contrived a subject not an expletive and produced a sentence like the following:

Nobody can conceive any direction in which a transfer may not be made.

The result is clumsy; for simple purposes like identification expletives may provide the smoothest, most economical structure.

2. Expletives permit the writer to assemble parallel details, especially materials too complicated to serve well in the subject, which usually should be followed by a verb without much intervening matter. Consider the following:

But there was a class of residents which appears to be perennial in that University, composed out of the younger masters; a class of men who, defective alike in age, in wisdom, or in knowledge, were distinguished by a species of theoretic High Church fanaticism; who, until they received their natural correction from advancing age, required from time to time to be protected against their own extravagance by some form of external pressure.

—JAMES ANTHONY FROUDE

If the subject, *class*, were to appear in its usual position at the beginning of the sentence it would be separated from the verb by more than fifty words of elaborate modification; and when the verb finally appeared it would be only *was* or perhaps some such wordy device as *was in existence*. The expletive construction allows the subject to come after the verb but near it; *there was* in effect introduces the subject and then allows it to have the major emphasis of the sentence.

3. The expletive variation can provide continuity from clause to clause or give special emphasis. Whitney's first clause differs somewhat from the *there*-patterns and derives from a possible kernel: *To exhaust the variety is impossible*. The sentence labors a bit because so many words intervene between subject and verb, but it would work. In the context, however, Whitney prefers the expletive pattern because he can carry it on in the last two clauses—where he cannot use the direct pattern—and can preserve parallel patterns throughout the sentence.

The feel of the basic pattern persists strongly enough in these variations so that the noun after the verb is traditionally thought of as the subject. Since *be* has different forms to agree with its subject, this identification of the subject can become practically important: *There* is *one house on the hill*, but *There* are *two houses on the hill* (see 17j).

The Passive 14-2

Usually the agent or actor should be mentioned first in a sentence, so that we know who or what we are talking about. Sometimes, however, the agent or actor is less important than the action or the result; sometimes the actor is unknown or should not be mentioned; and sometimes continuity requires that some word other than the name of the actor appear first. The passive construction provides for such variations. Compare:

The rebels fired the first shot.
The first shot was fired by the rebels.

In the first, the more direct sentence, the actor, *rebels,* is the subject, with *shot* as object. The second reverses the pattern, and *shot* becomes the subject in the passive sentence. Either pattern would work, of course, depending on the context and the emphasis desired. Compare the following, however:

In June somebody completed the new road.
The new road was completed in June.

The second, passive, sentence omits the subject *somebody,* and for most purposes this passive sentence would be preferable to the active. The useless subject *somebody* can be omitted.

Passive constructions are frequently misused and overused, but they have important functions. Sometimes, as in the sentence above, the word that would have to serve as subject in the kernel sentence is better omitted. Suppose, for example, we wish to mention the publication of a book in 1623, but we have no reason to name the publisher. We want the publishing to be the main action, but if we use the subject–verb–object pattern, we are faced with something like this:

A person or persons whom we do not wish to mention just now published the book in 1623.

In this sentence, the receiver of the action, *book,* is more important than the missing actor. We therefore solve the problem by putting *book* into the subject position and using a passive form of the verb.

The book was published in 1623.

For a statement as simple as this, however, a separate sentence is usually inappropriate; the writer might better reduce the idea embodied in this sentence to a modifier and go on to another idea.

The book, *published in 1623,* has provided the basis for all subsequent editions of Shakespeare's works.

Sometimes circumstances make the passive construction convenient, or even imperative. The actor may be known, but there may be reasons for not mentioning him. A newspaper reporter might be telling the truth if he were to write:

John A. Scrogum murdered Joseph Meek at 7:45 this morning in the Hot Spot Lunch.

This statement is libelous; the reporter and the newspaper which publishes the sentence can be sued for accusing a man of murder who has not been legally convicted. Accordingly, the reporter would probably write something like the following:

Joseph Meek was shot and killed at 7:45 this morning in the Hot Spot Lunch.

The actor has now been removed, and the statement is legally publishable.

Or the actor or agent may not be known. A historian writes:

The world of St. Paul was steeped in guilt and wretchedness.

He does not know who steeped it; the agent, even if it could be determined, would be much too complicated for expression in a single sentence. Or consider:

Nations which have lost their moral self-respect are easily conquered.

This generalization does not depend at all on who conquers these nations; no one actor could be specified. Occasionally, a passive construction is desirable for stylistic reasons; for instance, a writer may wish to avoid inserting complicated material between the subject and verb. Compare the following

The hearing was opened by the chairman of the committee, who was known for his ruthlessness in smirching the reputation of innocent witnesses and for his cleverness in beclouding the issue by his own witticisms and innuendoes.

The chairman of the committee, who was known for his ruthlessness in smirching the reputations of innocent witnesses and for his cleverness in beclouding the issue by his own witticisms and innuendoes, opened the hearing.

The first version has the advantage of keeping subject and verb together. A verb in a dependent clause may be thrown into the passive in order to continue the subject of the main clause, as in the following:

Carlo, although he was known to have communist leanings, maintained his position because he always met his payrolls.

The passive, then, has very definite uses. It is properly used when

(1) the subject is not known;
(2) the subject is known, but for some good reason cannot, or had better not, be mentioned;
(3) the receiver of the action is so much more important than the actor that emphasis properly belongs on the receiver;
(4) one of the elements of the actor-action pattern must be moved from its normal position for stylistic reasons.

Except in these special situations, the passive usually weakens English prose. Consider the following passage, in which most of the verbs are passive:

Zoroaster's spirit was rapidly caught by the Persians. A voice which was recognized by them as speaking truth was responded to eagerly by a people uncorrupted by luxury. They have been called the Puritans of the Old World. Never, it is said, was idolatry hated by any people as it was by them, and for the simple reason that lies were hated by them.

Compare this passage with the following written by James Anthony Froude:

The Persians caught rapidly Zoroaster's spirit. Uncorrupted by luxury, they responded eagerly to a voice which they recognized as speaking truth to them. They have been called the Puritans of the Old World. Never any people, it is said, hated idolatry as they hated it, and for the simple reason that they hated lies.

Froude's version keeps the actor-action pattern everywhere but in the third sentence and the parenthetical *it is said* of the fourth—in which the actual subjects of the action are unknown. Obviously, his paragraph is more direct, more economical, and more effective.

14 *Guide to Revision*

Revise inappropriate expletive or passive sentences, putting them into standard subject–verb order.

Variations on basic kernel sentence patterns have developed to serve special purposes. When varied sentences occur only because the writer has begun with the wrong subject (see 12-2, 12-3) or forgotten to revise, the writing is likely to be dull and roundabout. Many writers find the following a good rule: test the possibility of revising any sentence that varies from the basic patterns. Many sentences, of course, withstand the test and prove to be best in their varied form, but the attempt to change is often revealing—often, in fact, forces the writer to be more precise or more specific.

Expl   Postponed Subjects; Expletives   **14a**

Overuse of the postponed subject is one of the sins of student writing. The construction is by its nature roundabout; often it is wordy, and it obscures the parts of the sentence which are potentially strongest, the subject and the main verb. Many a page of weak writing is weak because sentence after sentence, which should begin with the name of some concrete thing, begins with *it* or *there*. Consider the following:

It is a fact that it is hard to get people to see that there is a lot of sport in skiing.

Several weaknesses mar this sentence, but the needlessly postponed subjects cause most of them. The writer might better have said

Skiing can be a good sport, though few people know it.

A writer who finds himself beginning many sentences with *it* or *there* can appropriately ask himself: Have I any good reason for not beginning this sentence with its logical subject?

ORIGINAL

It was after a long argument that we decided to push on. It was soon agreed among us, however, that we had made a mistake. Within an hour there were two sharp attacks which scattered our rear guard. It was obvious that we should have stayed at the fort.
[*The needlessly inverted sentences slow and obscure the passage.*]

REVISION

After a long argument we decided to push on. Soon, however, we agreed that we had made a mistake. Within an hour two sharp attacks scattered our rear guard. Obviously, we should have stayed at the fort.
[*Normal order strengthens and shortens the passage. For variety some writers might prefer to leave the last sentence:* It was obvious that we should have stayed at the fort.]

His escape set England again on fire. There were Llewelyn wasting the border, the Cinque Ports holding the sea, the garrison of Kenilworth pushing their raids as far as Oxford.
[*Postponement of the subject weakens the second sentence and blocks the continuity of ideas from one sentence to the next.*]

His escape set England again on fire. Llewelyn wasted the border; the Cinque Ports held the sea; the garrison of Kenilworth pushed their raids as far as Oxford.
[*With normal order restored, the reader can see that the second sentence develops the general idea of the first.*]

14b   Passive Sentences   Pass

Usually a statement tells who or what acts (the subject) and what it does (the verb). Inversion through use of the passive verb throws stress on the receiver of the action and draws attention away from the actor–action pattern. It makes the receiver of the action the subject and the center of attention. Such inversion is justified only in special circumstances. Used indiscriminately it weakens writing; a sentence like the following is painfully awkward:

The lake where the meetings of our gang are held is reached by an old road that was found by me when I was hidden out there by the kidnappers.

Less cluttered sentences may be equally harmful to direct communication, especially when they occur frequently and do not provide special emphasis warranted by the context. A student writer can find few better ways to improve his style than to practice using active instead of passive verbs, to hesitate every time he finds himself using a passive form, to ask himself whether the passive form is justified, and, if it is not, to try recasting the sentence in actor–action order.

ORIGINAL

That there were many difficulties whereby women were unable to use the new union lounge was the attitude which was stated by the first speaker. It was her contention that women were resented in the lounge by the men students and that this resentment was clearly made known by the men in their actions. A different point of view was introduced by the second speaker, by whom it was stated that the reason for the inability of the women to make full use of the lounge was caused by the attitude of the women themselves. The views which were expressed by this speaker were the objects of sharp criticism from the other members of the panel.

The trouble was caused by John's insistence that he begin.

REVISION

The first speaker insisted that women were unable to use the new union lounge because men students resented having women there and made their resentment clearly known. The second speaker introduced a new point of view, that women were unable to make full use of the lounge because of their own attitude. The other members of the panel sharply criticized the views of this speaker.

[*The original has many weaknesses, but basic to most of its difficulties is overuse of unwarranted passive sentences. The revision still needs development, but it improves the passage, mainly by recasting sentences in the actor–action pattern.*]

(1) John's insistence that he begin caused the trouble.

ORIGINAL (*Cont.*)

[*Nothing here warrants departing from normal order, since the actor–action elements are present and important.*]

REVISION (*Cont.*)

(2) John caused the trouble by insisting that he begin.

Exercise 14

A. Revise each of the sentences below by converting it to usual word order and using active verbs.

1. The pink corsage was worn by Wilma on the left shoulder of her orange dress.
2. The election was arranged by a group of dishonest party hacks so that the success of the reform movement was prevented.
3. A very rigid censorship was imposed by the commanding officer on war news.
4. For the first time officeholders could be criticized by the people.
5. By using a spectroscope it is possible for many metals to be identified by a laboratory technician.
6. The man in the street is granted by the Constitution the right to say what he pleases without fear of prosecution.
7. Important information about military matters should not be revealed by the newspapers.
8. After working for fifteen minutes, the ground was finally cleared and leveled by the men enough for the sleeping bags.
9. Provisional governments were set up by the military forces as soon as an area had been conquered.
10. Citizens of the United States were guaranteed freedom of speech by the First Amendment to the Constitution.
11. If the petition is signed by enough people, it will be considered by the assembly.
12. Drifting down the river out of control, a series of dangerous rapids was approached by the boat.
13. The enemy was driven into the sea by our reinforcements.
14. Although still eager to write a great epic, many prose pamphlets had to be turned out by Milton.
15. The ball was thrown accurately by the first baseman, but it was

Exercises

missed by the catcher, and the runner was waved home by the third-base coach.

16. The introduction of the speaker was made by the past president of the club.

17. Undeterred by the stories in the papers, a trip around the lake after midnight was contemplated by Jane and her roommate.

18. At the end of the passage our progress was arrested by a pile of huge boulders.

19. Tickets were bought by Mr. Sims from a scalper for twice their value.

20. A small shop was opened on Fifth Avenue by two of my classmates where clothes could be designed by them to suit both the figure and the purse of the average girl working in an office.

B. Revise each of the following sentences by removing the expletive and recasting the sentence in normal order with a subject followed by a verb.

1. There were more than a dozen cats waiting for the children to feed the birds.

2. There was no reason why Wayne had to doubt his mother's word.

3. There was a tall white stallion standing all alone at the edge of the cliff.

4. It is in his book *The Diary of a Writer* that Dostoevsky describes how a mother hen defended her chickens from a brutal and sadistic boy.

5. If there is the desire to help, there are always lots of ways for a father to be saved money by the student.

6. It was when I was waiting in a registration line and I was talking with a graduate student that the realization came to me of how complicated a university is.

7. That was the time when there was an opportunity for me to buy my first colony of bees.

8. There were two chaperons in attendance at the dance, but still the uninvited guests soon outnumbered the invited ones.

9. It was because so many students had forgotten to register for the examination that there were new rules passed by the academic council.

10. It is obvious that there should be more courses in fine arts taken by the average student.

C. The following paragraph has been altered from the original, largely by including more passive and more expletive sentences. Revise it, changing any sentence patterns which seem to you inappropriate. Your instructor can supply the paragraph as Rachel Carson originally wrote it.

[1] Of all the elements present in the sea, probably men's dreams

have been stirred by none more than gold. [2] There is gold there—in all the waters covering the greater part of the earth's surface—enough in total quantity so that every person in the world could be made a millionaire by it. [3] But how is it possible that the sea can be made to yield it? [4] The most determined attempt to wrest a substantial quantity of gold from ocean waters—and also the most complete study of the gold in sea water—was made by the German chemist Fritz Haber after the First World War. [5] There was the idea conceived by Haber of extracting enough gold from the sea so that the German war debt could be paid, and there was from his dream the result that there was the German South Atlantic Expedition of the *Meteor*. [6] The *Meteor* was equipped with a laboratory and filtration plant, and between the years 1924 and 1928 the Atlantic was crossed and recrossed by the vessel, with the water being sampled. [7] But the quantity found was less than had been expected, and there was far greater cost of extraction than there was value of the gold recovered.

D. Mark every sentence in one of your themes in which you vary from usual word order. Then revise these sentences to the actor–action pattern and judge whether or not the change improves the theme.

Coordination
and Parallelism

For
Guide to Revision,
see page 242.

For most purposes the basic sentence pattern requires development; coordination, revealed in parallel structure, provides means to develop complicated ideas.

I see the kitty is a sentence, but few writers who have progressed beyond nursery school find much use for it. As indicated above (see 12-2), such kernel sentences are expanded in three ways, one of which is coordination. With it, the writer can relate and order ideas—parts within sentences, sentences in paragraphs, or paragraphs in longer compositions. In the sentence a pattern of coordination may be as simple as *John and Mary* or *ham and eggs*, a structure that any child can handle. In fact, childish talk is likely to be a combination of the basic and the coordinational sentence patterns —"I took my fish pole, and I took Rover, and I took my Daddy, and I went fishing." That is, *coordination* is bringing like things together, combining them; the term *parallelism* is often used to indicate the patterns which reveal coordination. Naturally, they are not all as simple and easy to manage as *ham and eggs*. The author of the following was a New York newspaper man, and presumably a practiced writer; he certainly knew the patterns of coordination, but he here failed to use them carefully:

Among the items in the collection are the only known document bearing the signatures of Queen Elizabeth and Sir Walter Raleigh and a cigar-store Indian.

The writer probably attributed more skill to the Indian than he intended. Coordination can be used for development with most important elements of the sentence; the various patterns and their adaptations warrant study.

Coordination of Clauses   15-1

Among the grammatical groups that can be coordinated within the sentence are varieties of the basic sentence pattern itself. Consider the following:

The sun had set. A cool breeze was blowing across the lake. The tiny cabin was still too warm to be comfortable.

Here are three sentences, each of which can be considered independent, one concerning the sun, one the breeze, and one the cabin. More revealingly, the three can be considered as parts of one idea, that in spite of certain cooling agents the cabin was still too hot. Obviously, the three sentences had better become one, somewhat as follows:

Although the sun had set and a cool breeze was blowing across the lake, the tiny cabin was still too warm to be comfortable.

The subject–verb patterns of the three short sentences are preserved here, but the patterns work together to make a single sentence. That is, clauses of like nature can be coordinated; consider the following:

Marriage and hanging go by destiny. Matches are made in heaven.
Marriage and hanging go by destiny; matches are made in heaven.
Marriage and hanging go by destiny, but matches are made in heaven.

In the first version, the two ideas stand as independent sentences, although they are obviously to be taken together. In the second version the ideas are still independent—neither relies on the other —but their interrelation is emphasized by their being joined into one sentence with a semicolon between them. What were formerly sentences have become independent clauses. The English writer Robert Burton understandably preferred the idea in this form. The third version also contains two clauses which could serve as independent sentences, with the contrast between them emphasized by the signal word, *but*. For the punctuation of such sentences see 25b, 25c.

Not all clauses can be coordinated because they are not all of like nature; that is, they have different uses and follow different clause patterns. Conventionally, clauses are divided into two sorts, *independent* and *dependent* or *subordinate*. Grammatically, the distinc-

237

tion is not always sharp in English; but of course clauses can coordinate only with other clauses like themselves, independent with independent, dependent with dependent. For purposes of sentence structure the distinction is sharp enough, since we recognize like patterns. Observe the following:

If you have any ideas about how we can improve our product

or

you know any ways of improving our service,

I advise you to keep quiet about them.

Two dependent clauses connected by *or* are coordinate, and their working together is made clear by their parallel form and position.

15-2 Coordinating Lesser Sentence Elements

Often ideas which might be expressed in a sentence or a clause may be reduced to a phrase or a word coordinated with another phrase or word. Consider the following:

In the Indian Parliament a member may call his colleague a simian.
In the Indian Parliament a member may not call his colleague a baboon.

Obviously, the sentences are alike except for one part of the complement. The whole can be said with one sentence having a coordinate complement:

In the Indian Parliament a member may call his colleague a simian, but not a baboon.

Buffon was using a similar sort of coordination, although he coordinated more parallel complements, when he wrote:

The human race excepted, the elephant is the most respected of animals. . . .
We allow him the judgment of the beaver, the dexterity of the monkey, the sentiment of the dog, and the advantages of strength, size, and longevity.

Using a sentence for each of the elephant's virtues would expand the statement to a paragraph. In these sentences, only the complements are coordinated, but most elements of a sentence can be used coordinately, and most sentences of any complexity have more than one sort of coordination. For instance, H. L. Mencken recorded his disapproval of zoos as follows, without, of course, italicizing his coordinate elements:

The sort of man who likes to spend his time watching *a cage of monkeys chase one another,* or *a lion gnaw its tail,* or *a lizard catch flies,* is precisely the sort of man whose mental weakness should be *combated* at the public expense, not *fostered.*

Coordination and Parallel Structure 15-3

Coordination can be more or less elaborate. When a zookeeper remarked that "We need good, strong cages to protect the animals from the public," he was using coordination very simply to join the words *good* and *strong*. The same device can knit together extremely complicated structures; for instance, in the sixteenth century, balanced and contrasted constructions became a fad, and when John Lyly wrote the following he was gaining a number of effects and also having fun with language:

This young gallant, of more wit than wealth, and yet of more wealth than wisdom, seeing himself inferior to none in pleasant conceits, thought himself superior to all in honest conditions, insomuch that he deemed himself so apt to all things that he gave himself almost to nothing but practicing of those things commonly which are incident to these sharp wits, fine phrases, smooth quipping, merry taunting, using jesting without mean, and abusing mirth without measure.

—Euphues

The style is exaggerated, but the passage illustrates how intricately words, phrases, and clauses can be balanced against one another in writing.

However complicated or simple the coordination may be, the pattern of the sentence should be clear; that is, the coordinated elements should be parallel in form or position or both. As a minimum, the coordinated elements should be alike grammatically. In the phrase *good, strong cages,* only the most common grammatical devices are required. *Good* and *strong* are words of similar type; they both describe the cage. They have the order of words in a series; that is, they stand side by side, and the comma between them indicates that they are a series. These evidences of parallelism assure us of their coordinate meaning.

More complicated coordinate ideas may require more complicated structures. In the quotation from Mencken, for example, the first series of clauses coheres through the repetition of *or*, and in the quotation from Lyly this device of repeating a signal word goes further. Lyly might have written *of more wit than wealth, and yet more wealth than wisdom.* These phrases would be understandable, but the reader might hesitate as to which of the elements the word *and* coordinates. As Lyly did write the sentence, repeating the word *of*, misunderstanding is scarcely possible. Such use of signal words supplements grammatical parallelism.

Word order also helps to support coordination. Signal words especially need to be placed carefully. Compare:

You are either *late* or *early*.
Either *you are late* or *I am early*.
You are either *late* or *I am early*.

The first two sentences are clear because the signal words *either* and *or* appear just before the two expressions to be coordinated. The third is not clear because *either* is out of position. The following howler from a student paper illustrates a similar danger.

To be polite he first poured some of the wine into his glass so that he would get the cork and not the lady.

The intention of the writer is clear enough; in speech he could have made himself understood by emphasis. In writing he would need to put the parts of his compound subject together.

To be polite he first poured some of the wine into his glass so that he, and not the lady, would get the cork.

The requirements of handling coordinate material may be summarized as follows:

1. Coordinate elements must usually be in parallel grammatical form, independent clauses with independent clauses, subjects with subjects, complements with like complements.
2. Coordinate elements must appear in the proper order, usually in series, with appropriate punctuation.
3. Coordinate elements may need to be joined with signal words indicating coordination: *and, but, or, nor, yet,* and some correlative groups like *either . . . or, neither . . . nor.* The signal words need to be placed so that the elements to be parallel are clearly distinguished.
4. If necessary to indicate coordination, other kinds of signal words (*of, the, in, to, if, who,* for instance) should be repeated in parallel structures.

Abbreviation of Parallel Patterns   15-4

Coordination, as examples above indicate, may promote economy, since parallel patterns are so well established that entire structures need not be repeated:

He knew the rules and (*he knew the*) regulations.

Coordination makes expression of the italicized repetition unnecessary. The stability of English word order allows similar shortcuts in other patterns. Parts of verbs, for example, need not be repeated in a parallel passage:

In a few minutes the stakes had been driven and the canvas (*had been*) spread on the ground.
The children started to work just as their parents had (*started to work*).

Even when the idea is not expressed in the form later required, it need not always be repeated:

They did all they could (*do*).
He ran as fast as he could (*run*).

Similarly, connectives need not be repeated in parallel constructions:

They fought on land and (*on*) sea.
He had not learned how to read or (*how to*) write.

Usually, however, such economies work only when the ideas to be carried over establish a form that will fit the second part of the parallel pattern.

Patterns of Comparison   15-5

Parallel patterns may express comparison, usually with function words like *than* or *as*. These patterns are so well established that they permit ideas to carry over even though they would have to be understood the second time in a different form:

Plants grow more rapidly in California than (*plants grow rapidly*) in New York.
Plants grow more rapidly in California than they do (*grow*) in New York.
She was treated more politely than he (*was treated*).

The joke was as old as the hills (*were old*).

The sentences are clear and also economical. Like other patterns of coordination, however, these constructions serve only when the elements to be compared are parallel in form.

My cousin was older than *any other freshman.*

It is easier *for a camel to go through the eye of a needle* than *for a rich man to enter into the kingdom of God.*

His teeth were sharper than *a tiger's* (*teeth*).

In each example the items compared are in parallel form and are comparable in meaning.

Paral   **15** *Guide to Revision*

Revise to make appropriate use of coordination or to put coordinate elements in parallel form.

By using compound subjects, verbs, complements, or modifiers, rather than series of independent simple sentences, the writer can show which ideas enjoy equal status and can avoid needless repetition. Items to be considered coordinate, however, should be parallel in form. Notice the following sentence:

The play was lively, witty, and the audience responsive though not very many of them.

A diagram reveals at once that the coordinated elements are not parallel:

	(1) lively	
	(2) witty	
The play was	(3) the audience	(1) responsive
		(2) not very many of them

Audience is not parallel with *lively* and *witty;* nor are the coordinated modifiers of *audience* parallel. The writer probably intended a pattern like the following:

(1) The play was	(1) lively
	(2) witty
(2) The audience was	(1) responsive
	(2) small

The play was lively and witty, and the audience was responsive though small.

Paral a   Parallelism in Coordination   15a

Parallelism requires that the balanced expressions correspond in form. When two or more words are joined by *and, or, nor, but,* or *for,* or are in a series, they should, in general, all be the same parts of speech or words of the same class (for grammatical forms, see Glossary). Balanced phrases or clauses should correspond in structure.

ORIGINAL	REVISION
Today a secretary has to be attractive in appearance and a high intelligence.	(1) Today a secretary must be attractive and intelligent.
[*Attractive is here a modifier,* intelligence *a noun. Revise by making both modifiers or both nouns.*]	(2) Today a secretary must have an attractive appearance and high intelligence.
Buffalo Bill could ride like the wind and who shot a bottle cap thrown into the air.	Buffalo Bill could ride like the wind and shoot a bottle cap thrown into the air.

When items occupy parallel positions in a series, they should have consistent forms, even though the series is long.

ORIGINAL	REVISION
Mary enrolled for painting, harmony, music appreciation, and to study art history.	Mary enrolled for painting, harmony, music appreciation, and art history.
[*The final item of the series is not parallel.*]	[*The final item appears as the name of a course, like the others.*]

Often parallelism will be apparent if similar structures appear side by side, but in more complicated sentences words which signal

243

similarities should be repeated. A student wrote the following excellent sentence:

Bacon's "idols" dwell in the minds of men, but their temples are in London, in Moscow, and in Washington, for in these world capitals clouded thinking is condoned, perpetuated, and to some extent originated.

The signal is wisely repeated to make the parallelism certain.

ORIGINAL

I told him that he should have an agreement about his situation at home, he needed a room to himself with a good light, and specified hours when he could have freedom to study.
[*Failure to repeat the signal word* that *leaves the sentence confused. The reader starts to read* he needed *without understanding that he has begun the second of three things* I told him.]

REVISION

I told him that he should have an agreement about his situation at home, that he needed a room to himself with a good light, and that he should be allotted specified hours when he could have freedom to study.
[*The three clauses which follow* I told him *are now marked off by the repeated signal word* that.]

ORIGINAL

The only enemies of the sloth are the eagles, jaguars, and the large boas.
[*Inconsistency in the use of articles in a series is not always confusing, but it breaks the rhythm of the sentence and destroys the parallel structure.*]

REVISION

(1) The only enemies of the sloth are the eagles, jaguars, and large boas.
[*The first* the *is understood for all items of the series.*]

Expressions not parallel in sense should not appear in a pattern suggesting parallel structure. Difficulty arises especially when parallel passages are woven together in a sentence and not kept separate.

ORIGINAL

On the first day we visited the Metropolitan Museum, the Planetarium, and rode the ferry to Staten Island.
[*Museum, Planetarium, and* rode *are not parallel in meaning, and should not appear in parallel form.*

REVISION

On the first day we visited the Metropolitan Museum and the Planetarium and rode the ferry to Staten Island.
[*Insertion of* and *in place of the first comma breaks up the illogical series and makes the parallels clear.*]

Penicillin was found to cure most diseases more quickly, effectively, and less dangerously than did the sulfa drugs.

(1) Penicillin was found to cure most diseases more quickly and effectively and less dangerously than did the sulfa drugs.

ORIGINAL (*Cont.*)

[*Again the series is not a series as it stands. The sentence can be revised either to avoid the illogical series or to make it logical.*]

New Orleans is exciting, surprising, and which I should like to visit again.

REVISION (*Cont.*)

(2) Penicillin was found to cure most diseases more quickly, more effectively, and less dangerously than did the sulfa drugs.

New Orleans is exciting and surprising, and I should like to visit it again.

Paral b; Inc   Filling Incomplete Parallel Patterns   15b

Coordination discourages needless repetition, but omission of words not previously expressed or of words necessary to make items parallel often obscures meaning.

ORIGINAL

The liquor was confiscated and the barrels dumped into the sea.

[*The reader must supply a verb between* barrels *and* dumped, *but the verb suggested by word order is* was, *which does not fit the plural* barrels.]

Many of the soldiers saw only what hundreds of tourists always had and always will be seeing.

The water cask was nearly empty by noon and drained for evening rations.

[*Drained must be preceded by* was *understood, but the* was *after* cask *is a complete verb; it cannot be understood as part of the verb* was drained.]

REVISION

The liquor was confiscated, and the barrels were dumped into the sea.

Many of the soldiers saw only what hundreds of tourists always had seen and always will be seeing.

(1) The water cask was nearly empty by noon and was drained for evening rations.

(2) The water cask was nearly empty by noon; we drained it for evening rations.

The preposition can be omitted in parallel passages only when the expressed preposition fits logically into the place where it is to be understood (see also 17c). The preposition should not be carelessly omitted from clauses in which it is separated from the verb.

ORIGINAL

D'Artagnan was interested and skillful at fencing.

[*No connective follows* interested; at, *which does not make sense, is the only word available.*]

REVISION

(1) D'Artagnan was interested in and skillful at fencing.

(2) D'Artagnan was interested in fencing and skillful at it.

245

15c   Coordination in Comparisons   Paral c; Comp

Comparisons frequently fit a word-order pattern so well fixed that parallel elements need not be completely repeated, and when a shorter construction becomes established, it, too, provides a pattern and the basis for further economy. Consider the following:

It was easier to take a cab *than it was easy to take* a bus.
It was easier to take a cab *than to take* a bus.
It was easier to take a cab *than* a bus.

One idiomatic pattern in English involves a special problem. Sentences like the following are common colloquially:

That night the team was as good if not better *than* any other team in the league.

But the connective *than* cannot be logically understood after *good,* where *as* is required. Standard English, therefore, requires some kind of completion of comparisons of this sort.

In another troublesome colloquial pattern, expressions like *so beautiful, most wonderful, biggest, finest, prettiest* appear as vague indications of enthusiasm.

It was *such* a lovely party.
He was the *nicest* man.

These expressions begin a comparison, and in standard written English either the comparison should be finished or modifiers should be used which do not imply a comparison.

ORIGINAL	REVISION
I knew her better than Mary. [*With parts of the comparison omitted, two meanings are possible.*]	(1) I knew her better than Mary did. (2) I knew her better than I knew Mary.
The people had been as kind if not kinder than my own family. [*Than cannot serve both comparisons. Revision (2) is accurate, though stiff; (1) lacks logical connectives, but follows a familiar pattern.*]	(1) The people had been as kind as my own family, if not kinder. (2) The people had been as kind as, if not kinder than, my own family.
The heroine was so charming. [*The writer probably did not intend a*	(1) The heroine was charming. (2) The heroine was so charming

246

ORIGINAL (*Cont.*)

comparison but added the intensifier under
the impression that it made his statement
more convincing.]

REVISION (*Cont.*)

that I paid no attention to the other
characters.
[*If the writer has a comparison in mind,
he should complete it.*]

Patterns in comparison which appear complete may be incomplete in fact because they have been completed with a word which cannot logically work with the words in the remainder of the comparison.

ORIGINAL

During the war the value of the Negro troops was found to be on a par with white service forces.

[*The sentence compares* value *and* forces, *which are not logically comparable. The writer probably intended to compare the value of one force with the value of the other, or to compare the two forces.*]

The foreman insisted that his job was harder than a laborer.

[*Job* and laborer *are not comparable.*]

His ears were longer than a jack rabbit.

But the battle against eating pumpkin seeds in school continued, as gum chewing does in most American schools.

[*The words put into parallel positions,* battle *and* gum chewing, *are not comparable.*]

Cyrano is more popular than any of Rostand's plays.

[*Cyrano* cannot be more popular than itself, *and* any of Rostand's plays *includes* Cyrano.]

REVISION

(1) During the war the Negro troops were found to be on a par with white service forces.

(2) During the war the Negro troops were as valuable as the white forces.

[*Troops and forces can be logically compared. The idea of value can be retained by making it the basis for comparison.*]

(1) The foreman insisted that his job was harder than a laborer's.

(2) The foreman insisted that his job was harder than that of a laborer.

His ears were longer than a jack rabbit's.

(1) But the battle against eating pumpkin seeds in school continued, as does the battle against gum chewing in most American schools.

(2) But the eating of pumpkin seeds in school continued, as gum chewing does in most American schools.

Cyrano is more popular than any other of Rostand's plays.

[*Cyrano can logically be compared with the other plays of Rostand.*]

Exercise 15

A. Combine the materials of each of the following groups of sentences into a single sentence using parallel structure.

1. In this corrupt system we see the cruelty of the totalitarian kind of government. There we also see the craft of this type of government. And we see there its ambition.

2. Upon the chair hung a neatly folded suit. There was also a crumpled red tie there. A crushed gardenia was on the same chair.

3. Every person in the tournament knew bridge thoroughly. Each one was intelligent in his playing. A firm determination to win was in every player.

4. Seated on the steps were a tan spaniel and brindle boxer. Angela, the Manx cat, was also there.

5. A good nurse possesses a willingness to do more than her required tasks. She is also constantly alert to guess her patient's wishes.

6. The brown pup seemed to possess intelligence. None of the other dogs in the litter seemed so intelligent.

7. A nationalistic rather than a sectionalistic attitude developed in the West. This was partly because the West needed a national government to protect it from the Indians. It also looked toward the national government to provide aid in the development of transportation facilities. Furthermore, foreign affairs could be handled by a strong national government.

8. Without the mariner's compass, Columbus could not have discovered America. Neither could Vasco da Gama's trip to find a sea route to India have occurred. Magellan's sailing around the world would not have taken place without it, either.

9. Jean spent an hour with the tea committee. After it she knew that she had never before known how intricate planning a tea could be. She did not believe that the event was worth the trouble it took. She would never be on another tea committee, she was sure.

10. A course of study in music may prepare a student for concert performances. It may also provide preparation for a career in teaching. And many students gain preparation for occasional recreational activity through their entire lives.

B. Recast each of the following sentences so that items intended to be coordinate are parallel in form and meaning, or remove unwarranted parallel structures.

1. After college I plan to teach in a school with good equipment and should be medium sized.

2. Escalators should not be used by barefooted persons, pets, or for transporting strollers or wheelchairs.

3. He is a person of great integrity, vision, and has the rare ability to stimulate the best efforts of his associates.

4. He stated in his complaint that the defendant owned a large dog that walked the floor most of the night, held noisy midnight parties, and played a radio so that sleep was impossible until 1:30 in the morning.

5. The typical hero wears light clothes as opposed to the "bad man" dressed in black.

6. I still remember the smell of burning candles, incense, and Greek chanting.

7. It was smooth reading, interesting, and yet avoided being superficial.

8. The professional players were more skillful, accurate, but less enthusiastic than their amateur opponents.

9. The dean told Alice that she should find a better place to study, she needed to spend less time at the movies, and ought to attend class more frequently.

10. She seemed pretty, clever, perceptive, and the courtesy required of an airline hostess.

11. We found the two gamblers in the dressing room and talking to the captain of the team.

12. On the shelf were sets of the novels of Dickens, Thackeray, and an old volume of Jonson's plays.

13. To survive without a guide in the north woods one has to be well trained as a woodsman as well as excellent physical condition.

14. She told her mother she wanted either a wedding in a church with flower girls, organ music, long trains, or a quick elopement to a justice of the peace.

15. I much prefer listening to concerts on the radio rather than to sit in the heat and discomfort of our auditorium.

16. His career, unlike most people who played a musical instrument, ended when he left school.

17. His job consisted mostly of planning and constructing roads, bridges, and various forms of surveying.

18. From the air the stream looked languid, twisted, and flowed on its course like some giant caterpillar en route to its cocoon.

19. She dreamed that she had gone to the concert wearing a scarlet bathrobe, black riding boots, and carrying a silver fox muff.

20. He accused the senator of being a fool and too stupid to know the real issues.

C. Supply or delete words to clarify patterns of coordination in the following sentences.

1. We found worms in the corn, tomatoes, and the broccoli.

Exercises

2. When I looked into the cell I disliked Dandy Jack as much as the police officer.

3. He learned respect and obedience to the new officers.

4. People say that reading a book a week increases your vocabulary and your manner of speaking.

5. The girls found the cabin so beautiful, and Aubrey was such a handsome man.

6. Her gray hair adds rather than detracts from her appearance.

7. There were great scientific advances, but precious little chance to use them until government regulations had been removed.

8. I have and will continue to be a defender of liberty.

9. She looked as old or older than Methuselah.

10. After an hour of this conversation, I decided that I disliked Mary's cousin as much as Mary.

D. Revise the following sentences to complete or improve patterns of comparison.

1. In *Othello* the structure is somewhat different from the other tragedies.

2. At first Mrs. Ellison seemed to be the nicest person.

3. She liked Picasso better than any painter.

4. Because cars are so well built, the driver drives much faster than he can safely handle the car.

5. The lecturer compared his life with a medieval peasant.

6. His arms dangled down longer than a baboon.

7. Wordsworth's *Prelude* was written, not like Rousseau wrote his *Confessions,* to reveal himself, but for the happiness and moral betterment of men.

8. The vampire leered at the little girl, showing teeth as white and sharp as a wolf.

9. His career was more brilliant than any musician who had graduated in his class.

10. Geology, unlike most professional men, seems to have entered into a period of shrinkage in job opportunities.

Subordination; Modification

For
Guide to Revision,
see page 257.

Sentences develop through addition, primarily by the addition of sub-ordinated materials, usually modifiers.

A child, with a few strokes of a crayon, can draw something identifiable as a man, but his creation is not a finished likeness. A portrait painter does more. He makes his outline more accurately, adds details to distinguish his subject, and heightens some effects by subduing others. Similarly, a child can communicate with a simple kernel sentence like *Willie eats bananas,* but an adult user of the language would probably need a particular statement that would distinguish Willie from a monkey and specify more accurately Willie's individual behavior. He might retain the kernel sentence, but he would add to it, providing subordinate details that would modify the central pattern. He might say something like

Sometimes, when he is tired of his regular baby food, Willie eats very ripe bananas crushed to a paste and mixed with a little milk.

The sentence has been developed by modification, one of the three main ways of expanding kernel patterns (see 12-2).

We have already observed how subordination of some material affects communication generally, in extended discourse as well as in brief sentences (see 3-2). In sentences, subordinated materials work as modifiers—limiting, restricting, specifying—sometimes modifying subject, verb, or complement, sometimes an entire predication, sometimes another modifier. Structures for subordination or modification, like those for coordination, allow a writer to combine for economy but, more important, to clarify relationships. The following might be written as separate sentences, or strung together with *and* into a rambling coordinate sentence:

We are offered a penny for our thoughts.

251

We consider what we have been thinking.
Many things have been in our minds.
From these many things we can select a few.
The things we select do not compromise us too nakedly.

The skillful writer would subordinate some material, selecting the idea he wanted to stress and subordinating the others to it. He might end with something like the following sentence, from which the above ideas were taken:

When we are offered a penny for our thoughts we always find that we have recently had so many things in mind that we can easily make a selection which will not compromise us too nakedly.
—JAMES HARVEY ROBINSON, *Mind in the Making*

The whole has been shortened, sharpened, and clarified with a complex of modifiers.

16-1 Modifiers of Nouns

Noun modifiers, traditionally called *adjectives,* appear as complements in one type of kernel sentence (*Sugar is sweet; The proposal looks good*), but other varieties can be derived from these and other kernel sentences. Generative grammarians would call the modifiers with their nouns transforms of kernels. The following words regularly precede the nouns they modify:

Kernel	*Modifier and Noun*
The plan seems dangerous.	The *dangerous* plan
The boat looks leaky.	The *leaky* boat
The university is Cornell.	*Cornell* University
The boy grows.	The *growing* boy
The boat is a house.	The *house* boat
The coat is for the house.	The *house* coat
The builder builds houses.	The *house* builder
The man works in the house.	The *house* man

As the last four sentences indicate, modifiers may have different meanings distinguishable by comparing the kernels from which they can be derived. Out of context *the orange crate* is ambiguous, depending on whether it derives from *The crate is painted orange* or *The crate is for oranges.*

Other modifiers of nouns, phrases and clauses, regularly follow the nouns they modify:

The man *in the moon* looked tired.
The end *of the road* was near.
The captain *of the ship* found the boat *which had broken away.*
I was the first person *the board interviewed.*

Word order may vary from the patterns indicated here. For example, *appositive modifiers,* which repeat in different words the expressions they modify, follow what they modify:

My brother, *a private detective,* took charge of the investigation.

Sometimes adjectives, usually more than one, gain special prominence in a position immediately after the noun they modify.

The convertible, *red and shiny,* looked like a fire engine.

In this shifted position, modifiers are usually set off by commas, which mark the change from usual order. Sometimes, also, variations in order change meaning or emphasis. Compare:

Our hearts were *gay.*   *Gay* were our hearts.
They found the *deserted* village.   They found the village *deserted.*

Modifiers of Verbs and Other Modifiers 16-2

Adverbs, which modify expressions other than nouns, do not always have fixed positions in the sentence order. Single-word modifiers of verbs, for instance, may appear in any of several positions, sometimes without much shift in meaning or emphasis. They occur most frequently immediately after the verb (*He drove slowly down the street.*) They may appear within complex verbs (*She was* always *losing her gloves.*) Or they may precede the verb (*I* soon *recovered*). Some modifiers, especially those that indicate direction, regularly appear after the verb but either before or after an object (*Take* back *what you said,* but *Take that* back). Sometimes one position is obligatory, or almost so (*Set the clock* ahead, not *Set* ahead *the clock*).

A few limiting modifiers (like *only, nearly, very, just, almost, merely, ever, hardly, scarcely, quite*) are expected to modify whatever expressions immediately follow them, especially if they accompany other modifiers:

They supplied *too* little *too* late.
Very *quickly* we were *thoroughly* disgusted.

Compare the following:

Only Williams could hope to win the hundred dollars.
Williams could *only* hope to win the hundred dollars.
Williams could hope to win *only* the hundred dollars.

16-3 Modifiers of Sentences and Clauses

Fitted into such word-order patterns, modifiers tend to limit specific expressions. Some modifiers, however, are not intended to modify a single word; they modify all of an actor–action pattern and do not function in fixed positions. They are best considered as sentence modifiers.

Before lunch, he read two novels.
He, *before lunch,* read two novels.
He read, *before lunch,* two novels.
He read two novels *before lunch.*

Since it modifies the entire action of the sentence, *before lunch* can occur in various positions, although it is least awkward at the beginning or end. Such sentence or clause modifiers are movable, relating to the entire sentence pattern and not to individual words.

Sentence modifiers, however, are movable only within limits. Consider the following:

Walking in the park the man found a mushroom.
The man *walking in the park* found a mushroom.
The man found a mushroom *walking in the park.*

In the first sentence, *walking in the park* modifies the action of the entire sentence. In the second, however, the phrase identifies the man. In the third, it has moved into the position of a fixed modifier of *mushroom* and causes either awkwardness or absurdity. Sentence or clause modifiers do not usually occupy fixed positions, but there are relatively few points at which they can appear without ruining or altering the sentence. Often they work best at the beginning of the sentence, where they do not interrupt the subject–verb–complement pattern or fall into fixed positions for modifiers of specific expressions.

Subordination and Sentence Style 16-4

Subordination can provide both economy and accuracy in sentences. Notice the obvious immaturity of the following:

Beechwood is a park. It is in my home town and is a cool, shady park. I knew it as a child. Then I went on many picnics there.

The repetitions indicate that all four sentences would combine into one.

When I was a child, I went on many picnics to Beechwood, a cool, shady park in my home town.

The final sentence becomes the basis of the new sentence, and all the other sentences are subordinated as short modifiers.

Now consider the following sentences:

Calling a spouse vile names is grounds for divorce, *and this is true if the names are put into language composed only of signs.*
Calling a spouse vile names *which are couched in the language of signs* is grounds for divorce.
Calling a spouse vile names *by using the language of signs* is grounds for divorce.
Calling a spouse vile names *in sign language* is grounds for divorce.

Notice what has happened to the idea of using signs for marital epithets. In the first sentence, this idea requires all the words after the function word *and;* that is, it is an independent clause and a rather complicated one. In the second sentence the idea has been reduced to the italicized dependent clause. In the third sentence this idea has been subordinated still further to the italicized group of words introduced by *by,* and in the last sentence the idea has become *in sign language.* The groups of words which express this idea in the last three sentences can all be thought of as modifiers; they all show subordination, but the subordination is progressive. Naturally, the Spokane court which made this ruling preferred the last sentence, in which the modifiers show the greatest evidence of subordination.

Deciding what to subordinate in what patterns is one of the

most complicated and difficult tasks of writing. Compare the following, all of them descriptions of the same phenomena:

The girl in the green hat	The green hat on the girl
The girl wearing a green hat	The girl's green hat
The girl who wears a green hat	The green hat which the girl is wearing

The two things being considered, the girl and the green hat, appear in all the expressions, with the physical relationship maintained; the hat presumably remains on the girl's head. In those on the left the hat is grammatically subordinate to the girl; in the others the girl is subordinate to the hat. That is, either the girl or the hat can be selected as the object to be talked about and the other can be subordinated to it. The writer makes his choice not because either item is necessarily more important than the other, but because for his immediate writing purposes he wants to relate the items grammatically in a certain way. He wishes to say something about the girl and uses the hat to distinguish her, to point out which girl he means, even to suggest what kind of girl she is. Or he wishes to say something about the hat and to use the girl to specify which hat. In other words, the writer's purposes determine which items he subordinates. In the following the subordination differs; so does the meaning:

The green hat is ugly.   The green on the hat is ugly.

Contexts, then, and the author's desire for particular emphases and meanings determine what should be subordinated; for certain purposes almost any idea can be placed in a subordinate position.

Some sorts of details, however, are more likely to profit from subordination than are some others.

That night in a drafty hall at Red Lion Square, having escaped from an importunate hostess who wanted me to meet her niece, I heard a little, greying old man, England's leading living novelist, Thomas Hardy, read Greek poetry with an understanding and love that bespoke a lifelong devotion to the classics.

One might notice the sorts of material that are here subordinated; they include the following: time (*that night*), place (*in a drafty hall at Red Lion Square*), incidental information (*having escaped* . . .), details of description (*little, greying old*), identification or apposition (*England's leading living novelist, Thomas Hardy*). Such details are usually best subordinated; they provide attendant circumstances, offer explanations, fill in minor bits, and keep the relationships of the main predication clear in light of other predications. Of course, a very minor notion may provide the sentence's grammatical framework (see also 12-2):

Not until long after my vacation was over and I had returned to my studies at Oxford did I realize that the quiet little gray man whom I would occasionally overhear as he trudged the hedgerowed lanes muttering Greek poetry was England's leading novelist, Thomas Hardy.

The main pattern of the sentence is *I did realize* plus a long subordinate clause used as the complement and carrying most of the meaning of the sentence.

Choosing the appropriate details to subordinate requires taste and long practice, but all good writers have learned to do it.

Guide to Revision **16**

Sub
Mod

Use subordination to make modification clear or to make sentence style more mature.

Sub   Adequate Subordination   16a

Inadequate subordination characterizes the kind of writing sometimes called "primer English" because it suggests a schoolboy's reader. Strings of short sentences, excessive use of *and* and *so* to join clauses, clumsy repetitions and repeated use of *this* and *that* as subjects are usually symptoms of inadequate subordination.

ORIGINAL

Margot Macomber must have been a very beautiful woman. She had everything except wealth. When she married Francis Macomber she acquired this wealth. Although she was married to Francis, she was very untrue to him.

One day they went on a hunting expedition to Africa. They took a white man as a guide. His name was Wilson. Of course, Margot had to have his attention, and she did. Francis felt very sorry for himself. He knew that she would never leave him because of his wealth. He would never divorce her because of her beauty.

One day Francis and Wilson went out hunting lions. They came upon one and wounded it. It ran into the brush and hid. Getting the lion out would be a very dangerous job. Wilson and Francis began moving into the brush looking for the lion. All of a sudden, the lion jumped out of the brush. Macomber became frightened. He turned and ran. Wilson stood his ground and shot the lion, killing it. Francis knew that he would be the laughingstock of the party.

Some time later, they went on a buffalo hunt. They came upon a herd of buffalo. A buffalo was wounded and ran into the brush. Previous incidents seemed to be repeating themselves. Francis saw a chance to redeem himself. He began going through the brush. All this time, his wife had been watching him from a distance. All of a sudden, the buffalo jumped up and charged Francis. Francis held his ground and aimed at the animal's nose. In the meantime, Margot saw the animal charge too. She brought a heavy rifle to her shoulder. Then there was

REVISION

Margot Macomber was a very beautiful woman who had everything except wealth. When she married Francis Macomber, she acquired that. Although she married Francis, she was untrue to him, and during a hunting expedition to Africa, she sought the attention of their white guide, Wilson. Although Francis felt very sorry for himself, he knew that his wealth would keep Margot from leaving him and that her beauty would keep him from divorcing her.

One day while Francis and Wilson were out hunting, they wounded a lion and let it get away to hide in the brush. They moved into the brush after him, although getting him out was dangerous. Suddenly the lion jumped out. Macomber, frightened, turned and ran. Wilson stood his ground and killed the lion. Francis knew he would be the laughingstock of the party.

Some time later they went after buffalo, found a herd, and wounded one, losing him in the brush. As the earlier situation re-occurred, Francis saw a chance to redeem himself and began to go into the brush. Suddenly the buffalo jumped up and charged Francis. He held his ground and aimed at the buffalo's nose. Margot, who had been watching from a distance, saw the charge, too, and raised a heavy rifle to her shoulder. Two shots sounded. Francis and the buffalo both toppled to the ground dead. When Margot saw that Francis was dead, she became hysterical, realizing that Francis was really the man she loved.

[The theme purported to be a character sketch of Margot Macomber, but turned out to be merely a plot sketch revealing some curious misinterpretations of Hemingway's story. The revision is still a

ORIGINAL (*Cont.*)

the sound of two shots. Francis and the buffalo both toppled to the ground dead. When she saw that Francis was dead, she became hysterical. She began to realize that Francis was really the man she loved.

[*The theme above deserved the F it received—in spite of its lack of grammatical errors. The style is that of a small child telling the story of Red Riding Hood in his own words.*]

REVISION (*Cont.*)

naïve misreading of the story, but it illustrates how much the style can be improved and clarified simply by subordinating some elements to others. For the most part the revision does nothing beyond reducing independent sentences to dependent clauses, phrases, or single words.]

Sentences that wind on and on, held together by connectives like *so* and *and*, can usually be improved by selecting one part of the sentence as a main clause and subordinating other elements to it.

ORIGINAL

Louise was tired of listening to the concert and it was dark enough that her grandmother could not see her and so she slipped out into the lobby.

[*The relationships between the three clauses are not accurately marked for the reader by linking them with* and *and* so.]

REVISION

Since Louise was tired of listening to the concert, she slipped past her grandmother in the dark into the lobby

[*With ideas subordinated to a main subject verb framework* she slipped— *the sentence is clearer and more economical.*]

There was a garage just around the corner and nobody wanted to be responsible for the keys so we took out our luggage and put the car in the garage.

Since nobody wanted to be responsible for the keys, we removed our luggage and put the car in a garage just around the corner.

Perhaps the most frequent sign of inadequate subordination is the repeated subject, especially the word *this* needlessly and often vaguely carrying on as the subject of a new sentence. Usually the two sentences should be joined.

ORIGINAL

When Lord Byron was at Cambridge, he published *Hours of Idleness.* This was in 1807. The volume was Byron's first book of poems.

[*Repeated subjects suggest inadequate subordination.*]

REVISION

In 1807, when Lord Byron was at Cambridge, he published his first book of poems, *Hours of Idleness.*

[*The combination says everything in the original more clearly and more economically.*]

259

ORIGINAL (*Cont.*)

Dramatics develops assurance. This is very valuable.

REVISION (*Cont.*)

Dramatics develops valuable assurance.

A minor detail may assume the main position in the sentence so awkwardly that the subordination seems illogical or upside-down. Often a shift in subordination may make the sentence fit its context more logically.

ORIGINAL

Andrea stepped confidently into the hall. Joe pulled the rug out from under her, when she fell down.

[*Either reversed subordination (1) or coordination (2) seems more likely in the context.*]

REVISION

(1) Andrea stepped confidently into the hall. When Joe pulled the rug out from under, she fell down.

(2) Andrea stepped confidently into the hall. Joe pulled the rug out from under her, and she fell down.

16b Position of Modifiers Mod

Usually, fixed modifiers can appear in only one position for a given purpose. In any other position they have a different meaning or become ludicrous.

ORIGINAL

He gave the book to his father that was bound in leather.

[*The final clause should modify the book, but it does not appear in the usual fixed position immediately after what it modifies. Moreover, the word father intervenes, and thus the man rather than the book seems to have the leather binding. The word order can be changed (1, 2), or the sentence revised (3, 4). Usually misplaced modifiers are symptoms of wordiness; the cure is cutting and revising.*]

REVISION

(1) He gave the book that was bound in leather to his father.

(2) He gave his father the book that was bound in leather.

(3) He gave the leather-bound book to his father.

(4) He gave his father the leather-bound book.

[*Obviously the last two revisions are preferable to the longer versions above.*]

In order to understand the importance of the magazines, we investigated their sources of popularity.

[*The sense of the sentence suggests that their was probably intended to modify popularity.*]

In order to understand the importance of the magazines, we investigated the sources of their popularity.

[*The single adjective is placed in its fixed position before the word it modifies.*]

ORIGINAL (*Cont.*)

The youngest girl only thought of new clothes.

[*The context might make the sentence clear, but a reader could be temporarily misled to take* only *as a modifier of* thought—*suggesting that the girl only* thought *of clothes, did not, for instance, buy any.*]

REVISION (*Cont.*)

The youngest girl thought only of new clothes.

[*In some colloquial idioms* only *appears before the verb even though it modifies the complement:* He only paid me a quarter. *Here the sentence is clearer with the modifier in its usual position.*]

Since the same words or groups of words can be used as either fixed or movable modifiers, the reader must depend on word order to see how they apply and what they mean. He interprets according to his expectations of word-order patterns. From the sentence

The man *in the boat* was a tyrant.

the reader understands automatically that *in the boat,* in a fixed position, is a modifier specifically locating the man. If the phrase is moved, the reader interprets it as a movable modifier which applies to the entire sentence, and he understands the sentence differently.

In the boat, the man was a tyrant.

The first sentence makes clear that the man was a tyrant, presumably all the time. The second preserves a little respect for him, limiting his tyranny to his time in the boat. So long as the sentence modifier is kept out of a fixed position, it may be moved, with changes in emphasis but no alteration of essential meaning.

In the boat, the man was a tyrant.
The man was a tyrant *in the boat.*

The writer must be sure that modifiers intended to apply generally are not put where they apply to a specific word. Negative sentences especially cause trouble. Compare:

Nobody was ever punished *because the camp was run so carelessly.*
Because the camp was run so carelessly, nobody was ever punished.

With the clause at the end, the sentence is ambiguous; it can mean either what the second version says or that the careless management of the camp brought no punishment.

ORIGINAL

He fired three shots at the lion with a smile of triumph on his face. [*Often a sentence modifier may appear at either the beginning or the end, but at the end it may fall into a fixed position.*]

REVISION

With a smile of triumph on his face, he fired three shots at the lion. [*In this sentence the reader has no trouble locating the smile.*]

ORIGINAL

Closed accounts are not to be deleted in order that numerical sequence will be preserved. [*The reader cannot be sure whether deleting or keeping the closed accounts will preserve numerical sequence.*]

REVISION

So that numerical sequence will be preserved, all closed accounts are to be retained. [*Changing the negative sentence to positive clarifies at least one possible meaning.*]

Modifying words that serve also as connectives (*however, therefore, moreover, consequently,* sometimes called *conjunctive adverbs*) appear at the beginning of a clause when they modify its entire action; placed within a clause they throw stress on the words they follow. Preceding clauses or sentences usually indicate which sentence parts need emphasis and therefore indicate where conjunctive modifiers should be placed.

John was afraid to look at me; *however* he was eager to look at Alice.
John was afraid to look at me; he was eager, *however,* to look at Alice.

The position of *however* in the second sentence stresses *eager* and accents the contrast between *eager* and *afraid.*

ORIGINAL

He ate baseball, slept baseball, and dreamed baseball; and when he thought he thought baseball. Therefore, a mere football game could hardly make him blink an eye. [*Therefore has stress at the beginning of the sentence, which it probably does not deserve; thus it fails to emphasize a significant contrast.*]

REVISION

He ate baseball, slept baseball, and dreamed baseball; and when he thought he thought baseball. A mere football game, therefore, could hardly make him blink an eye. [*Placed as it is here, therefore emphasizes football game and the contrast between football and baseball which is crucial for the sentence.*]

Movable modifiers can be so misplaced that they apply with equal ease in more than one way. They "squint," seeming to look in more than one direction at once. The difficulty arises when an adverbial modifier follows a word which it would normally modify but also precedes another word which it can modify.

ORIGINAL

The person who lies frequently gets caught.

[Frequently *can be taken to modify either what precedes or what follows it; it "squints." If it modifies the whole sentence, it should precede it (1). Sentences (2) and (3) are possible if they convey the writer's meaning. The sentence might well be recast (4).*]

She told me as soon as the dance was over she would marry me.

REVISION

(1) Frequently, the person who lies gets caught.
(2) The person who lies gets caught frequently.
(3) The person who frequently lies gets caught.
(4) Anybody who lies frequently is likely to get caught.

(1) As soon as the dance was over, she told me she would marry me.
(2) She told me she would marry me as soon as the dance was over.

DM   "Dangling" Modifier   16c

Sentence modifiers which do not themselves contain subjects, especially verbal modifiers, tend to be related to the subject or to the nearest noun. Compare:

Eating lunch on the lawn, the children were amused by the speeding cars.
Eating lunch on the lawn, the speeding cars amused the children.

The first is clear, but the second is ludicrous because the subject, *cars,* cannot logically supply the sense of a subject for the verbal *eating*—cannot tell what was eating. Similarly, the modifier that opens the following sentence dangles:

Sitting on the bridge, the huge steeple looked like part of a toy village.

The subject, *steeple,* seems to govern *sitting,* but the huge steeple could scarcely be sitting on the bridge. The sentence can be revised by using as a subject whatever was sitting on the bridge (*Sitting on the bridge,* we *could see* . . .). The sentence can be revised, also, by providing the modifier with a subject of its own (*As* we *sat on the bridge, the huge steeple* . . .), or by changing the modifier in some other way so that it does not rely on anything in the main clause (*From our position on the bridge, the huge steeple* . . .).

Since introductory modifiers readily refer to the subject, confusion may result if the subject is postponed or the sentence is passive (see 14-1, 14-2). Notice the following:

Finding something important, there are complete details to be recorded by the secretary.

When finding something important, complete details were recorded by the secretary.

The modifiers make sense only if the reader can tell who was doing the finding. Usually the name of the actor used as the subject of the sentence, in the position just after the modifier, supplies such information. In sentences like the above, in which the actor is not the subject, the modifiers dangle. Compare:

When the staff found something important, the secretary recorded complete details.

When they found something important, the staff dictated complete details to the secretary.

These revisions name the actor in the normal position in the actor–action pattern. In English the feeling for this pattern is sufficiently strong so that it will work even though the subject is only implied, as in a command:

To avoid a cold, wear a piece of red flannel around your neck.

If normal order is not followed, the modifier dangles:

To avoid a cold, a piece of red flannel may be worn around the neck.

The initial modifying phrase is so common in the pattern of the English sentence that an introductory modifier without its own subject may still seem relatively clear in itself and be useful because it is economical.

Talking with students, the same questions arise time after time.

Since *talking* is so nearly complete in its meaning—like *fishing* or *swimming*—that it relies but little on the subject, *question,* the sentence is reasonably clear. Or consider:

When lunching at the Union, conversation must be sacrificed for speed.

The conversation is not lunching, of course, but the sentence is not confusing, and the use of an impersonal *one* or *a person* would not improve it.

ORIGINAL

Having rotted in the damp cellar, my brother was unable to sell any of the potatoes.

[*The modifier applies automatically to the main action as it is expressed, to the subject–verb of the sentence. The result is the absurdly unsanitary state of the decomposing brother. The modifier should apply to an actor–action pattern of which* potatoes *is the subject, but* potatoes *is not in the subject position.*]

Convinced that people of the state were not well-informed about the university, pamphlets were printed describing the space-age educational program.

[*The sentence is not obviously absurd, but it is unclear because the reader needs to know who was convinced, and* pamphlets *does not tell him accurately.*]

REVISION

(1) Having rotted in the damp cellar, my brother's potatoes were unfit for sale.

[*Word order is changed so that the subject referred to by the modifier becomes the subject of the sentence.*]

(2) Since the potatoes had rotted in the damp cellar, my brother was unable to sell any of them.

[*The modifier is changed to a clause, which can include its subject,* potatoes.]

(1) Convinced that people of the state were not well-informed about the university, the committee published pamphlets describing the space-age educational program.

(2) Since the committee was convinced that people of the state were not well-informed about the university, it published pamphlets describing the space-age educational program.

Concluding verbal phrases, like introductory ones, often depend on the main sentence, usually on the name of the actor, to complete their meaning. If the word to be understood as a subject for the verbal is not expressed or is obscured in a passive construction, the modifier dangles.

ORIGINAL

The grain fields had been burned by the invaders, thus causing suffering in the valley.

[*The sentence seems to say that the fields caused the suffering; the intention obviously was to say that* the burning of the fields, *not expressed in the sentence, caused it.* Invaders *cannot complete the meaning of* causing *because it is put into a dependent position in the passive sentence.*]

REVISION

(1) Because the invaders had burned the grain fields, there was suffering in the valley.

[*The dangling expression, since it is really the most important idea of the sentence, is made the main clause.*]

(2) By burning the grain fields, the invaders caused suffering in the valley.

(3) The inhabitants of the valley suffered because the invaders had burned the grain fields.

ORIGINAL (*Cont.*)

He hit a home run in the eighth inning, resulting in the winning of the game.

[*The modifier has nothing to modify, but the confusion arises from obscuring the predication* He won the game *in the modifier.*]

ORIGINAL (*Cont.*)

(1) His home run in the eighth inning won the game.

(2) By hitting a home run in the eighth inning, he won the game.

(3) He won the game with a home run in the eighth inning.

16d   "Split" Constructions   Split

Normally modifiers should not be allowed to split constructions by separating closely related sentence elements, particularly if the separating element is long or complicated, although sometimes separation is unavoidable or is desirable for special effects. Subject and verb, parts of the verb, verb and complement, parts of a verbal, or elements of a series should be separated only with caution.

We may, if the weather clears, go to Birmingham.

Separation of parts of the verb *may go* might be desirable to put special emphasis on *may,* but usually the modifier, *if the weather clears,* would appear at the beginning of the sentence. Or consider the following in which subject and verb are separated by long modifiers:

The *driver,* confused by the snow icing on his windshield wiper and the tires skidding on the ice and his wife yanking at his elbow, *yelled.*

The unnecessary division of the basic pattern obscures meaning.

ORIGINAL

He expected that they would in the shortest possible time agree to our terms.

[*The long modifier obscures the pattern by separating words that logically belong together.*]

REVISION

He expected that they would agree to our terms in the shortest possible time.

[*The modifier should be placed where it does not interrupt the main sentence movement.*]

Similarly, placing a modifier between *to* and the remainder of an infinitive may falsify emphasis.

He promised to *firmly* hold our position.

The meaning is clear, and *firmly* would "squint" before *to,* but the sentence gains strength if *firmly* is moved.

He promised to hold our position *firmly.*

On the other hand, a split infinitive sometimes becomes almost a necessity. Herman Melville in *The Confidence Man* prefers to split an infinitive for the sake of clarity in modification.

The sick man seemed to have *just* made an impatiently querulous answer.

Placed either before *to* or after *made* the modifier *just* would change meaning, carrying something of the sense of *only.* Usually, however, the split infinitive should be regarded as a deviation from normal word order, warranted only by special circumstances.

ORIGINAL

I expected to quickly remove my incomplete, and to never again for any cause whatever get another.

[*Revision of the first split infinitive is advisable and revision of the second is imperative.*]

REVISION

I expect to remove my incomplete quickly and never again to get another for any cause whatever.

[*Revision both tightens the sentence structure and promotes ready comprehension.*]

Adj; Adv   Adjective and Adverb Form   16e

Some words are used as either adjective or adverb, but only colloquially as adverbs; others are restricted to only one of these uses. (For further distinctions, see *Adjectives* and *Adverbs* in the Glossary.)

ORIGINAL

Jack can sure sing.

[*Sure has developed a special meaning in this colloquial use.*]

When I called, they came quick.

She played her piece real good.

None of the work was done satisfactory.

REVISION

Jack can surely sing.

Jack can sing very well.

[*More formal expressions do not translate the original exactly.*]

When I called, they came quickly.

She played her piece very well.

None of the work was done satisfactorily.

After a linking verb a single-word modifier modifies the subject, a noun, and should be an adjective. Difficulties develop because some verbs can be either transitive or linking. *Tastes,* for example, can be a transitive verb (*He tastes wine*) or a linking verb (*The wine tastes good*). *Good,* in the second sentence, is an adjective modifying *wine.* To say *The wine tastes well* would be nonsense. We cannot speak of the skill of wine in tasting. We could say *He tastes well* or *He tastes the wine well,* a compliment for a professional wine-taster. To say *He tastes good* implies cannibalism. As a kind of rough test, the writer can sometimes substitute a form of *be* for the verb. If *be* can be substituted without creating nonsense, the original verb is a linking verb and should be followed by a subject complement, not an adverb.

ORIGINAL

The dog smelled badly.
[*Unless the writer intends a reflection against the dog's ability as a bloodhound, he needs the adjective.*]

She looked well in her new dress.
[*This suggests that she either is skillful at looking or has recovered her health.*]

He looked timidly standing all alone before the judge.
[*Compare* He looked timidly about the room, *in which the adverbial form is properly used.*]

REVISION

The dog smelled bad.
[*Since* is *could be substituted for the verb without making nonsense,* smelled *acts as a linking verb.*]

She looked good in her new dress.
[Good *modifies* She *and produces the meaning probably intended.*]

He looked timid standing all alone before the judge.
[*Timid* describes the man, not his way of looking; was *could substitute for* looked.]

Comparative and superlative forms are sometimes indicated by an ending, sometimes by a function word; but both signals are more than enough.

ORIGINAL

Stanley's singing was more better than his dancing.

REVISION

Stanley's singing was better than his dancing.

Extravagant superlatives may trap a writer into making statements he cannot substantiate and ultimately make his writing weaker and less convincing than more soberly qualified prose. Careless use of superlatives may lead to incomplete constructions (see 15c).

ORIGINAL	REVISION
The Rush Memorial represents Gutzon Borglum's most artistic achievement.	(1) Some critics consider the Rush Memorial Gutzon Borglum's most artistic work.
[*A judgment of this sort can be no more than an opinion and is likely to impress the reader as an unreliable one.*]	(2) The Rush Memorial is impressive in its mass and artistic in its conception.
The Byington Parkway is the most modern highway in all the world.	The Byington Parkway embodies many of the most recent developments in highway construction.

Some modifiers have meanings that are not logically subject to comparison (*opposite, final, dead* in the sense of deceased, *waterproof, entirely, diametric,* for example). Strictly speaking, *fatal* cannot be thought of in degrees; a wound is fatal or not fatal. Colloquially, however, the function words indicating comparison (*most* and *more*) are often used to mean *more nearly* or *very* and are used with such words. Furthermore, colloquially many such words are losing their traditional meanings and assuming meanings which are comparable. Many of these new meanings have not been accepted for standard usage.

ORIGINAL	REVISION
The new fan-jet is a most unique advance in aeronautical science.	(1) The new fan-jet is unique.
[*Unique originally meant* single *or* sole, *but it has come colloquially to be a rather vague—and overused—modifier meaning* extraordinary.]	(2) The new fan-jet represents a radical departure in engine design, since it relies upon a newly discovered principle of fuel consumption.
He was the most outstanding scholar in the school.	He was the outstanding scholar in the school.
[*Although* outstanding *has developed a meaning like "excellent" or "distinguished," it often seems redundant when compared.*]	[*Without* most, *the modifier is more economical and more forceful.*]

Although colloquial usage has never supported the distinction, formal practice restricts use of the superlative to comparisons among not fewer than three.

ORIGINAL	REVISION
Between the flatboat and the sponson canoe, I should say that the flatboat offers the best chance of shooting the rapids.	Between the flatboat and the sponson canoe, I should say that the flatboat offers the better chance of shooting the rapids.

Exercise 16

A. Combine each of the following groups of sentences into a single sentence:

1. Henry Purcell was a composer. He was English. He lived in the seventeenth century.
2. Many of the new dance steps are difficult. Anyone can learn them, however. That is, anyone can learn them if he has a good sense of rhythm.
3. *Charley's Aunt* is still a popular play. It was first presented, however, in 1892. And it is implausible and farcical.
4. Many flowers come out in the spring. They include violets, anemones, bloodroot, and trilliums. This is in the Middle West. These flowers appear about May. They cover the ground in woods and parks.
5. I am not a very good swimmer. This is because I have always been afraid of the water. I have spent many hours on the beach, however.
6. In *Jane Eyre* Charlotte Brontë describes abuses of education. These were in a real school. Miss Brontë had once attended the school, and it was at Cowan Bridge.
7. The oboe is a difficult instrument. This is because it has a double reed. This is hard to blow.
8. First all the girls in the camp had to take exercises. Then all the girls had breakfast and had to clean up the bunks. Then all the girls of the camp reported for swimming. I liked swimming better than any other activity.
9. In 1864 Atlanta was one of the most important cities of the South. This was so for the reason that the Confederacy had developed it as an important railroad center. It was also developed as a manufacturing center. This was done in the belief that it was far from the center of military activity. It would therefore be safe.

10. I grew up in a small town. It was in the South. I have not visited this town for many years. To be exact, I have not been there for eight years. It is still, however, the place I think of as home.

B. Revise any sentences among the following which you think might be improved by subordinating different elements. Be able to explain the effect of any changes you make.

1. I was still very young, although I thought it was getting to be time for me to make up my mind about whether I wanted to be a teacher or a librarian or an airline stewardess.
2. Although we had been warned against hiking over the rocky slope in the dark, we started before daylight. The sun peeped over the horizon just as I fell and sprained my ankle.
3. After three months of haunting casting offices and leaving her phone number with producers, Jane decided to go back to St. Louis. The telephone rang when she was almost too disgusted with New York to answer it.
4. Jack was seven years old, although he had never seen grass growing. He had never been outside the area about four blocks square which surrounded the dingy apartment house.
5. The man who was peeping in the window and who was immediately noticed by me, was on the outside.

C. The sentences below probably do not say what their writer intended. Revise them, paying particular attention to modification.

1. No one is allowed to dump anything along this road except a city official.
2. He is asking the reader to adopt his point of view as well as the lady to whom the poem is addressed.
3. *The Secret Life of Walter Mitty* by James Thurber is the typical story of a daydreamer.
4. He knew that the boat had been sunk because he had seen the battle.
5. My home is a good place for a boy who likes horses to grow up in the United States.
6. The old man was not arrested because he had befriended the natives.
7. Clarity was their basis of effectiveness.
8. Joan decided that she would not marry him at the last possible moment.
9. They should not move the old road so that the trees will shade travelers.
10. The nurse brought in Robert, Jr., to see his father in his bassinet.

D. Revise the following sentences so that modification is clear and logical:

Exercises

1. When hardly more than a baby, a gang of older boys threw me into the creek and told me to sink or swim.
2. Being very dark, we were unable to find our way about the cellar.
3. Knowing that the whole future of the club was at stake, the investigation found us reluctant to say a word.
4. At the age of nine my father's interest in languages was already developing.
5. Every promise had been broken by the new governor, causing widespread dissatisfaction.
6. On approaching the village the gold spire was the only evidence of civilization that we could see.
7. Although only pretending to shoot, the gun suddenly went off with a loud roar.
8. Having had no sleep for two nights, the dirty haystack actually seemed inviting.
9. Being afraid of his own shadow, we were not much disturbed by his threats.
10. Trying to climb in the dormitory window at night, the Dean of Women caught her and recommended her suspension.

E. Revise the following sentences by reducing italicized expressions to shorter modifiers, by making clauses into phrases or phrases into shorter phrases or single words:

1. He avoided tall girls *because of the fact that he was only five feet two in height.*
2. He did not believe *in the factor of hereditary influences.*
3. Hybrids are formed by crossing two species *which are pure before they are crossed.*
4. *Smoking when a person is in bed* is prohibited.
5. The will, *which can never be conquered,* sustains the rebel.
6. *When twelve o'clock had rolled around,* I was ready to eat.
7. *When breakfast had been finished,* the boys got out their fishing tackle.
8. The children's voices rang out *in loud tones.*
9. She was *the kind of girl that is a blonde type.*
10. She specializes in answers *that are in the negative.*

F. Combine the sentences below with the *introductory modifier* suggested for each, leaving the modifiers as they are but revising the sentences so that the combinations are clear and logical. Notice that the sentences as they now stand have passive verbs. Most of the sentences join logically with the modifiers if you make the verb active.

1. While trailing his line carelessly beside the boat. A five-pound bass was caught by Jim.

2. Having turned off the light. Ominous shadows were seen by Marie lurking in every corner.

3. After walking for an hour. The old cabin was finally seen by our leader.

4. After watching for an hour. The rare birds were finally seen by us.

5. Unable to get materials. A new product was put on the market by my father's company.

6. Playing the last ten minutes with a broken finger. The game was finally won by Jack with a free throw.

7. While flying a kite in a storm. Information about electricity was discovered by Benjamin Franklin.

8. While raking the yard. Her left knee was twisted.

9. To prove that there were no hard feelings. A dinner was given for us by the winning team.

10. Working without rest for two afternoons. The cabin was finally cleaned by the Boy Scouts.

G. Below are groups of slightly varied sentences. Comment on distinctions in emphasis or meaning you can discern among the versions in each group.

1. *a*) With the field glasses the girl found the dog.
   b) The girl with the field glasses found the dog.
   c) The girl found the dog with the field glasses.

2. *a*) Suddenly the clown jumped up and slapped the acrobat.
   b) The clown suddenly jumped up and slapped the acrobat.
   c) The clown jumped up and suddenly slapped the acrobat.

3. *a*) The past, at least, is secure.
   b) The past is secure, at least.
   c) At least the past is secure.

4. *a*) The Duke still lives that Henry shall depose.
   b) The Duke still lives that shall depose Henry.
   c) The Duke that Henry shall depose still lives.

5. *a*) Hope springs eternal in the human breast.
   b) Hope springs eternally in the human breast.
   c) Eternal hope springs in the human breast.

6. *a*) The law smiles in your face while it picks your pocket.
   b) While it picks your pocket, the law smiles in your face.
   c) While the law smiles in your face, it picks your pocket.

7. *a*) In the long run, we are sure to lose.
   b) We are sure to lose in the long run.
   c) We are, in the long run, sure to lose.

8. *a*) This was a better way of making a living.
   b) This was a way of making a better living.
   c) This was a way of making a living better.

9. *a*) Just before noon we decided that the program was too long.
  b) We decided that the program was too long just before noon.
  c) We decided that the program just before noon was too long.
10. *a*) Although he hated everyone there, John stayed at the party.
  b) John stayed at the party, although he hated everyone there.

H. Supply for the blanks in the following sentences appropriate modifiers; some sentences may require modifiers of more than one word:

1. When the doctor arrived, the patient was looking very _____ .
2. Both the tires are old, but put on the _____ of the two.
3. Neither cup is full, but yours is _____ than mine.
4. Alice's dress is unique, but mine is more _____ than hers.
5. He may not be simple-minded, but he always acts _____ .
6. She came to our pledge party, but we decided that she was too _____ for us.
7. Walter Johnson was one of the _____ baseball pitchers this country ever produced.
8. The apartment was old and in a poor part of town, but it looked _____ .
9. I watched both girls and decided the _____ one was probably a snob.
10. I ran to the window and looked _____ down into the street.
11. He was out of the hospital, but he was still looking very _____ .

I. In the sentences below, decide whether each italicized modifier is appropriate or inappropriate. If it is inappropriate, select a better form.

1. Our "open-house" was the *most unique* party I can remember.
2. Your collie may be smart, but she looks *mean*.
3. Before we were halfway down into the Grand Canyon my mule became *lame*.
4. The dog yipped, looked around as though for some protection, and ran *lame* toward his kennel.
5. Janice and Lorry lived in houses across the street from ours, but Janice's house was *more opposite* ours than Lorry's was.
6. Of the two sets, I should say that the *smallest* one has the *highest* fidelity.
7. When I saw that the cow moose had a calf with her I scrambled *lively* down the hill.
8. If I had had a shell in my gun, I could have shot that squirrel *easy*.
9. Mother was always an *easy* mark for any clever salesman.
10. Our old car did not have much power, but it rode *easy*.

J. Use the facts given below for a brief composition. Subordinate as many of the details as the material warrants.

Alice Marriott wrote an article.
The article is called "Beowulf in South Dakota."
Alice Marriott is an ethnologist.
Alice Marriott studies American Indian tales.
The New Yorker published the article.
The New Yorker is a sophisticated magazine.
The author was collecting stories from an old Indian.
The Indian lived in South Dakota.
One day the old Indian was bored and restless.
The Indian looked as though he did not want to tell more stories.
The Indian asked a question.
The Indian wanted to know why the white people wanted his stories.
The Indian wanted to know if the white people had no stories of their own.
The author said she wanted to compare the stories of the Indians with the stories of the white people.
The old Indian became interested.
He acted pleased.
The Indian said that the author's idea was a good idea.
The Indian said he wanted the author to tell him one of the white people's stories.
The author retold the story of *Beowulf*.
The author used Indian terms and Indian concepts.
The author made Beowulf a great war chief.
Beowulf gathered the young men of the tribe around him.
Beowulf and the young men went on a war party.
Beowulf and the young men attacked the Witch of the Water and her son.
The Witch of the Water lived under a great stone in a rushing, dangerous river.
A great fight took place under the water.
There was blood welling up through the water.
The water was as red as the sun rising.
Beowulf killed the Witch of the Water and her son.
The Indian liked the story.
The author had to tell it over and over.
The Indian told it to his friends and the friends talked about it.
The Indians talked about Beowulf.
The Indians sounded like a seminar in literature.
The Indian did not tell any more stories that day.

The author had to go home and wait until the Indians recovered from *Beowulf*.

The old man told the author many stories.

The storytelling continued for weeks.

Another ethnologist was trying to get the old Indian to tell him stories.

Ethnologists have methods of working and standardized ethical practices.

An ethnologist who tries to use another ethnologist's information is unethical.

Two ethnologists are likely to confuse an informant.

A confused informant gives unsatisfactory evidence to both scientists.

The old Indian said he liked the author.

The author was the friend of the old Indian.

The Indian offered not to tell the other ethnologist Indian stories.

The author went back to her university.

The author heard that the other ethnologist wanted to question the old Indian.

Two or three years passed.

The author was reading a learned journal.

The author found an article signed by the other ethnologist.

The article was called "Occurrence of a Beowulf-like Myth among North American Indians."

The author wondered whether or not she should tell what she knew.

(If you want to see what Alice Marriott did with the story, you will find the reference in 23-10.)

Coherence within Sentences: Function Words, Reference, Agreement

For Guide to Revision, see page 287.

Word order, function words, and various referential devices give English sentences coherence.

We have observed that paragraphs must be tied together and to one another (see Section 5), and that coherence among larger units relies upon sentences. Sentences, also, must cohere within themselves, and the immediately preceding sections of this book, discussing kernel sentences, their variations, and their developments through coordination and subordination, have treated devices which incidentally promote coherence. In addition, English has developed special means to knit sentences together, some of which can be most readily observed in their historical growth.

Growth of Structural Coherence   17-1

We have already seen that English has developed from an archaic ancestor, Indo-European, and that as part of this development it has moved from a language relying heavily upon inflection to one relying upon analysis or distribution. Notice the differences among three versions of a passage from Boethius's *Consolation of Philosophy:*

Latin of Boethius:

Tandem,	"Vincimur,"	arbiter	Umbrarum	miserans
At length	*"We are overcome,"*	*the judge*	*of Hades,*	*pitying,*

ait;	"Donamus	comitem	viro,	emptam
said;	*"Let us give*	*a consort*	*to the man,*	*bought*
carmine	conjugem."			
with song	*a wife."*			

Anglo-Saxon of King Alfred:

Tha	cleopode	se	hellwara	cyning,	ond	cwæth
Then	*spoke*	*the*	*of Hell*	*king*	*and*	*said:*
"Wuton	agifan		thæm esne	his	wif,	for thæm
"We ought	*to give back*		*to the husband*	*his*	*wife,*	*because*
he	hi	hæfth	gearnad	mid	his	hearpunga.
he	*her*	*has*	*earned*	*with*	*his*	*harping.*

Middle English of Chaucer:

At the laste the lord and juge of soules was moevid to misericordes, and cryede: "We been overcomen," quod he; "yeve we to Orpheus his wif to beren him compaignye; he hath wel y-bought hire by his faire song and his ditee."

A number of differences are apparent among the passages beyond those in vocabulary. Word order has replaced the endings of the Latin to reveal the subject–verb–complement pattern. The number of words has notably increased, twelve for Latin, twenty-two for Anglo-Saxon, and forty-two for Chaucer. Translation into modern English would require a few more words: *we been overcomen* would be *we have been overcome,* and *yeve we* would be *let us give.* The comparison illustrates a second characteristic of distributive grammar, that it sorts out and separates the signs of grammatical function from the signs of meaning. Whereas an inflected grammar, like that of Latin, puts the two kinds of signs into a single word, a distributive grammar, like that of modern English, tends to use one word to signal a grammatical relationship and another word to convey meaning.

Modern English, then, uses words in two ways, as signs of meaning and as signs of grammatical function. That is, the words in sentences can be roughly distinguished as *content words* and what we have called *function words,* or *relationship words.* Partly because English is still in process of becoming a language with a distributive grammar, words cannot be sharply classified as either content words or function words, and such classification is not necessary. Distinction between the two kinds of uses, however, is possible. Compare the following groups of sentences:

I *have* two apples.
I *have* eaten two apples.
Up is the right direction.
The balloon blew *up*.
He blew *up* the balloon.
The wind blew the balloon *up* the road.

In the first sentence, *have* is clearly a content word, a sign of meaning; but in the second it is a function word, a sign of the tense of the verb. In the second group, *up* appears in a variety of uses: first as a content word naming a direction, second as a part of a verb *blow up* which works as a sign of meaning, third as a part of the same verb representing a different meaning in its transitive use, and fourth as a function word joining *road* to the sentence. Since most function words formerly had other uses and since they did not lose entirely their old uses when they began to fill new functions, they have now developed remarkable variety and adaptability. In the following sentence, nearly half the words, those in italics, act as function words.

Although the room contained many women *who would have* died unhesitatingly *for their* children, *when a* mouse appeared, courageous mothers *who had been* sitting *on* chairs found themselves standing *on the* tops *of* piano benches *or* clinging *to* strange men *for* protection.

Although relates the words before the first comma to the rest of the sentence, but it also suggests that the clause it introduces presents a seeming contrast to the main assertion. *The* warns us that we are concerned with a specific room. *Who* relates the following words to the rest of the sentence, especially to *women,* and implies that the idea involved in *women* will serve as the subject of a dependent clause. *Would have* has little meaning but specifies the form of the verb. *For* is best thought of as part of the verb, but it shows the relationship of *children* to the remainder of the sentence. To see how hard it is to reduce some function words to a meaning, try to find a definition which will fit this *for* and the *for* toward the end of the sentence. *When* warns us that a dependent clause is coming and that the action in the clause determines the time of an event expressed elsewhere in the sentence. *A* introduces one particular mouse, but with the understanding that this mouse might as well have been any mouse. *In, of, on,* and *to,* like *for,* may be parts of the verb, but they also show how words like *tops, tables,* and *piano benches* are related to other parts of the sentence. *In* and *on* have meanings of their own; they modify our conceptions of space relationships. But what is the meaning of *of?* *And* and *or* join other words; *and* suggests that two words are to be taken together, *or* that there is an alternative between the ideas expressed in two words. And so on.

Function words may give the sentence additional coherence by specifying grammatical ideas beyond those conveyed by word order. For example, we can often know that we are dealing with a question only because certain words signal questions. Compare:

He spoke.
Who spoke?

We recognize the second as a question only because *who* serves partly as a function word. Or compare:

Jack *has* told a lie.
Jack *was* told a lie.

Only the fact that *has* and *was* signal different relationships distinguishes the active kernel sentence from the passive variation of it. The following differ only by a function word:

He had no basis for his charges.
Although he had no basis for his charges. . . .

The first is a sentence; the addition of a function word makes the second not a sentence but a possible modifying clause.

Since function words or relationship words have recently shifted within the language and are still shifting, they cannot be sharply classified. As this book is being written, for example, *like* and *as* are shifting in usage. Function words are sometimes grouped as *determiners, auxiliaries, relatives, intensifiers, conjunctions,* and *prepositions,* with subdivisions among these, but distinctions are not always sharp. Two of these groups, however, are especially important to sentence coherence.

17-2 Conjunctions

Conjunctions serve generally to reinforce coordination and subordination, the two main processes whereby the kernel sentence pattern expands or develops. Theoretically, a *coordinating conjunction* joins like or equal or coordinate elements, joining either complete patterns or parts of patterns. A *subordinating conjunction* functions only with complete sentence patterns, joining a dependent clause to another element. Although distinctions between the types of conjunction are not always logical, *and, but, for, or,* and *nor,* and often *so* and *yet* are conventionally recognized as coordinating conjunctions; they may join independent clauses or other sentence elements in parallel construction.

I jumped into the car without trouble, *but* Mary slammed the door on her fingers.

Although it was Sunday *and* although I knew I ought to get up for church, I turned over to take another nap.

The pavement was icy *and* treacherous from a night of raining *and* freezing.

Conjunctive adverbs, like coordinating conjunctions, connect parallel clauses, but at the same time modify within a clause. Observe the following:

I wanted one of the then fashionable dirndls; *however,* I got Jinny's old plaid skirt.

She was in no mood to take advice. I was angry, *however,* and I told her what I thought of her leaving the party.

The second *however* links the sentence to a preceding sentence. Other conjunctive adverbs include the following: *thus, then, nevertheless, nonetheless, moreover, likewise, similarly, also, furthermore, consequently, therefore, hence,* and *besides.*

Subordinating conjunctions present unusual opportunities for exactness, along with corresponding dangers if the writer chooses them carelessly. Notice the following:

Although I tried to explain,
Because I tried to explain,   } Angela became furious.
When I tried to explain,
While I tried to explain,

The first two sentences imply quite different psychological states for Angela. The last two involve time, but with a difference, the third indicating only the time of Angela's anger, the fourth suggesting that it developed during the explanation.

Relative pronouns—who, whom, which, that—function as do subordinating conjunctions, relating a subordinate clause to the sentence. They differ because they also have semantic and grammatical functions within their clauses. In the sentence *He is the man who takes candy away from babies,* the relative pronoun *who* relates its clause to *man,* but it also refers to *man* as its antecedent and serves as subject in its clause. For usage problems, see *Relative Pronouns* in the Glossary.

17-3 Prepositions

Unlike conjunctions, prepositions function only within the basic sentence, joining a noun or noun substitute to some part of a sentence. The preposition and the noun following it constitute a *prepositional phrase,* which can function as almost any sentence element, usually as a modifier. Choosing prepositions accurately is not always easy because convention, often arbitrary, may dictate which prepositions determine which meanings. For example, British English requires the idiom *He lives in Oxford Street;* whereas American English requires *He lives on Oxford Street. Street* in England retains some of its medieval meaning and designates both the thoroughfare and the areas alongside it. Most users of the language cannot be expected to know such historical backgrounds for differences and accordingly must rely on their sense of idiom when they distinguish among speaking *to, with, for, of,* or *about* the devil. They must sense that they agree *with* a friend, *to* a proposal, *on* terms, and *about* somebody's character.

17-4 Reference

Ideas carry from sentence to sentence and paragraph to paragraph partly as they are repeated or echoed, either in the same words or in synonyms or substitute words (see 5-2 through 5-4). This device, which contributes to coherence within the sentence as well as between sentences, may be called reference, signifying the relationship between one expression and another which restates its idea or refers to it. The word referred to, especially by a pronoun, is called the antecedent (see Glossary).

Reference works in a variety of ways, as the following sentences illustrate (antecedents are in italics):

My *sister* said she had found the *book* that was missing from the shelves. (*She* refers to *sister* and *that* to *book.*)

I *have* more faith in her judgment than you do. (*Do* repeats *have* and can be said to refer to it.)

He offered *to phone the hostess and ask if I could come along with him,* but I have never liked such arrangements. (*Such arrangements* refers much less precisely to an antecedent understood from the long complement, but the meaning seems clear enough.)

He believes that *everyone who attends the dean's teas receives special favors,* but this is not true. (*This* refers to the idea of the entire clause.)

He annoyed many people by his *smugness and intolerance,* attitudes which developed from'his early training. (Attitudes restates *smugness and intolerance* in order to develop the sentence.)

Although these sentences vary widely, with verbs, nouns, or pronouns in reference patterns, they are all clear. Consider the following variation on the last sentence:

He annoyed many people by being smug and intolerant, attitudes which developed from his early training.

In this sentence, reference is not clear; *attitudes* does not logically repeat the meaning of *smug* and *intolerant,* which are modifiers and not names for attitudes or anything else. Reference reinforces coherence only when it is clear, when the reader can readily make a logical association between the reference word and its antecedent. Pronouns, being reference words by their nature, take their meaning from that of their antecedents and must refer precisely. A reader must be able immediately to relate a pronoun to its antecedent. In English, two kinds of signals help him: word order and word forms or inflections. Word order has assumed major importance in patterns of reference in English as inflections have tended to disappear. The pronoun, however, retains considerable remnants of earlier form changes, and these work also as signals of reference. That is, the writer can make reference clear both by word order and by selecting pronoun forms that agree in person, number, and gender with their antecedents. Often choice of proper forms, along with attention to meaning, establishes reference, as in the following example:

John showed *his* sister *his* copy of the book which *she* had written.

Since *she* is feminine in form it must refer to sister; the authorship is clear.

Notice, however, the difference if John had met his brother. **283**

John showed *his* brother *his* copy of the book which *he* had written.

Because of meaning and order we could probably guess whose copy is involved, but we cannot guess who wrote the book. Form distinctions are not enough to establish reference.

To insure clarity, then, the writer can profitably observe the following rule:

Be sure that every reference word has a clear antecedent, and that the form of the reference word and the order of words in the sentence make the reference immediately certain.

17-5 Patterns of Reference

Often we must rely on word order to establish reference relationships, and the patterns of reference in English sentences are variable enough to make vague and inaccurate references a hazard for the writer. In general the following principles apply:

1. The subject, as the most important noun or pronoun in a clause, and especially the subject of a main clause, tends to become an antecedent of a personal pronoun. Consider:

Shakespeare was two months younger than Marlowe; a record of his baptism April 26, 1564, has been preserved.

Even though *his* could apply sensibly to either *Shakespeare* or *Marlowe,* and even though *Marlowe* is nearer *his* in the sentence, the reader knows that *Shakespeare,* the subject, is the antecedent of *his.*

2. If the subject is obviously impossible as the antecedent of a personal pronoun, a complement tends to be the next choice.

She took the rooster out of the sack and put a rock in *its* place.

Its cannot refer to the subject, but it does refer to *rooster.* Notice that while the meaning helps clarify reference, the order is essential here. We could change the chicken's fate by transposing *rock* and *rooster.*

3. The less important the position of the word in a sentence, the greater is the difficulty of making the word an antecedent. Modifiers and other words in subordinate uses, however, may work as antecedents of pronouns in parallel structures.

I visited the library and spent an hour looking through the book. I found nothing in *it.*

It refers to *book;* pronoun and antecedent have parallel uses and positions.

4. A noun expression immediately before a relative pronoun tends to be its antecedent. Notice what happens when a relative pronoun is used in the sentence above.

Shakespeare was two months younger than Marlowe, a record of whose baptism in February, 1564, has been preserved.

The relative pronoun *whose* refers to *Marlowe,* and the date has to be changed to keep the sentence accurate.

Agreement or Concord 17-6

Although word order and function words establish sentence coherence, a few surviving inflections or form changes reinforce it. Older forms of English used inflections extensively to specify relationships between words, even requiring a modifier to change its form to agree with the form of a noun. Most inflections have disappeared from English; those that remain apply to only a few grammatical relationships, and clarity seldom requires the inflectional signals of agreement. No one would miss the meaning of *The man walk to work,* even though the sentence sounds like pidgin English. Since agreement is not often essential for communication, it is often not observed in nonstandard English; and in many constructions agreement is only partially observed in spoken English. Agreement is, however, characteristic of standard English, and writers need to know common practices.

The inflections in English involved in agreement are the following:

The different forms of personal pronouns which distinguish person (*I, you, it*), number (*I, we*), and gender (*him, her, it*).

The ending on nouns, or sometimes the form change, which distinguishes the plural number.

The *–s* ending on the third person present singular of verbs which distinguishes person and number.

The form changes of the verb *to be* which distinguish number and person (*am, is, are*).

These forms affect mainly two relationships in English, between a pronoun and its antecedent and between a subject and verb. In general, two principles apply:

A pronoun agrees with its antecedent in gender, number, and person,

285

but not in case. That is, if a pronoun refers to a feminine, singular antecedent (*woman* or *Evangeline*), a feminine, singular pronoun would be chosen (*she* or *her*); for case, see the Glossary.

A subject and its verb agree in number and person. That is, if a subject is third person and singular (*goat* or *salesmanship*), the inflected form of the verb is used (*is, does, works*).

One other relationship, that between two nouns, is sometimes important. In *The children washed their faces every morning, faces* is plural both to agree with *children* and to make sense.

In most sentences, agreement causes difficulty only to the most inexperienced writers, but some constructions cause trouble because the number of the antecedent or the subject cannot readily be determined. Is *committee* singular or plural? What of *everybody,* which is logically singular, but tends to carry a sense of the plural to most users of the language? And sometimes the sentence pattern is so obscured that the writer forgets or mistakes his antecedent or subject.

The dancer, with her ballet company, her orchestra, her stage crew, and her managers and directors, occupies the sixth floor.

Dancer, although separated from the verb by modifiers that are plural, is singular, and *occupies* is singular to agree.

For these special problems no single rule suffices, but surviving inflections give the writer an opportunity to specify number precisely. In general, modern English tends, in questionable instances, to determine the number of an antecedent or a subject according to the meaning intended, rather than according to set rules or "logic." If the sense of the subject is singular, the verb is singular; if the sense of the subject is plural, the verb is plural.

Guide to Revision **17**

**Ref
Agr**

Improve coherence by precise use of function words, clear reference, and accurate agreement.

Modern English relies so heavily on word-order patterns to reveal relationships within sentences that supplementary devices may cause trouble. Because they are not always essential to some kind of understanding, function words, patterns of reference, and signals of agreement are sometimes used carelessly. Precise writing requires careful use of these secondary devices. Function words are pivotal; one function word can change the whole tenor of a sentence.

Because I love you, I must leave you.
Although I love you, I must leave you.

Function words must be chosen to reveal precisely the intended relationship, but since function words vary subtly and in numerous ways, choosing individual words and types of words may involve usage. For common examples, see Glossary.

Conj a   **Coordinating Conjunctions**   **17a**

Coordinating conjunctions join coordinate elements, and show how they are related. *And* joins like elements of thought or adds a similar element; *but* emphasizes a contrast; *or* offers a choice.

ORIGINAL	REVISION
The sea was like glass, and that was the last calm day we had at the beach. [*Probably, a contrast is intended.*]	The sea was like glass, but that was the last calm day we had at the beach.
You can play all sorts of games, and if you want to, you can spend the afternoon under a tree reading a book. [*A choice seems intended.*]	You can play all sorts of games, or if you want to you can spend the afternoon under a tree reading a book.

In order to avoid lengthy sentences modern writers sometimes put coordinate ideas in separate sentences, beginning the second sentence with a coordinating conjunction.

> The wolf is today what he was when he was hunted by Nimrod. But, while men are born with many of the characteristics of wolves, man is a wolf domesticated, who both transmits the arts by which he has been partially tamed and improves upon them.
>
> —R. H. TAWNEY, *Religion and the Rise of Capitalism*

Although the sentences might have been combined, the separation sharpens the contrast between ideas, because *but,* the sign of the contrast, is in the position of emphasis at the beginning of the sentence. This device is easily overworked. It is useful only when the writer needs the special emphasis given to the coordinating conjunction by the initial position, or when the sentence beginning with *but* is to be contrasted to more than one preceding sentence.

ORIGINAL	REVISION
At first I thought I would decorate the table with flowers. But I found that the roses had gone to seed.	At first I thought I would decorate the table with flowers, but I found that the roses had gone to seed.
[*Opening the second sentence,* but *is unduly emphatic.*]	[*Within a compound sentence,* but *is appropriately inconspicuous.*]

17b   Subordinating Conjunctions   Conj b

Subordinating conjunctions do more than indicate that one part of a sentence is dependent; they also specify the particular way in which it is dependent. Compare:

Although she was his wife, she stayed at a hotel.
Because she was his wife, she stayed at a hotel.
Before she was his wife, she stayed at a hotel.
Until she was his wife, she stayed at a hotel.
After she was his wife, she stayed at a hotel.
While she was his wife, she stayed at a hotel.
Whenever she was his wife, she stayed at a hotel.

Because they indicate different kinds of relationships between the ideas in the clauses, the various conjunctions give the sentences different meanings. Subordinating conjunctions need to be chosen with care to define relationships precisely (see also 13b).

ORIGINAL	REVISION
While Father did not approve of alcoholic beverages, he always had some in the house for guests. [While *is loosely used as an equivalent of* although *or* because. *Strictly used it means that one event takes place at the same time as another.*]	Although Father did not approve of alcoholic beverages, he always had some in the house for guests. [*The subordinate clause mentions a concession, and the concessive conjunction,* although, *has accordingly replaced* while.]
Since my mother was a little girl, she was not allowed to sit at the table [Since, *often, refers to time, but it is also used in the sense of* because.]	Because she was only a little girl, my mother was not allowed to sit at the table.
I did not know but what she was afraid to come in.	I did not know but that she was afraid to come in.
He had heard as how anyone could make a living panning gold.	He had heard that anyone could make a living panning gold.
I washed my face so as I would be allowed to go in for dinner.	I washed my face so that I would be allowed to go in for dinner.
I arrived on time so I could leave early.	I arrived on time so that I could leave early.

At the beginning or end of a sentence a conjunctive adverb may become falsely emphatic (see 18b).

ORIGINAL	REVISION
Clubs for girls can fill useful social functions. However, they should not take up all of a girl's time. Then, they merely interfere with a girl's achieving social maturity. Nevertheless, there is a time in a girl's life when a club can be helpful, and even exciting. [*Childish sentences like these cannot be cured by merely removing excessive conjunctions.*]	If a girl allows her clubs to consume all her time, they may only interfere with her achieving social maturity. Nevertheless, there is a period in a girl's life when a club can be helpful, even exciting. [*The structure has been made simpler and more direct, and with the change several conjunctive adverbs have been dropped.*]

Prep   Prepositions   17c

Prepositions determine many intimate relationships within the sentence; the writer should know the meaning of prepositions and should choose them with care. In addition, the use of certain prepositions with certain words and for particular usages has grown with custom; our usage of prepositions is not always based on apparent logic. It is often idiomatic, but it is no less exact for that.

ORIGINAL

REVISION

He went in the house and stopped at the mirror.

He went into the house and stopped before the mirror.

I had never heard about him or of his famous rescue.

I had never heard of him or about his famous rescue.

Some prepositions must be composed of more than one word, but involved prepositions are to be avoided if a simpler construction will suffice.

ORIGINAL

REVISION

I found the keys in back of the water pitcher.

I found the keys behind the water pitcher.

He spoke in regards to the paving of the alleys.
[*When the construction is appropriate, the word is* regard, *not* regards.]

(1) He spoke about paving the alleys.
(2) He discussed paving the alleys.

17d   Reference   Ref

The relationship between a reference word and its antecedent, whether a single word or an idea, must be readily discernible and plausible. Consider the following sentence:

People in America believe that everyone should share the good and the bad, but this principle does not apply here.

The sentence turns on the reference of the word *principle* to the clause *that everyone should share the good and the bad.* The sentence is clear. But compare the sentence from a student theme from which the above was revised:

Our country's democracy believes in everyone's sharing the good and the bad, and in this case the assumption would not hold true.

The words mean something as individual words, but they do not combine to make a clear sentence. Part of the trouble is that subjects, verbs, and complements do not work sensibly together, but further trouble arises from the key word, *assumption,* which does not logically refer to any previous idea—no assumption has been made. Whenever ideas are repeated or referred to more than once in the progress of a sentence, the writer must be sure that he uses terms which can logically work together.

Ref Indef **Indefinite Pronoun Reference** **17e**

Pronouns present reference problems, especially when words like *this, that, it,* and *which* refer to a general idea.

I had thrown a loaf of bread at the Marquis, which hit him on the cheek, and *that* made me feel good.   —ROBERT GRAVES

No particular noun can be labeled as the antecedent of *that,* but the meaning is clear, with *that* referring to the entire action which is described in the first part of the sentence. This use of the pronoun, however, is subject to considerable abuse, especially in student writing. Too often the construction disguises careless thinking; the pronoun is used to stand for an idea which the writer assumes the reader understands, but which he has not made clear to the reader and may not have made clear to himself. The construction may also reveal failure to subordinate (see 16a). Before using a pronoun to refer to a general idea, the writer must be sure that the reference is clear and that the sentence would not be improved with a different construction.

ORIGINAL

Some critics have accused Chaucer of Frenchifying English, which has been disproved.
[*Which has no certain antecedent.*]

The constant reminder of Norway and home made Beret become nostalgic, which was one of the causes of her insanity.
[*The antecedent is only implied; the sentence would be clearer with an expressed antecedent.*]

REVISION

Some critics have accused Chaucer of Frenchifying English, but the accusation has been disproved.
[*No antecedent is necessary.*]

(1) The constant reminder of Norway and home made Beret become nostalgic, and her nostalgia provided one cause of her insanity.
(2) The constant reminder of Norway and home caused Beret's nostalgia, which promoted her insanity.

Sentences sometimes begin with a dependent clause followed by a pronoun referring to a noun in the clause.

If this article makes a few people take democracy seriously, it will have served its purpose.

It is a clear restatement of *article*. This construction has perhaps led to the colloquial popularity of a similar pattern in which the pronoun lacks an antecedent and in which the vague reference handicaps the reader and, in effect, produces an unworkable predication (see 13a).

ORIGINAL	REVISION
If they are taken into the army, it means they will not graduate. [It *lacks an antecedent. Even the loose idea which the reader might supply for* it, *their induction into the army, does not make a good subject for the main clause.*]	If they are taken into the army, they will not graduate. [*Usually, as here, vague reference is a symptom of roundabout writing. The vague pronoun usurps the position of the real subject of the sentence,* they.]
If there were some way to get all people to use the same dialect, it would be much simpler. [*Not even a vague idea can be supplied as an antecedent for* it.]	If there were some way to get all people to use the same dialect, communication would be much simpler. [*Revision supplies a subject to replace the vague* it.]

Impersonal constructions become ambiguous when the sign of the impersonal construction can be mistaken for a personal pronoun. *It*, used for either purpose, readily becomes ambiguous.

ORIGINAL	REVISION
My Chevrolet has a Mercury motor which makes it hard to shift gears. [It *should be impersonal, but it appears at first to be a personal pronoun with* Chevrolet *as its antecedent.*]	(1) My Chevrolet has a Mercury motor; with this combination I have trouble shifting gears. (2) I have trouble shifting gears because my Chevrolet has a Mercury motor.
The building of the Mississippi River jetties should be a good research topic, but it is going to be hard to find the technical details of construction. [It *is impersonal, but seems to refer to* building.]	The building of the Mississippi River jetties should be a good research topic, but I expect trouble when I try to find the technical details of construction.

Colloquially *they* and *it* are used as indefinite pronouns to refer generally to "people" or "society." Except in reference to weather

(It *is cold today*), this indefinite use, often indirect or vague, is inappropriate in serious writing.

ORIGINAL

In the paper it says the weather will change.
[*Nobody knows who* it *is.*]

While she was in the hospital her hair turned white, and now *they* say she dyes it.

REVISION

The paper says that the weather will change.
[*Omission of the vague pronoun provides a solution.*]

While she was in the hospital, her hair turned white, and now, apparently, she dyes it.

Ref Ant — Reference and Position of Antecedents — 17f

Unless form clarifies the reference, a pronoun usually refers sharply only to a noun expression in an important position in the sentence or in a use parallel to its own. If the word order does not clarify the reference, the sentence must be revised or an antecedent provided.

ORIGINAL

I should like to find out how authors were affected during the depression and how it changed their styles of writing.
[*Presumably* depression *is the antecedent of* it, *but this relationship is not at once apparent, because* depression *is not the subject, does not occur immediately before the pronoun, and is not in parallel structure.*]

In Hemingway's book *For Whom the Bell Tolls,* he tells about an American teacher in the Spanish Civil War.
[He *must refer to a person, but* Hemingway's *is not a person. It helps identify* book.]

REVISION

(1) I should like to find out how authors were affected during the depression years, and how the depression changed their styles of writing.
(2) I should like to find out how the depression affected authors, and how it changed their styles of writing.
[*In (1), it has been removed for a noun; in (2) it refers to* depression, *the subject of a preceding clause.*]

In this book *For Whom the Bell Tolls,* Hemingway tells about an American teacher in the Spanish Civil War.
[*With the pronoun in the dependent position and* Hemingway *as the subject, the reference of* his *is clear.*]

W Ref — Word Reference — 17g

When specific terms are restated generally, when general terms are broken into parts, or modifiers follow the word they modify,

293

word reference may be inaccurate. The writer, as he moves forward in the sentence, seems to forget the words he has used and to refer to them only imprecisely.

ORIGINAL

The field of interior decorating holds vast opportunities for the women who want to apply themselves to the task.
[*A* field *is not a* task, *and the faulty reference helps make the sentence ambiguous.*]

Of all the regulations for women, I hated most being in by nine o'clock.
[Being in *is not a regulation; the general term does not logically include the specific one.*]

He started out as a senior economist, very difficult for a person without much experience.
[*The writer probably did not mean to say that the economist was difficult, but that his work was.*]

When she applied the next time, she was appointed head dietician, vacated only the day before by a sudden resignation.
[Vacated *requires something to modify;* dietician *will not serve. The position, not the dietician, was vacated.*]

REVISION

(1) Interior decorating holds vast opportunities for women who want to apply themselves.
(2) Women who become interior decorators have vast opportunities.
[*Here, as often, confusion can best be cured by deletion.*]

I hated most the regulation for women requiring us to be in by nine o'clock.
[*The restatement is avoided.*]

He started out as a senior economist, doing work very difficult for a person without much experience.
[Work *provides a plausible idea for* difficult *to modify.*]

(1) When she applied the next time, she was appointed to the position of head dietician, vacated only the day before by a sudden resignation.
(2) When she applied the next time, she was appointed head dietician, filling a position vacated only the day before by a sudden resignation.

Writing may become confused when modifiers patterned to restate an idea reveal a shift in the writer's attitude.

ORIGINAL

Bowling Green, the name of my home town, is in the southern part of Kentucky.
[Bowling Green *can be either a name or a town, but the town, not the name, is in Kentucky.*]

REVISION

Bowling Green, my home town, is in the southern part of Kentucky.

Some modifiers resemble pronouns in that they refer to an antecedent at the same time that they serve their own grammatical function. Words of this sort include *the* and *such, there, here, other, another, this, that, these,* and *those,* when they are used as modifiers.

ORIGINAL

He meant no harm by his pranks, but this result did not always come of his mischief. Such result came from one affair.
[*Both* this *and* such *require antecedents but do not have them.*]

REVISION

He meant no harm; his pranks were only mischievous, but they sometimes ended unhappily.
[*The sentence has been recast and the awkward construction removed by simplified word order.*]

I feel that harbor dredging will be a very interesting subject. Since I have lived there for fifteen years, I am well acquainted with it.
[There *has no antecedent.*]

I feel that harbor dredging will be a very interesting subject, and I am well acquainted with it, since for fifteen years I have lived where I could observe operations.

We saw a little adobe house and rode over. The man and his wife greeted us pleasantly.
[The *suggests a man who has been mentioned before.*]

We saw a little adobe house and rode over. A man and his wife greeted us pleasantly.
[A *indicates that the man is being introduced; the false reference disappears.*]

A substitute verb or verbal (see 12-5), usually some combination with *to do,* must refer clearly and logically to another verb.

ORIGINAL

He expresses the revolt against bondage and the desire to be free. His argument centers around the possibility to do so.
[*The only verb in the first sentence that could work as an antecedent for* to do so *is* expresses, *and reference to it does not make sense.*]

REVISION

He speaks of revolting against bondage and being free. His argument assumes the possibility of doing so.
[*The original is so unclear that accurate revision is difficult, but the rearrangement provides parallel antecedents in* revolting *and* being.]

If he has any time for fooling around after class he will do so.
[*He cannot* do *fooling around.*]

If he has any time to fool around after class, he will.
[*With the form changed, no substitute is necessary.*]

Agr   Agreement   17h

Errors of agreement usually occur because the writer fails to identify an antecedent or a subject, has trouble deciding on its number, or confuses it with its modifiers. Usually meaning determines the number.

Two *hours* of his last twelve *were gone.*
Two *hours is* a long time.

In the first sentence *hours* is plural, according to the sense of the sentence, but in the second sentence, in spite of its plural form, *two hours* specifies a singular unit of time and is therefore in agreement with a singular verb. Usually form and meaning are the same, and often when a subject plural in form is used in a singular sense it is imprecise. Consider

Late *hours was* responsible for his illness.

The sense of the subject is singular, but revision would make the meaning more exact.

Keeping late hours *brought on* his illness.

Indefinite pronouns like *everybody, anybody, everyone, each, somebody* are traditionally considered singular, as specifying one of a group. They have been used so often, however, with a plural sense—to mean "all people," for example—that colloquially they have long been used as plurals. Even in formal writing, *none* is used as either singular or plural, depending on the sense intended, and words like *everybody* are occasionally considered plural when they clearly have a plural sense. Generally, however, in serious writing such pronouns are considered singular; pronouns referring to them are singular in form and verbs of which they are subjects are also singular. Confusion becomes acute if the verb and pronoun do not interpret the subject in the same way—that is, if an indefinite pronoun is followed by a singular verb and then referred to by a plural pronoun.

ORIGINAL

When everybody has given their opinion, the committee can decide. [Everybody *has a singular meaning here and is used with a singular verb. The pronoun referring to it should be singular.*]

Anybody knows it is to their advantage to have a college degree.

REVISION

When everybody has given his opinion, the committee can decide. [*The singular* his *has replaced the plural* their.]

Anybody knows it is to his advantage to have a college degree.

In written American English, a collective noun is treated as singular unless the meaning clearly shows that the parts in the collection, not the collection as a whole, are being considered. Colloquially, however, plural verbs and pronouns are common even when the sense of the noun is not clearly plural (*The staff* were *willing to work late*). Certainly, in writing, the verb and any pronouns referring to the subject should agree.

●

ORIGINAL

The company moves forward to their position in the line.
[*The company, thought of as a unit, is singular.*]

REVISION

The company moves forward to its position in the line.
[*The singular pronoun* its *has replaced the plural* their.]

The company considers John one of their best men.
[*Their can be replaced with the singular form (1), or it can be given an antecedent (2).*]

(1) The company considers John one of its best men.
(2) The managers of the company consider John one of their best men.

The committee have voted to lay the motion on the table.
[*The committee acted as a body and is singular in meaning.*]

The committee has voted to lay the motion on the table.
[*The singular* has *replaces the plural* have.]

The committee differs, some supporting the motion, some opposing it, and some calling it irrelevant.
[*Here the various members of the commitee, not the committee as a unit, are the subject.*]

The committee differ, some supporting the motion, some opposing it, and some calling it irrelevant.
[*The plural* differ *indicates the plural sense of the committee.*]

Agreement with Compound and Alternative Subjects

A compound subject usually is plural, even though its parts are singular. *Corn and lettuce* combine into a subject as clearly plural as a plural form like *vegetables*. The meaning of the subject, however, usually determines its number, and occasionally compound subjects join to form a noun expression whose sense is singular. Compare:

Ham and eggs are among his most profitable products.
Ham and eggs is a good dish.

The compound is plural in the first sentence, but in the second it names a single item for a menu.

ORIGINAL	REVISION
Adrian and Harry rides the trolley to school and walks home. [*Two people are riding, even though each part of the subject is singular.*]	Adrian and Harry ride the trolley to school and walk home. [*With* ride *and* walk *in the plural, subject and verbs agree.*]
A horde of little Mexicans and one lone donkey was trooping down the road. [Donkey *is singular, but the horde* and *the donkey were trooping.*]	A horde of little Mexicans and one lone donkey were trooping down the road. [Were *agrees with* horde *and* donkey.]

Either, neither, or, nor, usually separate alternatives and do not combine elements as compounds. Logically alternative subjects govern verbs and pronouns individually: *Virtue or honesty is its own reward.* Colloquially, however, such subjects are not always regarded individually (*Neither of them were afraid*), and competent writers sometimes feel that the sense of alternative subjects is plural. Usually, if both alternates are singular, a singular verb or pronoun follows; if both are plural, verb and pronoun are plural. If one is singular and the other plural, usage varies. Many writers make the verb or pronoun agree with the item nearest it:

Either the boys or their father is going to help.
Either the dog or the chickens were doomed.

Most writers, however, would avoid either sentence.

ORIGINAL	REVISION
Either French dressing or mayonnaise go well with tomatoes. [*The subject is singular,* dressing *or* mayonnaise, *not both.*]	Either French dressing or mayonnaise goes well with tomatoes. [*The singular* goes *has replaced the plural* go.]
Neither Columbus nor Henry Hudson achieved their ambitions. [*The subject, being alternative, is singular.*]	Neither Columbus nor Henry Hudson achieved his ambitions. [*The singular* his *has replaced the plural* their.]
Neither the captain nor the radar men was aware of the approaching bomber.	Neither the captain nor the radar men were aware of the approaching bomber.

Agr Fol   Agreement When Subject Follows Verb   17j

Subject–verb–complement order is so well established in English that speakers may have trouble recognizing a subject that follows the verb and fail to make the verb agree with it. Colloquially, an introductory *there* or *it* is frequently taken for a singular subject and followed by a singular verb, even when the real subject is plural. In standard writing, however, the verb takes the number of its subject, even though the subject may follow it.

ORIGINAL	REVISION
There was left only one seat in the balcony and one behind a post. [*The subject is compound and thus plural.*]	There were left only one seat in the balcony and one behind a post. [*The plural* were *has replaced the singular* was.]
Behind the tree was two squirrels. [Squirrels *is the subject.*]	Behind the tree were two squirrels.

A similar problem arises when the subject and complement of a linking verb differ in number; is the subject the word following or the word preceding the verb? Usually the basic word order pattern prevails, and the verb agrees with the word preceding it:

Oranges were his main product.
His main product was oranges.

ORIGINAL	REVISION
The answer to our problems are well-trained soldiers. [*The verb should agree with* answer. *This sentence will be awkward unless the linking verb is replaced (see 13b).*]	(1) The answer to our problems is well-trained soldiers. (2) We need well-trained soldiers.

Agr Cons   Consistency in Pronouns   17k

Unnecessary shifts from one person to another (see 13d) can produce awkward constructions, especially in impersonal constructions, which do not develop gracefully in modern English. Constructions like *we find, they say,* and *you go* are common, but ambiguous. The indefinite *one* is less ambiguous but can become awkward, especially when the possessive *one's* is required. For all but the most formal writing, however, *one* can be combined with *he* and *his*.

ORIGINAL

When one is aboard, you will almost always find somebody who can speak your language.

[*The shift from* one *to* you *is a shift of person.*]

I think everybody should be careful of one's grammar.

REVISION

When one is abroad, he will almost always find somebody who can speak his language.

[*The third person forms,* he *and* his, *are consistent with* one.]

I think everybody should be careful of his grammar.

17l Agreement in Dependent Clauses Agr Dep

A clause or phrase used as a subject is considered singular and is followed by a singular verb.

What you are looking for is in the closet.
To know birth and death is to know life.

Within a clause the verb agrees with its subject, but when the subject is a relative pronoun it takes its number from its antecedent. In a few types of sentences, therefore, the number of the verb form chosen may reflect different meanings in different contexts. Compare:

The court is concerned mainly with the group of delinquent children responsible for the vandalism. John is one of those children, who *seems* unaffected by punishment.

The courts have to deal with many different types of children. John is one of those children who *seem* unaffected by punishment.

The writer must be sure that the verb form reflects the intended meaning.

ORIGINAL

My father was one of the many businessmen who was ruined by the depression.

[*The subject of* was ruined *is* who, *which almost certainly is intended to refer to* businessmen *and thus is plural.*]

REVISION

My father was one of the many businessmen who were ruined by the depression.

[*The plural form* were *replaces the singular* was; *only in an unusual context would* one *be the antecedent of* who.]

17m Agreement with Modified or Separated Subjects Agr Mod

When a subject is modified, a writer may carelessly mistake the modifier for part of a compound subject or may make the verb agree with the modifier rather than the subject. Colloquially, however, a subject modified by a prepositional phrase is sometimes used as a compound: *The captain with most of the crew were standing on deck.*

ORIGINAL

Orrie, with his little sister, were squatting in the middle of the puppy pen.
[Orrie *is a singular subject, modified by* with his little sister.]

Jim, as well as his brothers, plan to enter the university.

REVISION

Orrie, with his little sister, was squatting in the middle of the puppy pen.
[*The singular* was *has replaced the plural* were.]

Jim, as well as his brothers, plans to enter the university.

Sometimes the subject and verb are so widely separated by modifiers or other material that the writer forgets the number of the subject.

ORIGINAL

The employer of all sorts of people, highly trained scientists, ignorant laborers, callow youths, and lovesick stenographers, have to have wide understanding of human nature.
[*The subject,* employer, *requires a singular verb.*]

REVISION

The employer of all sorts of people, highly trained scientists, ignorant laborers, callow youths, and lovesick stenographers, has to have wide understanding of human nature.
[*The singular* has *has replaced the plural* have.]

Agr N Agreement of Nouns in Number 17n

When one noun refers to another, clarity requires that it agree with it in number.

ORIGINAL

Women are treated as an equal, however, when they work in the fields.
[*Several women can scarcely be treated as one equal.*]

The men wear long robes, which somewhat resemble a dress.

REVISION

Women are treated as equals, however, when they work in the fields.

The men wear long robes which somewhat resemble dresses.

Exercise 17

A. Combine each of the pairs of clauses below into five different sentences, varying meanings or shades of meaning by varying conjunctions or conjunctive adverbs. You may change the order of the clauses and make necessary changes in forms of the words.

1. Mary asked me to go skating   I developed a headache
2. I slid down the drain pipe   I heard somebody scream upstairs
3. I have fast reaction time   I like sports
4. I have to ride the subway to school   I study the advertising on the car cards
5. The boat heeled over   He worked at the sails

B. If the italicized function word in each of the sentences below is faulty, choose a better form, or revise the sentence.

1. He told me to move into the light *so as* he could watch the expression on my face.
2. I wrote a letter *in regards to* the advertisements for hair tonic.
3. Wilma liked to swim in the warm pool, *while* Joan preferred the invigorating water of the ocean.
4. *Being as* I have never learned to play bridge, I do not enjoy Mrs. Blackwell's parties.
5. *While* I do not like to complain about my guests, I do object to anybody who comes in with his shoes dripping mud.
6. I had expected to love Venice, *and* when I got there I could not stand the smell of the canals.
7. Mother always said that childhood is *when* you have the best time.
8. *While* I don't usually eat green onions, I sometimes do.
9. The reason I do not approve of federal aid for education is *because* we must protect our liberties.
10. We spent our vacation in the Big Smokies, *and* we knew it would be cool there.

C. Revise the following sentences, correcting any examples of illogical word reference.

1. Many students spend all their time in extracurricular activities, and I am glad I am not in that category.
2. His long punts and accurate passes, qualities which made him feared by all opponents, helped us to win the championship.

3. He was always boasting about his conquests in love, and I have never admired this characteristic.

4. The girls decided to restrict membership in the club to members of sororities, an attitude which seemed to me undemocratic.

5. Of all the people in our neighborhood, the sadness of one case affected me most.

6. The field of chemistry is exciting for anyone who undertakes this great adventure into science.

7. All the men were looked on as a brother in the camp.

8. An important part of a student's life, especially a man, is activity in student government.

9. College, the word dreamed about by so many high school students, was not what I had expected it to be.

10. The other secretaries all conspired to give me the most unpleasant jobs, aspects I had not anticipated.

11. I believe that Hoover Dam, which is the topic for my paper, is one of the greatest sources of power in the world.

12. On inspecting the engineering field you will find that not only are improvements made but inventions are brought forth by these gallant young explorers.

13. Although there are many faults in the unicameral system of legislation, there are not enough to make it an unprofitable change.

14. If the state chose to give money to public and parochial schools alike, nobody could criticize it for this affair.

15. Some feel that they do not have the ability to study, and others feel that they have better things to do. The latter include marriage, traveling, or work.

D. Revise the following sentences so that all pronouns or other reference words refer clearly to logical antecedents:

1. Television requires little mental activity, and in my opinion this is what we need.

2. When Admetis discovered that the veiled woman was his wife, it certainly had a significant effect on his thoughts.

3. Some of Cortez's horses were so outstanding in battle that it caused the Indians to consider them gods.

4. In the pterodactyl the hind legs were poorly developed, and thus we do not see any of them walking or crawling around on land.

5. If anything wrong has been done, I hope they put them in jail.

6. In the time of Shakespeare there existed much anti-Jewish prejudice and their religion set them apart from the rest of the people.

7. The chest had been her mother's, and she remembered the sorrow she had felt when she left for America.

8. The only used trailers we found for sale had been lived in by families with children which had been all scratched up.

9. At the club they said that all matches had been postponed.

10. The children had scattered small pieces of bread among the ducks which they had been eating all afternoon.

11. Later several experimenters added more keys to the clarinet to give it range, and this is why its popularity increased.

12. Glass-making flourished in very early times; it was made and used by the Egyptians before 1400 B.C.

13. In the first chapter of Miss Langer's book she talks about symbols.

14. Too often people make the mistake of thinking that education is not as valuable as experience, and that is why I am in school.

15. Macbeth fears that Banquo knows that he has killed Duncan, the king, and this necessitated his death.

E. Notice carefully the occurrences of *this* in the paragraph below, and revise so as to remove any vague reference.

Acetylene is usually only mildly poisonous and it is commonly available; this makes it a handy way of getting rid of vermin. It has other properties aside from being poisonous and convenient, and this is not always remembered. A Swedish garage owner recently provided an example of this. While he was driving to work, he became aware that a rat was chewing the cushion of the rear seat of his car, and hearing this, he stopped to kill the rat. This did not help much, because the rat scrambled under the back of the seat, which could not be removed although the seat could have been. Knowing this, the garage owner drove to his place of business, determined to poison or to smoke out the rat. This was sensible, and the garage owner got out his acetylene welding kit with a good fresh tank of gas, thinking this would kill the rat or get him out. It got him out. Shortly after the car was filled with gas, the garage owner saw his roof flying seventy-five feet into the air, this presumably being due to a short circuit in the automobile which had ignited the acetylene. Along with the roof went much of the owner's automobile, and parts of five others. This was not the only damage the owner saw around him. Six men had to be hospitalized because this was so unexpected that people stood still in the street staring while pieces of garage fell on them. The rat has not been seen since. Neither has the cushion. In spite of this, the garage owner is not taking out a patent on his rat exterminator.

F. In the following sentences select for each blank the appropriate present tense form of the verb in parentheses:

1. A sales lot full of old cars, some with battered fenders and bashed grills, some badly needing paint, and some with broken glass and missing chrome, _____ (*resemble*) a portable junk yard.

2. Neither Darwin nor his critics today _____ (*understand*) the full implication of the theory of evolution.

3. In the United States, everyone who _____ (*want*) an education can have it.

4. Clarence is one of those men who never _____ (*do*) tomorrow what can be put off until next week.

5. Clark, with all his little brothers and sisters, _____ (*be*) trying to squeeze through the closing subway door.

6. Each of them, in spite of the most stubborn resistance to education, _____ (*find*) that he cannot entirely escape learning something.

7. If either of you _____ (*like*) the sweater, you can have it.

8. If either Helen or Judy _____ (*like*) the sweater, I will give it up.

9. He was one of those lucky soldiers who _____ (*seem*) always to be where there is no battle.

10. There _____ (*be*), after all is said and done and your life has mostly run away, only two rewards which make life worth living.

G. In the following sentences choose a pronoun to agree in number with the collective noun which is its antecedent:

1. The herd of wild burros follows (its, their) path up the canyon.

2. The gang held (its, their) regular meeting Wednesday after school.

3. The Chamber of Commerce cast (its, their) ballots for various candidates for beauty queen.

4. The team took (its, their) positions about the field.

5. The Security Council will endeavor to reach (its, their) decision today.

6. The convention of nurses kept busy brushing (its, their) respective teeth.

7. The fraternity bowling team has just won (its, their) first victory.

8. The cordon of policemen tightened (its, their) net around the hide-out.

9. The committee approved the minutes of (its, their) last meeting.

10. If one is in a national park (you, he, they) can find drinking water if (you, he, they) will ask a ranger.

Style

A good style must, first of all, be clear. . . . It must be appropriate.
A good style must have an air of novelty, while concealing its art.
Style is the man himself.
He that will write well in any tongue . . . must speak as the common people do, but think as the wise men do.
Let your matter run before your words.
A man's style is as much a part of him as his face, his figure, or the rhythm of his pulse.
All styles are good save the boresome kind.
The style of an author should be the image of his mind, but the choice and command of language is the fruit of exercise.
Style is the physiognomy of the mind.
There is no way of writing well and also writing easily.
I confess to you I love a nobility and amplitude of style, provided it never sweeps beyond its subject.
The secret of the style of the great Greek and Roman authors is that it is the perfection of good sense.
A man's style in any art should be like his dress—it should attract as little attention as possible.

Since the dawn of sophisticated culture men have been talking about style in writing; the first two quotations above are from Aristotle, and most of them are more than a century old. The quotations suggest that thinkers have offered various solutions to the problem of style, but they suggest, also, some general agreement about the nature of style in writing. Style is the name we give to the particular combination of characteristics that gives any piece of writing its distinction, that differentiates it from other writing. Style is the "character" of writing. Style therefore includes almost everything that we have discussed in this book and most of what is to be discussed later—especially the material on language in Sections 20-21. It is partly as a kind of summary, then, that we here look at some of the general topics that a writer must consider as he develops a style.

One of the statements quoted at the beginning of this chapter is Arthur Schopenhauer's "Style is the physiognomy of the mind."

Although it cannot be taken too literally, the statement emphasizes the central characteristic of a good style: it has something to say. Fundamental in style are content, matter, meaning, information; obviously, to some degree, style is the man. For this reason, many intelligent, mentally alert, well educated people write interestingly, even brilliantly, without ever having studied language or composition formally. The habits of mind that produce clear thinking also promote a good writing style. Many a scientist writes well, not so much because he has studied writing as because he has studied bugs or atoms. For the student, therefore, the preceding chapters of this book are almost all fundamental to the cultivation of a good style, because they are concerned mainly with the handling of content—finding a theme idea, collecting information to develop it, thinking logically about it, and so on. But some scientists who know much about bugs or atoms also write abominably. A good style requires knowledge of a subject; it also requires knowledge of language—what it is, how it works, how it can be used. Style is the man, but a good style is the wise man using words and sentences so that they reveal him faithfully.

A writing style develops, of course, in many ways, but especially from reading. Renaissance writers like John Lyly acquired much of their ornate styles from reading Latin; nineteenth century writers often reveal their early reading in the Bible. Probably the best single thing a student can do to improve his writing is to read. In fact, he can profitably read writers whom he admires and make a conscious attempt to learn from them, analyzing their sentences, their diction, their tone. Writers often learn by direct imitation, learning what they can from another writer and then going on to create their own styles. Chaucer, for instance, as a young man admired the French poets of his day and imitated them until he could do as well as they in their own manner—in fact, the French poets like Machaud whom he imitated are now mainly remembered because they influenced Chaucer. Then he found out about the great Italians of his time, Boccaccio and Petrarch, and imitated them. But he did not become truly himself until he had outgrown both his French and Italian teachers and had begun to write in his own style. Robert Louis Stevenson describes how he "played the sedulous ape"; that is, he imitated writer after writer, deliberately, until he had mastered their ways of writing. "That," Stevenson concludes, "is the way to learn to write . . . Before he can tell what cadences he truly prefers, the student should have tried all that are possible; before he can choose and preserve a fitting key of words, he should long have practiced the literary scales."

"Perhaps," Stevenson goes on, "I hear someone cry out: But this is not the way to be original! It is not; nor is there any way but to be born so." Originality is a virtue much admired in writing, but a student cannot write originally by imitating what seems clever in some other writer. Trying to make characters talk like those of Damon Runyon or Hemingway will not in itself produce originality, nor will attempts to reproduce the superficial characteristics of an unusual style—to omit periods or capital letters, to write in incomplete sentences, to affect nonstandard diction. Originality is not mere novelty or trickery. Especially unimpressive are old favorites of student writing such as the character sketch of "my best friend" which turns out in the end to be a description of a dog or a horse, or the theme that spends five hundred words telling why the writer could not find a topic, or the narrative that ends with the revelation "and then I woke up." Most students, however, are born with originality, at least with individuality. The originality emerges in writing when the student thinks and learns enough about his topic to make the ideas he presents his own. Tricks and devices are likely to be less original than clearly conceived material presented with sincerity, directness, and simplicity.

A good style, then, emerges primarily as the writer reads discerningly, develops and controls his thoughts, learns standard patterns for handling ideas in sentences and larger units of composition. Efforts to develop a style mechanically or artificially almost always fail. A few general approaches to problems of style, however, can profitably be considered. Section 18 considers mainly some devices for emphasis, particularly as they affect sentence structure. Section 19 considers the importance to style of point of view, tone, and appropriateness.

Emphasis and Style

*For
Guide to Revision,
see page 320.*

The skillful blending of rhetorical devices can give writing appropriate emphasis.

Exploding bombs are notably emphatic, but they do little of the work of the world and produce little of lasting beauty. Good writing seldom requires bombs. Forceful prose gains its power not from unlimited fireworks but from steady use of standard patterns with variations to produce special effects when they are appropriate. Excessive or unwarranted variation has the effect of no variation at all. Some stylistic devices, however—variations in sentence length, structure, and rhythm—can strengthen writing.

Sentence Length 18-1

The most obvious difference among sentences is that some are longer or shorter than others. Similarly the most obvious difference between modern American prose and the prose of two centuries ago is that the modern tends to run to shorter sentences, although the apparent difference is deceptive because habits of punctuation have changed so that writers now often use periods where their predecessors used colons or semicolons. Even in contemporary prose, however, sentences vary in length as one can observe by comparing the following two paragraphs from Ernest Hemingway's *A Moveable Feast* which concern the American writer F. Scott Fitzgerald and his wife Zelda at a time when she was near a nervous breakdown. Hemingway and Fitzgerald, being unaware of Zelda's illness, assumed she was just behaving badly and drinking too much.

Zelda had a very bad hangover. They had been up on Montmarte the night before and had quarreled because Scott did not want to get drunk. He had decided, he told me, to work hard and not to drink and Zelda was treating him as though he were a kill-joy or a spoilsport. Those were the two words she used to him and there was recrimination and Zelda would say, "I did not. I did no such thing. It's not true, Scott." Later she would seem to recall something and would laugh happily.

Sentences are short, and even the longer sentences are mainly short sentence patterns strung together. The writing is choppy, but intentionally so. The most staccato passage is that quoted from Zelda, and the style of the whole is appropriate as a reflection of the character of the conversation behind the scene; the style itself contributes something to the meaning of the passage.

That Hemingway does not always write this way is clear from the previous paragraph:

> Scott Fitzgerald invited us to have lunch with his wife Zelda and his little daughter at the furnished flat they had rented at 14 rue Tilsitt. I cannot remember much about the flat except that it was gloomy and airless and that there was nothing in it that seemed to belong to them except Scott's first books bound in light blue leather with the titles in gold. Scott also showed us a large ledger with all of the stories he had published listed in it year after year with the prices he had received for them and also the amounts received for any motion picture sales, and the sales and royalties of his books. They were all noted as carefully as the log of a ship and Scott showed them to both of us with impersonal pride as though he were the curator of a museum. Scott was nervous and hospitable and he showed us his accounts of his earnings as though they had been the view. There was no view.

The sentences are longer, more subtle in structure and more crowded in detail than those of the other paragraph. The only notably short sentence is the final one, and it is short for a purpose. It provides a kind of epigrammatic close, giving the paragraph a sudden, dramatic, ironic turn at the end, establishing the attitude of the entire paragraph, the disapproval of Fitzgerald's display of shallow pride. Concentrating the final blow in four words accents the shock.

Differences in sentence length obviously affect style, but the differences do not occur because writers have consciously set out to write either long or short sentences or because they have consciously mixed the lengths to gain some kind of variety. Sentence length depends on the material to be presented, the audience addressed, and the purposes of the writer. Sometimes sharp changes in sentence length can produce special effects; short sentences can nail an idea down, accent a climax, provide a transition, or concentrate attention.

Sentence Variety 18-2

Since sentence length normally depends on what is said to whom and why, and since these needs vary, adequate sentence variety usually follows naturally. The notion that variety is inevitably a virtue, that student writers should consciously set out to regulate sentence length or to avoid repeating a subject or a structure, does more to muddy writing (see Section 5) than to develop a style. The expository writer, particularly, seldom needs the kinds of special effects Hemingway employs in narrative fiction; exposition is likely to go along without monotony but with no dramatic attempts to provide variety. Consider the following, for example, the conclusion of an introductory section in a book on literary scholarship:

> Despite these formidable barriers—the necessity for discovering authentic records in the first place, and then peeling off the successive layers of embroidery with which later generations have adorned them—the scholar persists in trying to find out the truth. From the time that Chaucer, according to a contemporary legal document, was accused "de rapto meo" by a lady with the enchanting name of Cecily de Chaumpaigne, literary biography has been thickly sprinkled with ladies whose relationships with men of letters require exegesis. "Cherchez la femme" is a motto of the literary detective as much as it is of the fictional criminologist; and scholars would not be human if they did not betray a certain zest in running down the often delectable details. But they must draw a careful line between the episode which, however sensational it may have been, lacks real relevance to the literary productions of an author, and that which can be an important clue to his personality or a profound influence on his later life and his work. In the following pages we shall see an example of each type.
> —RICHARD D. ALTICK, *The Scholar Adventurers*

The sentences, except the last, are of middle length, not notably different in structure. The last sentence, making a transition, is appropriately short. But like most modern expository prose the passage has adequate variety, which develops naturally from the variety in the material.

Emphasis and Sound; Sentence Rhythm 18-3

Most modern prose is intended primarily for silent reading, but sound patterns echo even in silent reading and a sense of underlying intonation or rhythm is part of total comprehension. A device like alliteration, for example, the repetition of initial sounds (*flight of fancy*), may bind a phrase together but may also become obtrusive with overuse. An unexpected rhyme may call attention to itself (*He couldn't brook the book's attitude*) and hinder understanding. Some writers even avoid combinations of sounds that are hard to pronounce. Certainly the rhythm of prose, the pattern of accents in the sentences, is part of stylistic effect. Notice, for instance, the following from a seventeenth century prose writer.

How all the kinds of Creatures, not only in their own bulks, but with a competency of food and sustenance, might be preserved in one Ark, and within the extent of three hundred Cubits, to a reason that rightly examines it, will appear very feasible. There is another secret, not contained in the Scripture, which is more hard to comprehend, and put the honest Father to the refuge of a Miracle; and that is, not only how the distinct pieces of the World, and divided Islands, should be first planted by men, but inhabited by Tigers, Panthers, and Bears. —THOMAS BROWNE, *Religio Medici*

The passage, in the rhythmic style common in its time, has almost the regularity of verse. Modern prose tends to be less mannered, less regular, but tends also to cultivate subtlety and variety of rhythm. The skillful writer has developed an ear for prose as for poetry. The late President John F. Kennedy, addressing the Canadian Parliament, probably did not analyze the rhythms in the following very carefully, but he certainly knew what he was doing:

Geography has made us neighbors. History has made us friends. Economics has made us partners. And necessity has made us allies. Those whom nature hath so joined together, let no man put asunder.

Obviously, there are two sorts of rhythm here. The first four sentences are short, blunt, and highly parallel. Ordinarily so skillful a writer as Kennedy would never use four childishly simple sentences one after the other, but here he had a purpose. He wanted those four salient facts to strike his hearers like blows, and probably he wanted the rhythm to become just a bit monotonous before he changed it. When he does change the rhythm the effect is dramatic, and partly because the new rhythm is a parody of the marriage ceremony, as though he were the officiating priest solemnizing the sacrament joining two great nations.

The next day Kennedy said essentially the same thing again, but he said it in a different way and with different rhythms.

In the effort to build a continent of economic growth and solidarity, in an effort to build a hemisphere of freedom and hope, in an effort to build an

Atlantic community of strength and unity of purpose, and in an effort to build a world of lasting peace and justice, Canada and the United States must be found, and I am certain will be found, standing where they have always stood, together.

In a sense this sentence is like the earlier passage; the four parallel clauses beginning with *in* suggest the four staccato sentences, but here instead of establishing something the rhythm seems to suggest that the speaker is building up to something. He is; the final word, *together,* climaxes and clinches the whole.

Detailed study of rhythm, an aspect of rhetoric, is too elaborate and difficult for this book, but even a beginning writer can be aware that rhythm is important in prose and can train his ear to be sensitive to the cadences of good writing.

Emphasis Through Structure 18-4

A kernel sentence, composed of a subject, verb, and sometimes complement, serves most of the utilitarian needs of language—to greet friends, get food, ask directions. Adult communication concerned with complex problems, however, relies on longer sentences composed of various parts. Inevitably the parts must be organized, must develop in accordance with some pattern. Two patterns are natural: (1) The kernel can be completed at once, with various modifying and coordinated elements following it; or (2) some elements of the kernel can be withheld while modifying elements build up until the final word closes at once the kernel and the sentence. Compare the following:

> Tolerance, good temper, and sympathy are no longer enough in a world which is rent by religious and racial persecution, in a world where ignorance rules, and science, who ought to have ruled, plays the subservient pimp.
>
> In a world which is rent by religious and racial persecution, in a world where ignorance rules, and science, who ought to have ruled, plays the subservient pimp, tolerance, good temper, and sympathy are no longer enough.

The first version, with subordinate material appended to an initial kernel, exemplifies what we have called the *cumulative sentence;* E. M. Forster wrote the sentence this way. The second version, changed so that modifiers appear first and the kernel is postponed for a final climax, exemplifies the *periodic sentence.*

Patterns, of course, can be combined, and not all sentences

313

follow models like these; but the sentences illustrate two general kinds of emphasis characteristic of complex English sentences. For a language like English, relying heavily on word order, the cumulative sentence may provide the natural emphasis—making a statement and then appending qualifications. The cumulative sentence seems to have grown naturally in English; the author of *Beowulf* used it extensively, as did Chaucer and other early writers. The periodic sentence, however, also has a long tradition in English, fostered by the school rhetoric founded on classical Latin and Greek. Both types of sentence—the cumulative sentence, apparently native, and the periodic sentence, assiduously cultivated—have uses in modern writing.

18-5 The Periodic Sentence and Special Devices

Classical rhetoric mainly described oral prose as exemplified in ornate speeches for formal occasions or persuasive speeches addressed to judges or political audiences. Since Latin and Greek seldom used word order or position for grammar, classical orators could place words anywhere they pleased for emphasis, and accordingly orators devised what were called "colors of rhetoric," cultivating figurative language and elaborate displays of word patterns. These patterns, including balance, contrast, climax, and the tricolon, fitted readily into the periodic sentence. English and American orators have imitated such sentences; notice the following from Lincoln's Gettysburg address:

> But, in a larger sense, we cannot dedicate—we cannot consecrate—we cannot hallow this ground.

With a tricolon, three parallel elements—*cannot dedicate, cannot consecrate, cannot hallow*—the sentence builds a climax from human dedication to divine hallowing, closing sense and structure at once. The next sentence is balanced as well as essentially periodic, as the following printing suggests:

The world will	little note	
(nor)	long remember	what we say here
(but)		
it can never forget		what they did here.

The oration comes to a crashing conclusion with a period that builds through a tricolon and a tricolon within a tricolon:

```
that we here highly resolve
    that these dead shall not have died in vain
    that this nation, under God, shall have a new birth of freedom
    (and)
    that government        of the people
                           by the people
                           for the people
                           shall not perish from the earth
```

The longer sentence quoted from Kennedy (see 18-3) makes similar use of balance, developing to a climax as a periodic sentence.

Most modern writers do not compose orations, particularly not orations modeled upon the classics, but notice the following from Macauley's review of Boswell's biography of Samuel Johnson:

> Johnson grown old, Johnson in the fullness of his fame and in the enjoyment of a competent fortune, is better known to us than any other man in history. Everything about him, his coat, his wig, his figure, his face, his scrofula, his St. Vitus's dance, his rolling walk, his blinking eye, the outward signs which clearly marked his approbation of his dinner, his insatiable appetite for fish sauce and veal pie with plums, his inextinguishable thirst for tea, his trick of touching the posts as he walked, his mysterious practice of treasuring up scraps of orange peel, his morning slumbers, his midnight disputations, his contortions, his mutterings, his gruntings, his puffings, his vigorous, acute, and ready eloquence, his sarcastic wit, his vehemence, his insolence, his fits of tempestuous rage, his queer inmates, old Mr. Levitt and blind Mrs. Williams, the cat Hodge and the negro Frank, all are as familiar to us as the objects by which we have been surrounded from childhood.

Macaulay was admired for sentences like these, and they do assort numerous details into a neat order, but most modern prose is more relaxed. Restrained use of parallelism continues, however, and good modern writers find use for the periodic structure, as in the following description of the birth of an Americanism:

> When head, wings, and claws were added by Gilbert Stuart, the celebrated painter, the result was by a stroke of genius called a *gerrymander*.

The Cumulative Sentence   18-6

Nevertheless, periodic sentences, even sentences as inconspicuous as this one, do not do the work of most modern paragraphs, however useful they may be for variety and for special effects. For whatever reasons—and the reasons are probably rooted in the nature of the English language and in the needs of modern society—good American writing relies heavily on cumulative sentences.

Such structures appear readily in fiction; consider the following:

> He took all his pain and what was left of his strength and his long gone pride and he put it against the fish's agony and the fish came over onto his side and swam gently on his side, his bill almost touching the planking of the skiff and started to pass the boat, long, deep, wide, silver and barred with purple and interminable in the water.
>
> —ERNEST HEMINGWAY, *The Old Man and the Sea*

This sentence carries with it a great weight of detail, but it does so with ease and with no sense of strain. Instead of building to a climax the sentence moves like waves, instinct with life, and with crests and valleys. Sentences likes these, because they can move in varied rhythms, team well together. Notice the following paragraph from later in the same book:

> The two sharks closed together and as he saw the one nearest him open his jaws and sink them into the silver side of the fish, he raised the club high and brought it down heavy and slamming onto the top of the shark's broad head. He felt the rubbery solidity as the club came down. But he felt the rigidity of bone too and he struck the shark once more hard across the point of the nose as he slid down from the fish.

These sentences could, of course, be cast into periodic form, but a succession of formally wrought periods would ill consort with the story of an old man catching a fish. Hemingway's sentences not only carry the detail better, and move more easily from the sharks to the club, to the man, and back again to the sharks, but they suggest better the time and the place, the temper of a tale more concerned with suggesting than with persuading.

Similar structures serve, also, for modern nonfictional prose. The following describes a teenage delinquent on trial for having participated in the gang murder of a helpless old man:

> It was not hard to see evil in Jack Koslow, the oldest defendant. So manifest was his sickness of soul that he could have posed as one of the tormenting demons that populate Hieronymus Bosch's vision of hell. His skin had been described as "sallow," but that gave no hint of its dead green-whiteness, in eerie and surprising conjunction with thick hair that was dark red and wholly without shine, receding from his forehead in a high crest. His features were delicately ugly; a long thin curved nose with a sharply articulated ridge; a thin, downturned, and usually derisive mouth, lips colorless, the upper extending slightly above the lower; weak but bony chin; a white, undeveloped neck. His eyes were strangest of all. They were dark brown and seemed pupilless, and their look was hooded as if by a transparent extra lid. When Koslow walked in and out each day manacled to his guard, you could see

how tall and thin he was, and how his narrow head hung forward from his body like a condor's.   —MARYA MANNES, *But Will It Sell?*

The fourth sentence, the one beginning "His features were delicately ugly," may profitably be compared with the sentence quoted above from Macaulay describing Samuel Johnson, which begins, "Everything about him, his coat, his wig, his figure, his face, his scrofula," continues for a half a page of typewritten copy, and closes, "are as familiar to us as the objects by which we have been surrounded from childhood." Of course this conclusion is not true; nobody since Boswell has known Johnson that well, but even if we concede Macaulay his innocent hyperbole, the fact remains that his periodic conclusion was concocted for the structure of his sentence, and the whole long list of Johnsonian qualities impresses us as brought together for effect. Macaulay sounds as though he were composing in his study, which doubtless he was; Miss Mannes sounds as though she was sitting in the court room, acutely examining Koslow feature by feature, detail by revealing detail. We believe her, as we do not believe Macaulay, partly because we sense that we see these horrible scraps of evidence as she saw them. Yet she achieves a climax at least as devastating as was Macaulay's; the sentence closes with Koslow's "white, undeveloped neck," and we realize that this young scavenger upon the body of society has never worked, and that the aimlessness of his life has something to do with his congenital evil. These effects of Miss Mannes are deliberate; the "white, undeveloped neck" foreshadows the conclusion of the paragraph, when we see how Koslow's "narrow head hung forward from his body like a condor's." Such climaxes are the more effective because they are not flaunted as they would be in periodic sentences, but are slightly veiled beneath the shifting patterns of cumulative structures.

Inversion   18-7

Some less elaborate rhetorical devices have had their uses, and still have. One of the commonest is inversion; a word is drawn out of its normal place in the sentence, and since modern English makes much use of normal order, the change, even a slight change, strikes us forcibly. The following provides an extreme example:

> By foreign hands thy dying eyes were clos'd,
> By foreign hands thy decent limbs compos'd,

> By foreign hands thy humble grave adorn'd,
> By strangers honoured, and by strangers mourn'd!

Usual order is changed in each clause in a curious way so that each involves a kind of double inversion. The usual pattern would be:

Subject	*Verb*	*Complement*
Foreign hands	closed	thy dying eyes.

The poet, Alexander Pope, has followed two procedures for varying word order. He has reversed subject and object, making the verb passive:

Thy dying eyes were closed by foreign hands.

Then he has gone a step further and moved the modifier, which would have been the subject of the action in a conventional sentence, into the position of emphasis at the beginning. The result is stress on the initiator of the action, *foreign hands*—even more stress than normal word order would provide. Repetitions of this pattern throughout the clauses multiply the stress. The first three clauses build on the importance of *by foreign hands* so that the meaning of *by strangers* is sharp and clear. The result is that the reader remembers most vividly, even in the presence of death itself, the circumstance that only strangers were present at the death.

Emphasis so strong as this would not be appropriate in most prose, but unusual order may enforce continuity (see 5-3) or provide special emphasis, as in the following passage from a monologue in Virginia Woolf's novel *The Waves:*

"I have signed my name," said Louis, "already twenty times. I, and again I, and again I. Clear, firm, unequivocal, there it stands, my name. Clear-cut and unequivocal am I too. Yet a vast inheritance of experience is packed in me. I have lived thousands of years. I am like a worm that has eaten its way through the wood of a very old oak beam.

18-8 Emphasis by Subordination

Periodic and cumulative sentences, as examples above indicate, differ in the location of subordinated material. The periodic sentence keeps subordinated material toward the opening of the sentence; the cumulative sentence tends to append subordinate material. The writer's decisions about what to subordinate, therefore, can regulate emphasis both by influencing structure and by influencing meanings. Subordination (see 3-2 and 16-4) offers the writer a useful means for combining the following relatively simple ideas:

I was twelve years old.
I got my first long pants.
I took the girl next door to the movies.

Most obviously, perhaps, the first idea might be subordinated to the others as an indication of the time, with the last two ideas sharing equally the stress of the sentence:

When I was twelve years old, I got my first long pants and took the girl next door to the movies.

A change in the subordinating word would vary both meaning and emphasis.

Although I was only twelve years old, I got my first long pants and took the girl next door to the movies.

Centering attention on the second idea could produce a sentence like the following:

Since I was now twelve years old and about to take the girl next door to the movies, I was allowed to buy my first long pants.

Or both the first two ideas might be subordinate:

When I was twelve years old and in my first long pants, I took the girl next door to the movies.

The trip to the movies becomes the event which the writer wants primarily to talk about, and the acquisition of the pants drops out.

Subordination should vary with the sentences which precede and follow. The last version above, for example, might be appropriate in a paragraph narrating a story about the friendship of a boy and girl. The context might suggest even wider variations in the pattern of subordination. Consider:

When I had my first long pants and had taken the girl next door to the movies, I was twelve years old.

This unusual emphasis might be logical if the preceding sentence had read:

The actual date of my twelfth birthday meant nothing to me.

Or a different preceding sentence might suggest the wisdom of a parallel pattern of subordination following it.

At the age of eleven, I tore my knickers trying to catch a toad with which I hoped to frighten the girls at the Sunday School picnic. At twelve, I wore my first long pants to take the girl next door to the movies.

The second sentence fits the pattern of the first, draws the contrast between the events, and enforces the continuity (see 5-3).

Em

18 Guide to Revision

Revise for emphasis and variety, using devices appropriate to the material and the purposes of the writer.

Modern English prose can be powerful and varied, and it usually gains its effects through skillful use of standard sentences, especially the cumulative sentence. Often recasting a sentence by grouping subordinated materials, sometimes also varying subordination, will clarify both sense and emphasis.

ORIGINAL

Karen, because she was so changeable and was sometimes openhearted and friendly but sometimes selfish and calculating, was a source of continuing bafflement to me, although she did have a way that I found completely charming, in spite of being uncertain of herself.

REVISION

Karen baffled me, sometimes openhearted and friendly, sometimes selfish and calculating, always uncertain of herself, and yet occasionally exhibiting a warm charm that I found completely disarming.

[*With a clear opening statement followed by cumulating details, the sentence falls into a pattern.*]

Em a   Inverted Sentences   18a

Shifting subject, verb, or complement from its usual position can achieve special effects, but unless these effects are justified, normal word order should remain. Inversion not required by the context or warranted by special intentions of the writer makes writing confusing, falsely rhetorical, or affected.

ORIGINAL

REVISION

We were never happy about the climate in New York. Cold were the winters; hot were the summers.

[*This inversion, unless the writer is attempting some kind of half-humorous exaggeration, sounds absurd*]

We were never happy about the climate in New York. The winters were cold, the summers hot.

[*Usual order is more direct, and there is no artificially induced special emphasis.*]

I was only a child, inexperienced and trusting. Little did I know what was in store for me.

[*The second sentence is trite, but the staleness is obvious because the inversion is unwarranted. The unusual word order makes the sentence overdramatic.*]

I was only an inexperienced and trusting child, unaware of what was in store for me.

[*Restoration of usual word order removes most of the affectation from the sentences, although the reader is still suspicious of the significance attached to the facts.*]

Em b   Minor Words to Provide Emphasis   18b

Relatively unimportant words in key positions may provide false emphasis.

ORIGINAL

REVISION

This nation must return to the ideals which inspired its founding. Yes, we must re-examine our goals.

[*The insertion of words like* yes, *indeed, well, now can overemphasize insignificant parts of the sentence.*]

This nation must return to the ideals which inspired its founding. We must re-examine our goals.

[*Even with the* yes *omitted, the sentence is oratorical enough in its tone.*]

Well, first I thought I ought to see what was in the cave. Now, I was not really afraid to look, but I decided there was no hurry.

I thought I should first see what was in the cave, but although I was not really afraid to look, I decided there was no hurry.

18c   Rhetorical Questions   Em c

The rhetorical question is an inversion of regular sentence order
for the sake of emphasis, a statement in question form. Sometimes
the answer is assumed to be so obvious that the reader will supply
it automatically and will be convinced of the entire implied statement. Sometimes the writer supplies the answer. In either instance
the device—another favorite in oratory—provides strong emphasis
and should be used only when the situation warrants unusual stress.

ORIGINAL

There are five reasons for joining
a sorority in college. What are those
reasons? The first is. . . .

[*The question dramatizes a prosaic
statement, which should be clear without
repetition in inverted order.*]

REVISION

There are five reasons for joining
a sorority in college, of which the
first is. . . .

[*Omission of the rhetorical question
makes the emphasis more appropriate to
the meaning.*]

Exercise 18

A. Revise each of the sentences below, moving the italicized modifier to a
different position. Then explain any changes in meaning or emphasis
effected by the shift in word order.

1. The girl *with the broken arm* grabbed the new doll.
2. The children promised to *carefully* chew every bite.
3. *In complete confusion* the speaker finally found his audience.
4. *Happily* the old man watched the children singing.
5. The hill is not really pretty *because of the big rocks on it.*
6. We found the girl *breaking into the back room.*
7. He ordered them *at once* to dump the ammunition into the sea.
8. I decided I would get up *when my roommate threw a glass of water on me.*
9. The room looked filthier than any stable I had ever seen *by daylight.*
10. She *nearly* threw away all her diamonds.

B. Rewrite the following selection from a student theme, improving its style in any way you can and paying particular attention to opportunities for clarifying relations between ideas by subordination:

On the night of the flood four of us drove across the river away from home to see what damage had been done. We drove around on the other side for about an hour and a half. We finally decided to start home. We came back to the bridge. There was about three feet of water over the road. We had to get across for classes the next day, so we had to find some way to cross to the other side. After considerable debate we decided to drive across. We had gone about a fourth of the way and the ignition got wet. The car stalled in about two feet of water. The water started pouring in under the doors. The heat of the engine dried the ignition, and the car started again. We went about half way and stalled again. This time we were in about three feet of water. The water poured in. We talked about pushing the car across. The three boys got out and pushed. I steered. The water was deep, and so they could not push the car. They got back in. I thought maybe the water would get deeper. It was very exciting. The water was swift. Finally a large truck came in behind us. He pushed us across. We still could not start the car, and so we had to leave it. The water was still rising. We came back the next day. The car was still there and the water had not come to it again. We tried to start it. It would not start. We pushed the car for three or four blocks. It did not fire at all. We pushed it to a garage, and the mechanic said the carburetor was full of mud. The river water was very muddy in the flood. We left the car at the garage to be cleaned.

C. Revise for emphasis and clarify the faulty sentences in the following student theme; often sentences can appropriately be combined.

(1) When our Constitution was written, the thing foremost in the people's mind was to have freedom of speech. (2) People were tired of listening to the government tell them what to say and what not to say. (3) They had come over here to escape from a society where there were always government agents, and the people could be persecuted by them. (4) Town meetings were broken up unless the speakers were told by a government official exactly what to say.

(5) After the Constitution took effect, freedom of speech began to be used by the people in its true meaning. (6) Opinions could be voiced by anyone on any subject. (7) No longer did a person have to be afraid of landing in jail or getting deported from the United States. (8) Often there were soap-box speakers, and they stood on boxes in the streets or in the city squares and gave speeches. (9) Sometimes public officials were attacked by these speeches. (10) These speeches were finished without punishment by the speakers.

(11) It seems that nowadays nothing can be said by a citizen, or he will be in danger of being thrown in jail by the government. (12) If a person talks against our government or any high official in it, he may be labeled

a Communist. (13) I wish a different system could be found by the Government to enforce its laws. (14) Yes, what people say should not be used as evidence against them. (15) If it were not, there would be for us more of the kind of freedom of speech we used to have.

D. The following paragraph is the next one after the description of Koslow in 18-6, and the *his* in the first sentence refers to Koslow. Rewrite the paragraph in three ways: (1) using only short sentences, (2) using only long or relatively long periodic sentences, incorporating balance if you can, and (3) using only long, cumulative sentences. You need not rewrite sentences that fit the type you are using in any given paragraph; that is, the final sentence as Mannes wrote it is periodic and need not be changed in version (2) unless you want to. When you have written three versions of the paragraph, compare them with Mannes's original for their effects as pieces of writing, and embody your results in a written paragraph.

Melvin Mittman, seventeen, was physically his antithesis. His body was barrel-thick and strong, and his shoulders wide, his head square, his features blunt. He had an upturned, broad-based nose, small, thick-lashed eyes under glasses, dense hair growing low on his brow, and a strong round chin. Throughout the trial until the verdict, when he wept and buried his face in his hands, he was expressionless. You would not have picked him out of a group, as you would Koslow, as having something "wrong" with him; he seemed just stolid and enclosed. Yet where Koslow's hands were white and thin and smooth as a girl's, lacing and interlacing during the trial and drumming little dances, Mittman's hands, abnormally short and thick, with hair on the fingers, made one inevitably imagine them pounding flesh.

E. As the sense for sentence patterns has become stronger in English, writing has become more economical. The following, from Chapter 2 of Exodus in the King James Version of the Bible, is the famous story of the birth of Moses, which followed the order by Pharaoh that all male Hebrew children be killed. The writing represents good English prose of about 350 years ago. Retell the story as best you can in modern English. Then compare the versions, noticing where you have been able to be briefer and terser than the original by omitting parts of constructions which the authors of the King James Version thought essential.

1 And there went a man of the house of Levi, and took to wife a daughter of Levi.

2 And the woman conceived, and bare a son: and when she saw him that he was a goodly child, she hid him three months.

3 And when she could not longer hide him, she took for him an ark of bulrushes, and daubed it with slime and with pitch, and put the child therein; and she laid it in the flags by the river's brink.

4   And his sister stood afar off, to wit what would be done to him.

5   And the daughter of Pharaoh came down to wash herself at the river; and her maidens walked along by the river's side: and when she saw the ark among the flags, she sent her maid to fetch it.

6   And when she had opened it, she saw the child: and, behold, the babe wept. And she had compassion on him, and said, This is one of the Hebrews' children.

7   Then said his sister to Pharaoh's daughter, Shall I go and call to thee a nurse of the Hebrew women, that she may nurse the child for thee?

8   And Pharaoh's daughter said to her, Go. And the maid went and called the child's mother.

9   And Pharaoh's daughter said unto her, Take this child away, and nurse it for me, and I will give thee thy wages. And the woman took the child, and nursed it.

10   And the child grew, and she brought him unto Pharaoh's daughter, and he became her son. And she called his name Moses: and she said, Because I drew him out of the water.

11   And it came to pass in those days, when Moses was grown, that he went out unto his brethren, and looked on their burdens: and he spied an Egyptian smiting a Hebrew, one of his brethren.

12   And he looked this way and that way, and when he saw that there was no man, he slew the Egyptian, and hid him in the sand.

13   And when he went out the second day, behold, two men of the Hebrews strove together: and he said to him that did the wrong, Wherefore smitest thou thy fellow?

14   And he said, Who made thee a prince and a judge over us? intendest thou to kill me, as thou killedst the Egyptian? And Moses feared, and said, Surely this thing is known.

15   Now when Pharaoh heard this thing, he sought to slay Moses. But Moses fled from the face of Pharaoh, and dwelt in the land of Midian: and he sat down by a well.

16   Now the priest of Midian had seven daughters: and they came and drew water, and filled the troughs to water their father's flock.

17   And the shepherds came and drove them away: but Moses stood up and helped them, and watered their flock.

18   And when they came to Reuel their father, he said, How is it that ye are come so soon to-day?

19   And they said, An Egyptian delivered us out of the hand of the shepherds, and also drew water enough for us, and watered the flock.

20   And he said unto his daughters, And where is he? why is it that ye have left the man? call him, that he may eat bread.

21   And Moses was content to dwell with the man: and he gave Moses Zipporah his daughter.

Point of View, Tone, and Style

For
Guide to Revision,
see page 337.

*A style grows partly from the point of view of the writer and the attitude
he takes toward his subject and his audience.*

Parodies provide a ready means of studying style, since parodies
are verbal caricatures which criticize a style by exaggerating, often
to absurdity, some of its qualities. Of the following paragraphs, the
first provides an example of a distinctive, though not necessarily
distinguished, modern style, and the second is a critical parody of it.

. . . They rushed down the street together, digging everything in the early
way they had, which later became so much sadder and perceptive and blank.
But then they danced down the streets like dingle-dodies, and I shambled
after as I've been doing all my life after people who interest me, because the
only people for me are the mad ones, the ones who are mad to live, mad to
talk, mad to be saved, desirous of everything at the same time, the ones who
never yawn or say a commonplace thing, but burn, burn, burn like fabulous
yellow roman candles exploding like spiders across the stars and in the
middle you see the blue centerlight pop and everybody goes "awww." What
did they call such young people in Goethe's Germany? Wanting dearly to
learn how to write like Carlo, the first thing you know, Dean was attacking
him with a great amorous soul such as only a con-man can have. "Now,
Carlo, let *me* speak—here's what *I'm* saying . . ." I didn't see them for about
two weeks, during which time they cemented their relationship to fiendish
allday-allnight-talk proportions.   —JACK KEROUAC, *On the Road*

I was just thinking around in my sad backyard, looking at those little
drab careless starshape clumps of crabgrass and beautiful chunks of some
old bicycle crying out without words of the American Noon and half a
newspaper with an ad about a lotion for people with dry skins and dry souls,
when my mother opened our frantic banging screendoor and shouted, "Gogi
Himmelman's here." She might have shouted the Archangel Gabriel was
here, or Captain Easy or Baron Charlus in Proust's great book: Gogi Him-

melman of the tattered old greenasgrass knickers and wild teeth and the vastiest, most vortical, most insatiable wonderfilled eyes I have ever known. "Let's go, Lee," he sang out, and rubbed raw by a cheap handkerchief and a dreary Bandaid unravelling off his thumb. "I know the WAY!" That was Gogi's inimitable unintellectual method of putting it that he was on fire with the esoteric paradoxical mood. I said, "I'm going, Mom," and she said "O.K.," and when I looked back at her hesitant in the pearly mystical UnitedStateshome light I felt absolutely sad, thinking of all the times she had vacuumed the same carpets.   —JOHN UPDIKE, *On the Sidewalk*

This style does not follow the advice of Samuel Butler that a style should "attract as little attention as possible." The tricks are so obtrusive that parody is relatively easy. But the parody reveals, by what it selects to ridicule, characteristics of Kerouac's style.

The parody, even though it does not refer specifically to the paragraph of the original, concentrates on the subject matter—the preoccupation of the original with "madness" for life or a "great amorous soul." But the parody also makes fun of the attitude of the original toward this abstract subject matter, its tone. By exaggerating at the same time the excessive enthusiasm of discussion and the triviality of what is discussed, the parody implies that the tone is inappropriate. In the absurdity of the "beautiful chunks of some old bicycle crying out without words of the American Noon" the parody indicates that the actual facts of the original do not justify the frenzied manner in which they are described. In small details, the parody catches the rhythm of the original and picks up characteristics of style—tricks like the compounded adjectives, the self-conscious images, or the pretentious and vague literary allusions.

Aspects of style can seldom be separated from one another. Sentence structure, paragraph patterns, diction, are all elements of style; a style is the particular combination of choices among these elements made by the individual writer. But the choices are governed especially by what has been called the writer's stance, the position he takes for a particular writing task. For, in a sense, a writer is never "just himself" when he writes; he becomes a "voice" speaking to a reader. He moves out of himself, looking at his material in a way that suits his purposes. Sometimes, in literature, the writer becomes an actual character in his novel, the narrator who may have very little in common with the author in real life. The writer takes a stance or assumes a voice much less obviously in straight expository prose, but to some degree, at least, he plays a role here, the role of the writer of the particular piece, having attitudes reflected in the tone of the writing.   **327**

19-1   Point of View

Compare the following passages describing the same scene from the reign of terror that followed the French Revolution:

The call to plunder was received with enthusiasm, and in the morning of the 25th of February a troop of women marched to the Seine and, after boarding the vessels that contained cargoes of soap, helped themselves liberally to all they required at a price fixed by themselves, that is to say, for almost nothing. Since no notice was taken of these proceedings, a far larger crowd collected at dawn of the following day and set forth on a marauding expedition to the shops. From no less than 1200 grocers the people carried off everything on which they could lay their hands—oil, sugar, candles, coffee, brandy—at first without paying, then, overcome with remorse, at the price they themselves thought proper.

—NESTA H. WEBSTER, *The French Revolution*

And now from six o'clock, this Monday morning, one perceives the Bakers' Queues unusually expanded, angrily agitating themselves. Not the Baker alone, but two Section Commissioners to help him, manage with difficulty the daily distribution of loaves. Soft-spoken, assiduous, in the early candle-light, are Baker and Commissioners: and yet the pale chill February sunrise discloses an unpromising scene. Indignant Female Patriots, partly supplied with bread, rush now to the shops, declaring they will have groceries. Groceries enough: sugar-barrels, rolled forth into the street, Patriot Citoyennes weighing it out at a just rate of elevenpence a pound; likewise coffee-chests, soap-chests, nay cinnamon and clove-chests, with *aqua-vitae* and other forms of alcohol,—at a just rate, which some do not pay; the pale-faced Grocer silently wringing his hands!

—THOMAS CARLYLE, *The French Revolution*

The passages differ in various ways, but they differ perhaps most obviously in point of view—that is, in the position in space and time from which the writer looks on his subject. The first writer assumes that she is looking back on events of the past, describing them objectively. The second pretends that he is on the scene as the events happen and asks the reader to join him in watching the events as they occur. As part of his rhetorical stance, the writer adopts a point of view in space and in time and also in the person he assumes himself to be; usually he needs to maintain this position consistently throughout his composition.

The writer of a treatise on philosophy may not need to worry much about the position in space he assumes. In a description, however, and in some other expository composition, location may be **328** important. The writer of a description needs to decide where he is in relation to the scene he is describing. He may, of course, pretend simply that he is located in some spot of heavenly omniscience from which he can describe everything. Or, for a sharper sense of reality, he may pretend to stand in a specific place, from which he can logically describe only what would be within his range of vision.

A position in time is necessary in any kind of writing, and maintaining it consistently can be difficult, requiring the writer's constant attention as well as care in the tense of verbs. In a narration the writer is likely to assume either that he is looking back from the present, as in Webster's paragraph on the French Revolution above, or to pretend that he is recording events as they occur, as in Carlyle's paragraph. An expository composition, such as a term paper on Shakespeare, may involve a variety of times such as those implied in the following:

1. Shakespeare *was* thirty-eight years old when the first edition of *Hamlet* appeared in London.
2. He *had earned* a reputation as one of the leading dramatists of his day.
3. *Hamlet has been discussed* and *criticized* more than any of the other plays.
4. It *is* a favorite on the modern stage.
5. In the play Hamlet *is faced* with a decision.
6. Ironically the only course consistent with Hamlet's character and satisfactory to the audience *leads* to disaster.

The first sentence indicates the basic attitude of the writer; he is in the present writing of events in the past. The second mentions what has occurred *before* the past time of the first. The third concerns what has occurred continuously and indefinitely in the past. The last three treat the play as it exists at the time the writer is discussing it.

There is a story that Harold Ross, long editor of *The New Yorker,* had a favorite criticism of a cartoon: "Who's talking?" He would often demand that the artist open the speaker's mouth wider or otherwise indicate who was responsible for the words in the caption. The writer may have more trouble than the cartoonist in showing who's talking, but he has to do it. Usually the writer uses the third-person approach for objectivity: *Student government requires. . . . The new teacher entered. . . .* He may want to assume a more personal relationship and describe events or facts in the first person as he saw them: *I observed student government. . . . My new teacher saw me. . . .* He may, although it is out of fashion except in some newspapers, avoid *I* by using the editorial *we,* a device for shifting the responsibility for a statement by suggesting that the entire newspaper accepts it:

We believe that student government requires. . . . In a slightly different sense, *we* is often used—as it is in passages in this text—to indicate people in general: *We use pronouns to stand for nouns.* In a narrative the writer may speak objectively but recount events from the point of view of a main character: *George soon discovered that student government.* . . . The possibilities are numerous; the writer should be consistent enough to keep the reader from confusion.

19-2 **Tone—Attitude Toward Material and Audience**

Tone, though a useful term, is almost as difficult to define as *style.* It is metaphorical in its meanings, used in reference to all the arts but basically connected with sound. That is, the tone of a paragraph has much the same importance as the tone of voice in which something is spoken. "Yes," spoken in different tones, can have differing effects—questioning, skeptical, affirming, hesitant, doubtful. In the same way, a composition has different effects, expresses different attitudes, depending upon its style. *Tone* is used here to refer to the quality of a piece of writing which reveals the writer's attitude toward his subject matter and toward his audience.

Compare the following passages from two student themes, written about the same central idea—that some types of advertising should be discontinued.

The general public has great faith in the printed word. People tend to believe what they read in supposedly reputable newspapers and magazines. Advertising, therefore, which makes false claims about the values of a product or the consequences of failing to use it may cause real hardship and may eventually even harm the standing of the company.

In the living room I found my mother in tears; she had been snubbed by the Tuesday Afternoon Bridge Club. Sadly I watched her fingering the white blouse in which tattle-tale gray persisted in spite of the new soap. My sister was revising the second paragraph of her suicide note; she had not had a date for a week in spite of using all the proper soaps and toothpastes and mouthwashes. She faced the question why romance had passed her by, and there were no more answers in the advertisements.

The first theme is serious and objective, an attempt to make a reasoned, logical statement; the second is ironic, exaggerated; it employs ridicule, reducing to absurdity the kind of advertising its author resents. The themes differ in *tone*—that is, in the attitude the writer takes toward his material and toward his reader.

Varieties of Tone   **19-3**

Since tone reflects attitudes, it can vary almost infinitely. Compare, for example, the following brief passages on the same general topic—the weather.

What happens in this particular case—and it accounts for half our winter days—is simply that the cool ground of the wintry continent chills this moist, warm air mass—chills it just a little, not enough to change its fundamental character, and not all the way up into its upper levels, but in its bottommost layer and that only just enough to make it condense out some of its abundant moisture in the form of visible clouds; it is quite similar to the effect of a cold window pane on the air of a well-heated, comfortable room—there is wetness and cooling right at the window, but the bulk of the room's air is not affected.

—WOLFGANG LANGEWIESCHE, *What Makes the Weather*

And spring? Ah! there is no spring in the Delta, no sense of refreshment and renewal in things. One is plunged out of winter into: wax effigy of a summer too hot to breathe. But here, at least, in Alexandria, the sea breaths save us from the tideless weight of summer nothingness, creeping over the bar among the warships, to flutter the striped awnings of the cafés upon the Grande Corniche.   —LAWRENCE DURRELL, *Bathazar*

Clearly the pieces differ in tone. Partly, of course, the differences grow from the content, but the content, the selection of materials, is determined partly by the writer's attitude. The first is informal and familiar, but its tone is mainly objective; its purpose is to inform the reader of facts. The second is concerned more to convey an impression, a "feeling" about the day, and its style and tone are different, more "poetic," more dependent on images.

Precise description of the varieties of tone is almost impossible. The writer may approach his material and his audience seriously, or he may adopt a joking or whimsical manner or both. He may promote confidence with a judicial calm, or he may stimulate action with eager enthusiasm. He may be objective, formal, informal, ironic, jovial, confidential, flattering, wheedling, belligerent, conciliatory. Aristotle describes tragedy as written in "lofty language," and the impact of poetic drama depends greatly on the formalized, nonconversational quality of verse. An encyclopedia article normally attempts an impersonal tone. The following are only a few of the more obvious approaches that may determine tone:

1. *Objective.* A telephone directory or a compilation of statutes reveals little of the opinions or prejudices of its writer, but it has

tone; that is, it assumes an objective, noncommittal attitude toward its materal and its readers. Many other types of writing approach a similar tone, offering material as impartially as possible. Scientific works, textbooks, histories, newspaper accounts, factual magazine articles, or informative bulletins are likely to be primarily objective in tone.

2. *Formal.* Serious writing often, though not always, promotes a formal author–reader relationship, the writing acquiring a dignity and decorum dictated more by literary tradition than by the habits of ordinary speech. Consider the following selection from Emerson's essay *Self-Reliance:*

> Trust thyself: every heart vibrates to that iron string. Accept the place the divine providence has found for you, the society of your contemporaries, the connection of events. Great men have always done so, and confided themselves childlike to the genius of their age, betraying their perception that the absolutely trustworthy was seated at their heart, working through their hands, predominaing all their being.

The tone of planned, formal expression appears in the vocabulary, in the patterned, balanced rhythm, in the elevated manner. The tone suits Emerson's subject and purposes; a similar manner would be embarrassingly inappropriate for a student theme pleading for softer seats in the gymnasium.

3. *Informal.* Much modern writing gains the allegiance of the reader by an intimate, genial manner. Charles Lamb's essay *Old China* establishes an informal tone at once:

> I have an almost feminine partiality for old china. When I go to see a great house, I inquire for the china-closet and next for the picture-gallery. I cannot defend the order of preference, but by saying that we have all some taste or other, of too ancient a date to admit of our remembering distinctly that it was an acquired one.

Lamb chats with his reader, observing neither forms nor ceremony. His essay may have a serious purpose, but it remains friendly, informal.

4. *Emphatic, enthusiastic.* Especially in fiction, writers may heighten style and overstate for emphasis. Observe an emotional scene in Charles Dickens' *Bleak House:*

> I saw before me, lying on the step, the mother of the dead child. She lay there, with one arm creeping round a bar of the iron gate, and seeming to embrace it. She lay there, who had so lately spoken to my mother. She lay there, a distressed, a sheltered, senseless creature.

The context may justify the highly rhetorical, figurative style, although out of context the passage sounds inflated. Such a tone conveys emotion, but unjustified, it rings false.

5. *Understated.* Another description of death, from Ernest Hemingway's story *My Old Man,* describes the death of the narrator's father in a different tone:

> Then Gilford rolled over to one side off my old man and got up and started to run on three legs with his off hoof dangling and there was my old man laying there on the grass flat out with his face up and blood all over the side of his head. I ran down the stand and bumped into a jam of people and got to the rail and a cop grabbed me and held me and two big stretcher-bearers were going out after my old man and around on the other side of the course I saw three horses, strung way out, coming out of the trees and taking the jump.

In contrast to the heightened style of Dickens, the passage from Hemingway describes the same sort of scene with almost exaggerated restraint, using colloquial language, emphasizing facts rather than describing emotions. Modern writers, especially, use understatement, letting the facts rather than the style convey the desired emotion.

6. *Ironic.* The following is from *Pickwick Papers;* it may be compared with another excerpt from Dickens above.

> Rising rage and extreme bewilderment had swelled the noble breast of Mr. Pickwick, almost to the bursting of his waistcoat, during the delivery of the above defiance. He stood transfixed to the spot, gazing on vacancy. The closing of the door recalled him to himself. He rushed forward with fury in his looks, and fire in his eye.

The two passages by Dickens differ in tone. In *Bleak House* the tone is dramatic and tense, in keeping with the narrator's discovery of the dead mother. In *Pickwick* the scene shows a humorous character reacting to a belligerent little doctor who has just said, "I would have pulled your nose, sir." The incident is dramatic but not tragic, and the tone is ironic. That is, the reader understands from the context that he is not to interpret words literally—that the breast of Mr. Pickwick is more "noble" in size than in courage, that the "fury" in Mr. Pickwick's look or the "fire in his eye" is more ludicrous than frightening. Irony may vary from this sort of tolerably subtle whimsy to bitter sarcasm. It may be the tone of a sentence like a young man's "Aren't you afraid we'll be early?" to a girl who has kept him waiting in the dormitory hall until the play is half over. It may be the tone of an entire essay like Swift's famous *A Modest Proposal,* suggesting that if Irish children are to be starved they had as well be butchered. Writing may be ironic whenever a statement in its context suggests a sense different from—often opposite to—its literal meaning.

The possible variations on these or other approaches are infinite; good writing requires a tone appropriate to the writer, his material, and the reader. Usually what seems most "natural" to the writer works best, but once the tone is established it should be maintained.

19-4   Appropriateness of Style and Tone

A writer adjusts his style and tone to be appropriate both to his subject and to his audience—to the circumstances in which he is writing. The style of a columnist ridiculing the foibles of bargain-hunting shoppers differs from that of a sociologist trying to explain why a juvenile delinquent may kill for fun. An editorial writer for a college newspaper may discuss a post-game invasion of the girls' dormitory as a serious blow to the school's reputation, or he may take an ironic or serious approach; a writer for the audience of a metropolitan paper is more likely to treat the subject lightly. Neither writer, however, would be likely to comment humorously on a large-scale violation of a national border that carried threats of war. An economist would use quite different approaches in a paper prepared for a learned society analyzing the financial structure of a beach community, in a report to a corporation on the same community as a site for a shopping center, and in a letter to his wife suggesting that the community would be a pleasant place for a vacation. Situations and purposes for writing vary so much that any "rules" for appropriateness are dubious, but the following observations may be useful to the student writer.

1. *Suitability.* Creative writing may reflect only the author's sense for significance, but most expository and argumentative writing must be suited to the audience. Much writing, most newspaper writing, for example, should be understandable by all adults. The writer of popular works should avoid rare words and complex constructions, and even in semipopular writing he should explain any terms not in common use. But popular writing is not the only kind of useful writing. Most good writing for children will bore intelli-

gent adults. Conversely, a theoretical physicist would be justifiably irked if, in reading a learned paper on his speciality, he was constantly interrupted by explanations of matters familiar to every graduate of Physics 1—but not to every layman. Good professional music criticism may baffle even a learned reader who does not know music; much good philosophy written for philosophers will inevitably be unreadable for many of us. Most writing should be guided by the audience for which it is intended; usually, student writing is directed toward a semipopular audience, but the student should learn, also, to do more specialized writing upon occasion Many college students are preparing for careers in which their most important writing will be specialized or technical.

2. *Maturity and taste.* The student writer needs to remove himself far enough from his subject matter to view it objectively, with perspective. The student whose theme describes with a straight face the glories of a 4-H fair—"the most important moment of my life"—is often unintentionally humorous.

3. *Sincerity and simplicity.* Conscious efforts to adopt a style usually fail. They sound insincere, affected, or merely pompous. The kind of sports writing, for example, that relies on calling a baseball a pill or the old apple is likely to sound false and weary, not clever and racy. The theme that tries to be impressive by referring to Shakespeare as the bard or the swan of Avon is likely to sound trite and juvenile. Sinclair Lewis in *Babbitt* burlesques the affected high style of some society-page prose:

'Twixt the original and Oriental decorations, the strange and delicious food, and the personalities both of the distinguished guests, the charming hostess and the noted host, never has Zenith seen a more recherche affair than the Ceylon dinner-dance given last evening by Mr. and Mrs. Charles McKelvey to Sir Gerald Doak. Methought as we—fortunate one!—were privileged to view that fairy and foreign scene, nothing at Monte Carlo or the choicest ambassadorial sets of foreign capitals could be more lovely. It is not for nothing that Zenith is in matters social rapidly becoming known as the choosiest inland city in the country.

Or for a sample of a style that is perhaps more subtly bad, consider the following from a contemporary mystery novel:

The black gabardine suit she wore instead of the electric-blue gown seemed to have been stroked to her form by a sensitive young sculptor who fell in love with his creation and let his sensual imagination run wild. She walked toward him with slow grace, and he saw the tautness that made her red mouth seem completely imperious, in the firm mold that some mistake for courage.

And for a moment he was trapped again, like a small boy looking at the grandest, most sparkling and magnificent red wagon he has even seen. She was the chrome and polished enamel, the speed and the powerful promise of the low-slung car shining through the window from the plush interior of the showroom.   —WILLIAM L. ROHDE, *Murder on the Line*

The effort in the writing shows; neither the prose nor the lady is as seductive as the writer apparently intended; the description does not ring true.

For most purposes the student writer does best to write sincerely, naturally, simply, directly.

4. *Objectivity and emotion.* Directness and sincerity become a virtue of style and tone especially when the writer tries to convey emotion. As in life buckets of tears do not measure the depth of grief, so in writing multiple superlatives do not reveal sincerity of emotion. If emotion is there, it will be conveyed best by a straight and objective presentation. Writing that tries to milk more emotion than the facts warrant is *sentimental*—false in its emotion.

5. *Humor.* Humor usually profits from a straight face. Notice, for example, the style of the following brief excerpt from James Thurber's reminiscences about university days:

One day General Littlefield picked our company out of the whole regiment and tried to get it mixed up by putting it through one movement after another as fast as we could execute them: squads right, squads left, squads on right into line, squads right about, squads left front into line, etc. In about three minutes one hundred and nine men were marching in one direction and I was marching away from them at an angle of forty-five degrees, all alone. "Company, halt!" shouted General Littlefield. "That man is the only man who has it right!" I was made a corporal for my achievement.
—My Life and Hard Times

The writer lets the humor grow from the facts.

Guide to Revision 19

Revise the composition to make point of view and tone consistent and to provide an appropriate style.

As a larger problem the development of an interesting and adaptable style involves long study and practice, but for immediate results revisions to make the point of view and the tone consistent and appropriate often improve style.

PV   **Consistency in Point of View**   19a

The reader is confused unless the writer maintains a position in space and time and speaks consistently with the same voice, in the same person.

ORIGINAL	REVISION
From my corner I could see the long platform of the subway stretching dimly beside the tracks. A girl clicked through the turnstile and sat at once on the bench beyond the change booth. The street was empty and quiet. For a moment there was no rumble of trains, no sound of voices—a frightening silence. [*The third sentence shifts the point of view by making the reader change the position he has assumed to imagine the scene.*]	From my corner I could see the long platform of the subway station stretching dimly beside the tracks. A girl clicked through the turnstile and sat immediately on the bench beyond the change booth. For a moment there was no rumble of trains, no sound from the street above, no voice—a frightening silence. [*The revision retains the detail of the original, but presents it from the point of view already established.*]

Consistency in time requires appropriate tenses in verbs (see Glossary under *Tense*).

ORIGINAL	REVISION
The play begins with a scene on the castle walls of Elsinore. Horatio, a friend of Hamlet, met the soldiers	The play begins with a scene on the castle walls of Elsinore. Horatio, a friend of Hamlet, meets the soldiers

337

ORIGINAL (*Cont.*)

who were on watch and learned from them about the ghost that had appeared. Then as the soldiers were talking, the ghost, dressed in full armor, appeared again.

[*The writer, as he proceeds, perhaps begins to think of his experience in reading or seeing the play rather than the play itself. After one sentence he changes tense.*]

REVISION (*Cont.*)

who are on watch and learns from them about the ghost that has appeared. Then as the soldiers are talking, the ghost, dressed in full armor, appears again.

[*The revision consistently considers the play as a piece of literature still in existence which can therefore be referred to in present time.*]

Shifts in person may involve conventions in the use of pronoun forms or case (see Glossary under *Pronoun*).

ORIGINAL

If you want your campfire to be both safe and useful, you have to build it carefully. You have to begin by selecting a good place for the fire. One should be sure that there are no trees within ten feet of the site and that all leaves and brush have been cleared away.

[*The writer begins with* you *as his subject but shifts in the third sentence to* one, *for no apparent reason.*]

I looked out over the pines toward the tiny lake a thousand feet below us. You could hardly see the cabin where we had spent the night.

After the textbook had been mastered, he had no trouble with chemistry.

[*The impersonal passive construction shifts awkwardly to the active with the subject* he.]

REVISION

If you want your campfire to be both safe and useful, you must build it carefully. Begin by selecting a good place for the fire. You should be sure that there are no trees within ten feet of the site and that all leaves and brush have been cleared away.

[*Changing* one *to* you *keeps the point of view consistent. The writer might, of course, have used* one *and* he *instead of* you.]

I looked out over the pines toward the tiny lake a thousand feet below us. I could hardly see the cabin where we had spent the night.

After he had mastered the textbook, he had no trouble with chemistry.

19b Appropriateness in Tone Tone

A student who writes in sober ecstasy of the world-shaking importance of a home-run he hit to win a junior-league baseball game is likely to create more unintentional humor than genuine respect for his batting eye. The lecturer who takes a tone of patronizing condescension to a group of college students misjudges his audience by treating them as children and annoys more than he informs. The writer who offers commonplace or trivial ideas in a formal, rhetorical manner is likely to appear more pompous than wise; he should establish and maintain an appropriate tone.

ORIGINAL	REVISION
Graduation from high school is a very important event, often shaping much of a person's future career in life. It is a time of commencement, not of ending. But it also is a time when a person realizes the importance of the hard struggle that has carried him successfully through four years of heartbreaks and triumphs. When those wonderful words of congratulation ring out after the awarding of diplomas, every graduate knows a thrill which he will never forget. It is truly a wonderful moment.	To the high school graduate, commencement may seem the most important event in life. The parade in white dresses and blue suits or caps and gowns, the music with all the ringing discords of which a nervous school orchestra is capable, the grim, freshly scrubbed faces, the earnest platitudes of the student orations, all convince the graduate that this is the real turning point of his life. He leaves certain that he will never forget a moment of what has occurred, and a year later he may actually remember something of it.
[The tone of overstatement and high seriousness is not justified by the occasion, and the passage does more to reveal the immaturity of the writer than to convince a reader.]	*[A lighter tone, with factual details replacing the overstatement, leads to a less naïve paragraph. Other approaches, would have been possible.]*

Humor may be the salt of society, but its savor is delicate; a remark that produces a laugh or a smile in one reader elicits bewilderment in another and something approaching nausea in a third. A joke which sends Junior into hysterics may make his parents hope only that someday Junior will grow up. Attempts at humor often fail because the writer relies on overworked tricks— stale quips or slang intended to suggest a blasé style, attempts at exaggerated, thesaurus-inspired wit (In elucidating that toothsome phenomenon characterized among the ranks of the intelligentsia as granulated cow. . . .), or irony with a question mark to explain the joke (The instructor started his clever? lecture). These devices can be, and have been, successfully used, but they usually amuse the writer more than the reader.

ORIGINAL

When the light of day next osmosed through our hero's casement it discovered the would-be Romeo and mighty guzzler with a disturbance in that portion of his anatomy known as the cranium that was so perceptible that it resembled nothing so much as the activities of a jackhammer. In short, he was, to use the vernacular, hanging over.

[*Some readers may find this mildly amusing the first time through, but a discerning person is likely to be disgusted at a cheap attempt to show off.*]

REVISION

Jeffrey was half awake with the pain throbbing in his temples. He fought his way under the covers, but he could not escape the sense of smothering. He tried with his right hand to block off the sun from the window, but he could not get things quite right. His head kept pounding, and his eyes hurt.

[*The revision is not very funny, but it is not disgusting, and it says much more than did the original.*]

Some variety in style and tone is inevitable, even desirable, but in general a writer should adopt a tone suited to his subject and maintain it. A writer or speaker may assume an easy, conversational manner to introduce his subject and become more terse, more dramatic, more persuasive as he moves into the body of his composition. A conclusion may differ somewhat in tone from the evidence that has preceded it. A violent shift in tone may be deliberate and striking, but skillful writers generally avoid sharp shifts of tone, and they never shift tone without good reason.

ORIGINAL

. . . Tying flies requires patience, practice, and skill, but there is a special thrill in hooking a trout with a fly you have made yourself.

And now if you are not completely bored by my lesson on how to tie a fly, let us go on, dear reader, to what the flies are to be used for. Flyfishing. . . .

[*After a straightforward discussion, the writer shifts to what is perhaps an attempt at mild humor or "lightening" the paper.*]

REVISION

. . . Tying flies requires patience, practice, and skill, but there is a special thrill in hooking a trout with a fly you have made yourself.

Catching a trout, however, requires not only a well-made lure but a good deal of skill in using it. Flyfishing. . . .

[*A more direct transition introduces the new topic equally well and avoids the awkward shift in tone.*]

Exercise 19

A. Following are two paragraphs, the first a selection from a novel and the second a selection from a parody of the style of the novelist. Write a discussion of the parody as a representation or criticism of the novelist's style. Is the parody fair? What specific qualities of the novelist's style does the parody exaggerate?

1. Sight of the old gilt clock had made Arthur Winner think of his father—indeed, the room was full of such mementos. A little-disturbed museum, its collection, informal and unassuming, preserved evidences of that many-sided mind, of the grasp and scope of interests, of perceptions so unobtrusive as to be nearly private, of quiet amusements and quiet enjoyments. Seeking Arthur Winner Senior's monument, you could look around you. You could ask yourself, for example, how many lawyers—or, to give the point proper force, how many small-town lawyers, born and brought up in fairly-to-be-called rural county seat like Brocton—would, fifty or more years ago, have had the interest—let alone, the taste, the eye—to pick over, unaffected by then current ideas of what was fine or beautiful, of what was rare or valuable, the then next thing to junk—the secondhand, the old-fashioned, the discarded—and select, exchanging a few dollars for them, exactly the items that the antique trade (at that time hardly born) was going to look on as prizes half a century later. Would you guess one in a thousand, or one in ten thousand?
   —JAMES GOULD COZZENS, *By Love Possessed*

2. Author Winner sat serenely contemplating his novel. His legs, not ill-formed for his years, yet concealing the faint cyanic marbling of incipient varicosity under grey socks of the finest lisle, were crossed. He was settled in the fine, solidly-built, cannily (yet never parsimoniously, never niggardly) bargained-for chair that had been his father's, a chair that Author Winner himself was only beginning to think that, in the fullness of time, hope he reasonably might that he would be able (be possessed of the breadth and the depth) to fill. Hitching up the trousers that had been made for his father (tailored from a fabric woven to endure, with a hundred and sixty threads to the inch), he felt a twinge of the sciatica that had been his father's and had come down to him through the jeans. Author Winner was grateful for any resemblance; his father had been a man of unusual qualities; loyal, helpful, friendly, courteous, kind, obedient, cheerful, thrifty, brave, clean and reverent; in the simplest of terms: a man of *dharma*.
   —FELICIA LAMPORT, *James Gould Cozzens by Henry James Cozened*

B. Following are selections from varied types of prose, some modern, some earlier. Describe what seems to you the "stance" of the writer of each, the point of view and the tone; then discuss how the tone is revealed in each paragraph. Since the passages are taken from their contexts, you may wish to check your judgment by consulting the whole works.

1. Although I had been baffled in my attempts to learn the origin of the Feast of Calabashes, yet it seemed very plain to me that it was principally, if not wholly, of a religious nature. As a religious solemnity, however, it had not at all corresponded with the horrible descriptions of Polynesian worship which we have received in some published narratives, and especially in those accounts of the evangelized islands with which the missionaries have favoured us. Did not the sacred character of these persons render the purity of their intentions unquestionable, I should certainly be led to suppose that they had exaggerated the evils of Paganism, in order to enhance the merits of their own disinterested labours.

   —HERMAN MELVILLE, *Typee*, Chapter XXIV

2. In taking up the clue of an inquiry, not intermitted for nearly ten years, it may be well to do as a traveller would, who had to recommence an interrupted journey in a guideless country; and, ascending, as it were, some little hill beside our road, note how far we have already advanced, and what pleasantest ways we may choose for further progress.

   —JOHN RUSKIN, *Modern Painters*

3. Of recent years there has been a noticeable decline of swearing and foul language in England; and this, except at centres of industrial depression, shows every sign of continuing indefinitely, until a new shock to our national nervous system—such as war, pestilence, revolution, fire from Heaven, or whatever you please—revives the habit of swearing, together with that of praying. Taking advantage of the lull, I propose to make a short enquiry into the nature and necessity of foul language: a difficult theme and one seldom treated with detachment.

   —ROBERT GRAVES, *Lars Porsena*

4. "And who is this? Is this my old nurse?" said the child, regarding with a radiant smile a figure coming in.
   Yes, yes. No other stranger would have shed those tears at sight of him, and called him her dear boy, her pretty boy, her own poor blighted child. No other woman would have stooped down by his bed, and taken up his wasted hand, and put it to her lips and breast, as one who had some right to fondle it. No other woman would have so forgotten everybody there but him and Floy, and been so full of tenderness and pity.

   —CHARLES DICKENS, *Dombey and Son*, Chapter XVI

5. THE KING? There he was. Beefeaters were before the august box; the Marquis of Steyne (Lord of the Powder Closet) and other great officers of state were behind the chair on which he sate. *He* sate— florid of face, portly of person, covered with orders, and in a rich curling head of hair. How we sang, God save him! How the house rocked and shouted with that magnificent music. How they cheered, and cried, and waved handkerchiefs. Ladies wept; mothers clasped their children; some fainted with emotion. People were suffocated in the pit, shrieks and groans rising up amidst the writhing and shout- ing mass there of his people who were, and indeed showed themselves almost to be, ready to die for him. Yes we saw him. Fate cannot de- prive us of *that* . . . that we saw George the Good, the Magnificent, the Great.

—WILLIAM MAKEPEACE THACKERAY, *Vanity Fair,* Chapter XLVIII

6. I suppose you could call it a frame. But it wasn't like no frame that was ever pulled before. They's been plenty where one guy was paid to lay down. This is the first I heard of where a guy had to be bribed to win. And it's the first where a bird was bribed and didn't know it.

—RING LARDNER, *A Frame-up*

7. John B. Smith takes the stand.

Q. Mr. Smith, are you familiar with the clichés used in football?

A. Naturally, as a football fan. . . .

Q. Mr. Smith, as an expert, what lesson do you draw from the game of football?

A. Life is a game of football, Mr. Sullivan, and we the players. Some of us are elusive quarterbacks, some of us are only cheer leaders. Some of us are coaches and some of us are old grads, slightly the worse for wear, up in the stands. Some of us thump the people in front of us on the head in our excitement, some of us are the people who always get thumped. But the important thing to remember is—Play the game!

Q. How true!

—FRANK SULLIVAN, *Football is King*

8. Animals talk to each other, of course. There can be no question about that; but I suppose there are very few people who can understand them. I never knew but one man who could. I knew he could, how- ever, because he told me so himself. He was a middle-aged, simple- hearted miner who had lived in a lonely corner of California, among the woods and mountains, a good many years, and had studied the ways of his only neighbors, the beasts and the birds, until he believed he could accurately translate any remark which they made.

—MARK TWAIN, *Jim Baker's Blue-Jay Yarn*

9. It is true to nature, although it be expressed in a figurative form, that a mother is both the morning and the evening star of life. The **343**

light of her eye is always the first to rise, and often the last to set upon man's day of trial. She wields a power more decisive far than syllogisms in argument, or courts of last appeal in authority. Nay, in cases not a few, where there has been no fear of God before the eyes of the young--where His love has been unfelt and His law outraged, a mother's affection or her tremulous tenderness has held transgressors by the heart-strings, and been the means of leading them back to virtue and to God.

—T. L. HAINES and L. W. YAGGY, *The Royal Path of Life*

C. Revise the following passages so that the point of view is consistent:

1. At the beginning of the play Romeo was very much in love with Rosalind. He seemed almost amusing as a lovesick youth. Then he meets Juliet, and at once he is madly in love with her. The sudden change was not convincing to me.

2. No matter how carefully one plans, you can always count on forgetting something.

3. The six main streets of the town spread out like spokes of a huge wheel, whose hub was the courthouse circle where I walked. As I crossed Central Avenue, I could see traffic lights blinking off to the north for eight or ten blocks. A dozen girls in blue jeans and bright shirts giggled by me, bound for the first show at the Circle Theater. The theater was open; gaudy ushers swished along the aisles, and a small crowd waited for the picture to begin. I walked on past the theater entrance, past a bookstore whose window display suggested that it specialized in office equipment rather than books, and then I turned up Grand Avenue to the northwest.

4. When I first read the story I thought Hemingway was interested mostly in the two killers who come into the restaurant and inquire about Ole. They are revealed through their clipped speech and their attempts to bully the boys in the diner. Most of the story seems to concern them. Nick did not speak very often.

5. If you expect people to take you seriously, you must take time to think about what you say. It is not enough to speak with conviction or pound the table with enthusiasm. One must know what he is trying to do and have a plan for doing it.

6. After he ate the soup and finished the huge salad, he began to regain his cheerfulness.

7. *Huckleberry Finn* is more than a children's book. Huck, of course, is interesting to children. He was always doing something exciting. I can remember still how interested I was when I first read the book. But the novel has ideas in it that appeal also to an adult mind.

8. A person who wants to get something out of his classes must do more than simply the required work. You can often get a degree by doing just the minimum, but you cannot get an education that way.

D. In the 19th century, two contemporaries wrote philosophies of clothes. One, ecstatic, philosophical, and violent, was the work of Thomas Carlyle. The other, moral, pedantic, doctrinaire, was an editorial by Louis A. Godey, editor of *Godey's Lady's Book*. The "paragraph" below has been made by mixing selections from these two accounts. Naturally, the tones of the two are quite different. Judging by the tone, try to sort out the sentences so that you get two consistent accounts. The sentences occur in the same order they had in the original versions. The following might be used as a topic sentence for the matter from Carlyle: "Man's earthly interests are all hooked and buttoned together, and held up, by Clothes." The following would serve as a topic sentence for the passages from Godey: "The Bible, as our readers well know, is the standard of authority by which we test the right or the wrong of ideas and usages; nor can we comprehend the full import of clothing or its advantages unless we look at the evil results that follow neglect of or disobedience to this law of necessity for the human race, ever since 'the Lord God clothed' the first man and woman before sending them out of Eden."

(1) Clothing has nine distinct phases of teaching the philosophy of its usefulness. (2) It gives covering, comfort, comeliness; it marks custom, condition, character, and civilization; it symbolizes Redemption through Christ, and the holiness of the saints in Heaven. (3) Society sails through the Infinitude on cloth, as on a Faust's mantle. (4) Strange enough, it strikes me, is this same fact of there being Tailors and tailored. (5) The Horse I ride has his own whole fell; the noble creature is his own semp-ster, and weaver, and spinner. (6) A clothing of rags symbolizes wretched-ness, wickedness, ignorance, imposture, or imbecility. (7) While I—good Heaven—have thatched myself over with the dead fleeces of sheep, the bark of vegetables, the entrails of worms, the hides of oxen and seals, the felt of furred beasts. (8) Nakedness is savagery, or shameless sin, or extreme misery. (9) Heathenism has no darker shadow on its God-forsaken horizon than the half nude millions on millions of its worshipers; until these people are clothed, neither China nor India can become Christian countries. (10) Day after Day I must thatch myself anew; day after day this despicable thatch must lose some film of its thickness, till by degree the whole has been brushed thither, and I, the dust-making, patent Rag-grinder, get new material to grind on. O subter-brutish! vile! most vile! (11) Wherever Christian civilization prevails, as in Europe and America, dirt and disorder in a household or in dress are proofs of ill-conditioned or ill-trained people. (12) For have not I too a compact all-enclosing Skin, whiter or dingier? Am I a botched mass of tailors' and cobblers' shreds, then; or a tightly-articulated, homogeneous little Figure, automatic, alive? (13) The dress must be decent before we can have confidence in the character of any person. (14) For my own part, these considerations, of our Clothes-thatch, and how, reaching inwards even to our heart of hearts, it tailorizes and demoralizes us, fill me with a certain horror at myself, and mankind. (15) We feel and judge thus intuitively, because the instincts of humanity tell us that without decent

clothing there cannot be real delicacy of feeling or true dignity of mind, unless the 'miserable' suffers from the sins of others. (16) And this does not weaken the force of our moral of dress—that there is or has been wrong doing wherever we see people badly or indecently clothed. (17) There is something great in the moment when a man first strips himself of adventitious wrappages; and sees indeed that he is naked, and, as Swift has it, 'a forked straddling animal with bandy legs'; yet also a Spirit and unutterable Mystery of Mysteries.

E. Biblical scholars recognize that the Old Testament we know is made up of several older versions edited into one by breaking up the earlier accounts and running them together. Two of these versions are called *P* and *JE*, *P* standing for a version which we suppose to have been the Priests' Code, and *JE* for a more popular account which combined two versions, in one of which the Lord is called Javeh, and in the other Elohim. Thus, whatever the reason for the Bible's appearing in this form, many of the Old Testament stories are told twice, and naturally the style differs in the two versions. For example, here are two accounts of early days in the Garden of Eden in the King James version, but with modern punctuation and paragraphing. The first is from *JE*.

Now, the serpent was more subtil than any beast of the field which the Lord God had made, and he said unto the woman, "Yea, God hath said, 'Ye shall not eat of every tree of the garden?' "
And the woman said unto the serpent, "We may eat of the fruit of the trees of the garden, but of the fruit of the tree which is in the midst of the garden, God hath said, 'Ye shall not eat of it, neither shall ye touch it, lest ye die.' "
And the serpent said unto the woman, "Ye shall not surely die."

Now try to describe this passage. For what sort of reader does it seem to be intended? What is the content? How would you characterize the style? Next, study the following passage from *P*.

This is the book of the generations of Adam. In the day that God created man, in the likeness of God made he him, male and female created he them; and blessed them, and called their name Adam, in the day when they were created. And Adam lived an hundred and thirty years, and begat a son in his own likeness, after his image, and called his name Seth. And the days of Adam after he had begotten Seth were eight hundred years, and he begat sons and daughters.

Now try to describe the audience, the content, and the style of this passage and contrast it with that from *JE*.

The following is a continuous passage from Chapter Eleven of Genesis, which contains material from both *P* and *JE*. Identify the passages from each and determine where the break or breaks come. Enumerate as many differences in style as you can with which you distinguish the two versions.

And the whole earth was of one language, and of one speech, and it came to pass, as they journeyed from the east, that they found a plain in the land of Shinar, and they dwelt there.

And they said one to another, "Go to, let us make brick, and burn them thoroughly," and they had brick for stone, and slime they had for mortar. And they said, "Go to, let us build us a city and a tower, whose top may reach unto heaven, and let us make us a name lest we be scattered abroad upon the face of the whole earth."

And the Lord came down to see the city and the tower, which the children of men had builded, and the Lord said, "Behold, the people is one, and they have all one language, and this they begin to do. And now nothing will be restrained from them, which they have imagined to do. Go to! Let us go down and there confound their language, that they may not understand one another's speech."

So the Lord scattered them abroad from thence upon the face of all the earth, and they left off to build the city. Therefor is the name of it called Babel, because the Lord did there confound the language of all the earth, and from thence did the Lord scatter them abroad upon the face of all the earth.

These are the generations of Shem: Shem was an hundred years old, and begat Arphaxad two years after the flood. And Shem lived after he begat Arphaxad five hundred years, and begat sons and daughters. And Arphaxad lived five and thirty years, and begat Salah, and Arphaxad lived after he begat Salah four hundred and three years, and begat sons and daughters.

If you wish to check the accuracy of your guess, the break comes between the ninth and tenth verses in the King James numbering. If you care to pursue this study and make a more elaborate distinction between the styles of *P* and *JE*, the following include suitable passages in the King James numbering; the Douay version differs slightly: Genesis 5:1-28 (*P*); 5:29 (*JE*); 5:30-32 (*P*); 6:1-8 (*JE*); 6:9-22 (*P*); 7:1-5 (*JE*); 7:6 (*P*); 7:7-24 (*JE*); 8:1-5 (*P*); 8:6-12 (*JE*); 8:13-20 (*P*); 8:21-22 (*JE*); 9:1-17 (*P*); 9:18-27 (*JE*); 9:28-29, 10:1-7 (*P*); 10:8-19 (*JE*); 10:20 (*P*); 10:21 (*JE*); 10:22-23 (*P*); 10:24-30 (*JE*); 10:31-32 (*P*).

Words

She speaks poiniards, and every word stabs.
—William Shakespeare

Words are the most powerful drug used by mankind.
—Rudyard Kipling

Deliver not your words by number, but by weight.
—H. G. Bohn, Handbook of Proverbs

Ford Madox Ford reports that when he heard of the death of Joseph Conrad, his long-time friend and collaborator, he saw again in his mind the two of them driving past "a ramshackle, commonplace farm building in an undistinguished country over slight hills on a flinty byeroad and heard Joseph Conrad saying to him, 'Well, Ford, *mon vieux,* how would you render that field of wheat?' " He goes on to recount that they had spent many hours through many years in that way, jolting through "a country of commonplace downlands," asking themselves how they would describe a field of wheat under the conditions of the moment. Should one say, "Fields of wheat that small winds ruffled into cat's paws"? No, that was too literary. But what ideas and what words should one use? Then there was that "ten-acre patch of blue-purple cabbage." What should one do about that?

Here we have the picture of two distinguished writers, spending great chunks of their lives asking each other what words to use to describe a field of wheat or a patch of cabbages. Quite surely they wrote well partly because they studied words and the power of words. Conrad said his purpose was "above all things to make you see," but he understood that before he could make anyone else see, he had to see. Unless a writer sees sharply, he cannot make others see sharply. Unless he hears vividly, he cannot make others hear. How does snow look when it falls in large flakes, widely spaced, in no wind? How do the brakes of a car sound when the driver jams them on suddenly to avoid a crash? What is the difference between the smell of roasting turkey and roasting goose? If one goes to his wardrobe in the dark and finds the particular garment he wants by feel, what in the texture of the cloth identifies it? What is the taste of Roquefort cheese?

A writer who will ask himself questions like these is likely to write better because he has more to say, although he still needs words with which to say it. He needs vocabulary. The Anglo-Saxons had a revealing term for vocabulary; they called it a "word hoard," a treasury of words that each man owned and on which he could draw at any time he wanted to speak. They seem to have understood that if a man is to be rich intellectually, he needs a great store of words; the more words he acquires the richer he becomes. Modern psychologists agree with the Anglo-Saxons about this. They have found more direct relationship between the size and accuracy of vocabulary in one test, and general intelligence in another, than between general intelligence and anything else.

Modern man needs words as the tools with which he speaks and writes. To express himself well, a writer must have many words in his word hoard and must be able to select just the right word for each purpose. Let us postpone the question of selection and ask first how the writer can develop a rich treasury of words. The writer can learn words by many means, but perhaps most easily by listening to intelligent conversation and reading intelligent writing. We increase our vocabularies mainly by the same means with which we started them as children, by hearing, seeing, and using words. Most people who have large vocabularies have learned the greater part of their words by reading, particularly by reading carefully and using a good dictionary. In the long run little else can help a student so much as the habit of reading widely and critically, and if he does not have the habit, he can acquire it.

Everyone builds some vocabulary in this way: He learns as he matures, although the learning is mainly unconscious. The process is slow, especially for someone who has not already developed good reading habits, but the process can be speeded up, converted to conscious learning. A student can deliberately learn new words, and force himself to use them, and he can increase his holdings in the words he knows by learning new uses for them and new powers in them. Usually, the most satisfactory improvements in vocabulary come from increased interest in language and livelier knowledge of it. This section of the book is intended to help students learn language by learning about language; having fun with language can be a profitable occupation.

20

Language, the Means
of Being Human

Knowledge of language provides a sound foundation for the use of language.

Henry Ward Beecher once observed, "When we talk about ourselves we almost invariably use Latin words, and when we talk about our neighbors we use Saxon words." No doubt the witty divine was having fun, including fun with language, but he had a point. Many Latinate words are considered polite and even complimentary; many native English words seem salty, terse, even insulting. We use our language the way we do partly because languages grow their own natures, partly because they reflect the history and culture and mental processes of the people who have used the language, and partly because they reflect the history of the language itself. A user of language does well to know something of the nature of language and something of the history of his own language.

20-1   The Miracle of Language

How does language work? Nobody knows exactly. Some things we know, things like the following: one of the authors of this book sits before a typewriter, thinking about language and what can best be said about it, and hitting the typewriter keys. A student sits before the book, looking at it, probably because he has been told to, possibly because he hopes the book will help him to write better, or at least to get a better grade in a course. If both the writer and the reader have done their jobs moderately well, ideas will appear in the student's mind which roughly approximate those that were in the writer's mind. Here, surely, is a marvel and a mystery, and this miracle can occur although the author writes on one continent and the reader studies on another; it can take place even if the writer has been dead for centuries. We do not know in detail how this marvel comes about, but we know it relies on language. For the marvel to work, the writer and the reader must know the same language, and the written form of it. If the marvel is to work well, both the writer and the reader must be so familiar with the necessary linguistic symbols that they use them unconsciously; the writer will seldom think about the words he is using, and the reader almost never will. To a degree this process can be described; the language contains symbols for meaning—whatever we mean by *meaning*, and we shall have to ask that question—and ways of using these symbols. In English, although not in all languages, these symbols are what we call words, and the way we use the words we call grammar and rhetoric, and sometimes prosody. All users of a language have a mutual agreement, a sort of unwritten contract, that certain linguistic symbols can be used in certain ways; given that mutual understanding and human minds, extensive and relatively precise communication becomes possible.

No one knows who invented language, when or how. The most nearly primitive peoples of whom we have any record have possessed languages already so developed that in some ways they have decayed. Guesses about the origin of language have been more contradictory than convincing; various learned thinkers have argued that language grew from cries of love and fear, from imitation of babies' prattlings, from mimicking the sounds of nature, from the accompaniments of gestures, from the love of naming things, and many more. No doubt all of these had effects, but the arguments about the origin of language became so varied and volatile that the whole discussion grew more humorous than enlightening, with people making up funny names for the theories: The Bow-Wow theory, the Mu-Mu theory, the Woo-Woo theory, the Whistle and Grunt. Of course somebody started language somewhere sometime; perhaps many people started in many places many times, and the "somebody" is more likely to have been plural than singular. Perhaps something like the following provides the best guess, and it must possess some truth even though it lacks details: language is so complicated, varied, and subtle, that it probably was never "invented," in the way we use that word, in any one time and place. It is apparently so native to man that it began to spring up wherever vertebrates became human, and men were quite possibly not anything we would call human until they had some language; thus language and mankind grew simultaneously in a sort of hen-and-egg relationship. Animals, birds, bees, dolphins, chimpanzees, and perhaps even earthworms can communicate in limited ways, but only man has a communications system sufficiently adequate to be called a language; apparently all man has language, and for all we know he has always had it, ever since he could be called human. Language and humanity may be only two aspects of the same thing; language may be a way of defining man.

20-2 The Ancestry of English

Where did English come from? This answer is easier, and although it has been known only relatively recently, it has revolutionized our thinking about language. A schoolgirl can now know fundamental principles of language that were not dreamed of by the most learned scholars two centuries ago. Of course learned men tried to study language; they could always try to describe languages in their own times, but, generally, they had too little knowledge of other languages, living and dead, to develop sound theories for the study of language. The ancient Greeks studied their contemporary native language and wrote excellent grammars of it—we have the conventional eight parts of speech from them—but the Greeks knew no languages from much earlier times. In the Hebraic tradition the notion seems to have been that Jehovah started talking with Adam as soon as He had made him; we are not told what language they used. Later we are told that the Lord, to keep people from building a tower to the sky, "confounded their languages" and scattered them abroad upon the face of the earth, sending their confounded languages with them. This account is now valued more for its theological than for its philological import, but even a man as late and learned as Noah Webster assumed that the diversity of modern languages stemmed from the dispersal at Babel. He guessed that western European languages came from a tongue spoken on the plains of Chaldee, and that this language was best represented in Celtic. We now know that both of these were bad guesses, and that a student of language needs to rely on only a few consecutive bad guesses to be fantastically wrong, but until about Webster's day nobody knew enough to be very right.

Some facts were known. Obviously, Latin had borrowed words from Greek, but Latin was a different language from Greek. On the other hand, French and Italian had grown from Latin. Latin had changed, subtly and slowly from Classical times, until it had become Italian in its native peninsula, and Latin as it was spoken in what had once been Gaul changed so much that it had become what is known as French; meanwhile, the Latin spoken in the Iberian Peninsula had changed still differently so that it became what is called Spanish and Portuguese. All this occurred in historic times, and the evidence has been sufficiently preserved in manuscripts so that no real doubt exists as to what, in general, happened. Scholars might have made something of this had they wished; after all, if Italian had Latin as its parent, did it not probably have a grandparent as well, the parent of Latin? And if so, might not all languages descend from a single parent language, as all men presumably descended from Adam and Eve, or from some group of arboreal apes?

Scholars might have so reasoned, but apparently they did not think much along these lines prior to the nineteenth century. Then new observations caused men to look closely at language; everybody knew that many English words resembled Latin words because English had borrowed words from Latin. Similarly, Latin words were like Greek words because Latin had borrowed from Greek. But now Englishmen in India, educated men who knew Latin and Greek, observed that the ancient Indic tongue, Sanskrit, resembled Latin, Greek, and Old English in the verb *be*, in the numerals, and in many other common words, far too many to be explained as accidents. And yet, English and Latin had never had any contact with Sanskrit in historic times, and Greek had had too little to matter much. Why were these languages so much alike? Once this question had been asked, the evidence started pouring in from all sorts of places. For example, here is a comparison put together by the great nineteenth century American philologist William Dwight Whitney:

English	Lithuanian	Celtic	Latin	Greek	Persian	Sanskrit
three	tri	tri	tres	treis	thri	tri
seven	septyni	secht	septem	hepta	hapta	sapta
me	manen	me	me	me	me	me
mother	moter	mathair	mater	meter	matar	matar
brother	brolis	brathair	frater	phrater		bhratar
night	naktis		noctis	nuktos		nakta

From evidence like this, the modern theory of the growth and descent of languages has been developed and made plausible. By examining evidence which has survived for languages living and dead, we have been able to reconstruct earlier languages, and from these, still earlier languages. For example, if we did not have records of Latin, we could reconstruct Latin at least approximately because we can guess the forms that would account for modern Romance languages. If we did not have the Latin word *oculus* (English *eye*), we should know that some such word must have been there to account for *oeil* in French, *ojo* in Spanish, and *occhio* in Italian. Similarly, we know some words that must have been in the ancestor language of English, Greek, and Sanskrit to account for the words that have come down to us. Of course this is only conjecture, but conjecture that can be worked out in such detail and with such consistency that no person learned in languages doubts its essential truth. It has even found remarkable confirmation. By these methods scholars had reconstructed an ancient language, which they called Indo-European, which must have been spoken perhaps four or five thousand years before Christ in what is now east central Europe. Meanwhile, among the languages that nobody knew how to read was one impressed into numerous clay tablets known to have come from the Hittites. Eventually, but only recently, scholars learned to read Hittite; when they could, they discovered that Hittite was closely related to Indo-European, and that the forms in Hittite confirmed the forms already obtained by reconstruction in Indo-European.

20-3   Indo-European and Its Descendants

What do we know of these Indo-Europeans? Directly, very little; even the name, Indo-European, has been made up for them. History is no help; we have little history from before 5000 B.C., and none at all from then barbaric central Europe. Archaeology does not help much; presumably the Indo-Europeans were seminomadic and built no buildings that would endure. Their tools, if we have them, cannot be identified as theirs. Written records do not help; presumably the Indo-Europeans could not write; at least no scrap of writing has survived from them. But we do have their language, at least approximately, and from language much can be inferred. We know, for example, that they had words for bears, wolves, and pine trees; they had no words for alligators, elephants, and palm trees. Accordingly, we assume they lived in a cold climate. They had horses; they rode them, and drank their milk, but did not use them as draft animals. They had something with which to dig in the earth and promote growth, but they did not drag it like a plow. Accordingly, we assume they were seminomads with some herds, practicing a little dibble agriculture, but hunting and fishing, also. They spoke a highly inflected language, with some sixteen case distinctions for nouns in more than a dozen classes, and many conjugations of verbs; even adjectives were declined in three ways.

During the half-dozen millennia before Christ they underwent a population explosion, and spread in almost all directions, although especially west, south, and southeast. Possibly their acquisition of the horse gave them a fighting advantage over their neighbors. Whatever the cause, they initiated one of the most significant population movements of all time. Working east and southeast, they broke into the subcontinent of India, perhaps about 1500 B.C., where they established the Indo-European language which we call Sanskrit, ancestor of modern Indic. Another branch, speaking what we call Iranian, has given us modern Persian. Armenian and a number of minor languages fit in here somewhere. Some barbaric Indo-Europeans whom we call Hellenes worked into southern Russia and eventually down into the Balkan peninsula; by this time places like Crete, the Nile valley, and the Tigris–Euphrates valley were highly civilized. The Hellenes became civilized, too, in time; we know them as the Greeks. Meanwhile, peoples speaking a branch of Indo-European which we call Italic worked past the Alps and down into the Italian peninsula; they gave us Latin, and by descent, the Romance languages. People we call Celts or Kelts, near-relatives of the Italic group if we may judge from the similarities of the languages, spread west through northern Europe, and even took over the offshore islands, now England and Ireland. Another group, speaking what we call Proto-Germanic or Teutonic, followed them, overran them almost everywhere, and spread north into the Scandinavian peninsula. Those who migrated less, who spoke what we call Balto-Slavic, account for modern languages like Russian, Bulgarian, and Lithuanian, which has preserved the old Indo-European inflection system to a remarkable degree.

Thus the branches of the Indo-European language family account for most of the languages of Europe, some of the most important in Asia, and all the languages likely to survive in Australia and in North and South America. Extensive charts appear in most good dictionaries; for our purposes the concise chart on p. 356 will suffice. It should not be taken literally. The figure of speech of the family, by which we describe linguistic relationships, works well enough if

SIMPLIFIED CHART OF THE INDO-EUROPEAN LANGUAGE FAMILY

The chart emphasizes Western languages, especially those leading to English.

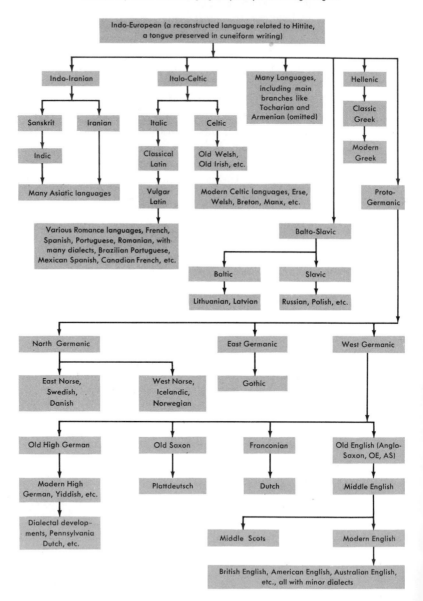

we remind ourselves that it is a figure of speech, not an accurate statement. A parent language does not give birth to a daughter language, as a mother bears a child, at a certain time and place. Rather, dialects of a language drift apart, usually because the speakers have drifted apart, and since language is always changing, it changes differently in the two groups. These two groups of speakers will have differing experiences, which will be reflected in language change, and the groups will coalesce in varying degrees with other linguistic communities. For a time the two ways of speaking can be thought of as two dialects of the same language, but eventually they change so much that the speakers of one group cannot understand the speakers of the other, and we must recognize two languages, which of course will already have developed dialects.

The Growth of English 20-4

When history dawned over northwestern Europe, England and Ireland were inhabited by the Celts, a relatively unsophisticated people, mostly hunters and fishers. The Romans readily conquered those who lived outside the swamps and mountains, and brought them a measure of civilization, but the Romans left about A.D. 400, and Germanic peoples moved west to fill in the power gap. They brought their own Indo-European language with them, a language which was not much more influenced by Celtic than was English in America by the native American languages. These invaders came from two important tribal groups, the Angles, who came apparently *in toto,* and the Saxons, who left enough of their number behind to form Saxony on the Continent; there were also a few people known as Jutes, of whom we know little. All these peoples spoke Low-Germanic dialects, the dialects that existed along the North European coast; their language is often referred to collectively as Anglo-Saxon, which we shall call Old English to distinguish it from Middle English and Modern English.

These recently arrived Germanic peoples took several centuries to defeat the Celts, to stop fighting one another, and to import much Mediterranean culture through France. They had been in some contact with the Romans on the Continent; one of their own crude roads they called a *weg,* our word *way,* which means a place one could go. The fine paved roads the Romans built they called by the Latin name, our word *street.* An inlet in the coast they called a *hafen,* our word *haven,* a place one was safe, but they had learned to call the marine installations the Romans built a *port* (Latin *portus*). In time they were converted to Christianity and began to borrow Greek, Latin, and French words associated with the church. They developed commercial and cultural connections with the Continent and borrowed more words, but not many. For a time they were overrun by some of their northern Germanic neighbors, the Norsemen, Danes and Norwegians, mostly; but these people eventually settled down, having brought with them other sorts of Germanic dialects which influenced the native speech, notably in the north and northeast. Then, as every schoolboy knows, the Normans conquered England in 1066.

The direct effects on the language of this conquest were not so great as are sometimes supposed, but the indirect effect was permeating. Although the invaders were few in number, and most Englishmen went right on talking English, French became the official language—the language of the court and culture, the language of big business; Latin remained the learned language. The Normans ruled, and words for government were Norman French, even *government* itself. The Normans directed commercial, educational, and ecclesiastical affairs, and words like *commerce, education,* and *ecclesiastics* stem from the French-Classical tradition, but common words like *learn* and *book* come from Old English, probably because native children were doing one with the other. Meat appeared on a wealthy Norman's table named with the Norman equivalent of our words *beef, veal, pork,* and *mutton,* but meat on the hoof was presumably tended by natives, who called the animals the Old English equivalent of *cow, calf, swine,* and *sheep—hog* and *pig* probably come from Norse and Dutch, but the principle is the same, for the common people were doing the work. Thus, learned or specialized words were borrowed, but the words that expressed the stuff of life continued to be native—*man, wife, child, house, bed, eat, live, die, love, fight.* Almost all the words language works with were native—*the, a, an, and, but, who, that, he, it, in, on, by.* Practically the only exceptions are *they, their,* and *them,* which seem to have come in with the Norsemen, and by 1066 can be thought of as native; they were not French. The result is that although borrowing from French, Latin, and Greek had begun before the Norman conquest and had somewhat increased after the Conquest, no great surge in borrowing took place until some two centuries after William won at Hastings; and of the hundred commonest modern English words only about ten per cent are borrowed.

Then the flood set in. By the fourteenth century, burgeoning England was developing close connections with the Continent, both commercial and cultural, and in that century more words were borrowed from French than in all the half-dozen centuries preceding. During the Age of Elizabeth another great wave of French and Latinate words swept in. By that time English had borrowed so many Gallicisms that it was running out of French to borrow; but when we could no longer borrow French words for armor, we borrowed Italian words for music, Latin words for botany and zoology, Greek words for physics and chemistry, and then French words again for food and fashions. We are still borrowing words from Latin and Greek and the Romance languages at a lively rate, especially in science and technology. The result is that a large percentage of the words in any English dictionary will be borrowed, mainly from Latin and Greek and the Romance languages; but the commonest words, the most useful words, are mainly native. They usually account for more than half of any piece of prose. To show how this goes, native words in the next sentence you read will be printed in italics. *The* result *would* differ *somewhat with the* subject *and the* author's style, *of* course; *if this* book *were about* philosophy, *the* borrowed *words would* probably *be more* numerous; *if it were about feeding pigs, they would be fewer; but the* results *could not be* changed *much, no* matter *what the* subject *nor how the* sentence *was written.*

The language changed also in structure. We have noted that Indo-European was a highly inflected language; the Indo-European forms and classes tended to combine in the Germanic languages, as they have in the Romance languages, but Old English still retained some eight classes of nouns—depending on how many subclasses you recognize—and about as many conjugations of two sorts of verbs. The adjective was still declined in two ways. But the language was already becoming notably analytic; apparently a speaker had to use the inflectional endings to be correct, but not much to be understood. After the Norman conquest English grammar changed relatively rapidly; apparently languages change rapidly when they are fighting for their lives. For the next four hundred years or so, endings weakened and mostly disappeared, while analytic devices developed rapidly. For example, Old English had no form for the future at all; now we have many, made up by analytic means—*shall go, will go, am going to go, expect to go, am planning on going,* and the like. Such changes have continued ever since, and are presumably continuing still, but since about the time of

Shakespeare these changes seem to have slowed. While the grammar of the language was changing, the sounds, also, were changing relatively rapidly, as was the vocabulary, for, as we have already seen, this was the great period of borrowing. Accordingly, we recognize three stages of the language which can be distinguished roughly as follows: Old English, from the beginnings (the earliest written work supposedly comes from about A.D. 675) to about 1100; Middle English, reflecting the period of great change, about 1100 to about 1500; Modern English, about 1500 to the present, often broken into Early and Late Modern English, dividing at about 1700. The names are abbreviated OE (Old English), ME (Middle English), and Mod.E. (Modern English).

We have noted that the sounds also changed. As a matter of fact, most of the individual sounds did not change much, but the whole pattern of sounds changed enough so that Old English today sounds like gibberish to any but a student of the language, and even Middle English is not very intelligible. Many of the dialects can be understood only by a specialist. Most consonants remained unchanged; Old English had a consonant often spelled *h* which sounded something like *khkhkh*. It has disappeared, leaving behind it spellings like the *gh* in *thought, though,* and *enough.* Most of the so-called short vowels like those in *hill* and *get* have remained unchanged. Most of the so-called long vowels and diphthongs, however, have changed, and a phonetician would describe these changes by saying that the sounds have moved forward and upward in the mouth. Vowels are made at different points in the mouth, depending in part on the position of the tongue; the sound heard as the first vowel in *mawkish* is low-back; the vowel heard in *meek* is high-front. This same vowel heard in *mawkish,* then, has moved toward *meek* but has not moved far enough to become the vowel in *meek.* For example, Old English had a word often spelled *rad,* which was pronounced about as a modern speaker would expect to say *rawd,* if there were such a word; it is our word *rode.* Similarly, the Old English word for *judgment,* pronounced like our word *dome* has come to be our word *doom.* In a word spelled *hat* and pronounced like our word *hot* the vowel moved forward so that the word became our *hate.* A word pronounced like our word *hay* and spelled *he* became our modern word *he.* Sounds that were already high and to the front became diphthongs; a sound like that in the word *moose* broke into a diphthong so that the word is now *mouse.* Similarly, a sound like that in our word *leek* became the diphthong in *like.*

Roughly speaking, the vowels in Old and Middle English are about what those correspondingly spelled vowels would be in German or Spanish; the stressed or long vowels have moved forward and upward in what is called the Great English Vowel Shift.

Naturally, this description of sound changes in English is simplified; details and exceptions have been omitted. One other change must be noted, however; the stress in many words has shifted, and sounds have been lost or changed with shifts in stress. For example, every reader of the *Canterbury Tales* will recall that Chaucer rhymes words for *flower* and *liquor.* He could do this since the word for *flower* was then pronounced so that it would rhyme approximately with our word *poor;* the French word for *liquor,* spelled something like *licour,* ended with the same sound, and like many words from Old French, had an accent on the last syllable. But the pattern of English is to put the accent on the first syllable; the accent in Old French *licour* has moved forward in English *liquor,* which no longer rhymes with *flower* although it did 600 years ago. Especially in American English the tendency is to reduce all vowels in unaccented syllables to a neutral vowel like that heard in *of* or the second syllable of *sudden.*

Semantic Change 20-5

Having seen how our vocabulary came into being, we are prepared to see what it has become. How many words do we have? Nobody knows, because we cannot agree on what a word is; and even if we could, we are gaining new ones and losing old ones, and nobody has ever collected them all in one place. Nobody could count them fast enough to get an answer, and it would be wrong as soon as we could write it down—*sputnik* became an English word almost overnight. But we can approximate. Large general dictionaries of English enter about a half-million words, and there must be some hundreds of thousands of obsolete, slang, and highly specialized words. Most words have several uses; many have dozens. We can probably assume that there are or have been more than two million named uses in English. Now the curious fact is that most of these words have come to us in one way or another from Indo-European. True we got *John* from Hebrew, *chemistry* from Arabic, *kimono,* from Japanese, *woodchuck* from Algonquin, and a scattering of others from non-Indo-European languages; but the great bulk of our words came to us directly from Indo-

European through Old and Middle English, or they were borrowed from languages that got them directly or indirectly from Indo-European. All the languages from which we have borrowed much have been Indo-European—Latin, Greek, French, Italian, Spanish, the Scandinavian languages, Dutch, German, even Indic and Russian, from which we are now beginning to borrow more. Did Indo-European have a large vocabulary? No, rather remarkably not, for so important a language. It was, after all, the language of a relatively unsophisticated people who did not need many names for things because they did not have many things; furthermore, they made so much use of decliners and classifiers that a syllable or two that embodied the core meaning could be made to serve many purposes. A relatively few hundred of them have been identified, and we have no reason to suppose there were more than a very few thousand. How have a few hundred Indo-European bases been blown up into hundreds of thousands of named uses in English? Obviously, if we say that these words came from Indo-European, *came from* must usually mean *grew from.*

We might look at sample words. Recently *backlog* has grown rapidly; manufacturers have backlogs of orders, judges have backlogs of cases, jobbers have backlogs of goods. But a century ago, apparently, nobody used the word in this way; a backlog was a device for radiant heating. It was put at the back of a large fireplace, with the lighter wood, including the forestick, in front of it so that the flames would make the front surface of the backlog glow and radiate heat. (The curious reader will find a description of such a fire in Whittier's *Snowbound.*) But the great backlog might burn for days, and perhaps for this reason became a figurative indication of something in reserve.

Neither did the parts of this word mean what they mean in *backlog.* The old Norse word *lag* did not mean wood; it is related to our verb *to lie,* and it meant *the lying thing.* That is, the *lag* or *log* meant the fallen tree after it was lying on the ground, and then the trunk of a fallen tree in any position. Nor has *back* always meant back. It comes from an Indo-European base **begh,* meaning to bend (the asterisk indicates that the base is reconstructed), and as such it became the name for the part of the body that bends. The bending, however, is on the side away from the face or front of the human body, and thus anything opposite the front could become the back—but not always, for the backbone of a quadruped is at the top, and correspondingly the back of a handsaw is at the top in sawing. Once *back* had developed the meaning of opposite to the front, it acquired all sorts of other uses; to *back up* is to go toward the rear, but to *back somebody up* is to support him, presumably from the rear. Any good modern dictionary is likely to have columns involving *back*, from *back and fill* to *backyard*.

As the word *back* is lived with, it grows to fit human needs. Having by generalization acquired the general force of *opposite-front* or *to-the-rear*, it can become specialized again in a great variety of words and phrases like *back stroke, backhanded, backorder;* and by more figures of speech a bumptious kind of person becomes a *back-slapper* and an old fashioned person can be *backnumberish*. The sorts of mental processes involved in these developments are too numerous to examine here, but anyone who will study what has happened to words will see that they grow as the human mind works. They employ generalizing from a particular example and specializing or particularizing from the general; along with these relatively pedestrian growths in use are sudden leaps in meaning involving figures of speech.

Indo-European Bases and Modern Cognates

Since words have descended into many languages, including Modern English and languages from which English has borrowed, dozens of words may go back to an Indo-European base, and they may retain similarities that help a writer to know more words and to use them with keener sense of their worth. Consider the descendants of the Indo-European base **derew-*, which meant tree or oak. This word descended into Proto-Germanic along with many others, and became OE *treow*, our word *tree*, which used to mean *wood* as well as a standing tree. It also became the name for things made out of "tree" in the sense of *wood;* that is, OE *treg* became our word *tray*, and OE *troh* became our word *trough*. It also became OE *treowe*, our word *true;* apparently the Old English people thought that being faithful was standing like a tree, very much as we now say *true as steel*. The Old English people also developed a verb with the idea, OE *trimian*, to make firm as a tree, which gives us modern *trim*.

Meanwhile, the same Indo-European base **derew-* was descending into other languages, from which we borrowed. Old Norse developed the word which we borrowed as *trust*, very much as we developed *true*. Latin had a word from **derew-* which we write as *durus*, meaning hard; before the day of metals, wood was considered hard. Figuratively, *durus* gives us words like *obdurate* meaning stubborn; and Scotch *dour*, meaning hard, unbending, severe, and, through French, *duress*, meaning hardship. It is probably related, also, to Latin *durare*, meaning to last, which gives us dozens of words like *endure* and *durable*. All these words are what we call *cognates* of the words that come to us through Old and Middle English; that is, they were "born together," (Latin *co-gnatus*, which means born together).

Indo-European bases are symbols to conjure with. Once a writer knows that words like *truth, trust, dour, obdurate,* and *trim* all go back to an ancient word for *tree* and are associated with the reliability, hardness, and enduring qualities of a tree, he can use these words with more grasp and he can more readily learn words like *induration, duramen,* and *durative* which may be strange to him. The following is a list of Indo-European bases and some of the cognates that have descended from them. For almost any of these bases an industrious student could find hundreds of modern English words—try the cognates of any of the words spelled *can,* for example. The root ideas are given in parentheses.

*ar- art, arm, armada, armor, article, articulate (to join)

*au- ear, auricle, auricular, auriculate, auscultation (to perceive)

*aues- east, easter, aurora, aurum (to shine)

*bhudh-/men- bottom, profound, foundation, fundament, funds (soil)

*deigh- dough, duff, figure, effigy, lady (to knead)

*deik- toe, digit, diction, token, teach (to point)

*dekm- hundred, decade, century, cent, reckon, read, riddle (ten)

*ed- eat, ate, edible, edibility, comestible, obese (to eat)

*edont- tooth, teeth, dentist, dentistry, orthodontist, edentate (tooth)

*gan(dh)- can (noun), canister, canasta, canal, channel (reed)

*gene-/*geno- can (v), know, gnome, agnostic, could, uncouth, quaint, acquaintance, cognition, ignorant, connoisseur (to know)·

*glogh- gloss, glossary, glottal, epiglottis, gloze (thorn)

*kali-/*gel- cold, cool, chill, gelid, gelatin, glacier, glace (cold)

*kel- hall, hold, hull, hill, hole, hulk, conceal, color, Colorado (to cover)

*kuon- hound, canine, cynic, canary, cynosure, kennel (dog)

*lauh-/*lewp- leaf, loft, lodge, lobby, lobbyist (peel off, bark roof)

*leip- life, live, leave, liparoid, lipolytic (to endure)

*leuq- light, luminous, lunar, Loki, de luxe, luxury, lucid (shine)

*mel- meal, mill, malm, mollusk, mollify, Molinari (to grind)

*oqw- eye, oculist, optical, ophthalmologist, ogle (to see)

*pater- father, Pope, paternal, expatriate, padre, patron (pa-pa)

*ped-/*pod- foot, pedal, pew, pedestrian, gastropod (to go)

*penqwe- finger, quintet, five, Quinquagesima, quintessence, pentagon (five)

*pou- fowl, pullet, pauper, foal, fowler, puerile (small)

*pu- foul, putrid, pus, putrefaction, filth, defile (to stink)

*que- head, capitol, chapter, hump (to bend)

*(s)que- hide, hat, hood, hut, hoard, cuticle (to cut)

*rewos- room, rural, rustic, roister, ream, reamer (wide)

*sequ- say, see, seer, saga, saw (to see)

*slab- (from *leb-) sleep, labor, lapse, laboratory, elapse, collapse, elabora-
tion, collaboration, relapse (to glide)

*wegh- way, vehicle, vehement, via, impervious, invoice, wain, wagon, con-
vex, voyage, deviation, obvious (to go)

*wer- ward, ware, revere, guard, warden, warranty, guarantee, aware, guard-
ian, reward, Ed, Teddy, disregard, wardrobe (to keep safe)

*wer-/*werbh- word, verb, verbal, verbatim, verve, verbosity, rhetoric, rhetorical (to say)

*werk- work, organ, playwright, wrought, erg, organize (to do)

Exercise 20

A. Recall that certain common words are likely to be native words from
Old English through Middle English; check 20-4 to find out which
sorts of common words are most likely to be native. Some borrowed
words have become common, *factor, faith,* and *circumstances,* for example.
Of these *factor* has become popular only very recently; *faith* became
popular early. Perhaps you can guess why. Now examine the following
list of words and divide them into two lists, one which you would guess
to be native words from Old English, and one which you would guess
to be borrowed. Then check the accuracy of your guesses against a
good dictionary. Try to account for the words about which you are
incorrect. CAUTION: words that appear in Middle English may have
come from Old English (Anglo-Saxon) or they may have been borrowed,
especially from Latin, French, or Old Norse; be sure you count as native
only those from Old English or Anglo-Saxon.

an, and, aggression, alembic, aria, as, ate, barbiturate, best, blaze, brain, brontosaurus, carve, church, churn, cook, common, council, cyclometer, demoralize, dog, earth, emphasize, enthymeme, expose, fat, father, filterability, flexion, for, game, give, glaciation, hand, habitual, hen, her, hypocrite, in, interest, iota, it, king, know, labyrinth, land, like, language, lay, legislature, lung, man, manage, mimicry, mow, not, nominative, odoriferous, paternal, piano, pick, prosody, pure, read, refutation, revenge, ring, scissors, scorpion, she, smoke, snake, spectroscope, the, that, to, transcendental, translate, turquoise, up, uxorial, who, why, yacht.

B. Consult the list of Indo-European bases in 20-6, and select any three. Then find twenty-five cognates in Modern English derived from each of these bases—for the more common of the bases it is possible to find up to a thousand apiece, counting phrases and rare or slang words. For additional information the best books to consult are Eric Partridge, *Origins,* 2nd ed. (New York, 1959), and *The Oxford Dictionary of English Etymology* (Oxford, 1966). *Webster's New World Dictionary of the American Language* will give further information on the Indo-European bases. The *New English Dictionary on Historical Principles* (*Oxford English Dictionary*) gives the history of each word. The *Century Dictionary and Cyclopedia* is a good place to look for phrases and specialized words. There are many slang dictionaries, both English and American.

C. Recall that words have changed their meanings, and look up 20-5 to see how they have changed. Then look up five meanings for each of the following words, and mark them G (for generalization), S (for specialization), or F (for figure of speech), depending on how the meaning seems to have developed:

1. bank	4. hand	7. pipe
2. chair	5. home	8. run
3. general	6. man	9. under

D. Select two or three of the dictionaries listed above and in 21-1, preferring those which you have already found useful for etymological study. Then look up the following words, and write a brief paragraph about each, summarizing the most interesting facts you have discovered about the history of the word. Be sure to use at least one book which provides Indo-European bases. The most readily available are Partridge, *The Oxford Dictionary of English Etymology,* and *Webster's New World Dictionary,* all cited above.

atlas	futhark	neighbor
bond	head	pants
canary	infantry	piano
defense	light	quick
explode	melancholy	stable
foot	mercury	travel

Vocabulary, Meaning, Word Choice

*For
Guide to Revision,
see page 381.*

Every successful writer needs an adequate vocabulary; we write with words.

Almost everyone has at least four basic vocabularies. He uses a relatively small number of words which we may call the *speaking vocabulary*, composed notably of words that come readily to the speaker's tongue. A dull person may use only a few hundred words in this way; even a moderately articulate speaker uses only a few thousand. Every literate person has a second vocabulary, a *writing vocabulary*, which includes the words in the speaking vocabulary, plus other words that he can call up. A good writer may employ a vocabulary of ten thousand, twenty-five thousand, perhaps fifty thousand words. A poor writer, on the other hand, may suffer from a vocabulary little larger than his speaking vocabulary. Every literate person has also a *reading vocabulary*, including words he would not speak in conversation or use when he writes but would know when he sees them written. For most people the reading vocabulary is much larger than either the speaking or writing vocabulary—fifty thousand, seventy-five thousand, a hundred thousand words, perhaps more. The fourth vocabulary, the largest of all, we may refer to as the *acquaintance vocabulary*. It includes the other three, but it includes, also, a considerable number of words which the owner has seen or heard before although he can do little more with them than guess their meaning in context. Vocabularies of this sort can be very large.

From the description of these four vocabularies, the student has probably guessed at least one way to improve his oral and written expression. Since speaking and writing vocabularies are relatively small and reading and acquaintance vocabularies relatively large, he has only to move words from his reading and acquaintance vocabularies into his speaking and writing vocabularies.

21-1 Word Hoards and Dictionaries

In any deliberate attempt to improve vocabulary, the most useful aid is usually a good dictionary. At this writing, four desk dictionaries are much the best in their class. They are *Webster's New World Dictionary of the American Language,* published by the World Publishing Company, *The American College Dictionary,* published by Random House, *Webster's New Collegiate Dictionary,* published by the G. & C. Merriam Company, and the Funk and Wagnalls *Standard College Dictionary,* published in a text edition by Harcourt, Brace & World. Students should know also the bigger dictionaries. *Webster's New International,* published by the G. & C. Merriam Company, the best one widely used in this country, is available in two editions. The second edition (1934, often with later dates on title pages) was widely admired; the third edition (1961) has been criticized as being too permissive, but if the student will use it as a description of American English, not as a usage book, he is likely to find it excellent; for common problems in usage, see the Glossary. Two British dictionaries of about the same size are excellent in various ways: the H. C. Wyld *Universal Dictionary* and the *Shorter Oxford.* In many ways the most interesting American dictionary is the *Century Dictionary and Cyclopedia,* which runs to ten volumes. It is old but a mine of valuable material. The great dictionary of the language, of course, is the *New English Dictionary on Historical Principles,* usually called the *Oxford English Dictionary.* For Americanisms it should be supplemented with the *Dictionary of American English,* and the more recent *Dictionary of Americanisms.* No student should be content with meager dictionaries. Why starve when we have the Lord's plenty? A writer will remember words longer and use them more accurately the more he knows about them. Furthermore, using a book like the *Oxford English Dictionary, The Oxford Dictionary of English Etymology,* or Eric Partridge's *Origins* can be downright exciting.

Any user of a dictionary should learn how much information he has available. He should examine the table of contents and preface and learn where to find foreign words and phrases, new words, proper names, abbreviations, and other special materials. He should learn the pronunciation system and find the list of abbreviations used in the book. A good desk dictionary should be adequate for at least the following uses:

1. *Spelling.* Dictionaries record preferred current spellings for words and indicate how words can be divided between syllables and whether compounds are usually written as single words or with hyphens.

2. *Pronunciation.* Dictionaries reprint each word with special marks to indicate the location of accents and the sounds of individual letters. The marks, called diacritical marks, are explained in the introduction, and examples may appear at the bottom of pages

3. *Word origins.* Every dictionary adequate for student use describes, using abbreviations explained in its introduction, the origins of words. Knowledge of derivations can be extremely useful in learning and remembering words.

4. *Grammatical information.* The dictionary indicates, with abbreviations, the grammatical uses for which a word is considered suitable.

5. *Usage.* Dictionaries endeavor to distinguish words which have general use from those which have not by indicating that certain words or certain usages of the word have limited currency; for common usages, see the Glossary.

6. *Definition.* Most important of all, a dictionary endeavors to define words. A good desk dictionary should define most meanings of all but rare and highly specialized words.

Increasing a Writing Vocabulary   21-2

A student familiar with his dictionary can increase his vocabulary with the following simple procedures.

1. *Learn words which you will use.* You may be able to baffle your friends if you know the meaning of *ento-ectad,* but words completely strange to you are hard to learn, and unless you use them you are likely to forget them. Learn words which you encounter and recognize but cannot define or use.

2. *When you learn a word, learn enough about it to make it yours.* Notice its various uses. Try to learn details about the origin and history of the word, where it came from and what has happened to it in English and American speech. For this, the *Oxford English Dictionary* is excellent; the *Century* and the others mentioned in 21-1 are also good.

3. *Learn words by groups.* If you will learn related words together, you can learn several words, sometimes a dozen, as easily as

you can learn one, often more easily. Suppose you were to look up the word *pictograph.* You would find that it is related to the words *picture* and *graph,* both of which you probably know, though you may have to find out what the Greek root *graph* means. Any good dictionary ought to have twenty or thirty more words related to *picture* in adjacent columns; make out a list and learn them all as a group. In learning words by groups, knowing foreign languages helps. Latin and Greek are especially useful. Even if you do not know these languages, you can learn a few Latin and Greek prefixes; a list of common ones will be found in Exercise 21C.

4. *Once you have learned a word, use it.* Many a good student, presented with a word he does not know, will look it up and immediately forget it. Do something deliberate to keep your words. Find a way to use them in conversation or in your next theme. Make up a list of words, put the list in your purse or pocket, and glance over it at some odd time every day for a week.

21-3   The Meaning of Meaning

Successful use of any vocabulary requires understanding the way words convey meaning. Strictly speaking, no word has meaning as a physical object can have length. The bars of metal in the Bureau of Standards, for instance, which determine our inches and feet, keep the same length at a given temperature, no matter who measures them, so long as the measuring is accurately done, but no words are kept at a controlled temperature in the Bureau of Standards. Words exist only in people's minds, and all minds are different. No word has a "meaning" that it inevitably calls up in everyone.

Theoretically Humpty Dumpty is justified in telling Alice, "When *I* use a word, it means just what I choose it to mean— neither more nor less." No authority can keep him from using the word *glory,* as he does, to mean *there's a nice knock-down argument for you.* Practically, however, Humpty is not communicating much. Words have no mystical connection with a particular "meaning," but communication is possible because at any time in history by common agreement people associate certain words with certain thoughts. We can communicate because we agree, closely enough for practical purposes, to let certain words symbolize certain ideas.

People can agree about meaning because words relate to things in the real world and are, relatively speaking, common and enduring, but the use and choice of words is complex because words are related to things through various human minds. A word is a symbol a human being uses to reveal his idea about something.

A writer or speaker can use *daisy* as a symbol to express his thought about a thing, a particular flower growing in a meadow, a referent. Speakers of English, by general agreement, use this symbol when they think of this particular kind of flower. The symbol would not work if the writer were thinking of a four-footed animal that brays or of a carved representation of George Washington. Neither would it work if he were writing in French or German. Conversely, any users of the language, readers or listeners, could interpret this symbol similarly.

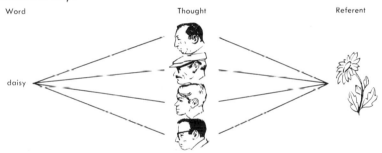

Furthermore, a writer may have various thoughts about a referent he sees growing in a meadow, and he may choose a word quite different from *daisy*.

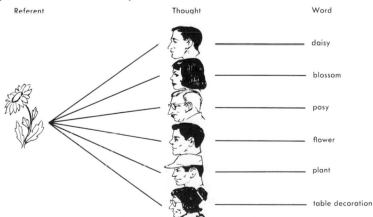

Each of these words—or any of many others—has the same referent, but each conveys a slightly different thought about the referent. *Plant* indicates that the writer is distinguishing the referent less precisely than does *flower; posy* suggests something about the attitude of the writer; *blossom* and *table decoration* indicate special attitudes toward the referent. These differences illustrate some of the distinctions involved in word choice, distinctions between concrete and abstract words, between denotation and connotation, between different meanings in different contexts. They may even represent differences in the same person from day to day or minute to minute as his mood changes.

21-4   Symbols and Word Choice

Modern philosophers, developing a theory of symbolic transformation, suggest that the symbol was the tool with which man built civilization, the device with which he made himself human. Man, living in a complicated and seemingly confused world, was able to reduce his universe to something like order by using symbols. Symbols, which could attach to thoughts as well as to physical phenomena, enabled man to grasp relationships, to see wholes. Man is a symbol-making animal; by his ability to deal in symbols he became unlike other creatures, which seem not able to use symbols, but only to respond to signs.

Man's discovery of symbols made language possible. We have already noticed that words are symbols, that a sequence of letters can stand for a thought about a flower and things associated with a flower, but the process which created language continues to operate, and words, acting as symbols, readily develop new symbolic significances. Take, for example, a favorite remark among stock brokers, "The bulls make money and the bears make money, but the pigs seldom do." Taken in the sense that we might call "literal," a bull meaning a male bovine and a bear a large ursine quadruped, the sentence makes no sense; neither of these makes money. But, of course, a bull is not here a bovine; *bull* is a symbol for an investor or a gambler who hopes to make money through a rise in the value of stocks he buys. Metaphorically, the word has developed new symbolic abilities which have become so crystallized that any good modern dictionary will list something of the sort as a meaning of the word. *Pig* is also a symbol, and in the sentence above we can guess readily what it means, but in this sense, a buyer who endeavors to make as much profit as possible, the word will not be found in dictionaries. That is, man's ability as a symbolmaker persists; man readily extends words to new symbolic uses and understands complex symbolic uses of words. Writers take advantage of man's continuing ability to make symbols.

Specifically, the symbolic power of words permits the writer to be both concrete and general, specific and abstract, at the same time. He can choose a specific detail which has the vividness of the concrete, but one that has general symbolic overtones. In conversation we rely on symbolic associations even though the symbols have become trite. We use *whistlestop* instead of describing abstractly a provincial town; we speak of a person who would kick small dogs or would poison wells. Often, of course, such specific comments are accompanied by more general ones, but the well-selected specific detail may give the desired impression more vividly and convincingly—perhaps even more accurately than the general description. Katherine Brush, in introducing a character, mentions two specific details but makes no general statement about the person:

> Miss Levin was the checkroom girl. She had dark-at-the-roots blonde hair and slender hips, upon which, in moments of leisure she wore her hands, like buckles of ivory loosely attached. —*Night Club*

Somerset Maugham makes a general comment about a room he is describing, then illustrates with two specific details which become symbols:

> It was a room designed not to live in but for purposes of prestige, and it had a musty, melancholy air. A suite of stamped plush was arranged neatly round the walls, and from the middle of the ceiling, protected from the flies by yellow tissue paper, hung a gilt chandelier. —*Rain*

Abstract and Concrete   21-5

Drawing a picture of the referent of the word *daisy* is relatively easy, and the resulting picture may also portray the referent of the word *flower*, but a picture of the referent behind the "full" meaning of the word *flower* would be more difficult. It would have to include not only daisies but also irises and begonias and violets and the blooms on thistles, in fact everything in the writer's experience which made up the idea he was expressing by the word. Or consider drawing a picture of the referent behind the word *beauty*. The picture of the daisy might be a part, but hundreds of other bits from the writer's experience would be necessary, and a picture would become virtually impossible.

Obviously, *flower* is more general than *daisy*, and *beauty* is more general than *flower*. *Beauty* can also be said to be *abstract*, whereas *daisy* is *concrete*. Roughly, one can say that abstract words refer to generalities or to ideas, and that concrete words refer to things or objects. Or, in terms of the discussion above, concrete words stand for a thought of a referent which can be pictured or specified; abstract words go back to referents so complex or general that they cannot be visualized. These statements, however, require two qualifications. First, *abstract* and *concrete* are relative terms, like *general* and *specific* (see 4-2). Compare the following:

There was *something* on the table.
There was a *creature* on the table.
There was a *tarantula* on the table.

Creature is more concrete than *something, tarantula* more concrete than *creature*. The ideas become more specific; the words become more concrete and increase in exactness and suggestiveness as they do so. Second, just as the general develops out of the specific, abstract expressions grow from more concrete ones. *Color* stands for a thought which would be hard to express if we had only more concrete terms like *red, yellow, blue, green.*

Consider the following sentence proposed by George Orwell to illustrate how some writers might translate a passage of the Bible:

Objective consideration of contemporary phenomena compels the conclusion that success or failure in competitive activities exhibits no tendency to be commensurate with innate capacity, but that a considerable element of the unpredictable must invariably be taken into account.

Although the sentence exaggerates deliberately, it suggests how abstractions can obscure ideas. Compare the passage from Ecclesiastes which Orwell has "translated":

I returned, and saw under the sun, that the race is not to the swift, nor the battle to the strong, neither yet bread to the wise, nor yet riches to men of understanding, nor yet favour to men of skill; but time and chance happeneth to them all.

Instead of one general statement, the original uses five specific examples; instead of abstractions like *consideration, phenomena, conclusion, success,* and *failure,* the original uses more concrete words like *race, battle, bread,* and *riches.* Almost always, clear and accurate writing uses concrete words whenever possible.

Denotation and Connotation; Slanting   21-6

Roughly speaking, a word's communication of a thought about a referent is the word's denotation, what is sometimes called its "dictionary meaning." *Flower* and *table decoration,* therefore, have different denotations; but *flower* and *posy* can hardly be distinguished in denotaton. Still, no botanist today would write that "the begonia bears monecius posies"; he would feel that the word *posy* is unsuited to scientific description. On the other hand, one might wish to suggest that certain wallpaper was old-fashioned by saying, "It was all cluttered up with pink posies." That is, each of these words can do something more than point to a particular thought. This power of a word to do more than designate, to make emotional and interpretive suggestions, is the word's *connotation.* Connotation is an essential part of the meaning of a word, to be distinguished from denotation only in analysis.

Connotation is always individual. To a garden lover, the word *flower* may suggest hours of pleasure in the sunshine, a sense of pervading joy, or even ecstasy. To someone else it may suggest Georgia O'Keefe's paintings, or if one has been ill from mimosa, it may even suggest nausea. But to a considerable degree, even though the basis of connotation is personal, most people share much of the connotative power of a word, for most of us have somewhat similar heritages and experiences. The word *home* connotes something different for each of us, but most people share feelings about the word, and would distinguish them from other feelings associated with *house.* Thus, to a degree, the emotional qualities of words can be used for communication, and the connotative power of words is so great that most good writers make conscious use of connotation.

In general, the connotations of words serve to emphasize certain characteristics of a referent or to reveal attitudes toward it. *Statesman* and *politician* may describe the same person, refer to the same referent.

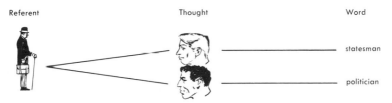

Referent	Thought	Word
		statesman
		politician

The thoughts expressed by the words differ, however; the words have become associated with emotional suggestions so that *statesman* emphasizes wisdom, dignity, vision, and integrity, and *politician,* especially in American use, suggests intrigue, time-serving, and self-seeking. Through their connotations, the words present different views of the referent. Connotational meanings, therefore, are exploited especially in any writing or speaking which seeks to persuade, to move, or to stimulate emotion.

Concern for propaganda and analysis of propaganda have made our society alert to the emotional qualities of words, especially as used in politics or advertising. Compare the following statements, which describe the same incident:

Senator A ranted interminably this afternoon in a bigoted attack on the new budget.

Senator A delivered a full and detailed address this afternoon in a spirited criticism of the new budget.

In their emotional content the words in the first are clearly "slanted" or "loaded" against the senator; words in the second seek to move the reader to approve the speech. To suggest that "emotional" words should not be used is absurd, but the writer should be aware of their limitations and their weaknesses. From neither of the statements above does the reader know what Senator A did. The connotations of the words outweigh their denotations. Many similar words in English, especially words like *freedom, communist, authority, terrific,* or *civil liberties,* have developed such varied connotations that they can be used only with care and skill if the writer is to avoid distortion. Furthermore, misleading use of the emotional power of words is as false as any other kind of verbal lie because the connotations of a word are part of it. The writer who intentionally distorts the truth through his choice of "loaded" or "slanted" words should be challenged on his integrity rather than his skill with language.

21-7 Figurative Language; Metaphor

Irresponsible exploitation of connotations can distort truth, but skillful management of emotional meanings can make language more precise, more interesting, more intense. The importance of connotations can be seen especially in figurative language, in a device like the metaphor. Metaphor, or comparison in language, is more than embellishment; it is part of language itself. We use metaphors constantly in conversation (*He ran like a deer; he is a little devil*). Words develop through metaphors; we speak of the *hands* of the clock, the *foot* of the bed, the *head* of the household, the *legs* of a chair. Sails *belly,* and crowds *thunder* applause as the *shell shoots* across the *line.* We no longer think of the italicized words as figures of speech, but they developed as metaphors, and words are developing in this manner constantly, as we saw in Section 20. Metaphor, then, is a device by which connotations of words provide precise and vivid meanings. Consider the following relatively elaborate comparison from *Romeo and Juliet,* which uses one of the words considered above.

> This bud of love, by summer's ripening breath,
> May prove a beauteous flower when next we meet.

The metaphor is complex, but essentially it uses the word *flower* to express the referent usually denoted by *love.*

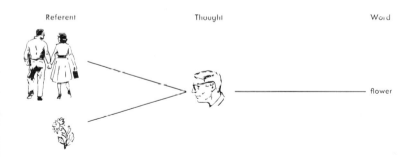

Referent   Thought   Word

flower

By using the word *flower* rather than the word *love,* Shakespeare emphasizes parts of both the connotational and denotational meanings of love. He makes us think of the "flowerlike" significance of love, its ability to grow, its beauty, its relation with time. The metaphor, in its context, allows the writer to exploit the emotional meanings of the words

Words in Their Contexts 21-8

Words affect, and are affected by, the words they accompany. The writer needs to choose his words with care, selecting so that in both denotation and connotation they are appropriate in their contexts. Consider, for example, the following sentences:

My *love* is like a red, red rose.
The *love* of money is the root of all evil.
Greater *love* hath no man than this, that a man lay down his life for his friends.
Friendship is *Love* without his wings.
The score was forty-*love*.
God is *love*.

The word *love* appears in each sentence, but the meanings differ. The context, the company the word keeps, indicates its meaning.

The writer must choose his words with their contexts in mind. The lists of discriminative synonyms in dictionaries suggest how words fit different contexts (look up, for example, *joke, wit,* or *wise*). Even synonyms cannot be changed at random; for example, dictionaries list *exonerate* as a synonym for *clear*. Substituting *exonerate* would sharpen meaning in a sentence like *The attorney hoped to clear the ex-convict,* but it would not serve in a sentence like *Mary cleared the dishes from the table.*

21-9   Precision, Vigor, and Economy in Word Choice

As the discussions above indicate, choosing words with precise meaning and appropriate tone is not easy, but choice of the exact word often distinguishes good writing from mediocre. Almost any piece of good prose, such as the following, will illustrate:

For Cooper was distressed by the new American world he found and bitterly resented many of its changes. He felt that America had retrogressed a century in these seven years, or perhaps he had stayed away too long, for he remembered Jefferson's saying that Americans might find themselves aliens if they spent more than five years out of the country. He had gone abroad in the days of the stagecoach, and the railroads were running on his return, while the scholarly John Quincy Adams had given place to Jackson and the piping times of ultra-republicanism. He was not prepared for the tawdry vulgarity that assailed him in the New York streets, or the flaring red of the bricks and green of the blinds, and this "rainbow capital" seemed to him a mean provincial town that could hardly compare with the second-rate cities of Europe. The scramble for money depressed him, and the general self-complacency, as if the "perfection of the people" had really been achieved, the mania for change and speculation, the "gulpers" in the dining-rooms, the pigs that ran wild in the gutters and the rowdy press. For the yellow journals of the eighteen-thirties abounded in violent epithets, "offal," "garbage," "liar" and "bilious braggart," and Cooper himself was presently styled a "spotted caitiff" and a "leprous wretch," a "tainted hand," an assassin and a jackass. The most respectable editors, Bryant, for instance, assaulted one another on the streets. Cooper was disconcerted too by the coldness of the ordinary American manner, in contrast to the warmth and cordiality he had known in France, the lack of aesthetic sensibility, the timidity and wariness, so different from the freedom and frankness he had known of old. For when he referred to the bad pavements and the poor lighting of the town, his friends led him aside and begged him to be careful. It was unpatriotic to criticize American things. It was disloyal to suggest that the Bay of Naples could be mentioned in the same breath with the harbour of New York. It was shocking to compare the Alps with the Rockies. Yet, for all the bragging one heard in New York, there was little independence of mind, and England still did most of the thinking for the country.

—VAN WYCK BROOKS, *The World of Washington Irving*

Study of this passage reveals that certain words do a great deal. Some of the vividness of the picture James Fenimore Cooper found on his return grows from details, the pigs in the New York gutters, the author of *Thanatopsis* assaulting a fellow editor, but part of it grows from Brooks' choice of words. The country had "retrogressed a century" since the "days of the stagecoach." Modifiers make precise distinctions: "*piping* times," "*tawdry* vulgarity," "*flaring* red," or "*rowdy* press." Brooks uses words out of the day to picture the day, the "gulpers" in the dining rooms, and epithets for Cooper like "leprous wretch." One might notice the variety of words Brooks uses to indicate different degrees of disturbance in Cooper; sometimes he is "depressed," sometimes "disconcerted," and he "bitterly resented" the changes. One might notice, also, the impact of the word *led* in the passage, "his friends *led* him aside and begged him to be careful," and the nice distinction among *unpatriotic, disloyal,* and *shocking*.

English works best when used efficiently. People in dreadful need of communication can usually make themselves understood in few words. "Help!" "Fire!" "Murder!" say more than "I am in need of assistance," "There is a conflagration," and "A person is being illegally dispatched." Of course complicated ideas and fine distinctions require elaborate treatment; they cannot be considered in few words, but the fewer the better, so long as the expression is adequate. Good writing results from a plenitude of ideas and an economy of words, not from a desert of ideas and a flood of vocabulary. Most writers, especially most beginning writers, should throw out words, and even well-constructed sentences may improve with the removal of nonessential or redundant words. The following will bear more than normal attention.

1. *Cutting deadwood.* Good writers resolutely cut out the words doing no work. Notice the italicized words in the following sentences:

It happened that she was elected *to the position of* secretary *and this was* [of] the oldest club *that existed* in the city.

Although he had always considered his sister *to be of the* awkward *type,* he found her *to be* a good dancer.

With the italicized words omitted, the sentences are clearer and sharper.

2. *Direct expressions.* Often shorter, more direct routes to meaning can be discovered. Notice, for example, the substitutions suggested in brackets for the italicized words in the following sentences.

Mary's tears *had the effect of making* [made] Jim regret *the accusation which he made hastily* [his hasty accusation].

By the time the end of the month rolled around [By the end of the month] *it seemed to us a certainty* [we knew] that our first business venture would *be a success* [succeed].

A well-chosen verb or adjective may say as much as a wordy clause.

3. *Economy in modifiers.* Every modifier added to a sentence decreases the impact of the others. Words like *very, really, surely, actually, merely, simply, great,* and *real* tend to accumulate in careless composition. Consider whether the modifiers italicized in the following sentence should be omitted.

As I crept *hesitantly* out of the *dark,* dingy, *grimy* hotel and felt the *blazing,* withering sun on my back I was *very* sure I did not *really* want to *actually* spend a month in the city.

Often the effect of modifiers can be embodied in telling nouns or verbs. *Liar,* for most purposes, says everything in *a person given by nature or habit to disseminating untruths; canter* or *gallop* says more than *ride at a rapid pace.*

Brief writing is not necessarily good writing; expression in a complicated world must usually be detailed, and details require words, many of them. Even publishers, who have to pay printing bills, often advise authors to "write it out," but granted that the writer uses words enough to express himself, the fewer words the better. Notice the following:

Spring comes to the land with pale, green shoots and swelling buds; it brings to the sea a great increase in the number of simple, one-celled plants of microscopic size, the diatoms. Perhaps the currents bring down to the mackerel some awareness of the flourishing vegetation of the upper waters, of the rich pasturage for hordes of crustaceans that browse in the diatom meadows and in their turn fill the waters with clouds of their goblin-headed young. Soon fishes of many kinds will be moving through the spring sea, to feed on the teeming life of the surface and to bring forth their own young.

—RACHEL L. CARSON, *Under the Sea Wind*

This is good writing, not because it is brief, but because it is economical. Miss Carson is saying something more than that the mackerel, after hibernating off the continental shelf, mysteriously wake up every spring; she is fitting the annual migration of the mackerel into the impelling cycle of the seasons; explanation requires detail, and details require words. The student might try going through this passage, endeavoring to remove one word without damaging the effect. In the last line, for instance, *teeming life* could be reduced to *life*, but the account would suffer. Note how much is implied in a passage like "hordes of crustaceans that browse in the diatom meadows." Word economy is not sparing words; it is putting them to work.

Guide to Revision 21   W

Choose words as precisely as possible to fit their contexts.

Problems in word choice may vary from gross confusions of unfamiliar words to the necessity of drawing fine distinctions between synonyms. Mrs. Malaprop, a character in Sheridan's *The Rivals,* made herself famous and added the word *malapropism* to the language by misusing words she did not understand. When she complimented herself on a "nice derangement of epitaphs" and said that someone was "headstrong as an allegory on the banks of the

Nile," she certainly did not mean to say *derangement, epitaphs,* or *allegory*. Slips in word choice may be as destructive of prose as were Mrs. Malaprop's, but less easily observed. They may result from ignoring connotations of a word, from failure to utilize concrete terms, from cluttering prose with needless verbiage or from failure to distinguish synonyms like *splash, slop,* and *spatter* which may be equally concrete but differ in meaning.

ORIGINAL	REVISION
The capture of the ridge had seemed an inhuman feat. [*Confusion with* humanly impossible *or* superhuman *may account for the inaccuracy.*]	Capturing the ridge had seemed impossible.
The inheritance brought them only transitive pleasure.	The inheritance brought them only transitory pleasure.
Dr. Brinkley ran a fowl with other regulations concerning his practice.	Dr. Brinkley ran afoul of regulations concerning his practice.

Words similar in spelling or meaning are easily confused; distinctions between many common words must be learned (see Glossary and 26-2).

ORIGINAL	REVISION
The critic's statement inferred that he had plagiarized.	The critic's statement implied that he had plagiarized.
Every affect has a cause.	Every effect has a cause.
Most everybody went to the party.	Almost everybody went to the party.
There were less women than men in the class.	There were fewer women than men in the class.
When he entered, her face turned a livid red.	When he entered, her face turned a vivid red.

21a   Wordiness   Wordy

Wordy writing is seldom wordy in only one way. Often a writer can revise a wordy passage best by thinking it through again from the beginning and trying to express the idea as simply and directly as possible. Good thinking, expressed in simple structures with carefully chosen words, will automatically remove wordiness.

WORDY	CONCISE
Although the story is in the supernatural class, Hawthorne manages to put over his point and show the effects on a person when he is confronted with the fact that everyone contains a certain amount of evil in their physical make-up.	Hawthorne uses the supernatural to suggest that there is some evil in everyone. *[The original version was cluttered; with the verbiage cleared away, the writer can make the sentence direct and precise.]*
But if you get right down to the facts in the case, we cannot reorient this tract of real estate, nor can we determine what disposition is fated to be made in the future of this acreage fresh from God's hand, and last but not least we cannot render a decision as to whether or not this section of the earth's surface is to be employed for purposes other than those of the divine.	But in a larger sense, we cannot dedicate, we cannot consecrate, we cannot hallow this ground. —ABRAHAM LINCOLN, "Gettysburg Address"

Spec   Concrete and Abstract Words   21b

Some words are more concrete than others. They refer to real things, even to particular objects. A blow is more specific than an insult, a right hook to the ear more specific than a blow. General and abstract words have their uses, but on the whole, vigorous writing is specific, concrete writing. Many a dull writer has only to substitute concrete words for his more abstract words to become interesting.

ABSTRACT	MORE SPECIFIC
When we were in some fighting it was hard to know what was going on because so many things were happening that usually you did not know much about it until after it was over. You were excited, and though maybe you would know the things which were occurring, it was hard afterward to know just what had happened, especially around you.—Student theme.	Who know the conflicts, hand to hand—the many conflicts in the dark, those shadowy-tangled, flashing moonbeamed woods, the writhing groups and squads, the cries, the din, the cracking guns and pistols, the distant cannon, the cheers and calls and threats and awful music of the oaths, the indescribable mix; the officers' orders, persuasions, encouragements; the devils fully roused in

ORIGINAL (*Cont.*)

REVISION (*Cont.*)

human hearts; the strong shout, *Charge, men, charge;* the flash of the naked sword, and rolling flame and smoke?—Walt Whitman's diary, slightly repunctuated.

I always used to like to go out camping when I was younger because Father was always doing funny things, and that always made us have a lot of fun. Father was always a funny man and he would do things you would not expect your father to be doing, and usually his things didn't work.

Camping with Father was always fun, because he was sure to come lugging some contraption he had just invented, a chipmunk-repeller, which was supposed to keep chipmunks from devouring the soap— and did not—or an electrically driven decoy duck, which would get short-circuited halfway across the lake.

Abstract words are sometimes used as if they had no meaning at all, as blankets to cover meaning in the vicinity of the writer's idea. Such words go in and out of fashion, but the following are among those currently popular: *angle, area, aspect, breakdown, circumstances, claim* (verb), *picture, point, facet, factor, setup, situation, deal, phase, basic, regard, fundamental, force, rate* (verb), *worthwhile, unique, put over, put across, over-all,* and *outstanding.* Blanket words are closely related to jargon and often appear in roundabout and wordy sentences.

ORIGINAL

REVISION

The question in this regard is directly related to the basic circumstances of the situation.

The question is basic.

The abnormal condition within Hamlet's mind is a governing factor which is the foremost force in molding his character traits.

The turmoil in Hamlet's mind altered his character.
[*This may not be true, but it approximates what the student apparently meant to say.*]

21c   Colored, "Slanted," or Prejudicial Words   Slant

In an oration once popular in high-school contests, Regulus addressing the Carthaginians referred to "the slimy ooze that stagnates in your veins," contrasting it unfavorably to the blood of the Romans. Obviously Regulus was not trying to be objective in his typing of Carthaginian blood. Similarly, when a mother says, "Now take your nice medicine," she is not necessarily describing objectively her own impression of the medicine. As they are here used *slimy, ooze, stagnates, nice* are colored, calculated to influence feelings, not to communicate truth. The connotations of words always influence their effect. Usually colored words are combined with ideas calculated to appeal to fears and prejudice. Notice the following:

Rush me airmail without cost or obligation to me all the exciting facts about your amazing new "Pay-check Protective System" that pays me $400.00 a month for life with other valuable benefits. I understand that the remarkable dividends of this plan will give me money to help pay bills, keep me out of debt, and take care of my family's needs.

At times a writer may wish to play upon the emotions and the prejudices of others, but most writing is the better for being objective. Often, slanted words are so obvious in their intent that they fail to make even a convincing emotional appeal.

ORIGINAL

In high school there were some radicals who always stabbed any new worthwhile project in the back just because they were rats at heart. [*Apparently, the writer is trying to discredit by calling names, but he is mainly discrediting himself.*]

My mother is a perfect angel with a saintly face and the most perfect disposition in the world. [*Words like* angel *and* saintly *have some emotional force, but are vague enough to be unconvincing.*]

REVISION

There was one faction in our high school which tried to block any change that my group instituted. [*The attitude of the writer has changed, and relatively objective words have replaced colored words.*]

Mother is seldom cross, never angry without good reason, and always helpful; years of smiling have left little wrinkles at the corners of her mouth. [*Concrete terms clarify the passage and strengthen the appeal.*]

Fig   Metaphorical Writing   **21d**

Comparisons and figures of speech may make language brighter, more specific, more precise. Many words have their meanings because they are old metaphors no longer recognized. *Outskirts* comes to us from the days when women wore more skirts than most women do now, and the "outskirts" were of course on the circumference. Much of the most vigorous, charming writing is metaphorical writing.

PROSAIC

Falstaff is so big and fat that he sweats a great deal when he walks too fast.

METAPHORICAL

Falstaff sweats to death
And lards the lean earth as he walks along.

—SHAKESPEARE, *Henry IV*, Pt. 1

My roommate has a funny-looking face because his nose is short and kind of flattened.

My roommate's nose looks as though he always has it pressed up against a window pane.

The long mountains came down to the abrupt coast, and you could see them rather mixed up, running every which way. Some were angular, and some were rounded, and they all looked sad and depressing. Back from the shore where they were high the peaks were all snow-covered, and even nearer there were patches of snow and glaciers on them.

These long mountains . . . lie, one after another, like corpses, with their toes up, and you pass by them, . . . and see their noses, tipped by cloud or snow, high in behind, with one corpse occasionally lying on another, and a skull or a thigh-bone chucked about, and hundreds of glaciers and snow-patches hanging to them, as though it was a winter battlefield.

—WORTHINGTON C. FORD,
Letters of Henry Adams

A metaphor can be a useful instrument. So can dynamite. Either can be dangerous. Avoid mixed metaphors, and avoid shifting metaphors so quickly that your reader is thinking about one figure of speech when you have gone on to another.

ORIGINAL

A creative person who has no political crystallization, not merely cuts the production end of his work, but loses a vital gut that is part of the social continuum.
[*Doubtless the man who published this to advertise an obscure magazine thought he was both profound and witty.*]

REVISION

A creative artist who ignores contemporary politics limits himself as a creator and to a degree cuts himself off from society.
[*This is prosaic, perhaps, but understandable, and at the worst, not silly. The artist is no longer whacking off his production while disemboweling himself, and all because he has not undergone crystallization.*]

Since then the snowball of knowledge has swept relentlessly on, stamping with each year another rivet of reliability and craftsmanship into the name of the House of Melarkey.—*London trade advertisement.*

The House of Melarkey has advanced with the times, in experience, in craftsmanship, in reliability.

Some mixed figures, like those above, result from a misguided striving to write well. Worse are the mixed metaphors caused by careless use of language.

ORIGINAL	REVISION
He is always getting on band wagons, going off in all directions, and ending up clear out in left field.	He is impetuous.
We keep clipping the wool off the goose that lays the golden eggs, and instead of getting on the beam we pump her dry.	Taking excessive profits inevitably destroys the source of those profits.

Dir   **"Direction" in Words**   **21e**

Words may have meanings which will make sense in only one "direction." That is, if you mean that Irene likes jewels, you can say *"Jewels have an attraction for Irene."* You cannot say *"Irene has an attraction for jewels"* without meaning something quite different, without using *have an attraction* with what might be called "false direction."

ORIGINAL	REVISION
The Elizabethan audience had a great fascination for wars and duels.	Wars and duels fascinated the Elizabethan audience.
I have a very inadequate feeling when I think of writing about this book.	I feel inadequate when I think of writing about this book.
Nor does an enemy of the prairie dog ever manage to approach the "town" unawares.	No enemy of the prairie dog can approach the "town" undetected.
Once action is put forth the problems become disintegrated; therefore, let us build up our weaknesses.	Prompt action will solve many problems; therefore let us overcome our weaknesses.
Necessary financial reimbursements sent to the above address will receive my prompt attention.	I shall promptly pay any bills sent to my address.

Exercise 21

A. On the following pages are reproductions from *Webster's New World Dictionary of the American Language,* College Edition, the *American College Dictionary,* the *Standard College Dictionary,* and *Webster's New Collegiate Dictionary.* Try to learn what you can about the contents of a good dictionary by comparing these pages in detail, beginning with the entry for *year.* Notice especially certain sorts of evidence.

1. *Word-list.* The dictionaries differ in the words they have used as entries. Can you see why? We may assume that the editors of all the dictionaries knew all the words, but that some felt that the available space was better used for one sort of information, some for another. How do the word-lists differ? (It is possible, of course, that the editors of a dictionary missed a new word, or that the word or its use had not become common at the time the dictionary was edited. Some dictionaries have been re-edited more recently than others.)

2. *Definitions.* How do the definitions compare? Are those in some dictionaries clearer and easier to understand than others? Are some more exact or accurate than others? Is there any difference in the way the editors of the various dictionaries have gone about defining words? Have some used devices in definition that the others did not use? Do some include uses of words not recognized in others? Have some wisely omitted uses?

3. *Compounds and phrases.* Do the dictionaries differ in the compounds and phrases they have felt worth including? For example, only one includes *yearbook* in the sense of a student annual, and none enters *year-end* as a modifier.

4. *Etymologies.* Which dictionaries have the best etymologies? Which are the most detailed? The clearest? The most interesting? Are some too long and detailed?

5. *Grammar and Usage.* Do the dictionaries differ in their treatment of spelling, pronunciation, grammar, and the like?

Now write an account of your findings, 300–500 words long, citing specific evidence. You will not be able to answer all the questions above with appropriate detail, but assemble evidence, choose a theme idea, and support it with the evidence you have found.

year (yĭr), *n.* **1.** a period of 365 or 366 days, divided into 12 calendar months, now reckoned as beginning Jan. 1 and ending Dec. 31 (**calendar year**). **2.** a period of approximately the same length in other calendars. **3.** a space of 12 calendar months reckoned from any point: *he left May 15, to be gone a year.* **4.** a period consisting of 12 lunar months (**lunar year**). **5.** (in scientific use) the time interval between one vernal equinox and the next, or the period of one complete apparent circuit of the ecliptic by the sun, being equal to about 365 days, 5 hours, 48 minutes, 46 seconds (**tropical year, solar year, astronomical year**). **6.** the true period of the earth's revolution round the sun; the time it takes for the apparent traveling of the sun from a given star back to it again, being about 20 minutes longer than the tropical year, which is affected by the precession of the equinoxes (**sidereal year**). **7.** the time in which any planet completes a revolution round the sun. **8.** a full round of the seasons. **9.** a period out of every 12 months, devoted to a certain pursuit, activity, or the like: *the college year.* **10.** (*pl.*) age. **11.** (*pl.*) old age: *a man of years.* **12.** (*pl.*) time, esp. a long time. **13. a year and a day**, a period specified as the limit of time in various legal matters, as in determining a right or a liability, to allow for a full year by any way of counting. [ME *yeer*, OE *gēar*, c. D *jaar*, G *jahr*, Icel. *ār*, Goth. *jēr*]

year·book (yĭr′bŏŏk′), *n.* a book published annually, containing information, statistics, etc., about the year.

year·ling (yĭr′lĭng, yûr′-), *n.* **1.** an animal one year old or in the second year of its age. **2.** *Horse Racing.* a horse one year old, dating from Jan. 1 of the year of foaling. —*adj.* **3.** a year old. **4.** of a year's duration. [f. YEAR + -LING¹ Cf. G *jährling*]

year·long (yĭr′lông′, -lŏng′), *adj.* lasting for a year.

year·ly (yĭr′lĭ, yûr′-), *adj., adv., n., pl.* **-lies.** —*adj.* **1.** pertaining to a year, or to each year. **2.** done, made, happening, appearing, coming, etc., once a year, or every year. **3.** continuing for a year. **4.** lasting but a year. —*adv.* **5.** once a year; annually. —*n.* **6.** a publication appearing once a year.

yearn (yûrn), *v.i.* **1.** to have an earnest or strong desire; long. **2.** to be moved or attracted tenderly. [ME *yerne*, OE *giernan*, c. Icel. *girna*]

yearn·ing (yûr′nĭng), *n.* **1.** deep longing, esp. when tinged with tenderness or sadness. **2.** an instance of it. —**yearn′ing·ly,** *adv.* —Syn. **1.** See **desire**.

yeast (yēst), *n.* **1.** a yellowish, somewhat viscid, semi-fluid substance consisting of the aggregated cells of certain minute fungi, which appears in saccharine liquids (fruit juices, malt worts, etc.), rising to the top as a froth (**top yeast** or **surface yeast**) or falling to the bottom as a sediment (**bottom yeast** or **sediment yeast**), employed to induce fermentation in the manufacture of alcoholic liquors, esp. beer, and as a leaven to render bread, etc., light and spongy, and also used in medicine. **2.** a commercial substance made of living yeast cells and some meallike material, used in raising dough for bread, etc. **3.** a yeast plant. **4.** spume or foam. **5.** ferment or agitation. —*v.i.* **6.** to ferment. **7.** to be covered with froth. [ME *yeest*, OE *gist*, c. G *gäscht, gischt*] —**yeast′-less,** *adj.* —**yeast′like′,** *adj.*

yeast cake, living yeast cells compressed with a little starch into a small cake. In **dried yeast cake**, yeasts are inactive; in a **compressed yeast cake** they are active and the product is perishable.

yeast plant, any of the minute, unicellular ascomycetous fungi constituting the genus *Saccharomyces*, and related genera.

yeast·y (yēs′tĭ), *adj.* **1.** of, containing, or resembling yeast. **2.** frothy or foamy. **3.** trifling or frivolous.

Yeats (yāts), *n.* **William Butler,** 1865–1939, Irish poet, dramatist, and essayist: Nobel prize, 1923.

Yed·do (yĕd′dō′), *n.* former name of **Tokyo.** Also, **Ye′do′.**

yegg (yĕg), *n. U.S. Slang.* a criminal, esp. one who robs banks, safes, etc. Also, **yeggman.** [orig. obscure; ? var. of *yekk* beggar, a term once popular in California Chinatowns]

year (yir) *n.* **1.** The period of time in which the earth completes one revolution around the sun, consisting of 365 or 366 days divided into 12 months and now reckoned as beginning January 1 and ending December 31; also, a similar period in other calendars. See ASTRONOMICAL YEAR, LUNAR YEAR, SIDEREAL YEAR. **2.** Any period of 12 months, usually reckoned from a specific date or time: a *year* from now. **3.** The period of time during which a planet revolves once around the sun. **4.** A specific period of time, usually less than a year, given over to some special work or activity: the school *year.* **5.** *pl.* Age, especially old age: active for his *years.* **6.** *pl.* Time: in *years* gone by and *years* to come. Abbr. *y., yr.* — **year after year** Every year. — **a year and a day** *Law* A time designated for the purpose of ensuring a full year's lapse. — **year by year** Each year; with each succeeding year. — **year in, year out** From one year to the next; without cessation. [OE *gēar*]
year·book (yir′bŏŏk′) *n.* **1.** A book published annually, presenting information about the previous year. **2.** *U.S.* A book compiled by the graduating class of a high school or college, and containing photographs of and information about its members, accounts of activities, etc.
year·ling (yir′ling) *n.* A young animal past its first year and not yet two years old; especially, a colt or filly a year old dating from January 1 of the year of foaling. — *adj.* Being a year old.
year·long (yir′lông′, -long′) *adj.* Continuing through a year.
year·ly (yir′lē) *adj.* **1.** Occurring, done, payable, seen, etc., once a year; annual. **2.** Continuing or lasting for a year: a *yearly* subscription. — *adv.* Once a year; annually.
yearn (yûrn) *v.i.* **1.** To desire something earnestly; long; hanker; pine: with *for.* **2.** To be deeply moved; feel sympathy. [OE *giernan, geornan.* Akin to OE *georn* eager.]
yearn·ing (yûr′ning) *n.* A strong emotion of longing or desire, especially with tenderness. — **yearn′ing·ly** *adv.*
year-round (yir′round′) *adj.* Open, operating, or continuing for the entire year: a *year-round* health resort.
yeast (yēst) *n.* **1.** A substance consisting of minute cells of ascomycetous fungi (genus *Saccharomyces*) that clump together in a yellow, frothy, viscous growth promoting fermentation in saccharine liquids, with the production of alcohol and carbon dioxide, as in the brewing of beer and the raising of bread. **2.** Such a substance mixed with flour or meal, and sold commercially. **3.** A yeast plant (which see). **4.** Froth or spume. **5.** Mental or moral ferment or agitation. — *v.i.* To foam; froth. [OE *gist*]
yeast cake A mixture of living yeast cells and starch in compressed form, suitable for use in baking or brewing.
yeast plant Any of a family (*Saccharomycetaceae*) of fungi that form yeast.
yeast powder Dried and powdered yeast used as a leavening agent.
yeast·y (yēs′tē) *adj.* **yeast·i·er, yeast·i·est 1.** Of, resembling, or containing yeast. **2.** Causing or characterized by fermentation. **3.** Restless; unsettled; frivolous. **4.** Covered with or consisting mainly of froth or foam. **5.** Light or unsubstantial. — **yeast′i·ness** *n.*
Yeats (yāts), **William Butler,** 1865–1939, Irish poet, dramatist, and essayist.
Ye·do (ye·dō) A former name for TOKYO.
yeel·in (yē′lin) *n. Scot.* A yealing.
yegg (yeg) *n. Slang* A burglar or safe-cracker. Also **yegg′·man** (-mən). [Origin unknown]
Ye·ka·te·rin·burg (yi·kə·tyi·ryin·bŏŏrk′) A former name for SVERDLOVSK. Also *Ekaterinburg.*
Ye·ka·te·ri·no·dar (yi·kə·tyi·ryi·no·där′) A former name for KRASNODAR. Also *Ekaterinodar.*
Ye·ka·te·ri·no·slav (yi·kə·tyi·ryi·no·släf′) A former name for DNIEPROPYETROVSK. Also *Ekaterinoslav.*
yeld (yeld) *adj. Scot.* Not giving milk; barren: also *yald, yauld.* Also **yell** (yel).
Ye·li·za·vet·grad (yi·lyi·zə·vyit·grät′) A former name for KIROVOGRAD. Also *Elizavetgrad.*

year (yêr), *n.* [ME. *yere;* AS. *gear;* akin to G. *jahr;* IE. base **jē-* (< **ei,* to go, as also in L. *Janus,* orig., god of the speeding sun, *janua,* door); basic sense "that goes, passes"], 1. *a)* a period of 365 days (in leap year, 366 days) divided into 12 months and regarded as beginning January 1 and ending the following December 31. *b)* a period of more or less the same length in other calendars. 2. the period of time, 365 days, 5 hours, 48 minutes, and 46 seconds, spent by the sun in making its apparent passage from vernal equinox to vernal equinox: also **astronomical, natural, equinoctial, solar,** or **tropical year.** 3. the period of time, 365 days, 6 hours, 9 minutes, and 9 seconds, spent by the sun in its apparent passage from a fixed star and back to the same position again: the difference in time between this and the astronomical year is due to the precession of the equinoxes: also **sidereal year.** 4. a period of 12 lunar months: also **lunar year.** 5. the period of time occupied by any planet in making one complete revolution around the sun. 6. a period of 12 calendar months reckoned from any date: as, we shall return one *year* from today. 7. a particular annual period of less than 365 days: as, a fisherman's work *year,* a short school *year,* etc. 8. *pl. a)* age: as, he seems old for his *years. b)* time; especially, a long time: as, he died *years* ago. Abbreviated **y.** (*sing. & pl.*), **yr.**
  year after year, every year.
  year by year, each year.
  year in, year out, every year.
year·book (yêr'book'), *n.* a book published yearly, especially one giving statistics and data of the preceding year; annual: abbreviated **Y.B.**
year·ling (yêr'liŋ, yûr'liŋ), *n.* 1. an animal one year old or in its second year. 2. in *racing,* a horse one year old, reckoned from January 1 of the year of its foaling.
year·long (yêr'lôŋ), *adj.* lasting or continuing for a full year.
year·ly (yêr'li), *adj.* 1. continuing or lasting for a year. 2. done, happening, appearing, payable, etc. once a year, or every year: as, a *yearly* event. 3. of a year, or each year. *adv.* annually; every year.
yearn (yûrn), *v.i.* [ME. *yernen;* AS. *gyrnan* < *georn,* eager], 1. to be filled with longing or desire. 2. to be deeply moved, especially with pity or sympathy.
yearn·ing (yûr'niŋ), *n.* [*yearn* + *-ing*], deep or anxious longing, desire, etc.
yeast (yēst), *n.* [ME. *yest;* AS. *gist;* akin to G. *gischt,* spray, froth & OHG. *jesan,* to ferment; IE. base **jes-,* to foam, boil up, seen also in Gr. *zeein,* to boil (cf. ECZEMA, ENZYME)], 1. a yellow, frothy substance consisting of a mass of minute fungi which germinate and multiply in the presence of starch or sugar and form alcohol and carbon dioxide during a process of fermentation induced by an enzyme: used in making beer and as a leavening agent in baking. 2. any of the family of fungi that form yeast; yeast plant. 3. yeast mixed with flour or meal, usually made up in small cakes. 4. foam; froth. 5. *a)* something that agitates or causes ferment; leaven. *b)* ferment; agitation. *v.i.* [Rare], to froth or ferment.
yeast cake, a small cake made by mixing yeast with flour or meal: sold commercially for use in baking, etc.
yeast plant, yeast (sense 2).
yeast·y (yēs'ti), *adj.* [YEASTIER (-ti-ĕr), YEASTIEST (-ti-ist)], 1, of, like, or containing yeast. 2. frothy; foamy. 3. light; superficial; frivolous. 4. in a ferment; unsettled; restless.
Yeats, William Butler (yāts), 1865–1939; Irish essayist, poet, and dramatist; received Nobel prize in literature, 1923.
Yed·o, Yed·do (ye'dô'), *n.* Tokyo: a former name.
yegg (yeg), *n.* [said to be from name of famous safecracker], [Slang], a criminal; especially, a safecracker or burglar.

From *Webster's New World Dictionary of the American Language,* College Edition. Copyright 1966 by The World Publishing Company, Cleveland, Ohio.

21

Exercises

year \'yi(ə)r\ *n* [ME *yere,* fr. OE *gēar;* akin to OHG *jār* year, Gk *hōros* year, *hōra* season, hour, L *ire* to go — more at ISSUE] **1 a :** the period of about 365 ¼ solar days required for one revolution of the earth around the sun **b :** the time required for the apparent sun to return to an arbitrary fixed or moving reference point in the sky **2 a :** a cycle in the Gregorian calendar of 365 or 366 days divided into 12 months beginning with January and ending with December **b :** a period of time equal to one year of the Gregorian calendar but beginning at a different time **3 :** a calendar year specified usu. by a number **4** *pl* **:** a time or era having a special significance **5** *pl* **:** AGE; *also* **:** the final stage of the normal life span **6 :** a period of time (as the usu. nine-month period in which a school is in session) other than a calendar year

year·book \-,bùk\ *n* **:** a book published yearly as a report or summary of the statistics or facts **:** ANNUAL

year·ling \'yi(ə)r-liŋ, 'yər-lən\ *n* **:** one that is a year old; as **a :** an animal one year old or in the second year of its age **b :** a racehorse between January 1st of the year after the year in which it was foaled and the next January 1st — **yearling** *adj*

year·long \'yi(ə)r-'lòŋ\ *adj* **:** lasting through a year

¹**year·ly** \'yi(ə)r-lē\ *adj* **1 :** reckoned by the year **2 :** occurring, appearing, made, done, or acted upon every year or once a year **:** ANNUAL

²**yearly** *adv* **:** every year **:** ANNUALLY

Yearly Meeting *n* **:** an organization uniting several Quarterly Meetings of the Society of Friends

yearn \'yərn\ *vi* [ME *yernen,* fr. OE *giernan;* akin to OHG *gerōn* to desire, L *hortari* to urge, encourage, Gk *chairein* to rejoice] **1 :** to feel a longing or craving **2 :** to feel tenderness or compassion **syn** see LONG — **yearn·er** *n*

year of grace **:** a year of the Christian era ⟨the *year of grace* 1962⟩

year–round \'yi(ə)r-'raùnd, 'yiə-'raùnd\ *adj* **:** effective, employed, or operating for the full year **:** not seasonal ⟨a ∼ resort⟩

¹**yeast** \'yēst\ *n* [ME *yest,* fr. OE *gist;* akin to MHG *jest* foam, Gk *zein* to boil] **1 a :** a yellowish surface froth or sediment that occurs esp. in saccharine liquids (as fruit juices) in which it promotes alcoholic fermentation, consists largely of cells of a fungus (family Saccharomycetaceae) and is used esp. in the making of alcoholic liquors and as a leaven in baking **b :** a commercial product containing yeast plants in a moist or dry medium **c** (1) **:** a minute fungus (esp. *Saccharomyces cerevisiae*) that is present and functionally active in yeast, usu. has little or no mycelium, and reproduces by budding (2) **:** any of various similar fungi (esp. orders Endomycetales and Moniliales) **2 :** the foam or spume of waves **3 :** something that causes ferment or activity

²**yeast** *vi* **:** FERMENT, FROTH

yeasty \'yē-stē\ *adj* **1 :** of, relating to, or resembling yeast **2 a :** IMMATURE, UNSETTLED **b :** marked by change **c :** EXUBERANT **d :** FRIVOLOUS

yegg \'yeg\ *n* [origin unknown] **:** SAFECRACKER, ROBBER

¹**yell** \'yel\ *vb* [ME *yellen,* fr. OE *giellan;* akin to OHG *gellan* to yell, OE *galan* to sing] *vi* **1 :** to utter a loud cry, scream, or shout **2 :** to give a cheer usu. in unison ∼ *vt* **:** to utter or declare with or as if with a yell **:** SHOUT — **yell·er** *n*

²**yell** *n* **1 :** SCREAM, SHOUT **2 :** a usu. rhythmic cheer used esp. in schools or colleges to encourage athletic teams

¹**yel·low** \'yel-(,)ō, -ə-(w)\ *adj* [ME *yelwe, yelow,* fr. OE *geolu;* akin to OHG *gelo* yellow, L *helvus* light bay, Gk *chlōros* greenish yellow, Skt *hari* yellowish] **1 a :** of the color yellow **b :** become yellowish through age, disease, or discoloration **:** SALLOW **c :** having a yellow complexion or skin **2 a :** featuring sensational or scandalous items or ordinary news sensationally distorted ⟨∼ journalism⟩ **b :** MEAN, COWARDLY

²**yellow** *vt* **:** to make or turn yellow ∼ *vi* **:** to become or turn yellow

³**yellow** *n* **1 a :** a color whose hue resembles that of ripe lemons or sunflowers or is that of the portion of the spectrum lying between green and orange **b :** a pigment or dye that colors yellow **2 :** something yellow or marked by a yellow color: as **a :** a person having yellow skin **b :** the yolk of an egg **3** *pl* **:** JAUNDICE **4** *pl* **:** any of several plant diseases caused esp. by viruses and marked by yellowing of the foliage and stunting

yellow bile *n* **:** a humor of medieval physiology believed to be secreted by the liver and to cause irascibility

yel·low·bird \'yel-ō-,bərd, -ə-,bərd\ *n* **1 :** any of various American goldfinches **2 :** a small mostly yellow American warbler (*Dendroica petechia*)

yellow daisy *n* **:** BLACK-EYED SUSAN

yellow–dog \,yel-ō-'dòg, -ə-'dòg\ *adj* **1 :** MEAN, CONTEMPTIBLE **2 :** of or relating to opposition to trade unionism or a labor union

yellow–dog contract *n* **:** an employment contract in which a worker disavows membership in and agrees not to join a labor union during the period of his employment

yellow enzyme *n* **:** any of several yellow flavoprotein respiratory enzymes widely distributed in nature

By permission. From *Webster's Seventh New Collegiate Dictionary,* copyright 1965 by G. & C. Merriam Company, Publishers of the Merriam Webster Dictionaries.

B. Your instructor will assign one of the following words to each member of the class:

above, *prep.*	lake, *n.*	sail, *v.*
appreciate, *v.*	legal, *adj.*	sick, *adj.*
apron, *n.*	make, *v.*	sun, *n.*
bedlam, *n.*	manufacture, *v.*	street, *n.*
bully, *n.*	noun, *n.*	tap, *n.*
cotton, *n.*	nobody, *p.*	tender, *adj.*
dead, *adj.*	over, *prep.*	tool, *n.*
find, *v.*	paper, *n.*	up, *adv.*
goose, *n.*	paternal, *adj.*	up, *prep.*
head, *n.*	quick, *adj.*	veal, *n.*
idle, *adj.*	read, *v.*	water, *n.*
judge, *v.*	red, *adj.*	wiggle, *v.*
kick, *v.*	road, *n.*	yank, *v.*

Look up your word in each of the following dictionaries: *A New English Dictionary on Historical Principles* (*Oxford English Dictionary*), *Dictionary of American English, Dictionary of Americanisms,* Wyld's *Universal Dictionary of the English Language, Century Dictionary and Cyclopedia,* and *New International Dictionary of the English Language,* if possible, both the second and the third editions. Use the questions in A above, and add to them the following:

Which dictionaries give examples of the use of the word? Which dictionaries give such systematic lists of examples that they constitute a history of the word in English or American speech?

Using your notes, prepare an oral report on your word, or write a 300–500 word paper, as your instructor directs.

C. The following are some of the more common prefixes from Latin and Greek used in modern English:

ab- (abs-)	contra-
ad- (ac-, af-,	de-
ag-, al-, an-,	di- (dis-)
ap-, ar-, as-,	ex- (e-, ef-)
at-)	ex- (ec-)
ambi- (ambo-)	extra-
ante-	hyper-
anti- (ant-)	in- (il-, im-, ir-)
arch-	inter-
bi-	intra-
cata-	intro-
circum-	mal-
com- (co-, col-,	multi-
con-, cor-)	neo-

Exercises

non-	se-
ob- (oc-, of-, op-)	semi-
para-	sub- (suc-, suf-, sug-,
per-	sum-, sup-, sur-,
peri-	sus-)
post-	super-
pre-	supra-
pro-	syn- (sy- syl-, sym-)
proto-	trans-
pseudo-	tri-
re-	uni-
retro-	vice-

Be sure you know the use and meaning of each prefix, verifying in a good dictionary those about which you may be uncertain. Then choose five prefixes, and find at least ten words in which each of these occurs.

For more extensive lists of prefixes and suffixes, see Arthur Garfield Kennedy, *Current English* (Boston, 1935), pp. 337–45.

D. Look up each of the following words in a good desk dictionary and study the discriminative synonyms listed. For each word and each of its listed synonyms write a sentence putting the word in a suitable context.

1. assume	8. law	15. relevant
2. beg	9. lift	16. see
3. change	10. material	17. smell
4. crowd	11. object	18. stick
5. deceive	12. power	19. think
6. debase	13. proud	20. wordy
7. guide	14. rebellion	

E. Correct the false direction of words in the following sentences:

1. Many results may be obtained which make their scientific value skeptical.
2. Shirley instilled an unreasonable fear of spiders as a small child.
3. You never know what your weaknesses are until you are applied to them.
4. When a point is trying to be made, a reader must watch the evidence.
5. The people who want more rigid rules for the girls in the dormitories are attributed to the older generation.
6. Jake yielded a very profitable income from these products crossing his bridge.
7. They were inculcated with the idea that they were well informed.
8. Enterprising publishers have now started bringing out a dearth of older detective stories.

9. These fads usually are addicted to the younger set.
10. Students are required to take some courses because it is known that the course will be profited by the students.

F. Each of the sentences below is followed by words which can be synonyms for the italicized words in the sentence. Indicate which could be substituted in the sentence and explain changes in meaning that would result.

1. Many members of the audience were *moved* to tears. (*incited, prompted, impelled, instigated, actuated*)
2. The general was not willing to pay the *price* of victory. (*value, charge, cost, expense, worth*)
3. Mary felt no *fear* as she faced the microphone. (*dismay, alarm, horror, anxiety, dread*)
4. The president did not have enough *power* to enforce the rules. (*potency, puissance, strength, energy, force*)
5. Her *pride* would not allow her to dress as the other girls in the house did. (*vanity, haughtiness, superciliousness, egotism, vainglory*)
6. *Examination* of the evidence showed that the jury had been wrong. (*inquiry, inquisition, scrutiny, investigation, proposition*)
7. The judge had no *sympathy* for law-breakers. (*pity, commiseration, condolence, tenderness, agreement*)
8. His devices were so *transparent* that nobody was deceived. (*translucent, lucid, diaphanous, limpid, luminous*)
9. The entire *company* joined in the song. (*group, throng, assemblage, flock, circle*)
10. Her dyed hair and *gaudy* clothes shocked the congregation. (*ostentatious, pretentious, tawdry, garish, flashy*)

G. Revise the following passage by replacing the italicized words with other words which make us see, hear, taste, smell, or feel:

When I *entered* the *enclosure*, the *affair* was *going on*. I *found a place*, and was *feeling pretty good* if a *little uncomfortable* because of *the circumstances*, when I saw a *person* approaching me. She was a *female*, and *seemed to be in an agitated condition*. Her face looked *kind of funny*, and she *moved in a peculiar way*. She started *saying things* in an *odd kind of voice*, and I *realized* that she was in an *intoxicated condition*. Her *way of standing* was *unusual*. Then some *other persons approached*, including a *man*, who seemed to think he *was important around there*. He *spoke to me*. I also, was *in an agitated state* by now, so that I was *not sensitive to all that was transpiring*, but I heard *certain sounds from various people*. *Somebody* with a *repulsive face* was *admonishing* me. *One individual inquired* if I *was not aware* that I was an *improper person* to be *in these surroundings*. He *had a threatening attitude*. I *replied* that I *was unaware of the circumstances*, but that I would *accede to their wishes and retire*. As I took my *departure* I heard them *expatiating upon me*.

21

H. The metaphors and similes in the following sentences vary in complexity. Study each one in terms of the referent–thought–word relationship discussed above (21-3). Then decide as specifically as you can which parts of the referent are emphasized or changed by using words metaphorically.

1. The moon was a ghostly galleon. . . .—Alfred Noyes
2. This man was hunting about the hotel lobby like a starved dog that has forgotten where he has buried a bone.—O. Henry
3. A wit's a feather, and a chief a rod;
   An honest man's the noblest work of God.—Alexander Pope
4. An honest God is the noblest work of man.—Samuel Butler
5. A pun is not bound by the laws which limit nice wit. It is a pistol let off at the ear; not a feather to tickle the intellect.—Charles Lamb
6. Like our shadows,
   Our wishes lengthen as our sun declines.—Alexander Pope
7. I wonder why anybody wanted to wing an old woman in the leg.
   —Hilda Lawrence
8. So 'tis not her the bee devours,
   It is a pretty maze of flowers;
   It is the rose that bleeds when he
   Nibbles his nice phlebotomy.—John Cleveland
9. All of Stratford, in fact, suggests powdered history—add hot water and stir and you have a delicious, nourishing Shakespeare.—Margaret Halsey
10. Our two souls, therefore, which are one,
    Though I must go, endure not yet
    A breach, but an expansion
    Like gold to airy thinness beat.—John Donne

The Research Paper

Nothing's so hard but search will find it out.
—Robert Herrick

Truth means facts and their relations, which stand towards each other pretty much as subjects and predicates in logic.
—Cardinal Newman

It is the quest after truth, not its possession, that falls to our human lot, that gladdens us, that fills our lives—nay, that hallows them.
—August Weismann

Truth fears nothing except being hidden.
—Latin Proverb

Research, investigation directed to the discovery of new knowledge, both initiates and supports much in today's society. More than ever before, research influences human lives, discovering facts and principles that lead to changes in diet or transportation, in clothing or weapons. Governments and private foundations annually invest millions of dollars in research projects on widely varying subjects—nuclear physics, linguistics, plant pathology, hallucinatory drugs.

Research as conceived by scholars and scientists on this scale requires experience and background and time. The student in the beginning writing course can seldom hope to complete a project that will contribute substantial new knowledge to the world. He can, however, profitably practice some basic methods of research, to prepare for more advanced investigation and to learn more about objective, factual writing.

Investigative methods are particularly the business of people in college. Most of what colleges teach has been discovered by the same means that have become standard in research; and to understand the past, to grasp the world in which he lives, the student needs to appreciate research, the tool with which others have learned what he is now learning. Moreover, much college activity requires knowledge of basic research procedures—whether the student is working in a laboratory, evaluating historical evidence in textbooks, or observing and ordering psychological or sociological phenomena. The student needs research skill to continue his own education.

He also needs knowledge of research to participate in the affairs of the world. Investigation is the basis of most serious intellectual activity, not only in the arts, in the sciences, and in the learned professions, but also in commerce, technology, government, and education. The lawyer preparing a case works through previous judgments, using indexes and summaries, and applies the information he collects to his particular case. The sales manager proposing a new campaign investigates past records of his own company, campaigns of other companies, and general economic and sociological conditions, isolating material that will help him plan his own project and predict its results. Techniques vary with materials and the purpose of the investigation, but the essential process behind much of the world's activity is research of a sort—acquiring knowledge about a subject and applying it to new circumstances.

An elementary research or investigative project, then, like that assumed for the next three sections, is especially important as an introduction to practical problems—of college education and of the world—in disciplining and ordering thinking and in writing objectively. In such a project the student learns how to use a library, a valuable but not widely practiced skill; he learns orderly methods of taking and preserving notes to develop working evidence, not a jumble of bewildering details; he learns to evaluate and select evidence, so that he records what he needs in the form that will do him the most good; he learns techniques for the economical recording of information; he learns how to document, so that his arguments are supported and a reader can appreciate this support; he learns how to think from evidence to generalization, and again back to confirming evidence. And especially, although perhaps less obviously, he learns how to write factually and objectively—that is, he practices the kind of rhetoric which is probably most useful in modern society. Most of the writing that most modern men have to do deals with facts, or supposed facts, or evidence we hope may be facts. Learning to recognize and deal with facts provides the foundation for objective writing, but this sort of writing requires special techniques. The objective writer must learn to deal with quoted material, to so control it that he maintains his own intellectual integrity while keeping his reader informed as to sources. He must learn to write with restraint; the admonitions, especially in Section 2, concerning the writer's commitment and the necessities of at once restraining and fulfilling his commitment, are unusually important in objective writing. He must learn to write so that he reveals his own evaluation of material; in this world little is certain, and thus the objective writer is likely to deal with a tissue of probabilities. He must learn to find his way and to lead his reader among these uncertainties.

The so-called research paper has also the advantages of being a long paper, a longer paper than most college freshmen have ever written before. Thus, it provides an opportunity to practice some of the procedures expounded in earlier portions of this book—notably in Section 7—which students may not have used much for relatively brief papers.

Taking Notes;
Plagiarism

Taking adequate, orderly, thoughtful notes encourages careful reading and competent writing, while preparing the student to maintain his intellectual integrity.

Among the special skills required in research and objective writing, note taking is one of the most important. The writer needs a way of recording results of his investigations, of collecting material systematically and economically, so that it will be readily available and accurate. Occasionally, of course, documents must be copied entire. This was formerly an onerous job, but devices like Thermofax and Xerox have made mechanical copying so cheap and easy that anything to be quoted extensively can be reproduced. These facsimile printing devices have revolutionized some scholarship, and are useful to almost all serious students, but they have limitations. Getting material to the reproducing device, arranging for copies and waiting for them, can be time-consuming, and the writer has still to digest the evidence in the copied document. Thus, the well-tried procedures for taking notes still have their uses. Three sorts of notes which are often combined in practice and all of which may be combined with direct quotation need consideration: summary, paraphrase, and précis.

22-1   Summary and Paraphrase

Usually a summary provides the briefest general-purpose note. The following might serve as a summary of the fifth paragraph of the discussion above entitled "The Research Paper."

Gorrell and Laird say an elementary research project has at least two practical uses: (1) to teach useful techniques of investigation like using the library and evaluating facts, and (2) to teach skills especially necessary in objective writing like handling quotations.

A summary may have several uses. It can remind the writer of material to which he may wish to return later; often, especially during the early part of an investigation, a research worker may be uncertain how much detailed material he will need from any one source. A summary can also provide all the material needed for many purposes; for example, it records enough of a source to which the writer will refer only generally. Even the shortest summary, however, requires the following: (1) careful reading of the entire passage, (2) thinking through the entire passage to extract its essence, and (3) careful writing, even though sentences may be skeletonized. Contrast the following with the summary above:

> Gorrell and Laird say an elementary research or investigative project provides training in disciplining and ordering thinking and writing, since the student learns how to use the library and not collect a jumble of be wildering details.

Superficially, this looks all right. It seems to make sense, but it is no summary at all. Apparently, the student skimmed through the first two sentences, shamelessly or carelessly lifting passages without putting them within quotation marks, and missed what the authors had to say because he never understood the paragraph as a whole.

In general, a paraphrase is somewhat more detailed. The following might serve as a paraphrase of the same paragraph.

> Authors say elementary research projects teach both investigation and resulting factual writing. The first includes use of library, keeping notes in order, techniques of note taking, evaluation of evidence, and working with evidence. The second is important because student uses rhetoric most applicable to our times and learns special practices useful in objective writing handling quoted materials, using restrained style, and dealing with uncertainties.

The paraphrase differs from the summary above. The summary was prepared by thinking through the paragraph, deciding what the authors meant to emphasize, and restricting the statement to this central idea. The paraphrase is a little more elaborate. The student thought through the paragraph, but he also worked through it, included in his statement all the secondary ideas in the original, and kept them in their original order while expressing them in his own words. The paraphrase preserves more of the original than a summary but is still relatively brief, and the writer can later incorporate it into his own writing without fear of plagiarism because he has already written it in his own words.

Often the summary is best used with direct quotations. Notice the following summary of the same paragraph:

> The research paper can teach both "disciplinary and orderly thinking" and "writing objectively." The first includes learning to use a library, "orderly methods of taking and preserving notes," evaluating and selecting evidence so that the student "records what he will need in the form that will do him the most good," documentation, and thinking from evidence to generalization and "again back to confirming evidence." In writing the student practices "the kind of rhetoric, which is probably most useful in modern society," including such techniques as handling quotations, writing with restraint, and revealing the writer's degree of uncertainty as he works with a "tissue of probabilities."

Such a paraphrase can have several advantages. It may preserve key passages exactly; it may preserve some of the flavor of the original, picturesque or well chosen bits, and in some kinds of writing it may reflect evidence of another time or place. We might notice, however, that this particular paraphrase was damaged by carelessness. If the note taker trusts it he will make errors, since he did not check his original and consequently made four mistakes in copying.

22-2   The Précis

The word *précis* is French, related to our word *precise* and to a Latin word which meant "cut off in front." A good précis embodies the idea of both words; it is "cut off" in the sense that it is intended to give the essence in brief compass of a longer piece of writing, and it should be as precise as a relatively brief restatement can be. Its origin suggests its character. The précis arose from reports sent by diplomatic representatives abroad; if the student, therefore, will put himself in the position of a representative of the State Department in a foreign country he should recognize the qualities of a good précis. Consider, for instance, the position of a diplomatic attaché in a South American capital who fears a revolution accompanied by an attack from a neighboring country. The State Department will want his opinion of the situation, but it will also need evidence divorced from opinion, because any decision must take into account both of the countries, factions within the countries, international organizations, and a host of other governments, along with a variety of interests, including our own. Decisions will be made in Washington, and those who decide will need accurate and proportioned understanding of the situation in Latin America. Right decisions require reliable information, but time may not permit lengthy reports—revolutions may not wait. Accordingly, the attaché prepares précis of important documents, and as he writes he must be as objective and penetrating as possible, endeavoring to reflect his originals accurately, without distortion or bias, and losing nothing vital, as a small mirror can reflect a large room without distortion or omission. In words, the accuracy of the mirror is not possible, but for a précis, precision is still the ideal.

The précis has uses outside the diplomatic corps. In the classroom it requires the student to read carefully enough to transfer the essential thought of a piece of writing into his own words, an exercise which forces both close reading and precise writing. The précis can also provide a record of a document which the student wants to preserve in some detail, for review for a class or for use in a research paper. A précis of Section 20-3 of this book, "The Ancestry of English," might read as follows:

Knowledge of the origins of English, acquired only recently, has revolutionized current thinking about language. Although scholars two centuries ago worked with language, describing the language of their own times, they knew too little of languages other than their own to develop general principles. The Greeks, for example, had good grammars of Greek but only limited knowledge of other languages. The Biblical tradition—tracing language from Adam to the Tower of Babel to modern tongues—dominated other thinking, even that of Noah Webster.

Earlier scholars did have some knowledge of languages around them. They had observed the origins of French, Italian, Spanish, and Portuguese in Latin and the borrowings of Latin words from Greek. Scholars did not, however, make full use of this knowledge. Particularly they did not speculate about what had happened before historic times, before Latin; at least they did not before the nineteenth century. During the nineteenth century, however, new observations led to new questions which led to new knowledge about language. The key observation was that the ancient Indic language, Sanskrit, resembled Latin and Greek in a number of ways, even though there was no reason to think that the languages had influenced one another in earlier times. This observation was extended to the observation that similarities extended through several languages; a set of comparisons by the American philologist William Dwight Whitney includes: *three,* English; *tri,* Lithuanian; *tri,* Celtic; *tres,* Latin; *treis,* Greek; *thri,* Persian; and *tri* Sanskrit. Evidence like this led to modern theories of the growth and descent of languages.

403

The method used to develop notions of language growth is essentially to reconstruct earlier languages on the basis of conjectures about what must have existed earlier to account for what exists now. For example, to account for the modern *oeil,* French; *ojo,* Spanish; and *occhio,* Italian, scholars could have predicted the existence of a word like the Latin *oculus,* eye, even if they had not known it. By the same methods, figuring out what must have existed to account for the development of modern words, scholars reconstructed a hypothetical ancient language called Indo-European, presumably spoken some thousands of years before Christ in central Europe. Even though recent discoveries of similarities between ancient Hittite and the conjectured Indo-European language have led to new theories, Indo-European remains important as a reconstruction of an early ancestor of English.

This précis reduces the original to a little less than half its length, omitting much of the illustrative material such as most of Whitney's table of cognates. Sometimes a longer, more detailed précis is required. Especially useful is the précis augmented with carefully selected direct quotations; the précis above could be built up with quotations so that the beginning would read as follows:

Knowledge of the origins of English have recently been so revolutionized that a "schoolgirl can now know fundamental principles of language that were not dreamed of by the most learned scholars two centuries ago." Older scholars, while working with languages of their own times, knew too little of earlier languages to develop general principles.

22-3   Fact and Opinion in Notes

No matter what kind of notes he takes, the writer planning an objective paper must understand and record the basis on which each piece of material can be evaluated. That is, he must know whether information is a confession of faith or belief, an opinion fabricated from thin air, a judgment based on expert observation, or a factual report that can be tested objectively. Compare the following comments about a heavy rain storm:

I believe that last night's storm was divine punishment to the farmers of this county for their sins.

Crop damage from last night's storm, according to insurance company estimates, will run to more than $2,000,000.

According to weather bureau reports, the storm last night brought 2.2 inches of rainfall in ten hours.

The first is obviously belief or opinion; no means of verification is available. The others, with the qualifications specified, are factual; they could be checked. As already indicated (see 4-1), fact cannot be strictly separated from judgment or opinion; the last two comments above are approximations and involve the judgments of the insurance company and the weather bureau. The objective writer, however, especially concerned with "facts," must be aware of the type of information with which he is dealing.

For an example, consider a passage in a book by a modern American critic-historian; he is discussing Thomas Jefferson.

> Scarcely leaving his native province, he had become a great humanist there and one of the most cultivated men the world could boast of,—and all this thanks to the kind of advantages that he shared with thousands of other young men and that any Virginian of means might have had as well. . . . He had developed early the eager curiosity that marked him as an architect, an inventor and a linguist, for he was also more or less familiar with the languages of forty Indian tribes.
>
> —VAN WYCK BROOKS, *The World of Washington Irving*

Let us assume that an investigator, using this passage, has taken the following note:

> Jefferson had become one of the most cultivated men in the world; his eager curiosity developed early, and helped make him an architect, an inventor, and a linguist.

Assertions recorded in this note are not equally factual; consider the three following: (1) "Jefferson was one of the most cultivated men the world could boast of," (2) his "eager curiosity" developed early, and (3) he was an inventor. The last should be subject to documentation, and in fact Brooks does document it in a footnote, where he notes that Jefferson invented "a plough, a sundial, an adjustable bookcase, a portable reading and writing desk, a phaeton, a swivel-chair, a lock-dock for laying up vessels, a chaise lounge, a leather buggy-top, a folding ladder, a hexagonal lantern, a two-way dumb waiter, and a sheltered weather vane," along with a device to open and shut double doors. Since documentary evidence could be produced for all of these inventions, presumably, we may say relatively factually that Jefferson was an inventor.

The other statements are not equally subject to verification. All normal children are curious, but how does Brooks know that Jefferson's curiosity was developed, not inborn, how early it was, or whether it was unusual enough to be called "eager curiosity"?

Probably he does not, but he certainly could have found—and doubtless he did—that Jefferson, as a young boy, gave much more evidence of curiosity than do most youngsters at that age. Brooks could not have been so sure about the state of Jefferson's curiosity as he was about Jefferson's standing as an inventor, but roughly speaking the statement can probably be called factual.

What about Brook's assertion that Jefferson was "one of the most cultivated men the world could boast of"? How can one determine degrees of cultivation factually? Is it likely that Brooks had studied intimately the lives of all men in the eighteenth century, the state of learning of individual Tibetan monks, for example? Obviously, this is an opinion, although an opinion based upon sufficient evidence so that it is plausible.

All this subtle variation in fact and opinion would probably be inferred by anyone reading the book because Brooks endeavors to write factually. He reports that Jefferson as a boy "pored over Virgil stretched out under an oak tree," and we are confident that these details came out of a document, and he usually qualifies when he makes generalizations, saying that some of Jefferson's courtesy "he may possibly have owed to the example of Franklin," and as evidence he cites Jefferson's praise of Franklin's manners. This judicious weighing of fact and opinion has disappeared, however, from the investigator's injudicious note, which jumbles all statements together as though they were equally factual. He might better have written something like the following:

> Brooks considers Jefferson "one of the most cultivated men" of his day, and attributes his abilities as architect, inventor, and linquist in part to an "eager curiosity" which had developed early.

By clearly attributing the opinions to Brooks and making use of direct quotations, the writer produces a more useful note.

22-4 Taking and Preserving Notes

For the preparation of a paper, the student sometimes needs to make a précis, paraphrase, or summary of a book or article to which he can refer later. More often, however, he must assemble brief notes from widely scattered material, and the success of his project depends on his working out a system for orderly handling of such notes. The wrong way to take notes is to write them down consecutively in a notebook. They soon become a jumble. They occur in whatever order they occurred in the book from which the information was taken—usually not the order which the investigator will require. They are unidentified. They cannot be classified, particularly if the investigator writes on both sides of a sheet of note paper. As a result, the investigator knows only that he "has that somewhere" and has to spend half his time hunting for notes he cannot find. Most research workers find that cards or uniform slips provide the most practical means of taking and preserving notes; they permit the most flexible system, and in the end are the most economical. The procedure takes a little time to learn, and using it makes the recording of material a little slower, but in the end it more than pays for itself. The investigator should begin by providing himself with cards or slips; usually three-by-five bibliography cards prove to be too small. Four-by-six cards will serve many purposes, but some writers prefer half-sheets of paper; if slips are used, the paper should be heavy enough to be handled easily, and slips should be cut uniformly so that they can be filed. The following are fundamental rules for using the system:

1. *Copy notes directly onto the cards.* Copying notes into a notebook and then transcribing them to cards wastes time and encourages error.

2. *Write only one piece of information on a card.* If a card contains only a single piece of information, it can be classified by subject with cards containing similar information, no matter from what source it comes. Thus the investigator has all his material on one aspect of his subject filed together.

3. *Identify the source of the information on the card.* Any note— summary, paraphrase, précis, or brief comment—must be precisely identified. Many research workers use the following system: they record the author's name and an abbreviated form of the title. A reference to page 166 of the first volume of Christopher Ward's *The War of the Revolution* might be identified on the note card as Ward, *Revolution*, I. 166.

4. *Be sure to indicate clearly on the note cards any passages taken verbatim from the source.* Apparent plagiarism results if the investigator fails to mark a direct quotation on his note card, forgets that the passage was written by somebody else, and writes it into his paper as his own work. Whenever even a two- or three-word phrase is taken directly from a source, it should be enclosed in quotation marks on the note card.

5. *Indicate with key words the nature or use of the material taken.*
When the card is complete, it should be filed according to subject.
For this purpose, the investigator should adopt a number of words
under which material can be filed; usually these words are headings
of his outline.

The following card contains material on the importance of
clothing and supplies in the Revolutionary War. Clothing and
supplies, of course, are subjects of all the cards and need not be
entered on any of them. One important subtopic of the subject,
however, is the importance of uniforms. Thus *uniforms* becomes the
first key word to identify the note. *American* subdivides the cards
concerning uniforms, and *from France* further identifies this note.

Note restricted to one subject; other notes
from the book appear on separate cards.

Key words classify note
by subject matter and
indicate how it can be
filed.

Quotation marks en-
close material taken
in the author's words.

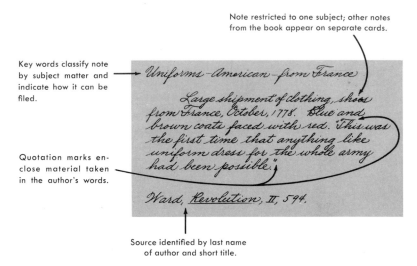

Source identified by last name
of author and short title.

22-5   Recording Material in Notes

Labor involved in collecting material may be routine; the investigator has only to use sound methods. The selection of material
is not routine. It requires understanding, alertness, and self-train-
ing. Consider the following passage from Mark Twain's *Roughing It.*

He [Hyde] said it was pretty well known that for some years he had been
farming (or ranching, as the more customary term is) in Washoe District,
and making a successful thing of it, and furthermore it was known that his
ranch was situated just in the edge of the valley, and that Tom Morgan
owned a ranch immediately above it on the mountainside. And now the

trouble was, that one of those hated and dreaded landslides had come and slid Morgan's ranch, fences, cabins, cattle, barns, and everything down on top of *his* ranch and exactly covered up every single vestige of his property, to a depth of about thirty-eight feet. Morgan was in possession and refused to vacate the premises—said he was occupying his own cabin and not interfering with anybody else's—and said the cabin was standing on the same dirt and same ranch it had always stood on, and he would like to see anybody make him vacate.

"And when I reminded him," said Hyde, weeping, "that it was on top of my ranch and that he was trespassing, he had the infernal meanness to ask me why I didn't stay on my ranch and hold possession when I see him a-comin'! Why didn't I *stay* on it, the blathering lunatic—by George, when I heard that racket and looked up that hill it was just like the whole world was a-rippin' and a-tearin' down that mountainside—splinters and cordwood, thunder and lightning, hail and snow, odds and ends of haystacks, and awful clouds of dust! Trees going end over end in the air, rocks as big as a house jumping 'bout a thousand feet high and busting into ten million pieces, cattle turned inside out and a-coming head on with their tails hanging out between their teeth!—and in the midst of all that wrack and destruction sot that cussed Morgan on his gatepost a-wondering why I didn't *stay and hold possession!* Laws bless me, I just took one glimpse, General, and lit out'n the country in three jumps exactly."

Let us assume that the investigator wishes to make use of this passage in a paper intended to reveal the peculiar qualities of Mark Twain's humor. He might make a summary like the following:

'T. makes a rancher called Hyde give very funny account of how another ranch landed on top of his. Good picture of way landslide came down mountain, using exaggeration and wild details.

A note like this is almost worthless for most purposes. It is too general to be of much use; Twain's humor has disappeared from it. Compare:

T. makes rancher named Hyde tell how in a landslide "Morgan's ranch, fences, cabins, cattle, barns, and everything" slid down and "exactly covered up every single vestige of his property, to a depth of about thirty-eight feet." Morgan refused to vacate, saying cabin "was standing on the same dirt and the same ranch it had always stood on," and asked Hyde why he had left when he "see him a-comin'." What Hyde had seen was "just like the whole world was a-rippin' and a-tearin' down that mountainside," bringing with it "odds and ends of haystacks . . . trees going end over end in the air, rocks as big as a house jumping 'bout a thousand feet high and busting into ten million pieces, cattle turned inside out and a-coming head on with their tails hanging out between their teeth! " In the face of this, Hyde "lit out'n the country in three jumps exactly."

The quotation has been reduced to less than half, but the most picturesque details have been preserved. Furthermore, the material can be used without fear of plagiarism because material which has been quoted exactly has been kept within quotation marks.

Selection of material, then, depends first of all on the purpose of the investigator. He can select sensibly because he knows what he is looking for. A few basic rules, however, may help him take notes adequately and efficiently.

1. *Adopt a system and follow it scrupulously.* The investigator must doggedly resist the temptation to "just jot this one down in my notebook," or to "just remember this one until I get a chance to write it down."

2. *Avoid taking unnecessary notes.* Hours spent collecting material not pertinent to the paper may be educational, but they do not get the job done. Some material important for a general understanding of the subject will soon become so familiar that the investigator will not need it in his notes. The sensible research worker reads generally upon a subject before starting to take notes, and skims through a book before collecting material from it.

3. *If in doubt, take the note.* Taking just the right material, just enough material and no more, is hardly possible. The investigator will save time by taking too much rather than too little. Copying a few extra words takes a few minutes, but trying to get a book after it has been returned to the library and someone else has borrowed it may take hours.

4. *Take concrete, specific, exact material.* Occasionally generalities are useful, but, on the whole, the more specific the notes, the better. Facts, figures, dates, statistics, verbatim quotations, or factual digests are useful. Most beginners collect too much general material, not enough concrete, objective material.

5. *Distinguish sharply between material which you quote and material you digest; if you quote, quote exactly.* Knowing when to take material verbatim and when to summarize is difficult. In general, however, the investigator may find that he wants word-for-word accounts of the following: material that has been very well phrased; material which is extremely important for the discussion; and controversial material, especially if the writer expects to examine the statement and comment upon it adversely. Scrupulously enclose any quoted material within quotation marks.

6. *On the whole, avoid long quotations.* When long quotations are necessary, a facsimile reproduction may save time and errors.

7. *Be accurate and neat.* Type or write legibly; take especial pains with titles, figures, the spelling of names, or with any material in which blunders cannot be caught by context.

8. *Double check every note card.* A wrong page number or an omitted title can cost hours of time and frustration in locating a quotation, and if the final paper contains misquotations, misspellings, or mispunctuation in copied material, the reader cannot be expected to trust much else in the paper.

Plagiarism and Intellectual Maturity   22-6

At least one matter that has entered into the previous discussions in various ways calls for more detailed treatment: plagiarism. It is the academic and literary equivalent of burglary, taking another person's property and treating it as though it were one's own. It is not restricted to reporting research, but at least in student writing it is most likely to appear there, particularly insofar as it is concerned with intellectual maturity. Some plagiarism involves unadulterated dishonesty; the student, being overworked, lazy, or incompetent, copies printed material or another student's work and submits it as his own, knowing quite well what he is doing, but hoping he will not be caught. He is a petty criminal, and he deserves the contempt that society reserves for petty criminals as well as the treatment that the law endeavors to provide for them. But this book does not purport to be a treatment of morals or ethics, and most student plagiarism, particularly in papers resting upon library investigation, stems not so much from dishonesty as from intellectual immaturity. Since intellectual maturity is surely one of the goals of higher education, it warrants careful attention.

That many students grow up intellectual copycats is not to be wondered at; they have been taught no better. With young children this is inevitable; small children have to be told, and they may learn most readily by repeating what they are told. They have to assume that everything they are told is true, and they early learn that, relatively speaking, it is likely to be. But of course a time comes when they ought to outgrow this childishness. Sometimes they are not much encouraged to do so; they go on through the secondary schools praised if they can produce a "correct" answer, even though the answer is something they have parroted out of a book or a lecture without knowing what it means and without being expected to know. They continue to take matter out of textbooks and to record it in lecture notes, and again, they may be encouraged to regurgitate this jumble uncritically in examinations. Many examinations are calculated to encourage original thinking, but under the pressure of an examination, routine correctness may be preferred to judgment, and even an intelligent student may go on for years without discovering that higher education is training the mind, not stuffing the mind with relatively reliable statements which can be reproduced on stated occasions. Thus, the student may be slow to recognize that at last he is being treated as an adult and that he is expected to act like an adult and assume the responsibilities of an adult.

Thus, intellectual honesty and intellectual maturity go together. Most students want to be intellectually honest, but they may not know how; they may not have trained their minds to distinguish what they believe they know from what they are accepting because they assume that a writer knows. Or they may not have become much aware that they should not steal another man's phrasing and treat it as their own. They may never have learned to paraphrase intelligently and carefully; they may not even have learned to be careful to distinguish their own material from other people's material, and thus they become unwitting criminals, but criminals all the same.

Perhaps an example may be instructive; the following is from Alexis Carrel, *Man the Unknown*.

The life of all great mystics consists of the same steps. We must accept their experiences as described by them. Only those who themselves have led the life of prayer are capable of understanding its peculiarities. The search for God is, indeed, an entirely personal undertaking. By the exercise of the normal activities of his consciousness, man may endeavor to reach an invisible reality both immanent in and transcending the material world. Thus, he throws himself into the most audacious adventure that one can dare. He may be looked upon as a hero, or a lunatic. But nobody should ask whether mystical experience is true or false, whether it is auto-suggestion, hallucination, or a journey of the soul beyond the dimensions of our world and its union with a higher reality. One must be content with having an operational concept of such an experience. Mysticism is splendidly generous. It brings to man the fulfillment of his highest desires. Inner strength, spiritual light, divine love, ineffable peace. Religious intuition is as real as esthetic inspiration. Through the contemplation of super-human beauty, mystics and poets may reach the ultimate truth.

The following is one student's paraphrase of the passage:

All the great mystics go through the same steps, and we have to accept their experiences. For people who have lived a life of prayer the search for God is personal, and they get outside the world around us. Mysticism is the greatest adventure that one can dare, and although a mystic may be called a hero or a lunatic, he is concerned with a higher reality. Mystics are splendidly generous people, and religious intuition is as real as esthetic inspiration.

This is a weak paraphrase, mainly because it does such scant justice to Carrel, but secondarily because it could scarcely be used without some plagiarism. The student has not understood the passage, but he has recognized that it contains intelligent comment. Accordingly, he has gone through it, picking up familiar words and stringing them together so that they make a sort of sense, although certainly not the sense that Carrel intended. When he changed "mysticism is splendidly generous" to "mystics are splendidly generous people" he was misunderstanding the use of "generous" and hence the whole sentence. He ignored whole passages, probably because they made no sense to him, but he incorporated verbatim the sentence "Religious intuition is as real as esthetic inspiration," probably in a sort of desperation, and because the comparison appealed to him; but by using it as the closing idea he distorts the meaning of the whole. Furthermore, when he comes to write his paper he would probably be attracted by these words and write them into his paper without indication that they constitute a direct quotation.

Now notice another purported paraphrase:

Only those who have themselves led the life of prayer, that is, the mystics, are capable of understanding its peculiarities, because the search for God must inevitably be a personal undertaking. A man who endeavours to reach an invisible reality both immanent in and transcending the material world throws himself into the most audacious adventure that one can dare. Nor should anyone ask whether mystical experience results from auto-suggestion, hallucination, or a journey of the soul beyond worldly dimensions in its unions with higher reality. Mysticism, being splendidly generous, brings its fulfillment in inner strength, spiritual light, divine love, and ineffable peace, and mystics may share with poets the ultimate truth.

In one sense this is much better; the student has gained some grasp of what Carrel is saying, and if he has stolen unabashedly, he has at least had the taste to steal Carrel's best passages and not to corrupt them much. But, obviously, if he treats this paraphrase as his own notes and makes any use of it, plagiarism of a good many sorts is inevitable.

An adequate paraphrase of a paragraph like this may well be beyond the student's ability, but any student should be able to take better notes than these paraphrases represent if he will consider the following injunctions:

(1) Endeavor to understand a passage as a whole before attempting to paraphrase any of it.

(2) State in your own words anything you summarize, and note carefully that your wording is not colored by the original.

(3) When you can provide no adequate summary of your own, or when the wording of the original is so good that you wish to preserve it, scrupulously surround it with quotation marks.

The following paraphrase may not be adequate, but it could be used without plagiarism:

The activities of mystics, although they may strike more worldly people as strange, or even as insane, have their justification in that mystics, like poets, "may reach the ultimate truth." We must assume that mystics are describing their experiences to us honestly, and that only those who have experienced a mystical life can understand it. The mystic "throws himself into the most audacious adventure that one can dare"; mysticism is "splendidly generous," and the mystic's end is to "reach an invisible reality both immanent in and transcending the material world," and thus to cultivate "inner strength, spiritual light, divine love, and ineffable peace."

Exercise 22

A. Read carefully the following selection from Bergen Evans, *The Natural History of Nonsense* (New York: Knopf, 1953), pp. 258–59:

In the *New York Evening Mail* for December 28, 1917, Mr. H. L. Mencken diverted himself by greeting what he called "A Neglected Anniversary." On that day seventy-five years before, he averred, one Adam Thompson, an adventurous cotton broker in Cincinnati, had created quite a splash by lowering his naked form into the first bathtub installed in America. His act had precipitated a storm of protest. Bathing was universally condemned as an affectation and a menace to health and morals. Medical societies expressed their disapprobation, state legislatures imposed prohibitive taxes to prevent the custom from spreading, and the city of Boston—then as now zealous to protect its citizens from harmful contacts—passed a special ordinance forbidding it. There was strong public resentment when President Fillmore had a tub installed in the White House, but ultimately his example carried the day and bathing came to be tolerated if not practiced by our grandfathers.

This story in its author's words, "of spoofing all compact," was "a tissue of heavy absurdities, all of them deliberate and most of them obvious," but it was seized upon with avidity by all sorts of people and related as one of the most sacred facts of our history. Quacks used it as evidence of the [end of p. 258] stupidity of doctors. Doctors used it as proof of medical progress. Bathtub manufacturers used it as proof of their foresight, and assorted reformers used it as proof of the public's lack of it. Editors used it as proof of their own knowledge. It appeared as a contribution to public welfare in thick government bulletins. The standard reference works incorporated it. It was solemnly repeated by master thinkers, including the president of the American Geographical Society and the Commissioner of Health for the City of New York. Dr. Hans Zinsser communicated it to his readers as one of the esoteric facts of medical annals, and Alexander Woollcott shared it with the radio public as one of those quaint bits of lore with which his whimsical mind was so richly stored.[1]

By 1926 Mencken, "having undergone a spiritual rebirth and put off sin," felt that the joke had gone far enough. He confessed publicly that his story had been a hoax and pointed out what he felt should have warned the critical reader against accepting it as a fact. His confession was printed in thirty newspapers "with a combined circulation, according to their sworn claim, of more than 250,000,000," and the gullibility of the public (which had consisted largely in believing these same papers) received many an editorial rebuke.

[1] H. L. Mencken: "Hymn to the Truth," *Prejudices. Sixth Series* (New York: Alfred A. Knopf, Inc.; 1927), pp. 194–201. See also Vilhjalmur Stefansson: *Adventures in Error* (New York: Robert M. McBride & Company; 1936), Chapter 8; and Curtis D. MacDougall: *Hoaxes* (New York: The Macmillan Company; 1941), pp. 302–09.

Prepare note cards, with key words suggesting the content, and with indications of the source, for the following:

1. A note card for a paper to be entitled "Mencken, Master Spoofer," in which you reduce the first paragraph to about half, but retain the most interesting passages in direct quotation. Make clear that you are quoting Evans' summary of Mencken.
2. A note card for the same paper, in which you recount Mencken's confession and quote both Mencken and Evans.
3. A note card for a paper to be called "Learned Gossip," in which you try to show how rapidly learned errors may spread. This note might in effect be a paraphrase of the second paragraph.

4. A note card to yourself for the same paper in which you record the information so that you can look up treatments of the bathtub hoax by Stefansson and MacDougall.

5. A note card for a paper to be called, "Bergen Evans: Modern Mencken."

B. Study carefully the following paragraph from Edward Sapir's *Language:*

Strictly speaking, we know in advance that it is impossible to set up a limited number of types that would do full justice to the peculiarities of the thousands of languages and dialects spoken on the surface of the earth. Like all human institutions, speech is too variable and too elusive to be quite safely ticketed. Even if we operate with a minutely subdivided scale of types we may be quite certain that many of our languages will need trimming before they fit. To get them into the scheme at all it will be necessary to overestimate the significance of this or that feature or to ignore, for the time being, certain contradictions in their mechanism. Does the difficulty of classification prove the uselessness of the task? I do not think so. It would be too easy to relieve ourselves of the burden of constructive thinking and to take the standpoint that each language has its unique history, therefore its unique structure. Such a standpoint expresses only a half truth. Just as similar social, economic, and religious institutions have grown up in different parts of the world from distinct historical antecedents, so also languages, traveling along different roads, have tended to converge toward similar forms. Moreover, the historical study of language has proven to us beyond all doubt that a language changes not only gradually but consistently, that it moves unconsciously from one type towards another, and that analogous trends are observable in remote quarters of the globe. From this it follows that broadly similar morphologies must have been reached by unrelated languages, independently and frequently. In assuming the existence of comparable types, therefore, we are not gain-saying the individuality of all historical processes; we are merely affirming that back of the face of history are powerful drifts that move language, like other social products, to balanced patterns, in other words, to types. As linguists we shall be content to realize that there are these types and that certain processes in the life of language tend to modify them. Why similar types should be formed, just what is the nature of the forces that make and dissolve them—these questions are more easily asked than answered. Perhaps the psychologists of the future will be able to give us the ultimate reasons for the formation of linguistic types.

Criticize the following attempts to paraphrase this passage:

1. Trying to put the thousands of languages and dialects spoken on the surface of the earth into a limited number of types makes it necessary to ignore certain contradictions in their mechanisms, and hence classification becomes a useless task. In assuming the existence of compara-

ble types, therefore, we are gainsaying the individuality of all historical process. Perhaps the psychologists of the future will be able ultimately to put the languages of the world into types.

2. Although Sapir recognizes that speech, like all human institutions, is too elusive to be ticketed, he believes that endeavoring to type sorts of speech develops constructive thinking. He points out that historical study of language has proven that a language changes not only gradually but consistently, and that accordingly, we must assume that similarities in language in different parts of the globe represent powerful drifts that move language, like other products, to balanced patterns, in other words, to types.

Now try to write a more adequate paraphrase of not more than a hundred words.

Collecting Material

Careful, orderly, systematic investigation saves time and promotes the accuracy necessary in any objective writing.

A research paper is a creative project. As a record of the writer's thinking and organizing and relating of ideas, it requires imagination and judgment; it is not merely a mechanical reproduction of mechanically collected data. Since the job is complex, however, systematic procedures will help save the writer from confusion and inaccuracy.

23-1 Choosing a Subject

A subject for research should have at least these four qualifications: it must be within the range of the student's capabilities; it must be conducive to objective treatment; it must be sufficiently restricted to permit detailed work, and it must be chosen with a view to the limitations of the library and other sources of information. The first of these limitations will exclude many technical subjects, since the specialized knowledge required even to read the available publications may require years of preparation. The study of an American Indian language would require a knowledge of phonetic and phonemic structural analysis; discussing the nature of matter would require a knowledge of both higher mathematics and atomic physics. Many aspects of most subjects, however, can be studied by any literate person.

A research paper should be objective, and objectivity requires rigid restriction of the subject. Objectivity, of course, is always relative; it represents an ideal, not an achievable reality, but the writer can endeavor to be objective, and some subjects are more amenable to objective treatment than are others. *Why I Believe the Republican is the Best Party* is not a likely subject for research. The writer is not prepared to be objective; he has already made up his mind. Neither is he likely to provide much evidence; psychologists may some day have evidence on how political opinions are formed, but the writer is probably not prepared to study the subject in an objective way.

Furthermore, even subjects amenable to objective study cannot be studied objectively unless they are restricted. Unless he restricts his subject the writer may never get beyond his introduction or a few generalities whose validity he has never tested. This, of course, is the same problem discussed earlier (see 1-4), but in choosing a subject for research it becomes acute because beginning students seldom suspect how much material is available on almost any subject. Below are subjects obviously too broad, with suggestions for restricting them:

Physics	Some Dangers in Disposing of Atomic Waste in Desert Areas
Nursing	The Care of the Wounded at Gettysburg
Architecture	The Early Impact of LeCorbusier on American Architecture
Shakespeare	The Background and Meaning of "Hoist with His Own Petard."

The last qualification will not be important for most subjects, provided the student has a good library at his disposal. The holdings in well established libraries are so great that the beginning student, although he may at first have difficulty locating the most useful material, will soon find himself buried in information and wondering how he can reduce his subject further. Libraries in small or new colleges, however, may be inadequate, and may force the student to abandon an otherwise promising subject, and some libraries, especially in institutions with a technical or professional bias, may be so restricted that the general collection of books is inadequate. Some subjects carry their own restrictions; material of military importance may be restricted for reasons of security, and rare manuscripts or old newspaper files may not be available for general use. On the other hand, the student may wish to take advantage of special materials locally available. He might, for example, write the history of his home town, using materials collected in the state historical society, or he might write the biography of a figure prominent in his community, using local newspaper files.

Locating Material 23-2

For most investigations, the student will find his main sources in libraries. Although librarians labor to have their materials in good order and readily available, libraries are inevitably complicated because the world's knowledge is complicated; thus, the problem of finding material usually resolves itself into the problem of using the research tools in a library. Printed material is classified according to the manner of its publication. For purposes of arrangement, printed material is divided into books, periodicals, and pamphlets and bulletins. The investigator should learn to use appropriate tools to locate all the material of each sort that may be pertinent to his study.

Most important material is eventually published in book form and is most readily available in that form. The best tool for locating books is usually the card catalog in the library, which for most libraries lists all available books (but *not* the articles in periodicals nor the pamphlets). Books in the library will be entered alphabetically by the last name of the author if the author is known, by the first letter (except *a, an,* or *the*) of the title, and by the subject of the book. For instance, Eric Partridge's *The World of Words* will be cataloged under *Partridge, Eric,* as author; under *World of Words, The,* as title; and under *Language and languages, English language— History, Americanisms,* and other divisions of learning as subject. If a book has more than one author, it will be entered once for each author; sometimes a book will be entered for an editor; usually a book will be entered for more than one subject, since most books discuss more than one. The subject cards in a library catalog can be helpful, but they can never be exhaustive, and the investigator must expect to use a card catalog as a means to start his search, not as the source of his final list of appropriate books. The research worker should always look up several synonyms of his subject. For instance, if he is working on *words,* he should also try *language, speech, vocabulary, diction, etymology, usage* and the like.

23-3 Classification of Books; Catalogs and Bibliographies

So that they can be easily located, books in libraries must be arranged according to some system. Many American libraries use the Dewey Decimal System or a variation upon it. Large libraries often use the Library of Congress numbering system or a system adapted to their peculiar needs. The numbering and the classifications vary, but the theories of the systems are similar.

By the Dewey Decimal System, for example, all books are divided into ten groups (except fiction and biography, which are classified under *F* and *B*, respectively), the first group being general books and the nine others, books in nine general areas of knowledge which supposedly include all subjects. Each of these groups is in turn divided into ten, and this subdivision again into ten. Thus the top row of the number for Partridge's book would be 410. The number means that this book falls within the broad subject of language, 400 in the Dewey system; 1 as the second digit indicates the English language, and 0 as the third digit indicates that the book is general. The second row of the call number identifies the individual book, with a capital letter for the author's name, numbers to identify the book within the latter group, and the initial of the first important word of the title (*P259w*). A third line of the call number may add the date of first publication. Thus the call number of Partridge's book would be:

410

*P*259*w*

1944

This call number is put on the spine of the book itself and recorded on all catalog cards of the book; every book in the library can be identified and located by a call number.

Library cards provide a variety of information about the book and its author. A typical author card looks like the following:

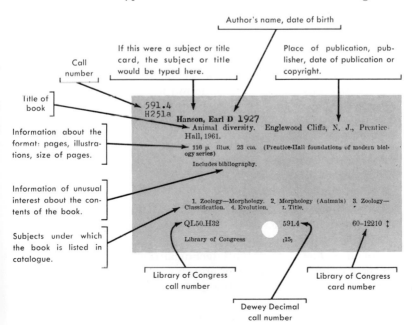

Author's name, date of birth

If this were a subject or title card, the subject or title would be typed here.

Place of publication, publisher, date of publication or copyright.

Call number

Title of book

591.4
H251a

Hanson, Earl D 1927
Animal diversity. Englewood Cliffs, N. J., Prentice-Hall, 1961.

Information about the format: pages, illustrations, size of pages.

116 p. Illus. 23 cm. (Prentice-Hall foundations of modern biology series)

Includes bibliography.

Information of unusual interest about the contents of the book.

1. Zoology—Morphology. 2. Morphology (Animals) 3. Zoology—Classification. 4. Evolution. I. Title.

Subjects under which the book is listed in catalogue.

QL50.H32

591.4

60–12210 ‡

Library of Congress

[15]

Library of Congress call number

Dewey Decimal call number

Library of Congress card number

23-4   Printed Catalogs and Bibliographies

Books not available in the local library may be obtained from other libraries, borrowed by interlibrary loan, or if they are important and in print, purchased. For these purposes, printed catalogs of the great libraries and printed bibliographies are indispensable. At this writing the most useful, since it is recent, extensive, and all in one series, is *Author-Title Catalog: Library, University of California* (Boston: G. K. Hall & Co., 1963), 115 vols. The catalog of the Library of Congress is available in some libraries on cards and has also been printed with supplements which bring the whole up to more than two hundred volumes. The catalog of the British Museum has also been issued in supplements, though not yet brought down to date; it is excellent for older books, for British and Continental books, and for rare books. The *Cumulative Book Index* lists current books in English; in annual and cumulative five-year volumes it is known as the *U. S. Catalog of Books in Print.* Other bibliographies can be found through *Bibliographic Index: A Cumulative Bibliography of Bibliographies, 1938*—(New York, 1939—). Some libraries have a union card catalog made up of cards for books in many libraries. Bibliographies for many subjects may be located conveniently through Constance M. Winchell, *Guide to Reference Books,* 8th ed. Chicago, 1966.

The student should also be alert for bibliographies and bibliographic footnotes in books. These are often the best sources because they are prepared by experts in particular subjects. A good beginning bibliography can usually be found in an authoritative encyclopedia.

23-5   Periodical and Newspaper Indexes

With rare exceptions, magazine articles are not included in the card catalogs of libraries or in the general bibliographies, and must be located through special indexes. Magazine articles may be extremely important, more important than the writer who knows only popular magazines is likely to expect. There are scholarly, technical, scientific, and professional journals in all subjects of any consequence. They print highly technical material, some of which is never reprinted in book form, and they report the latest findings before this material can possibly be incorporated in books. Thus, extremely important information appears first in periodicals, and some very important material is available only in periodicals.

Many periodical indexes are "cumulated"; that is, they are constantly re-edited and republished in accordance with a system which keeps them up to date. For instance, the *Reader's Guide to Periodical Literature*, which indexes relatively popular magazines, appears every month. In February of any year, the library will receive a number which indexes the January issues of magazines, and in March a number which indexes the February issues. In April, however, a large number will arrive, in which all the issues of January, February, and March have been re-edited into one list. Thereafter one month numbers will continue, but the July issue will cumulate the articles for six months. The following January a number will cumulate the entire preceding year. Similarly, there will be two-year, three-year, and five-year cumulations, by which time the book has become so large that the cumulation begins all over again. In this way, the index can be kept constantly up to date, while the user need not thumb through the numbers for each month. Not all indexes are cumulated so frequently as is the *Reader's Guide*, but the principle is the same. The investigator should be sure, however, that he uses all the copies of the index to cover the time in which he is interested, and that the periodicals he needs are indexed in the periodical index he is using; there will be a list somewhere, usually in the front of any volume. Most periodical indexes use a highly skeletonized style; the user should consult the list of abbreviations.

The following are the most useful indexes to periodical material published in English:

Poole's Index to Periodical Literature, 1802–1907. A pioneer work indexing leading English and American periodicals, this set is still valuable for its date; for more recent times it has been replaced by the next two items.

Reader's Guide to Periodical Literature, 1900___. The most useful general index in English, although it includes fewer serious or specialized periodicals than the *International Index*.

International Index to Periodicals, 1907___. Unusually useful for investigative papers of the sort under consideration, since it includes extremely important American and foreign periodicals in the sciences and humanities. It does not index highly specialized or technical journals.

Indexes to special subjects. Almost every field of study and every subdivision of a large field of study has a specialized periodical index. Many of these are published in an issue of a periodical; for example, the most widely used current bibliography of the study of language and literature is that published in an annual number of *PMLA* (the *Publications of the Modern Language Association*), and bibliographies of periods are likely to appear in journals of more restricted interest. Specialized indexes, not all of which are cumulated, include the following:

Agricultural Index, 1916___. Includes pamphlets.
Annual Bibliography of the Modern Humanities Research Association, 1924___.
Art Index, 1929___.
Book Review Digest, 1905___. Indexes reviews, with excerpts; not cumulated.
Dramatic Index, 1909___.
Education Index, 1929___. Includes both professional and academic journals.
Engineering Index, 1906___. Indexes, also, many subjects related to engineering.
Essay and General Literature Index, 1900___. Invaluable for locating essays by subject, fiction by theme, and the like.
Industrial Arts Index, 1913___. Indexes a large number of trade, technical, and industrial periodicals, many of them obscure. Includes pamphlets.
Official Index of the Times (London), 1906___. Cumulation has varied; now quarterly; for earlier references, see *Palmer's Index to the Times Newspaper,* 1868___.
New York Times Index, 1913___. Cumulation available, but not in all libraries.
Public Affairs Information Service, 1915___.

(For additional indexes, see Winchell, *Guide,* 23–4, above.)

23-6   Bulletins and Pamphlets

Bulletins and pamphlets vary, both in the manner of their publication and in their value; accordingly, libraries handle them variously. Some bulletins come out more or less regularly and in series. For example, the Bureau of American Ethnology publishes what are called *Bulletins,* which may run to hundreds of pages of original research not elsewhere available. On the other hand, a pamphlet issued to describe the beauties of a lake resort may be almost worthless. Accordingly, such questions arise as when is a pamphlet a pamphlet and when is it a book or a periodical, which so-called pamphlets are worth cataloging, which are worth keeping but not worth cataloging, and which should be thrown away? No simple statement can be made about pamphlets. Some are treated as though they are books, and are cataloged in the regular way and appear in the card catalog. Practice varies, especially with the purposes of the library. In a university library having an active anthropology department, the Bureau of American Ethnology *Reports* and *Bulletins* are likely to be cataloged. In a public library they are likely not to be. If they are not cataloged as individual volumes, they are likely to be cataloged as a series with authors and titles on a central card under the name of the series. As indicated above, some pamphlets are listed in periodical indexes, even though they are not periodicals. Government bulletins—and they include quantities of extremely important material—appear in the *United States Document Catalogue.* Many libraries collect documents by subject, especially on local topics.

Reference Books 23-7

Some books are so useful for ready reference that most libraries keep them on special reference shelves or at a reference desk. The most important works in all fields, including reference works, can be located through Winchell, *Guide to Reference Books,* cited in 23-4. Some reference works are so useful that everyone should know them without reference to Winchell.

Dictionaries. For the most important dictionaries of English, see 21-1.

Encyclopedias and specialized dictionaries. Encyclopedias and specialized dictionaries are good to start with but not to finish with. They should be used mainly to acquire a reliable introduction, for brief bibliographies, and to verify routine details. They should not be used as crutches to avoid serious investigation. Useful general encyclopedias include the following:

Encyclopaedia Britannica, 14th ed., 1929, 24 vols. This work is in continuous revision, so that important articles may be quite recent; some articles are signed. Scholarly articles in the eleventh edition are still valuable, as are some in the thirteenth. For many purposes this is the best general encyclopedia in English.

Encyclopedia Americana, rev. ed., 1945, 30 vols. In many ways similar to the *Britannica;* less detailed on most subjects.

New International Encyclopedia, 2nd ed. 1914–16, rev. 1922–30, 25 vols. Older and briefer than the two previous items and with fewer signed articles, but useful.

Encyclopedias are available in most important European languages, some of them excellent. In addition, some encyclopedias, although limited by area or a sectarian approach, are yet sufficiently inclusive so that they serve for general reference work. They include the following:

Catholic Encyclopedia, 1907–22, 17 vols.

Encyclopedia of the Social Sciences, 1949–50, 13 vols.

Hastings' *Encyclopedia of Religion and Ethics,* 1908–27, 12 vols. and index.

New Schaff-Herzog Encyclopedia of Religious Knowledge, 1949–50, 13 vols.

Encyclopedias and handbooks of more specialized subjects can save time and trouble:

Bartlett's *Familiar Quotations, 13th ed., 1955.*

Grove's *Dictionary of Music and Musicians,* 5th ed., 1954, 9 vols.

Handbook of Chemistry and Physics, 1914___.

Harper's Dictionary of Classical Literature, 1897.

Mencken's *A New Dictionary of Quotations,* 1942.

Oxford Companion to American Literature, 4th ed., 1965.

Oxford Companion to English Literature, 3rd ed., 1946.

New Oxford History of Music, 1957.

Mythology of All Races, 1916–32, 13 vols.

Collections of biographical accounts in English include the following:

Dictionary of National Biography (called *DNB*), 1882–1949, 22 vols. Treats important British figures no longer living.

Dictionary of American Biography (called *DAB*), 1928–1936, 20 vols. and index. Supplements, 1944, 1958. *American* refers to the United States.

Briefer accounts are included in the following:

The International Who's Who, 1935___.

Who's Who, 1849___. Biographical accounts of British subjects and some others of great prominence.

Who's Who in America, 1899___. For living citizens of the United States. For names not in the general volume, see *Who's Who in New England,* 1915___; *in the East,* 1943___; *in the Midwest,* 1949___; in the West, *1949___*.

Who Was Who, 1897___. Useful for those not included in *DAB;* supplements roughly by decades.

Similar works are available in the native language for most large countries. More specialized dictionaries of biography include the following:

American Men of Science, 11th ed. 1965.

Century Dictionary and Cyclopedia, 1911, 12 vols.

Current Biography, 1940___.

Directory of American Scholars, 4th ed., 1964, 4 vols.

Twentieth Century Authors, 1942___.

Webster's Biographical Dictionary, 1943.

Almanacs and Yearbooks. Some publications bring within ready compass statistics and miscellaneous information about a variety of subjects of general, and especially of current, interest. Most of them are revised annually, with statistics brought down to date for the previous year or the most recent compilation. They include the following:

Facts on File, 1940___. A weekly digest under headings like *Sport, World Affairs.*

Statesman's Yearbook, 1864— . Standard; strong international bent, with emphasis on political and commercial subjects.

Statistical Abstract of the United States, 1878___ . The most extensive body of general statistical information readily available in English.

World Almanac and Book of Facts, 1868___ . Perhaps the best of a number of almanacs published by newspapers; another good one is that published by the *Chicago Daily News.* Every student should have one on his desk.

Encyclopedias publishing annual supplements, surveys for the year, include the following: *Encyclopedia Americana, Encyclopaedia Britannica, New International Encyclopedia.*

The Trial Bibliography   23-8

The first step in any investigation is the preparation of a trial or preliminary bibliography. Through this bibliography the investigator discovers what has already been learned about his subject, and accordingly, what is left for him to do. It provides him with a general view of his subject and its relationships, with the titles of important relevant works, and with an orderly way of working. Since he now has a list of the best known, he can start with the more general and the more important.

For a trial bibliography, the investigator should make intelligent use of available bibliographical and reference tools. First, he should look up the subject in general works, in encyclopedias, for instance. Next, he should consult the card catalog, using first the subject entries, and checking general works in a preliminary way for bibliography. Anyone who has written on the subject should be looked up in the card catalog as an author; if a man writes a book on a subject, he may include information on the same subject in another book, although too little to warrant a subject card in the catalog. Meanwhile, the investigator should be considering other sorts of publications. Is the subject of such nature that there would be magazine articles on it? If so, what index would cover the most likely periodicals? Would there be pamphlets or documents on the subject?

For instance, let us assume that a writer has realized that the United States has a remarkable system of roads and has decided to learn more about road building. He looks up *roads, transportation,* and *road building* in several encyclopedias. He discovers that modern methods of building roads have developed in the last two centuries, and he then looks up social histories, like Traill's *Social England,* and books on transportation. In some of these he finds extensive bibliographies and bibliographical footnotes, and he makes cards for these (see 23-9). In one of them he notes that when Josiah Wedgwood's dishes became popular all over Europe, Wedgwood built private roads, because the public roads were so bad that he had to pack his dishes on muleback, and when packs slipped off mules, that was the end of the dishes. The writer becomes interested and tries to find out all he can about Wedgwood and his ware. In the *DNB* he finds biographies of Wedgwood and bibliographical suggestions for further investigation. He discovers an elaborate series of British local histories, called the *Victoria County Histories,* and he surmises that the county history for Wedgwood's shire will tell him something about the roads of the area and probably refer to more detailed studies which will include Wedgwood's roads. By now the writer is well on his way to locating the material for an investigative paper on the manner in which ornamental vases contributed to the revolution in road building. From now on he has only to use reference works intelligently and faithfully.

Two things the investigator should avoid. He should not begin by asking the librarian, "Is there anything in the library on building roads?" Any good library contains hundreds, thousands of works on building roads, but the librarian does not have time to prepare a list of them. That is the investigator's job, not the librarian's. Similarly, the investigator should not try to get his work done for him by writing an authority for information; he should not write the county engineer, "Please tell me all you know about building roads." Most of what an investigator wants to know is in published form; his job is to find it.

23-9   Bibliography Cards

As fast as the investigator locates titles that may be pertinent to his subject, he should prepare his bibliography. Most competent investigators use a system something like the following:

They provide themselves with small cards or slips of paper of uniform size; three-by-five-inch cards are customary. They use one card and only one for each book, article, or pamphlet. On it they write the name of the author first, exactly as it appears on the title page except that the last name is put first. They record the bibliographical information in accordance with a style like that described below. They often add the library call number for the book, for their own convenience, and any brief comment that may be useful later. A bibliography card for a book looks like this:

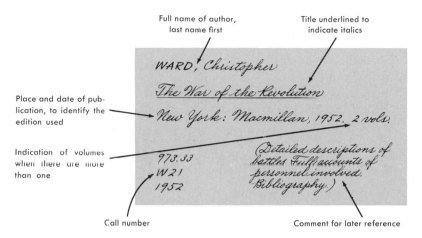

Full name of author, last name first

Title underlined to indicate italics

Place and date of publication, to identify the edition used

Indication of volumes when there are more than one

Call number

Comment for later reference

Some bibliographies include other information. Most bibliographies omit the publishers especially for books out of print or books published more than fifty-six years ago and hence out of copyright.

A bibliography card for a magazine article looks like this:

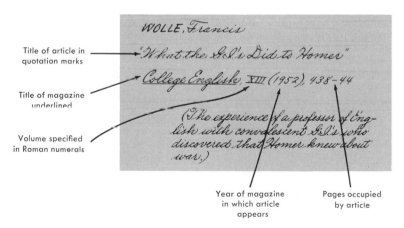

Title of article in quotation marks

Title of magazine underlined

Volume specified in Roman numerals

Year of magazine in which article appears

Pages occupied by article

The month of issue and the number of the magazine are sometimes added.

A bibliography prepared on cards of this sort can be expanded indefinitely without becoming confused. The cards can be kept in a file drawer for ready reference; they are usually filed alphabetically by the author's last name (alphabetically by the first important word of the title if the work is anonymous.)

23-10 Bibliographic Form

A bibliography of the principal works consulted, including all those cited in the paper, is customarily appended to a long documented composition. The entries should follow a standard form, and the form should be used in entering information on cards of the preliminary bibliography. Styles for bibliographies vary in details according to the field of investigation and the publication for which the paper is written. All publications of any consequence have a style sheet, which formalizes practice; if a writer knows he is writing for a specific publication, he should acquire the style sheet of that publication and follow it. Described here is one of the standard styles. Others vary in details, some using commas rather than periods between items or inserting parentheses around publication data, but the student should become familiar with the common practice of taking a style and following it scrupulously, even though on another occasion he may be asked to follow a different style. The recommendations below, which follow the style sheet adopted by the Modern Language Association, are widely used for literary and humanistic studies.

Some bibliographic entries, especially those in elaborate series, become complicated, but the basic entry is as follows: last name of author, comma; remainder of author's name and collaborators, period; title of book, underlined (for print, in italics), period; place of publication, comma; date of publication, period. The following is a typical bibliographic entry:

Hockett, Charles F. *A Course in Modern Linguistics.* New York, 1958.

If the publisher is included, the style becomes as follows:

Hockett, Charles F. *A Course in Modern Linguistics.* New York: Macmillan, 1958.

If the work runs to more than one volume, the number of volumes and the inclusive dates should be given as in the following:

Baker, Ernest A. *The History of the English Novel.* 10 vols. London, 1924–39.

The following entry provides a form for a work having more than one author and for a work having a subtitle:

Bernbaum, Ernest, Samuel C. Chew, Thomas M. Raysor, Clarence D. Thorpe, and René Wellek. *The English Romantic Poets: A Review of Research.* New York, 1950.

If the edition is not the first, this fact may be noted as follows:

Baugh, Albert C. *A History of the English Language,* 2nd ed. New York, 1957.

Works for which the author is not given on the title page may be listed under *Anon.* for anonymous, but are usually entered by title; if the author is known but his name does not appear on the title page, it may be inserted within square brackets, and with a question mark if the identification is uncertain, as follows:

[Wesley, John?] *The Complete English Dictionary.* Bristol, Eng., 1764.

The same rule usually applies if an anonymous work has an editor, but an edition, particularly one cited for the editor's notes, may be alphabetized under either the title or the editor, as follows:

Beowulf and *The Fight at Finnsburg.* Ed. Fr. Klaeber. New York, 1928.
Klaeber, Fr., ed. *Beowulf* and *The Fight at Finnsburg.* New York, 1928.

A similar style serves for translations, as follows:

Translations from the Chinese. Trans. Arthur Waley. New York, 1919.

If the date of publication cannot be determined, it may be replaced with n.d., for *no date.* If it is not on the title page, most styles permit using the copyright date as the date of publication. If the date is not given but is known, it may be inserted within square brackets, and if it is uncertain it may be followed with a question mark. Some publications in series are sufficiently complicated bibliographically that no brief statement will provide for all contingencies, but much can be inferred from the following entry:

Young, Karl. *The Origin and Development of the Story of Troilus and Criseyde,* Chaucer Society, 2nd Ser., No. 40. London, 1908 [for 1904].

For other examples, see *The MLA Style Sheet,* compiled by William Riley Parker (New York, 1951), pp. 14–17.

For articles and selections, this standard bibliographical form is adapted to account for the name of the article, which is enclosed within quotation marks, and the name of the book or periodical, in italics, as follows:

Wolle, Francis. "What the G.I.'s Did to Homer," *College English,* XIII (1952), 438–444.
Lewis, C. S. "Hamlet: The Prince or the Poem?" *Hamlet: Enter Critic,* ed. Claire Sacks and Edgar Whan. New York, 1960, pp. 170–187.

The article and the periodical are treated as a continuous description, with commas instead of periods, and page numbers in the periodical or the book are included. If the volume number is given, the abbreviation for pages is not used. For a periodical the number or other identification may be included, and must be included unless the whole volume of the periodical is paged consecutively, as follows:

Marriott, Alice. "Beowulf in South Dakota," *The New Yorker*, XXVIII, No. 24 (1952), 46, 48–51.
Updike, John. "Recital," *The New Yorker* (June 10, 1961), p. 29.

If pages are interrupted, they may appear as follows: 6–18, 81, 90.

23-11 Footnote Form

Footnotes do not become a problem until the student starts to write, but for simplicity they may be reviewed here, since footnote form closely follows bibliographic form. In general, the two differ in four ways: (1) the name of the author is not reversed, since no alphabetizing is involved; (2) the page or pages referred to must be included; (3) the footnote carries a superscript number, and (4) the style presumes that the footnote is a sort of a statement, and hence the punctuation is changed so that terminal periods do not appear within the footnote citation—periods will, of course, appear after abbreviations and between sentences in a discussion footnote. The basic bibliographic note given above would appear in a first footnote as follows:

[1] Charles F. Hockett, *A Course in Modern Linguistics* (New York, 1958), pp. 46–53.
[1] Charles F. Hockett, *A Course in Modern Linguistics* (New York: Macmillan, 1958), p. 219.

If the author's complete name has been given in the text, it may be omitted from the footnote, as follows:

[1] *A Course in Modern Linguistics* (New York, 1958), p. 89.

If the work runs to more than one volume, the volume must be identified, but the abbreviation for page or pages is not used:

[2] Ernest A. Baker, *The History of the English Novel* (London, 1939), X, 63.

Other details, such as editors and translators, are inserted as in the bibliographic form, but separated from each other and from the remainder of the citation by commas. Similarly, the footnote form for articles in periodicals and for briefer pieces within a collection reflects the bibliographic form, as follows:

27 Francis Wolle, "What the G.I.'s Did to Homer," *College English,* XIII (1952), 441.

13 C. S. Lewis, "Hamlet: The Prince or the Poem?" *Hamlet: Enter Critic,* ed. Claire Sacks and Edgar Whan (New York, 1960), p. 183.

35 Alice Marriott, "Beowulf in South Dakota," *The New Yorker,* XXVIII, No. 24 (1952), 46, 48–51.

If he knows the source of a reprinted article or monograph, the writer may well include this in his footnote, as follows:

13 C. S. Lewis, "Hamlet: The Prince or the Poem?" *Hamlet: Enter Critic,* ed. Claire Sacks and Edgar Whan (New York, 1960), p. 183; repr. from *Proceedings of the British Academy,* XXXVII (London, 1942), 1–18.

If the writer is relying on material not available to him, but cited in a secondary work which is available, he may cite as follows:

28 Thomas Campbell, *Essays on English Poetry* (London, 1848), p. 39; cited in Albert C. Baugh, *A History of the English Language,* 2nd ed. (New York, 1957), p. 224.

For simplicity in dealing with periodicals which do not follow the familiar pattern of volume numbers and consecutive pagination, or which have relatively complicated subdivisions with pagination within the subdivisions, an acceptable form is as follows:

47 "The Problem of Atomic Energy" (editorial), New York *Times,* March 4, 1951, Sec. 4, p. 8.

Common dictionaries and encyclopedias arranged alphabetically may be cited without the conventional bibliographical details as follows:

39 *Encyclopaedia Britannica,* 14th ed., under "Jonson, Ben."

40 Sidney Lee, *DNB,* under "Marlowe, Christopher."

All these forms serve for the first citation from a given work; thereafter the citation is abbreviated for convenience. Currently, the best practice is to use the author's last name, a shortened title, or both, mentioning this abbreviation in the first footnote from the work. For example, if an article concerns the works of one figure, the title may be reduced to *Works* and footnotes handled as follows:

17 *The Complete Works of Chaucer,* ed. Fred N. Robinson, rev. ed. (Cambridge, Mass., 1957), p. xii; hereafter cited as *Works.*

21 *Works,* p. 547.

Similarly, a work may be cited by the abbreviated title, or if only one work is cited from an author, by the author's name. The first work cited above might well be abbreviated Hockett or *Linguistics*.

¹ Charles F. Hockett, *A Course in Modern Linguistics* (New York, 1958), pp. 46–53; hereafter cited as Hockett.

⁵ Hockett, p. 275.

Earlier practice encouraged reference to a work already cited by one of the following abbreviations: ibid., loc. cit., and op. cit., usually not now printed in italics. Modern practice is to discourage use of these abbreviations, since they can be confusing and save little or no space; if they are used they should be employed as follows:

¹⁴ Albert C. Baugh, *A History of the English Language*, 2nd ed. (New York, 1957), p. 38.

¹⁵ Ibid., p. 65.

²² Baugh, op. cit., p. 91.

²⁴ Baugh, loc. cit.

The abbreviations must be used with the following restrictions. *Ibid.* is the abbreviation for *ibidem,* meaning "in the same place," and hence can be used only to refer to a single citation in the immediately preceding footnote. *Op. cit.* is the abbreviation of *opere citato,* meaning "in the work cited," and hence can be used for a work recently cited, but for a different page in that work. *Loc. cit.* is the abbreviation for *loco citato,* "in the place or passage cited," and hence does not include a page number and can be used only if the citation refers to the same page or passage identified in the previous citation.

Highly specialized writings, notably scholarly, scientific, and technical studies, usually employ letter abbreviations for standard journals and reference tools; *Webster's New World Dictionary of the American Language* becomes *WNWD* and the *Library of Congress Catalog* becomes *LC.* These abbreviations are permissible only if they are indicated in a footnote as above, if they are included in a list of abbreviations in the book or periodical, or if the work is intended for a very restricted body of readers, all of whom can be expected to know the abbreviations. Usually they are appropriate in student writing only if they are individually identified in the first footnote citation to the work.

For reference, the prescriptions for footnotes in the Modern Language Association *Style Sheet* are reprinted below, minus the footnotes:

For Books

a. *Author's or authors' names* in normal order, not as though they were being alphabetized, followed by a comma. By always giving names in the fullest form known to you, or at least the most usual form, you may save your reader many minutes of searching in a library catalogue, e.g., for "H. M. Jones."

b. *Title of the chapter or part* of the book cited, enclosed in quotation marks (not underlined), followed by a comma inside the final quotes. This detail is rarely necessary except in references to articles in collections, Festschriften, etc.

c. *Title of the work,* underlined, followed by a comma unless the next detail is enclosed in parentheses. Some abbreviation of the title is permissible in cases of books with unusually long titles; but the first few words should always be cited intact, and any later omissions *within* the portion cited should be indicated by three periods (. . .). Always take the title from the title page, not from the cover or running title. If there is a subtitle, underline it as well and, if necessary, supply appropriate punctuation (usually a colon). If there are typographical peculiarities in the title (e.g., an italicized name of a play), you may normalize them, using quotation marks or roman for something there italicized.

d. *Editor's or translator's name* in normal order, preceded by "ed." or "trans." (without parentheses), followed by a comma unless the next detail is enclosed in parentheses. If the editor's or translator's work rather than the text is under discussion, give his name *first* in your reference (followed by a comma, followed by "ed." or "trans." without punctuation) and the author's name *after* the title, with a comma and "by."

e. *Edition used,* whenever the edition is not the first, in Arabic numerals (e.g., "4th ed."), followed by a comma unless the next detail is enclosed in parentheses. Unless you are concerned with your author's changes of opinion, or with differences in text, you will of course have used the latest *revised* edition or will inform your reader of your inability to do so.

f. *The series* (if unnamed on the title page), not underlined and not in quotation marks, followed by a comma, followed by the number of this work in the series (e.g., "VII" or "Vol. VII" or "No. 7"), followed by a comma unless the next detail is enclosed in parentheses. If, however, your reference is to part of a collection or section of works named on the title page, the more general title is also underlined and may be introduced by "in."

g. *The number of volumes* with this particular title, if more than one (e.g., "3 vols.") and if the information is pertinent. It is usually not pertinent when your reference is to a specific passage rather than to the book as a whole.

h. *Places(s) and date(s) of publication,* within parentheses, the place followed by a comma; but if the publisher's or bookseller's name is also supplied, it follows the place of publication, preceded by a *colon,* and followed by a comma. Except in articles with a bibliographical slant or purpose, or except when acknowledgment for permission to quote must be made, it is usually pointless to add the name of the publisher, for this information rarely aids in identification of the book. Some scholars, however, regularly include the information for all works still in the copyright period (i.e., published within the last 56 years), assuming a legitimate interest by the reader. In listing places avoid ambiguity (e.g., Cambridge—Mass. or Eng.) or vagueness.

i. Volume number, if one of two or more, in capital Roman numerals, preceded and followed by a comma, unless it is necessary to give the date of a single volume (in parentheses, followed by a comma). Use the volume number alone (without "Vol.") if the page number follows, e.g., "III, 248–251."

j. Page numbers in Arabic numerals (unless the original has small Roman numerals), preceded by a comma, followed by a period unless an additional reference is required, e.g., "p. 47, n. 3." The numerals are preceded by "p." or "pp." only for works of a single volume.

Articles in Periodicals

a. Author's name in normal order, followed by a comma. Here it is not so important as in the case of books to give the name in the fullest possible form, but if only initials are given, give them all (and, in typing, leave a space between them).

b. Title in full, enclosed in quotation marks (not underlined), followed by a comma inside the second quotation marks.

c. Name of the periodical, abbreviated in accord with good usage, underlined, followed by a comma.

d. Volume number (without "Vol." preceding) in capital Roman numerals, followed by a comma unless the next detail is enclosed in parentheses. Volume numbers of newspapers and weekly or monthly magazines may be omitted and the complete date given instead—with commas, not parentheses.

e. Issue number or name (e.g., "Autumn") if the pagination of the issue is separate and if, the month of publication is not also given.

f. The year (preceded by the month, if needed; see *e*), enclosed in parentheses, followed by a comma. The year should always be given unless it has been noted in your text, for it tells the reader at once how recent the study is and serves also as a useful check on the volume number in the act of location. If the volume covers more than one year, give only the year of the number involved.

g. Page number(s) in Arabic numerals, without "p." or "pp." preceding, followed by a period unless an additional reference to a footnote is needed.

Exercise 23

A. Using the style recommended and information in the examples above, correct the following as bibliographic entries:

1. Bough, A. C. (Second Edition) Hist. of the Engl. Lang. 1597, N.Y., U.S.A.

2. A Course in Linguistics by Charles F. Hackett, published by the Mac Milan Company, Inc., in New York early in 1958

3. Sacks, Claire and Wham, Edgar (They are the editors of the whole book), the book is *Hamlet: Enter Critic,* New York, 1960. but the article is by C. S. Lewis and called Hamlet: The Prince of the Poem? (question mark is in original), Pages 170–187.

4. Otto Jespersen, *Language,* its nature, development, and origin, (New York, the MacMillan company, 1922, pp. 85.

5. G. N. Clark, "Social and Economic Aspects of Science in the Age of Newton. Economic History 3. 1937. pp. 362–79.

6. Davidson, Martin: *The Stars and the Mind,* a study of the impact of astronomical development on human thought, 210 pages long. (London: 1947)

7. August Goll, *Criminal types in Shakespeare, Journal of Criminal Law and Criminology* 29, (1938) 492–516.

8. Ruth Leila Anderson, *Elizabethan Psychology and Shakespeare's Plays,* University of Iowa Humanistic Studies (1927) III, number 4.

B. Assume that you have footnote references to the works in Exercise 23A in sequence as follows:

Jespersen, p. 96; Jespersen, p. 181; Clark, p. 371; Anderson, p. 16; Jespersen, pp. 186–190; Lewis, p. 171, Davidson, pp. 73–75; Baugh, p. 89.

Prepare the appropriate footnotes.

C. Below are nineteen titles of reference works and twenty questions which have answers in the books. For each question indicate which reference book would be likely to supply the answer.

1. *World Almanac*
2. *Statesman's Yearbook*
3. *Encyclopaedia Britannica*
4. *Dictionary of National Biography*
5. *Dictionary of American Biography*

6. *Catholic Encyclopedia*
7. *Statistical Abstract*
8. *Facts on File*
9. Hastings' *Encyclopaedia of Religion and Ethics*
10. *Harper's Dictionary of Classical Literature*
11. *Dictionary of Americanisms*
12. *New English Dictionary on Historical Principles*
13. Winchell, *Guide to Reference Books*
14. *American Men of Science*
15. Bartlett's *Familiar Quotations*
16. *Who's Who in America*
17. *New York Times Index*
18. *The Cambridge History of English Literature*
19. *Grove's Dictionary of Music and Musicians*

1. What is the educational background of the present Secretary of Housing and Urban Renewal?
2. Who is currently head of the government of Venezuela?
3. Where is the original of the Magna Carta?
4. When did the term *sans-culotte* develop with a political meaning?
5. What is the title of a standard bibliography of English history?
6. Where were the Olympic Games held in 1956 and who won the women's 80-meter hurdles in the meet?
7. What beliefs are associated with the god Krishna?
8. Who discovered electric welding?
9. What is the story told of the Virgin of Guadalupe?
10. Is it true that Watt became interested in steam engines while watching his mother's kettle?
11. Who wrote, "Ring out wild bells to the wild sky"?
12. What were the twelve labors of Hercules?
13. Who were the Nobel Prize winners of 1961?
14. Is there a prepared bibliography on diamond cutting?
15. How does it happen that Buddhism has become common in China but has lost popularity in India?
16. What college or university did the head of your department of chemistry attend as an undergraduate?
17. What was the sixteenth century meaning of the word *fond?*
18. What Greek plays deal with stories of the family of Atreus?
19. What is the history of the word *Tammany?*
20. Where can you find a good nineteenth century article on the English poet Thomas Hood?

D. By using conventional reference aids, answer the following questions and specify where you found each answer.

1. What was Tennyson's first published book?
2. Where did the word *Yankee* come from?
3. Of what New York periodicals was Noah Webster once editor?
4. What is the most recent history of India in your library?
5. Is there a concordance of Omar Khayyám? If so, when was it published?
6. Locate and name two recent magazine articles on trout fishing.
7. When was the word *gig* current to refer to a rowing boat used for racing?
8. How many students attended the University of Wisconsin last year?
9. What is the source of the quotation "Great wits are sure to madness near allied"?
10. What was the height of the winning pole vault in the most recent Western Conference outdoor track meet?
11. What is the height of the tallest mountain peak in Europe?
12. What is the origin of the word *pamphlet?*
13. In Jewish religion, what is the length of the knife to be used in Shehitah, or the ritual slaughtering of animals?
14. What was the maiden name of the wife of one of the senators of your state?
15. Who are the authors of a bibliography of the writings of Washington Irving published in 1936?
16. Of what type is the government of Liberia?
17. What is the most recent article published on extracting salt from sea water?
18. In Greek mythology, is there any difference between Pallas and Athene?
19. What percentage of American hosiery was produced in the Southern states last year?
20. What is the native name of the Friendly Islands?

E. Make bibliography cards for three periodical articles, using information in the *International Index to Periodicals* or the *Reader's Guide to Periodical Literature.* Use the list of abbreviations for the index to translate the entries into standard bibliographical form on your cards.

Section
24

Writing a Research Report

*Evidence should be organized for clarity, and the report should be written
with grace and objective restraint to reveal the significance of the material.*

A serious investigation usually leads to a report; in fact, the
purpose of the investigation may be to provide a report, which is
likely to be a relatively long composition. Reports of research involve the principles of organizing longer papers discussed in Section 7, and the student preparing an investigative report may do
well to review that material as well as discussion of the paragraph
(see Sections 1 through 5).

24-1 Style in the Investigative Paper

The handling of materials in any research report should be objective and relatively impartial, and the style should reflect this
objectivity. If the writer has opinions to express, he should label
his opinions clearly. Research reports mainly employ the third person, although good practice now allows the use of the first person
to avoid excessive use of the passive voice where circumstances require some discussion of the author and what he did—for instance,
in describing how equipment was set up, or why an investigation
was conducted in a certain way—but a research report should be
couched in generally objective terms.

The need for writing skill becomes acute in almost any research
report, and developing the essential technique gives the young
writer excellent training. The reader of any difficult or controversial report wants always to know whether the author is sure he is
right, whether his evidence is sound. But writers cannot always be
sure; they do not always have adequate evidence. Thus, the writer
should make clear what he knows certainly and why; he should
also make clear what he is saying because the evidence is extremely
good, although inconclusive; and he should identify any observations which are guesses, which he has made just because they are

his best guesses, subject to revision. Keeping the reader constantly aware of the writer's own estimate of the conclusiveness of his statements is not easy, and it can become cumbersome, although it need not be. Writing need not be pedestrian because it is exact and careful, and part of the secret of a good objective style grows from learning to keep the reader informed, unobtrusively, of the writer's own estimate of his material. The devices for doing this are legion, too numerous to be detailed here, but the beginning writer will do well to study competent pieces of serious writing, in magazines like *Harper's* and *The Atlantic,* for instance, and in scholarly and scientific journals.

Another problem bothers almost every beginning research worker: what should he do when the authorities disagree? They do disagree. Most important problems cannot be settled certainly and finally, and even for minor questions the evidence is often contradictory. If the writer finds no reason for preferring one of his disagreeing sources, he can present the evidence on all sides and cite all authorities in his footnotes. If he thinks one argument is better than the others, he can present it and then cite opposing evidence in the text or in a footnote. Even if he is sure that one side is right, he should cite opposing opinions in footnotes.

Since evaluating evidence and dealing with inconsistencies are parts of the same problem, they may appropriately be considered together. Notice the following, an excerpt from a popular discussion of American English.

That this meaning of the word *lumber* was brought to America is evident from its survival in some local dialects as well as from a good deal of early legislation. The *Boston Records* for 1663 show that the inhabitants were cautioned to "take care that noe wood, logges, timber, stonnes, or any *other* lumber be layed upon the flatte to the annoyance of any vesseles," and a similar law was passed in 1701 against encumbering any street, lane, or alley. Certainly in a pioneer community with building going on constantly, cut timber would inevitably be piled in the streets from time to time, and the circumstance that this was so often the offending impediment seems to have led to a specific association of *lumber* with cut or milled wood, in contrast to uncut logs or possibly standing trees, as is suggested by the report of Sir Edmond Andros, written in 1678: "The Comodityes of the Country to ye westward are wheat . . . pipe staves, timber, lumber & horses."

—ALBERT H. MARCKWARDT, *American English*

Since the book is intended for popular reading, Marckwardt does not provide footnotes, but the passage indicates that documentation is essentially a quality written into the prose itself, a characteristic of style to which the footnotes are only an important appendage. Exact documentation is not possible, because without footnotes Marckwardt's sentences would become too cluttered with details if he were to provide all bibliographic information, but the essential documentation is there. The writer quotes his sources exactly, and he gives enough evidence of source so that we are convinced he is founding his observations upon carefully selected fact, and we are even provided with rough citations. Marckwardt mentions these sources urbanely, making no great to-do about them; but any examination of his terminology will reveal that he is constantly assessing his evidence and making us quietly aware of when he feels confident and when he is making a plausible guess. He starts by saying that the survival of the meaning in America "is evident," and he indicates that he has two sorts of evidence, survival in dialects and direct legislation. He then cites two specific instances in which building materials cluttering up streets or the waterfront were called *lumber;* here he makes flat assertions, but he is very careful what he asserts. He says the "inhabitants were cautioned," and he apparently assumes we will presume that the caution was needed. He points out that the caution might well be needed in a pioneer community. So much for his background; he is now ready for his main conclusion, the reason for his paragraph— how did a word which meant something like *rubbish* come to mean "cut or milled logs"? He believes he has the answer, but the answer is only inferred; he has no direct, reliable evidence for it, and accordingly he makes his proposal, but cautiously: "The circumstance . . . seems to have led to a specific association. . . ." He has some collateral evidence, but this also is not conclusive, and accordingly he uses the phrase "as is suggested." That is, though Marckwardt does not in this passage have the advantage of being able to use footnotes, he has written the essence of his documentation and his estimate of the worth of his evidence into the text itself; this is sound practice, even when the writer is addressing readers who welcome footnotes.

The next passage is from a documented history of the English language, with the footnote numbers changed to avoid confusion:

According to the same chronicler[1] William the Conqueror made an effort himself at the age of forty-three to learn English, that he might understand and render justice in the disputes between his subjects, but his energies were too completely absorbed by his many other activities to enable him to make much progress. There is nothing improbable in the statement. Certainly the assertion of a fourteenth century writer[2] that the Conqueror considered how he might destroy the 'Saxon' tongue in order that English and French might speak the same language seems little less than silly in view of the king's efforts to promote the belief that he was the authentic successor of the Old English kings and in the light of his use of English alongside of Latin, to the exclusion of French, in his charters. His youngest son, Henry I, may have known some English, though we must give up the pretty story of his interpreting the English words in a charter to the monks of Colchester.[3] If later kings for a time seem to have been ignorant of the language,[4] their lack of acquaintance with it is not to be attributed to any fixed purpose. In the period with which we are at the moment concerned—the period up to 1200— the attitude of the king and the upper classes toward the English language may be characterized as one of simple indifference. They did not cultivate English—which is not the same as saying that they had no acquaintance with it—because their activities in England did not necessitate it and their constant concern with continental affairs made French for them much more useful.　　　—ALBERT C. BAUGH, *A History of the English Language*

[1] Ordericus Vitalis, ed. Prevost, II, 215.

[2] Robert Holkot, on the authority of John Selden, *Eadmeri Monachi Cantuariensis Historiae Novorum siue sui Saeculi Libri VI* (London, 1623), p. 189.

[3] The story was considered authentic by so critical a student as J. Horace Round ("Henry I. as an English Scholar," *Academy*, Sept. 13, 1884, p. 168), but the charter has since been proved by J. Armitage Robinson to be a forgery. Cf. C. W. David, "The Claim of King Henry I to Be Called Learned," *Anniversary Essays in Medieval History by Students of Charles Homer Haskins* (Boston, 1929), pp. 45–56.

[4] We do not know whether William Rufus and Stephen knew English. Henry II understood it although he apparently did not speak it (see below, p. 144). Richard I was thoroughly French; his whole stay in England amounted to only a few months. He probably knew no English. Concerning John's knowledge of English we have no evidence. As Freeman remarks (*Norman Conquest*, II. 128), the royal family at this time is frequently the least English in England and is not to be used as a norm for judging the diffusion of the two languages.

We may note some similarities and some differences between Marckwardt's and Baugh's paragraphs. Most notable, perhaps, is that they read very much alike. Marckwardt has no footnotes, and Baugh's treatment can be read without them. Both paragraphs read smoothly; like Marckwardt, Baugh can keep his reader constantly aware of where his evidence comes from and how much he, as a scholar, trusts it. He is constantly evaluating this evidence; he is aware that chroniclers have varied in statements about William the Conqueror and his attitude toward English. He notices the testimony of one chronicler that William at forty-three tried to learn English and he observes that "there is nothing improbable in the statement," but recognizing that chroniclers are not always reliable, he makes no commitment himself. He records but declines to accept the opinion of another writer, partly because the person lived long after William, partly because William's own actions seem to belie the statement. He rejects out of hand a legend concerning William's son; the chronicle reporting it has been proved a forgery. As for the knowledge of English possessed by other twelfth century figures, he offers his own guess as "simple indifference." He does not labor his uncertainty; he does not say, "Of course this is just an opinion, and every man is entitled to his own opinion, but I have read a good many chronicles and scholarly studies, and I have tried hard to produce a fair answer, and for what it is worth, this is my best estimate." He implies all this, however, when he says "the attitude . . . may be characterized. . ." That is, scholarly writing that carries footnotes is much like scholarly writing that has no footnotes; it should be clear, orderly, well balanced, factual, judicial, and urbane, and the reader should be able to follow it with or without the footnotes.

On the other hand, footnotes provide the scholarly writer distinct advantages; we might observe how Baugh exploits them. He can, of course, be more precise; he can cite works exactly, giving the edition, the volume and page; he can quote long titles intact, can cite more than one source for a fact, and all this without interrupting the flow of his prose. He can save space and the hurried reader's time by banishing some details to the footnotes. For example, he rejects the story of Henry I besting the monks of Colchester in a few words because he can provide the details in the footnote. He has examined the evidence and has found it so convincing that he need not equivocate; if the reader is not content to trust Baugh as a scholar, he probably will be convinced when he reads the footnote; if not, he has the references, and can pursue the question. Baugh does not need to defend his position in the text; but Marckwardt, having no footnotes, presumably would not have felt he could be so cavalier. What about those people who had read the story of Henry I in some old history book and had believed it all their lives? Doubtless, without footnotes, the writer would have felt he had to interrupt his account to explain why he doubted this story; the footnote permits the writer to make his decision and get on with pertinent parts of the discussion.

Somewhat different is the last footnote, because it allows Baugh to introduce material which, without footnotes, he would probably have omitted as a digression. Some writers use footnotes even more extensively for this purpose than does Baugh; Van Wyck Brooks, for example, in a charming series of books on early America, uses footnotes to provide quantities of engaging supplementary information. This sort of thing can be carried too far; a scholarly writer should not use footnotes for any sort of gossip that comes into his head, but notes do permit a research worker to pass on bits which he has turned up that are not quite germane to his central purpose.

Documentation 24-2

What should be documented? The ability to use footnotes deftly, to determine what requires documentation and what is so clear or obvious that no support is necessary, marks a judicial mind and a good research worker. In general, a research writer may think of his composition as a building set upon pilings; he needs a piling, that is, a footnote reference, under every key point in the structure. These points must be supported so that they are absolutely solid; the points in between need no support, but are held up by internal structure. Statements on which the writer's argument rests must be supported from beneath; the others should not be cluttered with footnotes. In general, footnotes can be profitably used for the following (for footnotes form, see 23-11):

1. *The source of a significant quotation.* In carefully documented writing, any direct quotation used as evidence should be identified with a footnote. Material quoted for embellishment need not be identified in a footnote. For instance, suppose a writer begins a discussion as follows:

"In the beginning was the word"; whether or not we now accept this statement literally, words have been at the beginning of many ideas, and hence they have been at the beginnings of what grew out of the ideas.

The quotation from the New Testament does not require a footnote. Most readers would recognize it, and in any event it is only a stylistic device. If, however, the passage were used as evidence of the Greek veneration of language, it should carry a footnote.

2. *The source of information not sufficiently familiar so that most readers would know it or be able to find it readily.* The date of Shakespeare's death or the name of the twenty-fifth president of the United States needs no footnote; anyone who does not take the writer's word for

such details can find them in dozens of reference works. All major assertions in a serious discussion, however, should be supported by footnotes.

3. *Controversial matter and opposing views.* Any serious investigation is likely to lead the writer into fields where opinions differ. Whether he takes sides or not, the writer should be sure that both sides are represented in footnote references.

4. *Details or statistics that would interrupt the paper.* Statistics, figures, tables, or other supplementary data are sometimes placed in footnotes, where they are available for reference but do not interrupt the progress of the discussion. With discretion, details too good to miss but not quite on the subject may be added in footnotes. Additional evidence intended for the unusually skeptical critic may be placed in footnotes.

24-3 Conventions of the Research Paper

Footnotes are usually numbered consecutively through a brief paper or through a chapter of a long work. They are not now usually indicated by asterisks, daggers, and other printer's marks, because this system does not admit sufficient flexibility. Neither are footnotes now often numbered by page; the numbers in the copy do not correspond with the numbers on the printed page, and mistakes are easy. Customarily a superior figure (made on the typewriter by turning the platen half a line) is placed in the copy directly after the word, passage, sentence, or paragraph to which the footnote refers. A similar number appears immediately before the footnote. The footnote begins, like any paragraph, with an indention, and like any sentence, with a capital letter. Footnotes are placed in one of three positions: (1) especially in papers not intended for publication they may be placed at the bottom of each page with a rule above the first note on the page; this system is convenient enough for the reader, but somewhat irksome to the typist, who must estimate the space he needs at the bottom of each page; (2) they may be placed at the end of a brief paper, at the end of a chapter or a book; this arrangement is convenient for the writer and the typist, but may be maddening to a reader or an editor, who has to read with four stacks of manuscript in front of him; (3) they may be placed immediately after the line containing the citation, and ruled above and below; this method takes a bit more space, but is growing in popularity, especially for material intended for print, because it is the most convenient for the typist and a reader or editor.

Graphs, tables, and other illustrations or tabulated inserts are imperative for many technical papers, and much complicated material is best shown in visual or tabular form. The writer should always consider whether a table or an illustration will not make his meaning clearer. Inserts of this sort should usually be labeled for ready reference in the text. Use *plate* to refer to a full page (Plate IX), *figure* for an illustration in the text (Figure 8), and *table* for a tabular or graphic arrangement (Table 3)

Some abbreviations and standardized signals can be employed to save space in footnotes; formerly Latin words and their abbreviations were used for this purpose, but the practice of using English is growing. Even if the Latin is used, modern practice permits dispensing with italics. A list of these symbols can be quite long (see *MLA Style Sheet,* pp. 20–22), but a student writing an investigative paper is not likely to need any but the most common. For most purposes, those in the following list will suffice:

p., pp.—page, pages.

l., ll.—line, lines.

v., vv.—verse, verses.

vol., vols.—volume, volumes.

no., nos.—number, numbers.

cf.—compare.

n.—note, footnote.

supra—above; preferred to *Ante;* the English is now often preferred.

infra—below; preferred to *Post;* the English is now often preferred.

c.—copyright; used when the date of a copyright is known but the date of publication is not.

c., ca.—circa, about; used in approximate dates (ca. 1888).

ff., et seq.—and following; used to complete a citation to pages; not the best practice—inclusive page reference (pp. 86–93) is preferable.

passim—at intervals through the work or pages cited.

sic—thus; may be used after an obvious error in a quotation to indicate that the error was in the original; best used sparingly; when inserted in a quotation, should be enclosed in brackets.

n.d.—no date.

ed.—editor, edited, edition.

tr.—translated by, translation.

rev.—revised.

447

24-4   Samples of Research or Investigative Reports

Below are portions of two investigative papers of the sort commonly required in composition courses, written by students but somewhat revised for style. They illustrate two of the different ways of handling footnotes recommended in 24-3 and also two ways of using what have come to be known as "controlled research" pamphlets. These pamphlets, developed within recent years, present some distinct advantages: they avoid overburdening the library and discommoding students who cannot obtain books for which there is sudden demand; and they permit more careful study of the techniques of handling evidence, since the whole class is working on a common body of limited material. Many courses in composition now rely exclusively on one of these pamphlets to provide materials for one or more research projects; other courses use these pamphlets, but encourage the student to extend his subject by some work in the library. Still other courses, based on the theory that no student ever learns enough about how to use a library, require the student to dig out all the material himself, with no help from a special collection.

Of the selections which follow, that entitled "Young Man on a Horse" was written entirely from one research pamphlet; that entitled "A Yet Unexorcised Ghost" started with a research pamphlet and a paperback copy of the play, but the students were then required to continue their investigation in the library. For style as to the inclusion of publishers in the footnotes, and in the placing of the footnotes, the student should follow the form prescribed by the instructor. The first selection should offer suggestions for papers written from research pamphlets; the second suggests procedures for papers involving library reference, whether or not the paper starts from a pamphlet of controlled research materials. The papers themselves are printed on even-numbered pages; the facing odd-numbered pages contain comment on such matters as organization and style.

Page from *A Yet Unexorcised Ghost* as it would
appear typewritten

The critics apparently do not agree, and so far as I
have been able to discover, they have produced five different
sorts of answers, some of which subdivide into alternate
answers. He may have been, as he purported to be, King
Hamlet's soul,

Doom'd for a certain term to walk the night,
And for the day confined to fast in fires,
Till the foul crimes done in my days of nature
Are burnt and purged away. (<u>Hamlet</u>, I, v, 9-13)[1]

Even so, was he a Roman Catholic soul in Purgatory, or a
Church of England soul?[2] Granted that he is the soul of a
deceased king, is he on a personal mission of revenge, of
kingly justice, or is he the emissary of some higher power
who has sent him to intervene in affairs of state?[3] The
Ghost may be a devil,[4] as Hamlet himself recognizes:

The spirit I have seen
May be the devil: and the devil hath power
To assume a pleasing shape; (II, ii, 627-29)

---

[1] I employ here, and throughout, the spelling and line
numbering in <u>The Complete Works of Shakespeare</u>, ed. Hardin
Craig (Chicago, 1951), hereafter referred to as <u>Works</u>.

[2] The distinction is extensively drawn in Lily B.
Campbell, <u>Shakespeare's Tragic Heroes</u>: <u>Slaves of Passion</u>
(New York, 1952), p. 121, hereafter referred to as Campbell.

[3] The latter interpretation has been presented in I. J.
Semper, "The Ghost in Hamlet," <u>The Catholic World</u>, CLXII
(1946), 313.

[4] Robert H. West, "King Hamlet's Ambiguous Ghost,"
<u>PMLA</u>, LXX (1955), 1107-17.

YOUNG MAN ON A HORSE

by

Agnes Arnold

It was the third day at Gettysburg, midafternoon. Major General George E. Pickett's rebel-yelling Confederates had stormed Cemetery Ridge, and were boiling over a stone wall and a rail fence which had provided some protection to Brigadier General Alexander S. Webb's troops, holding the Union center. If they succeeded, if the charging men in gray could stay there, if they could establish a front around the clump of trees to which they had marched across open fields, the Union forces would be split, the Army of the Potomac cracked and faced with disruption or extinction. Nothing adequate for defense would stand between General Robert E. Lee and his undefeated Army of Northern Virginia and the populous Northern cities, Philadelphia, New York, Boston. If Pickett's men had stayed on Cemetery Ridge, Lee could quite probably have dictated, from either New York or Philadelphia, the terms on which the United States of America was to become two countries rather than one.

A half hour later, the decimated remnants of Pickett's men who "had moved across that field of death as a battalion marches forward in line of battle upon drill"[1] were fleeing, those who could run or crawl. Perhaps the most dramatic account of what turned the tide is that of Frank Aretas Haskell, a young Wisconsin civilian turned lieutenant, writing to his brother, H. M. Haskell.[2] Lieutenant Haskell was returning from an attempt to deliver a message when he stopped to view what he called the "tremendous" conflict, and observed that there was "no wavering in all our line." His account continues,

> Wondering how long the Rebel ranks, deep though they were, could stand our sheltered volleys, I had come near my destination, when—great heaven! were my senses mad? The larger portion of Webb's brigade—my God, it was true—there by the group of trees and the angles of the wall, was breaking from the cover of their works, and without orders or reason, with no hand lifted to check them, was falling back, a fear-stricken flock of confusion! The fate of Gettysburg hung upon a spider's single thread.[3]

---

[1] George E. Pickett, *Soldier of the South: General Pickett's War Letters to His Wife,* ed. Arthur Crew Inman (Boston: Little, Brown, 1928), p. 70, hereafter referred to as Pickett; repr. *The Third Day at Gettysburg: Pickett's Charge,* ed. Alan M. Hollingsworth and James M. Cox (New York: Appleton-Century-Crofts, 1959), p. 97, hereafter referred to as *Third Day.* This paper is written entirely from documents reprinted in the latter work; when pagination can be inferred in the original publication, exact pages will be given; otherwise they will be given only for *Third Day.*

[2] *The Battle of Gettysburg* (Wisconsin History Commission, November 1908), pp. 122–30; *Third Day,* pp. 66–70.

[3] *Third Day,* p. 68.

COMMENT

Miss Arnold uses an extensive introduction. Usually, such a long introduction would be quite inappropriate in a paper of moderate length, but her approach may be justified because it provides a dramatic opening to a semi-popular presentation and at the same time allows her to introduce material that is to prove useful in the body of her paper.

The author is not yet ready to state her main idea, but she is centering attention on the central figure.

Miss Arnold was instructed to accumulate footnotes at the bottom of each page.

The first part of the first footnote will serve as a typical example of a reference to a book which includes the publisher; since the author expects to use material from this book again, a short form is provided, and since this is the only piece of writing to be cited from Pickett, the name of the author provides the easiest form for brief reference. If the author were citing two books by Pickett, an appropriate shortened form would be "Pickett, *Letters*." The second half of the footnote introduces the collection of documents assigned, to which the student is restricted. The footnote can be taken as a model for reference to a book having no author; a shortened title serves for subsequent citations. Many collections similar to *Third Day* have page numbers in the text to indicate the end of each page in the original; they thus permit exact references to the original by using only the reprint, but this device is not employed in *Third Day*. If the author were writing for publication she would be expected to consult the original, but here she is working within the restrictions of a class exercise.

In footnote 2 the author can refer to the original and the reprint since the reference is to the whole passage.

For footnote 3 the author is able to cite only *Third Day* exactly, since the ends of pages are not marked in the reprint. The instructor may indicate that, to save time, references may be restricted to either the original or the reprint, although strict scholarly practice would require providing both.

Haskell goes on to tell how "a great magnificent passion" overcame him as he saw how "the damned red flags of the rebellion began to thicken and flaunt along the wall," and he dashed to stem "the tide of rabbits," commanding them to face about and fight, and beating with his sword on their "unpatriotic backs." Soon General Webb came sweating up on foot and "did all that one could to repair the breach," but his men were "falling fast." The Confederate flags "were accumulating at the wall every moment" now, and Webb had only three small regiments with which to oppose them. "Oh, where is Gibbon? where is Hancock? [4]—some general—anybody with the power and the will to support that wasting, melting line?"

Haskell had no troops under him, but he was aide to General Gibbon,[5] and thus had a sort of derived authority, so long as nobody asked questions. He set about trying to find help. The most copious body of reinforcements would have been the First Army Corps, which had not as yet been engaged, commanded by Major General Abner Doubleday,[6] but Haskell concluded that Doubleday was "too far and too slow," and he recalled, also, "on another occasion I had begged him to send his idle regiment to support another line battling with thrice its numbers, and this 'Old Sumpter Hero' had declined." [7] What about Hall?—Colonel Norman J. Hall, of the Seventh Michigan Infantry, commanding the third brigade, was stationed immediately to Webb's left.[8] His men had been under heavy attack, but "the fire was constantly diminishing now in his front." [9] Haskell located Hall, sword in hand, who agreed to "move my brigade at once," and soon five regiments were marching to the rescue of Webb's three. But this was not enough—how about Harrow? Brigadier General William Harrow was in command of the whole second division, and in addition—although Haskell did not know this at the time—he was now in command of the entire Second Army Corps,[10] since both Hancock and Gibbon had been severely wounded. Harrow could not be found, presumably because he had gone back to headquarters to relieve Hancock and Gibbon, but Haskell did not stand on ceremony. He managed to get men from the Nineteenth Maine, the Fifteenth Massachusetts, the First Minnesota, and the Thirty-second New York Militia to follow him, and "all that I could find I took over to the right at the *double quick.*" Arrived he saw that the Union troops had been pushed well

---

[4] Major General Winfield S. Hancock was in command of the Second Army Corps, of which Brigadier General John Gibbon was second in command, and in direct command of the second division; Webb commanded the second brigade within this division. Generals Hancock and Gibbon were thus Webb's immediate superiors, as well as Haskell's. *Third Day,* pp. 152–53.

[5] *The War of the Rebellion: A Compilation of the Official Records of the Union and Confederate Armies,* series 1, vol. XXVII, part 1 (Washington, D.C., 1889), p. 30, hereafter referred to as *Official Records; Third Day,* p. 62.

[6] *Third Day,* p. 151.

[7] *Third Day,* p. 69.

[8] *Third Day,* pp. 42–43, 47, 153.

[9] *Third Day,* p. 69.

[10] *Third Day,* pp. 43–44, 152.

COMMENT

How much should a writer quote? Miss Arnold has elected to quote verbatim the description of the flight from the wall, partly because it is a dramatic scene dramatically recorded, but also because some of the later discussion is to hinge on this scene. She could, of course, have gone on quoting, but the whole passage would run to several hundred words, and much of it is not germane to her eventual purpose. Accordingly, she gives her own running account, but she inserts within it words, phrases, whole sentences from the original which preserve the flavor of Haskell's account, although she has reduced the original by about ninety per cent. One might notice that Miss Arnold is identifying all sources within the text of the article, but making no great to-do of her documentation. The identification is started unostentatiously in the sentence on p. 450 beginning "Haskell was. . . ." by inserting the words "what he called the 'tremendous' conflict." No citation is necessary here because we get to it in the next sentence, and the two passages are related by "His account continues." After the quoted passage no further citation is necessary, because "Haskell goes on to tell" lets us know that the remaining details come from the next page or two.

If Miss Arnold were here trying to make a parade of her knowledge, she could seed this passage with footnotes, but she wisely restricts them to the quotations that involve a change of page reference.

Miss Arnold continues to keep the story dramatic by quoting bits from Haskell's account, but moves the story rapidly by relying mainly on her own summary. This procedure is the more appropriate because the essay depends in part on what Haskell did, how much of a hero he was; and since the writer's case is to hinge on the validity of Haskell's account as against Webb's official report, details are necessary but are best in Haskell's words. She could, of course, have reproduced Haskell's entire letter, but long undigested accounts are not usually so useful as more succinct versions with brief quoted passages.

The observation that Haskell was to learn only later why he could not find Harrow might have been relegated to a footnote, as could that about Hancock and Gibbon having been wounded. But on the whole the text should be readable without the footnotes, and apparently the author felt that her audience would want to know this much about Haskell's dilemma and the reasons for it.

Footnote 4 is informational; we need to know who these officers are. The author has worked out their relationships by studying the data supplied in the appendix.

Footnote 5 provides an example of a reference to a complicated title. Titles of this sort are not common, but they are relatively more common in scholarly and scientific writing than in most prose, and they are sometimes complicated enough so that they do not fit into a standard style. When in doubt the writer should give enough bibliographic details to identify the specific volume certainly.

If the author were using abbreviations in footnotes, she could use *ibid.* in footnotes 7 through 11. The instructor had designated a style not using abbreviations like *ibid.* and *op. cit.*

up the ridge, that in their confused milling they were suffering terribly from the Confederate troops firing from the wall from which Webb's regiments had fled. Haskell endeavored to organize a charge on the wall, but with some difficulties, as his description reveals: [11]

> My "Forward to the wall" is answered by the Rebel counter-command, "Steady men!" and the wave swings back. . . . These men of Pennsylvania, on the soil of their own homesteads, the first and only to flee the wall, must be the first to storm it. "Major—*lead* your men over the crest, they will follow." "By the tactics I understand my place is in the rear of the men." "Your pardon, sir; I see *your* place is in the rear of the men. I thought you were fit to lead." [12]

Under Haskell's urging, a color-sergeant dashed toward the wall and was shot down, but others followed him, gained the wall, breached it, and soon Pickett's charge was thrown back. The battle was won, and although nobody knew it yet, the issue of the war was determined.

Such was the high tide of the Confederacy as Haskell professed to have seen it, but his part in saving the day at Gettysburg for the Union forces found no reflection in the report of General Webb, whose troops he had relieved. On the surface, Webb's report appears to be brief, factual, and reliable. His command suffered in the bombardment, he reports, and then sustained the brunt of Pickett's charge. He continues,

> The Sixty-ninth Pennsylvania Volunteers and most of the Seventy-first Pennsylvania Volunteers, even after the enemy were in their rear, held their position. . . . but the enemy would probably have succeeded in piercing our lines had not Colonel Hall advanced with several of his regiments to my support. . . . The conduct of this brigade was most satisfactory. Officers and men did their whole duty. . . . I saw none retire from the fence.[13]

Webb makes no mention of Haskell.

One cannot help wondering why. Was Haskell so in love with his own Homeric account of the battle that he grossly distorted it? His being able to hear the commanders on both sides of the fighting above the thundering of thousands of men firing at each other rather suggests that he may have imagined some of what he reported. Was he handsomely making himself a hero for the family back home? Did he have an exalted notion of himself? Or did Webb deliberately suppress any mention of Haskell? He did mention Hall, but Hall was a general, and obviously protocol required mentioning

---

[11] *Third Day,* p. 70.

[12] I have not been able to identify this major. The regiments referred to were the 69th and 71st Pennsylvania, but the skeletonized outline of the Union command provided in *Third Day,* pp. 151–55, includes no majors for these units. Captain William Davis, reporting for the 69th Pennsylvania, reported that "our major" was wounded. *Official Records,* p. 432. The major, of course, had a point; troops were being constantly disrupted by the loss of their officers, who were obviously prime targets. For example, Pickett retired with only one field officer unhurt, he lists seven colonels and nine lieutenant colonels killed or seriously wounded. Pickett, p. 71; *Third Day,* p. 97.

[13] *Official Records,* pp. 428–29; *Third Day,* p. 46.

COMMENT

Again Miss Arnold has elected to quote a considerable passage, partly because it will prove germane to the central idea of the paper. One might notice the way she introduces this passage, keeping attention on what Haskell is doing and identifying the quotation with the phrase "as his description reveals."

Here the writer encounters a somewhat different problem. As will appear below, she has become convinced that Webb was a liar, even though he may have been a sort of white liar, trying to protect the reputation of his troops, and his manner of doing this may have made him look rather less trustworthy than, in fact, he was.

Now the author is ready to state her main idea. It is announced by the topic sentence, "One cannot help wondering why," which directs the reader's attention to the main problem of the paper, although not too belligerently. The author makes her point and lets us know where the article is going without saying "I shall now endeavor to prove to you. . . ."

Footnote 12, like footnote 4, illustrates how footnotes can be used to present information which would be useful to a reader intending to pursue the subject of the paper in detail, although it is not essential to the main narrative and might break continuity if included in the text.

superior officers; was Haskell's performance sufficiently routine for a lieutenant so that it did not warrant individual notice? Or did Webb have some reason for belittling Haskell's assistance? After all, if we are to accept Haskell's account, he saved Webb's forces from defeat and probably from destruction; he may well have saved the day for the Union forces, and he quite probably saved Webb himself from death or capture. Webb may have had both psychological and professional reasons for preferring to ignore Haskell's services.

Closer examination of the available documents may cast some light on these questions. First we might notice that at least two details in Webb's report are suspect. He says, as we have seen, that "officers and men did their whole duty," and "I saw no one retire from the fence." The first of these statements cannot be true; Captain Davis, reporting for the Sixty-ninth Pennsylvanians, was doubtless making the best of the situation when he wrote, "our troops, with few exceptions, met them bravely," [14] and Colonel Smith, reporting for the Seventy-first, mentioned that a captain and a private, "are under sentence of court martial," an admission which surely suggests they had done something less than their duty. Webb's other observation is even more suspect; when he says, "I saw no one retire," he must be deliberately using language to deceive. Possibly he did not see them; Haskell says the general arrived after "the larger portion of Webb's brigade" had fled. In the smoke of battle he may not have seen them, or he may have been appropriately bringing up the Seventy-second Pennsylvania, which had been held in reserve; he may have told the truth when he said he did not *see* them, but he certainly knew they had retired. If he did not know it, he must have been one of few men in both armies who remained in ignorance; Union commanders on both sides of him reported the retirement as one of the routine details of the battle, and Confederates, both in Pickett's charge and out of it, recorded the Union retirement.[15] Webb must have colored his account to protect the reputation of his men, and quite possibly of himself.

If so, one may raise the question, also, as to whether Webb did not gloss over some of Haskell's exploit for similar reasons. We know that Webb was not in all details a reliable reporter; was Haskell? Here we might consider at least two sorts of evidence: what corroborative evidence does Haskell's report receive from the reports of other observers, and how reliable does Haskell seem to be, particularly when he is dealing with his own achieve-

---

[14] *Official Records,* p. 431.

[15] Particularly convincing is the highly circumstantial account in a personal letter from a Confederate officer. He records that "Armisted's men rushed across the wall and pursued the enemy . . . we pushed up to the wall, and could almost see the Yankee gunners leaving their places and running in our lines for safety." Charles T. Loehr, "The Old First Virginia at Gettysburg," *Southern Historical Society Papers,* XXXII (1904), 35–37; *Third Day,* p. 94. One might notice, also, Hall's sketch of the battle lines at this point, which show Webb's troops drawn well back from both the stone wall and the rail fence. *Official Records,* pp. 437–41; *Third Day,* p. 49. Hancock's official report recorded that "the most of that part of Webb's brigade posted here abandoned their position"; presumably he had received Webb's report when he made his. *Third Day,* p. 78.

COMMENT

After a paragraph that presents us with the alternatives, a paragraph which becomes, in effect, a topic sentence for the whole paper, the writer makes clear how the article is to be organized.

Here the author faces one of those problems that may baffle young writers—what should one do when the evidence is contradictory? Of course, what the young writer does not know is that there is almost always some contradictory evidence, even on such matters as when a person like Shakespeare was born. For many of these questions the evidence has been sifted, and readers are given results of the sifting of evidence; whereas the writer is now faced with the problem of doing the sifting. Did Webb's men run, or did they not? In this case the decision is easy: Webb's superior said they retired, even after receiving Webb's report; his fellow officers said the men retired; the attacking Confederates said the same thing, and so did people who wrote letters and had no notion that they were giving evidence. They were just telling their friends what happened. Only Webb seems to have tried to suggest that his men did not retire, and he does this in such a way that one suspects he is twisting words to tell the literal truth while telling what amounts to a lie. Accordingly, the writer says confidently that Webb's men did retire, and addresses herself to the crucial problem of whether it is possible that Webb did not know this.

The author has now established her first point, that Webb was not above distorting evidence if he had good reason to do so. But that he distorted evidence to protect his men does not establish that he distorted evidence to belittle Haskell. Here we need more direct testimony, and the author recognizes that we have evidence of two sorts: (1) Webb is not an entirely reliable witness, but is Haskell any better? and (2) do the reports of other witnesses confirm Haskell's account of himself in any entirely convincing way? Since the second is more objective, she starts with that, reviewing the testimony, or lack of it, in the reports of officer after officer who either mentions Haskell or would have been in a position to see what he did.

ments? As for the first, a modern reader of the contemporary reports gains the impression that a large part of the Union army was recounting Haskell's exploits, and if so, the information must have come to Webb's attention, for the general's report is dated more than a week after the battle,[16] whether or not he noticed Haskell in the fighting. . . .

---

[16] *Official Records*, p. 428; *Third Day*, p. 45.

A Yet Unexorcised Ghost

by

James Assuras

Centuries have elapsed, if we are to take the plot of *Hamlet* for fact, since the troubled shade that purported to be the spiritual remains of the elder Hamlet was satisfied with Claudius' death and laid to rest. But not so, Shakespeare's ghost in *Hamlet;* he still stalks the halls of criticism and puzzles the mind of at least an occasional playgoer. Now and then a critic cries out against this "most unnatural murder" in killing off the essential nature of a poor ghost no longer able to defend himself. Even we who merely view the play may be reminded that although the play seems to end in a way partially calculated to please the Ghost, was it truly his will to have the court heaped with corpses, including those of his wife and their son? Had the Ghost, a supernatural being, plotted this blood-bath? If so, was he a servant of justice, albeit rough justice? Was he a devil inducing people to commit murder and die without time to repent? Was he a soul on his way to heaven or hell who could slip back to earth occasionally to tidy up his unfinished earthly affairs? In short, who or what was this ghost, provided he was anything more than a convenience for the plot, a convenience that Shakespeare did not bother to think much about?

The critics apparently do not agree, and so far as I have been able to discover, they have produced five different sorts of answers, some of which subdivide into alternate answers. He may have been, as he purported to be, King Hamlet's soul,

> Doom'd for a certain term to walk the night,
> And for the day confined to fast in fires,
> Till the foul crimes done in my days of nature
> Are burnt and purged away. (*Hamlet,* I, v, 9–13) [1]

---

[1] I employ here, and throughout, the spelling and line numbering in *The Complete Works of Shakespeare*, ed. Hardin Craig (Chicago, 1951), hereafter referred to as *Works*.

COMMENT

Appropriately, Mr. Assuras has compressed his introduction and his statement of his problem into his first paragraph. He lets us know that the Ghost in *Hamlet* presents one of those perennial uncertainties, and he indicates the lines along which he expects to investigate it. He does not anticipate his conclusions, if he is to reach any, quite probably because he cannot make brief, certain inferences. Had he had such conclusions, he might have preferred to announce them at once; for example, he might have begun, "The Ghost in *Hamlet* has long presented a vexed question, but new evidence has come to light which allows us to assert with some confidence that the Ghost was a benevolent Episcopalian ghost sent in answer to a prayer by the Archbishop of Canterbury." Of course, the evidence permits no such conclusion, but theoretically, a paper like this can be arranged either inductively or deductively.

Citations to most works must refer to a specific page in a given edition, and often one edition and only one will be standard, and by common agreement all references will be to that edition. There is no such edition of Shakespeare, but if the work is divided into chapters and verses, into acts and lines, or into some other recognizable divisions, page references are not necessary.

Even so, was he a Roman Catholic soul in Purgatory, or a Church of England soul?[2] Granted that he is the soul of a deceased king, is he on a personal

[2] The distinction is extensively drawn in Lily B. Campbell, *Shakespeare's Tragic Heroes: Slaves of Passion* (New York, 1952), p. 121, hereafter referred to as Campbell.

mission of revenge, of kingly justice, or is he the emissary of some higher power who has sent him to intervene in affairs of state?[3] The Ghost may be

[3] The latter interpretation has been presented in I. J. Semper, "The Ghost in Hamlet," *The Catholic World,* CLXII (1946), 513.

a devil,[4] as Hamlet himself recognizes:

[4] Robert H. West, "King Hamlet's Ambiguous Ghost," *PMLA,* LXX (1955), 1107–17.

> The spirit I have seen
> May be the devil: and the devil hath power
> To assume a pleasing shape; (II, ii, 627–29)

He may also be a figment of Hamlet's diseased mind, the results of melancholia,[5] and this explanation has the advantage that it accounts for

[5] This is, of course, having too much "black bile," something more than melancholy in the modern sense; see *The Oxford English Dictionary* (1933), under *melancholy;* Alban H. Doran, "Medicine," *Shakespeare's England: An Account of the Life and Manners of His Age,* ed. Sir Walter Raleigh, et al. (Oxford, 1916), I, 422; Virgil K. Whitaker, *Shakespeare's Use of Learning: An Inquiry into the Growth of His Mind and Art* (San Marino, Calif., 1953), p. 264, hereafter referred to as Whitaker; Walter Clyde Curry, *Chaucer and the Mediaeval Sciences,* rev. ed. (New York, 1960), pp. 7–20, 147–48, hereafter referred to as Curry; W. W. Greg, "Hamlet's Hallucination," *Modern Language Review,* XII (1917), 393–421; for a brief reference see Greg, "A Critical Mousetrap," *A Book of Homage to Shakespeare,* ed. Israel Gollancz (London, 1916), p. 180; repr. *Hamlet: Enter Critic,* ed. Claire Sacks and Edgar Whan (New York, 1960); the latter will hereafter be referred to as *Enter Critic.*

Gertrude's not seeing the Ghost, but what of Horatio, Marcellus, and his stout companions? Were they also melancholics? A fourth solution has been advanced in a brilliant essay by G. Wilson Knight,[6] that the Ghost is "the

[6] "The Embassy of Death: An Essay on Hamlet," *The Wheel of Fire* (London, 1930), pp. 35–50; repr. *Enter Critic,* pp. 157–69. See also Robert Ornstein, "The Mystery of Hamlet: Notes Toward an Archetypal Solution," *College English,* XXI (1959), 30, 35–36, repr. *Enter Critic,* pp. 196–99. A somewhat similar interpretation is implied in G. R. Elliott, *Scourge and Minister: A Study of "Hamlet"* (Durham, N. C., 1951), pp. 30–32.

Embassy of Death," a sort of symbolic character who sets the death motif which Knight believes dominates the play. Recently Maynard Mack has

COMMENT

The student was instructed not to include publishers in his bibliography and footnotes; footnote 2 may be taken as a standard reference to a book having a known author if the publisher is not to be included. For style if the publisher is included, see Miss Arnold's paper, above. Mr. Assuras was instructed, also, to rule footnotes into the text. Had he elected to place footnotes at the bottom of each page, his manuscript would have looked like the page reproduced on p. 449.

Footnotes 3 and 4 may be taken as samples of footnotes based upon articles, footnote 3 a reference to one page, footnote 4 a reference to more than one page.

No footnote is required for the second quotation from Shakespeare; the edition has been identified in footnote 1, and we have here the act, scene, and lines.

Footnote 5 is complicated, giving a number of references. A note of this sort can be useful to both writer and reader; for the writer, the footnote serves to provide bibliographic details for works to which he expects later to refer a number of times, and for the reader it provides a group of references should he care to embark upon his own study. In addition to examples of references to a book and to a magazine article, there are citations for an article in a book and for a standard reference work, *The Oxford English Dictionary*. Since this is a standard work, bibliographic details are not necessary; and since it is alphabetically arranged, page references are unnecessary; the writer need only say "under *melancholy*." He does identify the year, however, since there was an earlier edition of this work known as the *New English Dictionary*. Had the author been referring to a work like the *Encyclopaedia Britannica*, which has been edited many times, he would have needed to identify the edition.

For footnotes 6 and 7, the name of the author is mentioned in the text, since Knight and Mack are critics of some reputation, and the reader may well want to know who is espousing these theories; since their names are included in the text, they are not required in the citation. Mr. Assuras is here following sound practice; the text should be readable without the footnotes.

suggested that the Ghost represents reality.[7] We might review these theories

[7] "The World of Hamlet," *Yale Review,* XLI (1952), 502–23.

in order.

Assuming that the Ghost is a genuine spirit, we have first to ask if the shade is a benevolent or malevolent creature, and here the problem is greatly simplified if we can assume that the Ghost is a Catholic spirit, since that Church has laid down four clear criteria for identifying a benevolent ghost. . . .[8]

[8] Campbell, pp. 123–26.

BIBLIOGRAPHY

Campbell, Lily B. *Shakespeare's Tragic Heroes: Slaves of Passion.* New York, 1952.
Craig, Hardin, ed. *The Complete Works of Shakespeare.* Chicago, 1951.
Curry, Walter Clyde. *Chaucer and the Mediaeval Sciences,* rev. ed. New York, 1960.
Doran, Alban H. "Medicine," *Shakespeare's England: An Account of the Life and Manners of His Age,* ed. Sir Walter Raleigh, et al. Oxford, 1916, I, 413–33.
Elliott, G. R. *Source and Minister: A Study of "Hamlet."* Durham, N. C., 1951.
Greg, W. W. "A Critical Mousetrap," *A Book of Homage to Shakespeare,* ed. Israel Gollancz. London, 1916, pp. 179–80.
———. "Hamlet's Hallucination," *Modern Language Review,* XII (1917), 393–421.
Hamlet: Enter Critic. Ed. Claire Sacks and Edgar Whan. New York, 1960.
Knight, G. Wilson. "The Embassy of Death: An Essay on Hamlet," *The Wheel of Fire.* London, 1930, pp. 35–50.
Mack, Maynard. "The World of Hamlet," *Yale Review,* XLI (1952), 502–23.
Ornstein, Robert. "The Mystery of Hamlet: Notes Toward an Archetypal Solution," *College English,* XXI (October, 1959), 30, 35–36.
The Oxford English Dictionary. 1933.
Semper, I. J. "The Ghost in Hamlet," *The Catholic World,* CLXII (1946), 510–17.
Shakespeare, William. See Craig, Hardin.
West, Robert H. "King Hamlet's Ambiguous Ghost," *PMLA,* LXX (1955), 1107–17.
Whitaker, Virgil K. *Shakespeare's Use of Learning: An Inquiry into the Growth of His Mind and Art.* San Marino, Calif., 1953.

COMMENT

With his problem surveyed, the author turns to his first subdivision, and in footnote 8 he is able to take advantage of the fact that for most of the works he expects to cite he has already provided the bibliographic information.

The bibliography as here reprinted is restricted to the works cited thus far in the paper. The complete bibliography, of course, includes the remainder of the works cited, but does not include other books which the author consulted but which he did not cite directly. Occasionally, a writer may wish to include in his bibliography a work to which he is greatly indebted, although in such a general way that he has no occasion to use a footnote reference to it. Usually, however, such a work will appear in some footnote giving general references, or it can well be omitted from the bibliography.

The edition of Shakespeare is here entered under the editor because the writer expects to cite Craig's notes. If the work were entered under *Shakespeare,* a cross reference to Craig would be appropriate. As to the place of publication, several American cities appear on the title page of this Shakespeare, but they are only the various offices of the publisher. In such entries, usually only the first city is used. When a book is published in two countries, both cities may be used, as in the following: "William D. Bayles. *Caesars in Goose Step.* New York and London, 1940." Extending the number of cities in which a book is issued can become complicated and does not usually help in identifying the volume. For consistency, since he entered Shakespeare under Craig, perhaps he should have listed *Hamlet: Enter Critic* under Sacks and Whan, or at least provided cross references under the names of the editors. His inconsistency is perhaps defensible since he is not citing the editors and he uses the abbreviated title in footnotes. If Shakespeare's works had not been entered under Craig, they could have appeared as follows: "Shakespeare, William. *The Complete Works of William Shakespeare,* ed. Hardin Craig. Chicago, 1951." Since there are entries for two works by Greg, the second may be introduced with a long dash.

The Writing System

> At this moment the King, who had been for some time busily writing in his note-book, called out "Silence!" and read out from his book "Rule Forty-two. All Persons more than a mile high to leave the court."
> Everybody looked at Alice.
> "I'm not a mile high," said Alice.
> "You are," said the King.
> "Nearly two miles high," added the Queen.
> "Well, I sha'n't go, at any rate," said Alice: "besides, that's not a regular rule: you invented it just now."
> "It's the oldest rule in the book," said the King.
> —Lewis Carroll, Alice's Adventures in Wonderland

All peoples have language, and languages develop as speech. All literate peoples have writing systems, which reflect and in some ways amplify oral systems. Writing is often inadequate; it does no more than approximate the variety or subtlety of gesture or tone, by which a speaker may suggest that *yes* means *no* and *no* means *yes*. In some ways however, a writing system may be more precise and revealing than its corresponding oral system; in speech, *bare* and *bear* are not readily distinguishable, nor are *girls* and *girl's*, *queens* and *Queens*, although in writing the distinctions are clear for those who know the conventions. Whatever the virtues or the limitations of writing systems, however, literate peoples must have them, and once they are established they are likely to become more stable than the oral system, to develop rigid conventions, and to be used independently of oral speech.

Thus, much of our writing system is mainly conventional, although none the less important for that. Many of the "rules" represent codified good sense, what Alice thought of as "regular rules." Others smack of the judicial processes of the King of Hearts, but whether or not they are now "the oldest rules in the book," they have been established by convention, and conventions are necessary for clear communication. Ignoring conventions may even be dangerous. Anyone in this country who consistently drives on the left-hand side of the road will not stay long out of jail, a hospital, or the morgue. Anyone who drives on the right-hand side in England is in similar danger. A writer who fails to follow certain conventions, though he may be physically safe, is in danger of being misunderstood.

Furthermore, although the mechanical conventions surrounding writing are not the only conventions possible, sound reason stands behind each of them, and *in toto* they offer the writer useful standardized devices. Typed copy is double spaced because double-spaced copy is easier to read than single-spaced copy and because it allows room for editing. Margins are preferred because a crowded page looks messy. Manuscripts are written on one side of the paper because turning over pages leads to confusion and costly errors. Our conventions of capitalization are not the only possible ones; German capitalizes all nouns and Spanish capitalizes no proper adjectives, but our system has its uses. With it, one can distinguish at once an *opal* from *Opal, Hamlet* from a *hamlet.* Our system of punctuation permits the writer to make his meaning immediately and sharply clear, and he can do so because conventions are standardized and recognized. There is a difference between "The man who customarily wears a beret. . . ." and "The man, who customarily wears a beret, . . ." although the difference is made clear by nothing but commas. The conventions of writing and the mechanics which embody these conventions help a writer because they put useful tools into his hands.

Publishers and publications have style sheets which prescribe manuscript form, punctuation, capitalization, and even spelling; they may include details of style too specialized to be covered by general rules. A builder's manual may have a style sheet including special punctuation for unusual measurements; bibliographies often have style sheets which permit elaborate abbreviation of the information concerning the format of a book; a chemistry-journal style sheet will include abbreviations for compounds. For details of style not covered below, *A Manual of Style,* prepared by the staff of the University of Chicago Press and frequently revised, has been standard practically since the first edition appeared in 1906. John Benbow, *Manuscript and Proof* (New York, 1943), is the manual for the American Oxford University Press. Useful for technical work is the *United States Government Printing Office Style Manual* (Washington, D.C.); it too, is frequently revised.

The following chapters discuss punctuation, capitalization, spelling, and details of manuscript form.

Punctuation

For
Guide to Revision,
see page 470.

Punctuation clarifies meaning and structure.

Punctuation can make a difference. Compare the following:

Open fire; at noon our own troops will be out of range.
Open fire at noon; our own troops will be out of range.
If she plans to be married, before she is twelve she should have started a hope chest.
If she plans to be married before she is twelve, she should have started a hope chest.
However, it may be the responsibility is entirely our own.
However it may be, the responsibility is entirely our own.
The doctor said he was depressed and humanity was disappointed.
The doctor said he was depressed, and humanity was disappointed.
The American soldiers who had been hiding in the old barn were all killed.
The American soldiers, who had been hiding in the old barn, were all killed.
Turn the heat on, Willie.
Turn the heat on Willie.

Punctuation does not always affect meaning so obviously—many of the sentences above should be revised to avoid ambiguity—but most adequate writing systems have developed some system of conventional marks which can clarify structure and meaning. That is, by punctuation the writer can suggest what the speaker can reveal with gesture, pause, tone, and pitch. Or, to use the terms of many modern grammarians, punctuation is to writing what suprasegmental phonemes (see Glossary under *Phoneme*) are to the spoken sentence. Imaginative use of punctuation can strengthen prose; conventional use of punctuation, according to codes refined by printers and editors, promotes accuracy and clarity.

25-1 Styles in Punctuation

Until a century or so ago, punctuation in English was primarily rhetorical; that is, marks or "points" were stage directions for speaking, indicating pauses in speech. In modern English, punctuation has become more standardized, working largely in a set of relatively consistent patterns to clarify meaning or help mark the grammatical structure of the sentence. The writer follows principles which make punctuation marks emphasize sentence patterns— for example, the comma used before *and* or *but* between independent clauses. Modern punctuation does not mainly mark the length of "pauses," although pauses and pitch changes clarify grammatical patterns in speech much as punctuation does in writing. Pauses and punctuation marks, therefore, often coincide, and the student may get help with punctuation problems by considering how an expression would be pronounced. For example, the question of whether or not to put commas around a modifier can often be decided by considering how the sentence would be pronounced to convey the intended meaning. Consider:

The two newspapers which had been competing for morning circulation were closed by the strike.

The writer thinking of the *which*-clause as restrictive would pronounce the sentence with no significant pause after *newspapers* and with rising inflection on *circulation;* he would use no commas. Thinking of the clause as nonrestrictive, he would in speaking pause longer after *newspapers* and would pronounce *newspapers* with rising inflection on the first syllable; he would use commas before and after the clause to signal its nonrestrictive meaning.

Even though practices in punctuation are less arbitrary today than they were when they depended greatly on the whim of the writer or even the convenience of the printer, fashions still vary— from writer to writer, country to country, and time to time. Some writers use a comma whenever its inclusion might clarify; others punctuate more lightly, omitting marks whenever they can without obvious danger of being misunderstood. Some newspapers insist on a comma before the *and* in a series, some do not; book publishers generally use it. Books printed in England commonly have no period after *Mr;* books printed in America do.

Punctuation and the Sentence Pattern **25-2**

Writing being as flexible as it is, and human minds being as various and variable as they are, punctuation practice is not likely to be completely stable, but punctuation of standard English expository prose is sufficiently standardized to make clear punctuation relatively easy. With some understanding of how punctuation works, and of the meaning of punctuation marks, the student can mark his writing with little trouble. To begin with, he needs to observe that punctuation is mainly confined to the four following general uses, most of them designed to help the reader focus attention on the main sentence pattern.

1. Punctuation marks the ends of main sentence patterns—of sentences or of independent clauses in sentences. The period, question mark, and exclamation mark, with different meanings, indicate the ends of complete sentences. The semicolon, and sometimes the colon or dash or comma, indicate secondary breaks, breaks between independent clauses within the sentence.

2. Punctuation tends to preserve the flow from subject to verb to complement by setting apart any elements which interrupt the thought of the pattern—nonrestrictive modifiers, parenthetical expressions, and the like. Usually the comma is used for such purposes, although semicolons, dashes, and parentheses sometimes mark sharper separations.

3. Punctuation separates coordinate elements not sufficiently separated by function words. Usually commas are sufficient for such separation, but sometimes a semicolon is used.

4. Punctuation has conventional uses—to clarify statistical material, to mark bibliographic materials, to identify quotations, and so on. Most of these uses have been established by custom and are mechanical habits or traditions to be learned.

Marks of Punctuation **25-3**

The following marks are used in punctuation in English; their major uses are described in this chapter in connection with the discussions of particular punctuation problems.

> The *period* marks the ends of sentences not to be distinguished as questions or exclamations (see 25a). It has also a few conventional uses, mainly to mark abbreviations.

? The *question mark* (interrogation point) is used at the end of a direct question—not an indirect one (see 25a).

! The *exclamation mark* is used at the end of a complete or incomplete sentence to indicate strong emotion or feeling (see 25a).

: The *colon* has mainly conventional uses, especially to introduce formal lists (see 25j); it sometimes separates independent clauses (see 25b).

; The *semicolon* mainly separates independent clauses, although it sometimes separates items in series (see 25b).

, The *comma* is the most common punctuation mark in English, with a wide variety of uses (see especially 25c–25i).

— The *dash,* made with two hyphens on the typewriter, sometimes marks sharp breaks between clauses and sometimes sets off parenthetical material more sharply than a comma would (see 25k).

" " *Quotation marks* enclose direct quotations, words reproduced as spoken or written (see 25i).

( ) *Parentheses* have mainly conventional uses, but they also sometimes mark material to be sharply set apart within the sentence (see 25l).

[ ] *Brackets* mainly have conventional uses to set off inserted materials. Since standard typewriters usually do not have brackets, brackets should be inserted by hand in typed material or made with the diagonal and underlining bars (see 25l).

... The *ellipsis,* three periods, marks an omission, usually from quoted matter (see 25a).

P   **25   *Guide to Revision***

Use punctuation to reveal the sentence pattern and to clarify according to conventions.

Most punctuation problems can be solved with a working knowledge of the marks of punctuation (see 25-2, 25-3). For more detailed statements, see the appropriate discussions below.

P a; . ? !   End Punctuation; Period Fault   **25a**

Structurally the period is the most important device for punctuation, since it marks the end of any sentence not to be distinguished as a question or an exclamation. Use of a period to mark an expression not a complete sentence, sometimes called the *period fault*, usually reveals a basic error in sentence structure, the use of an inappropriate sentence fragment (see Section 12). Usually, also, the *run-together* or *fused* sentence grows from more serious trouble than mere lack of a period (see 25b).

The period is used after an indirect question, in which the question is not phrased verbatim but is part of a statement.

I asked her, "Will you go?" (*Direct question*)
I asked her if she would go. (*Indirect question*)

ORIGINAL

The question was whether Morgan would attack the center or make the long detour around Old Baldy and attack on the flank?
[*The indirect question should be followed by a period. If the question were put directly, it would be followed by a question mark.*]

REVISION

(1) The question was whether Morgan would attack the center or make the long detour around Old Baldy and attack on the flank.
(2) The question was this: would Morgan attack the center, or would he make the long detour around Old Baldy and attack on the flank?

Three consecutive periods (. . .) make a punctuation mark known as the ellipsis, inserted in the place of material omitted from a quotation. When the omission comes after a completed sentence or completes a sentence, the period needed to mark the end of the sentence is retained. In such instances, therefore, four consecutive periods appear.

ORIGINAL

Genius is the activity which repairs the decays of things, whether wholly or partly of a material and finite kind. Nature, through all her kingdoms, insures herself.
—RALPH WALDO EMERSON

QUOTATION WITH OMISSIONS

Genius is the activity which repairs the decays of things. . . . Nature . . . insures herself.
—RALPH WALDO EMERSON
[*The four periods mark both the omission and the end of a sentence.*]

In American usage the period appears, also, after most abbreviations: p.m., Mr., pp., Ave., St., U. S. A., ibid., A.D. Any good dictionary will include abbreviations in the word list or in a special section (see also 26j).

EXCEPTION: The period is not used after letters standing for recently created government bureaus: NLRB, CAP, ANZUS; after letters which represent scholarly or technical journals: PMLA, CA, MLR; after letters of radio stations: KLRB, WUISB, KATO; after MS (plural, MSS) for *manuscript;* certain unions and associations: WAA, AEF, CIO.

The question mark is placed after a direct question, but not after an indirect question.

ORIGINAL

By Sunday I could stand no more, and I said, "Aren't you ever going to leave."

Perhaps I was not very polite, but what could I do.

REVISION

By Sunday I could stand no more, and I said, "Aren't you ever going to leave?"

Perhaps I was not very polite, but what could I do?

The question mark is occasionally used after inserted interrogative material.

Anyone who loves his country—and who does not?—will answer a call to duty.

The question mark is used, sometimes in parentheses, to indicate that a fact, especially a date, is approximate or questionable.

The Play of the Weather (1533?) continues the convention. John Heywood, 1497(?)–1580(?), wrote the play.

Used as an attempted witticism or to mark sarcasm, the question mark is out of fashion and likely to appear amateurish.

The next motion showed how wise (?) [*better omitted*] the committee really was.

A request or command which for politeness is phrased as a question may conclude with either a question mark or a period.

Will you please sign and return the enclosed voucher? *or* . . . voucher.

The exclamation mark indicates emotion or feeling. It is seldom used except in reporting conversation, particularly after interjections like *Ouch! Murder!* Some beginning writers endeavor to liven their compositions with exclamation marks. This device seldom works—any prose so feeble that it must be propped up with punctuation had best be revised. Modern practice is to use the exclamation mark sparingly.

ORIGINAL

"Help," she screamed. "My dress, in the cogs."

[*A girl being dragged into power machinery may be excited enough to warrant exclamation marks.*]

And then! Just think! Out of the cocoon came a pale green luna moth! And still damp!!!

[*This is overblown. It may please children, but scarcely adults.*]

REVISION

"Help!" she screamed "My dress! In the cogs!"

[*The revision does not bolster weak prose; it makes clear at once the drama of the sentences.*]

And then, out of the cocoon came a pale green luna moth, still damp.

[*The use of two or three exclamation marks together is best confined to comic books.*]

Independent Clauses; Fused or Run-together Sentence; Comma Fault or Splice

P b; RT; CF; CS

Independent clauses, independent sentence patterns, are usually separated in one of three ways:

1. They are treated as separate sentences (see 25a).

2. Joined in a single sentence, they are separated by a semicolon.

We always like those who admire us; we do not always like those whom we admire.

Man is certainly stark mad; he cannot make a worm, and yet he will be making gods by dozens.

3. They are joined in a single sentence by a coordinating conjunction (*and, but, for, or, nor, yet, so*), with a comma preceding it (see 25c).

Statesmen are not only liable to give an account of what they say or do in public, *but* there is a busy inquiry made into their very meals, beds, marriages, and every other sportive or serious action.

Notice that the semicolon is used when the second clause is introduced by a connective like *hence, then, therefore, however, nevertheless, in fact,* or *moreover.*

I do not have a taste for caviar; however, I should like to be able to afford to develop one.

Short, closely related clauses, especially when they appear in series, are sometimes joined with only a comma.

The rain falls constantly, the river continues to rise.

The camera rolls back, the boom moves out, the water ripples gently, and the only one now to make a move outside the lighted circle is the man with the little fog can and the fan.

Occasionally, a colon separates independent clauses when the second clause specifies or exemplifies the idea of the first (see 25k).

A sentence in which independent clauses are joined without punctuation is sometimes called a *run-together* or *fused* sentence. Use of a comma between clauses when a semicolon or period is needed is sometimes called a *comma fault* or *comma splice.* The error usually involves more serious troubles than punctuation; it is a symptom that sentence patterns do not adequately relate ideas. Correction requires more than addition of a semicolon; it requires rewriting, often reducing one independent clause to a subordinate element.

ORIGINAL	REVISION
The children tore the stuffed stockings from the mantel then they crept quickly back to bed.	(1) The children tore the stuffed stockings from the mantel; then they crept quickly back to bed.
[*The clauses can be made separate sentences, or separated with a semicolon (1); one clause can be subordinated (2); or one subject can be removed and the verb in the clause made part of a compound verb (3).*]	(2) After the children had torn the stuffed stockings from the mantel, they crept quickly back to bed.
	(3) The children tore the stuffed stockings from the mantel and then crept quickly back to bed.
The hawk circled gracefully for a moment it seemed unaware of the scurrying chicks below.	The hawk circled gracefully; for a moment it seemed unaware of the scurrying chicks below.
The two boys cleared away the brush, then they pitched their tent and spread out their blankets.	(1) The two boys cleared away the brush; then they pitched their tent and spread out their blankets.

ORIGINAL (*Cont.*)

[*The comma does not indicate a large enough break to signal the beginning of a new statement. The sentence can be revised by supplying a semicolon (1), by making one element dependent (2), or by constructing a single clause (3).*]

He had been, he said, a most unconscionable time dying, however he hoped they would excuse it.

[*A conjunctive adverb* (however, moreover, therefore, then, hence) *is a modifier and does not obviate the need for a semicolon to separate the clauses.*]

REVISION (*Cont.*)

(2) After they had cleared away the brush, the two boys pitched their tent and spread out their blankets.

(3) The two boys cleared away the brush, pitched their tent, and spread out their blankets.

(1) He had been, he said, a most unconscionable time dying; however, he hoped that they would excuse it.

(2) He had been, he said, a most unconscionable time dying; he hoped, however, that they would excuse it.

[*For position of the conjunctive adverb see 16a.*]

P c Independent Clauses with Coordinating Conjunctions   25c

Even when independent clauses have a coordinating conjunction (*and, but, for, or, nor, yet, so*) linking them, they are separated by a comma, which signals a new clause rather than a compound complement or verb. Notice that in the following sentence the reader would momentarily misunderstand if the comma were omitted.

She fed all the peanuts to the elephant, and the monkey had to be satisfied with popcorn.

Without the comma the reader would miss the structure of the sentence until he came to the second verb, thinking momentarily that the monkey had shared the peanuts.

ORIGINAL

Jack had been brought up on golf and tennis did not interest him.

[*The writer can supply a comma (1), or make one clause dependent (2).*]

REVISION

(1) Jack had been brought up on golf, and tennis did not interest him.

(2) Since Jack had been brought up on golf, tennis did not interest him.

The comma is not usual unless the conjunction introduces a clause; if it joins two verbs or complements the pattern is usually clear without punctuation (see 25m).

Jack spent his mornings playing golf and his afternoons swimming.

When long or complex clauses containing commas within them are joined, a semicolon may be needed in addition to a coordinating conjunction to mark the main division in the sentence.

ORIGINAL

Men have sworn at one another from earliest times, according to a Chinese classic on profanity, and to abstain from this natural exercise of the tongue is unhealthful but since elaborate swearing requires high intellectual ability, the ordinary swearer is cautioned to consider moderation.

[*Complicated clauses, containing commas within them, are joined here without punctuation.*]

REVISION

Men have sworn at one another from earliest times, according to a Chinese classic on profanity, and to abstain from this natural exercise of the tongue is unhealthful; but since elaborate swearing requires high intellectual ability, the ordinary swearer is cautioned to consider moderation.

[*A semicolon is needed to point out the major division of the sentence.*]

25d   Punctuation in a Series   P d

Commas separate words, phrases, dependent clauses, and sometimes very brief independent clauses (see 25b) when they are coordinated in a series of three or more.

She announced that she was staying in bed until noon, that she was not cooking lunch for anybody, and that she would decide later about dinner.

Some newspapers do not require a comma before *and* (*lettuce, endive and celery*), but most publishers and writers of standard English prefer the comma before *and* (*lettuce, endive, and celery*) on the ground that the omission of the comma is occasionally confusing.

Their menu includes the following: veal steak, roast beef, pork chops, ham and eggs.
She purchased the following: veal, beef, pork, ham, and eggs.

In the first sentence the reader may be uncertain whether or not the eggs are fried with the ham.

If all the items in a series are joined by connectives, no punctuation is needed (*lettuce and endive and celery*).

ORIGINAL

We distinguished highways, roads, trails, streets and alleys.
[*Acceptable in some informal writing; usually not preferred in standard English.*]

REVISION

We distinguished highways, roads, trails, streets, and alleys.

A combination like *bread and butter* within a series is treated as one element of the series.

ORIGINAL

We considered the following subjects: criticism, science, medical, and dental surgery, education, and educators, and law, and the courts.

REVISION

We considered the following subjects: criticism, science, medical and dental surgery, education and educators, and law and the courts.

Consecutive modifiers that tend to modify individually rather than to combine as a composite modifier form a series and are usually separated by commas. Compare:

The streetcar had badly constructed, old-fashioned seats.
The streetcar had grimy cane seats.

In the first, the adjectives seem to modify *seats* independently. As a rough test, insert the word *and* between them and see if the construction still produces a familiar pattern. If it does, as in *badly constructed and old-fashioned seats,* the modifiers are probably in series. In the second, however, *grimy* seems to modify all that follows it; the modifiers do not work independently in a series. *Grimy and cane seats* does not fill a familiar pattern for modifiers. As another rough test, reverse the order of the modifiers. Those in series can be logically reversed, *old-fashioned badly constructed seats;* those not in series cannot, *cane grimy seats.*

Numerals and common adjectives of size, color, and age seldom appear in series:

Twenty-four scrawny blackbirds; two little girls; a spry old man; a pretty little girl

ORIGINAL

I canned dozens of gleaming many-colored jars of fruit.
[*The modifiers are in series; and could sensibly be put between them.*]

REVISION

I canned dozens of gleaming, many-colored jars of fruit.
[*A comma should separate the items of the series.*]

ORIGINAL (*Cont.*)

He bought a worn, old horse.
[Worn *and* old *do not modify separately.*]

The only available room was a dirty, vermin-infested, sleeping porch.
[Dirty *and* vermin-infested *modify in series, but* sleeping *is not part of the series.*]

REVISION (*Cont.*)

He bought a worn old horse.

The only available room was a dirty, vermin-infested sleeping porch.
[*Only the two items in series are separated; each of them modifies* sleeping porch.]

The semicolon also substitutes for the comma to divide items in a series or list when the items are complicated and contain punctuation within them.

ORIGINAL

She told me that, in view of my prejudices, my poor health, and my interests, I would never be happy as a teacher, that I would find myself, at the end of a day, exhausted from policing dozens of squirming children, and that I would find my evenings, during which I hoped to practice music, given over to school plays, the school band and orchestra, and playing command canasta with the superintendent's wife.
[*Since the sentence is long and involved, and broken only by commas, the reader has difficulty seeing at once the organization.*]

The Council included the following representatives: President John A. Rickert, administration, Professor George P. Barrows, faculty, Avery Warren, student council, and Janice Worley, W. A. A.

REVISION

She told me that, in view of my prejudices, my poor health, and my interests, I never would be happy as a teacher; that I would find myself, at the end of the day, exhausted from policing dozens of squirming children; and that I would find my evenings, during which I hoped to practice music, given over to school plays, the school band and orchestra, and playing command canasta with the superintendent's wife.
[*Semicolons separate the three dependent clauses, and mark the main divisions of the sentence.*]

The Council included the following representatives: President John A. Rickert, administration; Professor George P. Barrows, faculty; Avery Warren, student council; and Janice Worley, W. A. A.

25e   **Punctuation of Nonrestrictive or Parenthetical Modifiers**   P e

When modifiers limit closely, especially when they supply the information that identifies or distinguishes subject or complement, they are called restrictive and are not set off by punctuation. Modifiers not essential to the subject–verb–complement combination, which supply incidental information (as this clause does), are called *nonrestrictive,* and must be set off by punctuation. Compare:

All the children who were in the front row received ice cream.
All the children, who were in the front row, received ice cream.

First of all, read the two sentences aloud. As we read the first, we raise the pitch of the voice on *row* and tend to pause after it. As we read the second, we raise pitch on the main syllable of *children,* drop it on *row,* and pause after both *children* and *row.* That is, we distinguish restrictive and nonrestrictive in speech by intonation. We can tell which are nonrestrictive by thinking how they sound, and the punctuation helps us see how they should sound. The punctuation in writing reveals the meaning as the sound patterns do in speech. Both the sound and the punctuation show that the first sentence suggests that, of all of the children, only certain lucky ones, those in the front row, were treated; *who were in the front row,* without commas, is read as restrictive. It restricts or limits *children* to the group it names, specifies certain children, but the second sentence says that all the children received ice cream. The clause is nonrestrictive, as the commas indicate.

Sometimes, as in the sentences above, modifiers can be interpreted as either restrictive or nonrestrictive, but usually the modifiers make sense with only one kind of punctuation. A nonrestrictive modifier can be recognized because it can be dropped out of the sentence without distortion of the main meaning.

The old house, badly out of repair, was hard to sell.

Omission of *badly out of repair* would not change the central idea of the sentence. But compare:

An old house badly out of repair may be no bargain.

Badly out of repair is required as part of the subject; it cannot be omitted without shifting the meaning. Punctuation on only one side of a nonrestrictive modifier is especially confusing because it separates essential parts of the main sentence pattern.

Following are some of the types of modifiers that are commonly nonrestrictive and therefore require commas:

1. *Appositive modifiers:*

My brother, chairman of the board, opposed the stock issue.

Chairman of the board adds incidental information but is not essential to the subject–verb–complement pattern. Sometimes, however, an appositive does restrict the subject and is not separated.

My brother John is chairman of the board.

John specifies which brother, restricts *brother.*

2. *Verbal modifiers:*

The catcher, having played twelve innings, was glad to be taken from the game.

3. *Adjectives following the words they modify:*

The three books, dirty and charred, were all he saved from the fire.

4. *Parenthetical expressions:*

He decided, however, not to throw the pie.
The cape, as the illustration shows, reaches nearly to the ground.

General modifiers of the sentence like *of course, for example, that is, however, indeed, therefore,* and *in conclusion* need punctuation to separate them from the main pattern of the sentence unless they modify restrictively. Parenthetical expressions which interrupt sharply or dramatically or which are not grammatically a part of the sentence are sometimes set off by dashes (see 25k), or parentheses (see 25l).

5. *Final qualifying clauses:*

Fools cause as much damage as criminals, although they are seldom punished.

Qualifying clauses, especially those beginning with *although,* are often nonrestrictive even when they follow the main clause. When they are nonrestrictive, they are usually set off by a comma; when they are restrictive, they are not punctuated.

Even clauses beginning with *because* or *since* may be nonrestrictive following the verb:

"Did you go to the picnic?" "I went, because I had to."

The modifying clause supplies additional information, not that required to answer the question. Notice again that intonation supplies a practical clue; when the word before the modifier would be accented in speech and followed by a fairly clear pause, the sentence is likely to require a comma to indicate that the modifier is nonrestrictive. When no special accent falls on the word before the modifier and the main stress of the sentence is on the verb of the modifying clause, the modifier is probably restrictive.

ORIGINAL

I bought the material, that Mother had picked out.
[*The modifier identifies or defines the material; it is restrictive.*]

That evening which has always seemed the most terrifying of my life the dining room ceiling fell on us.
[*The modifier is not essential; it adds incidental information and is nonrestrictive.*]

My grandmother, who still had a powerful voice went to the door and shouted.
[*The subject, grandmother, is separated from the verb, and the modifier is not set off.*]

We started running for the express station which was still several blocks ahead.
[*The punctuation is accurate only if the clause identifies one station of at least two.*]

Politicians, generally speaking consider the desires of their constituents.
[*The expression must have punctuation both before and after.*]

The discussion is, indeed, silly.
[*The punctuation is not wrong, but it probably sets off the modifier more than necessary.*]

REVISION

I bought the material that Mother had picked out.
[*The restrictive use of the modifier is clear without punctuation.*]

That evening, which has always seemed the most terrifying of my life, the dining room ceiling fell on us.
[*The nonrestrictive modifier must be punctuated to set it apart from the main parts of the sentence.*]

My grandmother, who still had a powerful voice, went to the door and shouted.
[*Commas should appear both before and after the nonrestrictive modifier.*]

We started running for the express station, which was still several blocks ahead.
[*In most contexts, the clause would be nonrestrictive.*]

Politicians, generally speaking, consider the desires of their constituents.

The discussion is indeed silly.
[*Probably the writer intends* indeed *to modify* silly *only, not to be parenthetical.*]

481

ORIGINAL *(Cont.)*

Aunt Agnes dyed her hair, painted her eyelashes, and plucked her brows although she always wore shoe-length dresses.
[*The* although-*clause had best be set off with a comma.*]

I went, because I had to.
[*In most contexts the* because-*clause would be intended as restrictive.*]

REVISION *(Cont.)*

Aunt Agnes dyed her hair, painted her eyelashes, and plucked her brows, although she always wore shoe-length dresses.

I went because I had to.

25f   Punctuation after Introductory Modifiers   P f

Introductory modifying clauses and other long or complicated modifiers are set off from the rest of the sentence by commas. The punctuation is especially necessary, even with a short modifier, if the reader might otherwise have difficulty identifying the point at which the modifier stops.

ORIGINAL

Before we had finished eating the salad and the fish were snatched away from us.
[*A comma would prevent momentary misunderstanding.*]

By daylight, we could find our way.
[*The comma does no harm, but the introductory modifier is short.*]

In the morning light filtered through the chinks in the ceiling.
[*Even though the modifier is short, the comma is needed to prevent misunderstanding.*]

Accordingly I resigned.
[*Though brief, the introductory element is set off in meaning and would be set off orally.*]

REVISION

Before we had finished eating, the salad and the fish were snatched away from us.
[*The comma marks the end of the modifier.*]

By daylight we could find our way.
[*The comma is unnecessary.*]

In the morning, light filtered through the chinks in the ceiling.
[*The comma separates the two words which might otherwise be linked by their meanings.*]

Accordingly, I resigned.
[*The comma is preferable.*]

Often introductory modifiers are like restrictive and nonrestrictive modifiers in that the intonation intended provides a clue to punctuation. Consider:

Meanwhile the dog ate our dinner.

Spoken, the sentence would probably carry a sharp rise in pitch on the first syllable of *meanwhile* and a pause after the word; a comma after *meanwhile* would enforce this intention.

Punctuation with Geographical, Temporal, and Metrical Material

P g   **25g**

The comma has a number of conventional uses to separate parts of geographical, temporal, or metrical material, or anything that takes a statistical form.

1. Commas are used between all elements of a date. When a year is part of a date, it has commas both before and after it. Parts of a single element, such as the name of a month and the figure indicating the day, are not separated. With abbreviations both a period and comma are often required.

They arrived by train at 10 A.M., Monday, January 9, 1967.
Tuesday night, July 6, 1820, the debate began.

2. Elements of addresses are similarly separated. When more than one element appears in an address, the last element is followed by a comma, unless the address is itself a separate unit, as in the address of a letter. Parts of elements, such as a street number and the name of the street following it, along with some code numbers, such as those in Zip Code, are not separated.

He gave 1162 West Avenue, Cleveland 9, Ohio, as his address.

3. Commas separate parts of measurements, divisions of a whole, and other statistical details. The last element of a series of divisions, like parts of a book, is usually separated from what follows, but the last part of a series constituting a measurement is usually not.

He was six feet, eight inches tall.
The sentence appears on page 11, line 28, of the new book.
She must enter in Act III, scene 2, before the music begins.

ORIGINAL	REVISION
Mary was born January 4, 1952 in Chicago, at 1227 Second Avenue.	Mary was born January 4, 1952, in Chicago, at 1227 Second Avenue.
He cleared the bar at six feet four inches.	He cleared the bar at six feet, four inches.

25h   Comma to Clarify or Emphasize   P h

The comma may be useful to separate words which might be erroneously run together, to mark omission of a word used in a double capacity, or to emphasize structure when a connective is omitted.

ORIGINAL	REVISION
Whatever is is right. [*The two uses of* is *are confusing without separation.*]	Whatever is, is right. [*The words are separated for clarity, even though the subject is not normally separated from the verb.*]
The next day he told me what he meant what he had intended to say.	The next day he told me what he meant, what he had intended to say.
An hour of lecture presumes two hours of preparation, an hour of laboratory none. [Presumes *is assumed between* laboratory *and* none.]	An hour of lecture presumes two hours of preparation, an hour of laboratory, none. [*The comma makes the structure clear.*]

25i   Punctuation with Quotations   P i; ''; Quot

Direct quotations, words actually said or previously written, are enclosed in quotation marks.

"Get out," she said.
After his service in Vietnam, he agreed that "the paths of glory lead but to the grave."

This use is sometimes extended to include short expressions which quote speech from a special level of usage or from a particular person, or which call attention to a way of saying something.

It was then the fashion for popular male choruses to describe themselves as "beatles," "zanies," or something else unpleasant.

The quotation marks are used because a quotation from some other speaking group is implied. Quotation marks are no longer generally used as indiscriminate apologies for slang or colloquial English. In most instances, the slang should be used without apology if it is appropriate and omitted if it is not.

Quotation marks are sometimes used to indicate that a word is used as a word, but italics are more common (see 26n)

The noun "boy" is the subject.

Quotation marks distinguish titles in two special circumstances: (1) when mechanical limitations, such as those in typesetting for a newspaper, make italics impractical; and (2) when a short work is to be distinguished from the larger work that contains it (see 26n, 23-10, 23-11).

Robert Frost's "Mending Wall" appears in *Poetry of America.*

Quotation marks appear before and after the quoted material. When a quotation runs for more than one paragraph, the mark of quotation begins every paragraph but closes only the last one. Long quotations may be printed without quotation marks, in smaller type and indented; in typescript, the passage is indented and typed single-spaced.

Single quotation marks ('), the apostrophe on the typewriter, enclose a quotation within a quotation.

The witness said, "I was just opening the door when I heard her scream, 'Drop that!' "

An indirect quotation is not placed within quotation marks, but a few words within an indirect quotation may be quoted directly.

In his quiet way, he said that he was "excessively annoyed" with the hoodlums next door.

ORIGINAL	REVISION
I am sorry, she said, but those weeds you are lying in are poison ivy. [*Material quoted directly should be set off by quotation marks.*]	"I am sorry," she said, "but those weeds you are lying in are poison ivy."

ORIGINAL (*Cont.*)

Shaw pretended to believe that all man's civilization is founded on his cowardice, on his abject tameness, which he calls respectability.

[*The latter part of the sentence is quoted directly.*]

REVISION (*Cont.*)

Shaw pretended to believe that all man's civilization "is founded on his cowardice, on his abject tameness, which he calls respectability."

[*The quoted matter has been placed within quotation marks.*]

I told "her she ought to stop wasting her time."

[*The quotation is not direct; the direct quotation was something like "You'd better stop wasting your time."*]

I told her she ought to stop wasting her time.

[*The quotation marks have been removed, since an indirect quotation is not enclosed.*]

She said I was in a hassel and that I had blown my top.

[Hassel *and* blown my top *are quotations from the character's manner of speech.*]

She said I was in a "hassel" and that I had "blown my top."

[*The characteristic words have been enclosed within quotation marks.*]

The old garden had been taken over by heather aster, the poverty weed.

[*Without quotation marks,* poverty weed *is taken as merely an alternative name.*]

The old garden had been taken over by heather aster, the "poverty weed."

[*Quotation marks might be used to show that the name is quoted from local speech.*]

When an expression like *he said* introduces a quotation, it is separated from the quotation by a comma.

I said, "I have always hated Pomeranians."

Sometimes a formal introduction to a quotation is followed by a colon (see 25j), but the comma is not used before an indirect quotation, that is, a quotation which is not verbatim.

I said that I had always hated Pomeranians.

ORIGINAL

Then Juliet asked "Why is your name Romeo?"

REVISION

Then Juliet asked, "Why is your name Romeo?"

Then Juliet asked, why his name was Romeo.

[*The quotation is indirect and should not be set off.*]

Then Juliet asked why his name was Romeo.

[*The comma of the original separates verb from complement.*]

The position of the quotation mark in relation to other punctuation used with it is determined partly by logic and partly by arbitrary convention. Commas and periods are always placed inside quotation marks. All other punctuation marks are inside if they punctuate only the quoted words, outside if they punctuate an entire sentence containing a quotation.

The rafters used a long handspike, which they called a "picaroon."
He asked me to open the "boot"; I did not understand.
"Are you ready?" I asked.
Do you know who said that "life is but an empty dream"?

ORIGINAL

An upright contraption, known as a "moon box", was used to show an artificial moon on the stage.
[*The comma always goes inside the quotation.*]

"Are you afraid of the dark"? the child asked.
[*Since the question mark punctuates the quoted material, it belongs inside the quotation marks.*]

REVISION

An upright contraption, known as a "moon box," was used to show an artificial moon on the stage.

"Are you afraid of the dark?" the child asked.

P j; : The Colon **25j**

The colon resembles in force the sign of equality in mathematics; that is, whatever comes before the sign is in at least one sense equal to what comes after it. It is most frequently used to precede a series which has already been introduced by a completed statement, often containing the word *following* or *follows*.

The common silk dress goods are the following: raw silk, taffeta, crepe de Chine, shantung, pongee, silk chiffon, silk organdy, satin, and silk velvet.

I found that there were four kinds of girls in college: those who came to get married, those who came to get an education, those who came because their parents made them, and those who came because they did not know what else to do.

The colon is not needed, however, when the series immediately follows the verb as a group of complements.

ORIGINAL

The common silk dress goods are: raw silk, taffeta, crepe de Chine, shantung, pongee, silk chiffon, silk organdy, satin, and silk velvet.

[*The list is a complement and should not be separated from the verb it completes.*]

REVISION

The common silk dress goods are raw silk, taffeta, crepe de Chine, shantung, pongee, silk chiffon, silk organdy, satin, and silk velvet.

[*The colon which breaks the continuity of the subject–verb–complement pattern is omitted.*]

In high school I competed in the principal girls' sports, that is: in hockey, swimming, and basketball.

[*The colon properly introduces a formal series; here* hockey, swimming, *and* basketball *are in apposition with* sports.]

In high school I competed in the principal girls' sports, that is, in hockey, swimming, and basketball.

[*The meaning is at once clear with a comma, and accordingly the lighter punctuation is preferable.*]

The colon is occasionally used between independent clauses when the second part of the sentence has been introduced in the first.

Two events occurred that spring to make Marie less happy in her new home: the mangy cat that had been her best friend was hit by a car, and the low spot near the garage which became a fine mud puddle after every shower was filled and leveled.

The colon is unusual in this use, however, unless the second part of the sentence clearly repeats or clarifies the first.

ORIGINAL

Almost everybody tries to come to Washington: everybody complains about the weather after he gets here.

REVISION

Almost everybody tries to come to Washington; everybody complains about the weather after he gets here.

The colon also has certain conventional uses, notably after the formal address of a letter (*Dear Miss Smith:, Dear Sir:*), in statements of time (*8:35*), and in citations from the Bible (*Genesis 5:1-3* or *Genesis V, 1-3*). For other conventional uses of the colon, see *A Manual of Style,* cited above.

25k The Dash P k; —; Dash

The dash (—), made with two hyphens on the typewriter, is used to mark sudden breaks in the flow of the sentence. It stops the reader abruptly, a little like a closet door bumped into in the dark. Dashes are useful and versatile punctuation marks, but they should be used with care and restraint. Most commonly they have the following uses:

1. A dash may emphasize a sharp break or change in thought, separating sentence elements or marking a break at the end.

If he has any decency he will come and apologize—but has he any decency? He knew the soldiers would march up in formation, aim their rifles, and then—

2. A dash may emphasize a dramatic or striking interruption or set off parenthetical material (see 25f) when the writer desires a sharper separation than commas signify. Parentheses usually set off an insertion not grammatically part of the sentence (see 25e).

The new queen of the senior ball—and she was fully aware of her royalty—swept into the room.

The dash is especially useful if the modifier has internal punctuation.

Often had he sighed, in Africa, for its drowsy verdant opulence—those willow-fringed streamlets and grazing cattle, the smell of hay, the flowery lanes.

3. One English sentence pattern used occasionally lists a long series of subjects or modifiers followed by a dash and usually by a pronoun or other word summarizing the list.

A brown, crusty turkey, fluffy mashed potatoes, jars of jam, pickles, and olives, and mince and pumpkin pies—all these and more appeared before Linda, as if she were in a dream.

4. The dash is sometimes used between clauses when one clause introduces another, or it may introduce a list, less formally than a colon (see 25j).

Of the thoughts that flashed through my mind one persisted—if I screamed the children would wake up.
He bought samples of all the common silk dress goods—raw silk, taffeta, crepe de Chine, shantung, pongee, silk chiffon, silk organdy, satin, and silk velvet.

5. The dash has various conventional uses, especially before a citation at the end of a quotation.

"Nothing endures, nothing is precise and certain (except the mind of a pedant)." —H. G. WELLS, *A Modern Utopia*

It is used also in various kinds of informal tabular arrangements.

Humanities—fine arts, literature, language, philosophy.
Social sciences—history, political science, sociology, economics.

In current usage, other punctuation marks are avoided with a dash.

ORIGINAL	REVISION
These discoveries,—evolution, relativity, and now atomic fission,—have given us a new conception of the world. [*The comma is not necessary with the dash.*]	These discoveries—evolution, relativity, and now atomic fission—have given us a new conception of the world.

Writers too indolent to decide what they wish to say, and thus how to punctuate, sometimes try to save themselves trouble by using dashes for everything, hoping that the reader will do the thinking that the writer should have done. The device seldom works.

ORIGINAL	REVISION
Knowing only the most elementary principles of chemistry—I should never have attempted the experiment alone—However—I set up the equipment—and got out the necessary materials—not knowing how explosive they were—especially in combination— [*This is a jumble because the writer has not punctuated.*]	Knowing only the most elementary principles of chemistry, I should never have attempted the experiment alone. However, I set up the equipment and got out the necessary materials, not knowing how explosive they were, especially in combination. [*The dashes have been replaced by standard punctuation.*]

25l Parentheses and Brackets P l; ( ); [ ]

Parentheses enclose inserted material which does not fit into the grammatical structure of the sentence and which adds incidental information. In this book, for example, parentheses punctuate cross references or examples inserted into sentences. They can also enclose sentences or passages irrelevant to the main discussion.

The statue bears this inscription: "To our bountiful lady, Margarita Fernandez." (Señora Fernandez was an Indian woman who married a Spaniard and at his death inherited his mining wealth.) It is an outstanding example of Spanish baroque.

Parentheses have various special uses such as enclosing numbers or letters in an enumeration.

He cited reasons as follows: (1) no students had been allowed in the building in the past; (2) furniture was not well enough built to stand student use; and (3) students had adequate facilities without new quarters.

Punctuation goes inside the parentheses when it punctuates only the parenthetical materials, outside when it punctuates the whole passage. Parentheses are used only in pairs. In most contexts they are best used sparingly.

ORIGINAL	REVISION
He distinguished between the members of the family *Juniperus, Juniperus communis, Juniperus virginiana,* and the like, and the plants resembling juniper, such as retem, *Retama raetam.*	He distinguished between the members of the family *Juniperus* (*Juniperus communis, Juniperus virginiana,* and the like) and the plants resembling juniper, such as retem (*Retama raetam*).
[*The words separated by commas seem at first to be words in a series.*]	[*Parentheses clarify the sentence.*]
To write you need a sharp pencil and a quick mind (the first of which can be easily acquired).	To write you need a sharp pencil and a quick mind, the first of which can be easily acquired.
[*Clauses within a sentence are usually sufficiently set off with commas.*]	[*The comma is sufficient; for a sharper break, a dash would be preferable to parentheses.*]

Brackets are used to enclose matter inserted into a direct quotation.

ORIGINAL	REVISION
We hold these truths to be *self-evident* (the italics, of course, are mine), that all men are created equal. . . .	We hold these truths to be *self-evident* [the italics, of course, are mine], that all men are created equal. . . .
[*The parentheses imply that the inserted matter was part of the original and was there in parentheses.*]	[*The inserted matter has been enclosed within square brackets.*]

Brackets are used for parenthetical material within matter within parentheses, to avoid the confusion of parentheses within parentheses.

25m Inappropriate or Excessive Punctuation P m; No P

Punctuation is intended to clarify; sprinkled indiscriminately through writing, especially when it separates closely related sentence elements, punctuation distracts or obscures. The mistaken notion that any pause in speech suggests a comma in writing is perhaps responsible for some useless punctuation. Punctuation that separates subject from verb or verb from complement is especially misleading. Commas setting off parenthetical or nonrestrictive material do not separate subject and verb so long as they appear both before and after the expression, but a comma on only one side of such an expression breaks the continuity of the sentence.

ORIGINAL	REVISION
Hundreds of tattered men, came tramping back from the war. [*The subject,* men, *should not be separated from the verb,* came tramping.]	Hundreds of tattered men came tramping back from the war.
Even Pearl, who had worn loafers all her life bought a pair of high-heeled pumps. [*The comma after* Pearl, *on only one side of the modifier, separates subject from verb.*]	Even Pearl, who had worn loafers all her life, bought a pair of high-heeled pumps. [*When commas enclose the modifier, they set it apart and accentuate the subject–verb relationship.*]

Perhaps because final clauses sometimes modify nonrestrictively and are set off by a comma, students sometimes precede a clause used as a complement with a comma. Such a comma separates verb from complement.

ORIGINAL	REVISION
Mary was afraid, that someone else would wear a pirate costume.	Mary was afraid that someone else would wear a pirate costume.

The practice of using a comma before *and* between independent clauses should not be distorted into the notion that a comma always precedes *and*. Usually, a comma is not needed before *and* when it joins parts of a compound subject, verb, or complement.

ORIGINAL

My father, and John ran up the walk, and threw their arms around us.

REVISION

My father and John ran up the walk and threw their arms around us.

The need for a semicolon between long, complex independent clauses does not require that a semicolon appear whenever an independent clause has any internal punctuation.

ORIGINAL

Of course, I looked in the drawer for the flashlight; but someone had taken it.

REVISION

Of course, I looked in the drawer for the flashlight, but someone had taken it.

Exercise 25

A. Supply appropriate punctuation and capitalization in the following sentences. The meaning changes with various sorts of punctuation.

1. A certain truck carries the following signs this truck stops for a red light or a red head backs up 25 feet for a blonde and courtesy is our motto
2. He was playing left end you say so you say he was playing left end is that it
3. One avocado did not ripen I don't know why the other one did
4. He was the worst dean I ever heard of with the alumni his putting the whole Sigma Nu house on probation is still a favorite story
5. Two times two are four four times four are fifteen no four fours are sixteen or are they or is it is
6. I said rats if they are eating the cake I don't want any of it
7. So you think you're pretty good do you feel like taking off your glasses and settling this outside

8. The following have registered thus far Alice Melarkey Los Angeles Muriel Jones St. Louis Florence O'Brien Seattle Florence Schmidt Syracuse and Helen Adney Atlanta

9. A number of changes account for the movement of beef raising into the southeast wornout cotton lands heavily cropped for years will no longer raise a high production crop successfully and meanwhile Texas ranchers finding they have insufficient pastures in this the driest year in a decade are glad to acquire additional grazing land in the eastern gulf states

10. Joseph Joubert is credited with the following some men find their sole activity in repose others their sole repose in activity

B. The sentences below could be corrected by supplying adequate punctuation, but most of them would be improved by revision. Correct each by changing punctuation; then revise each by making one of the independent clauses dependent and compare the results.

1. I finished washing all the dinner dishes then Mary said she thought we might mop and wax the kitchen floor.

2. It was cold and rainy outside, however, the house was warm and dry.

3. I was in the hospital during the time I was there I fell in love with the head nurse.

4. I never learned the multiplication tables for this reason I have always been slow at mathematics.

5. The clerk opened the bank door at the time he did so the three robbers pushed their way into the bank.

6. The team lost the final game of the tournament, for this reason June cried herself to sleep that night.

7. My sister was beautiful and talented however she did not win a trip to Atlantic City.

8. The wounded were evacuated by helicopter, they could not do this if machine gun fire was heavy, however.

C. Punctuate the following sentences, paying particular attention to punctuation of nonrestrictive and parenthetical modifiers.

1. Then she started talking about a tepidarium whatever that is.

2. The atoll a coral reef which barely broke the water was nothing to turn to for protection particularly in stormy weather.

3. The tailored suit which I had brought home with me from Hadley's Bazaar a department store in New York City hung on me like a Hindu robe but everybody admired the outfit I had made a simple little dress I devised out of some coarse basket-weave that Aunt Lilly gave me.

4. That summer I was employed as assistant to the playground director

in Jordan Park the same park in which the previous summer I had refused to take part in the group games.

5. In our school Beeson County High School most of the students were interested in sports especially basketball and accordingly you did not ask whether a boy had anything in his head but only whether he was tall enough to hold his head six feet in the air.

6. Gladys who was the only daughter of a steel manufacturer used to make me angry and jealous showing off her new clothes.

7. She is the girl who won the 4-H scholarship.

8. After one hour saturate the curls with neutralizer for bleached, dyed, or overdry hair see insructions on the front of the folder.

9. What we called the "coasting hill" a long grade that wound past the cemetery and down through the school yard unfortunately crossed Lake Street at the intersection by the feed and grain store a crossing which was much used by farmers on Saturday our only coasting day.

10. The sorority which my mother favored was the only one that showed me any attention.

D. Supply the missing punctuation in the sentences below, and correct inappropriate punctuation; where two marks of punctuation are required, be sure you put them in the proper order. Some sentences are well punctuated as they stand.

1. Inside I saw: a cat, some kittens, and an old white-haired Negro.

2.   . . . the play's the thing
Wherein I'll catch the *conscience* the italics are mine of the king.

3. Janice (a quiet girl who went out little) was very anxious to have dates.

4. I turned and ran toward the subway station,—or thought I did, for it was snowing so that I could not see,—then I bumped into someone.

5. Maximilian had three courses before him he could try to become a genuine ruler of the Mexicans for the Mexicans; he could take his scraps of a French army and flee; or he could go on living in indolent luxury, which would probably be ended by a firing squad.

6. "The so-called Dixiecrats [dissident southern Democrats] hoped by this move to gain the balance of power."

7. Alice—the scrawniest little girl in our block—was growing up to be a beauty.

8. To distinguish the types of furniture, note the following: bamboo grows in sections and is hollow between the sections; rattan, a much stronger material, grows solid.

9. They had something they called a "booby-hutch," which was defined as "a carriage body put upon sleigh runners."

10. "They the Pueblo Indians make a kind of bread called guayave which the white people call a 'hornet's nest.'

E. Insert the correct punctuation in the following:

When I was in Cuernavaca Mexico on a vacation trip in July 1966 I heard a story of what became of one of Rivera's murals It seems that the proprietor of a fashionable restaurant ordered his walls decorated Since I do not wish to be libelous let us say that the restaurant was at 268 Morales Avenue which it was not The proprietor a small ingratiating excitable man considered various muralists interviewing them from the time he arose at 10 a m until he went to bed at 2 a m Finally he settled upon Rivera who was known to be fashionable with certain groups especially the foreigners The mural finished he awaited the approval of the dignified people in the town Members of the important old families who were eager to view the newest monument to local progress responded to his invitation They came in holiday mood and looked they left enraged They had seen their own faces painted upon the bodies of gangsters robbers cutthroats and quacks with small ceremony and no delay at all they rendered their artistic judgment If those pictures stayed up the most important people would stay out What to do The proprietor loved his murals for they had cost him much money he loved his business for it had brought him much money So he paced the floor which was new and only partly paid for and tore at his trim carefully waxed mustache At that he had an idea and with deft strokes painted bushy whiskers sprightly goatees and respectable muttonchops upon the faces of the abused citizens Should he not reason that whiskers that would render a mayor unrecognizable would also make him genial and as a result might he not be expected to eat the restaurant beefsteak But the device which the proprietor's mustache inspired was more ingenious than successful The outraged citizens were more outraged than ever not only had the proprietor insulted them by calling them bandits but he had further and doubly insulted them by implying that they grew bad beards As for Rivera he threatened to shoot the proprietor for desecrating art Torn between art and the artist between his patrons and their patronage the bedeviled proprietor saved at once his sanity and his business by having the whole room replastered.

Mechanics:
Spelling, Capitalization,
Printing Conventions,
Manuscript Form

*For
Guide to Revision,
see page 509.*

Accurate composition requires knowledge of the standard English writing system and of special writing conventions.

The English alphabet is a precious heritage and a handy tool, but it has inadequacies, some of which have grown into it. The learned men who worked out a way of writing spoken English adapted the Latin alphabet to the purpose, but the Latin alphabet was not entirely adequate for English. The Roman writing system had come west from early Semites, who had so few vowel sounds in their spoken language that, for economy, they did not mark them, and hence had no symbols for vowels. The Greeks, who transmitted the Semitic alphabet, converted a few symbols for consonants into symbols for vowels, but they never converted enough, and the Romans added only a few more. Accordingly, the Latin alphabet, which could not record all the sounds in Latin, was still less adequate for English, which has sounds not in Latin.

Some adaptations helped. A Latin symbol that looked like U was carved on stone with straight lines, so that two letters, *U* and *V*, were available to English. Doubled, this symbol gave yet another, *W*, called *double-U* in English and the equivalent of *double-V* in German. Similarly, when Latin provided no symbols for the initial sounds of words like *think, she,* and *chip,* digraphs or combinations of two letters *th, sh,* and *ch* were used to stand for the single sounds. In spite of such helps, however, we have too few letters for all the English sounds.

Furthermore, changes in English have complicated and confused the writing system. Old and Middle English existed in various dialects, which survived irregularly. *Girl, pearl,* and *world* now all contain the same sound, but they are spelled differently because they were once pronounced differently and the letters reflect the earlier sounds. *Meet* and *meat* were once pronounced differently and therefore spelled differently: the sounds have now fallen together while the spellings remain distinct. Old English had a sound rather like *khkhkh,* which was later written *gh;* the sound disappeared from the language, but the letters that designated it persist in words like *through* or *rough.* Similarly, many sounds written with the letter *g* disappeared—becoming first vowels, then parts of dipthongs, then nothing—but they have left spellings with *i* or *y,* as in *maid, day,* and *said.*

A major confusion comes from our extensive borrowing of foreign words, introduced without much change in spelling. Thus we spell one word *fait accompli* because it comes from French, another *blitzkrieg* because it was German, another *sputnik* because we have transliterated it from Russian. We have adopted *c* as a spelling for the sound of *s,* while keeping it in its English use as the equivalent of *k.* Meanwhile, we picked up more equivalents of Old English *c,* so that, although we have generally too few letters, we squander symbols writing this sound as *c, ck, k, ch, qu, que,* and, in combination, *x.* Since more than two-thirds of the words in most dictionaries have been borrowed from some language with sounds and spellings different from those in English, and since we have never systematically overhauled our writing system, spelling is far from regular.

In spite of the confusions we have inherited, however, the English writing system is not so senseless as it might be, or is sometimes supposed to be. Medieval scribes had no universal spelling rules, but they recognized some principles, two of which can be observed in the phrase *spelling rules* itself. *Spelling* has two *l*'s to indicate that the preceding *e* stands for a short vowel sound, and *rules* has an extra *e* to indicate the long pronunciation for *u.* Thousands of modern words have similar spellings because we have inherited the words and the principles from medieval scribes. In fact, modern systematic analyses of English indicate that more than 80 per cent of English words are spelled according to discernible principles. Other writing conventions, though not always logically originated, follow patterns. The apostrophe as a sign of the possessive, for instance, grew from a curious blunder. Renaissance grammarians supposed that a form like *the kingis book,* an alternate medieval form for *the kinges book,* should actually read *the king, his book.* They assumed that an *h* had been omitted and used an apostrophe to mark the omission. They were wrong, but the apostrophe has been adopted for the possessive with standard rules for its use. Capitals, hyphens, italics, and other devices supplement the writing system, often in arbitrary patterns, but detailed rules for their use can be found in any good style book.

Spelling and the Sound System   26-1

In an ideal spelling system, every phoneme—every working sound unit—would have a single symbol to represent it in writing. That is, every sound which for users of a language causes a difference in use would be represented by a different letter or some other mark. Because languages constantly change, this kind of correspondence—one phoneme, one symbol—is seldom realized, although a few languages, like Finnish, with relatively new writing systems, approximate it. English does not have such correspondence. Most speakers of English employ about thirty-five phonemes, twenty-four consonants and eleven vowels, although linguists vary classifications slightly. The English alphabet has only twenty-six letters. English writing does not distinguish the consonant sounds in the middle of *ether* and *either,* although these sounds are phonemes, distinguishing meaning. Neither does it distinguish the vowels in *bow,* as in *rainbow,* and *bow,* indicating the prow of a boat. Furthermore, using different symbols for the same phoneme suggests nonexistent difference between the second *bow* and *bough.*

Most of the time, however, English spelling presents no such difficulties. Take the word *melt;* practically speaking, it could be spelled only as it is. The first letter, *m,* indicates only the phoneme /m/, the sound created when the air column vibrates through the nose and the lips are closed. Similarly, *l* and *t* are used almost exclusively for /l/ and /t/, and these phonemes are usually expressed by no other symbols. The exceptions are few; *l* is still written in a few words in which it was once pronounced, like *chalk* and *would,* and in a few words the sound /t/ is written *th* as in *thyme.* The letter *e* has many uses, but as it appears here, along with no following vowel and in a word of one syllable, it commonly represents only one phoneme, the sound familiar in words like *get, met,* or *let.* Nearly half the phonemes of the language are spelled consistently with a single letter.

A few symbols and sounds are slightly complicated. Some symbols work in pairs to represent one sound; that is, they are what we call *digraphs. Ch* as a pair of letters working together represents a sound in *chug* and *much,* and it is about the only way you can represent this sound, although, especially in proper names, it may represent a sound more commonly spelled with *sh,* as in *Chicago* and *Charlotte.* Similarly, *ng* represents one sound and practically speaking only one sound; *ph* working as a unit represents one sound, although the same sound can be spelled *f.* The confusions here are not many, however, and can be readily learned; the sound /f/ can be written in more than one way, as *f, ff,* and *ph,* and even *gh* in *enough,* but the last two spellings are rare.

Even the complicated sounds can be broken down to make some sense. Take one of the worst, as it appears in *fish, fission, complexion, initiate, chaise, schwa, censure, conscious,* and some others. The commonest spelling is *sh,* and it is commonest because this was the spelling that represented the sound in native English words— *wish, dish, she, ship.* Since these words come from Old English they are usually short, common words. The other spellings are mostly in borrowed words, but they, too, fall into patterns. Many come from Latin, using a *ti* spelling—*condition, situation, negation, vitiate.* These words tend to be long, abstract, and rather formal. The spelling with *ch* usually comes from French or through French— even *Chicago,* although it was an Indian word, comes to us in a French spelling. *Sch* is the German spelling. Most other spellings— and they are few—represent some kind of softening or eliding of an older sound; for example, *fission* comes from a form of Latin *fissio,* where the two *s*'s represented a long or repeated sound, but the sound shortened and became more slack in English, which has a sound pattern different from Latin, while the old spelling remained.

The hardest sounds, of course, are vowels. Eleven or twelve different vowel sounds occur commonly in English, plus some combinations of sounds or diphthongs, and these are spelled with only six letters, *a, e, i, o, u, y*. Furthermore, these letters are not used consistently for the same phonemes. The letter *e*, for example, perhaps the most versatile of all, can appear in *get, greet, great, river, ride, covey, sieve, receive, complete, aye, new, changes, decay, unique*, and many others, with sounds and without them. Still, the common uses are few and can be understood historically. We have already seen that English borrowed the Latin short *e* and used the letter for the same sound in English that it had in Latin, in words like *get*. If scribes feared the reader might not know the sound was short, they doubled a following consonant, as in *getting*. They also borrowed the same vowel long, as in our word *street*, from Latin *sternere*, and although this sound has changed in English, the change need not concern us here. If an early scribe wanted the reader to know that the vowel was long, he added a second vowel, as in *street, speech;* or he might add another *e* after a following consonant, as in *ride, compete*. Thus, some *e*-letters always have been silent; others have become silent or nearly so, mainly because stress moved away from a stressed vowel. For example, *government* formerly had considerable stress on the last syllable, so that the vowel in *ment* was pronounced about like the *e* in *get*. Now, however, the stress is on the first syllable, and the vowel in the last syllable has been reduced to what we call *schwa*, a very slack, colorless vowel like the first syllable of *about*, or to nothing. Meanwhile, the sound that was once represented by *-er-* has fallen out completely in some dialects, so that many people, and cultured people at that, pronounce *government* as though it were spelled *guvmnt*. Thus, although *e* as a spelling is complicated, it mainly represents the short sound in *spell*, the long sound in *meet*, the neutral schwa in *decay* or a silent letter of which some were used to mark preceding long vowels. All these appear in patterns well known to all literate users of English.

The linguistic phenomenon by which a word once pronounced something like *go-ver-na-ment* is reduced to *guv-mnt* is called syncopation, leaving out something. It happens regularly in language; our word *eye*, one syllable, used to be something like *oculum*, three syllables. Syncopation complicates spelling as pronunciations change while spelling remains constant, reflecting earlier pronunciations. Thus a student who writes *airfiel* for airfield, *intrest* for *interest, exackly* for *exactly*, or *signifigance* for *significance* is probably producing a tolerably accurate representation of what he usually says. Since syncopation is normal, we cannot expect to cure such spelling errors by sounding out every letter in pronunciation; words like *phthisicky* or *colonel,* to mention only obvious examples, would cause trouble. We can recognize that the writing system differs from the oral system, and that it often reflects pronunciations of an early date, but that the sound system may help us understand the system of writing symbols. We can profit, for example, from the practices mentioned above, whereby the final *e* signals that an earlier vowel is long, and a doubled consonant that it is short. Knowledge of these practices distinguishes *dine* from *din* and *diner* from *dinner.* A student aware of these tendencies of the writing system would probably not misspell *getting, combine, helpful, referring, occurring, excellence, permitted, riding, Britannica, ninety, arguing, during* and similar words frequently missed. For variations on the rules, see 26h.

26-2 Analyzing Spelling Problems

Spelling ability is not necessarily an index to intelligence or education, but certainly the person who spells inaccurately works under a handicap. He is likely to be considered uneducated by anyone who catches him in errors, and he is likely to be limited in his writing, as he relies on simple but sometimes colorless words in order to be safe in his spelling. Some people are so eye-minded that they learn to spell unconsciously. By the time they have seen a word spelled correctly several times, they know it. Others have to work at spelling, not because they are slow or stupid but because their minds happen not to work in the way that records spelling automatically. But fortunately almost any intelligent person can learn to spell reasonably well if he will work at it. A "bad" speller is usually only a person who does not spell without learning, who has never been properly taught, or who has never tried hard enough to learn, and in an orderly way.

A student who has reached college and still has spelling difficulties can probably progress best by analyzing his individual errors and working systematically on the basis of his analysis. To begin, he needs to find out what words he misspells and, if possible, why he misspells them. He should first make a list of all words he has to look up in the dictionary in order to verify their spellings and of all words he misspells in his writing, indicating any repeated errors.

The lists should be drawn from as much of the student's normal writing as possible. For diagnostic purposes, the lists should record the actual misspellings, but should also include a correction of each error. Diagnosis is likely to reveal that any student's errors tend to be primarily of the same sorts—for instance, that he is careless, that he does not know the conventional letters for English sounds, or that he misspells the same few words over and over. He may find that he consistently makes several types of errors. From his list, however, he can discover which of the following kinds of common difficulties he needs to work at most.

1. *Habitual misspelling.* A student whose list includes mainly repeated mistakes on words like *receive, too, their, separate,* or *loose* for *lose* has a relatively easy problem. He has never learned the small number of common words with difficult spellings. He needs to memorize spellings of these difficult words, perhaps using a list like that in Exercise 26E.

2. *Carelessness.* If a list reveals that a student has spelled a book title four different ways in one paper, has omitted the final *e* in writing *inane,* and has spelled *Hemingway* correctly once but incorrectly twice, the student obviously needs to start being more careful. He may not have known the spelling of the title, but he could have looked it up and spelled it consistently. Even if the slips on *inane* and *Hemingway* got through a first writing, they should have been caught in revision.

3. *Errors in recording sounds.* As indicated in 26-1, spelling records sound, though not always obviously or consistently. The student who finds his lists consistently including errors like *Scananavian* for *Scandinavian, athelete* for *athlete, preform* for *perform, tradegy* for *tragedy, prejudice* for *prejudiced, thing* for *think, quanity* for *quantity, durring* for *during, refered* for *referred* or *wend* for *went* is having trouble with sounds and their spellings. He can correct many of his errors by learning more precise pronunciations—*pronunciation* rather than *pronounciation,* for example. He should study the English sound system and learn which letters are used for which sounds. He should study also the kinds of rules recorded in 26f-h for indicating vowel sounds.

4. *Confusion of similar words.* Words cause trouble when they have the same sound but different meanings—*sight, site,* and *cite; to, too,* and *two; rite, write, right,* and *wright; led* and *lead.* The cure for errors with such groups is to look the homonyms up in a dic-

tionary and learn enough about them to keep them separate. Words not pronounced identically but spelled similarly are confusing, especially if the difference in spelling involves only a transposition or doubling of a letter. The following frequently cause trouble: *angle, angel; casual, causal; chose, choose; lose, loose; desert,dessert; canvas, canvass; accept, except; affect, effect; principle, principal.*

5. *Errors from analogy or etymology.* Spelling by analogy or etymology can be very helpful, but analogies may lead a writer astray, especially if they rest upon false assumptions. One of the most common misspellings is *definate* for *definite*, probably because of the large number of English words ending in *ate*. The misspellings like *pronounciation* and *renounciation* result from the analogy with the corresponding verbs. The spelling *primative* is probably influenced by the more common *primary*. The frequent misspellings *Britian* and *villian* are probably made by false analogy with many English words having *i* and *a* in this sequence, as in *Parisian, gentian, Martian.* Even very accomplished spellers will make occasional errors of this sort, but awareness of the problem helps to solve it, and thorough acquaintance with the word will cure individual difficulties.

6. *Confusion with prefixes and suffixes.* The most numerous words that cause trouble through confusions are those that employ a syllable, often a prefix or a suffix, which can be spelled in several ways, or which differs but slightly from another sylable. Thus, *-ible* is confused with *-able,* and *-ents* with *-ence.* Is it *indistinguished* or *undistinguished, indistinguishable* or *undistinguishable?* Differences in meaning and use offer some help. The suffixes *-ents* and *-ants* are plurals, as in *residents* and *attendants; -ence* and *-ance* are evidences of an abstract noun, as in *residence* and *attendance.* Latin prefixes and suffixes tend to be used with Latin words, Anglo-Saxon affixes with Anglo-Saxon words. Thus we have *unable,* since both *un-* and *-able* come from Anglo-Saxon, against *indigestible,* since *in-, digest,* and *-ible* are Latin, but the rule is by no means consistent, as the confusion mentioned above in connection with words related to *distinguish* will illustrate. Frequently, *-able* follows words which are complete as they stand, whereas *-ible* follows syllables having no meaning without the suffix (*acceptable, marketable,* but *terrible*), even though a silent *e* has been dropped from the word (*drivable*). Some tendencies can be observed, also, in the letters that suffixes follow, but many students find learning the words easier than learning the tendencies and the exceptions. For what the tendencies may be

worth, here are the most common: -*able* usually follows hard *g* or *c* (*applicable*), *i* or *y* in the root word (*justifiable*); -*able* is common in words having a long *a* in a related word (*irritate,* and hence, *irritable*). The suffix -*ible* usually follows soft *c* or *g* (*tangible*), *miss* or *ns* (*sensible*); if the suffix can replace -*ion* in another word, without change of adjacent letters, -*ible* is usual (*perfection,* and hence, *perfectible*). The ending -*ar* is much less common than -*er* or -*or* (*grammar, calendar,* and a few others); -*er* is usual among words coming from Anglo-Saxon if the -*er* indicates a person's temporary or permanent occupation (*teacher, walker*); -*or* is the common ending, especially in words from Latin (*doctor, governor, motor*). Among the prefixes warranting unusual attention are the following:

per-	(meaning *through* as in *perfect,* carried through to the end)	pre-	(meaning *before* as in *prerequisite, predecessor*)
anti-	(meaning *against* as in *antitoxin, anti-Russian*)	ante-	(meaning *before* as in *antebellum, anterior*)
di-	(meaning *twice* as in *dibase, digraph*)	de-	(meaning *from* or *concerning, down* as in *depart, define*)

The endings -*cede,* -*ceed,* and -*sede* cause some confusion. The regular form in English is -*cede* (*concede, precede, recede*). The exceptions can be easily learned; one word ends -*sede* (*supersede*), and three end -*ceed* (*exceed, succeed, proceed,* but not *procedure*).

In modern English, especially in modern American English, all unaccented vowels tend to lose their quality and become a common vowel sound called *schwa,* the sound of the vowel in *the* when *the* is not pronounced like *thee.* Thus, for many American speakers the vowel in the final syllable of *resident* and *attendant* has the same sound, which is the same sound they use for the next to the last vowel sound in *accommodate.* Since one sound is here serving for *e, a,* and *o* (and it can serve, also, for *i, u, y,* and a number of others) phonetics will not help much directly. Indirectly, even in these special problems, however, recognition of the differences between the oral and the written systems of communication help make spelling easier to learn.

Capitalization 26-3

Whether or not we call capitalization a problem in spelling, capitals do help us to identify words. The radio announcer who says, "We shall now listen to an angel recording," seems to be predicting a miracle if we assume he is thinking of a lower-case angel, but if he is thinking of an upper-case angel—"We shall now listen to an Angel recording"—he is merely announcing a record of a particular brand.

Capital, or upper-case, letters were early introduced into the writing system, and they have always marked something important. In medieval manuscripts a big illuminated letter may open a chapter—*capital* and *chapter* are both related to the word *head*—and they have subsequently been used for the beginning of sentences, the beginning of lines of poetry, important words in titles, and the like. Since nouns were thought to be important, they were often capitalized—and still are in German—but in English practice only proper nouns are capitalized. This raises the subtle question, when is a noun a proper noun?

Superficially, the answer is easy: a proper noun is a name. But when does a noun become a name? The definition gives some trouble, not because the main distinctions involved in it are illogical, but because they are subtle enough to require clear thinking. For instance, Mrs. Hardy has a son, whom she names Thomas. Obviously, *Thomas Hardy* is a proper noun, the given name of one particular individual. Thomas Hardy writes some novels set in southwestern England near an imaginary town called Casterbridge. *Casterbridge,* also, is a proper noun. But suppose that a tourist wishes to visit the scenes of these novels, does he visit the Hardy Country or the Hardy country? Similarly, a river is named for Henry Hudson. Is it the Hudson River or the Hudson river? Does it flow through the Hudson River Valley or the Hudson River valley? There is a women's college on the bank of this river; is the president the President of Vassar College, since there is only one such president at a time, or the president of Vassar College, since presidents are of common occurrence? Are the subjects taught in this institution American literature or American Literature, History of the Americas or history of the Americas?

The confusions arise in several ways, but partly because every object on earth exists as an individual. Every pebble on the beach is a separate pebble, but one stone becomes the basis of a proper noun only if it is given a name, Plymouth Rock, for instance. On this basis one can answer the questions in the previous paragraph. The area described in Hardy's novels is the Hardy country, because there is no definite, designated area which has been officially so named, as there is an area officially named Connecticut. For the same reasons, it is Hudson River, but Hudson River valley. The president of Vassar College is president, not President, unless she should sign herself, with her title, which then becomes Mary E. Smith, President of Vassar College. The subjects taught are American literature and history of the Americas, but if these subjects become titles of specific courses, then as titles they would be written American Literature and History of the Americas. The question is not whether the noun is the name of an individual object, being, sort, area, or anything else, but whether the noun is a name given to a particular unit, not shared by other units of its sort.

Words derived from names and closely associated with them are usually capitalized. *American* derives from the name *America,* and although there are many Americans the word is capitalized. On the other hand, proper nouns that have become common nouns are not capitalized. In the early nineteenth century, sample forms for the British army were made out with the name *Thomas Atkins.* Eventually Tommy Atkins became the colloquial name for a British soldier; now *tommy* has become a common noun. Similarly, a Victrola was a trade name of an instrument manufactured by the Victor Company, but the instruments became so common that any record player could be called a *victrola.* Salad dressing made of oil and vinegar is called French dressing, because French cooks developed and popularized it and Americans borrowed it from France, but if salads increase in popularity we may yet put french dressing on them. We use the Bible in church, but the incoming freshman student is expected to study the student handbook, often called the "freshman bible." Thus some words which are proper nouns become common nouns, at least in some usages. If the writer is uncertain whether a proper noun has become common, he should consult a good dictionary.

Italic Type 26-4

Writing systems have generally made use of two styles of letters, those drawn for relatively formal purposes, and those written rapidly in a free-flowing hand. When written letters became the basis of printed letters, both styles were imitated; the formal letters, called *roman,* were made upright, and the informal letters, made slanting, were called *italic.* Both styles were long used for display purposes, but now they are being standardized, and the difference between them provides the writer with a good means of distinguishing some uses. In general, roman type is used as body type, the main type in which a book or magazine is printed; italic type is used for some special use. The following are the most common.

1. Italics may be used for emphasis or contrast, as in "The President's spokesman—*not* the President himself—said you acted like a nincompoop." This device can readily be overworked, and good writers use it only sparingly, many not at all.

2. Italics are used for foreign phrases not yet Anglicized, as in *savoir-vivre, Weltschmerz.*

3. Increasingly, it is used for words out of context, that is, words used for themselves not for their meaning or use in the sentence. In the following sentences—and in this sentence—*hamlet* is used out of context: *hamlet* is a noun. Etymologically, *hamlet* means a little enclosed place. Formerly, words used out of context were placed within quotation marks, and this practice is still acceptable in many style books, but italic type is becoming the standard means of indicating that a word is employed for itself, not for its meaning.

4. Increasingly, also, italic type is used for titles (see 26m). Older practice was to enclose titles within quotation marks, and this style is still in some use, but standard form usually requires that italics be used for all titles referred to in context. A shorter work within a longer work may be distinguished by placing it within quotation marks, as in the following:

Robinson's poem "Mr. Flood's Party" appeared in the volume *Avon's Harvest,* and was reprinted in *Collected Poems.*

For the more complicated citations required in footnotes and bibliographies see 23-10 and 23-11.

Guide to Revision   **26**

When writing for publication, use the publication's style sheet; otherwise, follow accepted standards for manuscript form, correct spelling, and mechanics.

Individual publications, newspapers, or college classes have special requirements for preparation of a paper, but any manuscript, whether submitted for publication, presented as a business report, or prepared to fill a class assignment, should be neat, standard in appearance, and conventional in spelling, capitalization, syllabification, and use of italics, abbreviations, and numbers.

The following rules are standard and fit the requirements of almost any publisher or reader:

1. Typewrite in black or write in black or blue-black ink on one side only of standard size (8½ × 11-inch) paper, unruled for typing, and ruled for handwriting with standard measure ruling, not the narrow ruling sometimes used for notebook paper.

2. Double-space between lines of a typewritten manuscript. Most editors refuse to look at unsolicited copy which is not double- or triple-spaced. Keep typewriter type clean and use a well-inked ribbon.

3. Make handwriting legible, distinguishing clearly between capital and small letters.

4. Leave generous margins on all sides of the paper—at least an inch and a half at the top and the left and an inch at the right and the bottom.

5. Indent about half an inch for each new paragraph—five spaces on the typewriter. In typing, leave one space after internal punctuation, two spaces after end punctuation.

Manuscripts submitted for publication usually carry a notation like the following in the upper right-hand corner of the first page:

> My Years in Jail
> John Doe
> 13 Skidrow Street
> About 92,000 words

Instructors specify requirements for papers submitted in class. Often brief papers are folded lengthwise and endorsed on what would be the front cover if the paper were a book. Longer papers are usually left flat, with information on the outside page. For class papers a notation like the following may be required.

> Mary Edmonton
> English 101, Sec. 24
> Theme VI
> October 10, 1966
> Professor John Hancock

26a   Spelling   Sp a

Spelling errors should be corrected, and the student should learn to read copy carefully on his own writing. But correcting errors is not enough. If a writer has trouble with spelling, he should remedy the cause. Most misspellings involve one of the causes discussed above (see 26-2); the writer is careless, he habitually misspells certain words, or he has one or more of several sorts of misspelling, which can be cured or greatly reduced with a little intelligent attention.

For the first, the solution is obvious—be careful. For the second, also, there are simple cures. Since relatively few words need be learned, they can be memorized. The writer can work from a list, eliminating words he knows. Furthermore, he can take advantage of some of our knowledge of how the mind learns. Anything repeated just before sleep is likely to be remembered in the morning. If the writer reminds himself just before going to sleep that *receive* is spelled *ei,* and does it on three successive nights, he is likely not to misspell it again. Anything repeated at intervals will be learned; a list of a few troublesome words can be repeated before every class, or every night while the writer is undressing. In a short time they will be learned for life, and the card with the list of words can be thrown away. A mnemonic device sometimes helps with particularly troublesome words. For instance, an old schoolboy device distinguishes *principal* and *principle* by suggesting that a high school *principal* might be a *pal* but a geometric *principle* could not. If the writer makes up his own device, it may work, no matter how silly it may sound. Often, learning many details about a word will make it easy to remember. The distinction between *affect* and *effect* is easier for the person who looks up the words in a good dictionary and understands all the differences between them.

Errors of the third sort are often more troublesome, but systematic work will decrease them. A first step is diagnosis of troubles (see 26-2). Some errors can be corrected by learning what are called "spelling rules," although strictly speaking these so-called rules are not rules at all. Those in the sections below have enough application so that anyone who has difficulty spelling should simplify his problem by learning them.

Sp b; Apos   The Apostrophe   **26b**

The apostrophe is used to indicate an omission of one or more letters or figures.

can't, isn't, o'clock, the gold rush of '49

It is used also to indicate omissions in reports of dialectal speech.

"I rec'leck how y'r paw come courtin' like 'twar yestiday," she said.

Avoid overuse of the apostrophe in recording dialect; apostrophes clutter the page and confuse the reader. A writer is usually wise to indicate with an apostrophe only the most noticeable omissions in pronunciation.

Some contractions give especial difficulty because they are readily confused with possessive forms of pronouns which do not require apostrophes. Note the following pairs:

Contractions	*Possessive pronouns*
it's (it is)	its (The cat carried its kittens.)
they're (they are)	their (They ate their lunch.)
you're (you are)	your (Mind your manners.)
who's (who is)	whose (Whose little boy are you?)

Contractions like *I've* and *don't* are not appropriate in formal writing, and are usually avoided in serious informal composition.

ORIGINAL	REVISION
You're supposed to pick it up by the back of it's neck.	(1) You're supposed to pick it up by the back of its neck.
[*The contraction* you're *requires an apostrophe; the possessive pronoun* its *does not.*]	(2) You are supposed to pick it up by the back of its neck.

"I'm go'n' t' d'vide m' w'rk int' a duz'n per'ods," he said.

[*Omission of letters requires apostrophes, but attempts like the above to record every variation in sound confuse more than clarify.*]

"I'm goin' to divide my work into a dozen periods," he said.

[*When dialect pronunciations are roughly the same as standard, they need not be respelled. Usually writers attempt to suggest, not reproduce, dialect.*]

The apostrophe is now most frequently used as a sign of the possessive or genitive case. To show possession in singular nouns and indefinite pronouns, provided possession is not shown by the preposition *of,* add an apostrophe and *s.*

Paul's temper, the cat's tail, anybody's opinion

For plural nouns which end in *s,* add only an apostrophe.

the soldiers' rifles, the schoolgirls' idol

For plural and collective nouns which end with a letter other than *s,* add an apostrophe and *s.*

the people's choice, all men's fate

Proper nouns ending in *s* follow the rule:

Frances's earring, Carl Zeiss's best lens

but may have the extra *s* omitted if it would cause an awkward series of sounds.

Xerxes' army, Moses' code, Keats' or Keats's poems

In compounds, the last part of the compound takes the possessive form.

mother-in-law's visit, anyone else's rights

In words showing joint possession, only the last takes the sign of the possessive.

Germany, France, and England's position; John and Robert's fight

A possessive form for each of two or more compound nouns indicates individual possession.

Harry and Bert's bicycle (they own it together)
Harry's and Bert's troubles (each has troubles of his own)

The apostrophe is often omitted in proper names which have become established.

North State Teachers College, Clayton County Old Folks Home

A few possessive forms, known as double possessives, use both the apostrophe and *of.*

a friend of my father's, a cousin of Ann's

Nouns of specification in time, space, quantity, or value follow the rule for the apostrophe in the possessive.

an hour's walk, a quarter's worth, at their wits' end

Pronouns, including the possessive forms ending *-s* and *-se*— *his, hers, its, ours, yours, theirs,* and *whose*—are used as possessives and do not have apostrophes.

ORIGINAL	REVISION
When June went to Ball State Teacher's College for a years work, she found that the warm wind's there made her hair curl.	When June went to Ball State Teachers College for a year's work, she found that the warm winds there made her hair curl.
[*The apostrophe should be omitted from the proper name.*]	[*Year's, a noun of specification, requires the apostrophe; winds, a plural, does not.*]
The Jones's dog chased the Macks's cat.	The Joneses' dog chased the Macks' cat.
[*The sense indicates that plural possessives are required.*]	[*The apostrophe after the regular plural forms the plural possessive.*]

Sp c; Hy; -   Compounding; Hyphenation   26c

When two words are used together to have a single meaning, they tend to combine in spelling, either as a single word or as a hyphenated word. The following examples illustrate how spelling differences signal differences in meaning:

The redcap wore a red cap.

The old stylebook was an old-style book.
The fairyland lady rented a room and became a fairy landlady.
He threw a big brown stone at the big brownstone.

Notice that in speech we distinguish the uses by stress; we stress the
first syllable of *redcap,* but *cap* in *red cap;* we stress *stone* the first time
it is used in the fourth example but stress the first syllable of *brownstone.* Often we can see a kind of logical need behind the development of compounds. Presumably the black board in the front of a
schoolroom was identified by its color so long that it naturally became a blackboard to distinguish it from any black board that happened to be around. But often no logic of any sort is observable. One
can rationalize that *post office* has remained two words because there
is no other meaning from which it has to be distinguished; but what
of *courthouse?* There are, actually, no consistent principles for spelling compounds, but one or two tendencies in practice are general
enough to be useful.

1. When two words function as an adjective or a verb with a
single meaning, they are regularly hyphenated.

He was only six feet tall, but he made a seven-foot jump.
One twentieth-century innovation was the pay-as-you-go tax plan.
We hot-roll all the metal and double-rivet the joints.
Macbeth was not caught red-handed, but he had a red hand.

Unless a compound adjective is formed from a word that has
already become a single noun (*a backhanded compliment*), it is almost
always hyphenated.

When the first of two modifiers modifies the second, however,
the modifiers are not hyphenated, especially if the first is an *-ly*
adverb.

The widely advertised camera took poor pictures.
The wide-lens camera was easy to operate.

2. With compound nouns, however, practices are much less
consistent, and the dictionary is often necessary.

> *a*) When the second word of a compound noun is stressed, the
> compound is seldom written as a single word (*high water,
> club steak, back road* but *headwaiter.*)
>
> *b*) Compound nouns are hyphenated only in special circum-

stances—especially when the first word of the compound is a possessive (*Dutchman's-breeches*), when the two words indicate parts of a joint idea with neither modifying (*secretary-treasurer*), and when a noun is joined to a word like *out* or *up* (*fade-out, slip-on,* but compare *fallout, breakdown, markup,* and *countdown* or *count-down*).

c) Compound nouns stressed on the first word follow no consistent pattern, except that they tend to combine with continuing use, especially if there is possibility of a confusion of meaning with a noncombined pair of words (*highway, limehouse, mailman, mailboat, iceman, coalbin, gasman;* but compare *garbage man, mail car, ice pick, coal oil, gas mask*).

Alternatives. If there are alternatives for the first element of a hyphenated compound, each of the alternatives may have a hyphen (*eight- and ten-paddle canoes, lower- and middle-income housing*).

Prefixes. Typically prefixes like *mis-, non-, dis-, anti-,* and *pre-* join words with no separation, but in a few circumstances hyphens are common. Hyphens usually separate a prefix ending with a vowel from a word beginning with the same vowel (*pre-eminent, semi-independent, re-elected,* but *co-ordinate* or *coordinate*). Hyphens sometimes separate other prefixes: (a) *ex* when it means former (*ex-president*), (b) a prefix with a proper noun (*anti-Nazi*), (c) most compounds with *self-* (*self-defense, self-taught,* but *selfsame*), (d) a prefix which leads to a combination that might be confused with another word (*re-cover* to distinguish from *recover*).

Numbers. Compound numbers from twenty-one to ninety-nine are hyphenated. A fraction used as a modifier is hyphenated unless one element of it is already a hyphenated compound. Fractions used as nouns are usually not hyphenated.

Twenty-seven cattle, nine hundred and ninety-nine, a four-fifths majority, four fifths of the class, a three-sixteenths drill.

Hyphens are used to join the figures in inclusive dates (*1790-92, 1850-1900*) and to join inclusive figures when these appear in tabular form (*500-1000, 10,001-10,025*).

ORIGINAL	REVISION
The car sank hub deep in the recently-graded road.	The car sank hub-deep in the recently graded road.

ORIGINAL (*Cont.*)

[Recently, *which modifies* graded, *should not be hyphenated.*]

Our slow baked bread has been slowly-baked.

The alloy is rust, weather, and heat-resistant.
[*Alternatives preferably include the hyphen with each alternative.*]

REVISION (*Cont.*)

[Hub-deep *is hyphenated; two words join to form a modifier.*]

Our slow-baked bread has been slowly baked.

The alloy is rust-, weather-, and heat-resistant.

26d   Plurals   Sp d; Pl; Sing

English vocabulary is made up mainly of (1) native words which have come from Old English, and (2) words borrowed from other languages. Roughly speaking, a piece of writing is likely to contain about equal quantities of each, a fact of interest for spelling. Although Old English formed plurals in a variety of ways, most such nouns were reduced eventually to a single system, so that native words generally form their plurals by adding *-s* or *-es*. To form regular plurals, add *s* if the sign of the plural is not pronounced as a separate syllable (*boy, boys; regulation, regulations*); after a consonant, if the sign of the plural is pronounced as a separate syllable, add *es* (*grass, grasses; class, classes*); if the singular ends in *e*, add *s* (*house, houses; bridge, bridges*).

Some few nouns were not regularized in Middle English and retain archaic forms (*ox, oxen; deer, deer; brother, brothers* or *brethren; child, children*). For such words, consult a good dictionary. Words ending in *o* formerly regularly added *es* (*tomato, tomatoes; Negro, Negroes*), but words recently borrowed usually have only the *s* ending in the plural (*radio, radios; banjo, banjos*). Thus words ending in *o* do not follow a reliable rule; exceptions must be learned. For nouns ending in *y*, see 26g. In nouns having a final *f* or an *f* before a final silent *e*, the *f* is often changed to *v* before the sign of the plural (*wife, wives; loaf, loaves*), but there are many exceptions (*sheriff, sheriffs; belief, beliefs*).

Words borrowed from other languages offer special problems. English speakers tend to change words slowly, to keep a word relatively long in the form in which it has been borrowed. Eventually, if the word becomes common, it becomes Anglicized with a normalized plural. The change does not greatly affect the plurals of words from German, French, and Spanish, most of which form plurals with -*s*, but words from Latin and Greek are somewhat complicated because they sometimes retain endings from the complicated classical declensional systems. Latin words ending in *um* usually form the plural by changing the *um* to *a* (*datum, data; agendum, agenda*); *us* is changed to *i* (*focus, foci; cactus, cacti*); *a* is changed to *ae* (*alumna, alumnae*). Foreign words eventually acquire a plural form by analogy with English; that is, the plural ends in -*s* or -*es*. Thus, for a time, there are two current forms; *focuses* is now more common than *foci*. Sometimes foreign plurals are not recognized for what they are, and are treated like singulars. Thus one hears *This data is unreliable*, although *data* is plural and *is* is singular; and one hears *The committee made up its agendas*, although *agenda* is already plural without the *s*. Eventually these blunders may become standard speech (our accepted plural *children* results from a similar blunder), but foreign forms are usually retained in writing.

Numbers, letters, and symbols become plural with the addition of *'s* (*two 2's; a row of x's*). Sometimes apostrophes are also used in the plurals of words spoken of as objects (*if's* and *and's*), but the current tendency is to form these plurals without the apostrophe (*pros and cons, but me no buts*). These are the only plural forms which use the apostrophe.

ORIGINAL	REVISION
High over our heads we saw dozen's of vapor trail's from the plane's. [*The apostrophe is used with possessives, but not with regular plurals.*]	High over our heads we saw dozens of vapor trails from the planes.
Be sure to dot your is and cross your ts. [*Numbers, letters, symbols, figures, and words out of context form the plural with 's.*]	Be sure to dot your *i*'s and cross your *t*'s. [*Notice also that italics show that the letters are used out of context.*]
Mrs. Appleby brought all the little Applebies with her.	Mrs. Appleby brought all the little Applebys with her.

Sp e   Spelling and Sound   26e

Errors in spelling frequently occur in words in which certain sounds are commonly unstressed or indistinct in everyday speech (see 20–4).

ORIGINAL	REVISION
We were suppose to get use to cold food.	We were supposed to get used to cold food.
Another performance would of been a failure.	Another performance would have been a failure.

26f Combinations of *i* and *e*   Sp f

When *i* and *e* are combined to indicate the sound of *e*, the old rhyme reminds us

> Put *i* before *e*
> Except after *c*.

Thus we spell *relieve*, but *receive*. Among exceptions, the most common can be kept in mind by remembering the following sentence: At his *leisure* the *sheik* will *inveigle* and *seize* the *weird* words *either* and *neither*. The standard spelling is *ei* when the symbol represents the sound of *a*, as in *weigh, neighbor*. In a few words having other sounds, *e* precedes *i*, as in *height, foreign, sovereign*.

26g Combinations of *y* with Endings   Sp g

A final *y* regularly changes to *i* before an ending beginning with a vowel (*ally, allies; cry, cries; lucky, luckier*). Exceptions mostly stem from obvious reasons. If *y* is preceded by a vowel, it usually is not changed (*monkey, monkeys; destroy, destroyer*). If the ending begins with *i*, the preceding *y* is not changed (*fly, flying, flies; fry, frying*). Proper nouns ending in *y* add *s* with no other change (*two Marys, all the family of Frys*).

26h Double Consonants, Double Vowels, Final Silent e   Sp h

In general, (1) consonants are doubled only after short vowels; (2) silent *e, o, a, i*, or *y* marks a preceding long vowel (see 26-1). The first part of the rule is complicated by the fact that some consonants are never doubled (*q, v, j, h, w, x*); others are seldom doubled except before an ending (*b, d, g, m, n, r, t*). Some consonants are usually doubled but not always (*f, l, s, c*—double *c* being spelled *ck*). Thus, we spell *cuff, hill, spell, hack, hiss*, BUT, *bed, dog, man, cur, get*. The second part of the rule involves various means of indicating a long vowel (*hoed, hose, speak, cede, read, day, maid*) and the fact that these same indications of a long vowel sometimes stand for a short vowel (*head, dead*). As usual, there are exceptions (*add, axe*).

A final consonant in an accented syllable having a short vowel is regularly doubled before an ending beginning with a vowel (*forgot, forgotten; omit, omitting; hug, hugged; slur, slurred*); in unaccented syllables the consonant is not doubled (*counsel, counseled; benefit, benefited*). Alternate forms (*traveller, travelling*) are often admissible but are discouraged in American spelling, which avoids unnecessary doubling. If the vowel in the syllable is long, a following consonant is not doubled (*ride, riding; eat, eaten*).

Final silent *e* is usually retained before an ending beginning with a consonant (*bore, boredom; love, lovely*) and dropped before an ending beginning with a vowel (*hate, hating; cure, curable*). Most exceptions, fall into patterns. If the final *e* is preceded by a vowel, it is usually dropped regardless, to avoid an awkward sequence of letters (*true, truly; argue, argument*) It may be dropped if it might lead to mispronunciation when retained (*whole, wholly*). If the final *e* is used to indicate that a preceding *c* or *g* has the soft sound, that is, if it occurs before *a, o,* or *u,* it is retained (*notice, noticeable; courage, courageous*). In the United States, however, *judgment* is preferred to *judgement,* since the *d* is sufficient indication that the *g* is soft.

Cap; lc   Capitals **26i**

Capital or upper-case letters have various uses as follows:

1. *The first letter of a proper noun* is capitalized (for proper nouns see 26-3).
2. *Words derived from proper nouns* usually begin with a capital (for exceptions see 26-3).
3. *The first word of a sentence or a line of poetry* begins with a capital letter.
4. *The pronoun I* is capitalized.
5. *References to deity* usually begin with capital letters.

> To God the Father, God the Son,
> And God the Spirit, Three in One.

6. *Initials and abbreviations* often require capitals (for details see 26j).

7. *The first letters of principal words in titles* are capitalized (see 26m).

8. Directions are not capitalized, but if a directional word is used as a proper noun it follows the rule for proper nouns (*the West, the Far East*).

ORIGINAL

During my Second Year in High School, I took American Literature, European History, Mathematics, french, and Home Economics, and a new course entitled social problems.

[*Words like* high school *and* literature *are not proper nouns, even though the writer is thinking of only one school and one literature.*]

I went to the Library and read a copy of the Library.

[*The first* library *is not a proper noun; the second names a magazine and follows the rule for titles (see 26m).*]

In the Autumn the ducks move South out of Canada, and hunting is good in some parts of the west.

[*Names of the seasons are not capitalized.*]

REVISION

During my second year in high school, I took American literature, European history, mathematics, French, and home economics, and a new course entitled Social Problems.

[Social Problems *is capitalized because it is a title given to a course, not a description of the material in the course.*]

I went to the library and read a copy of *The Library*.

[*The revised form makes clear the nature of each* library.]

In the autumn the ducks move south out of Canada, and hunting is good in some parts of the West.

[*Directions as such are not capitalized, but a direction is capitalized as a name.*]

26j   Abbreviation   **Ab**

In general, abbreviations are avoided in writing, except in footnotes, bibliographies, formal lists, compilations of statistics, tables, addresses, and the like. There are a few exceptions: common forms of address when used with proper names (*Mr., Mrs., Messrs., Dr., Jr., Sr., Ph.D., LL.D., D.D., S.J.;* but not *Rev., Sen., Gov., Prof.,* or *Pres.* in formal writing); times of day (*4:00 p.m.* or *4:00* P.M.); *Before Christ* and *Anno Domini* when used with a date (B.C., A.D.); a few common standard abbreviations when used in informal, technical, or business writing (*cf., e.g., no., etc.*); some government agencies (*NLRB, OPA, ICC, OEO*). Except in footnotes, bibliographies, addresses, tables, and the like, the following are spelled out: names of states and countries (*California, United States*); details of publication (*vol-*

ume, page, chapter); addresses (*street, avenue, road*); months and days of the week (*December, Sunday*); business terms (*company, manufactured*); and other words not specifically excepted (*Christmas, mountain, fort, saint*). Contractions (*don't, aren't*) are inappropriate in formal writing. Characters or symbols used for *and* are not acceptable in standard writing.

ORIGINAL

The pol. sci. assign. for Mon. is something about the U.N. meeting in N.Y.

Rev. McIntosh was in charge of the service.
[*The abbreviation is used only in newspaper writing and some informal writing.*]

Sen. Oldham announced a new govt. research grant to be administered by Prof. Jenkins.
[*First names should identify the persons when their names are first mentioned:* Senator John J. Oldham.]

Rome endured from 390 b.c., when it was sacked by the Celts, until 410 a.d., when it was sacked by the Germans.
[A.D. *and* B.C. *are always capitalized. They are conventionally printed in small caps, as in the revision.*]

REVISION

The political science assignment for Monday concerns the United Nations meeting in New York.

(1) The Reverend Mr. McIntosh was in charge of the service.
(2) The Reverend Ira J. McIntosh was in charge of the service.
[*Formally, two styles are acceptable.*]

Senator Oldham announced a new government research grant to be administered by Professor Jenkins.

Rome endured from 390 B.C., when it was sacked by the Celts, until A.D. 410, when it was sacked by the Germans.
[*Note that* A.D. *precedes the date and* B.C. *follows it.*]

Num   Numbers 26k

Numbers which can be expressed in two words are written out in standard writing; thus, all numbers one hundred or below are written out.

Exceptions to this rule are:

1. If several numbers are used in a passage and some of them are large, all of them are written in figures.

On a western highway, one passes through towns marked on the map with populations from zero up. For instance, traveling east on Highway 40, one leaves the San Francisco–Oakland metropolitan area, population 2,783,359; passes through Sacramento, 502,778; Verdi, 256; Mill City, 72; and Toy and Dad Lees, 0, since the Lees have moved.

2. Figures are regularly used in certain standard contexts: for street and room or apartment numbers in addresses (*1238 Ralston Street, 14 West Twenty-third Street*); to designate portions of a book (*Chapter 10, page 371*); for dates (*January 10, 1838*), and for decimals and percentages when using words would become complicated (*3.1416, 57%*).

Figures are not used to begin a sentence, and numbers are not written both as figures and as words, except in legal documents. For hyphenation in numbers see 26c.

ORIGINAL

1938 is remembered in our valley as the snowy year.

[*A figure should not begin a sentence.*]

REVISION

In our valley, we remember 1938 as the snowy year.

[*The sentence is rearranged to avoid the initial figure.*]

The 4 of us moved into a little garden cottage at sixty-two Longfellow Avenue.

The four of us moved into a little garden cottage at 62 Longfellow Avenue.

26l Division of Words Div

A somewhat uneven right-hand margin is preferable to numerous divided words, or words incorrectly divided. In copy to be printed, hyphenation is uncommonly inconvenient, since the printer may not be sure whether the hyphen marks only the end of a line, or the end of a line which breaks a hyphenated word. When necessary, however, words may be divided between syllables. Syllabification is complicated. In general, it follows pronunciation, and consonants attach to the vowels following them (*pa-per, re-gard*); two consonants which represent two sounds go one with each syllable (*mis-ter, har-dy;* but *soph-o-more*); prefixes and suffixes remain syllables by themselves (*ach-ing, ex-alt*), unless modern pronunciation has obscured a suffix (*chil-dren*). Double consonants are separated unless they are the ending of a word with a suffix (*rat-tle, swim-ming,* but *miss-ing*). Words of one syllable cannot be divided. Words should not be divided so that a single letter appears on either line. There are more rules and many exceptions; unless the writer is certain he should consult a good dictionary. When a word is divided, the hyphen appears at the end of the first line, not at the beginning of the second.

Titl Titles 26m

The title of a brief theme or other piece of writing should be centered on the first page, separated from the body of the composition by a blank line if handwritten, and by at least four spaces if typed. Principal words, usually all except articles and short connectives, are capitalized, but a title at the head of a manuscript is not underlined or enclosed in quotation marks. Titles of long manuscripts are placed on a separate title page.

When a title of a book, magazine, newspaper, play, poem, story, or moving picture appears within a manuscript, it should have capital letters to begin all words except prepositions, articles, and conjunctions, and should be underlined to indicate that it would be printed in italics (see 26n; for titles in footnotes and bibliographies, see 23-10 and 23-11). Mechanical limitations sometimes necessitate variations; for example, newspapers tend not to use italics because they complicate typesetting.

Ital Italics 26n

Italic type in printing, indicated in manuscript by single underlining of the words to be italicized, is increasing in popularity and respectability for titles referred to in a manuscript, for all foreign words and phrases not yet Anglicized (see 26-4), for words used out of context, and for words to which special attention is called. For most of these uses, quotation marks were formerly used, and for some of them quotation marks may still be used (see 25i).

Indiscriminate use of italics to emphasize certain words is to be avoided, but italics can be used for emphasis and contrast.

I said he was drunk? No! I said he was *not* drunk.

ORIGINAL	REVISION
Soon, very soon, we shall start for *sunny California*, hoping to have the *time of our lives.*	Soon, very soon, we shall start for sunny California, hoping to have the time of our lives.
[*Overuse of italics for emphasis destroys the emphasis.*]	

After Professor Lovejoy's lecture, it became "de rigueur" to have read "The Road to Xanadu."
[*Italics are preferable.*]

Man is the subject of the sentence.
[*Italics should point to* Man, *used out of context.*]

After Professor Lovejoy's lecture, it became *de rigueur* to have read *The Road to Xanadu.*

Man is the subject of the sentence.

Exercise 26

A. Correct mechanics in the following, noting any uses which would be acceptable in colloquial writing but inappropriate in formal writing.

I've just purchased in a 2nd hand book store a copy of *Appleton's Guide* to the United States for eighteen ninety-two. It's full of entrancing old things, but since for the past 8 or 10 years our Family has gone every Summer to the Adirondack mts., I was particularly interested in the description of those mts. The eds. point out that this section 30 yrs ago "was known even by name only to a few hunters, trappers, and lumbermen," but they're now able to give a detailed description of it. They correctly locate the area between L. Champlain and L. George on the East, and the St. Lawrence R. on the w. They also identify Mt. Marcy as the tallest mt. in the area, giving the measurement as five thousand three hundred thirty-four feet. They concede that this pk. is not so high as the Black Mts. of N.C., nor the White Mts. of N. Hampshire, but they point out that they're interspersed by more than 1000 lakes, the largest of which are more than 20 mls. long. These lakes're said to be infested with Trout weighing 20 lb. or more. Hunting was also A-1; for instance, the hunter could take woodcock from Sept. 1st to April thirtieth, & the fine for shooting game out of Season seems to have been only $25, which by our standards wasn't very high. The Publication also gave instrs. that a "lady's outfit" should include "a short walking-dress, with Turkish drawers fastened tightly with a band at the ankle." Travel in the area was apparently done by boats, built a few ft. long, carried by the guides on their shoulders from lake to lake and from river to river.

B. Correct the faulty use or omission of italics, quotation marks, and capitalization in the following:

Among the curiosities of literature and thought is the career of Lord Monboddo, a Scottish *baronet,* author of a book called Of the Origin and Progress of Language. He believed that human speech came from the speech of animals, and imported an *orangoutang* into scotland, assuming that the animal represented *the infantine state of our species.* The *chimp,* as the animal was called, was presumably a representative of "Pongo pygmaeus" or Simia satyris. Lord Monboddo taught the animal to play the flute, after a fashion, but in Monboddo's words, he *never learned to speak.* The lord patiently tried to teach the animal to say "hungry" and "eat," but without success. The learned Journals of the day, periodicals like the Quarterly Review and Blackwood's Edinburgh Magazine, ridiculed poor Monboddo, publishing articles with titles like Misguided Jurist and *This Monkey Business.* Not until long after the publication of Darwin's Descent of Man did students of modern thought realize that Lord Monboddo had been ahead of his day. Among the milder satirists of the radical jurist was Thomas Love Peacock, who made genial fun of Monboddo and his Orangoutang by inserting into his book Melancourt, a satirical novelette, a certain sir Oran Haut-ton, whose name was of course a pun upon the french haut-ton, that is, high-toned.

C. In the following paragraph, identify the specified forms to fill the blanks:

[plural of *beekeeper*] have long been intrigued by their [possessive plural of *bee*] peculiar habits. A _____ [possessive singular of *beekeeper*] year allows him some _____ [form of *month* indicating extent] leisure, when he is likely to wonder what a _____ [possessive singular of *bee*] mind is like, and spend long _____ [plural of *evening*] reading _____ [possessive singular of *Maeterlinck*] description of the social organization of the _____ [plural form of *bee* in the possessive with *of*] and _____ [possessive singular of *Fabre*] *Entymology,* available in _____ [possessive singular of *Mattos*] translation. Maeterlinck, alone, provides a long _____ [singular form of *evening* indicating extent] reading, or for that matter, several _____ [plural form of *evening* indicating extent] reading, and raises curious questions. Why, for instance, with _____ [possessive singular of *it*] reputation for industry, does a bee spend time on a sunny afternoon in what is called "play," when this time is _____ [appropriate possessive singular of *it*] for the using? The beekeeper was likely to answer, "Why, indeed? _____ [contraction of *they are*] strange _____ [plural of *creature*] and _____ [contraction of *there is*] no accounting for _____ [possessive of *they*] doings." But _____ [plural of *scientist*] work differently. The _____ [possessive singular of *scientist*] method requires the collection and study of _____ [plural of *datum*]; that is, in the case of the _____ [plural form of *bee* for the possessive with *of*], studying them when they are supposed to be at play. On any warm afternoon they can be observed before the hive in a sort of dance in the air, making figures like _____ [plural of *s*] and _____ [plural of *z*]. The beekeeper had assumed a few bees had become tired of industry, and danced around a little to feel better, but the _____ [possessive plural of *scientist*] _____ [plural of *record*] showed that these _____ [plural of *bee*] were returning workers, laden with honey, who with a series of _____ [plural of *signal* used with *of*] were informing their fellow workers where they got the honey. In short, the supposed "play" is the _____ [possessive singular of *bee*] way of giving directions, what might be called *The* _____ [possessive plural of *honeybee,* form suitable for a title] *Daily Market News.*

D. In the passage below italicized words include several compounds. Which should be (1) combined into a single word, (2) hyphenated, or (3) left as they are? For each, decide whether the current form can be determined by the rule or must be sought in a dictionary.

After the second *World War,* a German *displaced person* whom we shall call Hans found himself in a *base hospital* and also in a *semi rigid plaster cast.* He was *thirty one* years old, *brim full* of energy, was *naturally curious,* and had a *North German* horror of waste. He contemplated his cast with a *sadly jaundiced eye.* It was a *hand made* cast, intended to restrict his *inter costal* muscles, and it was *nicely calculated* to hold the *spinal column* while at the same time there was space enough to allow *abdomino thoracic* movement. In fact, by contracting his stomach muscles, Hans could enjoy a *side glimpse* of his own navel. There was enough space, he decided, to allow him to insert a *hen's egg.* He ordered a raw egg for his *mid morning* lunch, and proceeded to transform his cast into the equivalent of a *setting hen,* an *incubator cast,* if you will. That is, he tucked the egg under his cast, and it fitted nicely into his navel so long as he kept his *stomach muscles* contracted. But he was not a *mother hen* by nature. After *one day's* care, he relaxed and smashed the egg. He had the persistence of a *German born* scientist, however; he *back ordered* the egg, and was heard to remark, "I'll *mother hen* one of those things if I have to stay here until I've grown a *hen's nest* in my beard." Three weeks later he *hatched out* a little, downy, *baby chick.* He might, of course, have become a *duck incubator,* too, or started a *turkey flock,* even a whole barn yard, but he remembered that *turkey eggs* require a *five or six week* period, and he did not have room on his bed for a *duck pond.*

E. Dean Thomas Clark Pollock of New York University made an extensive summary of college misspelling, for which he used nearly 600 reports from college teachers, listing 31,375 misspellings, which included 4,482 different misspellings. Two salient facts emerge from this study: most words are misspelled very seldom, and most of the misspellings occur with relatively few words. More than a third of all the words were misspelled only once, but the 27 words misspelled more than 100 times each accounted for 5,097 misspellings; that is, less than 1 per cent of the words were involved in more than 16 per cent of the errors. Similarly, the 417 words misspelled more than 20 times accounted for more than half the misspellings. The moral of all this is that most young people who have trouble with spelling have their trouble with relatively few words, and learning to spell correctly may be easier than they think.

Following are the 308 word groups which account for twenty or more misspellings on Dean Pollock's list, printed in the order of the frequency with which the words were misspelled. They warrant careful study.

their	precede	argument	conscious
they're	referring	arguing	studying
there	success	proceed	varies
two	succeed	procedure	various
too	succession	achieve	category
to	its	achievement	embarrass
receive	it's	controversy	excellent
receiving	privilege	controversial	excellence
exist	environment	all right	grammar
existence	personal	possess	grammatically
existent	personnel	possession	repetition
occur	than	psychology	consistent
occurred	then	psychoanalysis	consistency
occurring	principle	psychopathic	prevalent
occurrence	principal	psychosomatic	intelligence
definite		analyze	intelligent
definitely	choose	analysis	realize
define	chose	equipped	really
separate	choice	equipment	led
separation	perform	affect	loneliness
believe	performance	affective	lonely
belief	similar	rhythm	prefer
occasion	professor	tries	preferred
lose	profession	tried	surprise
losing	necessary	weather	explanation
write	unnecessary	whether	fascinate
writing	began	forty	immediate
writer	begin	fourth	immediately
description	beginner	criticism	interpretation
describe	beginning	criticize	interpret
benefit	control	apparent	thorough
benefited	controlled	sense	
beneficial	controlling		

useful
useless
using
noticeable
noticing
probably
imagine
imaginary
imagination
marriage
prejudice
disastrous
passed
past
acquire
busy
business
Negro
Negroes
among
height
interest
origin
original
conscience
conscientious
accommodate
comparative
decision
decided
experience
prominent
pursue
shining
practical
woman
acquaint
acquaintance
exaggerate
incident
incidentally

effect
government
governor
prepare
recommend
appear
appearance
convenience
convenient
mere
opinion
possible
ridicule
ridiculous
summary
summed
attended
attendant
attendance
coming
difference
different
hero
heroine
heroic
heroes
opportunity
paid
quiet
villain
accept
acceptance
acceptable
accepting
dominant
predominant
foreign
foreigners
independent
independence
particular
technique

transferred
discipline
disciple
humor
humorist
humorous
quantity
accident
accidentally
character
characteristic
characterized
hypocrisy
hypocrite
operate
planned
pleasant
athlete
athletic
challenge
fundamental
fundamentally
liveliest
livelihood
liveliness
lives
philosophy
speech
sponsor
unusual
usually
across
aggressive
article
disappoint
suppose
curiosity
curious
desirability
desire
knowledge

ninety
undoubtedly
optimism
permanent
relieve
religion
together
you're
familiar
suppress
where
whose
author
authority
authoritative
basis
basically
before
conceive
conceivable
consider
considerably
continuous
dependent
extremely
finally
satire
careless
careful
condemn
maintenance
parallel
permit
weird
efficient
efficiency
friendliness
friend
fulfill
piece

temperament
carrying
carried
carries
carrier
happiness
response
further
laboratory
oppose
opponent
propaganda
propagate
therefore
hindrance
approach
approaches
physical
advice
advise
entertain
influential
influence
significance
exercise
involve
leisure
leisurely
sergeant
subtle
Britain
Britannica
completely
dealt
divide
excitable
favorite
interrupt
perceive
persistent
reminisce

suspense
amount
approximate
curriculum
disease
especially
fallacy
financier
financially
meant
politician
political
relative
scene
sophomore
guarantee
guaranteed
huge
indispensable
laid
length
lengthening
mathematics
remember
seize
several
substantial
tendency
whole
accompanying
accompanies
accompanied
accompaniment
hear
here
luxury
moral
morale
morally
phase
playwright

represent
schedule
source
capital
capitalism
certain
certainly
chief
counselor
counsel
council
divine
fictitious
primitive
regard
roommate
story
stories
strength
accustom
forward
pertain
safety
satisfy
satisfied
sentence
theory
theories
tremendous
vacuum
view
accomplish
arouse
arousing
despair
guidance
guiding
ignorance
ignorant
magnificent
magnificence

narrative
obstacle
shepherd
simply
simple
straight
synonymous
themselves
them
amateur
attack
attitude
boundary
clothes
expense
fantasy
fantasies
intellect
irrelevant
laborer
laboriously
labor
later
license
medieval
naturally
noble
peace
sacrifice
strict
symbol
actually
actuality
actual
adolescence
adolescent
against
appreciate
appreciation
experiment

Exercises

field	likeness	mechanics	omit
hungry	likely	medicine	persuade
hungrily	likelihood	medical	those
hunger	magazine	miniature	thought
interfere	maneuver	mischief	tragedy
interference			yield

Glossary of Usage
and Terms

*They're cur'ous talkers i' this country, sir; the gentry's hard work to
hunderstand 'em. I was brought up among the gentry, sir, an' got the
turn o' their tongue when I was a bye. Why, what do you think the folks
about here say for 'heven't you?' the gentry, you know, says 'heven't you'—
well, the people about here says 'hanna yey.' It's what they call the
'dileck' as is spoke hereabout, sir. That's what I've heard Squire
Donnithorne say many a time; 'it's the dileck,' says he.*
— GEORGE ELIOT, *Adam Bede*

The writer constantly makes choices; rhetoric may be described
as a study of linguistic choices—of the bases and effects of selecting
among various possible ways of putting ideas. Grammar contributes
to this kind of study of writing, since its function is to describe the
constructions. This book has been concerned with grammar as it
illumines techniques and problems of writing. A study of usage—
of the customary environments, the social limitations, the special
effects of various expressions—also contributes to a study of writing.
This book has been concerned with usage as it helps determine the
effect of the expressions the writer chooses—in questions of reference and agreement, for example. Special problems of usage, however, and a number of grammatical terms have not been pertinent
to preceding discussions; they are collected in the following Glossary for ready reference.

Varieties of Usage   27-1

The more English spreads throughout the world, the more varied it becomes. In spite of the standardizing influences of modern
communication media, the English of India, of Yorkshire, of Ne-
braska, and of West Australia differ considerably—in pronuncia-

tion, in idiom, in vocabulary. Expressions like "pure English," or "the Queen's English," or even "correct" English have never meant much, and they mean less today. Variations in language habits, in usage, can be classified in many ways, most of them overlapping; the following are some of the most important.

1. *Geographic dialects.* The term *dialect* is used to describe any kind of subdivision—any discernible variant—of a language, but it is especially associated with particular usages common to a region or area. Thus, in America we may speak loosely of a Southern dialect or a New England dialect, and linguistic geographers, investigating precisely, can discover dialectal differences within these areas, such as those that characterize various sorts of speech within a state like Texas. Differences in pronunciation—the vowels in *cow* or *either* or *can't*—and in vocabulary—*poke, sack, bag; skillet, frying pan, spider; earthworm, fishworm, angleworm*—are the most obvious.

2. *Cultural levels.* Differences in usage related to social and cultural relationships may be obvious, but complex and hard to specify—for example, the distinction between the language of the educated and the uneducated. Thus, *Who don't know English* might be called uneducated, *Who doesn't know English* educated. A similar widely used classification distinguishes standard from nonstandard English. Standard English is the language used by educated people, the language that commands respect and esteem, that provides social and professional status. Nonstandard, sometimes called vulgate, characteristic of the uneducated, is in social disrepute, like bad table manners; *ain't* and most double negatives are labeled nonstandard. Other kinds of cultural distinctions may be specialized—the cant of criminals or hobos, the slang of musicians, the shoptalk of railroad workers. Because of social attitudes we also can label some usages as obscene or affected or in poor taste.

Distinctions based on cultural or social levels are obviously difficult to establish, partly because cultural levels in our society are not sharply defined and partly because culture, society, and language are constantly changing. *Ain't* was once in good standing. A quarter of a century ago almost every editor excoriated *contact* as a verb; now the same editors may use the word without a second thought. Is *teen-age* now standard or educated English? One highly respected dictionary does not recognize it at all, and under its spelling gives only a British word meaning "brushwood used for fences and hedges." Meanwhile, other dictionaries enter it as both a noun and a modifier and do not suggest anything wrong with it. In England the word *bloody* is in bad odor, taboo in polite mixed company; in America it means only that something has blood on it.

3. *Functional varieties.* Probably more important, though less likely to stimulate popular controversy, are variations in usage to suit different purposes and different kinds of situations. That is, varieties may be distinguished within standard English. No one of these is "better" than the others, but one may be more appropriate. For example, contractions (*won't, aren't*) are certainly standard English, but they are appropriate in speech and some informal writing and not in formal writing. Three functional varieties are commonly distinguished, although they are only approximations. Formal English has the advantage of wide currency and permanent value; it is used in serious writing—in serious books, quality magazines, official statements. Informal English is more popular, more familiar, employing some devices generally associated with speech, common in newspapers and magazines and books directed to a wide public. Colloquial English is the language of speech, of familiar conversation, but it may also appear in personal letters or other writing intended to be conversational in tone.

Usage and "Correctness"   27-2

The complexity of such variations in language and the uncertainties of linguists in trying to categorize them contribute to the emotionalism that tends to develop around disputes on usage. Faced with the prospect of alternatives in language, usually reasonable people often react violently, either lamenting the seeming chaos and urging that some authority should set us right, or refusing to recognize the reality of variations and aggressively defending their own attitudes on the prepositional purity of *like* or the evils of the split infinitive. In reality, of course, arguments about what is "correct" are likely to be futile. The kinds of variations in language mentioned above, and others like them, are facts; they exist, whether we like it or not. They exist because users of a language change it, adapting it to fit their changing and increasing needs. Immutable standards of "correctness," therefore, even though they might be convenient, are impractical.

It does not follow that usage makes no difference, that anything goes. Usage makes a great deal of difference, but decisions on usage, unfortunately, require more than discovering a rule and following it. Selection among varying usages, like any rhetorical selection, requires the writer to try to anticipate results. Facts about usage—the company an expression usually keeps, the attitudes various kinds of people have toward it, even the emotional reactions it is likely to arouse—are the data, the information, on which the writer acts. He decides to say "I did it" rather than "I done it" because the expressions have different associations, and he wants one set of associations or does not want the other. He can anticipate the effects of each, and he makes his choice accordingly. He would have more trouble deciding whether to say *Two and two is four* or *Two and two are four*. Both versions are common; usage is divided. The writer can only use his best judgment in the light of what he knows about expressions among which he must choose; the more he knows about language, the more appropriate his choices are likely to be.

Writers and speakers, of course, do not think of all alternatives each time they utter a sentence and then consciously choose among them. They write and speak by habit. The practical problem for most students is to develop facility in standard English, especially in the sort of standard English appropriate for formal or some informal writing. This kind of English may not always be familiar, but it is necessary for the serious business of the world, and any student hoping to exert influence on affairs must command it. He needs to use standard English not because other people use it, or because someone has made a rule—any more than a carpenter cuts a board with a saw because other carpenters do or because someone has made a rule about saws. The carpenter uses the saw because it works better than a breadknife. Standard English is necessary because it works better for serious purposes. The following glossary, therefore, lists some common usage problems that should be understood by anyone competent with standard English. It lists also a few grammatical terms which have not been discussed in the text and which may be useful. For usages and terms discussed in the text but not included in the glossary, consult the Index.

a, an • The indefinite article (see *Article*). Sound determines the spelling of the indefinite article. *A* is used before words beginning with a consonant sound, even when a sound like /y/ is spelled with *e* or *u* (*a person, a history, a unit, a European*). *An* is used before words beginning with a vowel sound or a silent *h* (*an elbow, an hour*). Contemporary usage prefers *a* before a pronounced *h*, although *an historian* sometimes still appears.

Absolute construction • Usually composed of a verbal with its subject expressed, an absolute construction functions as a sentence modifier (see 16-3).

She rode on down the highway, *her hair flying in the wind.*

accept, except • To *accept* means "to receive"; *to except* means "to exclude."

He decided to *accept* the bribe.
They agreed to *except* the controversial paragraphs of the motion.

Except is also a function word to indicate an exception.

They all quit *except* Johnny.

Accusative case • See *Objective case.*

actually • Like *really*, frequently overworked as a broad intensifier.

A.D. • Abbreviation of *anno Domini*, "in the year of (our) Lord," used for dates after the birth of Christ when dates A.D. and B.C. could be confused. Being Latin, it preferably precedes the date (A.D. *43*).

ad • Informal shortening of *advertisement*, not appropriate in formal English.

adapt, adept, adopt • To adapt is to adjust, to make suitable.

The children *adapted* their habits to their new home.

Adept means "skilled, proficient."

She is *adept* at typing.

To adopt is to accept or to take as one's own.

The resolution was *adopted.*
He *adopted* the mannerisms of his teacher.

Adjective • Modifiers of nouns and pronouns are called adjectives; for confusion with adverb forms, see 16e and *Adverb;* see also *Comparison of modifiers.*

Adverbs • Modifiers of verbs or modifiers are classed as adverbs. For confusion of adverb and adjective forms, see 16d. The following statements describe some characteristics of adverbs and their relation to adjective forms (see also *Adjective; Comparison of modifiers*).

1. Most single-word adverbs end in *-ly*. Not all adverbs can be so distinguished, but most adverbs were formed by the addition of the word *like* to some other word, usually an adjective. When combinations such as *stormy-like* or *handsome-like* were shortened, they became *stormily* or *hand-*

somely. We now make adverbs by adding *-ly* to almost any modifier. A few adjectives have been formed by adding *-ly* to a noun (*homely, leisurely*).

2. Some adverbs existed in Anglo-Saxon and have survived in their early form; thus the ending *-ly* was not necessary to make adverbs of them (*well, however, down, ahead*).

3. A few words function as either adverbs or adjectives (*better, early, fast, much, more, late*).

4. A few words function informally or colloquially as either adverbs or adjectives, even though *-ly* adverb forms exist and are usually preferred in formal writing or speaking (*cheap* or *cheaply, close* or *closely, deep* or *deeply, even* or *evenly, loud* or *loudly, slow* or *slowly, tight* or *tightly*). Compare:

> It was a *slow* train.
> Go *slow* in this zone.
> You should proceed *slowly* with the reorganization.

5. A few words are frequently confused because of similarities in spelling and meaning.

Adjectives	*Adverbs*
good (kind, agreeable, satisfactory)	*well* (satisfactorily, in a pleasing or desirable manner)
well (fortunate, fitting or proper, in good health)	
real (authentic, genuine)	*really* (actually, in a real manner)
sure (firm, secure, dependable)	*surely* (certainly)
some (in an indefinite amount)	*somewhat* (to a certain extent or degree)

advise, advice • The first is the verb, the second the noun (*I advise you to listen to his advice*).

adviser, advisor • Both spellings are in current use; the *-er* spelling is perhaps more usual.

affect, effect • *Affect* is a verb meaning "influence." *Effect* is usually a noun meaning "result," but it may be a verb meaning "cause" or "bring about."

> The weather does not *affect* her disposition.
> The weather has no *effect* on her disposition.
> The envoys tried to *effect* a compromise.

agenda • In Latin, a plural, meaning "things to be done," with a singular, *agendum.* The word has come in English to mean "a list of things to be done" and has developed its own English plural, *agendas.*

aggravate • Used in formal English to mean "intensify" or "make worse." Used informally in the sense of "annoy" or "provoke."

> *Informal:* The children *aggravated* her.
> *Formal:* The children *annoyed* her.
> *Formal:* The new ointment only *aggravated* the disease.

agree • Idiomatically we agree *with* a person, *to* a proposal, *in* principle, *on* a course of action.

alibi • Formally used only in the legal sense, an indication that a defendant was elsewhere at the time of a crime; informally, "an excuse."

all (of) • Constructions with *all of* followed by a noun can often be made more concise by omission of the *of.* Usually *of* is retained between *all* and a pronoun.

He could not bribe *all of* them with *all* the money in the world.

all right, alright • *Alright* is a common and plausible misspelling for *all right,* but is not accepted in standard usage.

already, all ready • *Already* is a single modifier meaning "before some specified time." In *all ready, all* modifies separately.

The team was *already* on the field. They were *all ready* for the kickoff.

alumnus, alumna • An alumnus is a male graduate; *alumni* is the plural of *alumnus,* and is usually used for groups including both males and females. An alumna is a female graduate; *alumnae* is the plural form of *alumna.* The contraction, *alum,* is not acceptable in standard English.

among, between • The formal distinction that *between* is used of two and *among* of more than two has not been rigidly observed, at least informally.

The men divided the reward *between* Bob and me.
The book records differences *among* [or *between*] synonyms.

amount, number • *Amount* indicates a sum or total mass or bulk. *Number* refers to a group of which individual parts can be counted; it is a collective noun, singular when designating a unit, plural when designating individuals.

A *number* of friends were in the lobby. The *number* of his crimes is astounding. A large *amount* of wheat has been stored.

Analysis • In grammar, analysis is the principle by which relationships within the sentence are revealed by the position of words and by the use of relationship words. English makes great use of analysis in its grammar; thus *to the good girls* is grammatical, but *girls good the to* is not. For analysis in rhetoric, see 6-1, 6-2.

and which, and who • Standard only when the following clause is co-ordinate with a previous clause introduced by *which* or *who.*

Nonstandard: That was the first car I owned, *and which* I expected to cut down for a racer.
Standard: The car, which was the first I ever owned *and which* I expected to cut down for a racer, was . . . .

angle • Currently popular in a number of colloquial expressions, rapidly becoming trite; see 21b.

Slang: He knows all the *angles.* What's the *angle* on this?

Antecedent • A word or construction to which a pronoun or pronominal modifier refers is called its antecedent (see 17-4, 17-6, 17h).

anxious • Formerly restricted in meaning to "apprehensive," "worried"; still sometimes suspect formally in the newer sense of "eager."

Formal: He was eager [not *anxious*] to enter the game.

anybody, any body; anyone, any one • Combine the words to make the pronoun form; separate if the first portion is a modifier.

Anybody may come. *Any body* in the burning ruins. . . .
Anyone could do that. *Any one* infraction of the rule. . . .

anywheres • Nonstandard; omit the *s*.

apt • See *liable*.

area • Overused, usually redundantly, to refer to a subject or discipline.

He was a student *in* [not *in the area of*] agriculture.

around • Informal when used for *about*.

There were *about* [not *around*] a thousand people present.

Articles • *A, an,* and *the* function as determiners to point out nouns (see *a, an; the*).

The, called the *definite article,* often refers to something previously mentioned.

One evening Father remarked casually that we might soon go to see Niagara Falls. Thereafter, for days, all conversations led inevitably to a discussion of what we would do when we went to see *the* Falls.

The often identifies a particular object from others in its class. Compare:

He lost his eye in *an* accident.
He lost his eye in *the* accident I was telling you about.

The can replace a personal pronoun referring to part of the body.

Take the bow in *your* left hand and the bowstring in *your* right.
Take the bow in *the* left hand and the bowstring in *the* right.

Since *the* usually implies a reference to something previously mentioned, its use to introduce a noun new to the context may be confusing.

When we first entered the park, it seemed almost deserted. *A* [not *The*] man was sitting alone on a bench, and a pigeon pecked at a paper cup.

The would suggest that the man had been introduced previously. *The* has some special uses, as in "*the* man in the street," meaning the average person, and some generalized uses: "Take *the* ball in the left hand."

The *indefinite articles a* and *an* have developed from the numeral *one* and retain some of their earlier meaning. Usually they have the force of *any.*

Many noun expressions require no article. Plural nouns including all members of a class usually require no article.

On the whole, *Americans* like *dogs, cats,* and *children.*

Abstract and general nouns usually require no article.

The history of your town is part of the study of *history.*

Evening came down and soon we could see thousands of *stars*. *The night* was clear and bright.

as • Not standard as a substitute for *that* to introduce a noun clause.

I am not sure that I believe you [not *I do not know as I . . .*].

As is often imprecise when it is used as a subordinating conjunction indicating cause; in "As we were sitting on the beach, we had a good view of the race," *as* could mean "while," "when," "because," or "since." The more precise function word is usually preferable. For confusion of *like* and *as,* see *like*.

as to • Especially at the beginning of a sentence *as to* is standard English to emphasize or point out (*As to the recommendations, the less said, the better*). *As to* is usually awkward as a substitute for *about* or *of:*

He spoke to me *about* [not *as to*] the nomination.
He doubted *whether* [not *as to whether*] he should make any promises.

aspect • Overused; see 21b.

at • Redundant in questions with *where* (see *where at*).

athletics • Plural in form, but often considered singular in number.

auto • No longer much used as a colloquial shortening of *automobile; car* is a more common short form.

awful, awfully • Overworked as a vague intensive: *awfully good, awfully bad*. Since the words are overworked, their effectiveness is blunted. In formal English *awful* means "awe-inspiring."

bad • When used as subject complement, sometimes confused with the adverb *badly* (see 16d).

She felt *bad* [not *badly*] all day.

B.C. • Abbreviation of *before Christ,* used to mark dates that could be confused with dates in the Christian era. It appears after the date (*52* B.C.).

be • The verb *be* or *to be* is made up of forms from several older verbs, and is thus irregular. It has the following forms: infinitive, *be;* gerund and present participle, *being;* past participle, *been;* first person present in singular, *am;* second person present, *are* (*art,* used with *thou,* is archaic); third person present singular, *is* (*be* is preferred in relatively formal writing for the subjunctive or imperative: *if that be true; be thou me*); first and third person past singular, *was;* second person past singular and all past plurals, *were. Were* is also used in the subjunctive and conditional moods; see *Mood*.

because • Standard to introduce a modifier, not a noun clause (see 13b).

The reason I ride the elevator is *that* [rather than *because*] I am lazy.
I ride the elevator *because* I am lazy.

being as, beings as • Nonstandard usage for *since* or *because*.

Because [not *being as*] I live here, I know what I am doing.

beside, besides • *Beside* is used as a preposition, meaning "by the side of." *Besides* may be an adverb or preposition, meaning "in addition" or "except."

539

He had to sit *beside* the teacher. It was too late to go to the dance, and *besides* I was tired.

between • See *among.*

blame • Some writers still insist that formally at least "He blamed me for it" must be used rather than "He blamed it on me," but the latter is used widely in educated speech and in some writing. "He put the blame on me" is not.

blond, blonde • The feminine ending *e* of the French word is sometimes retained, with *blonde* used to refer to women; but *blond* is currently used for both sexes, and any distinction is disappearing.

broke • Used to mean "out of money," *broke* is not used formally; *financially embarrassed* as a substitute is trite and affected.

bunch • Overused to mean "group."

A group [not *a bunch*] of students . . . .
A large amount [not *a bunch*] of material . . . .

burst, bust • Standard principal parts are *burst, burst, burst. Bust* or *busted* in the sense of "burst" is nonstandard.

but, hardly, only, scarcely • Negative words not used in standard English with another negative (see *Double negative*).

He *had* [not *didn't have*] but one alternative.
He *knew* [not *didn't know*] only one answer.
I *hardly* [not *don't hardly*] think so.

but that, but what • Used for *that, but that* is redundant and *but what* is nonstandard.

He did not doubt *that* [not *but what* or *but that*] she would finally agree.

can, may • In formal English, *may* refers to permission (*Mother, may I go swimming?*) and *can* to ability (*I can swim across the pool*). Informally, *can* is commonly used for both meanings, and even formally *can* sometimes refers to permission to distinguish from *may* referring to possibility:

I *can* [I have permission to] go swimming.
I *may* [possibly I shall] go swimming.

Cant • English that rests upon the usage in occupations and has never attained common currency is often called cant. It can be very useful, but should be used with caution in formal composition.

Confusing: Give the stiff the gandy.
Clear: Tamp that railroad tie.

can't help but, can't hardly • A double negative (see *but, hardly, only, scarcely*).

I *cannot help thinking* [not *cannot help but think*] she is honest.

case • Overworked in expressions like "in this case" or "in the case of" (see *Jargon*).

Case • As a grammatical concept, case is the way in which nouns and noun substitutes work. Ancestors of English made extensive use of case, and the various cases were revealed by inflectional endings. Most of these endings have now been lost, and their functions have been absorbed by other grammatical devices. The ideas expressed by *at* and *to* in "at the street corner" and "to the campus" would formerly have been expressed by case endings. In the sentence "The coach gave Chuck a chance" we know that *Chuck* is the indirect object, *chance* the direct object because of their positions. Modern English has only two cases in the noun, genitive or possessive (see *Possessive case*) and a general case used for all other purposes. Some of the ancient case system is preserved in various pronouns (see *Pronoun*).

censor, censure, censer • *To censor* means "to examine," especially to examine printed matter for possible objections. *To censure* means "to reprimand" or "to condemn." A censer is a receptacle for incense, especially one used in religious ceremonies.

> Half the story was *censored*. The students condemned their treasurer in a vote of *censure*. Choirboys carried the *censers*.

certain • Redundant in expressions like "this certain person" or "in that certain instance." *Particular* is preferable where *certain* could be ambiguous, meaning either *some* or *reliable* (*certain examples*).

circumstances • Currently misused and overused in jargonic writing; use a more exact expression.

> He was *in great difficulty* [not *in very difficult circumstances*].

cite, sight, site • *To cite* means "to refer to." *Sight* means "view" or "spectacle." A site is a location.

> He *cited* an old legal document. The mountains below were a beautiful *sight*. We visited the *site* of the new building.

claim • Overused; see 21b.

Clause • In the older grammatical statement, any construction which could have been a sentence if it stood alone was called a clause if it was incorporated into a sentence. That is, a clause was any construction including a subject and predicate. Structural linguistics designates most verbal constructions as clauses, even though they do not contain finite verbs. Transformational grammar makes little use of the concept of the clause, but all kernel sentences and many transforms could be clauses. See 12-2, 12-3.

Clichés • See *Trite expressions*.

Collective noun • A collective noun indicates more than one (*a committee of citizens, an army of ants*). For agreement involving collective nouns, see 17h.

Colloquial • Derived from the Latin verb meaning "speak," *colloquial* refers to the functional variety of standard English mainly appropriate to conversation. The label is sometimes confused with *localism,* to which it is unrelated, and is sometimes mistakenly thought to designate nonstandard usages. It marks an expression appropriate in conversation but not in formal and some informal writing.

Comparison of modifiers • We recognize three degrees of modifiers, as follows: positive, implying no comparison (*fast car, beautifully landscaped*); comparative, implying that one exceeds another (*The boulevard is a faster street than the highway and is more beautifully landscaped.*); and the superlative, which implies the highest degree, at least within certain limitations (*The boulevard is the fastest road out of town, and the most beautifully landscaped*).

Modifiers are compared in two ways.

	Positive	*Comparative*	*Superlative*
Short adjectives	red	redder	reddest
	short	shorter	shortest
	greedy	greedier	greediest
	homely	homelier	homeliest
Long adjectives	beautiful	more beautiful	most beautiful
	superficial	more superficial	most superficial
Adverbs	slow	slower	slowest
	rapidly	more rapidly	most rapidly
	beautifully	more beautifully	most beautifully
	superficially	more superficially	most superficially

Short adjectives (all adjectives of one syllable and most adjectives of two syllables) and a few adverbs (especially those not ending in -*ly*) are compared by adding -*er* in the comparative and -*est* in the superlative. All long adjectives and most adverbs are compared by preceding the positive form with *more* and *most*. Adjectives of two syllables can be compared either way, and the distinctions are too subtle to be described by rule. The same person might say

He is *stupider* than an ox.

but write

I never saw a *more stupid boy*.

A few modifiers retain irregular forms.

Positive	*Comparative*	*Superlative*
good	better	best
well	better	best
bad	worse	worst
little	less	least
much	more	most
many	more	most
far	farther	farthest
far	further	furthest

complected • A nonstandard substitute for *complexioned.*

She was *light complexioned* [not *light complected*].

Complete sentence • A sentence used to be defined as "a complete thought," although no thought is complete, even though the author takes a whole book to explain it. A sentence is often called complete if it has a subject, a verb, and a complement if one is needed (see Section 12).

conscience, conscious • *Conscience* is a noun referring to a sense of rightness. *Conscious* is an adjective meaning "awake" or "aware" or "active mentally."

Let your *conscience* be your guide. I was not *conscious* of his fear.

'*contact* • Overworked as a verb synonym for *talk with, telephone, ask about, advise, inform, query, write to, call upon.*

continue on • Redundant as a verb with a separable suffix; omit *on.*

Contractions • Like other colloquial locutions, contractions are standard for intimate or nonchalant relationships. They have developed because they are convenient aids to speech, easy to pronounce, but they are not appropriate to formal writing (see *don't, its*).

Formal: We *do not* [not *don't*] as yet have accurate relative heights for the tallest mountains, partly because mountaineers *have not* [not *haven't*] agreed on a uniform method of measurement.

could of • Sometimes, because of its sound, mistakenly written for *could have.*

He *could have* [not *could of*] looked up the word in the dictionary.

council, counsel, consul • *Council* means "advisory board" or "group." *Counsel* means "advice" or, especially in law, "the man who gives advice." A consul is a government official.

He was elected to the administrative *council.* The dean's *counsel* always made sense. He was American *consul* in Brazil.

couple • Nonstandard as a modifier meaning "two" or "about two"; sometimes used informally followed by *of* (*a couple of people*).

I gave him *two* [rather than *a couple*] dollars.

cute • Overworked colloquially as a vague way of expressing approval.

He was an *attractive* [or *charming* or *pleasant* or *handsome* rather than *cute*] boy.

data • Originally the plural form of Latin *datum*, often considered singular in colloquial usage, but still plural in formal English. *Strata* and *phenomena* are plurals of the same sort.

Formal: These [not *this*] data *confirm* [not *confirms*] the theory.

date • A useful colloquialism, rapidly becoming standard, meaning "appointment" or "to make an appointment," or "the person with whom an appointment is made," especially if the appointment is social and with a person of the opposite sex.

deal • Currently overworked as a vague slang term for any transaction or arrangement or situation. A more specific term is preferable. *Great deal* is loosely used as an equivalent of *many.*

definite, definitely • Overworked as vague intensifiers in expressions like "a definitely fine party."

Dependent clause • See *Subordinate clause.*

Determiner • Articles (*a, an, the*) and some other words like numerals (*forty*, in *forty old golf balls*) are now often called determiners rather than modifiers or adjectives.

different from, different than • *From* is idiomatic when a preposition is required; *than* introduces a clause.

Direct object • Transitive verbs require objects, of which the most common is the direct object; in "Karen likes pizza," *pizza* is a direct object (see 12-6).

disregardless • Nonstandard; use *regardless.*

do • An extremely useful verb sometimes carelessly used in idioms in which it cannot function (see 15b).

Everyone has an ambition he wants to *fulfill* [rather than *do*].

don't • Contraction of *do not,* not standard after *it, he, she,* or a singular noun.

It *does not* [or *doesn't* in conversation, not *don't*] seem wise.

Double negative • Although a double negative is conceived in some languages as a device for enforcing the negative sense, two negatives are not used in the same negative statement in modern standard English.

We *did* [not *didn't do*] nothing wrong.
We did not see *anybody* [not *nobody*] on the pier.

Two negatives are used in the same statement in English to give varying emphasis to a positive idea.

It was *not impossible* to see their meaning. I was *not* totally *unimpressed.*

doubt • *Doubt that* implies a negative; *doubt whether* (informally *doubt if*) assumes that there is room for doubt.

I *doubt that* he will come [presumably he will not].
I *doubt whether* he will come [probably he will not, but he may].

due to • Like *owing to* or *on account of, due to* is originally an adjective modifier (*The delay was due to the icy roads*). Its use adverbially is not generally accepted as standard English, although it has long been common in introductory adverbial phrases (*Due to unavoidable circumstances, the delivery has been delayed*). *Because of* is the preferable adverbial idiom.

Because of [not *due to*] the icy roads, the bus was late.

each other, one another • Some careful writers distinguish, using *each other* to refer to only two and *one another* to refer to more than two.

effect • See *affect.*

either, neither • Usually singular in number (see 17h, 17i) and used to designate one of two, not one of more than two (see also *each other*).

Any [not *either*] of the three books has the information.

enthuse • Colloquial but overworked for *be enthusiastic* or *make enthusiastic*.

equally as • A wordy confusion of *as good as* and *equally*.

My cake was *as good as* Sue's. The cakes were *equally* [not *equally as*] good.

etc. • Abbreviation for *et cetera* meaning "and so forth" or "and the like," appropriate only when statistics or lists justify abbreviations. *And etc.* is redundant; *et* means "and."

exactly • Currently popular as a meaningless word. The person who asks "Exactly what is poetry?" probably does not want to be told "exactly," even if he could be.

except • See *accept*.

expect • Colloquial in the sense of "suppose" or "suspect."

I *suppose* [not *expect*] that his paper is finished.

Expletive construction • Expletive constructions employ an expletive to fill the subject slot in the sentence pattern (see 14a).

extra • Nonstandard in the sense of "unusually."

The coffee was *unusually* [not *extra*] good.

fact, the fact that • Often overused as a roundabout way of saying *that*.

He was aware *that* [not *of the fact that*] everybody disliked his plan.

factor • See 21d.

famed • Used for *famous* or *well known*, *famed* usually suggests journalese or amateur writing.

farther, further • A distinction, not universally made, prefers *farther* as the comparative form of *far* in expressions involving space, and *further* to mean "in addition." Modern dictionaries recognize the interchangeable use of the two words.

feature • Used to mean "emphasize" or "give prominence to," *feature* is becoming standard usage, but the word has been so overworked in this sense by journalists and press agents that it bears watching. In expressions like "Can you feature that?" the word is slang.

fellow • Colloquial when used as a synonym for *man, friend, person, individual*.

fewer, less • *Fewer* is used in distinctions involving numbers of individuals, *less* in relation to value, degree, or quantity.

There were *fewer* than ten students. The receipts were *less* than the expenditures.

field • Overworked and often redundant when used to refer to a realm of knowledge or subject.

He was an expert *in* [not *in the field of*] chemistry.

figure • Colloquial for *think, expect, suppose, conclude, believe*.

I did not *expect* [not *figure*] the course to be difficult.

fine • Nonstandard as an adverb.

She sang *well* [not *fine* or *just fine*].

fix • In standard English a verb meaning "make fast" and, more recently, "repair." The word is nonstandard as a noun meaning "predicament" and as a verb meaning "intend" or "prepare" (*I was fixing to go*).

folks • Colloquial for *people* or *relatives*.

Form • The word *form* can be confusing in modern grammar, since it has been used differently by the newer and older grammarians. In the older terminology *form* designated the makeup of a locution, its spelling or pronunciation. Thus *sang* and *sung* would be forms of *sing*. Many grammarians now use *form* to designate anything that differs from other linguistic units; *sing, sang,* and *sung* are three different forms (see *Form class*).

Form class • A term used in some modern grammatical statements to designate a set of words which can appear in the same position or slot in a given construction. Thus, all the words which could appear in the blank in constructions like *The ———— walked* belong to the same form class, have *privilege of occurrence* (which see) in the same position. Obviously many individual words belong to more than one form class. Major form classes are roughly equivalent to parts of speech.

formally, formerly • *Formally* means "in a formal manner"; *formerly* means "previously."

We had to dress *formally* for the party. She was *formerly* a singer.

Functional shift • In English many words shift readily from one use or function in the sentence to another. *Cow* is regularly classified as a noun, but consider the following:

The principal thought he could *cow* the rebellious students.
The road to the old mine was little more than a *cow* path.

In the first sentence *cow* is a verb, in the second a modifier. The word *fast* can function in several ways (*It was a fast trip; we fast during Lent; he ran fast; they broke their fast Sunday*).

funny • Overused and imprecise as a synonym for *strange, odd, unusual, perplexed*. A more exact word is preferable.

Generative grammar • A generative grammar is one that attempts to formulate the rules whereby sentences can be created in oral or written language. In modern English, the most extensively studied generative grammar is called transformational or transform grammar (which see).

Genitive case • See *Possessive case*.

Gerund • A verb form having some nominal use and ending in *-ing* (see 12–5).

get, got • Useful verbs and the basis of many standard idioms, but also used in many colloquial and slang expressions (*The song gets me; the pain got him in the back; better get wise*). Used to mean "must" or "ought to," *got* is colloquial and usually redundant.

We *must* [or *have to,* not *have got to*] finish by evening.

good • An adjective, not to be confused with *well,* the corresponding adverb.

The car runs *well* [not *good* or *pretty good*].

good and • Nonstandard as an intensive.

He was *very* [not *good and*] angry.

gotten • Alternative form for *got* as past participle for the verb *get.*

guess • Dictionaries record *guess* in the sense of "believe," "suppose," "think," but some writers restrict it to colloquial usage.

Hackneyed expressions • See *Trite expressions.*

had of • Nonstandard for *had* (see also *could of*).

I wish he *had* [not *had of*] told me.

had ought, didn't ought, hadn't ought • Nonstandard redundant forms for *ought* or *should.*

He *ought not* [or *should not,* not *hadn't ought to*] say that.

hang • Principal parts of the verb are *hang, hung, hung,* but to refer to death by hanging, they are *hang, hanged, hanged* in formal English.

We *hung* the new picture. The murderer was *hanged.*

hardly • See *but, hardly,* etc.

he or she • The combination is not usual as an equivalent for *one. He,* alone, is usually preferred.

healthful, healthy • A distinction gradually breaking down restricts *healthful* to mean "conducive to health" and *healthy* to mean "possessing health."

heap, heaps • Not common in standard written English in the sense of "a great deal."

heighth • Common misspelling for *height.*

hisself • Nonstandard for *himself.*

honorable • Used as a title of respect, mainly for people holding a political office. It is usually preceded by *the* and used only with a full name (*The Honorable John H. Jones* or *The Honorable Mr. Jones,* not *Honorable Jones* or *the Hon. Jones*).

human • Originally an adjective, *human* is now often used as a noun meaning "human being."

humor • Like almost anything else, wordiness can be turned to humor. The American pioneer was amused by a word he devised, *segastuate,* by which he meant "walk." In place of "Someone had jimmied the kitchen window," the following might conceivably be amusing: "It became apparent a party or parties unknown had gained entrance to the culinary regions by means of that instrument of ingress commonly known as a 'jimmy.'"

Usually, however, the use of circumlocutions in the hope that overblown words will be funny leads only to boredom. A writer should use the device with the greatest caution.

> *Wordy:* Tuneful canines, when you hear them yodeling their native woodnotes wild in the dead of night, remind one of the gentlemen of the press; to put it mildly they can sound like the last trumpet on the day of judgment.
> *Concise:* Dogs are born journalists; their voices are like extras of dismay.
>
> —*Christopher Morley*

IC cut • Structural linguistics works in part by what are called IC cuts (Immediate Constituent cuts). By this procedure, a piece of language is cut into its immediate constituents, the parts which comprise it (see pp. 187–88).

idea • A handy word which careless writers readily overuse. A more exact word is often preferable.

> My *purpose* [not my *idea*] is to become a nurse.
> The *theme* [not the *idea*] of the book is that crime never pays.

Idiom • Idiom is the result of custom in language. Usually it is logical, though not always; but to use the language a writer must learn idioms, whether they are logical or illogical. Native speakers have learned most idioms unconsciously, but writers with poor linguistic backgrounds have trouble. Furthermore, many idioms have become common only in nonstandard English; some are listed in this Glossary.

if, whether • *If* implies uncertainty; *whether* implies an alternative.

> *If* he will trust me, I shall tell him. I shall tell him, *whether* or not he believes me.

If is not used with *regardless.*

> *Even though* [not *regardless if*] he is a doctor. . . .

imply, infer • To imply is to suggest a meaning; to infer is to draw a conclusion from evidence.

> The attorney *implied* that the witness was lying.
> The jury *inferred* that the attorney was trying to discredit the witness.

in, into • *In* implies rest or motion within a restricted area; *into* is preferable to indicate motion from the outside to the inside.

> She lives *in* town. We drove *into* town.

in back of • Redundant; prefer *behind.*

in regards to • Nonstandard; use *in regard to.*

Incomplete sentence • Sentences are not easy to define (see *Complete sentence*), and to write them one need not be able to define them, but the term is often used for sentences left carelessly incomplete (see Section 12).

Independent clause • Any structure that could be a sentence and is incorporated into a sentence without being made subordinate is called an independent clause. All clauses not subordinated are conceived to be independent; see *Subordinate clause* and Section 12.

Indirect object • An object complement (see 12-6), usually in sentences involving asking, telling, giving and the like, specifying what receives the direct object.

Tam gave his nag [indirect object] a dig [direct object] in the ribs.
She told him [indirect object] the truth [direct object].

Indirect question • Indirect questions usually convert a direct question into a noun clause complement, frequently introduced by *whether*.

Direct: Mrs. Howard asked, "Are the others ready?"
Indirect: Mrs. Howard asked whether the others were ready.

Using the direct pattern in an indirect construction is not standard in written English

He asked *whether I was* [not *was I*] coming.

For verbs in indirect questions, see *Tense*.

individual • Loosely used, and often overused, as a synonym for *person;* best used as a noun to emphasize that persons are separate and unique.

Students are not merely names in a card file; they are *individuals*

infer • See *imply*.

inferior than • Nonstandard; use *inferior to*.

Infinitive • A basic verb form, the form in which verbs are entered in dictionaries and other formal lists (see 12-5).

Inflection • Inflection is the grammatical principle through which relations within the sentence are revealed by a change of form in a locution. Thus *sings*, *sang*, and *sung* are inflected forms of the verb *sing; he, his,* and *him* are inflected forms of the third person singular masculine personal pronoun. Languages which are ancestors of English made much use of inflection, but modern English grammar uses it but little; see pp. 184–85.

ingenious, ingenuous • *Ingenious* means "having or giving evidence of resourceful intelligence." It can be used of either persons (*an ingenious strategist*) or things (*an ingenious device*). *Ingenuous* means "naïvely frank." It is used only of persons and of things closely associated with them (*an ingenuous proposal*).

inside of • Redundant as a compound preposition; omit *of*.

Intensifier • Words like *very*, and sometimes words like *deeply* (*I am very sorry; he is deeply concerned*), which are often called adverbs, are now increasingly called intensifiers, since they intensify but do not much modify.

invite • A verb. Not acceptable as a substitute for *invitation*.

I asked Joe for an *invitation* [not an *invite*] to the dance.

irregardless • Nonstandard; use *regardless*.

it • Usually to be avoided in impersonal constructions, especially in locutions like "It says in the book . . .," in which *it* seems to have an antecedent but does not (see 17e).

its, it's • *Its* is the possessive form of *it*. *It's* is the contraction of *it is*.

Jargon, journalese • Jargon is vague writing using blanket terms (see 21-b), but it is notable in that the writer of jargon uses more words than he needs, apparently pleased with himself because the large, pompous words fill so many pages. He is not concerned with making the words say much. The writer of jargon says *the field of mathematics* rather than *mathematics, difficult in character or nature* rather than *difficult, in an intoxicated condition* rather than *drunk*. Favorite words of the jargon fancier include *case, factor, character, circumstances, conditions, situation, picture, line, persuasion, level, variety, degree, type, outstanding, worthwhile.*

> *Jargonic:* In the case of Jim, it was apparent that his condition was of a serious nature.
>
> *Revision:* Jim was seriously ill.
>
> *Jargonic:* There were several instances where Hamlet could have put the quietus on the King, but he failed to come through because the situations were not applicable to the circumstances in his case.
>
> *Revision:* On several occasions Hamlet could have taken revenge, but he wanted to kill Claudius in some act which would assure the King's going to hell.

A particular sort of jargonic writing has long been known as journalese because it reveals the flamboyant, careless superficiality which is characteristic of cheap journalism, though not of good newspaper writing. Avoid it by refusing to use words just to make an impression, by thinking clearly, and by endeavoring to say exactly what you think.

> *Journalese:* A new edition of State University hoopsters is slated to make its debut Saturday night to lift the curtain on the current hardwood season.
>
> *Revision:* State University's basketball team will play its first game of the season Saturday night.

Juncture • In phonemic analysis, *juncture* is the term for a pause and all that goes with it. Sets of symbols to reveal juncture are not standard at this writing, but one common system uses cross or plus juncture / + / or nothing between words, bar juncture / | / to indicate breaks often marked in punctuation by a comma, double bar / ‖ / or sustained / — / juncture for important breaks within a sentence, and double cross / # / or terminal juncture to close a sentence. Some systems use rising, horizontal, and falling lines. Junctures are suprasegmental phonemes, and thus indications of juncture are placed within slant lines, which are used to mark phonemes.

Kernel sentence • In transformational grammar a kernel sentence is a basic pattern from which all structures can be derived (see 12-1).

kind, sort • Singular words, which formally can be modified only by singular demonstrative adjectives, *this* or *that*. Plural forms, *those kinds* or *these sorts,* are used, and colloquially *kind* and *sort* are commonly treated as if they were plural (*these kind*).

kind of, kind of a • Colloquial as the equivalent of *somewhat, rather.*

lay • For confusion of forms of *lay* and *lie,* see *lie.*

lead, led • *Lead* is the present tense of the verb. Because of the identical pronunciation, the past tense, *led,* is often misspelled *lead,* the name of the metal.

He *led* [not *lead*] the horse to water.

less • See *fewer.*

let, leave • Both are common in a few idioms (*leave,* or *let it alone*), but in other idioms, especially when the verb carries a sense of permission, *let* is standard.

Let [not *leave*] them stay.
Let us [or *let's* not *leave us*] go soon.

liable, apt, likely • Interchangeable informally, but often distinguished in careful writing.

She is not *likely* [rather than *liable* or *apt*] to tell her teacher.

Strictly, *liable* means "responsible for" or "subject to."

He is *liable* for the damage he caused.

Apt means "has an aptitude for."

Marie is an *apt* pupil.

lie, lay • Three pairs of similar verbs have been so thoroughly confused in dialect and nonstandard usage that many people have trouble distinguishing between them in meaning and spelling, particularly in their uses with separable suffixes.

Lie (*lay, lain*), intransitive, but usually modified or combined with a suffix like *down,* indicates that the subject occupies a position.

The book *lies* on the table.
The book *lay* on the table yesterday.
The book *has lain* on the table in the past.

Lay (*laid, laid*), transitive except for a few special uses (*The hens lay well; lay on, Macduff*), means *place* or *put* and now appears mainly in a variety of special contexts (see a dictionary).

He *lays* brick in his spare time.
The men *laid* their plans carefully.
The soldiers *have laid* down their arms.

Sit (*sat, sat*), intransitive except for a few uses, especially with suffixes like *out* or *with* (*She sat out the dance; she sits a horse gracefully*), indicates that the subject occupies a place or seat or is in a sitting position.

He *sits* by the window.
He *sat* by the window last week.
He *has sat* there for a year.

Set (*set, set*), transitive except for a few uses (*The sun sets in the west; the hens are setting*), means *place* or *put,* often varied in combinations with words like *off, up, by.*

He *sets* the lamp on the table.

They *set up* the new organization yesterday.
Finally they *have set out* on their journey.

Rise (*rose, risen*), intransitive, often combined with suffixes like *up*, indicates that the subject moves.

He *rises* before dawn.
He *rose* before dawn yesterday.
He *has never risen* before dawn in his life.

Raise (*raised, raised*), usually transitive (but *John opened the betting, and Tom raised*), indicates that the subject acts on something, making it rise or appear.

He *raises* his hand when he wants to talk.
The committee *raised* a new issue.
His salary *has* not *been raised* for a year.

Notice the following:

Her clothes were *lying* [not *laying*] on the bed.
We decided just to *lie* [not *lay*] around on the beach.
The citizens *rose* [not *raised*] up in rebellion.

like, as • In formal written English *like* is used only as a preposition (*He ran like a deer*), and *as* and *as if* are conjunctions (*He ran as if he had seen a ghost*). Informally, however, with impetus from television advertising (. . . *like a cigarette should*), the distinction is disappearing (*He looks like he could use some sleep*). The confusion has perhaps aggravated a tendency to over-correction, misusing *as* as a preposition (*He ran as a deer*). Sometimes the distinction is useful to specify meanings; compare "He slipped into the house as a thief" and "He slipped into the house like a thief" or "He cried as a baby" and "He cried like a baby." In general, college writing requires limiting the words to their formal functions.

As [not *like*] I said, the meeting is canceled.

line • Jargonic or slang or redundant in certain current uses.

He sells books [not *Selling books is his line*].
I want to buy something *similar to* [not *along the lines of*] the dress in the window.
He was *deceiving her* [not *handing her a line*].

literally • An antonym, not a synonym of *figuratively*. The student who wrote, "I was literally dead when I got in," did not say what he probably meant.

loan • Now generally accepted as a synonym of *lend;* many careful writers, however, use *loan* only as a noun and prefer *lend* as a verb.

locate • Provincial as a synonym for *remember* or *take up residence*.

lot(s) of • Colloquial as a synonym for *many*.

love • Imprecise and sometimes affected as a synonym for *like*.

mad • Colloquial in the sense of "angry." Use *angry* or a more exact word like *vexed, furious, annoyed*.

Mass noun • A mass noun refers to a quantity (*a bushel of corn, a portfolio of stocks*) but is singular in form and in use. That is, it requires a singular verb unless it is itself plural (*bushel . . . was; bushels . . . were*).

math • Clipped form of *mathematics,* not appropriate in formal writing.

might of • Use *might have* (see *could of*).

mighty • As a synonym for *very,* not acceptable in formal English, although common in speech in certain areas.

She was a *very* [not *mighty*] pretty girl.

Mood • English verbs can express mood: the indicative mood states a fact, the interrogative asks a question, the imperative issues a command, the conditional marks conditions, the subjunctive expresses uncertainty, supposition, or desire. Usually auxiliary verbs indicate mood; most special forms have disappeared, but a few special subjunctive forms survive in formal usage at least, mainly in the following situations: (1) in main clauses to express a wish (*The Lord be with you*); (2) in *if*-clauses expressing a so-called "condition contrary to fact," that is, a supposition that is impossible or thought to be improbable (*If I were he, I would quit*); (3) in *that*-clauses expressing a wish, command, or request (*The major ordered that the prisoners be held for interrogation*). In formal uses the present subjunctive is sometimes used in *if*-clauses which are not contrary to fact (*If these data be verifiable, the hypothesis becomes untenable*).

The special forms for the subjunctive which survive are two: (1) the third person present subjunctive singular does not have the ending *-s* or *-es* (indicative, *he proves;* subjunctive, *if he prove*); (2) for the verb *to be,* the present singular subjunctive form is *be,* the past singular subjunctive form *were.*

If my brother *were* [not *was*] here, you would behave.
If I *were* [not *was*] you, I would tell the truth.
If I *had known* [not *would have known*] you were coming, I would have cleaned the house.

moral, morale • *Moral* is a modifier, concerning the preference of right over wrong; *morale* is a noun suggesting good spirits and a healthy attitude.

George Washington was a *moral* man. The victory improved the soldier's *morale.*

more than one • Logically plural, sanctioned by custom as singular except when the meaning clearly requires a plural verb.

More than one man is eager to marry her. If there are *more than one* apiece, they should be divided equally.

Morpheme • A morpheme is a working unit of language. A morpheme may be the same as a word; *boy* is a word, and it is also a morpheme, written in phonemics /bɔi/. *Boys,* however, is two morphemes, since the sound represented by *-s* in spelling and by /z/ in phonemics is a working unit of the language, indicating plural.

most • Nonstandard as a synonym for *almost.*

I am home *almost* [not *most*] every evening.

muchly • Nonstandard; use *much.*

must • Currently overworked as a noun.

myself • Perhaps to avoid choosing between *I* and *me,* or from sense of modesty, some speakers use the reflexive rather than the personal pronoun, but the form is not standard in formal writing.

Henry and *I* [not *myself*] decided to remodel the boat.
They invited Anne and *me* [not *myself*] to the luncheon.

nature • Jargonic in certain current wordy expressions (see Jargon).

The job was *difficult* [not *of a difficult nature*].

neither • Used of two; see *either.*

neither . . . nor • Used as correlatives.

She could *neither* set up her experiment *nor* [not *or*] conduct it.

nice • Colloquial as a synonym for *affable, agreeable, amiable, congenial, considerate,* and so on through the alphabet. Prefer a more exact word. Carefully used, *nice* means "precise," "exact," "discriminating."

nice and • Colloquial as an intensive.

The coffee was *pleasantly* [not *nice and*] hot.

Nominative case • See *Subjective case.*

none • As a subject, *none* takes a singular or plural verb depending upon the meaning intended.

not . . . as • Some writers on usage have objected to this construction. They prefer

He is *not so* [rather than *not as*] dull as his younger brother.

Either construction is now generally considered acceptable.

Noun • The older definition was that a noun is "the name of a person, place, or thing." This statement is too loose for close grammatical analysis; is *red,* which is the name of a thing, a noun or an adjective? *Running* could be called an action word and *perseverance* a quality, but they may work like nouns. Modern students prefer to say that a noun is the sort of word that can serve as a subject, or that a noun is the kind of word that can serve as head word in a construction like "the little old man," or that a noun is the kind of word that takes *-s* or *-es* in the plural. There are some exceptions (*child, children; deer, deer*); see *Proper noun.*

Noun as modifier • English words adapt readily to different functions (see *Functional shift*), and words that are usually nouns often modify (*rock garden, city jail, Sunday supper*). Excessive conversion, however, can muddy prose:

He applied to *the office of the committee for price stabilization* [rather than *the price stabilization committee office*].
He organized his theme *so that it had an introduction, development, and a conclusion* [rather than *according to the introduction, development, conclusion method*].

Noun clause • See *Clause.*

Noun phrase • The term *noun phrase* is used in at least two ways in English grammatical discussion. In the older use, a noun phrase was one of the types of prepositional or verbal phrase, as in "I have heard of the book." Older grammarians called *of the book* a noun phrase, object of the verb, although many more recent grammarians would make *of* part of the verb. In transformational grammar, and in some structural analysis, a noun phrase is any group of words having a noun as head word; thus *a very lively little pup* is a noun phrase. It is often abbreviated *N* or *NP*.

nowheres • Nonstandard; omit the *s*.

Object • The word *object* is variously used, sometimes to identify the direct object, sometimes to indicate any word or words that complete a transitive verb (see 12-6).

Objective case, object case • The objective case is presumably used for direct objects (*I detest him*), for indirect objects (*I told her the facts*), for other sorts of complements which do not refer to the subject (*They called it Boston*), and for objects of prepositions (*beside her*), but it can now be recognized by form only in certain pronouns; see *Pronoun*.

Objective complement • A complement (see 12-6), after the direct object, that provides another name for the object or otherwise amplifies the object.

The devil wanted to make Tam's *wife* [direct object] a *widow* [objective complement].

of • Confused with *have*. See *could of, might of*.

on • Sometimes redundant with dates.

I shall see you *Tuesday* (rather than *on Tuesday*).

on the part of • Often a clumsy equivalent of *by;* see *part*.

one • Used in English in impersonal constructions, although it sometimes seems stiffly formal. It may be replaced by *he*, and *one's* by *his*, for a second reference.

only • For the position of *only*, see 16-2.

-orama, -orium • Faddish suffixes overused in various advertising coinages: *seafoodorama, lubritorium* (for a filling station).

out of • Prefer *out* (*out the door;* not *out of the door*).

outside of • Redundant as a compound preposition (*outside the barn*, not *outside of the barn*). *Outside of* is colloquial in the sense of "except."

He failed all his examinations *except that in chemistry* [not *outside of chemistry*].

outstanding • Overworked; see 21b.

over with • Colloquial as a synonym for *done, finished with, ended, completed*.

overall • Useful as a synonym for *general*, but currently overused; accurately used in a phrase like "the overall length."

part, on the part of • Often used in wordy writing.

Wordy: There was some objection, *on the part of* the administration, to the moral tone of the skits.

Revised: The administration objected to the moral tone of the skits.

Participle • Participles are verbals, that is, they are verb forms, although they tend to function as adjectives (see 12–5).

Parts of speech • Traditionally words of the language are classified—on a variety of bases—into parts of speech: nouns, pronouns, verbs, adjectives, adverbs, prepositions, conjunctions, particles including interjections. This classification, derived from Latin grammar, has been criticized by modern linguists as inconsistent and inadequate, and some grammarians have substituted *form classes,* based on formal distinctions rather than meaning or function. Modern grammars, although modifying definitions, still use the traditional terms for parts of speech, but recognize the limited uses of the classifications, especially because English words move so readily from one use in the sentence to another (see *Functional shift*).

party • Not usually acceptable in composition as a synonym for *person;* used in legal papers (*party of the first part*) and by telephone operators (*Here is your party*).

past, passed • *Past* is the modifier or complement, *passed* the verb form.

His troubles were *past.* She had *passed* all the tests.

Personal pronoun • See *Pronoun.*

phase • Often jargonic; see *Jargon.*

phenomena • Plural; the singular is *phenomenon* (compare *data*).

phone • Informal; in formal composition use *telephone. Phone up* is colloquial; formally use *telephone, call on the telephone;* less formally, *call up.*

Phoneme • A phoneme is the smallest linguistic unit recognized by the users of a language. Phonemes are either segmental or suprasegmental; the suprasegmental comprise the oral pattern of sentences, the pitch, tone, and juncture. The segmental phonemes are those that can be broken up; these are the sounds often associated with letters. Thus the phoneme /t/ comprises the sounds usually symbolized by the letter *t.* In English, /t/ and /d/ are two phonemes, although they are only one in some languages. In English /r/ is one phoneme, but in Spanish sounds associated with the spelling *r* comprise more than one phoneme because different sounds distinguish one word from another. To distinguish phonemes from letters and from sounds in phonetics, they are put within slant lines.

Phonemics • The system of recording language in phonemes.

Phonetics • The study of linguistic sound, and also the system of recording language by using standardized symbols for sounds. Phoneticians usually use IPA (the International Phonetic Alphabet). Phonetic symbols are enclosed within square brackets [a].

Phrase • A phrase is a group of words working together for a grammatical use. The older grammar recognized mainly prepositional, verbal, and verb phrases (see *Prepositional phrase; Verb phrase*). More recent grammarians recognize as a phrase any combination of words clustering on a head word (see *Phrase structure*).

Phrase structure • In transformational and structural grammars, phrase structure is the study of groups of words that work together. The commonest phrases are noun phrases (abbreviated *NP*) and verb phrases (abbreviated *VP*). Thus in transformational grammar the following is a fundamental rule: $S \longrightarrow NP + VP$. This means "A sentence can be written as a noun phrase plus a verb phrase." This is, of course, roughly equivalent to the older statement that a sentence is made up of a subject and predicate. Phrases can be further broken down; *a very bad boy* becomes $NP \longrightarrow D + I + adj + N$, which means that a noun phrase can be written as a determiner (*D*) plus an intensifier (*I*) plus an adjective (*adj*) plus a noun (*N*)

picture • Currently overused in expressions like "I gave them the whole picture." More specific writing provides the cure: "I told them why I needed five dollars."

piece • Nonstandard in the sense "a short distance."

Pitch • Pitch in language is the highness or lowness with which a segmental phoneme or phonetic unit is uttered. Pitch is sometimes indicated by a sequence of numbers, 1–3 or 1–4, with the lowest number the lowest pitch, the highest number the highest pitch. Pitch can also be indicated by a line which rises and falls. The following is a common pitch pattern for some American English sentences:

I should know tomorrow.

plan on • Colloquial in some uses (*plan to go*, not *plan on going; plan to see*, not *plan on seeing*).

plenty • Not acceptable as an intensive (*excellent*, not *plenty good*).

point • Overworked as a blanket word.

He had many admirable *characteristics* [not *points*].

poorly • Used in some dialects, not in formal writing, in the sense "in poor health."

Possessive before gerund • A distinction in precise meaning can sometimes be obtained by using the possessive of a noun or pronoun to modify a verbal noun or gerund.

Compare: He saw *Alfred* [or *him*] drinking sloe gin.
He disapproved of *Alfred's* [or *his*] drinking.

In the first, the whole expression, *Alfred drinking sloe gin*, tells what he saw; in the second it is the drinking that is disapproved and it is identified as Alfred's.

The principal was not amused by *their* [not *them*] playing poker in class.
I was surprised by my *father's* [not *father*] believing in ghosts.

Possessive case • The possessive case, also called the genitive case, reveals possession (*Mary's hair*) and various other relationships (*our representative*, *the people's choice*). It appears in many pronouns (see *Pronoun*) and commonly in nouns, where it usually requires a phrasal form (*of father, of Father's*) or an apostrophe (*the boy's, the boys'*); see 26b.

Postponed subject • Through the device of an expletive (*there* or *it*) the subject of a sentence can be "postponed" so that it appears after the verb (see 14–1).

Predicate • In general, the predicate comprises all the sentence not the subject or closely related to it. In English sentences it usually follows the subject and makes a predication about the subject; that is, it completes the subject–verb–complement pattern. It may consist only of a verb, as in "Birds sing," but it usually comprises a verb and a complement, and whatever other words go with these. The concept of the predicate is not much used in either structural or transformational grammar, although in actuality the predicate would usually be the constituent to the right of the first IC cut, or the *VP* in $S \longrightarrow NP + VP$.

prejudice • A noun, not to be confused with *prejudiced*, a modifier.

He was *prejudiced* [not *prejudice*] against John.

Prepositional phrase • A preposition (see 17–3) with its object.

presence • The noun form corresponding to *to be present* (*The chairman requests your presence on the platform*); to be distinguished from *presents*, plural of *present*.

principal, principle • The two words should be distinguished. *Principal* can be a modifier meaning "first in importance" (*I answered his principal objections*), or a noun naming somebody or something first in importance (*a high school principal, the principals in the fight*). *Principle* is always a noun.

The law of the conservation of matter formulates a fundamental *principle* in physics. Machiavelli has been accused of having no *principles*.

Principal parts • From the principal parts, most forms of most verbs can be derived. For many hundreds of years all English verbs have been made on the pattern *fire, fired, fired; walk, walked, walked*. These are often called weak verbs. Older verbs, if they have not been changed to follow the pattern of the weak verbs, may retain a variety of older patterns and thus seem to be irregular. Of these so-called strong verbs, the following are most likely to give trouble.

Infinitive	*Past*	*Participle*
awake	awaked, awoke	awaked
be	was, were	been
bear	bore	borne
begin	began	begun
blow	blew	blown
break	broke	broken
burst	burst	burst
catch	caught	caught

Infinitive	*Past*	*Participle*
choose	chose	chosen
cling	clung	clung
come	came	come
dive	dived, dove	dived
do	did	done
drag	dragged	dragged
draw	drew	drawn
drink	drank	drunk
eat	ate	eaten
fall	fell	fallen
give	gave	given
go	went	gone
grow	grew	grown
have	had	had
know	knew	known
lay	laid	laid
lead	led	led
lend	lent	lent
lie	lay	lain
lose	lost	lost
pay	paid	paid
prove	proved	proved, proven
put	put	put
ride	rode	ridden
rise	rose	risen
run	ran	run
see	saw	seen
set	set	set
shine	shone	shone
sit	sat	sat
speak	spoke	spoken
steal	stole	stolen
swim	swam	swum
swing	swung	swung
take	took	taken
teach	taught	taught
throw	threw	thrown
wake	woke, waked	woke, waked
wear	wore	worn

Standard English requires use of these principal parts:

I must have *broken* [not *broke*] my glasses.
By noon we had finished the digging and *begun* [not *began*] to pour the concrete.

Privilege of occurrence • This term refers to the uses to which an expression can appropriately be put. For example, *the* has privilege of occurrence before *student,* but not, unless it is part of another structure, after *student.* That is, *the student* is a grammatical structure, but *student the* is not. Roughly speaking *privilege of occurrence* from a structural point of view describes the nature of what is often called a part of speech. Thus, *carbon* and *campus,* when used as nouns, have similar privileges of occurrence.

prof • Slang when used as a common noun (*I like the course but not the prof*). Acceptable in journalistic and informal writing as an abbreviation with a full name (*Prof. George B. Sanders,* but *Professor Sanders*). Best formal style requires that *professor* be written out in all titles.

Pronoun, types and forms • Pronouns function as nouns, but take their meaning from their antecedents, the expressions to which they refer (see *Antecedent*). Several types of words are classified as pronouns, and many of them preserve case distinctions (see *Case*), which indicate how they are used. Because form changes to indicate case are not characteristic of modern English, various problems in usage of pronoun forms have developed. For usage problems other than those considered below, see also *myself; what; who; whom; whose; Possessive before gerund.*

1. *Personal pronouns* have case distinctions as follows: Subjective or nominative case, used for subjects and for complements referring to subjects after linking verbs; objective or dative-accusative case, used for various sorts of objects, including objects of prepositions, and for subjects of verbals; and possessive or genitive case, referring to various personal relationships, including possession.

	First Person	*Second Person*	*Third Person*
Subjective			
Singular	I	you	he, she, it
Plural	we	you	they
Objective			
Singular	me	you	him, her, it
Plural	us	you	them
Possessive			
Singular	my, mine	your, yours	his, her, hers, its
Plural	our, ours	your, yours	their, theirs

The second possessive forms are used as subjects or complements, most frequently as subject complements (*The book is mine*).

In standard English subjective forms are always used as subjects of a sentence or clause:

Jim and *I* [not *me*] made the first team.
I told them that *he* [not *him*] and Nancy could divide the lunch.

To test usage with a double subject, drop out the noun; one would not say "Me made the team." *I* and *we* are customarily last in a sequence, other pronouns first:

Evelyn and *I* [not *I and Evelyn*] won the doubles.

In formal written English, subjective forms are still used for a pronoun complement following a linking verb (*It was I who finally spoke; the real victim is she*). The subject–verb–object pattern is so prevalent, however, that users of English tend to prefer the objective form whenever it appears after the verb. Informally, "It's me" or "The real fools are us" is common.

Related is the use of a personal pronoun after *tha ⌐r as* in a comparison. Formally, subjective forms are preferred, on the theory that the pronoun is subject of a shortened clause (*She is older than I* [*am*]; *I am as well qualified as she* [*is*]). Here also, pressures of usual word order make the objective forms common informally.

Standard usage of objective forms is consistent. The objective case is used for objects of verbs, for objects of prepositions, and for subjects or objects of verbals. Self-consciousness about the forms, a tendency to over-correct, and perhaps some notion that *I* is more elegant than *me* produce frequent infelicities with pronouns in objective positions. Errors in sentences like the following have the extra disadvantage of sounding pretentious or affected.

He told my wife and *me* [not *I*] that the tickets were ready.
We never liked the Broadnicks, neither *her* [not *she*] nor her husband.
Just between you and *me* [not *I*], no hair ever got that color naturally.
The manager promised *us* [not *we*] girls the new apartment.
The man sitting in front of John and *me* [not *I*] kept his hat on.

2. *Relative pronouns* introduce subordinate clauses but also refer to antecedents and function in noun positions in the sentence. In

Grandmother, *who* wore spit curls to her dying day, arrived looking like a squid.

who introduces the modifying clause but also refers to *Grandmother* and serves as subject in its clause. The other relative pronouns, *which* and *that*, keep the same form in all cases, although *whose* is sometimes used for the possessive of *which*. *Who* and *whoever* are used to refer to persons and sometimes animals, *which* for inanimate objects, and *that* for either. Some writers prefer *that* to introduce a restrictive clause and *who* or *which* for a nonrestrictive clause. See also *who, whom, whose.*

3. *Interrogative pronouns* signal questions; they include *what* and the forms used as relative pronouns.

Who is he? *Whom* do you see? *Whose* book is it?

4. *Intensive pronouns* and *reflexive pronouns* have forms developed from personal pronouns: *myself, yourself, himself, herself, itself, ourselves, yourselves, themselves* (not *theirselves*). Their names distinguish only their use; intensive pronouns emphasize; reflexive pronouns redirect the predication to the subject. Compare:

Intensive: I cut the rope *myself.*
Reflexive: I cut *myself.*

5. Indefinite pronouns (words like *anyone, everyone, anybody, everybody, anything, everything, each, any,* and *all*) and *demonstrative pronouns* (*this, that, these, those, such*) do not change form to show their use in their clauses. They are pronouns when they function as substantives; often the same words are modifiers. Compare:

Pronoun: Any of you may taste the jam.
Modifier: Any person here may taste the jam.
Pronoun: That is the man I saw through the window.
Modifier: I saw *that* man through the window.

For agreement with indefinite pronouns, see 17h.

Proper noun • In general a proper noun is a name; in "Spot caught a rabbit; he has a black spot on his back," *Spot* is a proper noun, *spot* is not. Proper nouns are capitalized (see 26-3).

proved, proven • *Proved* is the only form having historical foundation, but *proven* is also commonly accepted. The verb *prove* is often used carelessly of statements which are not proved; often *suggest, imply,* or *indicate* would be more accurate.

providing • In older usage, not admitted as a synonym of *provided,* a conjunction meaning "on the condition."

put across • Blanket term for *explain, prove, demonstrate, expound, argue, make clear, establish,* and the like (see 21b).

quite • Generally accepted, although often unnecessary, in the sense of "entirely" (*quite dead, frozen quite to the bottom*); colloquial in the sense "somewhat," "rather" (*quite cold, quite a big job*).

raise • For confusion of forms of *rise* and *raise,* see *lie. Raise* is now generally accepted as a synonym of *rear* in the sense "bring to maturity," but many writers prefer *rear* when referring to human beings.

rate • Currently overused and misused; slang in some usages (*He does not rate with us*).

re • In the sense of "about," used for formal purposes only in legal documents and skeletonized commercial writing.

real • Colloquial as an intensive (*It was a real nice clambake*). Use *really, very,* or a word expressive enough so that it needs no intensive.

really • A useful word frequently overused and misused so that it clutters sentences.

Ineffectual: He had been *really* traveling.
Revised: He was gasping for breath because he had been running.
Redundant: It was *really* true.
Revised: It was true.

reason is because • See *because* and 13b.

reason why • Usually redundant (*The reason why I like to swim. . . .*); omit *why.*

reckon • Dialectal and inexact as a synonym for *believe, suppose, assume.*

Redundancy • Excess words, especially those that double the meaning of neighboring words, are called redundant, and are usually the result of careless repetition or of inadequate knowledge of the full meanings of the words used. *Repeat again, continue on, return back,* and *diametrically opposite* are common examples of redundancy.

Redundant: He was the first originator of the theory that we all now unanimously accept that understanding should be substituted in the place of punishment.

Revision: He originated the theory, now unanimously accepted, that understanding should replace punishment. [The following of the original are redundant: *first, originator; all, unanimously; substituted, in the place of.*]

Redundant: In this modern day and age of the present, one can never return back to the old methods of home industry of earlier times.

Revision: One cannot return to old methods of home industry.

regard, regards • Often overused; see *Jargon. Regards* is nonstandard in constructions like *in regards to.*

Relative pronoun • *who, whoever, whom, whomever, whose, whosever, which, that;* see *Pronoun* and *who, whom.*

Repetition • Repetition is often an effective device for emphasis, and it is often necessary. Repetition of a key word, for example, is preferable to the use of ostentatious synonyms. A paper on Shakespeare is bound to repeat words like *drama* or *play* or *Shakespeare,* and to avoid repeating the author's name with clichés like *the Bard* or *the Swan of Avon* is more obvious than the repetition. Careless repetition, however, particularly of easily noticed expressions, makes writing wordy and amateurish. Moreover, repetition of words is often a symptom of some fundamental weakness—of inadequate subordination, for example (see Section 16).

Repetitious: Users of the library often use little care in handling books.

Revision: Users of the library often are careless in handling books.

Repetitious: He announced that if anyone wanted to argue that he should wait until the next meeting.

Revision: He announced that if anyone wanted to argue he should wait until the next meeting.

respectfully, respectively • *Respectfully* means "in a respectful manner" (*respectfully submitted*); *respectively* means "in the the specified order," "severally" (*The balloons were identified as 4b, 5a, and 2g, respectively*).

Retained object • In some passive constructions, the word that would serve as direct object in the kernel sentence is retained as object of the passive verb.

Kernel: The president awarded him [indirect object] the *medal* [direct object].

Passive: He [from indirect object] was awarded the *medal* [retained object] by the president.

reverend • Used in standard English with the first name or initials of the person described or with the title *Mr.* (see 26j); in formal usage preceded by *the.*

The Reverend William Dimity: the Reverend W. L. Dimity; the Reverend Mr. Dimity.

right • Informal as an intensive in expressions like "right away"; prefer *immediately, at once, promptly,* etc. A localism in the sense of "very."

It was a *very* [not *right*] good fight.

rise • For confusion of forms of *rise* and *raise,* see *lie.*

said • Pseudo-legal affectation as a modifier; if necessary, use *this, that, these,* and the like.

Having rejected *the motion* [not *said motion*], the committee adjourned.

same • As a pronoun used with *in, same* is sometimes useful in legal documents, but sounds affected in most writing.

Having made his bed he must lie *in it* [not *in same*].

scarcely • Not to be used with another negative (see *Double negative*).

There *was scarcely* [not *was not scarcely*] any butter.

seem • A useful word, often misused or overused, especially as a qualification in constructions like "it would *seem* that."

The evidence *suggests* [not *would seem to suggest*] that Shakespeare was once a schoolmaster.

seldom ever • Redundant; omit *ever.*

set • For confusion of forms of *sit* and *set,* see *lie.*

set-up • Slang in the sense of "an easy victory," and currently overused in jargonic writing to mean anything related to organization, condition, or circumstances (*I liked the new set-up*).

shall, will • The verbs *shall* and *will* are troublesome because they have a troubled background. In Old English *shall* and *will* were not signs of the future; the word for *shall* meant *ought to* and the word for *will* meant *willing to, to be about to.* These meanings have been preserved in *should,* which implies obligation, and *would* which implies willingness. But *shall* and *will* became indications of the future, just as words with the same meaning today (*I am about to go; I have to go*) are becoming future forms. For hundreds of years little effort was made to distinguish between *shall* and *will* as auxiliaries, and users of English apparently never have had any deep-rooted feeling for a distinction between them—a fact which may account for the distinction's being difficult. In the eighteenth century, a popular grammarian laid down rules for the use of *shall* and *will,* and most handbooks of usage since then have repeated his rules—though a few have turned them exactly backwards. At present, most people, especially in America, pay little attention to these rules. Partly because contractions (*I'll, we'll*) are so common in speech, *will* is used in all persons in most informal situations. A few people, however, attach great importance to the arbitrary distinction between the words, and the following rule is still observed in some formal English. *In the first person, use* shall *to denote simple futurity,* will *to denote determination and purpose; in the second and third persons, use* will *to denote simple futurity,* shall *to denote determination and purpose.* In general, s*hould* and *would* also follow this rule, except when the use would interfere with the basic meaning of these two words, *should* implying duty, *would* implying willingness.

I *shall* consider each of the arguments.
I predict that the people *will* reject the offer.

shape • Colloquial in the sense of "condition," "manner."

She was *well trained* [not *in good shape*] for the tournament.

should • For distinctions between *should* and *would,* see *shall, will.*

should of • Mistaken form of *should have;* see *could of.*

show • Slang as a synonym for *chance, opportunity;* colloquial as a synonym for *moving picture, play.*

show up • Not standard in either the sense "arrive" (*Jim did not show up*) or the sense "expose" (*He is no gentleman, and Mary showed him up.*)

sic • See 24-3.

sign up, sign up for, sign up with • Not acceptable in formal English.

Signal words • See 17-1.

sit • For confusion of forms of *sit* and *set,* see *lie, lay.*

situated • Often used redundantly.

The house was *in* [not *situated in*] the tenement district.

situation • Wordy and jargonic in expressions like "the team had a fourth-down situation."

size • Not generally accepted as a modifier (*this size of dress,* not *this size dress*).

Slang • Slang develops variously, notably because we like to play with words. We put old words to new uses or coin new expressions, largely for the sake of novelty or cleverness. The results vary. Occasionally a slang expression fills a genuine need, persists, and is accepted as part of the language. Often it is accepted by limited groups and remains current in nonstandard or standard colloquial use. Usually it has quick popularity and then disappears. Using slang—especially if you make it up yourself—can be amusing, and the result vivid, but for two reasons slang is limited in its usefulness. First, it is usually known to so few people, in such a restricted group geographically or socially, and for so short a time, that it can be used for only the most local and ephemeral purposes. Second, much slang is so general that it means almost nothing. The user of slang often does not know what he wishes to say, and the listener to slang does not know what, if anything, has been said.

> *Slang:* It's okay by all of us if the dean of women wants to throw the book at us, but she better have the straight dope before she makes her move.
> *Standard:* None of us will object if the dean of women enforces the rules, but she should learn the facts before acting.

Slot • This term has been popularized through modern grammars to indicate a position in a sentence pattern which can be filled by an appropriate word or words. For example, a sentence will have a subject slot and a verb slot, which can be filled by words or groups of words having the appropriate privilege of occurrence.

so • Avoid the excessive use of *so* to join independent clauses (see Section 16).

so as • Not to be confused with *so that* (see 17b).

some • Not standard to indicate vague approval.

It was *an exciting* [not *some*] game.

somebody's else • The sign of the possessive appears on the last word (see 26b). Use *somebody else's*.

sometime, some time • One word in the sense "occasion," "some other time"; two words in the sense "a period of time."

Come up to see me *sometime*. The repairs will require *some time*.

somewhat of • *Somewhat* is most commonly an adverb (*They were somewhat slow*); *somewhat of* is not a standard idiom.

somewheres • Nonstandard. Omit the *s*.

sort • See *kind*.

sort of, sort of a • Both are clumsy and colloquial as modifiers.

I was *rather* [not *sort of*] tired.
He was *an amateur* [not *sort of a*] plumber.

speak, speech • The difference between the vowels in the verb *speak* and the noun *speech* is fruitful of spelling errors.

state • Currently misused as a loose equivalent of *say, remark, observe, declare*. Carefully used, *to state* is "to declare in a formal statement."

The board *stated* that the coach's contract would not be renewed.
The coach *said* [not *stated*] that practice would be postponed until four-thirty.

stationary, stationery • *Stationary* is a modifier meaning "not movable" or "not moving"; *stationery* is a noun meaning "writing materials." They can be distinguished by remembering that letters are written with stationery.

Stress • Stress in phonemics refers to the force or tenseness with which segmental phonemes are uttered. Stress is part of the pattern of the sentence, of the suprasegmental phonemes. Stress is often indicated by the following system of symbols: no symbol, light stress; / ^ /, moderate stress; / ` /, relatively heavy stress; / ' /, very heavy stress.

Subject • In all grammars of modern English, the subject, under whatever terminology, is an important part of the sentence. In "Planes fly," the subject is *planes*. Often, the subject is the first word or group of words that by its nature could be a subject (see 12-3).

Subjective case, nominative case • The subjective case is used for subjects and for complements referring to the subject. It can no longer be recognized in the form of nouns; for the subjective case in pronouns, see *Pronoun*.

Subordinate clause • A subordinate or dependent clause is one that is made subordinate to an independent clause or to a part of a clause. Modifying clauses function as adjectives (*Joan is the only girl that got an A*) or adverbs (*Smile when you say that*). Noun clauses are classified as subordinate (*Whoever dissents should raise his right hand*).

Substantive • Any nominal word or construction may be called a substantive; see *Noun, Noun clause, Noun phrase, Pronoun, Verbal noun, Verb phrase.*

such • Overused as a vague intensive (see 15b).

It was *a very* [not *such a*] warm day.

suit, suite • *Suit,* the commoner word, can be either a verb (*suit yourself*) or a noun (*a tailor-made suit*). *Suite,* only a noun, has several specialized uses.

The ambassador and his *suite* occupied a *suite* of rooms.

suspicion • A noun, not appropriately used to supplant the excellent verb *suspect.*

sure • Colloquial as an intensive.

He was *certainly angry* [not *sure sore*].

swell • Not acceptable in formal English as a modifier; use *good, excellent,* or, preferably, some more exact modifier.

take and • Redundant and nonstandard in most uses.

He *whacked* [not *took and whacked*] down the hornet's nest.

take sick • A regionalism not generally accepted in formal English; prefer *become ill* or *sick* or a more exact expression.

Tense • English has developed verb forms and combinations of verbs to indicate subtle variations in tense or time. These are not always consistent with traditional names for tenses; the so-called simple present, *I prove,* for instance, usually indicates a customary action (*I go to class at eight*) or future action (*I begin classes next week*). Native speakers, however, have little trouble distinguishing the forms; troubles with tense usually occur because the writer shifts his point of view (see 19-1 and 19a). This should remain consistent, and when two or more times are distinguished within the sentence, the forms of verbs should reveal the order of events. In general the relationship of the tenses can be suggested by a formula like the following:

	The past perfect forms	are to	the other past forms
as	the past forms	are to	the present forms
as	the present forms and the future perfect forms	are to	the other future forms.

This works out somewhat as follows:

When the boss *had come* [past perfect form] I *received* [past form] my pay.
At noon, if the boss *has come* [past form] I *receive* [customary present form] my pay.
By noon, the boss *will have come* [future perfect form], and I *shall receive* [future form] my pay.
By noon, if the boss *comes* [present form], I *shall receive* [future form] my pay.

When a direct quotation is reported as an indirect question, the word order shifts and the time is sometimes pushed back.

Direct: "You *were* wrong," he said.
Indirect: He said I *had been* wrong.

Patterns are not consistent; in the following the tense does not change:

Direct: He asked, "Was Caroline on time?"
Indirect: He asked whether Caroline was on time.

The tense of a verbal is determined by the relationship of the time of the action of the verbal to the time of the action of the main verb. The present verbal is most common and is used when the verbal and the main verb refer to action at the same time.

We expected him *to burn* the papers.

Both verb and verbal refer to the past; the verbal is therefore present in form.

Smiling at his discomfort, she looks at the photographs.

Verb and verbal both refer to the present and both forms are present. The present form is also used sometimes with a function word like *after* to suggest action preceding that of the main verb.

After *smiling* at his discomfort, she closed the photograph album.

The past forms regularly indicate action previous to the time of the main verb.

We expected him *to have burned* the papers.
Having smiled at his discomfort, she closed the photograph album.

The burning and the smiling preceded the expecting and the closing. The simple past participle often describes a state of affairs caused previously but existing at the same time as that of the main action.

Reconciled, he continued to praise the photographs.

terrible, terribly • Overused and misused; colloquial as general intensives (*She is a terribly sweet girl*) and as blanket words signifying anything unpleasant (*I had been vaccinated and felt terrible*).

terrific • Recently misused and overused as a general synonym for anything *large, impressive, dramatic, significant, dexterous,* or *important,* it can now scarcely be used in its standard meaning, "causing terror."

that • Like *who* and *which, that* is often unnecessary to introduce a clause (*Everybody knew* [*that*] *he had failed*). Omission is confusing, however, when it causes temporary misreading:

Mr. Chamberlain *forgot that the umbrella* [not *forgot the umbrella*] had been torn.

For reference of *that,* see 17e.

that there • Nonstandard; omit *there.*

the • The definite article (see *Article*).

their, there, they're • Commonly confused in spelling. *There,* which can be remembered by its similarity to *where,* means "in that place" (*Lie there, Nipper*). *Their* is the possessive of *they. They're,* the contraction of *they are,* is not acceptable in formal composition.

these • Should be avoided as a substitute for *the* (see *this*).

these kind, these sort • See *kind.*

they • For the colloquial use of *they* to refer to people or society, see 17e.

this • Like *the*, *this* as a determiner indicates that the noun it precedes has been previously mentioned.

> On our way home from Sunday School, *a* (not *this*) man came up to me and took my hand, and then *he* (not *this fellow*) said. . . .

For reference of *this*, see 17e; for *this* as a symptom of inadequate subordination, see Section 16.

this here • Nonstandard; omit *here*.

tho • A variant spelling of *though* not preferred for formal composition.

those • Avoid *those* as an intensive with no reference.

> He looked back fondly on *his* [not *those*] old college days.

thusly • Affected or nonstandard for *thus*.

to, too, two • Distinguish the function word *to* (*to the game, learn to read*) from the adverb *too* (*too sick, too hot*), and the numeral *two* (*two seats on the aisle*).

toward, towards • Alternative forms; *toward* is more common in the United States.

trait • Redundant in *character trait;* use *trait* or *characteristic*.

Transform • In transformational grammar, all structures not kernel sentences can be derived as transforms of them. *Astrid was chased by a bear* is a transform of *A bear chased Astrid. Red dress* is a transform of *The dress is red.* See 13-6, 14-2, 14b, 16-1.

Transformation grammar, transform grammar • Transformation grammar is a generative grammar, in that it endeavors to provide rules by which sentences are generated. It relies upon kernel sentences and transforms of these kernels; see pp. 188–89.

Trite or hackneyed expressions, clichés • Many expressions in English cannot stand popularity. Idioms, of course, and standard expressions appear over and over without losing their effectiveness, but slang or other attempts at cleverness or vividness emerge after overuse with as little vigor as any other stale joke. Metaphors which do not enter the language as new words often become trite. The writer who first referred to a wife as a *ball and chain* may have been amusing on the comic-strip level; the thousandth person who imitated him was not amusing on any level. Expressions which have been so tarnished by time that their charm, and often even their meaning, is gone are called trite or hackneyed expressions or clichés. Trite expressions are dangerous partly because they paralyze the mind. As ready-made channels for thought they invite the ideas of the writer, who can then cease thinking. An editorial writer commented in a discussion of academic freedom in a university:

> Any teacher who disagrees with his dean's academic views is not playing on the team and should turn in his suit.

The "team" metaphor was worn out long ago, but the writer fell into the set pattern so easily that he failed to analyze his own remarks. The convenience of the trite expression led him into an argument by false analogy (see 10e).

Trite: When war first reared its ugly head, John Q. Public took it in his stride and played ball.

Revision: Faced with war, we did what had to be done.

Trite: In our day and age, in this great country of ours, progress has taken place by leaps and bounds.

Revision: America has progressed.

try and • *Try to* is preferred in standard English.

type • In formal English, *type* is a noun or verb, although colloquially it is often an adjective (*a ranch-type house*).

This type of research [not *this type research*] yields results.

unique • For the use of *unique,* see 16d.

up • Useful in verb-adverb combinations (see 12-4), *up* can frequently be separated from the verb, but often the sense is clearer and the construction smoother if *up* is kept close to the verb.

Awkward: He made his mind up.

Revised: He made up his mind.

used to • The *d* is elided in speech but not omitted in writing.

We *used to* [not *use to*] go to the beach every summer.

used to could • Nonstandard for *used to be able.*

Verb • See 12-4. For problems with forms of verbs see *lie, lay; Mood; Principal parts; Tense; Voice; shall, will.*

Verb phrase • In the older grammar, a verb phrase was any combination of words serving as a verb. Thus *has gone* and *will go* were verb phrases. In transformational grammar the word is used in larger senses; it can be used to indicate the verb and all that goes with it, and is thus equivalent to the word *predicate,* or it can be used to indicate the verb and its modifiers, but not the complement.

Verbal • Formed from verbs, verbals retain some verb functions but serve primarily as nouns or modifiers or parts of complex verbs (see 12-5). Verbals cannot serve as finite or complete verbs (see Section 12). For tense of verbals, see *Tense.*

very • The most useful intensive, but since it is usually only an intensive, with relatively little meaning, it is as likely to weaken writing as to strengthen it. Most good writers use *very* sparingly. Older practice was to forbid the use of *very* before a past participle without an intervening *much* (*very much pleased,* not *very pleased*). The distinction is still maintained in some formal writing.

Voice • A distinction in verb forms between the active, in which the subject of the verb is the actor, and the passive, in which the subject of the verb receives the action. The passive (*was eaten, has been seen*) employs a form of *be* as an auxiliary and is used in passive transforms of active sentences (see 14-2).

Kernel (*active*): The children stole the turnips.
Transform (*passive*): The turnips were stolen by the children.

wait on • Except in the sense of "serve," *wait for* is idiomatic.
We have been waiting *for* [not *on*] you.

want for • In most constructions, omit the *for*.
I *want* [not *want for*] you to meet her.

ways • Colloquial for *way* in the sense "a distance."
It was a long *way* [not *ways*] to the road.

we • The editorial *we, we* used for *I* or to stand for a newspaper, is generally confined to journalistic writing; *we* is common as an impersonal subject meaning "people in general," or "the writer and the reader."

weather • Frequently confused in spelling with *whether* (*I asked him whether or not we could depend upon fair weather*).

well • An adjective in the sense "in good health," "cured" (*The patient is now recovered, and is quite well*); an adverb corresponding to the adjective *good,* but not to be confused with it (see 16d).
She played her part *well* [not *good*].
The blueprints look *good* [not *well*].

what • Nonstandard as a relative pronoun.
I liked the places *that* [not *what*] he recommended.

What all occurs in some dialects (*What all they do I have to do*), but *all* is redundant.

when • Avoid the *when*-clause in a definition (see 13b).

where • Nonstandard or colloquial when substituted for *that.*
I noticed in the paper *that* Senator Jones is a candidate for re-election [not *I see by the paper* where *Senator Jones is up for re-election*].

where at • In most constructions, omit the *at.*
Where is he? [not *Where at is he?* or *Where is he at?*]

whether • See *if.*

which • For *which* after *and,* see *and which;* for the use of *which* to refer to human beings, see *Pronoun.*

while • Often carelessly used as a synonym for *although* or *and* (see 17b).

who, whom • Logically, relative and interrogative pronouns take their form from their use in their clause—*who* for a subject or subject complement, *whom* for an object. When the words occur out of the usual subject–verb–complement order, however, users of the language do not always make the case distinction. Compare:
I asked him *who* he thought he was hitting.
I asked him *whom* he thought he was hitting.

In these sentences the pronoun functions as object of *was hitting;* formal written usage would require *whom.* Since the pronoun is the first word in its clause, however, in the subject position, speakers tend to use *who,* the subject form. Formal writing might require:

> *Whom* did Tom invite? *Whom* do you see? I don't know *whom* he is taking to the party.

In nonformal situations *who* is common in such sentences. *Whom* is used consistently when the pronoun immediately follows a preposition.

> I wasn't sure to *whom* [not *who*] I was speaking.

Concern for correctness with such pronouns often causes exaggerated deference to *whom,* which is more disturbing than informal neglect for the case distinction. Notice the following:

> *Who* [not *whom*] does he think he is?
> I met the girl *who* [not *whom*] everyone said would win the beauty contest.
> I asked him *who* [not *whom*] he was.

whose • English no longer has a possessive form for *which. Whose,* the possessive of *who,* is now regularly used to avoid the often cumbersome *of which,* even though *who* is usually restricted to reference to people.

> I do not like a ring *whose setting* [compare *the setting of which*] reminds me of snakes.

Who's is the contraction of *who is.*

will • For the distinction from *shall,* see *shall, will.*

wire • Informal for either *telegram* or *telegraph.*

wise • Currently in vogue and overused as an informal suffix for almost everything (*The meal was good tastewise*). Often the uses sound as absurd as this example.

without • Nonstandard as a substitute for *unless.*

> I will not stay *unless* [not *without*] you raise my wages.

wood, woods • In the United States either is acceptable as a synonym of *forest.*

worst kind, worst way • Not acceptable in the sense "very much."

worthwhile • Overused blanket word; see 21b.

would have • Often awkward.

> If they *had* [not *would have*] done that . . . .

would of • Mistaken form of *would have* (see *could of*).

you • To be used with caution in impersonal constructions (see 17k).

you-all • Colloquial Southern form as the plural of *you;* not acceptable for formal composition.

Exercise 27

A. In the following sentences supply the proper form of the appropriate verb and explain your choice.

1. While I (*lie, lay*) hidden behind the sofa, the other members of the family filed into the dining room and (*sit, set*) down to dinner.
2. He had been (*lie, lay*) on his back for three weeks, and he was so weak that he could not (*rise, raise*) his hand.
3. The coat still (*lie, lay*) where we had left it in the morning.
4. When the peasants finally (*rise, raise*) in rebellion, issues which had (*lie, lay*) dormant for years assumed new importance.
5. The sun (*rise, raise*) at 6:30 a.m. and (*sit, set*) at 5:50 p.m.
6. After I had eaten, I (*lie, lay*) down on the couch and (*sit, set*) the book on the stand in front of me.
7. All the children (*lie, lay*) in the tall grass watching the ducks (*rise, raise*) into the air and head south.
8. The pitcher should be (*sit, set*) wherever you (*sit, set*) it this morning.
9. He decided to (*lie, lay*) the difficult problems aside.
10. They let the injured man (*lie, lay*) in the middle of the highway until the ambulance arrived.
11. (*Lie, lay*) the slices of eggplant in a dish, (*lie, lay*) a weight on them, and allow them to (*sit, set*) there overnight.
12. He (*lie, lay*) the canceled check in the drawer, and presumably it (*lie, lay*) there yet.
13. I have (*lie, lay*) in bed all morning, and now you say I must (*lie, lay*) here all afternoon.
14. He had (*lie, lay*) emphasis on this fact, that the land (*lie, lay*) adjacent to the river.
15. He (*lie, lay*) a wager that the billfold would be found (*lie, lay*) on the dresser.

B. For each blank in the following sentences select an appropriate form of the verb in parentheses:

1. If you are going fishing with me you _____ (*be*) quiet.
2. When I _____ (*eat*) my lunch, I took a short nap.
3. If you want to stay out after hours, you _____ (*ask*) permission.
4. While I was looking in the closet for my windbreaker, part of the ceiling _____ (*fall*) down.

5. Since you say you can see in the dark so well, why _____ you _____ (*stumble*)?

6. While I _____ (*set*) the table, you might boil some water.

7. Before you screw down the lid, be sure you _____ (*check*) the safety valve.

8. You _____ (*prove*) the theorem before you could have proved the corollary.

9. Mother told me that strange men _____ (*be*) not to be trusted.

10. When Uncle Joe came to dinner he always _____ (*bring*) us oranges.

C. For each blank in the following sentences select an appropriate form of the verb in parentheses:

1. If I _____ (*be*) you, I would take it back and get my money.

2. If it _____ (*be*) noon, I would go right now.

3. If the plant _____ (*be*) sitting on the piano, it must have left a mark in the dust.

4. If only Father _____ (*be*) here!

5. If anybody _____ (*save*) him, Dr. Worley would be the man.

6. If your father _____ (*be*) not carrying a gun, I would think him a a religious man.

7. Mary, I often wish you _____ (*be*) smarter than you are.

8. John, I often wish you _____ (*act*) smarter than you do.

9. Children, _____ (*can*) you not keep from squabbling if you would try?

10. If those children _____ (*can*) keep from squabbling, I would let them play together.

D. In the following sentences, select the appropriate forms of the verbal and explain the reason for your choice:

1. I was glad (to receive, to have received) your invitation.

2. It was the largest audience ever (to convene, to have convened) in Severing Hall.

3. When you get into the boat be sure (to fasten, to have fastened) your life belt.

4. The stairs are steep; be sure (to hold, to have held) the guard rail.

5. Father came along just when I was about (to be arrested, to have been arrested).

6. I was ashamed (to lose, to be losing, to have been losing) the game for our team.

7. If they were not doing their algebra, they ought (to be doing, to have been doing) it.

8. Those who were about (to die, to have died) took a glance at each other.

9. She was unwilling (to undergo, to have undergone) the operation.

10. He expected (to be, to have been) elected house manager.

E. Choose the appropriate pronoun form in the following sentences, and give the reason for your choice.

1. Ask Mary. Mother said it was (she, her) who took the cake.

2. Everybody thought Uncle Angus was stingy, but he left (we, us) girls a beautiful house.

3. The bartender told my cousin and (I, me) that we should go get a few years older.

4. When she had the ingredients jumbled in the pan, she stood staring as though she did not dare ask what (we, us) girls would have done.

5. Ask the patrolman (who, whom) he thinks he is arresting.

6. The quarrel between my sister and (I, me, myself) began when I was a child.

7. Mother promised a glass of lemonade to (whoever, whomever) could get back from the store first.

8. I cannot help wondering (who, whom) he thinks he is.

9. Aunt Amy asked Ethel and (I, me, myself) out for the weekend.

10. He was afraid to ask (who, whom) would be playing the piano accompaniment.

11. We heard voices coming over the water, and we knew it was (they, them).

12. The trouble between my roommate and (I, me) all began when she started chewing bubble gum.

13. (Who, whom) do you expect to find buried under the cellar steps?

14. You may nominate (whoever, whomever) you please.

15. Harry kept complaining about the rain, but after a while we agreed that (he, him) and (I, me) would start out.

16. When Father cooks, nobody feels sorry for (he, his, him) sweating over a hot stove.

17. He stabbed in the dark, without knowing (who, whom) he might hit.

18. The janitor was always nice to (we, us) girls.

19. (Who, whom) do you think will be the new basketball coach?

20. The stupidity of both Hester and (she, her) was remarkable.

F. Discuss the suitability of the italicized expressions in the following sentences for (a) campus conversation, (b) informal composition, and (c) formal composition.

1. My *girl-friend* knows so little about football she *thinks* "clipping" is charging six *bucks* for seats in the end zone.
2. A *stolid,* bald-headed gentleman was *staring* at me as though he thought he was *acquainted with* me, but was not *quite* certain.
3. *Here's* the *deal,* and you can *take it from me, it's a dilly.*
4. Whatever you want, she is *liable* to want something *of a different nature,* like *movieing* while you want to *shoot the breeze.*
5. *Irregardless* of my mother's warnings, I decided to *date* him.
6. I was so *enthused I figured I'd contact 'em first off.*
7. I *suggest* the *inclusion* of this *data* on the *agendas.*
8. She was *cute,* all right, but, *last but not least,* I *suspicioned* she *wasn't* the *swell dame* she was *cracked up to be.*
9. A *great number* of onlookers *blamed* the accident *on* Jim.
10. Maybe it's *okay lecturewise,* but, *man,* I don't *dig* it.

G. Substitute fresher, more expressive terms for the trite expressions in the sentences below. You may find that you must use more revealing words than those in the original, since trite expressions often become very nearly meaningless.

1. I slept like a log, and woke up at the crack of dawn, fresh as a daisy.
2. With her hair a sable cloud about her face, her peaches-and-cream complexion, her ruby lips, and her eyes like stars, she was as pretty as a picture.
3. Martha was a perfect baby, as happy as the day is long.
4. The wily southpaw zipped a fast one over the corner, and the old speed king had done it again. You can't hit 'em if you can't see 'em.
5. The last examination had put me out like a light, and accordingly, although I was down in the dumps—it was blue Monday for me— I determined to burn the midnight oil.
6. Crime never pays and true Americanism requires that we stamp it out, each and every time a crime wave raises its ugly head in this great and glorious land of ours.
7. And last but not least, in advertising you have to sell yourself; that is, to make it short and sweet, you have to hit the market smack on the nose.
8. We would willingly point with pride at the progress onward and upward in this land of the free; we have no inclination to drag a red herring across the trail to becloud the issue; but any lover of government of the people, by the people, for the people must view with alarm the state of the nation in this day and age, and unless we go

back to the principles of the founding fathers, we are in grave danger of having our cherished liberties gone with the wind.

9. He took the unwelcome news like a man. He became sober as a judge, but I knew he was true as steel, all wool and a yard wide, and that he would snap out of it.

10. He was tall, dark, and handsome, with lean flanks and piercing eyes, always smelling faintly of good English tobacco and well-oiled leather, every inch a man's man.

H. Remove redundant words and phrases from the following:

1. It was the consensus of opinion that the statements were directly antithetical.
2. Her rendition was absolutely perfect.
3. While the nations work against one another, the presence of war is constantly at hand.
4. We hold diametrically opposite views on most questions.
5. My mother, she thought I ought to go to the cheaper college, but the differences in cost were infinitesimally small.
6. The way this story was written made it seem to make me feel that it could really have actually happened to me.
7. A girl should be able to make a living in her special particular line.
8. In spite of all the illegal crimes he had committed, the leader of the gang went entirely scot-free.
9. It is the one and only unique sacred white Burmese camel in the United States.
10. Formerly in the olden days the girls of the parish had to crawl through a small stone window to prove they had behaved themselves.

I. The passages below are wordy, many of them because they contain jargon. Rewrite them, making the sense clear in good English, if the passage suggests any sense. Some sentences may mean almost nothing, for blanket terms characteristically fill space with words, not with meaning. If a sentence has no discoverable meaning, write a sentence which says what you imagine the writer may have intended to say.

1. Though the evidence in the case seems to be that the crisis has passed and the Giants are over the hump of the slump that cost them great gobs of ground in the pennant chase, the Giant high command did not permit the chinks in the Giant armor turned up by the losing skid to go unnoticed. Quietly, behind the scenes, they are attempting to mend their fences, and you may be sure they will leave no stone unturned in their effort to batten down the hatches.
2. Another advantage of the cow is her ability to relax, and humans would be better off if they had this fundamental feature.

Exercises

3. In this day and age the problem of drinking intoxicating beverages has had a much freer scope in recent years than was the case at an earlier period in time.

4. The person in search of worthwhile science fiction material can find the basic circumstances at every facet of modern literature.

5. Some critics commented on his lecture to the highest degree.

6. Everybody should be capable of practicing in some line of work. Being able to support yourself is very important in this respect.

7. Although this may not be the over-all case, it does include the majority of advertisements, and the factors in the movement are to the extreme.

8. Reading—the anesthetic of a tired mind; the broadening of one's educational frame of reference; the opening of new and unfound fields of thought; a must in everyone's life.

9. The big day rolled around, but Hamlet, who had the inclination for abruptness of action, curbed his burning desires, and therefore slowness of action resulted.

10. I told her that if she wouldn't get on the beam and stop blowing up the insignificant factors in the case she had better get out of the picture.

Appendix: Revising and Correcting the Theme

Every piece of writing requires revision: a college composition needs at least two revisions, one before it is submitted and a second after the instructor returns it.

A student learning composition is like a man thrown into mid-ocean to learn how to swim. He has to write while learning to write. While he practices organization he must remember to spell and punctuate, and while he checks pronoun reference he must watch the coherence of his paragraphs. Careful and repeated revision helps.

Check Chart for Revision   28-1

For a college theme, the student might well ask himself the following questions, checking against his paper as objectively as he can.

1. Did the subject prove too big or too little or unsuitable?
2. Have you focused the material about a main idea?
3. Have you made each paragraph a developed unit?
4. Have you developed your subject adequately and logically?
5. Are style and tone appropriate and consistent?
6. Are sentences clear and direct? Could any profitably be revised from a passive or expletive pattern?
7. Have you chosen words that mean what you want to say?
8. Have you corrected mechanics? Be sure of the spelling of each word, using a dictionary when necessary.

The following suggests how a revision of a first draft might look:

The ~~stock market~~ crash, *however,* ∧~~of 1929~~

was only the begi*n*ing ~~of the great de-~~

~~pression~~; in the summer of 1932 the de-

pression reach its lowest point, both

economically and psychologically. The

The opening sentence is moved to improve continuity in the paragraph.

first signifi*c*ant event ~~to start the~~

Spelling errors are corrected.

~~ball rolling for the epoch~~ of the great

Unnecessary words are deleted.

depression was the stock market crash in

October, 1929. ~~The clerks in wall Street~~

A comma is supplied.

~~brokers' offices worked late into the~~

~~night posting records of an unprecedented~~

A sentence not relevant to the main idea of the paragraph is dropped.

~~volume of sales.~~ ∧ ~~Apples,~~ began to ∧~~be sold~~ *sell apples*

on the street. ~~by~~ (unemployed citizens) In

Word order is changed to make the sentence active.

New York, as well as in other cities,

bread lines appeared, displaying the

extreme poverty suffered by some people.

As early as January, 1932, ~~there was a~~

demonstrat~~ion~~ *ed* at the national capital.

~~conducted by~~ (10,000 unemployed men) When

The sentence is shifted to regular actor-action order and moved to the end, where it provides a transition to the next paragraph.

destitute families lacked sufficient

funds even to buy a few pounds of coal,

~~they gave~~ ∧~~them~~ fuel. *a relief bureau had to provide* People began crowd-

The sentence is revised to correct vague pronoun reference.

ing into banks, fearing failures and hop-

ing to rescue any savings they had.

When the draft has been thoroughly revised, it should be carefully and neatly copied, and then the final version should be checked for typographical errors or blunders introduced in the process of copying.

Correcting the Theme   28-2

Even though the student has carefully revised his theme, the instructor is likely to add corrections and suggestions. Inside the front cover of this book is a chart of key numbers and abbreviations which may be used in correcting themes. An alphabetical list of the abbreviations will be found inside the back cover. A reference chart to the rhetorical sections of the book also appears on the inside front cover. To profit from his instructor's corrections, the student should correct his paper according to the following procedures:

1. If your instructor uses abbreviations to mark corrections, refer to the alphabetical list inside the back cover and find the number of the section to which each abbreviation refers.

2. If your instructor uses numbers as symbols, or after you have found numbers corresponding to his abbreviations, turn to the section of the book headed by each number indicated on the paper, locating sections by the numbers at the tops of the pages.

3. Study the section of the book to which the instructor has referred you, comparing examples in the Guide to Revision sections of the book with your own paper until you are sure you understand his recommendation.

4. Then rewrite each passage as it should be written.

The student should note that profitable correction often requires more than rewriting misspelled words or changing punctuation. The writer derives the greatest benefit from carefully reworking sentences and paragraphs. A mark like *Coh* or 5 in the margin of the paper, for instance, indicates to the student that the portion of his theme so marked lacks coherence; it tells him to strengthen continuity between ideas, to devote special study to Section 5 in the text, and to rewrite the passage so that it holds together. If the mark *Sub* or 16 appears in the margin of the paper, the student needs to devote special study to Section 16, where he will find a discussion of methods for improving sentence structure through subordination; it is possible that to achieve this improvement he will need to combine two or three sentences by reducing a clause to a phrase or a single word. The following selection has been marked with the abbreviations listed inside the back cover.

> The public is fooled every day by a
>
> *W Ref* — variety of people <u>ranging</u> from the glib
>
> medicine man to people working for <u>high</u>   *Hy*
>
> geared political machines. The <u>inteligence</u>   *Sp*
>
> *Agr* — of these people <u>vary</u> widely. The people
>
> they fool are often more <u>inteligent</u> than   *Sp*
>
> *C F* — they, however, their skills are so great
>
> that they overcome even the <u>inteligent</u>   *Sp*
>
> *Sp* — man. <u>Inteligence</u> is not acquired, but   *Dev*
>
> *Sp* — <u>knowlege</u> can be acquired, (due to) man's
>
> ability to learn. Salesmen often (state)   *Coh*
>
> *Sub* — as fact information about their products.
>
> Often these are untrue.

The opening for the theme is not promising, and frequent errors in structure and mechanics have been marked. To correct them, the student should check each abbreviation in the list inside the back cover. He will discover, for example, that *W Ref* indicates faulty word reference and is discussed under 17g in the text. He can find 17 quickly by using the numbers at the tops of the pages. *Hy,* the student will find, indicates faulty hyphenation and is discussed under 26c, and *Agr* refers to agreement of subject and verb and is discussed under 17. The fourth sentence is marked *Dev,* which refers to relevance of the development and is discussed under 4, but it contains an expression, *due to,* circled and not otherwise marked. Whenever no abbreviation or number is used with ·a marked passage, the student should look up the marked expression in the glossary (27) or index, where he will find an explanation or a reference.

A theme may also be marked directly with the numbers which appear in the margins of the book and at the tops of pages and are summarized in the chart inside the front cover. The following selection from the theme begun above has been marked with numbers.

> Many methods are used to influence people. These methods include as one of the most popular the use, of propaganda. *16 a*
>
> Pamphlets, newspapers, magazines, books, posters, billboards, radio, movies and *25d* television are all mediums for the spread of propaganda. For example, know-
>
> *16 c* *see also* *14 b* ing the kinds of things audiences want to hear, many facts are distorted by radio commentators There are many kinds of in- *14 a'*
>
> *4, see especially 4-2* formation which are distorted for propaganda purposes.

The student can look up 16a and find a suggestion that the sentences be combined, with one subordinated to the other. The reference to 25d points out an omission of a comma in a series, and 16c marks a dangling modifier. The instructor has also suggested that the writer see 14b, which refers to overuse of passive sentences. The reference to 4 calls attention to a weakness that is apparent throughout the theme, overuse of general rather than specific development. The instructor has used another kind of symbol here also, the hyphenated number 4-2. Hyphenated numbers head discussions of writing methods and procedures; sometimes an instructor may think that the writer could profit from study of these sections and will refer to them. A reference chart appears on the front endpapers.

Record of Themes and Recommendations for Revision   28-3

Avoiding errors alone will not make a writer competent, but a writer can improve if he will learn to understand his errors, will concentrate on correcting habitual mistakes. The chart on the following page is intended to help the student analyze his weaknesses, to give him a guide for special study, and to help him know what to look for in theme revision. Use the blanks at the bottom of the chart for other subjects marked frequently in your papers.

THEME NUMBER	1	2	3	4	5	6	7	8	9	10	11	12	13	14	15
GRADE															
Organization, 7															
Paragraphing, 2-3															
Development, 4															
Fragment, 12															
Run-together, 25b															
Postponed subject, 14a															
Passive sentence, 14b															
Predication, 13															
Parallelism, 15															
Subordination, 16															
Dangling modifier, 16b															
Reference, 17															
Pronoun form, 27															
Verbs, 12, 27															
Agreement, 17															
Words, 20-2, 27															
Adjective, adverb, 16d															
Punctuation, 25															
Manuscript form, 26															
Spelling, 26															
Possessive, 26b															
Hyphenation, 26c															

Index

Q

Ab	Abbreviation	**26j**	**Div**	Division of words	**26l**
Adj	Adjective form	**16e**	**DM**	Dangling modifier	**16c**
Adv	Adverb form	**16e**	**Em**	Emphasis	**18**
Agr	Agreement	**17h-n**	**Eq**	Equations with verb *be*	**13b**
An	Analysis	**6a**	**Ev**	Evidence	**10**
Apos	Apostrophe, Possessive	**26b**	**Expl**	Expletives	**14a**
Cap	Capitalization	**26i**	**Fig**	Figurative language	**21d**
CF	Comma fault	**25b**	**Frag**	Sentence fragment	**12**
Class	Classification	**6b**	**Gloss**	Refer to glossary	**27**
Coh	Coherence	**5**	**Hy**	Hyphenation	**26d**
Colloq	Colloquial expression	**27**	**Id**	Idiom	**27**
Comp	Comparisons	**15c**	**Inc**	Incomplete constructions	**15b**
Conc	Conclusions	**8c-e**	**Intro**	Introductions	**8b, d-e**
Conj	Conjunctions	**17a-b**	**Ital**	Italics	**26n**
CS	Comma splice	**25b**	**lc**	Lower case	**26i**
D	Diction	**21**	**Log**	Logic	**11**
Dash	Dash	**25k**	**M**	Mechanics, MS form	**26**
Def	Definition	**9**	**MI**	Main idea	**1b**
Dele, *ϑ*	Delete, wordiness	**21a**	**Mod**	Position of modifiers	**16b**
Dev	Development	**4**	**Mood**	Mood of verb	**27**
Dir	"Direction" in words	**21e**	**No P**	Inappropriate punctuation	**25m**